P9-DZY-351

DUTY

A FATHER, HIS SON, AND THE MAN WHO WON THE WAR

Books by Bob Greene

Duty

Chevrolet Summers, Dairy Queen Nights

The 50-Year Dash

Rebound: The Odyssey of Michael Jordan

All Summer Long

Hang Time

He Was a Midwestern Boy on His Own

Homecoming: When the Soldiers Returned from Vietnam

Be True to Your School

Cheeseburgers

Good Morning, Merry Sunshine

American Beat

Bagtime (with Paul Galloway)

Johnny Deadline, Reporter

Billion Dollar Baby

Running: A Nixon-McGovern Campaign Journal

We Didn't Have None of Them Fat Funky Angels on the Wall of Heartbreak Hotel, and Other Reports from America

Books by Bob Greene and D. G. Fulford

To Our Children's Children: Journal of Family Memories

Notes on the Kitchen Table: Families Offer Messages of Hope for Generations to Come

To Our Children's Children: Preserving Family Histories for Generations to Come

DUTY

A FATHER, HIS SON, AND THE MAN WHO WON THE WAR

BOB GREENE

WM

William Morrow
An Imprint of HarperCollins*Publishers*

Grateful acknowledgment is made for permission to reprint lyrics from "Like a Rock," lyrics and music by Bob Seger, copyright © 1985 by Gear Publishing Co. (ASCAP).

HarperCollins books may be purchased for educational, business, or sales promotional use. For information please write: Special Markets Department, HarperCollins Publishers Inc., 10 East 53rd Street, New York, NY 10022.

FIRST EDITION

Designed by Jackie McKee

Library of Congress Cataloging-in-Publication Data has been applied for.

ISBN 0-380-97849-0

00 01 02 03 04 QWM 10 9 8 7 6 5 4 3 2 1

For Tim Greene

DUTY

A FATHER, HIS SON, AND THE MAN WHO WON THE WAR

ONE

The morning after the last meal I ever ate with my father, I finally met the man who won the war.

It was from my father that I had first heard about the man. The event—the dropping of the atomic bomb on Hiroshima—I of course knew about; like all children of the post–World War II generation, my classmates and I had learned about it in elementary school.

But the fact that the man who dropped the bomb—the pilot who flew the *Enola Gay* to Japan, who carried out the single most violent act in the history of mankind and thus brought World War II to an end—the fact that he lived quietly in the same town where I had grown up . . . that piece of knowledge came from my father.

It was never stated in an especially dramatic way. My dad would come home from work—from downtown Columbus, in central Ohio—and say: "I was buying some shirts today, and Paul Tibbets was in the next aisle, buying ties."

They never met; my father never said a word to him. I sensed that my father might have been a little reluctant, maybe even a touch embarrassed; he had been a soldier with an infantry division, Tibbets had been a combat pilot, all these years had passed since the war and now here they both were, two all-but-anonymous businessmen in a sedate, landlocked town in a country at peace . . . what was my dad supposed to say? How was he supposed to begin the conversation?

Yet there was always a certain sound in his voice at the dinner table. "Paul Tibbets was in the next aisle buying ties. . . ." The sound in my dad's voice told me—as if I needed reminding—that the story of his life had reached its most indelible and meaningful moments in the years of the war, the years before I was born.

Those dinner-table conversations were long ago, though; they were in the years when my dad was still vital, in good health, in the prime of his adult years, not yet ready to leave the world. I had all but forgotten the conversations—at least the specifics of them, other than the occasional mentions of Tibbets.

Now my dad was dying. We had dinner in his bedroom—he would not, it would turn out, again be able to sit in a chair and eat after this night—and the next morning I told him that I had somewhere to go and that I would be back in a few hours, and I went to find Paul Tibbets. Something told me that it was important.

TWO

It wasn't the first time I had tried. In fact, I had been attempting on and off to talk with Paul Tibbets for more than twenty years.

I had left Columbus to become a newspaperman in Chicago when I was in my early twenties; as I became a reporter, and then a syndicated columnist, I traveled around the world in search of stories, and, as most reporters do, met any number of well-known people as I pursued those stories. As often as not, the people were only too willing to talk; celebrity is embraced by most upon whom it is bestowed, even those who protest that it is a bother. Whether a famous athlete or an ambitious politician or a movie star or a newsmaker just feeling the spotlight's heat for the first time, the people who get a taste of fame often seem to crave it in a way that can fairly be described as addictive. There can never be enough; when the light turns away for even a second or two, some of the most famous men and women in the world seem almost to panic. They need to feel it constantly.

Which is what made me so curious about Paul Tibbets. He had been the central figure in the most momentous event of the Twentieth Century; what he had done changed the world in ways so profound that philosophers and theologians will be discussing and debating it as long as mankind exists. "The man who won the war," of course, is shorthand—no one person accomplished that. But it is shorthand based on fact—Tibbets was the man put in charge of preparing a top-secret military unit to deliver the bomb, he was the person who assembled and trained that unit, and when the time came to do what had never in the history of mankind been done, to fly an atomic bomb over an enemy nation and then drop the bomb on a city below, Tibbets did not delegate. He climbed into the cockpit and flew the bomb to Japan.

But he was seldom spoken about; the war ended in 1945, and by the 1960s his was a name that few people seemed even to know. Part of this was doubtless because of the deep ambivalence many Americans felt about the end of the war. Yes, they were grateful that it had ended, and that the United States and the Allies had won. But the death and devastation from the bomb—the unprecedented human suffering caused by the unleashing of the nuclear fire—was something that people instinctively chose not to celebrate. Hiroshima was not the stuff of holidays.

So I would hear my father talk of seeing Paul Tibbets here and there in Columbus, and when I was a young reporter my journalistic instincts were to try to speak with him, to secure an interview. By this time—by the early 1970s—Tibbets was running a corporate-jet-for-hire service in central Ohio. I wrote him letters, I left messages at his office—not just once, but periodically over the course of two decades I tried. I never received an answer. He didn't decline, he didn't explain, he didn't offer reasons. He simply didn't respond at all. Never. Not a word.

By the autumn of 1998, my father had been dying for several months. It was a word my family avoided—"dying" was not something we said in his presence, or very often in the presence of one another—but we all knew it, and I think he knew it best.

I was covering a court case in Wisconsin, and during a break I called my office in Chicago and the person who gave me the message was as careful as possible in how she told me: "Your mother called and said your father has been taken to the hospital, but she said to make sure to tell you it's nothing to panic about. She said they're just taking a close look at him."

Within days that had changed. My sister, who lived in Nevada, had flown to Columbus to help my mom. My father was home from the hospital, but he was not feeling strong enough to talk on the telephone. Another phone call from my sister: "Daddy wants you boys to come."

That day. Right away.

"I think he wants to say goodbye," my sister said.

My plane sat on the runway at O'Hare in Chicago for hours, its takeoff delayed due to some mechanical trouble or other. My brother was able to get to Ohio more quickly from Colorado than I was from Illinois. No working phones on the plane; no way to get word out, or to find out what was happening in my parents' home.

It was well after midnight when I landed at Port Columbus. I didn't call my parents' house—I didn't want to wake my father if he was asleep, and if the news was very bad, I wanted to hear it in person, not over the phone—so I just got in a cab and gave directions. The lights were all burning, at an hour when they never did.

My mom, my sister, my brother. All awake.

"Go on in and talk to him," my mom said.

Some moments, not a word is required. And my father and I had never talked all that easily anyway. I walked into the bedroom, seeing him smaller than I ever remembered him, gray and all but motionless in bed. My father had always been a man who led with a joke; he could make the soberest moment funny, especially when he needed to deflect matters of gravity.

Not tonight.

"Hello, Bob," he said. "Thanks for coming."

Too direct. Too unlike him.

"You've never seen your old man like this, have you?" he said.

I didn't ask him how he was doing. Having to answer that one was not what he needed this night. *Thanks for coming.* That's how he was doing.

Back in July, just a few months earlier, if you looked closely enough you could see it in his eyes.

He wasn't saying anything out loud about feeling especially ill. He seldom did complain, during all the years that diabetes ruled his life. But at the reunion of our immediate family that we held at my parents' house in July, he would sit off by himself and sort of look into the distance. He was present—but for long spans, it seemed that he was barely there. There is a country song with the lyric: *I can't see a single storm cloud in the sky, but I sure can smell the rain. . . .*

The rain was somewhere behind his eyes. A dozen family members were in Columbus for the reunion, more than could fit into my parents' house, so some of us were staying at a motel next to the airport.

One summer morning, before it was time to go to the house, I noticed something across a two-lane access road that separated Port Columbus from our motel: a modest little museum in a converted hangar, a place with a sign saying that it was the Ohio History of Flight Museum. I walked over to take a look.

I was the only visitor. Three bucks to get in—there were antique planes in the hangar, and airplane engines, and photos of Ohio's relationship with air travel. Which is considerable. The Wright brothers came from Ohio, and John Glenn, and Neil Armstrong—from man's first successful powered venture off the ground and into the sky, to man's first step onto the surface of the moon, Ohio may be the state that has had the most significant influence on flying.

The man who had sold me my ticket was strolling around the empty place. I said to him: "Does Mr. Tibbets come around much?"

"Not that often," the man said. "Once in a while."

I supposed it figured. Paul Tibbets had been thirty years old when he flew the bomb to Japan. Now, if I was doing the calculations in my head correctly, he was eighty-three, the same age as my father. With all the renewed appreciation that the World War II generation was receiving, people were noticing something: The

Americans who fought that war didn't go around telling stories about themselves. It made a certain sense that Tibbets would be a sporadic visitor here at best.

Outside the roadside air museum, it was a warm and beautiful summer morning in central Ohio. Land of the free. . . .

On October 20, my mother's seventy-ninth birthday, I was back in Columbus. She was determined to have her birthday dinner the same place she had eaten virtually every meal for the last two months: in the bedroom she shared with my father. If he couldn't leave to eat, then she wasn't going to either.

We ordered from a deliver-in place. My father, with some effort, had been moved from his bed into a nearby chair, and for about twenty minutes he was able to sit up and join us. He seemed almost ashamed of his halting, shaky motions; he had always been a physically strong man, and the fact that it was now a task for him to move a spoon from the plate to his mouth was something he was more than aware we were noticing.

My mother told him that his friend Bill Ehrman, who lived in Hawaii, had called that day to ask how he was doing. My dad smiled at that; Ehrman was a man with whom he had served in the war, and I never heard Ehrman's name mentioned without seeing a look of pleasure on my father's face. His friends from the war years seemed to occupy a place in his life that no other people did.

After dinner he fell asleep immediately. The meal had been the last time I would see him outside his bed.

I went into the room in my parents' house where they displayed the only visible artifact from World War II: an oil painting of my dad as a young soldier, painted, or so I had always been told, by a fellow American soldier in Italy who enjoyed doing portraits of his comrades. Growing up, when I had looked at the painting of my father, he had seemed so seasoned, so experienced. Now, looking at the portrait, I realized that he had been in his twenties when it was painted. On this night—as I looked at the portrait, with him sleeping not so many feet away—I was fifty-one. The man in uniform in the painting still seemed older than I was.

It was the next morning that I went to see Tibbets.

I had written a column during the summer in which I mentioned my visit to the Ohio air museum. Soon after, I had received a call from a man named Gerry Newhouse, who said he was a friend of Tibbets. Someone in Texas had sent Newhouse a copy of the column from a paper down there, and Newhouse had showed it to Tibbets.

"He liked what you said about the World War II generation not going around bragging about themselves," Newhouse said.

I said that I had been trying to get a chance to meet Tibbets for the last twenty years.

"Well, I think he'd be happy to say hello to you," Newhouse said. "Do you ever get to Columbus these days?"

I said my dad hadn't been doing so well. I said I had a feeling that I'd be in town quite a bit.

When I was a teenager, all of my friends lived in houses, except for one: a boy named Allen Schulman, whose family lived in the only high-rise apartment building in Columbus at that time, a place called the Park Towers. It was big-time, for central Ohio; it actually had a doorman—a dapper young fellow by the name of Jesse Harrell. Jesse knew about everything we did, especially everything we did wrong.

Now, more than thirty years later, I arrived at the front door of the Park Towers. Gerry Newhouse had an office on the first floor; he and Tibbets were going to have lunch together that day, and they were going to meet at Newhouse's office before going to the restaurant. I had called Newhouse to say I was in town, and he had said to drop by.

At the front door was Jesse. I knew him before he knew me. Thirty years and more at that front door; the dapper young man was now sixty. "You ever see your friend Allen?" he said, and when I said that yes, sometimes I did, Jesse said, "He never comes back here. There's not a person in this building who was here when you all were kids."

He told me where Newhouse's office was, and I went back and introduced myself, and in a few minutes Tibbets arrived.

I'm not sure what I expected. He was a compact man with a full head of white hair, wearing a plaid shirt and well-used slacks. Hearing aids were in both of his ears; I sensed immediately that I would have to lean close to him in order to be heard. He could have been any of a thousand men in their eighties in the middle of Ohio. You wouldn't know him in a line at the grocery store.

I told him how pleased I was to meet him—and how long I had wanted to get the chance.

His answer offered a glimpse of the reasons behind his reticence.

"I've heard rumors about myself over the years," he said. "I've heard rumors that I had gone crazy, or that I was dead."

Evidently that is what people had assumed: that the man responsible for all that death must inevitably have gone out of his mind.

I didn't know where to take this—I didn't know whether it was an indication that he wasn't in the mood for conversation—so we just made some small talk for a short while, about Ohio and the Park Towers and the weather on the streets outside, and I told Tibbets that I knew he and his friend had lunch plans, and that I didn't want to hold them up.

"That's all right," Tibbets said. "I'm not that hungry yet. We can talk some."

THREE

"Do people know my name?" Tibbets asked.

He was repeating the question I had just asked him.

A soft, private look crossed his face.

"They don't need to know my name," he said.

The deed he had carried out was one of the most famous the world has ever known; it will be talked about in terms of fear and awe forever. He, though, even here in the town where he lived, was not as famous as the local television weatherman.

"People knowing my name isn't important at all," he said. "It's more important—it was more important then, and it's more important now—that they know the name of my airplane. And that they understand the history of what happened.

"Although sometimes I think that no one really understands the history."

And so we started to talk. Neither of us knew it that day, but it would be the first of many conversations—about the war, about the men and women who lived through it, about their lives, and the lives of their sons and daughters: the lives of those of us who came after them, who inherited the world that they saved for us.

As I sat with Tibbets that first day—thinking of my father in his bed just a few miles away—it occurred to me that Eisenhower was dead, Patton was dead, Marshall was dead, MacArthur was dead. And here was Tibbets, telling me in the first person the story of how the great and terrible war came to an end.

On this day—the day I met Tibbets—all of his stories were war stories. That would change; gradually the stories would expand in context, would begin to explain to me certain things not just about this man, but about the generation of men and women who are leaving us now every day. It is a wrenching thing, to watch them go. As the men and women of the World War II generation die, it is for their children the most intensely personal experience imaginable—and at the same time a sweeping and historic one, being witnessed by tens of millions of sons and daughters, sons and daughters who feel helpless to stop the inevitable.

For me, as my father, day by day, slipped away, the overwhelming feeling was that a safety net was being removed—a safety net that had been there since the day I was born, a safety net I was often blithely unaware of. That's what the best safety nets do—they allow you to forget they're there. No generation has ever given its children a sturdier and more reliable safety net than the one our parents' generation gave to us.

The common experience that wove the net was their war. And as I began to listen to Tibbets—to hear his stories, later to question him about the America that preceded and followed the war from which his stories came—I realized anew that so many of us only now, only at the very end, are beginning to truly know our fathers and mothers. It was as if constructing that safety net for their children was their full-time job, and that finally, as they leave us, we are beginning to understand the forces that made them the way they were.

Tibbets began to speak, and as I listened I thought I could hear a rustle of something behind the words—I thought I could hear the whisper of a generation saying goodbye to its children.

* * *

When I was very young, my father told me that he wanted me to come out to a local air base with him.

We went; by this time the war had been over for seven or eight years, he was not a soldier in uniform but a businessman in a suit of clothing. Which in a way, in the 1950s, made his garments just as uniform as what he had worn in the Army; he had automatically melded into the sea of men in suits who worked in the offices of the post-war United States.

That day, or so I recall, we went out to the air base, where it was stiflingly hot. The occasion was the unveiling of some sort of new fighter plane. A military honor guard stood surrounding the plane, which was covered in cloth prior to the unveiling. The young military men were perspiring heavily, unprotected from the sun.

There were some speeches from military officers, and some photo-taking with local elected officials, and on one side of the rope the honor guard stood at full attention, while on the other side those of us in the audience stood watching. Almost certainly the majority of the audience members were people very much like my father—men who had come back from World War II, who were civilians now, but who felt somehow obliged to be here to watch this ceremony. The introduction of a new plane that would protect America, and protect our hometown.

Suddenly, with no warning, one of the young soldiers who had been standing at attention fell face-first onto the hard runway. There had been no sign that he was about to lose consciousness; he had not swayed or called out for help. He just went straight down, his face making a sickening sound as it hit the cement.

"He remained at attention the whole time," I remember my father saying, with an admiring tone in his voice.

I recall being frightened for the young soldier; I recall thinking that he was dead. Only after medics had revived him and helped him to his feet, only after I could see for myself that he had fainted and was going to be all right, was I able to take my eyes off him.

But I can still see him falling. And I can still hear my father's voice, with something like pride in it, and a sense of identification: The soldier had remained at attention.

As Paul Tibbets began to tell me his story, I sat as close to him as I could. It became evident within minutes that when I wanted to ask him a question, I would have to speak loudly, and with care about pronunciation. His hearing—there was no mistaking this—was all but gone. So I looked him in the eyes, and listened to every word, and did my best to make sure he didn't have to ask me to repeat my own words twice.

"Sometimes I think that no one really understands. . . ." he said.

And so it began.

FOUR

The airplane, he said, had been named in honor of his mother.

"She's the one who said it was all right for me to fly," he said. "My father didn't. He hated airplanes, and he didn't want me to go near one. In my father's mind, I was supposed to be a doctor. He sort of waved me off, and when he understood that I really wanted to be a flier, he said, 'If you want to kill yourself, go ahead.' But my mother understood. She encouraged me."

Thus, when he was preparing for the flight that would change the history of the world, the name he chose for the airplane—the name that was painted on the nose—was her name: his mother's first and middle names.

"I thought it was a good name for the plane, because it was a name no one had ever heard before," he said. "I could be pretty sure that no other B-29 would be named *Enola Gay.*"

Some people, more than half a century later, still are appalled by what his government asked him to do. Some people are deeply proud and grateful. Others are ambivalent and, all these years later, confused. Tibbets himself is the only one who knows the whole story—and he has never talked much about it. His life—like the lives of so many of the men who served in the same war, and who unlike him will never be noticed by history—has been devoid of much publicity seeking or self-promotion.

Unlike the other men, though—men like my father, men whose names did not make the newspaper during their war—

Tibbets was, indeed, asked to do something monumental. I told him that I was interested in the specifics of it—the things that preceded the politics and the controversy: the details. When the 9,700-pound bomb dropped out of the belly of his plane and began its descent onto the city of Hiroshima, what did the plane do—how did the B-29 react to all that weight suddenly being freed?

"The seat slapped me on the ass," Tibbets said.

A blunt and purposely inelegant phrase—and a rather mild one to describe what happened at that particular moment in the story of mankind.

"We'd been all through it," he said. "We knew that if everything went as planned, the bomb would explode forty-three seconds after we released it from the plane.

"In order to get away from there quickly enough that we would not be directly over the blast, I had to make a diving turn to the right, away from the area at an angle of 160 degrees. We were flying with quite a center of gravity—when you drop something that weighs almost 10,000 pounds out of your airplane in an instant, you know there's going to be an effect of the plane bucking up when the plane gets that much lighter all of a sudden.

"So my hand was on the yoke and my feet were on the rudders, and our bombardier, Tom Ferebee, released the bomb over the bridge in Hiroshima that we had selected as the target. The seat slapped me on the ass, and I was putting the plane into that severe diving right turn so that we could get away from the bomb by the time it exploded. . . ."

He was careful and precise as he said the words. It's not that the tone of his voice was without animation, and certainly not that it was devoid of feeling; what struck me was just that the voice of history does not have to sound historic, that history has usually been built by people with voices that sound not so much different from your neighbor's, or your eye doctor's. The words that Tibbets was saying to me would more appropriately have been intoned by Edward R. Murrow, or by George C. Scott in a widescreen war movie. The reality was that the words had the matter-of-fact quality of something out of any American barber shop.

I asked how he—out of all the men in the service—had been the one selected to do this. Not just to fly the atomic bomb to Japan, but to assemble the whole operation. Because that is what happened—General Uzal G. Ent had asked Tibbets, who was at the time only twenty-nine years old, a lieutenant colonel, to start a new unit from nothing. He had been given full responsibility for putting together the mission, with orders to be prepared to fly when the bomb was deemed ready to function the way it was designed.

"Why was I chosen to be the one to do this?" Tibbets said. "I don't know. I was told, 'This is your job,' and I saluted and said 'Yes, sir,' and that was it.

"I think I had a reputation in the Army Air Corps as an innovative individual. The only airplane capable of carrying that bomb to Japan was the B-29, and I knew the B-29 better than anyone else in the service.

"There wasn't much of an explanation when I was given the job. In those days, they didn't explain. You were given a job to do, and you didn't question it. My job was to organize and train a unit capable of dropping atomic weapons, a unit to be self-supporting in all regards."

He assembled an 1,800-man force—the 509th Composite Group—at a remote site in Wendover, Utah, operating in the strictest secrecy. The men on the base did not know why they were there—did not know the exact nature of their mission. And then, in August of 1945, when the bomb was ready, Tibbets and his eleven crewmen took off from the island of Tinian in the Pacific Ocean and flew toward Japan.

"It had been explained to me that the bomb would have the power of twenty thousand tons of TNT," Tibbets said. "Who could envision what that meant? Twenty thousand tons? I knew that it was going to be a big, big bang, but I couldn't think much beyond that.

"We were all pretty quiet on the flight to Hiroshima. It took about six hours. The T-shaped bridge came into view just like it was supposed to, and we dropped the bomb, and I went into that turn. . . .

"I was prepared for the power, but not for the devastation. From a B-29 you really can't see down below you from the pilot's seat at the moment the bomb is dropping. The tailgunner saw the whole show, but I didn't see it until we were flying back over it.

"I looked at that city—and there was no city, there was nothing but the fringes of where the city used to be. There had been a city when we were making our approach, but now there was no humanity there. It was just something that had been . . . scorched. That word doesn't seem sufficient to describe what had just happened, but that's the only word I have. I could never have imagined anything being scorched like that city was scorched."

No one really knows the exact number of people who died in the instant the bomb—creating a peak temperature calculated to be more than a half-million degrees Fahrenheit—exploded; some estimate 100,000, some say the number of dead was probably much higher. With the mushroom cloud billowing above Japan and shock waves rocking his plane and the world having no idea what had just taken place, Tibbets was already flying the *Enola Gay* back toward his island air base.

"I had a pretty good idea that the war was over," he said. "I could not imagine how any rational leader would choose to continue to fight us knowing that we had this kind of weapon in our possession. I have two memories of the flight back:

"The memory of being so tired.

"And of believing that the war was finally over."

When I had left my parents' house to meet Tibbets, I had made myself a bet.

He had said he would be at the Park Towers at 11:30 A.M. I

made sure I was there by 11:15. I had a reason—the bet I had made myself.

I turned out to be right.

He didn't walk in at 11:29. He didn't walk in at 11:31.

He walked in at 11:30.

I knew he would. When Tibbets and his crew had flown the *Enola Gay* to Hiroshima, the plan called for the bomb to be released at 8:15 A.M. Hiroshima time.

There was no satellite navigation back then, no computers to guide the way. It was a six-hour, nearly 2,000-mile trip from the American air base on Tinian Island to Hiroshima. Tibbets and his crew made the trip by checking their watches and their flight plan.

He flew over the T-shaped bridge in Hiroshima and dropped the bomb at 8:15 A.M. plus seventeen seconds.

So I'd had a feeling that 11:30 it would be—and 11:30 it was. I found myself thinking about my dad, back in his bed, and about how he would have been just as prompt to keep an appointment—details mattered to him, details, it sometimes seemed, were everything to him. In a don't-sweat-the-small-stuff era, my father had always been a man who sweated the small stuff. And now I was sitting with the ultimate sweat-the-small-stuff aviator—the man who, on his 2,000-mile trip to try to end the war, had been late by all of seventeen seconds.

"We were off," Tibbets said to me now. "We weren't perfect."

I asked him about his precision.

"I think most people in the generation I come from are like me," he said. "I grew up being taught that there's only one way to do things—the right way."

But the task he had been asked to do by the United States government—the task of dropping the atomic bomb—yes, he had carried out that task virtually flawlessly, yet the ramifications of the request that had been made of him, the ramifications not only for the story of mankind, but for one man—for him, for Tibbets—personally . . .

"People thought that I should be weeping," he said. "Weeping for the rest of my life. They don't understand.

"I'll meet people, and when they find out who I am—when they find out that I'm the one who flew the *Enola Gay* to Hiroshima so that we could drop the bomb—sometimes they ask me: 'Why didn't you just tell them that you didn't want to do it?'

"That's when I really know that they don't understand. It's usually younger people who say that to me. Because in those days—during World War II—you didn't tell your superiors that you didn't want to do something. That's reason number one.

"Reason number two is more important. The reason I didn't tell them that I didn't want to do it is that I *wanted* to do it."

He told me that he had never lost a night's sleep in all the years since his crew dropped the bomb—"I sleep just fine"—and if anything upsets him, it is that some people still consider the use of the atomic bomb as an unnecessarily barbaric act.

"The biggest misconception is that the war was going to end soon anyway," he said. "That what we did was not necessary.

"Do you have any idea how many American lives would have been lost had we launched a ground invasion of Japan, instead of dropping the bomb? And how many Japanese lives? I sleep so well because I know how many people got to live full lives because of what we did."

At the time, though—on the flight to Japan—was he full of anger? Did his fury at what the war had done fill him with the fuel of vengeance and vindictiveness en route to his assigned target?

No, he said; he had felt no anger at all as he flew the B-29 toward Japan.

"My mother was a very calm, pacific individual, and I learned from her to be the same way. You get a lot damn further by being calm when you're doing a job. Our crew did not do the bombing in anger. We did it because we were determined to stop the killing. I would have done anything to get to Japan and stop the killing."

I asked if he had returned to Hiroshima in the years since the end of the war.

"I have no interest in doing that," he said. "Why should I go back? I've been there. I didn't go there as a sightseer. There are other places in the world to go and visit. I think it would be wrong for me to go back."

He said that he was pleased by how well Japan has done for itself in the years since 1945: "The people aren't to blame for what their government did during the war." When I brought up the almost unimaginable number of people who were killed by the bomb he and his crew dropped that day, his voice stayed even and unagitated, but his eyes fastened on mine and did not look away as he spoke.

"Please try to understand this," Tibbets said. "It's not an easy thing to hear, but please listen. There is no morality in warfare. You kill children. You kill women. You kill old men. You don't seek them out, but they die. That's what happens in war.

"Think about this: What would have happened if they had come over here? Take Detroit, for instance—if they had attacked Detroit, do you think they would have made sure that the workers in the industrial plants were in one place, and that the women and children were in another place? No, they would not have. This was World War II."

And if the atomic bomb had been ready to use a little earlier—before Germany was out of the war?

"If I would have been asked to do it, I would have done it in a second," Tibbets said. "You're damn right—if the Germans had not surrendered, I would have flown the bomb over there. I would have taken some satisfaction in that—because they shot me up."

He was referring to the many combat raids he flew over Europe before being assigned the Hiroshima mission. As he told me about all of this, I somehow had an unexpected thought about all the presidents of the United States who routinely invite well-known actors, popular singers, championship football and basketball teams to the White House for congratulatory get-togethers in commemoration of their victories. What about Tibbets? Did he ever, as he grows older, get invited to come to the White House for dinners or ceremonies?

"I went as a tourist one time, because my wife wanted to go," he said. "I stood in line with the other tour groups, just like anyone else. No one knew who I was."

There was one exception, he said. Right after the war, Harry Truman invited him to stop by.

"We met in an irregular-shaped room," Tibbets said. "I suppose it was the Oval Office. It was short and quick. He offered me a cup of coffee.

"Truman asked me if anyone was giving me a hard time—saying unpleasant things to me because of the bomb.

"I said, 'Oh, once in a while.'

"Truman said, 'You tell them that if they have anything to say, they should call me.

" 'I'm the one who sent you.' "

It had all been done in such utter secrecy—the development of the bomb even as the war in Europe slogged agonizingly on, the assembling of Tibbets' unit on the salt flats in Utah, the preparation on the island of Tinian for the raid itself—that I found myself thinking about whether something like this could be pulled off today: a mission of this staggering importance, planned and carried out in total silence.

"Not a chance in the world," Tibbets said.

I asked him what made him so certain of that.

"There's no chance a secret like that could be kept today," he said. "It would get out—it would get out in the name of freedom of information. The reason we were able to do it is that the mission was considered a matter of life-or-death secrecy. It wouldn't work in today's world."

And what would have happened if Tibbets had failed—if, with the people of the world ignorant of what was taking place, he and his crew had taken off for Japan and never made it to the target? What did he think would have become of him then?

"If I had failed?" he said. "I would have been court-martialed and in prison. Nobody knew I existed—no one knew our unit existed."

I could tell he knew I thought he was exaggerating—that I thought he would not have been sent to prison had the mission somehow gone wrong.

That's when he told me about Don Young—the flight surgeon who, in the predawn blackness of August 6, 1945, handed Tibbets a small cardboard box containing twelve cyanide capsules.

"One for each member of the flight team," Tibbets said. "In case we had to make an emergency landing, and were on the verge of being captured."

That didn't happen, of course; they didn't fail, and they weren't captured, and within days of the Hiroshima bombing a second atomic bomb was dropped on Nagasaki, and the long war was over. And now, here in central Ohio, Tibbets could go, as I was told he often did, to have his lunch at the Bob Evans restaurant on East Main Street—the same Bob Evans where my father would go at least once a week until he got so sick—and the people in the restaurant, almost all of whom were younger than he, would walk past his booth without giving him a glance, as if failing to consider that this man in his eighties could possibly have any connection with their own lives.

"I get called 'old man' all the time," he said. "It's true, I suppose. Physically, I've slowed down quite a bit."

I asked him if there were days when the United States—whose uniform he wore, whose freedom he did so much to preserve—sometimes began to feel like a place he hardly recognizes.

"It's really not the same country, in many ways," he said. "Talk to a bunch of kids in school—try to teach them something. There are times when you get the impression that they don't like to pay attention to anyone or anything but themselves. I know I sound like an old person when I say this, but there is a certain price to be paid—a certain peril—that comes with the lack of being raised in a disciplined environment."

It could have been my father talking—the words were of the sort he often spoke, the sentiments could have been his. I told that to Tibbets, and he said:

"I cannot communicate with people who are less than sixty years old. It's as if all of us in this country know the same words, but we don't use the words the same way. We speak different languages."

There were even times, he said, when he began to half-believe that he and his contemporaries may have more in common with the Japanese soldiers, fliers and sailors they fought against than with some of their current-day American countrymen.

"Those of us on the American side were over there risking our butts to meet the obligations that were set forth by the leaders of our country," he said. "The other side was doing the same thing. There's a certain common thread there."

He said he didn't think there would be another day like the one when he was asked to do what he did—to fly an atomic bomb somewhere and drop it on a city below. "No one can afford to do it," he said. And the very nature of global politics, and of global conflict, had changed.

But if such a day were to come? And if someone were to turn back the clock that rules his body?

He said he would be first in line to fight one more time for his country.

"If you could fix me up so that I could do the same things in an airplane now that I could do in 1945?" he said.

"If you could do that, and this country was in trouble, I would jump in there to beat hell."

FIVE

Before I left Tibbets that day, I told him the story: the story of how I had first heard that he lived in the same town where I grew up, the story of my dad coming home from buying clothes for the office and saying that he had seen Paul Tibbets in the same store.

And I told him how poorly my dad was doing. I said I'd be going back to his house, and that I planned to tell my dad where I had spent the morning.

"Even though you were so important in the war and he wasn't. . . ." I began.

"Don't say that," Tibbets said.

"I don't mean it in a bad way," I said. "I just mean that as much as the Army meant to him, no one outside of his friends and his family really ever knew he was there."

"That was the whole point," Tibbets said. "That's what being in the Army meant."

"But everyone knew about you," I said.

"That doesn't matter," Tibbets said. "Who knew about who doesn't matter."

I said goodbye to him, and thanked him for the visit. He asked me what my father's rank had been, and I said that when he left the Army after the war had ended he had been an infantry major.

He took out a pen and signed something and handed it to me. "Give this to your dad when you get back to his house," Tibbets said.

I put it in my briefcase and thanked him again, and it wasn't until I was in the cab that I looked at it.

To Major Greene, a World War II warrior, with best wishes from Brig. Gen. Paul Tibbets, USAF (Ret.)

I got back to my parents' house; he was still in bed, just as I had left him. I showed the signature to my mother, who carried it over to the bed and handed it to him.

He moved it toward his face and looked at it. First I saw the smile. Then the glistening, the shining in his brown eyes.

One of my first memories of my father—one of my first memories of asking him for something—had to do with a song.

"Sing 'Army now.' "

That's what my mother tells me I said—she said that when I was two or three years old, I would beg my father to sing that song for me.

You're in the Army now, you're not behind a plow. . . .

Apparently that was his ritual, when he would come home from work. My mom and I would be waiting, and in his business suit he would drive up to the house, and—at my urging—he would sing to me from the song. "You're in the Army now"—every soldier knew the song, every civilian, it was one of the last remnants of an era when not only did composers write songs about life in the military, but the songs became universally recognized.

So—I am told—"Sing 'Army now' " was my every-evening request. Number One on my hit parade—I couldn't get enough of it.

There is a photograph—a snapshot—that, according to the penciled notation on the back, was taken in 1949. That means that I was two; that means that my father was thirty-four. We had the same names; he was Robert B. Greene Sr., I am Robert B. Greene Jr. Both of us Bob Greene. He had returned to America, to Ohio, at the end of the war, less than five years before the picture was taken. In the photo he is in a suit and tie, wearing a fedora, a businessman supporting his family in a nation newly at peace. In the photo I am so small that I am barely visible. Bundled up against the cold, my face tiny, I am standing in front of my dad. We are posing by the garage of our home.

He's reaching down toward me, his hands just making it to the top of my head. He's smiling in the cold. Two years before, I hadn't been born; four years before, he was in Italy, in Africa, in uniform. So much motion for him, so quickly; so many changes.

Who knew about who doesn't matter. That's what Tibbets had said. All those soldiers, coming home to the country they had saved, and all of a sudden the country, and they, were on to the next page, the next chapter, moving forward, or trying to. What they had done in the war was yesterday. All those men. They had grown up in this country, and then gone away, and then they had been told that it was time to come home and start being someone new.

The hat on his head, the smile on his face, the tie around his neck. His son, in the picture, pressed against his knees. "Sing 'Army now,' " I would ask. And the businessman, home from a day at work, would comply.

You'll never get rich, by digging a ditch. . . .

There are shadows behind us in the picture, but from the front we are washed in winter sunshine.

That was before the walls went up. I suppose they always do—the walls between fathers and sons, the walls that separate one generation from the next. Fact is, from the time I was old enough to have any confidence in myself, I made it almost a point of pride never to ask my father for anything. Money, advice, perspective—I seemed to fear that it would be a sign of weakness to say that I needed him.

So I didn't. *Sing "Army now."* Who was that child who so unguardedly asked his dad to sing him that song every night? And who was the man who was only too pleased, even excited, to sing it to his son?

As he lay dying, I thought about that. Who was the man? *Who knew about who doesn't matter.* But now it did. I understood what Tibbets meant: Who knew about who didn't matter, they were all in the war, they were all doing the jobs they had been asked to do, they weren't doing it to become celebrated. They were doing it because nothing, at that point in the world's history, was more important.

Now, though, it did matter. The man dying in his bed, the man in the snapshot, home from the war, standing with his son—standing with me—who was he? He was fading in and out of lucidity as he died; who was this man, who had he been?

And then I remembered the tapes.

He and my mother had given us their life stories some seven or eight years before. My mom had written hers; my dad, who didn't like to write, had talked his into a tape recorder. They were gifts to my sister, my brother and me.

I had read my mom's story, had listened to my dad's, but I must confess that they didn't register quite so strongly at the time—my mother and father were both in good health then, they were both people I saw and spoke with all the time, and the life stories, while a wonderful keepsake, did not contain all that much urgency.

Now, though—my father's voice wispy and confused, his ability to maintain a cohesive narrative getting weaker by the day—I dug up the tapes.

There was his voice, strong and full. Telling the story of a life.

I was born on March 7, 1915, in Akron, Ohio. . . . Dad's parents were from very moderate circumstances, and from his very early days,

Dad had to work. As a matter of fact, he sold newspapers on the streets of Akron. . . .

He was more or less self-educated; he did not go to college, but he did study law in a very prominent law office by the name of Vorys. He got his diploma by taking the Ohio State Bar exam and passing it with flying colors, which was quite an accomplishment for a poor boy with only a high school education.

I believe the earliest thing I remember was when our house on Casterton Avenue was being built, and we lived in the Portage Hotel. I also can think of the drugstore, which was off the main lobby in that hotel, and the wonderful hot chocolate they served, and whenever I smell hot chocolate I think of the treats we used to have going down to that drugstore and getting a cup of that steaming good stuff. I believe I was four or four and a half years old.

Another thing I can remember very clearly was looking out of the window in our room or rooms, it was in the middle of the night and the fire alarm rang. Not in the hotel, but out on the corner, and down East Market Street dashed a steam fire engine drawn by about six horses, it was spitting smoke and fire and clanging bells and that was a very, very thrilling moment for me. I can see those horses coming around the corner now, those sparks coming off their hooves as they hit the pavement. . . .

Sometimes I think no one really understands," Tibbets had said. He had been talking about himself—about the mission he had been asked to carry out for his country, about the ferocious storm of emotions that still, fifty years later, the mere mention of his mission tripped.

My father lay sleeping. My mother—I could see her across the bedroom—had reclined on the other bed, and now she had drifted off too. I sat in the room, and I looked at both of their faces.

The need to understand—the duty to understand—can come

to you late. *Who knew about who doesn't matter.* Maybe not back then—maybe not when everyone was young. But whether you're a soldier the world never heard of, or the man who won the war, it matters in the end. In a way, it's all that does matter.

My father's breath and my mother's breath were the only sounds in the room.

SIX

The sole trip out of Columbus that my father and I ever took together—just the two of us—was when I was seventeen, and it was time for me to look at colleges. I had decided that I wanted to go to Northwestern University, if I could get in—it was said to have a good program in journalism—so one spring day in 1964 my dad and I got on a TWA plane at Port Columbus and flew to O'Hare International Airport in Chicago.

He had been making trips to Chicago all during his business career—not constantly, but enough that we in the family always assumed, without really thinking about it, that he knew the ropes, that Chicago was familiar territory to him—so I was a little surprised, when we got there, to sense that he was noticeably nervous.

This wasn't Ohio. This was big, intimidating, outsized. He rented a car at O'Hare, and we drove downtown—I could tell that the expressway traffic was much more daunting than what he was accustomed to in Columbus, he stared straight ahead as he drove and kept both hands on the steering wheel and occasionally registered startled disapproval as some Chicago driver would cut in front of him or speed past—and he didn't talk much. We got to a hotel called the Oxford House, on Wabash Avenue, and rode the elevator to our room and unpacked our bags.

It was so odd—his clothes in the drawers on one side of the dresser, my clothes on the other side, each of us sitting on one of the two beds, with no sounds of our family: no voices of my mother, my sister, my brother. He said that it was time to go down to dinner, so we ate in the hotel restaurant, and when we were finished it was still too early to turn in. He asked me if I would like to go to a movie.

We walked into the Loop—such an overpowering sensation, walking with my father through that burly, thick downtown, under elevated-train tracks and up crowded-even-at-night streets with famous names—State, Randolph, Washington—two guys from Ohio, one forty-nine, one seventeen, both feeling small and out of place, neither talking about it—and the lights from the marquees of all the movie theaters colored the night, and my father chose a marquee that was advertising *Seven Days in May.*

It was a military movie—actually, about a plot involving a military takeover of the United States—and many of the main characters were in Army uniforms, working at military installations. My father, sitting next to me in the theater in a coat and tie, almost twenty years removed from the military by this time, stared intently at the screen. When the movie was over we walked the famous streets again, back to the Oxford House. On the corners were newspaper boxes—all four Chicago dailies: the *Tribune,* the *Sun-Times,* the *Daily News,* the *American.*

That was quite a sight in itself—four newspapers, *four,* serving one town. To me it was almost intoxicating: the idea of a city with all that news, of there being so much news and so many people that four papers could exist and compete and, presumably, thrive. The main headline on each of the four papers on that night in 1964 said essentially the same thing, which was some variation of: MACARTHUR NEAR DEATH.

It caught my father's eye; we were walking past the news boxes, and he saw those big headlines, and he said, in a tone of soft surprise, as if speaking of an old friend, "Look at that. MacArthur's dying." I had only the vaguest idea of who General Douglas MacArthur was—a figure from the war, an eminent soldier—but I could not have told you much more than that. My dad bought a paper, and he started to read it as we stood on the sidewalk, and we went back into the hotel and up to our room and we got into our beds for the night.

He read his paper. He kept looking at the photo of MacArthur on the front page, and then he told me that we had to get up early in the morning to go up to Evanston and see Northwestern. He turned the lights off, and although he fell asleep right away, and started snoring, I had trouble sleeping. The Chicago street noise from down below was wafting up to our windows, I had never had to try to go to sleep with big-city traffic in my ears, and with my dad lost to the world in the next bed I was far away from almost everything I was used to. I looked over at him in his pajamas, and at the newspaper on the nightstand with the big black-and-white photo of the dying soldier, and it was a long time before I finally drifted off.

Now more than thirty years had passed. Now my father was the one who was dying, older than old should ever seem as he lay in that bedroom of our home in Columbus, and for him of course there would be no headlines as he faced death; no one outside our family was even aware. Not even my parents' closest friends, really; he and my mother had decided not to tell them just how bad it was.

I would look at him in his bed during those last months, and on some of the longest days and nights of his dying it would be hard to remember that he was ever young, that he was ever full of life and health and his special spark. But there were those tapes I had found—there were those stories, in his own voice, stories of another time.

So jarring—the sight of him asleep and dying, and, later, when I was alone with the tapes in a room with the door closed, his voice:

. . . I remember my first two-wheeler bicycle . . . It was brown and it was not very fashionable, and I know that I was terribly disappointed that I didn't get the popular bike, which was called the America.

For a later birthday I did finally receive my America, which made me very proud. I remember that a fellow by the name of Bob McLaugh-

lin wanted to ride my bicycle, and he said he would let me ride on the handlebars. So I let him drive me around, and by mistake my foot caught in the front wheel of the bicycle and broke some of the spokes. Well, I was scared stiff. I was afraid to tell my mother and father, and of course Bob McLaughlin would never tell them, but he lived way out on Portage Path. But I finally, I guess after a week or so, confessed this terrible sin of first letting somebody ride my bike, and secondly riding on the handlebars and thirdly causing damage to this beautiful thing.

To my great surprise, I didn't get hell. My mother and father simply had the front wheel fixed, and then off I went, never again to let anybody ride this bike. . . .

I would listen to my father's words on those tapes, talking about a boy I never knew—talking about himself. And meanwhile, as he lay dying and we saw him become terribly, heartbreakingly disoriented, there were times when entire days would go by when he did not say a single sentence that, in the world of the living, could be judged as making coherent sense.

On the last day I saw my father alive, my mother had a question for me.

"Have you said goodbye to him?" she asked.

She meant the real goodbye—the one that was going to have to last forever.

In those final months, my brother, my sister and I had been coming to Columbus, spelling each other as we sat with our parents. None of us could be there full-time, yet we knew that he wasn't going to get better—it wasn't a question of if the end was coming, but of when. So each time one of us left, we didn't know whether it was going to be the last time.

"Have you said goodbye to him?"

I hadn't, really; I had sat in the room with him, and listened as he talked, and when his disorientation was at its worst I had tried not to let him know just how far, in his dying, he had wandered from the person he used to be. There were certain hours—I think of one especially awful afternoon, when in an attempt to help him complete his bathroom functions, the four of us, my brother, my sister, my mother and I, had lifted him from the bed, and in the middle of this he had seemed to lose consciousness. . . .

I think of that now, and of how proud and self-sufficient he had always been, how confident of his strength, and it seems to me that we, all of us, were saying goodbye day after day, week after week, in ways more profound than words could convey. That by being there, by seeing him this way and looking his dying full in the face, we were saying the most complete and loving goodbye a family could possibly say.

But my mother meant something else. She meant: Have you sat next to him and told him what you think of him and let him know that this may be the last conversation the two of you ever have?

"I've been saying goodbye in my own way," I told her. She knew full well that my father and I were never any good at talking to each other about anything serious; I'm not proud of that and I'm not ashamed of it, it's just the way the two of us were, and I have a suspicion that we were far from the only fathers and sons in this world who were or are that way.

"Debby and Timmy have said goodbye," my mother said.

I knew that they had; I knew they had sat in the room with him and had done their best to have conversations that summed everything up. Whether he was comprehending what they said—and whether he remembered it even five minutes later—I am not certain.

"Go on in and say goodbye," my mother said.

I'd be leaving for the airport in half an hour. I went into the bedroom; outside those windows the trees had been deep green and full of leaves in the summer, when he had taken to his bed with this final illness, and during the months of his dying they had changed to the brown and orange trees of autumn, and now to the black bare branches of winter, all in the time he had been in the bed.

I looked at him and I knew he didn't want to be here for another spring.

We just sat. The door was closed, and no one else knew what was going on, and he clearly was in no mood for words and neither was I. I sat next to the bed and held his hand, and when he motioned that he was thirsty I held a glass of water to his lips, and there was ice on those branches outside the windows and I knew that this was the right way to do it, and I think he knew, too.

"You have to get on your airplane?" he said after a while.

"I do," I said.

I stood up and looked at him and I said, "I'll see you later."

He sort of smiled.

"You will?" he said.

"Of course," I said. "We'll be seeing each other."

He smiled again. He knew that I didn't mean in this world.

"That's good," he said. "I'll see you later, too."

My mother and sister were with him when he died. It happened on a Friday night in December; he fell asleep and he didn't wake up, and the after-midnight calls came to my brother and me. We were on the first planes we could get. The funeral was on a Monday.

During the months of his dying, I had been making notes about him—about his path toward death, and about the life he had lived, but mostly as I wrote things down I saw that they were questions. The world in which he had lived—the world that had existed prior to my birth—who had he been then, in that world? All of us know our parents as just that—as our mothers and fathers—but before we were born, they were someone else. Before they defined themselves as our parents, they were men and women whose universes had nothing at all to do with us.

And in my father's universe—the one closest to his soul—the central event, always, was the war in which he served. I sat at the funeral, looking at the casket, and I thought about the person he had been before I was even the remotest thought in his imagination.

I had found another passage on that tape he had made; it came early in his story, he was talking about a new elementary school in Akron that had been built when he was a young boy, and how when he was in the third grade all the students had been moved to that school—King School, it was called—and how handsome and sparkling it was in comparison to the forbidding, Gothic schoolhouse where they had gone before.

. . . One thing that I vividly remember about King School is that at the beginning of the school year we went to class despite the fact that the grounds were not completed as yet.

And in those days they didn't have bulldozers or any other backhoe type of heavy machinery to clear the ground. They had horses pulling great shovels. Well, one particular day, evidently the day was very hot, a poor horse died in harness and they let that poor horse stay in the schoolyard for days until it bloated up like a balloon. And I can still see that dead horse looking like it was ready to burst. Thankfully, they hauled it away one day, I guess to some burial place, long past due.

We must remember that this was in the early Twenties, shortly after the end of World War I. Even as a kid, I was fascinated with the war, and I always used to fantasize that I would be a soldier and I would return to Akron in triumph and one of the things that I would do would be to walk down the diagonal path that extended from Tallmadge Avenue to King School—I wanted to walk down that diagonal path to school as the conquering hero, coming home from the wars. . . .

I'll see you later," I had said to him.

All of a sudden, as I sat at the funeral, that seemed enormously important to me. "You will?" he had asked. "That's good. . . ."

I didn't know where or when. But when I got there, I wanted to have some stories to tell. Some stories that might make him know that I was doing my best, however belatedly, to understand.

SEVEN

With all the back-and-forth during the months of my father's dying, I did not write anything in the newspaper about my first visit with Paul Tibbets until a month after the funeral.

Back at work then, and, for the first time since summer, with the downturns of my father's health not on my mind—and with the new void left by his absence hitting me from all angles at unexpected moments—I went through the handwritten notes I had made during my hours with Tibbets. I thought that the story he had told me might make for reading that would interest people; I thought that, because of Tibbets' lifelong propensity for reticence and silence, there might be many people who literally had no idea who he was—and that those who did know might not even realize he was still alive.

And I was exhausted. The months of my father's leave-taking had affected me in ways that, as they had unfolded, I had been unaware. But—my father buried in Ohio, me back in Chicago, a job to do—I welcomed the chance to write something for which I had already done the reporting, something that, for a few days, did not require me to go out and talk to people. The way I was feeling, I did not want to listen to the voices of strangers, at least not quite yet.

The Tibbets notes were there—I had put them away after he and I had met, I had told virtually no one about our conversation—and as I looked at them, I decided to do a week's worth of columns about what he had told me. I shut myself in a room and wrote the stories—Tibbets' voice, as I had heard it.

The reaction staggered me.

* * *

It came from all over the world. The column is carried on the *Chicago Tribune's* computer-version site, so I had known for a while that the readership was not limited by the geographic boundaries of the Chicago area, or of the towns where newspapers carry the column in syndication. Still, until the stories about Paul Tibbets began to appear, I had no idea of just how wide the reach of the new technology was.

Every day, my computer at work was jammed with electronic messages about the interview with Tibbets; regular mail also poured in, and phone calls. That one three-sentence thought of Tibbets'—"I cannot communicate with people who are less than sixty years old. It's as if all of us in this country know the same words, but we don't use the words the same way. We speak different languages."—seemed to affect people. Some were his age, some weren't, but all understood what he meant. And they wanted to say so.

The most overwhelming sentiment in so many of the letters concerned something I had not thought much about before I had met Tibbets. It was about the lives that were *not* lost when the bomb was dropped; it was about the American families that were allowed to be born and thrive and grow to adulthood because the soldiers and sailors had not been sent on a bloody and disastrous land invasion of Japan.

Voices:

"At the time of Colonel Paul Tibbets' mission, I was a young nineteen-year-old Marine," wrote a man named Robert A. Guth.

> We had just finished some intense training for the final push against the Japanese homeland. Although our exact invasion location was secret, we found out later that we would indeed be sent in.
>
> At that time we heard scuttlebutt that an invasion of Japan would be very costly in casualties. I would have liked to thank President Truman at that time for his decision to order the bombing—and I

would like at this time to thank Paul Tibbets for his excellent mission.

I thank Colonel Tibbets and his crew, my wife Mary thanks them, our five children and fifteen grandchildren thank them.

It was an expression of gratitude that I would read and hear over and over. The point was unmistakable—so many people, most of them of Tibbets' and my father's generation, were absolutely convinced that untold numbers of American lives, including perhaps their own, would have soon been lost had Tibbets and his crew not flown their mission in August of 1945. These correspondents did not treat what happened in Hiroshima lightly; far from it, they made it clear that they understood in great detail the unfathomable extent of death and carnage that resulted from the bomb being dropped.

But they also seemed to feel that the bomb—in a complex and pervading sense—was their salvation, and the salvation of family members not yet born in 1945. A woman named Catherine E. Mitchell, seventy-three years old, of Biloxi, Mississippi, put it this way:

> I well remember that day when the bomb was dropped on Hiroshima. So often I have heard people saying that we should never have dropped that bomb. But those people were not living through the war.
>
> In early 1945, my husband was sent to the Pacific. The country was preparing for the invasion of Japan and we all knew it. Had the dropping of the bomb not happened, I know that my husband would not have returned home—so many American lives would have been lost.
>
> The younger generations cannot possibly understand what we went through and how we felt about our country being attacked [at Pearl Harbor]—you can't know until you live through it. My forty-six-year-old father was also in the Pacific with the Seabees then, and my twenty-year-old brother was finishing flight training.

I sincerely hope that the young people of today will never have to go through a war. I am glad that I did not have to make the decision [to drop the bomb], but I am glad that it was done.

From a man named E. R. Klamm:

I was a naval communications officer, and we headed a large convoy of ships in Guam, Tinian and Saipan for the eventual invasion of Japan. We weathered three different typhoons.

In August, during a lull in the weather, I was playing badminton on deck (staying fit) when a staffman brought me a communication. I read it and then resumed playing our game. Then, like a bolt of lightning, I suddenly returned to the communication.

Its wording was technical and complex, but I interpreted that it involved the use of a mega-explosive in bombing Japan. It triggered in my mind that it could stop the invasion of Japan. Hallelujah! Hallelujah! Hallelujah! Later aboard ship there was jubilation.

We never reached Japan. We did go to Korea and China. I then returned to the U.S. and the happiness of family life. I commend Paul Tibbets and his crew. I congratulate him for naming his B-29 the *Enola Gay,* in honor of his mother. *My* mother, and my wife, were happy on my return Thanksgiving Day, 1945.

From a twenty-five-year-old woman named Chantal Foster Lindquist:

Paul Tibbets' voice is stern and serene. The gravity of his act forces silence on the page.

I think most people my age don't understand the sacrifices our grandparents made during wartime. I remember, in high school, I wrote a paper about why we shouldn't have dropped the bomb on Hiroshima. I was adamant in my essay, but the moment I spoke with my grandfather, a Navy Seabee, and listened to his account of the war, I changed my mind.

His blue eyes flared when I said the bomb was unnecessary, and he leaned across the table to tell me how the bomb had saved his life. How he was so grateful to go home and see his family again. How he's pretty sure he would have been killed otherwise. And so in a way I realized I might not even be here if Paul Tibbets hadn't done his job.

Some of the letters were filled with a perspective that could be born only of that war and that time. From a "septuagenarian ex-city editor" named Brad Bradford:

> You quite properly focus upon the *Enola Gay*'s pilot. His command responsibilities must have been enormous.
>
> But please bear with me. . . . To bring the *Enola Gay* over target within seventeen seconds of the planned time, navigator Theodore Van Kirk had to have been virtually perfect with no chance to relax even for a minute on that two-thousand-mile run to Hiroshima. His was simply an almost miraculous exhibition of technical expertise.
>
> I was a B-29 navigator in Stateside training that August. Training that summer at Smoky Hill Army Airfield in Kansas, I was slated to head for the Pacific and fly cover for a land invasion of Japan. The Air Corps shipped my footlocker to Okinawa, but thanks to the flight of the *Enola Gay,* the Army decided it didn't need me there after all and returned it to Smoky Hill. I left active duty that December a Stateside-safeside WWII veteran. And I still have that footlocker as a reminder of the debt I owe Paul Tibbets and his crew.

There it was, in almost every letter—a legacy of the flight that was seldom spoken about publicly. One woman's words:

> My husband was with the 5th Marine Division and served on Iwo Jima. After the *Enola Gay* dropped the bomb on Hiroshima, my husband and the men he fought with did not have to invade the Japanese mainland. He came home to me instead.
>
> Ten years ago, my husband went into the bedroom to take a nap before dinner. When I went in to call him, he was dead. He was a

> wonderful husband and father, and our lives are very empty without him.
>
> I am writing to ask you if I could possibly have Mr. Tibbets' address. I would really love to write to him. I am aware [that he] remains out of the public eye. But maybe he would like to hear about the special man I shared my life with—because of the job he did.

Mixed in with my business mail, during that freezing January, were condolence notes—letters about my father's death, and about his life, from people who had known our family. Many had Columbus postmarks on the envelopes.

So each day, as I went through the volume of mail that inevitably comes in to someone who writes stories in newspapers, I kept an eye out for Columbus addresses. And one day, when I had found one such Columbus envelope and had put it aside, I opened it to find that it was not exactly what I had expected.

It was from Tibbets.

He had sat down at an old-fashioned typewriter to write the letter. For twenty years I had tried to meet him, with nary a word of response. Now, here was this. He had read what I wrote. This is what the quiet man who did so much to end World War II said:

"You made me think, after a word-by-word review, that maybe I am not too bad a guy. Thanks."

He wrote that he didn't know whether I would be coming back to Ohio any time soon, but that if I did, he would like me to let him know.

EIGHT

There's a General Something waiting for you in the lounge."

The clerk at the front desk of the hotel near Port Columbus barely looked up as she said the words. I had arrived at the airport and taken a cab to the hotel; this was my first trip back to Ohio since the funeral, a short visit to take my mother to dinner. The hotel is where Tibbets had said he would meet me before I went to my mom's house.

General Something. If he'd been the star of a network situation comedy, the desk clerk might have been able to work up a bit of interest in his presence in the hotel; if he'd been a football player or a singer, she might have known who he was, might have called her friends to excitedly tell them who she had just met.

But this old man—General Something—had stopped at the desk to tell her that someone might be looking for him, and to please refer the person to the hotel lounge, and evidently the name hadn't really stuck. I told her thanks; she said no problem.

Touch it?" Tibbets said. "No—I never touched it."

It was a little thing that had been on my mind since the last time I had spoken with him. It was probably a meaningless point—but I kept finding myself thinking about whether Tibbets had ever touched the bomb. All that terrible power riding in the plane with him, all that nascent death—I tried to imagine the night he climbed into the *Enola Gay* for the flight to Hiroshima, and every time I thought about that, I had a picture in my mind of

Tibbets stopping for a moment to touch the bomb he had been ordered to drop.

"I'm not sentimental or superstitious or anything else," he said. He was in the hotel lounge, just as the clerk had said he would be; he was finishing off a cup of soup. He's not a drinker, he told me; he doesn't mind being in bars, but he avoids alcohol.

"I could have touched it, when they wheeled it out," he said. "Tom Ferebee stopped and checked everything—he was the bombardier, that was his job. I had a team of professionals, and I trusted them. All I needed to know was: 'Will it work?' I trusted that it would."

I told Tibbets I had heard that some of the support team on Tinian in 1945 had written messages on the bomb before it was loaded onto the *Enola Gay.* The bomb was not fully armed until the plane was airborne; theoretically, there was no danger in approaching it and writing on it while it was on the ground. Still—walking up to the atomic bomb and fooling around with it. . . .

"I heard the same thing," Tibbets said. "That some of the guys had written something on it. 'To the emperor, with love'—I think that was it, something like that. It's probably true—they probably did write messages on the bomb. Didn't make any sense, really. Think about it—who the hell is going to read it?"

The otherworldliness of this was still sinking in on me. Here was Tibbets, who had turned eighty-four since I had seen him last, telling these stories while, on a TV set in the bar, an NBA game was on the color screen, and the handful of other patrons were staring at that game, following the action as if the outcome were a matter of life or death. A few feet away this elderly man whose identity was a complete mystery to the others in the bar narrated a tale almost beyond comprehension.

In the weeks since my father's death, when I had thought of Tibbets it wasn't only the flight to Japan about which I wanted to know more—the expertise of Tibbets and his crew was a matter of record, they got there and they got back and the war ended: They did their jobs. What puzzled me—what I also wanted to know more about—was how Tibbets was assigned to put together the unit at Wendover, Utah, that was responsible for the mission. He had, as far as I knew, at that time never run a business. Yet the Army—and the government—had told him, in the middle of a war, to in effect start a new corporation. The corporation would have 1,800 employees—and Tibbets would be the chief executive officer.

He was twenty-nine when he was instructed to do that. Yes, he could fly a bomber with great skill. But how do you learn to be the boss of 1,800 men when you've never been a business executive? Where do you get the knowledge and the confidence and the leadership skills to do that?

"I went to military school when I was a boy," he said. "I learned right away that I had to be good, and I had to be right. I decided when I was very young that I never wanted to do anything—any job at all—until I had thought it out first.

"How's it going to work? That's the first question I always asked myself about everything. And if I didn't know the answer, the next question was: How will I make it work?

"I have kind of an analytical mind. When I approach a problem, I'm thinking, what are the odds that this will happen the way I want it to? How will I make sure it will work? That's how I was thinking when I was given the assignment to put our unit together.

"If I had to be the head of that unit, it was going to be a question of commanding people—and I've always been able to judge people pretty well. I can judge who will succeed and who will fail. Yes, I was twenty-nine when I was given the assignment. But I was really thirty-five or forty. That's how I felt. That was my nature—I always felt older than I actually was.

"And I am an orderly man. When I stay in a hotel room, I fold up the towels. I usually make the bed before I leave. I don't have to; I know that the housekeepers will do it if I don't. But I don't like the idea of other people doing something that I can do myself. A sense of order is very important to me."

So had he made it his business to know each of the 1,800 men at Wendover? Did he fine-tune his command duties to that extent?

"No," he said. "I probably only knew a hundred or so of the men by name. I saw faces. I was so busy going back and forth to Washington, and to Los Alamos, that I couldn't know every man. I knew every guy in command of a unit on the base, of course. But what you're asking is how I learned to run the whole operation when I had never done anything like that before.

"The answer is this: At twenty-nine I was so shot in the ass with confidence that it wasn't a question of could I do it—there wasn't anything I *couldn't* do. By the time I got the assignment to put together the atomic-bomb unit, I had worked my way through the war in Europe and North Africa, and I was completely convinced that I could do anything. I had succeeded as a combat pilot over there because once I got into the air, *I didn't have anyone who I had to ask what I had to do.* I just did it.

"Maybe it came from the house I grew up in. From my dad. The old man was a short fellow with a small-man complex. A cocky rooster. He would tell you once, and you'd better listen and get it right. That must have stuck, in some way."

He took such pride in the punctiliousness of his organizational skills, the double-checking and triple-checking of every detail; I told him that I had read something about the Hiroshima mission that seemed to fit in. When I had read it, I didn't know if it was true or an apocryphal tale. But now it seemed right.

"What's that?" he said.

"What was the last thing you did before you dropped the bomb?" I asked.

"I don't understand what you're getting at," Tibbets said.

"The last thing you said to your crew," I said.

"In the plane?" Tibbets said.

"Yes," I said.

"I suppose I asked everyone whether they agreed that it was Hiroshima down there," he said.

That's what I had read; on this monumental day in the history of the planet, with the T-shaped bridge coming into sight, Tibbets had polled his crew to see if each man thought they were approaching the right city. It hadn't occurred to me—that the men in the plane, never having seen Hiroshima before, might be a little uncertain about where they actually were about to drop the world's first atomic weapon.

"Do you remember what you said—the exact words?" I asked.

"Probably, 'Do we all agree that this is Hiroshima?' " Tibbets said.

"Amazing," I said, trying to comprehend the moment. Like guys on a car trip to a state where they'd never visited. Is this the right exit? Except that this was the most somber journey that any men had ever taken.

"I don't see why it's amazing," Tibbets said. "It's the same thing I'd do on any kind of a job. You check, just to make sure. That's not amazing. That's just good sense."

A cheer came from over at the bar. Someone on the television screen had just made a basket to beat the shot clock.

The apocalyptic destructiveness of nuclear weaponry notwithstanding, the Paul Tibbets who flew the *Enola Gay* to Japan in 1945 wouldn't even be allowed to be a passenger in a commercial jetliner half-a-century later had he not changed his ways. Just one more small example of how the world has evolved: Tibbets was a smoker back then. All the time. Including in airplanes.

Including the *Enola Gay.*

"I smoked everything," he said. "Pipes, cigars, cigarettes . . . I would smoke on every mission. Pipes, mostly—I was using Bond Street tobacco. I had a Zippo lighter that I carried with me constantly."

"So you were lighting your pipe with the atomic bomb right beneath you," I said.

"Sure," Tibbets said.

"That didn't make you a little nervous?" I said.

"Why should it?" he said. "The bomb was inert."

"I don't know," I said. "Just the thought of that—an atomic bomb in the belly of your plane, and you're smoking away . . ."

"A cigarette lighter's not going to set off the atomic bomb," Tibbets said. "It didn't work that way. I was smoking my pipe and probably lighting it up when they were loading the bomb into the plane."

Of course, he and he alone knew what the bomb was. The other crew members had not been told—they were not informed of the exact nature of the mission until they were well on their way to Hiroshima. All those months in Wendover and then on Tinian—and the secret had been kept. Even from the men under Tibbets' command.

Before he could tell the men on board, he had to get the plane into the air. Which was no simple job—the runway that had been carved out of the jungle-like conditions on Tinian was not long enough to easily handle the B-29 as it had been reconfigured. With the heavy bomb underneath him, Tibbets knew that he would have to use virtually every foot of that runway before he lifted off.

"You had to take into consideration that airplane and all its problems," he said. "It was underpowered for what we had to do. If you were to lose an engine, you could not control that airplane.

"I know that some of the crew on the flight were getting very nervous as I kept the plane on the runway so long as we were taking off. There was a cliff-like drop at the end of the runway, and some of them were thinking about that. But I knew what I was doing. I was building up every possible bit of power that I could before taking the plane up. Remember—this was before jet engines. If I lost an engine, and if we were to crash . . .

"I needed every inch. The co-pilot thought he knew more about the airplane than I did—he thought I should take it up sooner. It was all business in there—every man had his own responsibility in the airplane to take care of. I wanted the men to know what was going on, but first we had to get up and off of Tinian.

"After we were up and the bomb had been armed, I decided it was time for no more secrets. I had to crawl through a twenty-six-inch circular tunnel to talk to the men in the back of the plane. I told everyone: 'This is what it's all about. We're carrying a weapon that we've been working with.' Bob Caron, the tailgunner, said to me: 'Colonel, we wouldn't be playing with atoms, would we?' I said, 'Sure. That's it.' They weren't startled. I think a lot of them had guessed, but they had known not to ask."

The fact that Tibbets was flying the plane—was that a part of his duties? He had been assigned to assemble and command the unit that would prepare for the flight. But did that mean he was assigned to fly the mission, too?

"The order was for me to organize and train a unit to drop these weapons," he said. "When I was looking for a place to assemble the unit, and I flew over those mountains in Utah and saw Wendover, I thought it was the most beautiful and isolated place I had ever seen. I knew I didn't have to look any further—boy, this was the place for me. *So* isolated—the most isolated place I could ever imagine. I saw Wendover from the air, and I thought that this is a place where it's easier to keep a secret than anywhere else I had seen in my life.

"I went back to General Ent and I told him, 'I've seen Wendover, and I want it.' He said, 'It's yours.' "

"You were twenty-nine," I reminded him.

"I was twenty-nine," Tibbets said. "You were asking me if it was part of my orders to fly the mission. Yes, it was part of my orders—from *me.* I had the authority to do anything I wanted, and I knew that I could fly that damn thing better than anyone else.

"So, yes, I issued the order—I was going to be the pilot. If anyone was going to make a mistake on this mission, it was going to be me."

As he approached Hiroshima, and Tom Ferebee released the

bomb and it detonated, as planned, some 1,800 feet above the city—the atomic bomb was not supposed to explode on impact, but well over the target—and the tumbling, rolling shock waves from the bomb reached the cockpit of the plane, Tibbets said he could taste it.

"It tasted like lead," he said. "It was like an electrical charge was running through the fillings in my teeth, and I could feel that electricity in my fillings and I had the taste of lead in my mouth. The feeling was like when cold ice cream touches one of your fillings, and the taste—the taste from that bomb is something I will never forget."

As he flew back toward Tinian, he was still smoking.

"No one asked me not to," he said.

He has stopped since. Doctor's orders. The atomic bombing of Hiroshima was the one most deadly act in the annals of man's time on Earth. But, in a twist the most inventive author could never have devised, in the years since World War II cigarettes have killed far more people than the bomb did that day—indeed, have killed far more people than all the military men who died in combat during World War II.

"Pilots smoked back then," Tibbets said. "Soldiers smoked back then. Everyone smoked back then. What did we know? The scientists hadn't told us yet."

Once in a while, as I talked with Tibbets, I half-forgot for a second that he didn't just suddenly materialize for the armed services when the atomic bomb project was being developed. The reason he was in the running for the job was because of his combat record in Europe. He flew twenty-five missions in B-17s, including being the lead pilot of the first-ever American daylight bombing raid against occupied Europe.

Still, occasionally he would drop a reference into our conversation that brought me up short. I had been asking him some technical question about the planes he flew in the war—I think this particular question was about the altitude at which the planes operated—and in trying to explain he said, "Well, when I was flying Ike to Gibraltar . . ."

"You knew Eisenhower?" I asked.

He gave me a look. "Yes," he said.

"Why were you flying him to Gibraltar?" I said.

"Because he had to get to the invasion of North Africa," Tibbets said.

"Oh," I said. Simple as that. Dwight D. Eisenhower had to get to the war, and Tibbets gave him a ride.

"How was he to fly with?" I asked.

"As nice a passenger as you'll ever find," Tibbets said.

Eisenhower, he said, was to be the overall commander of the operation, with Major General Mark Clark as his deputy. This was in November of 1942; Eisenhower was in England, the air was full of rain and fog, and there was much uncertainty about whether the planes could take off.

"We were standing on the runway," Tibbets said. "Eisenhower seemed like he wanted to get moving, but others were saying that the weather was just too bad. Eisenhower looked at me—were we going to take off or not?

"I said, 'General, if I didn't know the passenger who I'd be carrying on this trip, I'd make the decision to go.' Meaning if it was just me, I'd fly out of there.

"And Eisenhower said, 'I've got a war waiting on me. Let's go.' "

Tibbets said that a Jeep led his B-17 out onto the active runway, and that by the time he was airborne "I couldn't see three feet in front of me. I flew as low over the Channel as I possibly could—the last thing Eisenhower needed was for German radar to pick us up. I can't tell you exactly how low I was flying, because I don't know—but there was salt spray on the window of the plane."

And Eisenhower? "He was sitting on a two-by-four plank that

we had put between my seat and the co-pilot's seat. He had told us that he wanted to watch what was going on. And he sat there with us and talked with us as if this was the most regular thing in the world—him sitting on a two-by-four and us flying him to run the war.

"He had a thermos jug of coffee with him—it's funny how you remember the little things, but I remember that Eisenhower shared his coffee with us. It was a 1,200-mile flight, and by the time we landed in Gibraltar the invasion had started—the paratroopers were dropping.

"He was all business. He just got out of the plane, thanked us, and he was gone. He was just as fine as anyone could be. He was wearing four stars when he was with us, but he was one of the boys. I was only—what?—twenty-seven, I think, at that point. You try not to show that you're feeling anything. But this was Ike.

"Made me feel good—that he trusted me to get him there. That moment at the airfield in England is one that stays in your mind. You're standing in the rain with Eisenhower, and he's looking at the sky and you tell him that you can do it and he says those words. 'I've got a war waiting on me.'

"And you go."

I hadn't told my mother that I was stopping off to see Tibbets on my way from the airport—for some reason, at this point the fact that he had invited me to continue our conversations was something I wanted to keep to myself—and as he and I talked I realized that I'd better be on my way.

"I'm going to go take my mom out to dinner," I said to Tibbets.

"You go to your mother's house," he said. "That's more important than talking to me."

I told him the place I was thinking about taking her—the Top, it was called, a steakhouse that has been around Columbus since the

1950s, a place where she and my dad used to go when they were a young married couple in the years after the war—and Tibbets said that he used to go to the Top all the time, too.

He asked me how late I planned on staying up. I said that my mom tended to go to bed on the early side.

"Well, if you're not tired and you feel like talking some more, I'll be happy to meet you back here," he said.

"Right here?" I said. "Same place?"

"If you feel like it," he said.

I said I did. He looked at his watch and said that we should set a time. I made sure to make it late enough that I was certain to be back from dinner and from my mother's house; whatever hour we chose, I knew he would be there promptly as promised, and I didn't want to keep him waiting. The lounge was nearly empty and he was the oldest man there.

NINE

The diploma was on the wall of the spare bedroom my father used as his office.

"I thought he didn't put that up," I said to my mother.

"He decided he wanted to," she said. "He hung it on the wall the week after you gave it to him."

"You mean it was up there all the time he was sick?" I asked.

"Yes," she said.

"I guess with everything going on, I didn't notice it," I said.

There it was: a diploma from Ohio State University, dated the previous June. It had his name on it—it said that Bob Greene had been awarded an honorary doctorate.

My father never graduated from college. It always made him feel insecure; I think one of the reasons he was so meticulous in his language, why he paid such attention to grammar and word choice, was that he knew he was operating in a society in which so many other people had college degrees. My mother had graduated from Wellesley and had been selected for Phi Beta Kappa; my father had never made it through the University of Akron.

He didn't say much to us about it, ever. But I found a reference to it in the tape he had made. It wasn't for lack of desire that he had left college:

I went to West High School. Akron was a working man's town, and West High School was the educational place for working people's children. There were a lot of the kids of rubber workers who attended, and this was right in the middle of the Depression, so it was kind of sad to see some of those kids come to school literally dressed in rags.

It was a hard time for all, especially high school kids who couldn't have the pluses that went with being a teenager in the big city. In other words, the last two years of high school, my junior and senior years, when usually there were class rings and pins and yearbooks and that sort of thing, the Depression caused all that stuff to be cut way back. So those were kind of grim years.

After high school, instead of being able to go away to school, I went to what was called a streetcar school. I would get on the 22 streetcar on West Market Street and ride it downtown and then walk up the hill behind Polsky's department store to go to Akron University, which was also a hardbitten working man's school. Some of my old bad habits started anew—I would start to skip classes. Oftentimes I had a Spanish class on the first floor of a real old building, and I would sit in the open window and when our Spanish teacher, Señor Maturo, would turn around I'd slip out of the window and was gone. I was out of there for the day . . .

My dad, as I told you, was an attorney. A self-made man, actually self-educated after high school, and I would say rather stern. He was always a beautiful dresser and known as Nick throughout the whole city . . . He certainly looked healthy enough as he walked down the street with his walking cane and his derby and his Chesterfield coat. But when he was about fifty years old he suffered some very serious illnesses, he had a gall bladder operation that was almost fatal. At that time I was a junior at Akron University, and I had to drop out of school in order to get a job and help my parents out. I never went back to college. . . .

A year before my dad got sick for the last time—a year before his dying began—I received one of the great honors of my life.

I was invited to deliver the commencement address at Ohio State University. For a boy who grew up in central Ohio, the idea of speaking in Ohio Stadium—the legendary gray football stadium where the Ohio State Buckeyes play—was overwhelming, thrilling almost beyond description.

Ohio Stadium—the massive gray horseshoe on the Olentangy River, the stadium inside of which Coach Woody Hayes walked the sidelines, inside of which generations of Ohioans have gathered on football Saturdays for most of the last century—is the single most famous place in Ohio. When you grow up in the middle of Ohio, your world at times feels small and constrained and quiet. And then, one Saturday, your parents bring you with them to Ohio Stadium.

On that day you walk through the dull and dingy concrete bowels of the stadium, up a short flight of stairs and into a tunnel and then into the sunlight—and all of a sudden your world changes. You are still in the middle of Ohio, but for the first time in your life you are in a place so huge, so filled with color and noise, so exciting, that you instinctively have new knowledge of life's possibilities. Of size, and scale, and potential, of infinite horizons about which you had previously scarcely dared to dream.

Ohio Stadium, to me, had always borne more symbolic weight than the White House, than Buckingham Palace. Ohio Stadium, to me, was the end of the rainbow. The perfect place.

To be invited to be commencement speaker there had a meaning I could not come close to articulating. Spring graduation at Ohio State is said to be the largest in the United States; fifty thousand people gather for the ceremonies.

But that is not why the June morning in Ohio Stadium was going to mean so much to me.

And that is not why, when what happened inside Ohio Stadium happened, it hurt so much.

My mother and father, for more than fifty years, went together to Ohio Stadium every football Saturday. Their marriage was one of the closest I have ever observed; they did virtually everything together. They had a date with each other every night, whether they left the house or not.

And—especially after my sister and brother and I moved away from Columbus—those Saturdays in Ohio Stadium were the cement that connected the weeks and months and years of their life in Ohio. Think about that: going to that stadium together for more than fifty years.

They finally had to stop. My father, even before his final illness, didn't get around so easily. Ohio Stadium on a football Saturday was just too hard.

But on that June morning, they made plans to come to the stadium one more time. They came to see me speak.

I had my own plan that day.

I had come up with it the night before—I had arrived in Columbus from Chicago, had gone up to the Ohio State campus, and had found an open gate on the exterior of the stadium. I had walked inside, and had looked around.

I knew that I had never been any good at telling my parents private things about how I felt about them—at least not out loud, at least not face-to-face. This was my failing, not theirs.

But on that night, in the empty stadium, I decided what I was going to do the next morning.

Without telling anyone about it beforehand, I was going to ask the people who had come for commencement exercises to do me a kindness. I was going to let them know about my parents, and about those fifty years of football Saturdays that were now over. And I was going to ask the crowd to rise and honor my father and mother with a standing ovation—a standing ovation in Ohio Stadium.

The next morning was one of the worst rainstorms anyone in central Ohio could remember. The fifty thousand people showed up and took their seats in the stadium. For more than an hour, they waited in the downpour for the ceremonies to begin.

Standing with the official procession underneath the stadium, I thought about my mom and dad sitting in that unrelenting rainstorm. I didn't know what to do. We finally marched in; the rain only intensified. I tried to find them in the crowd, but couldn't.

Minutes into the ceremony, it was called off. The weather was just too severe. Graduation would have to be canceled.

I found them beneath the stadium—soaked to the bone. Broke my heart. Made me want to cry. Fifty years into my own life, and here they were, sitting for an hour in a rainstorm for the chance to watch me do something. What else matters in life? The people you can count on like that—what else matters?

A year passed. I was invited to come back again to deliver the commencement address. It was to be the last commencement in Ohio Stadium for a while—repairs were scheduled to begin on the mammoth old place.

My parents were in the crowd again. The morning began with rain, but it stopped by the time we marched onto the football field.

I looked into the stands. More than fifty thousand people, stretching all the way to the sky, were there. Ohio Stadium, on a joyous and sunny June day.

I told the crowd about my parents. I explained about the year before.

And I asked the fifty thousand to do me the favor.

They did. In Ohio Stadium—the place where for so many years the crowds have risen to cheer for the football teams—on this day they rose to cheer for my mother and father.

The roar filled Ohio Stadium. It will sound in my heart forever.

My mother and I stood looking at the diploma on the wall of his office. This was the first time I had been back in the house since his death.

"Do you think I should take this with me now?" I said.

"No," she said. "I think it should stay here."

I had meant for it to be a nice surprise—a gesture he would like. As I had gotten ready for the reunion weekend the summer he got sick—when all of us came to Columbus—I had packed the diploma to bring with me. Little more than a month had passed since the morning in Ohio Stadium; the honorary degree had been presented to me at the end of the commencement speech, and my name—our name—had been on it.

He had never had one of these. I was lucky enough—because of the years of work he put in—to be able to go to college; after that trip to Chicago we had taken when I was in high school, I had been admitted to Northwestern, and graduated from there. He paid for it.

So on the last night of our family's reunion, as we were all finishing dinner on the patio behind their house, I had said that I had something I wanted to give him. I handed him the package.

"What's this?" he had said.

"Open it," I had said.

He did.

"What am I supposed to do with this?" he said.

It wasn't exactly the reaction I had been hoping for.

"It's yours," I said.

His expression was dismissive—even disdainful. "Gee, just what I always wanted," he said, his voice full of sarcasm. At the time I thought that maybe he had had one too many drinks; later I concluded that the illness that changed his behavior toward the end had started to kick in.

Or maybe it just was what it was. Maybe he didn't want anyone else's diploma. Maybe I had made a big mistake by trying to give it to him. Especially in front of the rest of the family.

"Thanks," he had said, but had handed it back to me.

"I'm not taking it," I had said to him. "It belongs to you."

And now here we were—my mom and I, standing in the quiet house, the house from which he was gone. The diploma with his name on it—with our name on it—was on his wall.

"He put it up as soon as all of you left that weekend," she said.

I said that maybe we should head out to the Top for dinner.

* * *

How much has this place changed since you first came here?" I asked.

"Not at all, except for the prices," my mom said.

The Top, when it first opened in the Fifties, was—here is the only word for it—snazzy. A snazzy steakhouse, for all the young couples on the East Side of Columbus, back from the war and starting families. Forty years later the booths were the same, the decor was the same—I looked across the table, and I saw my mother, approaching eighty, and I tried to imagine her at thirty-five or thirty-six in this same booth, out for an evening with her husband. And I knew, as we sat there, that she wished I wasn't the person who was sitting across from her tonight.

"He still kept the 'Organize, Delegate, Supervise, Check' plaque next to his desk at home, I see," I said to her.

"Like he would ever forget the words," she said.

It was his credo—those four words, in that order, were, he said, what got him through his business career. Follow those words, he said, and you will be a success in your job.

Kind of a graduate business school for a guy who never had the good fortune to get to finish college. Four words. They seemed to have worked. They allowed him to do well enough at his job that he could send my brother and sister and me to good universities.

They were the first words in the eulogy at his funeral. We had made sure of that. Organize. Delegate. Supervise. Check.

The waitress came around, and my mom and I talked, and what I was hearing was his voice—his voice from those tapes he had given us. The part where he described going to work after he had to drop out of college to help his parents.

He had found a job at the most menial level at a scrap rubber company. He hoped to rise to something better, but he had to start somewhere:

I was an office boy, and a pretty poor one at that. . . . But the sales manager, a handsome Irishman by the name of Jack Costello, who never came to the office without a tremendous hangover but who despite all that operated at tremendous efficiency all the time, was a great help to me. He was about ten or fifteen years older than I, but he understood me and gave me an excellent grounding on how to conduct myself in business, whether in the office or on the road.

I shall never forget Jack Costello. One of the things he told me that I never forgot was, "Bob, when you're out on the road, which you will be, you're going to have an expense account and you can spend what you want on food and anything you need. But nobody ever got rich padding an expense account."

In the first place, I never knew what "padding" an expense account meant. I remember that he said to me, "Live well, but we do kind of frown on excesses like three dollar breakfasts and things like that." Well, up to that time I don't believe I had ever paid more than forty-five cents or fifty cents for breakfast, and so when I learned that three dollars for breakfast was a no-no, but that anything under that was acceptable, that, I believe, is when I started to gain weight. . . .

Suffice it to say that I mended my ways in the office and started acting like a grown-up, or almost, and then I was sent out onto the road. My travels consisted of driving into Pennsylvania, scouting the highways and byways and looking for junkyards where there might be huge piles of scrap tires. . . .

At the Top, my mom said that going out to dinner, even with her oldest friends, in these first months after his death was a chore at best—and painful at worst.

She looked over at the bar, and mentioned the name of a man they had known—a man who had a reputation for liking to spend time with women. She laughed.

"Daddy"—she was referring to my dad, not hers; often he was "Daddy" when she talked about him in front of my brother or sister or me, especially in the time after his death—"Daddy would say that if he ever wanted to find [this particular man], he knew that all he would have to do is come to the bar at the Top."

But that was in the days after he was established in business, a homeowner in Columbus. He'd had to start somewhere. In this old restaurant on East Main Street I kept hearing his voice:

. . . One of the most important, yet devastating, things that ever happened as far as my work record occurred about this time. Suffice it to say that it involved a mistake that I made, which could have cost the company an awful lot of money, and it was purely because of carelessness on my part. I won't go into any details on it, but it was the beginning of the end. My services were no longer required.

I went to Cleveland looking for a job, to no avail. So I was kind of down in the dumps, but fortune smiled upon me, providentially. One day I walked into the Dime Savings and Loan Company where I ran into an old friend of mine by the name of Bill O'Neill. He said, "What are you doing?" and I said, "I'm not doing a damn thing, I got my butt fired." And he said, "How would you like to go to work for the Philip Morris Company?" I said, "I would love it. When do I start?" He said, "What about tomorrow?"

So I rushed home and told Mother and Dad, who incidentally were very sympathetic about my firing and they wished me the very best, which made me feel very good because I felt as if I had let them down. The next morning I went to work for Bill O'Neill at the Akron sales office of Philip Morris. The office was in an old funeral home, actually it was simply a room, and they had done the embalming in that room. There was still the gutter in the floor where all the embalming fluid used to run out of the table on which the stiffs were laid. It was rather a macabre place, but regardless, Bill had his desk there and I had a little table or something.

My job consisted of calling on every store in Akron that carried cigarettes and tobacco. I had no car, but I had plenty of bus fare. So I would take the bus to the far ends of town, lugging a heavy sample case full of cigarettes and samples of pipe tobacco, get off the bus and start walking back in toward town, calling on every store, saloon and candy shop. I believe I was making eighteen dollars a week, and in those days that was not too bad. I got plenty of exercise and learned a heck of a lot about human nature.

And incidentally, having been fired made me make a vow to myself which has stood me in good stead to this day. And that vow was simply this: Grow up, be careful what you're doing, don't make mistakes and make yourself as indispensable to your boss as you possibly can. . . .

I asked my mom if coming to the Top had been a luxury for them back then—if going out for a big steak dinner in a restaurant was something they did all the time, or whether it was a treat to be budgeted for.

"This was sort of a gathering place," she said. "We came here whenever we could. When it was new, it was where all of our friends would come on a Friday or Saturday night. It was the hot new place."

I thought about him, coming out of the Depression, his future, like the futures of all those men who grew up in those years, far from certain. Were he sitting with us tonight—had this dinner been taking place ten or fifteen years before—I probably wouldn't have given a thought to the forces that brought him here. How he had managed to get himself started in the business world would not have been anywhere on my mind. I probably would have been talking about the day's news.

But tonight I saw my mom looking across the table at the seat I knew she wished he was in, and his voice was in my head. The young man trying to catch on with a company that might value him:

* * *

. . . I finally became fairly well known in Akron as being the Philip Morris representative, and I don't know how good your memory is, but the trademark of Philip Morris was a bellboy, a very beautifully uniformed midget who called out, "Call for Philip Morris." And so every time I came into stores, the people who I had dealt with used to make that call, which made me feel pretty good, being identified as the Philip Morris representative.

One day Bill O'Neill came to me and said there was an opening in Lima, Ohio, and would I like that job. Well, I said yes, and will I be making any more money, and he said yes, you'll be making a little more money and you're going to be your own boss. And we're going to give you a car, and you will have a territory that would comprise the northwest part of Ohio, down to Marysville and over to Grand Lake and St. Marys and so forth. That sounded very interesting, because that would be the first time I ever left home.

So I went home that day, my mother was home, and I said, "Mother, I've got a new job and I'm leaving this afternoon." Well, she couldn't believe it, because that was a pretty quick move, but I had no choice.

Bill O'Neill and I went for the long ride to Lima, so that he could get me established there. We took a newspaper, looked for rooms to rent, and found a lovely old house on Market Street in Lima, and I became a roomer. And a roomer I was, because I had a bedroom on the first floor, I think three towels, and the use of a bathroom on the second floor. I believe that was in the summer of 1938. I had my own car there, which was a really snappy maroon Ford convertible coupe, and then later I had a company car, which was a panel truck in which I carried a stock of cigarettes. Bill O'Neill left the next day after getting me all set up in Lima and said, "You're on your own." All of a sudden I think I grew up.

I didn't know a soul in Lima, not one soul, and the places to meet people were in the hotel bars. I was kind of a popular guy because part of my job was to give away samples of cigarettes, and everyone wants something for nothing. That stood me in good stead in the bars, especially the hotel bar where all of young Lima congregated.

Another big meeting place was Indian Lake, a resort south of Lima, where a lot of people went to hear big bands, which played every weekend. Now, these were the big bands of fame. And it was a wonderful thing to see hundreds of young people crowded around the bandstand and listening to the likes of Benny Goodman, Gene Krupa, the Dorseys and the like. Those days were never to be repeated, but of course we didn't know that.

And in the far distance was rumbling a war, because this was summer at the end of the 1930s, when all hell was breaking loose in Europe. . . .

The Top had not been crowded on this night; forty years down the road, the steaks were still good, but it's not the hot new spot in town. Never would be again.

My mom and I walked out and I took her home, and when she said she was ready for bed I headed back to the place where I'd been with Tibbets in the afternoon. For some reason I was very much in the mood to hear his voice.

I saw him before he saw me. He was walking quite slowly toward the lounge where we had sat before. I had made it a point to be a few minutes early; so had he.

So I followed him in—"Oh!" he said when he saw me. "Didn't know you were behind me!"—and we sat down, and I told him about my dad and that first real job, and about the "Call for Philip Morris!" thing—about how the store people, in the 1930s, would sing out "Call for Philip Morris!" when they saw the young salesman coming.

It was how he became a salesman, I told Tibbets—teaching himself, giving away free samples.

"That's how I started, too," Tibbets said.

"Being a salesman?" I said.

"No," he said. "Being a pilot. But I was giving things away just like your dad."

"How?" I said. "I don't understand."

The sound of this eighty-four-year-old man's words was something that felt exceedingly good to me right now.

"Well . . ." Tibbets said.

He stopped himself.

"Are you in a hurry?" he said.

"Farthest thing from it," I said.

TEN

"I dropped Baby Ruths," Tibbets said.

"What do you mean?" I said.

"Baby Ruths," Tibbets said. "The candy bars."

"You dropped them *where*?"

"Out of an airplane," he said. "Your father gave away cigarettes, I dropped Baby Ruths. It was how I first found out that I loved flying—it was the first I knew what I wanted to do with my life."

In the lounge, I asked him to tell me how it had happened.

"When I was twelve years old, my father was a wholesaler of confectioneries, and we were living in Miami, Florida," he said. "My dad distributed for the Curtiss Candy Company. They had a candy bar that was being introduced—Baby Ruth—that they wanted to promote to the public.

"Someone had the idea that a pilot should take a biplane up over the Miami vicinity, and throw Baby Ruth bars out of the plane over areas where there were a lot of people. So a pilot by the name of Doug Davis was hired. He showed up at my father's office the day before the flight. He said that he wanted tiny paper parachutes tied to each Baby Ruth, so that they would float to the ground rather than drop down real hard.

"I volunteered for the job. I sat there and I tied those paper parachutes to every Baby Ruth. It was tedious work. Then Davis told my dad that he needed someone to come up with him as he flew the plane—someone to throw the candy bars out. Kind of like a bombardier.

"I immediately said that I was the man for the job. My dad didn't want me to do it—he really didn't like the idea of flying. But I talked him into it, with the help of Doug Davis.

"The next morning we went to an airfield in a place that felt like a farmer's pasture. We loaded the open biplane with all the Baby Ruths with the paper parachutes I'd tied on. We climbed into the plane.

"Davis told me to get ready for our takeoff. We were going down the runway over some pretty rough ground—I remember the fence posts going by as we bumped past them. Then all of a sudden, the fence posts were gone, and the ground wasn't bumpy anymore.

"I said to Doug Davis, 'We're standing still.'

"And he said, 'No—we're flying.'

"I have never had a feeling like that in my life—the feeling of being off the ground, of flying through the air, above everything down below. Doug flew the plane to the Hialeah racetrack, where the horse races were going on. The grandstand was full; Doug banked the plane and told me to get ready, and he flew over the grandstand and called to me: 'Throw 'em!'

"I did—I started heaving those Baby Ruths out of the plane as fast as I could, aiming for the people below. Most of the parachutes worked—I could see the people in the grandstand looking up, and watching the candy bars float down, and trying to grab them. We made another pass over the racetrack, and I threw more of the candy bars, and then Doug flew us over to Miami Beach. We flew low over the beach and I threw the candy bars that were left to the people in their bathing suits who were on the sand next to the ocean."

As he told me this, I tried to imagine such a scene today—an open airplane flying at an extremely low altitude, buzzing a public gathering where large numbers of people are congregated, and someone in the plane throwing hard objects from the plane into the crowd. Not only would the pilot likely be arrested as soon as he landed—but attorneys would be lining up to file lawsuits on behalf of people who were struck by the falling objects.

But if that thought—the thought of a person tossing things out of an airplane at strangers below—was enough to give pause, then a second thought was even more provocative:

The thought of the boy—so excited and happy about dropping candy bars from a plane to hungry Floridians on the ground—ending up as a man who, half a world away from Florida, drops an atomic bomb on people standing on the ground below with no idea of what is about to transpire.

"Doug Davis flew back to the airfield after all the Baby Ruths were gone," Tibbets told me, his eyes somewhere else. "That was the day I knew. I had to fly airplanes. That was the day that changed my life. I knew I was going to fly."

My father had spoken with such obvious affection and wistful nostalgia about his beginning days in the work force; Tibbets' voice, as he told me about the Baby Ruth flight, had the same lilt as my dad's when he had described being a young man starting out.

I found myself wanting to know if Tibbets felt the same way about the places where he had done his later, more important work. Wendover, for example—the barren part of the Utah salt flats where he had assembled and trained the atom bomb flight team. Did he frequently go back there for visits?

"No," he said, a look of something close to contempt on his face. "I think I've been there three times since we left there."

"Why so few times?" I said.

"You ever been to Wendover?" he asked rhetorically, as if to say that had I ever been there, I'd know why he avoided it.

"Actually, I have," I said.

"Really?" he said, disbelieving.

"I can see why you stay away," I said.

Wendover—West Wendover is what the part in Nevada is called, just a few feet past the Utah line—is as desolate and remote a piece of land as you are ever likely to find. It feels separate from everything; the heat rises from the highway in waves you can see, the nearby Bonneville Salt Flats stretch to a blank horizon. The Nevada part of Wendover seems to exist for its casinos—for people coming from Salt Lake City, it is the closest place where gambling and its peripheral pleasures are legal. Utah residents drive for hours from Salt Lake City and beyond, across the melting highway through countryside all but devoid of scenery, looking for the state line. One of the first casinos they encounter is in fact called the State Line: supply and demand, hidden human needs fulfilled on the parched desert.

A novelist named Peter Rock, who set his book *This Is the Place* in Wendover, once said of the city: "It always seemed like a place where the dark lands begin. It's such a sad place. When I was writing the book, when I decided to set it there, I moved there. But after three days I realized I couldn't do it, so I left." When I was in Wendover myself, I met a schoolteacher who told me, "It's the children here I worry about. Not only that it's so far removed from the rest of the world out here, but so many parents work for the casinos, and are at work all night when the children are at home. . . ."

Wendover seems irrevocably distant from anywhere else, feels like a place no one would come to if they didn't have to: a place that easily confers privacy, unsolicitedly offers up secrecy. A place you would instinctively seek out if you didn't want to be seen.

"We had that place so beautified," Tibbets said. "The base we put together . . . I was really proud of what we built.

"I went back there in 1990, and the sight of our old base made me sick. A bunch of rundown shacks. Holes in the buildings. When I say it made me sick, I mean it—I was literally sick at my stomach, looking around. My old headquarters didn't exist."

What was his first thought, upon looking at the casinos rising near where he had trained his men? I told him that, from the guest rooms of some of the casinos, you can see the remnants of the base he had set up.

"It just felt bad," he said. "When I first saw what they had done in Wendover, it felt very bad. No casino has ever gotten a nickel out of me—I think people who gamble are a bunch of damn fools, throwing their money this way and that, watching those stupid wheels turn around.

"I didn't like it. I didn't like being around it. I just wanted to get out."

What about Tinian? What about that distant island in the Pacific, from which he had made the most important takeoff of his life—the most important takeoff of World War II? Had he gone back there to visit?

"I have not," he said. "I've been there, and I've seen it. In 1945. Not since. I'm a lousy tourist."

He looked at me with a smile and said, "You may have seen Wendover, but I know you've never seen Tinian."

"Actually, I saw it just the other day," I said.

In the 1940s, the United States struggled with almost unimaginable resolve to send men, machinery and weapons halfway across the globe and onto Tinian, so that Tibbets and his crew could stage the raid on Japan. Tinian was, and is, a speck in the Western Pacific Ocean, a piece of sea-surrounded land that was furiously fought for by American troops. It was because those troops were able to take Tinian and the other Northern Mariana Islands from the Japanese in 1944 that the U.S. airstrip could be built on Tinian. Soldiers, sailors and airmen were transported there—as was a certain B-29, as was the atomic bomb.

So far away, so remote and small in the middle of the ocean that it is difficult to find it on a map—yet the United States, battling hurriedly against space and time, moved all those men there.

And now, half a century later, I had gone to my office at the *Chicago Tribune* on the morning my series of stories about Tibbets began to appear, and among the e-mails about those columns was one from a man on Tinian.

His name was Jim McCullough; he wrote that he was the librarian for the elementary school on Tinian. He said that he was a regular reader of the column via the electronic version of the *Tribune*—he sits on Tinian, hits the keyboard, and there, in an instant, is the story I have written in Chicago. The concepts of distance, and time, and scope. . . .

"Tinian is a sleepy little island of about 2,500 people," he wrote in his e-mail. I began to correspond with McCullough, to ask him some questions about the island; he said that "While we [who were born in the U.S.] view Saipan and Tinian as one of the final stepping stones to victory in World War II, the Japanese see the islands as the location of one of the last gallant defenses of their homeland."

Life on Tinian, he wrote, is peaceful and pretty:

> It's like living in any small town Stateside. Except you can't get in your car and drive to the next town. Being in the middle of the Pacific Ocean has some disadvantages and some advantages. A disadvantage is that if you go anywhere—the beach, for example—there will be no one there and nothing going on. What a bore.
>
> On the other hand, one of the *advantages* is that you can go just about anywhere—the beach, for example—and no one else will be there. No surfers, boom boxes, wall-to-wall sunbathers to distract you from enjoying some peace and quiet. From each beach or hillside you get a magnificent view of endless blue.

McCullough wrote me that a casino (apparently you can't escape the things anywhere in the world, from Wendover to Tinian) had recently been built on the island, in an attempt to draw tourists from Japan and Korea. There are not many remnants from World War II, he said—and then he wrote something too strange to make up: "Most of the real [U.S. military hardware] such as trucks, Jeeps, buildings and aircraft wreckage was resold to the Japanese after the war as scrap metal."

I sent him a question about the airstrip itself—the runway from which Tibbets and his crew had taken off on that black August night in 1945, on their way to win the war.

Instead of answering me with words, McCullough went out onto the island with his camera. The next morning, when I got to work, there it was on my computer screen—a color snapshot of the island as it appears today. He had taken the picture and sent it to me over his computer.

"[The airstrip] is in very good shape, considering the time span involved," he wrote. "The top layer is broken up somewhat, so I would compare it to a large highway with pea-sized gravel scattered about. It is very easy and safe to drive on."

A safe and pebbly roadway—in a world that is tiny and incomprehensibly huge, all at the same time.

"So I have seen Tinian," I said to Tibbets.

"They're driving cars on the airstrip, the guy told you?" he said, shaking his head.

"He taps his computer key on Tinian, and in Chicago I'm looking at the airstrip," I said. "In seconds."

"As I recall, our trip took a little longer," he said.

As we talked, I looked at Tibbets and I thought about photographs of him I had seen from the war—photographs of him as a young pilot. I could still see that young man in his face—the young Tibbets' face was still there, underneath the years. It was like that portrait of my dad that had been painted in Italy—as old as he got, as sick as he got, I could always look in his face and see the young soldier in the portrait.

But I didn't know what my dad saw—I didn't know if, to my father, the young man was still in the mirror. I decided to ask

Tibbets what he saw—who was in his mirror every morning when he first woke up to start a new day?

"When I look in the mirror in the morning, I see myself," he said. "Let me put it this way—I figure that if another morning has come and I'm seeing something look back from the mirror, then I'm lucky that I'm looking at it."

"Do you like what you see?" I said.

What I meant was: Does the old man represent the young man pretty well? Is the life he has led reflected properly in the face in the mirror? But he answered in a way I hadn't anticipated.

"I've lost so much bone in my mouth," he said.

I didn't understand.

"I'm embarrassed to have my picture taken," he said. "My mouth goes in."

Apparently there had been some bone erosion above his upper lip. I hadn't noticed it—either before or right now. Even as he was saying the words, I looked at him and did not observe anything really wrong with his mouth.

"It's embarrassing to see me smile," he said. "That's why I don't smile very much in pictures."

You never know what another person worries about; you never know what another person thinks the world is seeing, and thinks the world finds lacking. I asked him, if he had a choice, whether that would be what he would change. Whether, if he could have something back, it would be the bone in his mouth structure that he seemed to feel was such a problem.

"No," he said. "My mouth, I can live with. But the hearing—the hearing is such an embarrassment for me. It's embarrassing as hell. I'm with people who I'm trying to have a nice time with—and I can't hear them. I have to ask them to say things over again. You've seen me do it with you—you'll say something to me, and I'll tell you that you have to say it again. It just makes me feel terrible. And then I'll have to do it again a few minutes later."

My father had the same problem as he grew older; conversations, especially in settings where there were many voices, such as in restaurants, were difficult for him to keep up with. He would become annoyed; especially with my brother or sister or me, if we were talking and he was missing sentences, he would occasionally get angry, as if we had somehow conspired to talk in a way that was designed to leave him out of the discussion. It was as if he—knowing how unclear our words were—believed that we knew it too, and were talking that way on purpose.

"It was all those years of pistons banging away next to my ears," Tibbets said. "From the airplane engines. There wasn't much I could do about it—and you don't realize at the time what effect it is going to have on your life. But that's what took my hearing away. That's what the doctors have told me."

"Would you be seventeen or eighteen again if someone could give you the chance?" I asked.

"No, but I'd like to be forty-five or fifty," he said. "By that time, I think I had a little sense. By the time I was forty-five or fifty, I appreciated the things around me more than I did before. But to be eighteen or twenty again? No way. I wouldn't want to be that age and have to think about raising a child today. Not in this world."

I asked him what physical changes he noticed as he grew older—what a man in his eighties observes about himself that's not visible to the outside world, but the man is conscious of every day of his life.

"I don't have the endurance I used to have," he said. "And I can't recover from being sick or hurting myself as quickly as I used to.

"But most of all . . . I could still *hear* when I was forty-five years old. A man has got to be able to *communicate* properly, and so many times I feel that I just can't, because of my hearing. You have no idea how much it bothers me. It bothers me every single day."

* * *

Thinking about that portrait of my dad, I tried to come up with anywhere else in his house where there had been a sign that he had been in World War II, and that it had been profoundly important to him. I couldn't think of anywhere—I knew there must have been places around the home in which he and my mom lived where there were artifacts from his war days, but if there were, I couldn't recall them.

I asked Tibbets about his home. How much war memorabilia did he keep around?

"None," he said.

"None, or very little?" I said.

"Nothing," he said. "There's not any indication in my house that I was ever in the service."

I knew that he was married for a second time, to a woman he had wed after being divorced from the woman who was his wife during World War II. I didn't know whether that had something to do with it—not having reminders of a first marriage in the home where a second marriage lives.

"That's not it," Tibbets said. "I just learned during the war—I had to move around so much, all the time, that taking things with me was a bother. The things that people call 'memorabilia'—it's not memorabilia at the time, it's just things you pack up and carry to the next place.

"I didn't want to carry all that stuff. So I didn't. Every time my orders said that I had to move on to the next place, I would just leave everything behind except for what I really needed to do my job."

But wouldn't some of those things be meaningful to him now—if he could have some artifacts from his war experiences in his home, would those artifacts not be evocative?

"It doesn't mean so much to me," Tibbets said. He pointed to his head. "I've got it all up here, anyway. I don't need to be reminded.

"I've gone into some people's houses—people my age, people

who were in the war—and you'd think there was a damned shrine in the house. Walls! Bookcases! All filled with things from their time in the service.

"I have never believed in that. I don't know what it is—do they want people to think that they're great big shots or something? That must be it. I don't want that. Not for me."

"So you think that's really why people do it?" I asked. "To impress visitors who come to their houses?"

"Oh, it's probably even worse than that," Tibbets said. "It would be bad enough if they set up these shrines to their war careers to convince other people of what a great job they did.

"But a lot of it is probably not to convince other people. It's to convince themselves."

Tibbets had made a note about something. I saw it on top of the table where we were sitting; the handwriting was neat, careful, almost pretty.

It had been that way when he had sent the handwritten greeting to my father. His penmanship was so lovely that it didn't necessarily seem to match the man. He was, after all, eighty-four; he also was a rough-hewn kind of guy, a combat-pilot/no-pretenses/anti-ornate person who, you might assume, expressed himself on paper with a direct and impatient scrawl.

But there it was: handwriting so elegant and delicate that it might belong to the most conscientious and eager-to-please schoolgirl at a top-echelon finishing school.

I asked him about it.

"I try to do things right," he said.

Simple as that. Pure Tibbets.

"My father had the best penmanship I ever saw," he said. "That is something I remember about him very well—how beautiful his handwriting was."

"Do you think a man's handwriting has anything to do with what kind of person he is?" I asked.

"Yes, very much so," Tibbets said. "More than anything else, if a man has good penmanship, it means that he's careful. He cares."

"He cares about what?" I asked.

"About himself," Tibbets said. "He cares what people think about him, and what conclusions those people might draw about him if they were only to see his handwriting."

I folded my arms over some pieces of paper where I'd written a few things down. I didn't want Tibbets to see the sloppy, rushed, all-but-indecipherable scrawl.

ELEVEN

We stayed late that night. I would ask him questions about the war, and he would search his memory and come up with bits and pieces of things that happened more then fifty years before; he would mention names and places and sometimes even specific dates, but there is one thing that he never talked about: being afraid.

So I asked him. What was he afraid of? Both now and then—what scared him?

"I'd have to tell you: nothing," Tibbets said. "What would there be for me to be afraid of?"

The answer to that one seemed beyond obvious: Back then, the German Luftwaffe and the Japanese air force would have seemed to present something to be mightily afraid of. Both—literally—were out to kill him. And now? As an eighty-four-year-old? People of that age have the right to be afraid of a lot of things. The uncertainty of their years, the thought of being eventually alone, the state of their health, something as elementary as walking down a city street at night.

"My mother told me, 'What is to be will be,' " Tibbets said. "I always took that to heart. In the war, and after the war. You can't change what's going to happen, so there's no use being afraid."

"Everyone's scared of something," I said.

"Well . . . I don't like snakes," he said. "But I wouldn't say I'm afraid of them."

"Do they spook you when you see them?" I said.

"No," he said. "I just don't like being around them. I've been in the Everglades, and I'd prefer not to be around those snakes, but they certainly don't put any fear into me."

"I can't believe that you feel just as safe on the streets at night now as you did when you were a young man," I said. I was recalling the look I often saw in my father's eyes, in his later years, when boisterous groups of young people would appear coming around a street corner. It bothered him that he, objectively, was now no match for them; it bothered him that in many ways he was dependent on their goodwill—or at least on their passivity.

"I'm more cautious now," Tibbets said. "But being cautious isn't the same as being afraid. It's just good sense.

"To me, fear paralyzes your mind. If you're afraid, you can't think straight. Literally—your thoughts become all confused if you're afraid. Do you think I could have flown those B-17 missions in Europe if I had allowed myself to be afraid? With all the decisions a man has got to make on missions like those?

"I don't care how old you are—being afraid can do nothing but cause you problems. I want to be able to think—I don't want to be a prisoner of some sort of fear. You've got a better chance to think your way out of a situation than to get out of it based on some kind of fear you're feeling."

He remained silent for a second or two, and then said:

"Bobcats."

"What about bobcats?" I said.

"If I was supposed to walk through a place where there were bobcats, I'd be afraid," he said.

"Why bobcats?" I asked.

"Bobcats are the dirtiest animals there are," he said. "If I had to be around bobcats, that would scare me to death."

"How about foxes?" I said.

"No, no," Tibbets said. "A fox is just a dog."

"Come on," I said. "A fox is definitely not a dog."

"Might as well be," Tibbets said. "A fox is no more dangerous to you than a dog would be."

This was a man who was not especially afraid of Hitler's fighter pilots, of the emperor's dive-bomber squads.

"I would do just about anything to avoid being around a bobcat," he said. "Take my word on this one—a bobcat is something to be afraid of."

I had never asked a pilot what it was like to sit in the back of a commercial plane when someone else was flying the thing. Tibbets clearly had always been a man who needed to be in control of every situation he was a part of. Did he feel differently about airplanes when he wasn't the one in the cockpit? Did something that filled him with such confidence—the act of flying—become something a little different on days when he wasn't the aviator?

Bobcats aside—as a passenger back in coach, did flying ever give him the jitters?

"Not a damn bit," he said.

He never noticed his hands and feet shifting involuntarily, in response to a motion the airplane in which he was a passenger was making—or not making?

"I know airplanes a little bit," he said. "I know that they're built to fly, to stay up in the air.

"And I know that the chances are good that the pilot up in front is a married man with a family. He's not up there to commit suicide.

"I know what he's doing up there, and what he's thinking. I'm as relaxed as can be, back in the passenger section. Flying the plane is not my job—it's his job. And he's not going to do anything that would kill himself."

"So you never notice little sounds when you're a passenger?"

"Yeah—but I know what they are," Tibbets said. "They're never a problem."

"You saw so many planes go down during the war," I said.

"Someone was shooting at them," he said.

* * *

The word he had used—*suicide*—brought my thoughts back to that small box of pills the flight surgeon had given him before the *Enola Gay* took off. One pill for each man—one pill for each member of his crew.

Because the mission had been a success, the decision about whether to take the pills had not come up. But I wanted to know whether Tibbets had given much thought to it at the time—to the question of killing himself had the Japanese military captured him.

"That wasn't the question I asked myself before we took off for Japan," he said. "The question I asked myself was, 'Are we going to come back or not come back?' I thought we were."

"Did the flight surgeon go over all the possibilities with you?" I asked.

"Not really," Tibbets said. "He just came out right before the flight and handed me the pillbox. He said, 'If you get shot down, these will do the job for you.' I took the box from him, but I wasn't really thinking about him, or about the box. I was ready to take off—ready to go.

"I remember him telling me that if we just bit into the pills, that's all it would take. He said, 'You will feel nothing.' Meaning that we would die painlessly."

"Would you have done it?" I asked. "If you had been captured, would you have taken the pill?"

"I don't know," he said. "I made sure it didn't come to that.

"But if we had been shot down, and the bomb hadn't detonated, and the Japanese had been ready to capture us and take us prisoner—I suppose I would have swallowed one of those pills. Think of the alternative—they would have done everything they could to get all the information out of us about the atomic bomb."

"Your crew members didn't even have much information about it," I said.

"The Japanese wouldn't have known that," he said. "In a way, the crew would have been better off dead than captured, because in captivity they'd be tortured until they gave up information about the bomb—and they wouldn't even have the information, but the Japanese probably wouldn't have believed them."

"You did know about the bomb," I said.

"I'm about the only one who did," Tibbets said. "Which makes me think that I would have taken the pill before the Japanese got the chance to start getting answers out of me."

"It would have worked that quickly?" I asked.

"That's what I was told," he said. "The flight surgeon assured me, 'You can swallow this thing and die within three minutes.' "

"Some assurance," I said.

"It was a cold-blooded fact," Tibbets said. "It was something I had to know. Same way I had to know how to fly the plane there and fly it back. If I had failed to do that, then I had to know how quickly the pill would kill me.

"It wasn't a choice, really. It was a cold-blooded duty."

Because he had not been put in the position of taking the pill, he flew the *Enola Gay* back to Tinian—only to find that the Japanese government and military leadership, even with all the carnage and death in Hiroshima, were refusing to surrender.

Which made the next step all but inevitable:

Do it again.

The question was, where? Which Japanese city would be the target for the second atomic bomb?

"Some people were saying Tokyo," Tibbets said. "To me, that made no sense at all. Yes, we had proven what the bomb could do. But let's say we had chosen to hit Tokyo—and we had killed the emperor.

"Who the hell were we going to make the peace with?"

So Tokyo was out. The second atomic mission—for which Nagasaki was selected as the target—was flown three days after the Hiroshima flight.

"Did you want to fly the second mission?" I asked Tibbets.

As I asked the question this was another moment—and there would be plenty of them during the times when I was in his presence—when the incongruity of the situation was almost too much to process. Elderly man sitting in a central Ohio bar, talking with a younger man who must raise his voice in order to be heard. Barroom close to empty, with the smattering of people who are present completely oblivious to the identity of the older man. If the other patrons are having any reaction at all, it is annoyance at the noise—they're trying to watch TV, and the younger man is speaking so loudly to the older man. Had the other people been paying attention, they would have been sucked into the surreal context of all this—they would have figured out that the elderly man was discussing not health problems, not sports, not family matters—but how he had dropped the atomic bomb.

"No, I didn't want to fly to Nagasaki," Tibbets said. "That was never the plan. I knew that I should fly the first one, to prove that it could be done. But I could not let my men think that I was trying to hog all the glory. So I knew that the second flight—if one was necessary—wasn't going to be mine.

"General Curtis LeMay was under the impression that I *was* going to fly the second mission. But Chuck Sweeney flew the Nagasaki mission, which had been my plan."

There it was again—the planning part. The macho aspects of flying a B-29 were almost a given with Tibbets—or, more exactly, with the young Tibbets. But, at least for me, it always circled around to the leadership qualities that had been expected of him. You, colonel—you're going to fly a nuclear weapon to Japan in an effort to win the war. And—oh—could you please be the chairman of the board of the unit that is responsible for this, too?

"It never occurred to me that being the leader was going to be a problem," Tibbets said. "When I was a kid, I was always the leader of the gang. I wasn't appointed—it never occurred to me *not* to be the leader.

"In the military, you ran into the situation all the time—you trained people to be leaders, but in your heart you knew that you can't do such a thing. Leaders can't be trained. Managers can—it is fairly easy to train a manager to do a manager's job."

"What's the difference?" I asked.

"Between a leader and a manager?" Tibbets said. "In the business world, it ends up being measured in salary, or title, or who has the best office. Career-oriented things. That's where you see the leaders and the managers split their ranks.

"But in the military—especially in war—the difference between leaders and managers is very simple. The difference can be the difference between life and death. So you'd better be certain that you have the real leaders in the positions where they are needed."

"You're convinced that it's nothing you can pick up by learning it?" I asked.

"I'm afraid not," he said. "You can't go to a businessman's school and walk out with it unless it's already inside you. They can give you an MBA—but they can't give you that."

I asked him—in the event that General LeMay had insisted that he fly the Nagasaki mission—whether he would have felt up to it. After all, he had carried out the culmination of the entire operation only days before—he had flown the long journey to Japan, had dropped the bomb, had flown back . . . might he not, objectively, have been too tired to effectively pilot the Nagasaki mission?

"Why would I be tired?" Tibbets said, with genuine curiosity in his voice. As if it were a trick question.

"Because of what you had just done," I said.

"I'd had a good night's sleep," he said. "Several of them, really."

"But you had to have been very, very tired," I said. "You just had to be."

"This was World War II," he said. "In my mind, it was illegal to get tired."

* * *

I had no doubt that Tibbets' ability to keep the details of the atom bomb project to himself had been absolute during those months of putting the 509th Composite Group together in 1944 and 1945. The information—the information that would change the world forever—flowed from his superiors to him, and stopped there.

But what of the 1,800 men who worked for him in Wendover—the men of the 509th, the men he had entrusted to make the mission a success? A cornerstone of his planning was his refusal to let them in on what exactly was going on—when they had signed on, it had been with the understanding that they would not be told exactly what they were trying to accomplish out on the salt flats.

Yet—human nature being what it is—had Tibbets not been afraid that even the little his men did know might get out, and compromise the whole project? Each man had to have figured out at least bits and pieces of the story of the atomic mission—each man might not have been aware of what the final picture would look like, but if enough individual observations were joined together, the story would be there. Had Tibbets simply taken it on faith that the men would obey him—that when he ordered them to tell no one anything about where they were or what they were doing, they would obey those orders without fail?

"Of course not," he said.

How, then, had he maintained secrecy?

"I told each man when he signed on that we would find out anything he might say to anyone outside our unit," Tibbets said. "I assured each man that we would know. I didn't say *how* we would know—but I told each man that this was no empty talk on my part.

"I set up a security organization for this very purpose. It was run by a man named Bud Uanna, and he had about thirty special agents working with him. Their job was to infiltrate what we were doing—to know everything.

"If one of our men received or sent mail, we read it. If a phone call came in, we listened to it. If a couple of guys were sitting around talking on the base, they were being heard. It had to be that way."

"But what about when the men left the base?" I said. "On the base, at least they were talking to each other. But off the base . . ."

"That was the key to everything we did," Tibbets said. "Shortly after the 509th was assembled in Wendover, I announced that I was allowing Christmas leaves for the men. They got to go home.

"I had a reason for doing this—and it had nothing to do with trying to be nice to them. Wendover was so isolated that there were really only two ways to get out—through the train station or the bus station in Salt Lake City, or through the bus station in Elko, Nevada.

"So the men left Wendover, and they went to Salt Lake City or to Elko. And if they had a drink in the bar of the train station, you can bet that the fellow on the next bar stool was one of our operatives. If they leaned back during the long bus ride out of Elko and the man in the next seat asked them what unit they were assigned to, you can bet that this man was working for us.

"And we found out who talked and who didn't. The men got home for their Christmas leaves—and the ones who had talked got telegrams, ordering them to report back to the base immediately. There was no indication in the telegram of why they had to come back.

"They got to Wendover, and I called them in. I would say, 'Did I not tell you to keep your mouth shut?' And if they would tell me that they *had* kept their mouth shut, I would tell them exactly what they had said, and when. How I knew was none of their business. It was my business.

"I wanted them to sweat. That was the whole purpose of this. I didn't want to go through it twice—I wanted to put so much fear in them that they would never talk about our unit again."

"So you never really believed, at the beginning, that they would keep silent the way you ordered them to?" I said.

"I knew very well that some of them were going to talk," Tibbets said. "You can't have that many men and have all of them obey. But if you put real fear in them—if you make them understand the lengths to which you will go to maintain security—then they won't do it again. Those who I did sense might do it again were shipped out. Some of them to Alaska, where there was no one to say anything to. But the rest were confined to the barracks for a while, and allowed to come out only to eat their meals in the mess hall, and after that it was up to them to keep quiet. Which they did."

"Did you let up on them after that first Christmas leave?" I asked.

"No," he said. "We never let up. We couldn't afford to. And we let them know it, in little ways.

"A man might call home, and his wife might tell him that she was pregnant—that she had gotten pregnant during his Christmas leave.

"And the next day one of us might see the man and say, 'Oh, your wife is going to have a baby. That's wonderful.'

"He'd know. We'd been listening to the phone call. We'd congratulate him on his wife's pregnancy, and it had nothing to do with offering best wishes. It had everything to do with letting him know that nothing got past us."

It sounded lonely. For all the swashbuckling aspects of the stories that Tibbets had been telling me—both the combat-pilot parts and the top-secret-commander parts—it sounded, to me, like just about the loneliest duty a man could have.

"Yeah," he said. "I felt pretty alone. A lot of the times I felt this real need to talk to someone about what I was going through—and there was no one I could talk to.

"Because of the orders I had been given, I really was alone with the knowledge of what we were doing and why. Most of the people who knew what I knew weren't with us in Wendover—they were in Washington, or Los Alamos. When I would fly there for meetings, I would be with people who knew the story. But then I would go back to Wendover—and even the people I trusted the most, even the people who worked with me the most closely, didn't know everything and couldn't know everything."

"Did you ever come close to cracking?" I asked.

"Look, we had a special job to perform," Tibbets said. "It had been told to me quite directly: If we were successful, we were going to hasten the end of the war. That was worth the loneliness.

"And please understand this: Any commander is lonely. When a man is in command, he sits in a position where he cannot have friend or foe. Regular human relationships do not figure into it. So you can't worry about what people think of you, and you can't lie awake and have sleepless nights. The job of being in command is lonely by definition.

"This one was just a little lonelier than most."

"And you were twenty-nine," I said.

"So were a lot of other guys," he said. "Twenty-nine didn't seem so young that year."

Which summed up something I had been thinking about all evening—really, since the day I had met Tibbets, but especially tonight, after dropping my mom off at the home she and my dad had shared, and coming back here to meet him.

They all seemed so much older at such a young age back then—the feeling I was having tonight was a permutation of what I had always felt when I had looked at the oil portrait of my dad in uniform, but it went well beyond that. The American men of their generation—or so it seemed—strove purposefully to come off as older than they really were. Maybe it was because of the war, or maybe it predated the war—but the emphasis on youthfulness that took over the American culture in the years after World War II seemed almost the mirror opposite of what had come before.

It was as if your dad, when he was a young man, wanted nothing more than to be mistaken for his own father. In mannerisms, and seriousness of purpose, and desire to join the society of adults—in just about every way, or so it appeared when looking back on them from a distance of fifty years, those young men were intent on being not so young at all.

Or was I wrong?

"Some elements of that are true," Tibbets said. "You can't generalize—it wasn't true of every man. But I think it was true of a lot of us.

"Maybe we had more of a reason to be serious. We were coming out of the Depression when the war began—we were serious even before we went into the service, because we grew up having no idea whether we would be able to go out and earn a decent living and support a family.

"That'll make you old inside—growing up worrying about that. Today . . . look, I don't want to be critical of young people who are growing up today. They have been handed a different set of circumstances than we were.

"But what I see, and I don't like, is this constant sense of *entitlement* that people who are younger than your dad's and my generation seem to have. Where did this belief that a person deserves *entitlements* come from? The queen of England may be entitled to something, but I can't think of many other people who are.

"Here's the difference—when I was running my company after I retired from the service, young people would come in to apply for jobs, and what do you think they always asked, right away? 'What are your benefits and workplace conditions?' That's what they would say. And they thought that's what they were supposed to say.

"I don't think we did that—I don't think that when your dad and I were looking for our first jobs, those were the words we said right away. What we said to a man we wanted to hire us was, 'I can do this for you.' 'I can help you out by doing this or that.' When you are raised during a little harder times . . .

"Well, you're a different person than if you were raised when things were easy. So, yes, I suppose we were different. With good reason."

TWELVE

When you are a child, you think your father can do anything. Anything in the world.

And, in every childhood, there comes a time when you first realize that you have been wrong. Your dad can't do everything. It was an illusion—an illusion willfully created by you.

Sometimes that realization arrives with great drama, at a life-changing juncture; more often it arrives quietly, in a moment that seems to mean nothing.

When I was four years old or so—maybe a year or two older—I asked my father to build me a rocket ship. He said he'd be glad to; he would build it in our garage. As soon as the weekend came, he would build it for me.

Waiting for Saturday, I was filled with excitement. I had the rocket ship in my mind, exactly as it was going to be: six or seven feet tall, made of wood (my dad had told me he would use wood), with a hatch through which I could climb in, and a seat in front of a steering wheel, and a control panel made of metal and glass. I knew the rocket ship wasn't going to go anywhere—I knew that it was just going to be one to get inside of and play with and pretend. But I couldn't wait for him to go out to the garage with me and for him to put it together.

Saturday came. He didn't forget. The two of us went out to the garage, and he pulled out his tool box and some pieces of lumber that were lying around.

He cut the lumber with a saw; he shaped it with a plane. He nailed a few pieces of the wood together, and there it was:

A toy rocket ship. About ten inches long. A rocket ship you could hold in one hand—a rocket made to a child's scale.

I don't know if my face showed anything that day. I'm certain I didn't say anything. But there was the rocket ship he had made me: not much bigger than a flashlight. It occurred to me that of course he hadn't known I was thinking of a big, elaborate rocket ship you could climb inside of; of course he hadn't been able to read my mind. And even if he had, he would not have been able to go out into the garage and make such a thing. It was beyond him—it was beyond what a dad could do.

That was the first time I knew: He could not do everything. I should not expect him to. My view of his abilities—like every child's view of his father's abilities, until a certain day arrives—had been overlarge.

Not his fault. Not my fault. Just the way the world works. And that first time gets you ready for what almost without question will come; that first time you realize your father can't do everything for you gets you ready for the day, many years down the line, when he can do just about nothing at all for himself. When the man you first assumed had no limitations turns out to have nothing but limitations, as he comes closer and closer to the day he will die.

They were raised during times that were a little harder, Tibbets had said; as far as work was concerned, the men of his and my dad's generation did not go in to a potential employer demanding things.

My father's voice—talking about the job offer that had gotten him out of Lima. A couple named Violet and Sam Shinbach, who lived in a suburb of Columbus called Bexley, were starting a company that specialized in metal plating. The company would do standard silverplating of household dinnerware, but the thing that was going to make it different, or so the Shinbachs believed, was their idea for bronze-plating baby shoes. They thought that parents might want to preserve their children's shoes as family heirlooms; this new firm of theirs, which they planned to call the Bron-Shoe Company, might offer prospects for the future for an employee who worked hard at the beginning. Or so my father seemed to believe:

One good thing I always remember, I didn't have any friends when I came to Lima, but when I left town a year and a half later these kids gave me a party at the Kirwan Hotel, in the bar, as a going-away gesture, and it was absolutely lovely. It was a good feeling to leave Lima knowing that I had some excellent friends remaining.

Violet and Sam Shinbach were in need of someone who had sales-promotion experience and ability, and having been with Philip Morris I seemed to fit the bill and I was available—cheap. So I left Lima to come to Columbus to join the then very tiny Bron-Shoe Company. There were exactly four employees.

Sam and Violet were good enough to let me stay at their house, where I had a bed underneath the stairway and all privileges of their home on Fair Avenue. This was the summer of 1940, and at the beginning of that summer I bought a new car on one of my trips back to see the folks in Akron, and it was a splendid Ford convertible coupe painted cigarette cream, which actually was a bright yellow. And my friends in Lima had immediately tagged and labeled the car as the flying omelette, and I indeed did fly around in that car the summer of 1940.

I was working pretty hard over the summer with Sam Shinbach, and at the end of the summer we went on a long business trip to the East Coast with Violet, and I started learning the business in earnest.

I shall not attempt to go into a history of the early part of World War II. Suffice it to say that the draft came along, and every able-bodied young man had to register for the draft, which of course I did. As the fall wore on they started to pick the numbers out of the big fish bowl in Washington, and lucky me, I was number one draft in the Bexley area. . . .

I hadn't been too crazy about the confinement of the Bron-Shoe job as compared with the freedom I had had with Philip Morris in the Lima area. But little did I know what was going to happen. I was called up, and on January 28, 1941, I entered the Army and was sent to Camp Shelby in Hattiesburg, Mississippi, that same day or a few days later. . . .

I have seen some impressive things in my life. I have never seen anything to match the way my mother cared for my father in the months of his dying.

When he became totally bedridden, virtually everyone to whom she went for advice—his doctor, our relatives, her friends, in the end the hospice people—told her the same thing: You must make some time for yourself. If you try to do everything, if you try to be with him every minute, you will exhaust yourself, deplete your strength and health, perhaps even shorten your own life. For his sake as well as your own, you must regularly step away—you must breathe.

She said yes. She said of course she knew that was true.

And then she didn't do it.

With the exception of when she took a shower, or went to the grocery to buy food, or had to leave the house for an essential errand, she did not leave him. He became more emotionally dependent on her than he ever had been; he became frightened and disoriented when she would leave the room. We had hired a man to come to the house every day to do the things she was not physically strong enough to do—lift him from the bed, assist him with the bathroom functions that must be tended to—there was time for her to give herself some peace. She didn't want it. She wanted to be with him.

As his confusion grew, he began to ask her the same questions, over and over. This was a man who never forgot a detail—and all of a sudden he was interrogating her about things that made no evident sense, and when she would offer some explanation to calm him, he would nod—and then, within minutes, ask the same questions once more.

And she would hold his hand and answer. Softly, lovingly, without rancor—she would go through everything again.

He would ask: What about the third floor? Was the third floor cleaned up? It was important—the third floor had to be straightened. Had she done it yet?

And she would explain with gentle patience: Their house did not have a third floor.

The mailman—had she given the mailman the notice yet? If the mailman came and she didn't give him the notice, he didn't know what they would do. Was she certain the mailman hadn't arrived yet?

And she would ask him what he wanted her to tell the mailman—and he would look off, not being able to think of it, and finally say that he guessed he was mixed up—he guessed it didn't matter. Then: Had the mailman come yet? Had she remembered to tell the mailman what he had asked her to tell him?

The white pipe that he wanted her to adjust; the geometric forms that he wanted her to explain. In his dying he became stuck on these things, things that defied logic, and she would sit and talk with him about them as if it were forty years earlier, and they were talking about their children, or their vacation plans, or their hopes. From the sound of her voice, you would think that these awful conversations were the most wonderful moments she could ever spend. She was talking with her husband.

She assured us that this was fine; she assured us that this was what she wanted. Often he would wake her up at 3 A.M. or 4 A.M. and start with his questions. The third floor; the mailman; the white pipe. She was getting no sleep, but she wouldn't leave the room. Don't worry, she told my brother and my sister and me; I sleep during the daytime, when he sleeps.

One night I called and there was something changed in the way she sounded. She was near tears. He had been asking her questions for twenty straight hours, she said; she would talk to him and soothe him and answer the questions, she would assure him that the fears upon which he was basing the questions were not real, and he would seem to understand—he would thank her. But the period between the bursts of questions had shrunk to virtually nothing; within seconds the same questions would start again. She was bone-weary, close to desperate.

She had gone out to the living room to lie down, just for a second, and had drifted off to sleep when I had called. She was telling me about all this, and the hollowness of her voice frightened me. In the background, I could hear him calling to her from the bedroom. Where was she? He needed to talk to her—he needed to ask her about some things. This was the ultimate terrible extension of Organize, Delegate, Supervise, Check: He was still doing it, except what he was supervising, what he was checking on, had only the most tenuous connection to reality.

"I'll be OK," she said.

I said I would get the next flight to Columbus. "Really, I'll be OK," she said. "This has just been a bad day." I said I'd be there anyway.

On the tape he made telling his life story, you have to jump past his induction into the Army to find his first reference to her.

It comes after he has been at Camp Shelby for a while; it comes as he is describing a trip to Columbus he had taken when the soldiers had been granted a leave.

In Columbus I had met a certain Phyllis Harmon, and I thought she was kind of nice. I had taken her to the movies on one of my previous trips to Columbus when I was first visiting Violet and Sam.

She seemed like an OK gal, but I didn't pay a hell of a lot of attention to her because I was still squiring around a girl named Nana Bowler, who lived up in Lima.

Well, I didn't think a heck of a lot about Phyllis Harmon until after I had been in the Army for about six months, and I believe she and I started corresponding with each other.

One fine day when I was on leave in Columbus, she volunteered to drive me to Union Station where I would catch a train to go up to Akron to see my folks. I remember the old blue/gray Pontiac she was driving, and I also remember she looked pretty damn good to me, and I said to myself, I think I'm going to marry that gal.

Little did I know that I really was going to. I believe that that little ride to the train station from Violet's house with Phyllis was the luckiest thing that ever happened to me. That fact has proven itself time and time and time again over the years.

I remember that once I was visiting my parents—this must have been when he was in his mid-seventies, getting noticeably older but not yet really ill—and I was staying in my brother's old room on the basement level of the house.

One of the lightbulbs in the bathroom down there had burned out—it was a special kind of bulb that had to be replaced in a specific way. I mentioned it to my parents at breakfast; my father said that he would take care of it.

We went down to the basement and he stood on top of a chair and asked me to hand him a new bulb and a tool of some sort.

"Don't let him stand up there and do that," my mother said to me, which was my thought exactly. I had no idea how to replace this particular bulb, but it was obvious that my dad—who had been having some trouble with his back and neck, as I recall—should not have been the one up on the chair performing this task.

"Let me get up there and do it," I had said.

"You'd screw it up," he said, which was true.

"Just tell me how to do it and I'll do it," I said.

"Give me the bulb," he said.

My mother whispered to me: "I mean it, you do it—he shouldn't be up there."

So I said, "Come on, get down—I want to do that."

And he—I can hear his words right now—said:

"I'm running this lash-up."

What a phrase. It sounds more Navy than Army—*running this lash-up.* In the middle of his seventies, so many years removed from military service, yet when he wanted to make a point, that's the language he reverted to. When, for example, he wanted to let us know that there was a person he didn't like—this could be someone our family had known for years, or a waiter in a restaurant whose attitude seemed lackadaisical—he would say to us: "I don't like the cut of that guy's jib." Again, Navy—which he was never in. But those were the references—military references.

He was kidding, at least a little bit, when he said them; he knew that changing a lightbulb hardly constituted a lash-up that had to be run, and he knew that the cut-of-his-jib line always made us smile. But when he used those phrases it was almost as if the words were not meant for us, but for himself. As if he were having a private conversation with himself that no one else was supposed to hear—or, more accurately, the emotional meaning of which no one else was supposed to be able to translate.

On the troop train to go down to Camp Shelby, Mississippi, all I could hear was a lot of griping about the Army, and not much foreboding, but a lot of dissatisfaction because it was kind of an uncomfortable ride down to Hattiesburg. Upper and lower berths, two people to a berth. . . .

After we got down to Camp Shelby, it was an entirely new world. The camp had recently been gouged out of cornfields and cotton fields, and consisted of miles and miles of perimeter tents with wood-and-coal-burning stoves in them. And that was our introduction to Army life. The first thing we noted was a cloud of black smoke over the whole area as far as you could see, a result of the soft coal that was being burnt in those stoves. It was the middle of winter, and while the camp was in

Mississippi it was still a very cold place, and the stoves were badly needed.

We lined up and were assigned certain companies. . . .

They were getting used to the cut of each other's jibs—young men who, weeks before, had been working in cities and small towns and farm communities all over the United States were now inextricably connected with one another. From the sound of my father's voice, it seemed that this lash-up was something that held unexpected revelations for him.

In the meantime, a strange phenomenon occurred. As you know, the favorite thing for a soldier to do is gripe, and believe me, this division made up of fifteen thousand recent civilians and a handful of regular Army officers and enlisted men did very little else but gripe. The weather was terrible, the jobs onerous, the drills and hikes very bone-wearying, and in all it was a hell of a way to live.

But the phenomenon I mentioned to you was just this—strangely enough, I started to like it. I don't know why, but it just seemed to me that I was free.

Although I had to obey orders and do everything a soldier must do, it was kind of a newfound freedom. Everyone was alike, nobody was given any privileges other than what they deserved or earned, and I was not fettered by a job that I did not like. So going into the Army, believe it or not, was kind of a relief for me. . . .

Listening to his voice—in the months after he was gone—made me think about the fine gradations in a man's life, the never-anticipated changes a man may encounter, changes that transform him from the person he was before into the person he will be forever after. Showing up for Army training in Mississippi and finding it liberating, finding it freeing . . . it's the kind of moment in a man's existence that they don't make movies about, I thought, but one that bears more quiet power than any dozen action films.

And then I thought about a man they did make a movie about. There were some questions I wanted to ask—about the movie, and about the man who was portrayed in it—the next time I saw him.

THIRTEEN

The movie—black-and-white—starred Robert Taylor in the role of Colonel Paul Tibbets. It was called *Above and Beyond,* it was produced by MGM and released in 1952, and you could see traces of *The Best Years of Our Lives* all over it—at least you could see how the MGM marketing department was trying to link it with *The Best Years of Our Lives.*

The Best Years of Our Lives had won the Academy Award for Best Picture of 1946. A beautiful, movingly lyrical film—it holds up even now—it told the story of three servicemen returning to the same small town after World War II had been won. The problems and eventual triumphs of the three characters—a bank executive played by Fredric March (who won the Oscar for best actor), a drugstore employee played by Dana Andrews, a kid just out of school played by Harold Russell (a young veteran who won the Oscar for best supporting actor and who, like the character, had lost his hands in the war)—captivated audiences all over the United States. How these men adjusted to the America they had left behind—and to their own families—touched emotions deep inside a nation that understood the plot only too well.

So when the story of the *Enola Gay* mission was brought to the screen, it was following in the steps of a proven feel-good movie about the U.S. after the American victory.

But how to make Americans feel good about the devastation and death that Tibbets and his crew had left behind in Japan?

And—more to the point—how to make Americans feel good about Tibbets' family life?

The preview for the movie is startling to view today. It begins on a note of romance, with the Tibbets character saying to his wife, Lucy (played by Eleanor Parker): "If I didn't have you, I wouldn't have anything."

"Oh, Paul," she replies passionately.

Almost immediately, though, the tone of the preview shifts. The deep, portentous voice of an unseen announcer informs the audience: "In his heart was locked the world's best-guarded secret. On his shoulders rested a responsibility greater than any man had ever carried. From here on he had no wife, no loved ones, no friends. Just duty—above and beyond." Next the audience sees Paul and Lucy Tibbets at the air base in Wendover. He is angrily speaking to her.

"Go home!" the Tibbets character says. "Stay home! And keep your nose out of this base!"

The Lucy character, not even trying to hide her contempt for her husband, says: "Is it really necessary to play it this big, Paul?"

"They told me not to bring you out here in the first place," Tibbets says. "Maybe they were right. . . . For the last time, stay out of my business!"

"It's my business, too!" Lucy says. "Now I'm beginning to understand a few things I couldn't face before."

"That's enough!" Tibbets says.

"Everything they say is true!" Lucy says. "You're not the man I married, not anymore. You're ambitious, you're cold, you're unfeeling. . . ."

Some "best years."

The studio—seeming to realize the problem it had on its hands—endeavored to market the movie to a female audience, in the hopes that enough women would want to see a motion picture about a troubled wartime romance that the film might turn a profit. The line used to promote the movie was: "The love story behind the billion dollar secret." MGM tagged endorsements by prominent women reviewers onto the end of the trailer:

" 'A love story with tenderness and heartbreak. Ladies, take a couple of hankies with you, you'll need them.'—Hedda Hopper, syndicated columnist."

" 'Picture of the month . . . a love story no woman will ever forget.'—Louella Parsons, *Cosmopolitan.*"

" 'The love interest is very real. Every woman should see it.'—Ruth Harbert, motion picture editor for *Good Housekeeping.*"

I knew that Paul and Lucy Tibbets had been divorced after the war; still, it was surprising to see the brittleness between them depicted on a movie screen. *Above and Beyond* didn't do much at the box office in 1952; you virtually never see it on television these days, and video stores don't regularly stock it. Yet as I watched the movie—looking at Robert Taylor on the screen playing the young Tibbets, thinking of the Tibbets at eighty-four whom I had been getting to know—I thought about something else, too: of my parents, and their closeness and love that had begun during the war, and that had lasted all those years.

For the last time, stay out of my business! . . .

You're not the man I married, not anymore. . . .

I could hear the echoes of the cinematic Paul and Lucy Tibbets, and I knew I had to ask him about it. Tibbets may have won the war; I couldn't help thinking that my dad was able to win something else, something that had eluded Tibbets.

I'm afraid that I treated Lucy very badly," he said.

I could tell that he didn't want to spend much time on this; he was as direct as always, but it was plainly far from his favorite subject.

"Look," he said. "I've told you about the secrecy that I was asked to maintain. I took that as seriously as a man can take anything. Please think back to 1944 and 1945. There were very few people in the world who were aware that we were well along in developing a bomb that could end the war. If I couldn't tell any of the men who were serving under me, I certainly couldn't tell my wife."

"I never knew how things like that worked during the war," I said. "Whether there was kind of an understanding that of course a man would tell the truth to the person he loved the most—of course he could trust her to keep the secret."

"You're right—you don't know how things worked," Tibbets said. "No, you didn't tell your wife things. What do you think I was explaining to you when I told you about setting up the operatives at the train stations and the bus stations? About listening in to the men's phone calls and reading their letters? If you were told not to say anything to anyone, that included your wife. You never knew who a guy's wife was going to talk to after she had talked to her husband."

"So how did you handle it?" I said.

"I wouldn't talk to her," Tibbets said.

"You mean about the mission?" I said.

"About anything, I'm afraid," he said. "Especially when she was in Wendover—I found myself shutting down completely. I couldn't talk to her about the things that were most important to me, so I found myself not saying very much of anything to her about other things, either. It wasn't fair to her—it also probably wasn't fair to me, being put in that position, but I know it wasn't fair to Lucy."

I was aware that Paul and Lucy Tibbets had had two sons who were very young during the war. I also knew that, in the years after the war and after the divorce, there had been a considerable emotional breach between the sons and their father, and that they did not see much of each other. Although there had been something of a reconciliation, the chasm in many aspects still remained, or so I had been told.

"Did the problems between you and your sons happen because

of what they lived through when things were bad with you and their mother?" I asked.

"I think so, to a large extent," Tibbets said. "I was not a good husband, and I was not a good father. I was so wrapped up in doing a good job in what I was entrusted to do in the war that I did not do a good job with the other things.

"I've told my boys: Your mother got a bum deal."

"You say that you don't think you were a good father, either?" I asked.

"No, I wasn't," he said. "Not the best."

"Why?" I said.

"I don't know," Tibbets said. "Don't ask me."

"But I am asking," I said.

"I was just . . . I was just distant from the boys," he said. "I didn't know how to show them any affection. I'm from the generation that, you know, if a man kisses a man—his son—that was considered a sissy thing."

"Did you know back then that you weren't doing so well with your sons?" I said.

"I didn't see them almost at all for years," he said. "I was flying those missions in Europe, and then there was Wendover—it's not like I had the chance to do well or not well with them. I wasn't there. I was in the war."

"When the war ended was it too late?" I asked.

"It might not have been, had I known how to be any other way," he said. "But I didn't. At the time, I thought that was how a father was supposed to be. I think I was probably wrong. But I didn't know. I didn't know how to do it."

I could sense his discomfort, just talking about it. So I shifted the subject. Instead of asking him about his relationship with his wife during the war—the relationship that had been portrayed in the movie—I asked him about the feeling of being depicted in a movie in the first place. What was that like, for a man who grew up in a movie-worshiping America—what had it been like, in 1952, to know that at least for a while, someone pretending to be you was being seen on screens in every downtown and neighborhood in the country?

"I found out right away that they took liberties," Tibbets said. "They made things up. Things about the flight—at first I felt like correcting them, but then they explained to me that this is the way the movies work. To make it more entertaining, and to make it move along. So I just accepted that, and watched it as a movie."

"Did you ever think you were similar to a certain movie star?" I said.

"Well, I liked Robert Taylor," Tibbets said. "He was a nice fellow."

"I'm talking about now," I said. "Is there anyone out there who you think has your personality?"

"Like who?" he said.

"I don't know," I said. "Maybe Clint Eastwood . . ."

"Well, I'm a stubborn man," he said. "I'm stubborn in my own way. I don't know if that's what you're asking, but I would say my stubbornness is the main thing about me.

"And I do like actors who don't use a lot of words. There's no use in wasting a lot of damn words when you can do something instead."

I brought up the *Best Years of Our Lives* comparison to *Above and Beyond.* I told him I'd noticed that *Above and Beyond* had even tried to emulate the inspiring symphonic sound that had served as the background music in *The Best Years of Our Lives.* It hadn't quite worked—Hugo Friedhofer had won an Academy Award for his heart-stirring score in *Best Years,* but the strings in *Above and Beyond* had merely felt weird and out of place. At least to me.

What had Tibbets thought of *The Best Years of Our Lives*?

"I never saw it," he said.

"You never saw it?" I said. "It was the best movie ever made about coming home from the war. How could you not see it?"

"I guess I wasn't interested," he said.

"What war movies have you seen?" I asked.

"Name some," Tibbets said.

"*Thirty Seconds Over Tokyo,*" I said.

"Never saw it," he said.

"*Saving Private Ryan,*" I said.

"I did not go," Tibbets said.

"*The Thin Red Line,*" I said.

"No," he said.

"You just don't like war movies?" I said.

"They're a bunch of bullshit," he said. "To make a movie about war, you have to glamorize it. You have to take the leading man and make him a hero."

"You'd think that would be pretty easy in a war movie," I said.

"That's not necessarily the case," Tibbets said. "In war, there are a bunch of bastards on *our* side the same as there are on the other side. Guys who are looking out for their careers—just like in industry. Guys who cut your throat if you get one-up on them."

"Not literally cut your throat," I said.

"No," he said. "In the same way people do it in business, though, people do it in the military."

"Did you at least like John Wayne movies about the military?" I said.

"Not really," he said. "At least Bob Taylor had served—by the time he played me in the movie, he had been in the Navy. John Wayne was a cowboy actor. Shoot 'em up.

"Maybe that's why he did so well when he was playing soldiers. A cowboy is a hero. People like cowboys. In a real war, you don't see many cowboys. A cowboy is a romantic kind of fellow.

"You don't find a lot of romance in a real war."

What had been on my mind—what I had been waiting for the right moment to talk to Tibbets about—wasn't war movies, and wasn't marital difficulties.

It was this:

Every time Tibbets spoke of his lingering thoughts about the aftereffects of the *Enola Gay* mission, it was with some variation of the I've-never-lost-a-night's-sleep line. He had been saying that for years; he had been saying that his conscience was clear, that he had done what his country had asked, that he had helped save many lives by bringing the war to an end.

And I believed him. For all the reasons we had talked about, and more, I knew that he was proud of what he had done and that he was honored he had been the man his country had asked to do it. It wasn't just American lives he had saved—not just the lives of the U.S. soldiers who would have been killed in a land invasion of Japan. He most likely had saved many Japanese lives, too—the lives of Japanese soldiers and civilians who would have died had the fighting moved on to Japanese soil. An argument can be made that many more Japanese lives would have been lost in conventional warfare once the land invasion began than were lost at Hiroshima and Nagasaki. The dying just would have stretched out over a much longer period of time.

And yet . . .

Some of the letters I received after my newspaper columns about Tibbets ran were from Japan; the columns appeared over there, so readers picked up their papers one day to see the stories about the man who had dropped the atomic bomb on their country.

The reaction from Japanese readers was not angry, or even resentful. Many said that they agreed Tibbets had been acting as a good combat pilot should, and that they understood, in the context of World War II, why his country asked him to do it. Some said that had Japan possessed the atomic bomb, the Japanese military leaders certainly would have tried to drop it on the United States; some said—as Tibbets had—that in the end, Japanese lives may have been saved by the bomb bringing a swift end to the war.

But the letters from Japan were not really about that. The letters were the Japanese readers' accounts of what happened. Some were firsthand, some had been passed down from older family members. They weren't about politics and they weren't even about warfare. They were human stories about what occurs when an atomic weapon is dropped onto an unsuspecting city.

Some of them kept me awake far into many nights. One in particular—it was a letter from a Japanese woman named Hideko T. Snider who had moved to the United States in the years after the war—stayed with me for days after I first read it.

I wanted Tibbets to know about it, too. This was not a woman who hated him, or who didn't understand why he did what he was asked to do. But I wanted him to know about her letter. So I brought it with me on my next visit to him:

> . . . On the morning of August 6th, 1945, I was a child in Hiroshima, just returned on the previous day from a far-away village where I was evacuated. We had no idea *Enola Gay* was on its way with its grave mission.
>
> When the bomb was let go in the mid air over the sky of Hiroshima, it unleashed the power so horrific that it defied a language of description. Even those of us who lived through it could not fathom our own experiences. Some people evaporated at the center. Hundreds and thousands were charred and naked with physical distinctions no longer recognizable. Their arms stretched forward, moving slowly, they fell to the ground and floated on the rivers. My brother, cousin and other cousins were among them. We were unable to rescue those buried alive under the collapsed buildings and burned to death. My mother was one of them.
>
> We did not know this was only the beginning. We did not know that the lethal power of radiation had penetrated to the marrow of our bones, destroying our organs and changing our DNA. People continued to die suddenly and strangely, bleeding from the mouth and often from every orifice. I nearly died myself, in a semi-conscious state running extremely high fever for days.
>
> The strange phenomenon continued with increased number of

> cancer deaths, first leukemia, breast and lung cancers not only among the survivors but among those who entered the city after the explosion, such as those searching for the family members. They, too, breathed the poison and were affected by it. . . .
>
> Strangely, the plants and flowers bore misshapen and misfigured offsprings. Three years after the A-bomb explosion, the banks of the river in Hiroshima were covered by 4-, 5- and 6-leaved clover. I know. I picked them up and kept them in my Bible. In Nagasaki, they detected the presence of radioactive poison in their water reservoir and in the soil more than 30 years later.
>
> It is an irony that my mother, who loved Wordsworth and even *Gone With the Wind,* never took a gun or spoke ill of the Americans or the British. My male cousin, who was only 12 and was burned alive by radiation, loved to watch the B-29 and its mechanical wonders. He used to climb to the rooftop to watch them at his own peril. There were many formations passing over our sky. . . .

It was the image of the boy—the image of the boy waving to the B-29s as they passed overhead—that haunted me. I had called Hideko Snider and spoken with her about it; she told me that apparently in the days and weeks before August 6, there had been a number of B-29 reconnaissance missions over Hiroshima, in which no bombs were dropped or shots fired. Many residents—like her twelve-year-old cousin—began not to fear the sounds of the B-29s; they thought they had learned that the planes were merely traveling by, on their way to somewhere else. Her cousin loved airplanes. From the roof he would wave hello toward the pilots.

And then the *Enola Gay* came.

I wanted to talk to Tibbets about the boy on the roof.

"So the boy was watching the other B-29s when they flew by," he said, his voice sounding different.

There were times when I was speaking with Tibbets that he

seemed like the young aviator of the 1940s—full of self-assuredness, bluster, literal combativeness. On this day, though, he was all of eighty-four.

I had recounted the story to him; he got quiet and there was a softness in his eyes. He said that, yes, there had been many flyovers of Hiroshima; yes, as far as he had been told, the citizens became so accustomed to the B-29s overhead that they assumed they were in no danger. That was the point—to lull the people on the ground so that on the day the *Enola Gay* arrived it would seem routine.

"Does it bother you at all, that story?" I said.

"Bother me to hear it?" he said. "Yes, it does. Of course it does.

"I can picture him doing it. He was encouraging the B-29s to fly on. I can see him up on the rooftop waving. . . ."

"I know you've lived with this for a long time . . ." I began.

Tibbets interrupted.

"You know, I was told that there were American prisoners being held captive near Hiroshima," he said. "The generals told me that the prisoners were there, but they said 'We don't know where.' They said that when we dropped the bomb, there was a good chance that we would be dropping it on American prisoners.

"And then they said to me, 'Will that bother you?' "

"What did you say?" I asked.

"I said no," Tibbets said. "I said it wouldn't bother me."

"Was that true?" I said.

"I had to make it be true," Tibbets said. "Because if it wasn't true, if I let it bother me, I might flinch. I might deviate from the job I was supposed to do. They asked me if I would be able to drop the bomb, even knowing what might happen.

"And I said, 'Yes. Of course.' "

"Were you at all sorry at the time that you were being put into that position?" I asked.

"That wasn't my business, to be sorry," Tibbets said. "My business was to hit them."

I told him that Studs Terkel had once written a fine book called *"The Good War."* It was about World War II—but what many people, even those who had enjoyed the book, had not noticed about it was that the phrase "The Good War" was in quotes. It was Terkel's way of making a point.

"His point was that no war is good, wasn't it?" Tibbets said.

"Yes," I said.

"He's right," Tibbets said. "There is no such thing as a war that is good."

I asked him if he thought that people who anguished over the suffering that was caused by the bomb he and his crew dropped—people like the woman who had written me the letter about the boy on the rooftop, people who sincerely feel that no victory was worth the human damage that Tibbets and his crew caused—were wrong to feel that way.

"No," he said in something close to a whisper. "They're not wrong. Why should they be?"

"Because of all the things you've told me," I said. "Because of the necessity of ending the war."

"Their relationship to that day is different than mine," Tibbets said. "I had a different relationship to that day than they do.

"But that doesn't make them wrong. I don't know who's wrong or what's wrong.

"I don't know that I'm right."

He looked at me.

"Do you understand what I'm trying to say?" he said.

I said I thought that I did.

And I said I had one other letter to ask him about.

It had come from a high school student—a seventeen-year-old boy by the name of Patrick J. Walsh. He, too, had read the newspaper columns I had written about my first visit with Tibbets; his letter was full of praise for Tibbets' bravery, and full of appreciation for the ending of the war that followed the mission. He wrote that if it were not for Tibbets and men like him, "our country would not be free from tyranny."

And then he ended the letter this way:

> I have just one question, Mr. Greene. I am an Irish-Catholic. I believe in God. I believe in the existence of heaven.
>
> I would like to know if Paul Tibbets ever thinks about going to heaven? I have asked myself this question, but have not come up with an answer.

So I did ask Tibbets, on behalf of the young man:

Did he ever think about it? Did he think he would be going to heaven?

He sat silent for a few seconds. Then he said:

"I never planned my life the way it happened. I never planned it so that I can go to heaven."

"What should I tell him?" I asked Tibbets.

"Tell him that heaven is here on Earth," Tibbets said. "Tell him that, yes, I think I will go to heaven.

"But tell him that your happiness is here. It's here, not in heaven. It's up to you to find it."

I asked him when the last time was that he cried.

"Don't ask me that," he said.

"You don't want to talk about it?" I said.

"I don't know when it was," he said. "I don't remember."

"I can drop the subject," I said.

"Just because I never was emotional and I never burst out into tears doesn't mean I don't feel certain things inside of me," he said.

FOURTEEN

Sometimes, when I was very young, my father would pick me up in his car after I had been playing at my best friend Jack Roth's house.

We played Army—we played war. We had seen the movie *To Hell and Back,* which starred World War II combat hero Audie Murphy portraying himself. In the movie, Murphy had seemed to run all over every overseas battlefield there ever was, mowing down the enemy, leaping for cover, tossing grenades and diving away from the explosions. He was who Jack and I pretended to be—he was the perfect representation of the courageous American soldier.

Jack's house had a little sloping hill just off to one side of the front yard. It was about as gentle as an elevation could possibly be—the rise from the sidewalk to the top of the hill was probably no more than a foot. But we were very small, too, so we would stand on the sidewalk and then charge up that hill, sometimes holding cap guns, sometimes holding sticks or overgrown twigs from Jack's parents' trees.

My dad would show up to bring me home for dinner, and he would stand beside his car and watch what Jack and I were doing. He never said much about it; he just stood and watched, as if it reminded him of something.

From his description of the first days of training at Camp Shelby, when he and the other draftees and enlistees had arrived at the base, in an America that did not seem all that expertly geared up to fight a war on foreign shores:

. . . To show you what kind of equipment we had, we used broomsticks for rifles and also to simulate 37-millimeter anti-tank guns. We used World War I underwear, wrap leggings and helmets. . . .

On we went with our training day after day until we finally went on what was called the Louisiana maneuvers. Many, many divisions packed up lock, stock and barrel and descended into the murky swamps and badlands of Louisiana where maneuvers which proved to be the largest in the history of the United States started to unfold. This was a very exciting time because we were all issued new equipment including real rifles and the new helmets. Of course that was a morale booster because before it was as if we were just playing soldier, but this time it looked like it was for real. . . .

The maneuvers were as close to actual battle as we could possibly be until later on we actually got into combat. . . . These were exercises in which live ammunition was used. . . . So here we are, we're running up and down the roads and byways of Louisiana not realizing that very, very shortly something bad would happen and would affect the lives of not only us, but everybody in the whole world. . . .

Less than ten years after the war ended, he would take my sister and me—my brother was just a baby, he was too young—to an amusement park called Norwoods.

This was in the days before the giant theme parks; Norwoods was as local as local could be. It was just a few minutes' drive from our house, with its front entrance on Main Street and its eastern boundary butting up against a tree line that led down to Alum Creek.

There was a not-very-tall ferris wheel, a merry-go-round, a "thrill ride" that mainly consisted of a two-minute trip through a lightless, overly warm room that featured one skeleton that lit up on mechanical cue, one recorded transcription of a woman screaming, one wooden hand, attached to a pulley, that came out of the wall at its assigned time, and, if memory serves, one hanging rubber mat with fringe on the bottom that swept across you as the car moved past.

There was more at Norwoods—bumper cars, Skee-Ball machines, the shortest miniature railroad in the history of amusement parks—but I think what I remember most was the smell of gunpowder.

It was from the shooting gallery—a place where men and older boys aimed rifles at moving targets that proceeded horizontally across their line of sight. There were white rabbit-shaped objects, and bull's-eye devices, and—I don't know why—figures that looked like horses. Why anyone would want to shoot a horse . . .

And it is difficult to believe, recalling Norwoods now, that the gunpowder was genuine; it is difficult to believe that real bullets were being fired in a place with so many children wandering around. But the smell was real; the scent of the gunpowder was so overpowering, so thick, that when you would get home from Norwoods your clothes would still smell like the shooting gallery.

There were exercises in which live ammunition was used, he had said. I think of him—still a relatively young man, he was in his thirties when, back from the war, he would take us to Norwoods—and I try to imagine what he was thinking as he heard the rifles going off, burst after burst, to the sound of laughter and shouts from the people trying to kill the metal rabbits. His clothes would smell, too; when we would get home for dinner—such a short drive from the place with the shooting gallery—his clothes, like his children's, would carry the memory of the gunpowder. And we would sit down and eat.

He had been on a weekend pass from Camp Shelby with some of his new Army buddies when the news came. They had been in New Orleans.

For a kid from Akron whose idea of someplace worldlier had been his fledgling life in Columbus, this had to have been something: on the town on Bourbon Street. A young soldier in training for a war that still seemed to be the immediate problem of other, far-distant countries—this wasn't bad: friends he'd just met, government paycheck in his pocket, the uniform of the United States on his back . . . this had to seem, if not fun, at least energizing, venturesome.

They got back to their hotel in New Orleans after an evening at the bars and nightclubs:

. . . So we got into the elevator and there was an awful lot of buzzing going on by people and someone said, Did you hear about Pearl Harbor? And I said, Who's Pearl Harbor? Because I actually had never heard of the place. . . .

There were squads of MPs rolling around New Orleans urging every soldier to get back to his post. Before packing up, somehow I got kind of sentimental and dashed off a wire to Phyllis saying that Pearl Harbor was bombed but I love you and so forth and so on. Now, that certainly doesn't sound much like me, but I did it and Mother will attest to it, as a matter of fact she might still have that wire somewhere. And after that day, nothing would ever be the same. . . .

In the house where I grew up, there were many occasions when someone in the family—my dad, my mom, my sister, my brother or I—would have to go down to the basement to look for something.

In the basement was a doored-off area we referred to as the darkroom—evidently the family who had lived in the house before we did used it for that purpose, to develop photographs. For our family, it was mostly a storeroom; the things we didn't really need to have easily on hand, things that didn't belong in an upstairs closet, were down in the darkroom.

His trunk was in there. It was a literal trunk—a military trunk, filled with things he had brought home from the war. We seldom opened it.

I think about the trunks that children take with them to summer camp, trunks that families buy to store possessions, and there's a smiling, good-time feeling to those items. They're luggage, meant to convey a sense of vacation, of relaxation.

My father's Army trunk always felt like something quite different. We were too young to know what it really meant; like the duffel bags that were down there, the trunk had been a part of his life when he was overseas—of that, we were aware. But it was almost as if he was consciously putting that World War II life of his away in the darkroom. Upstairs a family lived on a pleasant Midwestern street in a nation just as peaceful as the tree-lined block on which the house sat. Down in the darkroom were the trunk and the duffel bags. They had been to a few places, none of which we children would ever see—none of which the man whose possessions they held would ever want his children to have to see.

I recall that once my sister and I had opened the trunk, and had found some love letters—letters sent back and forth between my father and my mother while he was overseas. We thought they were mushy; we thought they were kind of embarrassing. We read a few of them—I think we must have giggled, we were at that age—and then we became a little bored and closed the trunk.

It was while he was in training to go overseas that he asked my mother to marry him. It was, of course, not done casually; he arranged to get a leave, and came from his military base in the South back up to Columbus to work on making it happen.

From his tape:

. . . Phyllis and I started badgering her parents to let us get engaged, and we were really turned down. I was supposed to go to [her stepfather's] office to "ask for Phyllis' hand"—believe it or not, that was still being done in those days.

I had to get my nerve up somehow, so like a damn fool I stopped in the Neil House bar and had about three quick shots, and I go up to his office shaky in my shoes.

He was very nice to me, I must have smelled like a brewery, but I think he was very understanding. . . . He said that he and [Phyllis' mother] had decided that because I was a second lieutenant by this time, and they had heard that the length of a second lieutenant's life in actual combat was twenty seconds—where they got this I don't know—but obviously they didn't want their loving daughter to be a widow twenty seconds into the game.

And so almost tearfully I left the office and reported back to Phyllis, who also was in tears, and we just felt that we had to keep on trying. Well, the bottom line was that just before July 14 they had given us permission to become engaged. . . .

In the last years of his life, he and my mother would often talk about coming to Chicago to visit, but they never did. They had come relatively often when I was first working there—a trip from Ohio to Chicago was not only no big deal, it was kind of joyful for them.

But one of the things that happened as he grew older was that the once-simple act of taking a short trip became cumbersome. He moved slowly; airplanes—which were much more cramped than the commercial aircraft of the 1950s and 1960s; the new planes felt as if they were designed to cram livestock in rather than to transport human beings in a gracious and civilized way—were considerable trouble for him to deal with.

It's not that he never traveled in the end; each year he and my mom would go down to Longboat Key, Florida, to spend a few winter months, and they would plan the transportation aspects of their trip well in advance. The actual day of getting from Columbus to Florida was usually an exhausting one for them; once they were there, they knew it had been worth the doing, because they had all winter to relax and not think about going anywhere else.

The short hops, though, became something out of their past. An easy trip never was, not anymore. It wasn't an especially dramatic change—it just sort of happened. One year, or so it seemed, they were a couple who were always traveling around, the next year they were a couple who, because of circumstances not of their own making, tended to stay in the city where they lived.

Back when they were first married—during the war, after they finally had persuaded my mother's parents how important this was to them—they set up housekeeping in Oregon, where my father and the men of the 91st Infantry Division were at that time being headquartered. Transportation for him then was not something to which he had to give much thought; he would not be choosing where he went or when he went there, and he and my mother knew that when the time to move quickly arrived, the arrangements would not be his to make.

. . . We were alerted, first a yellow alert and then a red alert, which meant we were at long last going overseas. Your mother and I would have the radio on every night and hear all the terrible things that were going on over in Italy. Little did we know that that would be our theater of operation. . . . I know it was a dark day for Phyllis and certainly a dark day for me and literally a dark day when I left.

We had a long train ride across the entire United States, and we finally arrived at Camp Patrick Henry, in Newport News, Virginia. It was from that spot we were to receive our final preparations to go overseas. We didn't know where we were going. Everything was top secret, so Phyllis had no idea where I was located and any hints that I would try to give at the infrequent times I could talk to her long distance were quite dangerous, because it was a mortal sin to give any information out about troop movements.

We were to be loaded onto Liberty Ships and go by convoys over the Atlantic to Oran, Algeria, which was our first stop. Now, convoys could only go as fast as the slowest ships. And we, on the Liberty Ships, were the slowest ships. They went about 10 knots, which made us sitting ducks for submarines and air attacks. We were surrounded by corvettes and destroyers, which maintained a constant lookout. And actually nothing happened until we went through the Straits of Gibraltar and then the depth charges were set off which indicated that there were submarines in the area.

A Liberty Ship was nothing but a hastily built tub, and the enlisted men slept on what were called standees. They were cots five feet high. A soldier was assigned one of these cots and his nose would press against the bottom of the cot on top of him, and so on for five layers. It was stifling, it was absolutely terrible, but it was the only way to move the troops. Eat in shifts, go to the toilet in shifts, shower in shifts, and all the time maintaining blackout. This went on for twenty days, and the only time we were allowed on deck was if it was all clear either at night or in the daytime. And believe me that was something to look forward to because it got awful smelly and awful fetid down in the bowels of that ship. . . .

If the little area in the basement of our house was referred to as the darkroom, then the room where we as children watched our family's first black-and-white television set was always called a name that had nothing to do with TV: It was the library.

It did indeed have bookshelves built into its walls; as small as the room—just down the hallway from the kitchen—was, you could imagine families who lived here before, in the pre-television era, sitting quietly on a winter's evening reading books before bedtime. At least before TV sets became the entertainment focal points of most American homes, a room like this one—a room devoted to books—likely did not feel elitist or stilted. A room like this was where the outside world entered your house; a room like this—

before TV—was the place where a family could read and discover a wider world.

My sister and brother and I would sit there and stare at *Rootie Kazootie* and *Ding Dong School* and *Super Circus*—would stare at the outside world being delivered onto a glass screen—and on the wooden bookshelves were the volumes our mother and father had collected over the years.

In the early 1950s, I recall now, so many places of honor in the family library went to books about the war. It was as if my father and mother felt an obligation to keep the narrative of the war in our home; these were not memorabilia specific to my dad, these were not his personal souvenirs. They were instead history—history that at the time the books first came out was still brand-new.

There were memoirs by Eisenhower and by Churchill; there were collections of war correspondence by Quentin Reynolds and other newspapermen who had been at the front. One book in particular I remember; by Ernie Pyle, the greatest chronicler of the fighting men, it bore a title that could not be improved upon. It was called *Here Is Your War.*

Seven or eight years before, all of this had been present tense. Now it was between hard covers: the literature of combat, on our safe little street. *Here Is Your War.* Your war. You, the man of this house.

His voice, on the tape, described the final stage of their troopship journey across the Atlantic Ocean:

. . . We finally got there in one piece and offloaded in Oran, and saw all the wreckage of the French battleships that were in the harbor. We got into trucks that took us out to the countryside. . . . We immediately started training there for the amphibious landings that were to come later.

It was here that we received our first casualties. The area around Oran and Port aux Poules was part of the battleground in the African invasion. And there were many minefields that were still very, very deadly and sure enough I lost three friends because of stepping on mines. And this really sobered us up, we were actually in a theater of war. . . .

He was serious about few people; from the time I was a boy, I could count on him saying something sardonic or amusingly cutting about just about anyone whose name I might bring up. It didn't matter whether the person was Elvis Presley or our milkman—my dad would make a joke out of the discussion, would go for laughs in his evaluation or description of whomever we were talking about.

Not only did he not impress easily—it was hard to impress him at all.

So I was more than a little surprised by his reaction when I mentioned Gary Griffin's dad.

Gary Griffin is the keyboard player for Jan and Dean, the '60s surf-rock duo. For most of the 1990s, I toured the country on summer weekends with Jan and Dean and their band, singing backup vocals during their concerts and eventually being promoted to lead vocals on "Dance, Dance, Dance" and "I Get Around." How this came to pass is a long and juvenile story, one that probably would be better to go into at some other time.

My father thought that the idea of his grown son singing surf music on stages around the United States was stupid beyond belief; it's hard to argue that he was wrong. But once, after we had played a show in Eaton, Ohio, and I had gone to Columbus the next day to visit with my parents, I mentioned to my dad that I had met Gary Griffin's father at the show, and that Gary's dad had been a Doolittle Raider. At the time, I am ashamed to confess, I did not know exactly what the Doolittle Raiders had done during World War II. I knew they had been a famed unit in the war, but that was about it.

So I had met Gary's dad—a self-effacing, friendly man, a

proud father who had come to watch his son make music—backstage at the show, and the next day I told my dad about it.

"Your friend's father was really a Doolittle Raider?" my dad had said.

I had said yes.

My dad—the man who was never serious about anyone—said: "If he was a Doolittle Raider, then that man is a hero."

I would one day find out for myself—but only after my father was gone.

FIFTEEN

I was having lunch with Tibbets on a Friday afternoon. I had called him at the last minute to say I would be in Columbus only briefly; we went to a restaurant called B. J. Young's, and I said I had a question for him.

"What's your opinion of the Doolittle Raiders?" I asked.

"They're the real thing," he said. "Why?"

I told him what my father had said about them.

"Your dad was right," Tibbets said. "If ever there were heroes, the Doolittle Raiders were it. But why are you bringing it up now?"

"Because I'm on my way to see them," I said.

Gary Griffin had gotten in touch with me, sounding a little harried.

The surviving members of the Doolittle Raiders—there had been eighty aviators, but now the number who were able to travel was down to seventeen—were being honored at the United States Air Force Museum at Wright-Patterson Air Force Base in Dayton, down the freeway from Columbus. A monument to the men was scheduled to be dedicated.

Gary's dad was in charge of this Doolittle reunion. He had been assured that a master of ceremonies befitting the occasion would be on hand.

But now, within a week of the event, there was no MC. Somehow, whoever was supposed to make certain that a Pentagon official or a leader of Congress would be on hand had not gotten the job done. The last living Raiders were making plans to come to Dayton for the dedication of their memorial—and there was no one to narrate the ceremony.

"My dad wants to know if you'll do it," Gary said.

I was stunned. Whatever the comical line was from a recent movie—"We're not worthy"—at that moment became personal. The Raiders must have wanted Colin Powell, or John Glenn, or Norman Schwarzkopf—they must have wanted someone on their own level. Not some guy who writes stories for newspapers.

I told Gary as much. "I'd feel embarrassed being up there in front of them," I said. "I don't have the right to appear at their ceremony."

"My dad's really in a pinch," Gary said. "Can he call you?"

I said of course. The next morning Tom Griffin called, and said, "Is there any way you can fly in from Chicago?"

I asked him whether the Air Force Museum was still trying to get one of the speakers whom the Raiders really wanted.

"I keep getting a little runaround," he said. "I finally found out that they had asked one of the local TV anchormen in Dayton to do it. But it turns out that he's on vacation."

I found myself shaking my head as I listened through the phone.

"I know it's asking a lot for you to come on such short notice. . . ." he said.

By this time I had read up on the Raiders. By this time I knew exactly why my dad and Tibbets would never kid around about these men. *I know it's asking a lot . . .*

"It's not asking a lot, Mr. Griffin," I said.

Meaning: You men, of all people, should never have to be put in the position of asking anyone to do anything.

It is almost impossible—even knowing the facts of what they were ordered to undertake—to comprehend the courage of the eighty men who, under the command of Jimmy Doolittle, took off from the deck of the USS *Hornet* on April 18, 1942.

In the months after the Japanese attack on Pearl Harbor, in which more than two thousand Americans were killed, morale in the United States about the war in the Pacific seemed to sink ever lower. There had been no effective response to Pearl Harbor; the leaders of the Japanese military appeared to believe that they were all but invincible.

American officials determined that a surprise bombing raid of the Japanese mainland was the way to turn things around. But how to do that—from where to launch the attack?

The only option was from the deck of an American warship. Bomber planes had never done this before. United States commanders concluded that such a feat was technically possible, if B-25s were modified specifically for this task, and if crews were trained to carry it out with no margin for error.

Sixteen five-man crews were selected. They had only three weeks to train for the mission—and the training did not include taking off from ships. None of the pilots, before the day of the raid, had ever attempted such a takeoff, and none had ever seen any other pilot do it. When they flew their B-25s off the deck of the *Hornet,* it would be their first such flights.

The plan was for the planes to drop their bombs on specific targets in Japan—and then to fly to China, and to land at a Chinese airfield friendly to the U.S. There could be no turning back; there was no way that a big, heavy bomber would be able to land on a carrier. The USS *Hornet* and its task force—four cruisers, eight destroyers, two oilers—would reverse course after the Doolittle Raiders took off, and head back to Pearl Harbor.

So on the day of the raid, the sixteen B-25s were lined up on the deck of the *Hornet,* their crews knowing that they had just enough fuel to get to China, and that returning to the *Hornet* was not an option.

And then the news came:

The launch of the bombers was supposed to have come from a point in the Pacific Ocean 400 miles from the Japanese mainland. But U.S. military officials intercepted a Japanese message that indicated the enemy had spotted the U.S. task force.

The Tokyo raid would either have to be called off—or begin earlier than scheduled. Which, ominously, meant much farther away from Japan than scheduled.

From the originally planned-for 400 miles away, the Doolittle crews knew they had barely enough fuel to make it to China. But from farther than that?

If they were ordered to fly, they might not make it out of Japanese airspace after dropping their bombs.

The *Hornet* was 640 miles away from Japan when the official order arrived from Admiral William F. "Bull" Halsey, who was on the USS *Enterprise:*

LAUNCH PLANES. TO COL. DOOLITTLE AND GALLANT COMMAND GOOD LUCK AND GOD BLESS YOU.

And they did it—knowing that they very well might have no chance of landing safely, they took off for Japan. Doolittle piloted the first plane in line, which had the greatest chance of crashing off the deck of the *Hornet*—it had the shortest amount of runway in front of it. He made it off the ship, followed by the next fifteen B-25s.

The men bombed Tokyo and other targets on the Japanese mainland, burning or destroying the Tokyo Armory, a tank depot, steel and gas works, factories and a harbor installation. In terms of real destruction, the Tokyo raid did not do much to significantly disable the Japanese war effort. But psychologically, what the Raiders accomplished was staggering. Finally, months after Pearl Harbor, the American people could be told that U.S. planes had hit Japan. The United States was striking back.

But the sixteen Doolittle planes were over Japan—and their fuel was running out. There was a storm over China, and thick fog. The planes managed to get past the Japanese mainland—but eleven of the five-man crews had to bail out. Four more crews crash-landed. The sixteenth Doolittle B-25 was able to land within the border of Russia—at which time the crew was taken prisoner, and held for more than a year.

So one B-25 was in Russia, its crew imprisoned. The other fifteen bombers had crashed or been ditched. Two men died as they bailed out; eight more were captured by the Japanese. Three Raiders were executed by their Japanese captors; five others were sentenced to life in prison. One of the five died of starvation in a Japanese prison camp; the other four endured forty months of mistreatment as POWs.

The other Raiders who bailed out made it safely to Chinese soil, and were treated well. The U.S. government, upon recovering these men, sent most of them back into combat; having survived the Tokyo raid, ten more of Doolittle's men were killed in action later in the war.

The Doolittle raid was regarded as the turning point in the war in the Pacific. And what those men did—taking off from the *Hornet* knowing what lay ahead—inspired Americans in a way that was desperately needed in the uncertain months after Pearl Harbor. Americans, in 1942, might not have always felt they had much to believe in—but they had the Doolittle Raiders. The Raiders represented the very best of how America wanted to see itself.

Each of the eighty raiders—some posthumously—was awarded the Distinguished Flying Cross, and Jimmy Doolittle himself was promoted to brigadier general, and was presented with the Medal of Honor by President Roosevelt. The Raiders, American citizens were being signaled, were the proof that no matter what the odds, the war could be won.

That was a long time ago, though. Doolittle had died in 1993; each year the number of surviving Raiders grew smaller. As they arrived in Dayton for the dedication of their memorial, they were well aware that few Americans knew who they were, or what they had done in 1942.

* * *

The night before the dedication ceremony, the seventeen Raiders arrived in Dayton from all over the country. There was a reception for them at an officers' facility at Wright-Patterson.

Gary Griffin and his girlfriend, Carol Huston, had planned a surprise for the Raiders. The kinds of songs Gary usually sang in public were along the lines of "Help Me, Rhonda" and "Shut Down"—I had seen him, with Jan and Dean, sing those songs to cheering, screaming crowds across the United States.

This night was going to be different. Carol is a singer and an actress, too—she starred as Andy Griffith's beautiful young female cohort during the last seasons of the *Matlock* television series—and in the weeks leading up to the Doolittle reunion she and Gary had been working on something.

So as the Raiders arrived for their welcoming reception, Gary and Carol were waiting for them. Gary, on stage, most often wears a Hawaiian shirt and a pair of jeans; tonight he was in a business suit, and Carol was in an evening dress. Gary was going to be playing the piano, accompanying Carol's vocals.

The Doolittle Raiders were in their seventies and eighties. Most of them, it was safe to assume, didn't go out much to concerts anymore. So this concert had been put together for them.

Gary hit the keys, and Carol sang "I've Heard That Song Before." She sang "White Cliffs of Dover." She sang "The Last Time I Saw Paris."

She and Gary had lovingly assembled a program of songs from the 1940s, from the years of the war—the years when these were new songs in the ears of the Raiders and their wives. The idea was to give them a show like one they might have enjoyed when they were young airmen and young airmen's wives. When they, and their world, were full of youth.

Carol sang "Where or When," and "One for My Baby," and "I'll Be Seeing You." She looked out into the eyes of the men and women in her small audience, and she saw emotions so intense that she had to look away.

She and Gary told the Raiders and their wives that there was one song they needed some help on. They asked the Raiders if they would sing along.

Every person in the room knew that it was far from certain how many more of these get-togethers there would be. The Raiders had been holding reunions since 1943, but as their numbers dwindled, the question of how long these could continue was a real, if mostly unspoken, one.

Gary hit the chord he was looking for and Carol sang the opening words of "We'll Meet Again."

We'll meet again,
Don't know where, don't know when. . . .

And in the audience, the Raiders and their wives joined in, singing together.

But I know we'll meet again
Some sunny day. . . .

I had taken my mother to dinner in Columbus before going over to Dayton in a driving rainstorm to get ready for the Doolittle Raiders ceremony.

It was to be a morning event; the dedication of the monument had been scheduled to be held outside, next to the monument itself. But the weather was still severe, and no one wanted to subject the Raiders to sitting out in it. The decision had been made overnight to hold the ceremony inside the museum's auditorium. It would be dry and warm—but the memorial would be nowhere in sight.

Something else would be missing, too. The Air Force Museum had arranged for a restored B-25—just like the one these men had flown off the deck of the USS *Hornet*—to fly over the memorial as the dedication was beginning. It was certain to have been an unforgettable moment—Doolittle's men sitting next to the memorial in their honor, while above them roared that B-25.

The flyover was rescheduled so that the Raiders could see the bomber as they were walking into the museum's main building. They had been at breakfast together; a van brought them to the museum, and just as they were getting out, the B-25, flying loud and low on the gray, damp morning, thundered above the roof of the museum. Most of the Raiders looked up toward it; some, having trouble getting around, chose to come inside the building and find a seat.

They walked into the auditorium—some of them helping their wives, who were in wheelchairs or who needed assistance getting down the aisle. The auditorium was not full for this ceremony, but a respectable number of people had shown up. The Dayton news media had been announcing that the ceremony would be open to the public, and some fathers had brought their sons to see the Raiders, and to hear about who they were.

When everyone was seated I introduced myself and read from a script I had been handed by a Wright-Patterson official:

"We ask everyone to stand at this time for the posting of the colors by the Wright-Patterson Air Force Base honor guard."

The color guard, marching crisply and handling the flag with great tenderness, came to the stage to present the colors.

I introduced Reverend Jacob DeShazer to give the invocation. Reverend DeShazer was one of the Raiders captured by the Japanese and sentenced to life in prison; upon his liberation at the end of the war, after Tibbets and the crew of the *Enola Gay* had dropped the atomic bomb on Hiroshima, he had dedicated himself to becoming a member of the clergy.

He blessed the gathering, and then Wilkinson Wright, the grandnephew of Orville and Wilbur Wright, welcomed the Raiders to Dayton. Retired Major General Davey Jones, one of the Raiders, spoke on behalf of the men and their families; Major General Charles Metcalf spoke on behalf of the Air Force Museum.

I did my best to tell them what I, and so many people, thought of them. I mentioned what my father had said about them, how they were just about the only people I had ever heard him talk about with a tone close to reverent respect, and I could see some of them looking at one another and nodding. I told them I had had lunch with Tibbets the day before, and that he had asked me to extend to them his congratulations and his best wishes; there were smiles and murmured conversations among them when his name was mentioned.

"The official announcement of this event says that we are here to honor you today," I said. "But that's not quite right. We are the ones who are honored today. We are honored to be in your presence. The monument is yours; the honor is ours."

I spoke a while more, without notes, just telling the men how I and so many others felt about what they had done, and then I read from the script:

"Everyone please stand while Reverend DeShazer joins us for the benediction, and the playing of taps."

The sound of a million military goodnights—the sound of a million military goodbyes—filled the room as taps was played, and then, still reading from the script, I said:

"Will everyone please remain standing for the retiring of the colors."

This was where the honor guard was supposed to return to the stage to retrieve the flag.

The Raiders and their wives—those who were able to stand—stood at attention and faced the flag.

And the honor guard didn't come.

Silence filled the room.

I looked at General Metcalf. He raised his eyebrows a little bit. I repeated it into the microphone. "The retiring of the colors."

No honor guard.

The flag was on the stage, the Doolittle Raiders were on their feet—and the honor guard had taken off. They were missing their cue; they were nowhere to be seen.

It would have been an awkward moment under any circumstances; here, it was terrible. These men, of all men, would have seemed to deserve a perfect military ceremony. To have every detail right—the way they tried to do it when they took off from the Navy ship in the Pacific that was going to turn around and leave them as soon as they were in the air.

At the back of the room, staff members of the museum looked frantically for the honor guard. They left the auditorium, they went to check the men's restroom. Nothing.

And the Raiders and their wives, men and women of seventy-eight and eighty and eighty-four . . .

They remained standing at attention, gazing at the flag of their country.

They probably didn't mind this as much as I did. After all, on the day they were supposed to attack Japan they were told that they'd have to fly from 640 miles instead of 400. And that they probably didn't have enough fuel to make it to China. Next to that, this little blip of a screwup at their dedication ceremony may not have meant much. If any group of men was used to things going wrong, it was these men.

I looked down off the stage toward them. One of them smiled and winked, as if to try to set me at ease.

"I hope that all of you know that you are our heroes," I said, and, with the flag still waiting on the stage for someone to come for it, I concluded the ceremony. I asked the rest of the audience to remain as the Raiders—slowly—made their way back up the aisles.

There was a lunch scheduled for the Raiders and their wives at a hotel on the base. It was a private event; I went to the same hotel to have a sandwich in the restaurant, and as I passed the door where the Raiders' lunch was being held Tom Griffin saw me and asked me to join them.

I said that I didn't want to intrude; he insisted that I come in. One after another, the Raiders came up to me to thank me for the words I had said about them. One after another, they told me how much they had appreciated it.

And I thought of that letter that Tibbets had sent me, early on:

You made me think, after a word-by-word review, that maybe I am not too bad a guy. Thanks.

As if these men should ever have to thank any of us—as if they should ever have to express a single word of gratitude to us who have followed them. I sat with these men—quiet, courteous men, men with not a bone of self-promotion or self-aggrandizement in their makeup. I watched as the men whose wives needed help getting to the table carefully moved the wheelchairs for the women they loved, patiently assisted their wives eat the sandwiches that the hotel had provided. They did what was expected of them in 1942, and they were doing what was expected of them now, because that is who they were and who they are.

There was a printed program for the dedication ceremony; inside the program were photographs of the Raiders taken in 1942, posing with their planes on the deck of the *Hornet.* I looked at the faces in the overly bright hotel function room, and I matched them with the faces in the program—kids' faces in the program, faces so young and proud and sometimes, or so it seemed, scared, faces peering over the tops of leather bomber jackets.

They weren't young now; the faces in this room were not the faces of kids, and while the faces still seemed proud, especially today, I did not see a single face in this room that appeared scared to me. I thought about that day when, at the request of their country, they had taken off for Tokyo knowing that there would be no turning back. These men in this room—they took off from that deck in the Pacific because the United States said that they must do it for the future well-being of their nation.

I was supposed to get back to Chicago. I said my goodbyes to the Raiders, and left Wright-Patterson so that I could make my flight. On the way off the base I saw a billboard advertising a local car dealership, encouraging Dayton-area motorists looking for a good deal to stop in at Airport Toyota.

SIXTEEN

I had seen a news item about an old sports star's uniform—I think it was the baseball jersey of a Hall of Fame player—going up for auction, with the expectation that it would bring in several hundred thousand dollars.

This didn't seem all that startling. The market for pieces of history, especially sports history, has been escalating rapidly in recent years. Whether it's Mark McGwire's record-setting home run ball from our current world, or Lou Gehrig's Yankee uniform from long ago, people are willing to pay big money to own a piece of the past.

So the next time I saw Tibbets, I asked him the question.

"Where's your uniform?"

"I have no idea," he said.

"You don't know where the uniform you wore in the service is?"

"I took everything to a thrift shop when I left the service and had it sold," he said. "I had no use for my uniforms once I was out—so whatever the thrift shop did with it, those are where the uniforms are."

"You know, I bet if you looked in your closet and found some of your old things, you'd be shocked at what the market might be for them," I said.

"There's nothing in the closet," he said. "I don't have anything left."

I told him about the prices that the clothing and equipment of sports celebrities are bringing in, and about how Americans are now collecting items like that the way art enthusiasts have always collected paintings and sculptures.

He shook his head, with a look that was a combination of amusement and disgust.

"Which uniform did you wear on your way to Japan?" I said.

"On the *Enola Gay?*" Tibbets said. "I just wore an old khaki flight suit. It was going to be a long flight, and I wanted to be as comfortable as I could."

"And what did you do with it when you got back from Hiroshima?" I said.

"Hell, I don't know," Tibbets said. "I suppose that when I got back to Tinian I turned it back in to supply. I didn't need it any more—the flight was over, and I was going to be leaving Tinian."

"So you never got anything for the uniform you wore," I said.

"I probably got a receipt from the supply sergeant," he said.

Sometimes, talking with Tibbets, I felt as if he regarded what he had been through as history with a lower-case h. For most of the rest of the world, the events he had been a part of were stories to be found in libraries between hard covers, or in documentary films with trumpets and bugles as a soundtrack. Tibbets, though . . .

Well, his was the receipt-from-the-supply-sergeant view of history. I thought I would ask him about some famous figures from the war years—men the rest of us thought we knew because of the mass-media portrayal of them.

"How about Audie Murphy?" I said, remembering that little hill on the side of my childhood friend's front yard.

"A showoff," Tibbets said.

"Pardon me?" I said, not really wanting to hear such a thing about my boyhood idol.

"Murphy was a showoff," Tibbets said. "He got a lot of medals—and he deserved them. He earned them in combat.

"But the guy wore them everywhere. He craved attention—he

wanted to be noticed and praised all the time. That's why he became a movie actor when he got back—he couldn't stand it when he wasn't the center of everything."

"Did you know Ernie Pyle?" I said.

"I was with him in North Africa," Tibbets said. "I watched him write his stories. He was a very quiet man, and very serious about his work.

"As you know, he was trying to write for the hometowns. Most of the war correspondents were writing the big picture, but Ernie knew that the Army was composed of a lot of hometown guys who went off to war. The guys who were really fighting the war—the guys no one ever heard of."

"Did the soldiers treat him differently than they treated the other war correspondents?" I asked.

"He was treated like a GI, which was the highest praise the soldiers could give him," Tibbets said. "Where the soldiers went, Ernie Pyle went. He went out and got dirty with them. He bled with them. And they loved him for it."

"What about Edward R. Murrow?" I asked.

"Never knew the man," Tibbets said. "I had heard him on the radio, obviously—everyone heard him on the radio. He told it so people could understand. That was very important—during the war, it wasn't so easy for the people back home to understand what we were doing over there. Murrow was so good because when he talked, what was going on became clear to his listeners.

"He told it *slowly.* He was careful with his enunciation. The war was hectic and it was fast, and Murrow knew that to make the people back home understand what it was all about, he had to be the opposite—he had to be slow and clear."

"Patton?"

"I knew him at Fort Benning, Georgia," Tibbets said. "He was what he was, and I had to admire him for that. Patton's model was Rommel—the dirty son of a bitch. Patton was a rough, tough SOB just like Rommel, and if you took him for that, he was very good at what he did. He led his troops, I'll tell you that."

"Was he anything like George C. Scott in the movie?" I asked.

"Well, he sure didn't talk like George C. Scott," Tibbets said.

I sat there recalling Scott's gravelly, almost belligerent voice.

"They sounded different?" I said.

Tibbets laughed. "Patton had an effeminate-type voice," he said. "Very squeaky."

"George Patton," I said, thinking that Tibbets was kidding me. "A squeaky voice."

"That's what he had," Tibbets said.

"Did it get in the way of his being a commander?" I said.

"Not at all," Tibbets said. "He didn't give a damn what people thought of him. What you got from Patton was *him,* it was no damn act."

"George Marshall?" I said.

"He was just the other way from Patton," Tibbets said. "He was a diplomatic man, a very intelligent man, well spoken.

"I flew him around for three weeks in '39 and '40. He was very much of a gentleman. I remember that I landed him at an air base in Anniston, Alabama. I was flying a two-seater airplane—just Marshall and myself.

"So we landed at the field in Anniston, and the people were waiting to take him to where he was going. He's wearing four stars, he's big, he's the one they were waiting for as our plane landed.

"But before they could lead him away, he said, 'Wait a minute. I don't want to leave until I'm sure that you're going to take care of Tibbets here. He needs to get some food and some sleep, and someone's got to make sure that his plane is refueled.'

"Now, I could have taken care of all of that myself, but it would have meant talking to people and asking them for favors, and it might have taken me a while. Marshall didn't want me to have to do it myself. I never forgot that gesture."

"Mark Clark?" I said.

"A great, great general," Tibbets said. "A Southern gentleman. Very soft-spoken, never got riled. Never got upset—or if he did, he didn't show it. He had innate politeness.

"He was more than a good general. He was a good man. Of all the military leaders in World War II, Mark Clark is the one who never got the proper credit publicly. He didn't seek it—and somehow he didn't get it.

"But we all knew. We knew what kind of a man Mark Clark was."

I asked Tibbets what sort of mail he got from the Pentagon these days. Was he still given the courtesy of being informed about various goings-on in the military?

"Not really," he said. "I get mail from the Pentagon, but it's the same kind of mail that all ex-servicemen get. Mass mailings."

"How's it addressed?" I said.

"On a label," he said. " 'General Paul Tibbets.' Some of it I read, some of it I know just to throw away without opening it."

"So no one makes any special effort to make you feel as if you're still a part of things?" I said.

"Hardly," he said. "I'm not a part of what they're doing. I'm on the outside looking in."

I knew that Tibbets had left the service with mixed feelings at best—after the war he had held a number of desk jobs, each of which filled him with increasing frustration about the military bureaucracy. He had risen as far as he was going to rise—brigadier general, never being promoted to two-star or three-star—and he had hated the idea of being evaluated by men he hardly knew, and of, in a peacetime military, becoming a half-forgotten cog in the machine.

He didn't like to talk much about it, but he said:

"You don't have to live under that kind of question mark. They would tell me something today, then change what they said tomorrow. . . ."

He shook his head.

"Anyway," he said, not wanting to dwell on the subject. "The mail I get from the Pentagon is no big deal. I'm on a mailing list. Guys who once served."

While he was talking about guys who once served, he said that he feels strongly that every guy should have to. Meaning: Bring back the draft.

"Yes," Tibbets said. "Every man ought to pay the price to live in this country. And that means helping to defend it. Discipline comes along with having to do that—and if you're going to grow up with the benefits of being an American, you should have to pay for it."

I told him that the draft must have disappeared from the American scene for some pretty good reasons—otherwise it would still be in place.

"You know what the reason is that the draft is gone?" he said. "It's very simple. People don't like the draft because they don't want to be told what to do.

"And to that I say, 'Show me how you can live without being told what to do.' It's the way the world has always worked, and not liking that fact doesn't change it."

"Do you think the draft is better for the person who is drafted, or just that it's better for the country and for the armed services?" I said.

"It's better for the person *and* it's better for the country," Tibbets said. "But don't assume that it's better for the armed services—it's not necessarily better for any of the branches of the service to have draftees.

"The services might very well be better off with men who choose to enlist. But the *country*—the country is better off when the draft is in place, because the young men who are drafted become disciplined. And they come out of the service—at least most of them—carrying that discipline inside of them. You don't think that's a good thing—in a country that right now has all these young men in gangs going around killing each other? You don't think we could use the discipline of the draft—for the good of the young men, and for the good of the country?"

"Well, speaking of that, one of the things that people always talk about is 'wanting to leave the country in good hands,' " I said. "Do you think that your generation feels you're leaving the country in good hands?"

"I don't know," Tibbets said. "There are times when I think I'd rather not know the answer to that one. But if you're asking me to think about it: If the ideal situation is to leave the country better, then I think my generation has lost the war."

"Why?" I said.

"My father's generation fought a war to save democracy," Tibbets said. "My generation fought to preserve our freedom from oppression. And sometimes I look around at what the United States has become, and I have to reach the sad conclusion that we may have won the battle—we may have won a lot of battles—but we haven't won the war."

"Because?" I said.

"Because of all the things you and I have been talking about," he said. "Because of the utter lack of discipline in every area of society. Anything goes. There is no center. . . ."

"And assuming that you're right, how do you think that can be changed?" I said.

"I would like to see determined and iron-assed people get into positions of influence in this country," he said. "Some people who wouldn't be afraid to say that there is a difference between right and wrong. I would like to see some standards set that we can be proud of."

"There was no television when you were growing up," I said. "I think it would be kind of hard for any political leaders to really be effective in setting the tone in a society where television is a fact of daily life. That's the difference between when you were growing up and when I grew up—and it's even more so today. The tone of society is set by what is broadcast into every home in the country every day. It has nothing to do with politicians—it's just there, out of the air and into the houses."

"I don't think television did us any good, I'll tell you that," Tibbets said. "And I'm not even talking about the same thing you're talking about—I'm not talking about the programs they put on the air."

"Then what do you mean?" I said.

"The main way television has changed the country is that it has kept people inside their houses," he said.

"It used to be, you knew all your neighbors. Now, people consider the people they see on television as their neighbors—they know the people on TV better than they know the people on their own blocks, or at least they think they do.

"I'm no different from anyone else—I've been as affected by it as anyone. I don't even know who lives three doors away from me."

"I'll bet that's quite a change from the way it was in the neighborhood you grew up in as a boy," I said.

"Of course," he said. "You would knock on any door in your neighborhood without giving it a second thought. That's what being a neighbor meant. Not necessarily that you were the greatest friends in the world—but that you were *neighbors.*"

"You might be able to do that now," I said.

"What?" Tibbets said.

"Knock on the door of someone down the street from you, or on the next block," I said. "Tell them who you are and that you just wanted to introduce yourself."

"I wouldn't do that," he said.

"Why?" I said.

"Because whoever's door I knocked on, I would assume that they didn't want to be bothered."

I told Tibbets about the sign I'd seen as I was leaving the Doolittle Raiders reunion—the AIRPORT TOYOTA billboard near the air base in Dayton.

"So?" he said.

"You don't think that's kind of odd?" I said. "The Doolittle

Raiders are meeting for the dedication of the memorial to their raid on Japan, and down the street the Toyota dealership is busy selling cars to the people of Dayton?"

"No," Tibbets said.

"Why?" I said.

"Because I drive a Toyota myself," he said.

It was one of those moments when I couldn't do anything but sit there and stare at him.

"But if that's the case," I said after a few seconds had passed, "then what was it all for?"

"What was what all for?" Tibbets said.

"What the Doolittle Raiders did when they flew off the *Hornet* toward Tokyo," I said. "What you and your crew did when you flew to Hiroshima. . . ."

"It's purely commerce," he said. "It's a competitive thing. I bought a Toyota because at the time I bought it I was looking at cars, and I thought it was the best one out there for me. I looked around and I decided that American carmakers were giving you what *they* wanted to give you, not what *you* wanted to drive."

"And you didn't think twice before you bought the Toyota?" I said.

"I like my Toyota," he said. "I don't hold any grudges. It was a good product, it was what I needed, so I bought it."

"Did it make you feel funny at all?" I asked.

"Not in the least," he said. "I have never held a thing in the world against a Japanese man or a Japanese woman. It was the system we were fighting against—what the government of Japan had put in place.

"But the people of Japan? I've never had a bad thought about them."

So here he was, at eighty-four, driving his Toyota around the freeways of central Ohio.

"Which is harder for you?" I said. "Driving the freeways here today, or flying a B-29 back when you were younger?"

"Driving the freeways is definitely harder," Tibbets said. "I have to be much more alert driving the freeways than I did flying an airplane."

"Just because of your age?" I said.

"No," he said. "Because we've got people driving cars that have no business being behind the wheel."

"Like who?" I asked.

"A lot of older people have no business driving," he said. "They can't see. Their eyesight is poor."

"You're not including yourself in that group, I assume."

"No," he said. "I'm a good driver.

"But on the road, I see so many aggressive drivers, and then I see these people driving with their telephones to their ears—they don't know what they'd do if they suddenly had to make a decision on the road while they're talking on the phone. It tears me up to see that."

"So compared to the flight of the *Enola Gay* . . ." I began.

"It is much more nerve-wracking for me on the freeways of Columbus than it was flying the *Enola Gay* to Hiroshima," he said. "Too many people make up their own rules of driving. It's like everything else you see today—people just think they have the right to make up their own rules, on the road just like anywhere else.

"I'm driving the right way, at the right speed. And they honk at me—like I'm impeding their progress."

"Do you think you're going too slow for them?" I said.

"I drive the limit," he said. "I don't set the speed rules—I obey them. I'm watching everything around me as I drive. Every curve on the road has a groove—people don't know that. But they're out there, driving any way they want."

"Still, though," I said. "You're probably exaggerating about the flight to Hiroshima being easier. Right?"

"No, I'm not exaggerating," he said. "Between Tinian and Hiroshima, there wasn't any traffic for me to have to deal with."

SEVENTEEN

My father felt the same way about drivers on the central Ohio freeways—and not just in his later years. When my sister and brother and I were children, sitting in the back seat as he drove somewhere with my mother in front next to him, he had a phrase that we turned into a family joke:

"These are treacherous driving conditions!"

He said it so often—he used it in so many road situations—that it lost just about all meaning. "Treacherous driving conditions" could refer to anything from a slight drizzle to a severe thunderstorm; from a lost-her-way woman slowing up the lane of traffic in front of him to teenagers passing him at eighty miles per hour and then cutting him off. "Treacherous driving conditions" could mean that the sun was too bright—but what it really meant was: Quit fidgeting back there.

He liked us to be quiet and still as we rode in that back seat. And I don't think he even noticed that, as the years passed, the driving conditions really did become treacherous for anyone riding in the car, and anyone in the vicinity of the car—not because of the weather, not because of speeders in adjacent lanes, but because of him.

He was too old. He had become a bad driver. Yet no one could tell him that—he insisted on driving wherever he went. This is something that millions upon millions of men and women in middle age must almost certainly go through with their suddenly elderly parents—the knowledge, on the part of the children, that the parents really should not be on the road anymore. And the great reluctance of the parents to even discuss this, much less give up the independence that driving represents.

So as Tibbets told me about his experiences on the freeways—he didn't use the phrase "treacherous driving conditions," but that was the message he was delivering—I thought about my father, and there was one difference:

I never knew Tibbets as a younger man. He was a man of eighty-four telling me about the freeways, just as he was a man of eighty-four telling me about World War II. With my father, my memories went all the way back to when he was in his thirties, when I was a small boy. Whatever the freeways eventually became for him, I could put that in the context of what the roads and highways—in the days when I was first in his sedan with him, before there had even been freeways—had been for him. I could, in my mind—for I seldom said this out loud to him—picture the roads as they were in his and my younger days, when the treachery had come exclusively from outside his car, and then picture him in his eighties, backing out of the driveway on nights when I knew that he shouldn't do it.

If there was one good thing about him getting so infirm in the end—and there weren't many good things—it was the relief that came with the knowledge that he wasn't going to be getting behind the wheel of a car. I imagined him and Tibbets driving alongside of each other on I-70, heading downtown, each of them wary of the other—each of them distrusting of the old man in the next lane.

Inside of a man, it must seem to happen so quickly—to go from vitality to something less. To go from complete confidence in what you can do . . .

On the tape of his life, his voice told of those initial days in North Africa, as the 91st Infantry waited to find out what was coming next. Treacherous conditions indeed.

* * *

The minefields were still there, and the booby traps were still there, which was a constant source of danger to everybody. . . .

There were all kinds of rumors about when the invasion of Festung Europa *would begin. That phrase meant Fortress of Europe, and Hitler had really prepared the west coast of France and all the other contiguous countries to repel the invaders when they did come. And as each day went by, the rumblings and rumors continued. . . .*

Sometimes, when we went on family vacations when I was a child, I would hear my father and mother discussing whatever hotel in which we were staying, and commenting on whether it was "American Plan" or "European Plan."

I didn't know precisely what those two things meant—I still don't—but from the way my parents talked about them, it was clear that the words referred to whether some of your meals came with the price of the room. When you're a kid, though, you pick up certain messages underneath the words—and the message I got from the American Plan/European Plan conversations was that my father must be a pretty worldly fellow.

How else would he know these things—the hotel plan that was used in Europe, the hotel plan that was used in the United States? He had to have an awfully sophisticated understanding of the ways of the world—at least to the ears of his son, that's the way it sounded.

And of course whatever worldliness he really did have—knowledge of the way things were done in Europe, knowledge of the way things were done in Africa—came almost entirely courtesy of a long trip that his employer, the United States Army, once sent him on.

It's a little-noticed aspect of what happened to the men of my father's generation and Tibbets' generation—but they were boys who grew up during the Depression, when there was absolutely no hope of going on any kind of a long vacation anywhere, much less across the Atlantic Ocean. And then, because of history's violent jog in the road, these small-town Depression boys were seeing places that even the most fabulously wealthy international travelers of previous generations never got to. These children of the Depression were—under the worst possible circumstances—cast to the most far-flung corners of the globe, to countries and cities that only a few years before they had been looking at on color-plate maps in their public-school geography books.

The man-made globes—the little globes, the ones that spun in the dens of American homes—must have looked so different to them when they got home from the war. Italy, Africa, Germany, France . . . Japan . . . these impossibly distant places were now a part of their lives forever. These young men had gotten out of town, all right—they had gotten about as far out of town as they ever might have dared to dream.

With a twist that even O. Henry might not have been able to come up with. See the world? You want to see the world, young man? All right, if you insist . . .

There were earlier twists, too—twists that transpired not at the end of the story, but at the beginning.

I had long been curious about how my father became an officer in the Army. He went in as a private and came out as a major; how had that happened?

It turned out to be one more instance of life's abrupt and unplanned detours. Because his family had not been able to send him out of Akron to go to college—because the working man's school up the hill was all that he could afford—he had followed the curriculum that Akron University required. He wouldn't make it all the way through school—his father's illness, and the need for him to help support the family, precluded that—but during his brief time at that commuter college, one of the classes that the school insisted all male students take had a ripple effect more powerful than almost anything else in his lifetime.

Let me digress just a bit, I have to go back to my Akron University days, which were not particularly fruitful as far as my education was concerned, but one thing happened that conceivably could have changed my life. One thing I do know, it sure changed my military career.

ROTC (Reserve Officers' Training Corps) was a required course at Akron U., and I took it and did well in it. One thing that I did was obey the orders given from a certain Sergeant Gee, and I got to be a pretty good cadet. Well, after I arrived in Camp Shelby and started basic training, I seemed to be about the only one in our training company who knew his right foot from his left foot and knew close-order drill. As a result of this I made buck sergeant after three weeks in the Army, which was some kind of a record in those days, and I attribute it all to ROTC because, as I said before, it taught me my left foot from my right foot—obviously very important in the Army. . . .

The continuum of a man's self-regard: from a boy who thinks that he has no command over life's vagaries, to a soldier who begins to understand that confidence is something that can be attained, to an older man who senses things starting to shift inexorably back in the other direction. . . .

In the early 1980s, when my brother got married in Colorado, the family gathered at a hotel complex in Keystone for the ceremony. My father had rented a car—he was still in his sixties, driving had not yet become a problem for him, even in our eyes—and one afternoon he and my mother took a ride down the mountain road to pick up some things at a grocery store.

When they returned, there was a sound in his voice I hadn't often heard before. Apparently as they were driving on the narrow road their car had been passed by some raucous young local guys who thought my dad had been holding them up.

Never one to hide his opinion of people—especially people

who annoyed him—he had given them an angry stare out the open window of his rented car. He wanted them to know that he thought they were driving like jerks.

And one of the guys in the car had rolled the window down and shouted at my father: "What are you looking at, you son of a bitch?"

Mountain road, sparsely populated part of Colorado, my mother in the passenger seat, outnumbered by young men he knew nothing about. . . .

"I just gave them a little nod and rolled the window up," he reported to us. "And I slowed down and let them go on."

He hadn't liked the cut of their jib—and it had turned out that they didn't much like the cut of *his* jib, either, and appeared ready to do something about it if he pushed things.

Discretion won out—as it undoubtedly should have. And the sound of his voice that day . . . it wasn't exactly that he sounded defeated, it was more a concession that he was reluctantly resigned to something. There are some battles not worth fighting; there comes a time in your life when you defer to people you once wouldn't have even wasted your spit on. There are wars and there are wars . . . and a man reaches a juncture in his days when he must realize that he's no longer a fighter.

He didn't say he was scared that day; it's not a word he would have chosen to use. But in his voice was the acknowledgment that he was glad the face-off had ended where it had—and maybe regretful that, with my mother in the car, he had initiated the incident with that first disapproving stare out the window.

Being afraid, at one time, was something he evidently used as fuel—being afraid was something he depended upon to propel him. In recording his personal history, he talked about the emotions that filled him in the months before he was sent overseas when, unexpectedly, he was selected to be trained as an infantry officer and sent to Fort Benning, Georgia, to see if he could make the grade.

* * *

. . . When I got there I was full of trepidation, because this was major league stuff, and the stories about the guys who busted out were legion. And I was just hoping and praying that it would not happen to me. . . .

One of the things I dreaded was the obstacle course, which we had to run every Saturday morning. I was never a particularly athletic guy, as you all know—I could hold my own in physical training and boxing and that sort of thing, but I really wasn't such a jock that I would break any records, and the obstacle course was a big fear of mine.

Well, I was very, very pleased when I found that I was far from being the last in the class as far as scoring in the obstacle course was concerned. As a matter of fact I was about in the top 15 percent, which was good enough for me. And so as I went through this obstacle course and the combat course, week after week, I eventually got stronger and stronger and had much more confidence in myself.

One of the things in the combat course was we had to crawl under barbed wire with live machine gun bullets being fired above our heads. This was very frightening, but it was all a part of training. . . .

When the last week rolled around, which was the most important week, I was named to command the whole class of potential officers at Fort Benning. And on July 14, 1942—what a feeling that was, not only to survive the thirteen weeks and to be called a ninety-day wonder, which is what we were called, but to realize that from that day on we would be officers. . . .

For all that had happened to the men and women of his generation—for all the places he had been, for all that he had been through—my father, and, I think, many of his contemporaries, regarded the world with a constant sense of distance.

"It's Akron calling," he would say when I was a child and his father or mother would phone Columbus on the weekend to say hello. The words themselves, and his phrasing of them—"It's Akron calling"—made it sound as if this was the most momentous, stop-the-presses telephone call that anyone had ever placed. The implicit sense of scale went way beyond the importance the call really carried.

And this was from a man who had been to Africa, to Italy, this was from a man whose country had sent him across the ocean. Maybe it was because he and the men of that generation returned from the war to a United States that was still mainly local—to cities with invisible walls around them in the years before the interstates opened. It remained relatively difficult to get from one place to another in the U.S. in the first years after the war—the roads and highways were still the old kind, the freeway entrance and exit ramps had not been constructed, even a car trip to another part of Ohio required planning in advance.

But later—after the interstates, after network television, after the worldwide computer network—he still spoke that way. I would telephone Columbus on a weekend to check in with my mom and dad, and if they had people over I could hear him put his hand over the mouthpiece of the phone and say to their visitors: "It's Chicago calling."

As if to silence them; as if, because the phone call was coming from a few states away, everything should stop, become hushed. It was long distance—it wasn't a call from right there in town. The world—or so his words and his tone of voice said—was very large.

I never quite understood the ever-present surprise in that tone. The world was, in fact, large—and no one had a right to know that any better than he. It certainly wasn't large because Akron was calling, or Chicago was calling; it was large in a manner that he and his friends and division mates had been shown ample evidence of when they were very young men.

His voice, speaking not of a long-distance phone call from the Midwestern United States to a house in Columbus, but of his first impressions of Naples, Italy, after the 91st had gotten its orders to march:

. . . There was no sanitation, and the Germans had taken everything with them, including the food the Italians had left, and there was very little clothing, furniture, everything you can imagine. The once beautiful city of Naples was a complete shambles.

We stayed there a few days, and then early one morning we loaded up on trucks and started the long trek northward to where, nobody knew. We got into the same situation that we found ourselves in in Africa. We had a chance to get off the trucks to rest. Some of the men were careless and wandered off into the bushes and that's where they were booby-trapped and stepped on mines and were terribly maimed or killed.

It was really war at this time. . . .

In the days after my father's death—the days leading up to the funeral, and then the days after he was buried—there were times when I was away from my mother's house for a few hours, and I picked up a phone to call her.

Usually she answered. But sometimes—if people were in her house making condolence visits, if she was busy doing something else—the answering machine clicked on to take the call.

And there was something I didn't really know how to tell her:

My father's voice was the one on the greeting tape.

"You have reached the Greenes. Neither Phyllis or I are available to take your call right now. . . ."

It was hearty, energetic, full of welcoming enthusiasm; he was always a pretty theatrical guy in his daily dealings with others, and it extended to the answering-machine tape.

But it was more than a little spooky. He was dead, and here was his voice, and if it was unsettling to me, his son, at least I understood that my mom had obviously not gotten around to taking care of certain things, which was why his voice was still there. But I thought of other people who might call—friends, relatives, his former business associates—and I really didn't want them to have to hear this. It was quite a shock—people call the house to say how sorry they are to learn of his death, and there his happy voice is, telling them to leave a message until he can get back to them.

My supposition was that my mom didn't know about it; I thought that she would be mortified if she knew that callers were hearing him greeting them. But I wasn't sure if I should bring it up to her, not only because it was one more thing I didn't want her to worry about—but because, in a strange way, I thought part of her might resist the impulse to change the tape.

It was one of the few things that remained from the way life had been in that house only a few days before. It had always been a house that belonged to the both of them, in every way—they thought of themselves as a couple, full-time, inseparable. *You have reached the Greenes. . . .* That's who they were, every bit as much as they were an individual man and an individual woman.

Getting rid of his voice on the tape might be a small detail, in the context of what she had just lost—but I knew that it would matter to her. His voice would no longer be speaking for them, in any way. I told my sister about it, and I'm not sure what she said to my mom, but within a day or two my father's voice had been erased and replaced by my mother's.

Not that I wasn't hearing his voice all the time, telling stories about a once-young man very far from home:

We continued the trek northward and found ourselves going through Rome, which had recently been liberated by part of the Fifth Army commanded by General Mark Clark.

We did receive quite an acclamation from the Italians, they just thought we were wonderful, but of course that's what they thought the Germans were when they first came in. So there we were on the way up what was to become Highway 65, but it had a different number at that particular point, and . . . again, this sounds like a storybook, but we were going to engage the Germans in battle. . . .

* * *

Sometimes I would hear young businessmen—usually white-collar types, stock traders and the like—speak of their jobs in terms of warfare.

"He's a killer," they might say admiringly of a colleague. "This is going to be a real battle," they might say as the deadline for a deal approached. "Hey, this is a war—don't forget it."

I never heard my father talk about business that way. He always—no matter what was going on at his office—spoke of business as just that: business. A job. He didn't pump it up into something like combat.

It made me think about whether the men of his generation—the men who had come back from the war in Europe, the men who had come back from the war in the Pacific—just instinctively knew better than to use those kinds of terms to describe something that was not even close to a war. Whether—out of respect not only for themselves and the men they had left behind, but out of dark respect for the very concept of war—they would have felt foolish using that kind of language to refer to the safe venue of the office-place.

He was gone, and I couldn't ask him about it. But I made a note to ask Tibbets. I was doing that a lot now—the questions I had never asked my dad about the world in which he had lived, I was taking to Tibbets, to see what he might have to say.

EIGHTEEN

Business is not a war and it never has been," Tibbets said. "Your job may not be a lot of fun at times, and you may not like the people you're competing with—both outside your company, and *inside* your company—but war? That demeans the word."

I had come to see him again in Columbus, and we were having lunch at a casual place just a few blocks from the apartment house where my father and mother had lived right after I was born. Tibbets told me that work was not the only part of contemporary life that is wrongly compared to warfare; he said there is another of life's aspects that is even more frequently placed falsely in that category:

"Look at sports," he said. "All the talk about how football is a war, how the football field is a battlefield. It's so ridiculous. You say that your father used to go to the Ohio State football games?"

"For fifty years," I said.

"I can almost guarantee you that he never acted like those people who paint their faces and their chests," Tibbets said. "Am I right?"

Of course he was—but then, in his later years, there was obviously no way a man my father's age was going to do that. I understood Tibbets' broader point—that even when my father was a younger man and just back from the war, he and the members of his generation likely accepted sports events, including the seemingly most crucial ones, as what they were: colorful entertainment.

"Your father knew, and I know, the difference between reality and fiction," Tibbets said. "Fiction is fine—as long as you don't get it mixed up with the things in life that are real.

"I don't think that any of us who came home from World War II made the mistake of confusing what happened there with what happens at a sports contest. Look, your dad probably hated to see Ohio State lose—he liked the team.

"But he was a realist—he knew that *he* wasn't playing. He wasn't down on the field, and he couldn't do anything about what was going on down on the field. Whether the team won or not, he was still going to get in his car and go home when the game was over—and then be back in the stands for the next game.

"It was a relief for us, to come back after the war and be able to attend the games. We didn't whoop and holler—we'd give our teams a good hand, but we understood that it was a game that we weren't playing in, that everyone, including the people on the field, was going to get to go home safely from it. It would have been sort of stupid to put the same kind of emotions into that that we'd put into the situation overseas that we'd recently been actual participants in."

I had brought a list with me—things about my father's life that I had been thinking about lately, things that I had never gotten around to asking him directly. I was looking for Tibbets' help in understanding some of them.

The importance my father had placed on being a major, for example. He had gone into the Army as a private—drafted—and when he left as a major, that had seemed to be one of the accomplishments in his life of which he was the very proudest. It was a running joke with my dad and his friends—they would call him "the major" ("Is the major home?" his friend Harry Hofheimer would ask my mom when he would call our house, all during the years of my growing up); they were kidding, but kidding on the straight. They knew that the rank mattered to him.

But why so much?

"Think of the Army as a company, as a business," Tibbets said. "Think of your father going in as a person at the most menial level—as a person sent down to the basement to work, sweeping the damn floor.

"That's what it was like when he was drafted into the Army. He was sent to the basement—he was a private, in the basement.

"And when he left the Army after the war, he was an executive. That's not something a young man ever forgets, even when he's no longer young. Why did it mean so much to him? Because at the first time during his life that it really mattered, he was recognized by the people he worked with. They recognized his talent and his ability."

"And what was the meaning of the rank?" I asked.

"The meaning was that the Army trusted him to tell other men what to do," Tibbets said. "They put that kind of trust in him.

"You only knew him when you knew him—after you were born. But he was someone before you were born—in the Army, he was a young man who went in with several million others. Was being a major a big deal to him? You're damn right it was. It ought to have been. Those millions of others didn't make it to major. He did."

Yet for all that pride in what he had become in the Army, my father was not an openly patriotic man—not in the sense that he was a flag-waver, or a maker of I-love-America speeches. That had always struck me as curious—that he and so many men like him, who had risked so much for their country, seldom talked about the affection they held for the United States. It just wasn't a subject that came up much.

Why?

"We didn't talk about it because we didn't see any reason to talk about it," Tibbets said. "Love our country? We were taught that, by our parents, and in our schools, and in our churches and synagogues. We grew up knowing that it was expected of us—to love this country and to treat it with loyalty and respect.

"Talk about it? That would be like talking about the air that we breathed."

"But the experiences that all of you had in defending the country . . ." I began.

"Look, I didn't know what my father did during his war," Tibbets said. "He was a captain. In World War I. But that's about all I knew, because it would have been ridiculous to say it out loud—to say that you had done a lot to help defend your country."

"Why ridiculous?" I said.

"Because everyone felt the same way that your father did and that I did," Tibbets said. "To love your country didn't make you something special—of course you loved your country, of course you would give your life for it if it came to that. You didn't need to tell people that—it was just the way things were."

"Was that the only reason?" I said.

"When we came home from the war, we were in the midst of millions of men who had just come home from the same war," Tibbets said. "And even if a man wanted to talk about what he had been through, he usually had enough sense to know that there were other men around him who had had experiences they did *not* want to talk about. So we usually made the choice not to bring it up.

" 'Patriotism' is a general word. It's vague. When you're fighting a war it is not a matter of patriotism in the general sense. It's about the death of friends.

"You watch friends get blown to pieces. And that is not a patriotic feeling. It's a revolting feeling.

"It's revolting to watch anyone die, and it hurts when the person is a friend of yours. You're talking to a guy one minute, and the next minute he's body parts and dead.

"It's shocking. It is a shock that doesn't leave you, and when you come back home you may not want to bring those things out. So you don't."

* * *

Once, when I was a young adult and my father was in his fifties or his early sixties, I was back in Columbus and I had lunch with him downtown.

We were walking down Broad Street, and at the southeast corner of Broad and Third my dad saw a man he knew—a business associate of some kind. He stopped the man and said that he wanted to introduce his son to him.

"Bob," my father said to me, "this is my old friend Johnny Johnson."

And the man corrected him. He said what his last name really was.

It was close—I don't recall now whether the man's name was Johnny Jackson or Johnny Jones, but I know that it wasn't all that far off from Johnny Johnson. But my father, I could tell, was mortified. He had committed a blunder, and quite publicly—and the next thirty seconds were uncomfortable for him, much more so than they were for me or for the man whose name he had gotten slightly wrong.

In the grand scheme of things, what had it meant? Nothing. A blown name on a busy city street. But when I thought about it in the years that followed—and I thought about it every time I passed Broad and Third—I tried to envision the battlefields of Europe, and then to juxtapose that visual image with the safe and civil streetscape of downtown Columbus. A mistake on the battlefield could cost a man his life—or the life of a friend. A little slip at Broad and Third? Gone with the next changing of the traffic light.

But was it? Or, to the men who came home, did the downtown streets sometimes seem as foreign as the hills of Africa and Italy? Had the war in Europe, the war in the Pacific, become, in a certain sense, these men's real hometowns? Had the war become their point of truest reference—the place they knew best?

And if it had, what was it like for them when they returned to city streets, and found the combatants wearing business suits instead of uniforms, in a different kind of conflict?

"Boy, you've been thinking about all of this a lot, haven't you?" Tibbets said.

"More than I would have expected," I said.

"Don't spend a lot of time thinking that part of us would have preferred to be back in the war," he said. "You're right that the war started to feel more real to us than our memories of what we had left back home. It was just like that—you've got it right.

"But it wasn't a reality that we wanted to keep alive. It never was that. Most of the guys wanted only one thing—to get out. To go back home and to start our lives over again."

"It just would seem to be such a harsh shift," I said. "To go from a place where the rules are the rules of warfare, to a place where your enemies—or at least your adversaries—are dressed the same way you are, and you have to relearn a whole new set of rules."

"It's like I was telling you before," he said. "Business was never war to us. We knew the difference, and we never confused the two.

"And no matter how annoying business could become, it was never an annoyance that we would trade in for what we faced during warfare."

I told him that story of my dad and the man whose name wasn't Johnny Johnson. It had felt, to me, like a lost skirmish played under rules of engagement that were at the same time stringently meaningful and totally irrelevant—rules of engagement my father had returned to after taking part in something that had been governed by a set of regulations quite separate.

I guessed that whenever I recalled that moment at the corner of Broad and Third, I had this twinge of a suspicion that the man in the oil painting back in our house—the young soldier in uniform—may have, at least on occasion, been surer of his footing in Italy in 1945 than on the concrete sidewalks of central Ohio thirty years later.

"I wouldn't give that too much thought," Tibbets said.

"I don't know why it sticks with me," I said. "And it's not like I think about it all the time."

"I'll guarantee you one thing," Tibbets said. "You've thought about it a lot more than your dad or that other guy ever did."

"Maybe it's not all that complicated a thought," I said. "Maybe it just comes down to the hunch that, given the choice, he would rather have been a soldier than a businessman."

"On that one, I can't tell you you're wrong," Tibbets said.

And I wanted to know about my father's music.

He liked Les and Larry Elgart; he liked Si Zentner; he liked Doc Severinsen in the days before Severinsen was on the *Tonight Show,* in the days when Severinsen was known as a great jazzman instead of a fellow in loud sport coats who, from the bandstand, traded jokes with Johnny Carson. He liked grown-up musicians with grown-up talent who made grown-up music.

And I got the impression that he had liked them even as a very young man—he had liked them on the day he had come out of the Army. It seemed to me to be symbolic of something that went well beyond music: It seemed to emblemize once again the notion that it was just about impossible to come home from World War II and seem like a kid. Prolonged adolescence—which became almost a way of life for generations born after the war—was a concept that would have had a hard time making it past years of fighting the Nazis.

Or so it had always seemed to me—and the music of my father's generation was a part of that. The men and women of that generation loved music that was older than their years.

"I think it was because there were changes going on at home while we were away at war," Tibbets told me when I asked him about it. "Rock and roll, the way I understand it, came along in the years after we came home and started raising our families. I think that rock and roll music was the outgrowth of the changes in society that were taking place while the men were away.

"After rock and roll, there was no going back to the music that was there before. We found that out quick enough. Speaking just for myself, rock and roll always disturbed the hell out of me. I couldn't stand it."

I told him that my father—who had despised Elvis Presley from the moment he had laid eyes on him—always appeared a little confused about Elvis after Elvis had joined the Army. All the terrible things my father had said about Presley—but how could he believe those things about a man who suddenly wore the same uniform that he had worn? How could he say that Presley represented everything that was wrong about American life, when Presley, just as my father had, answered the call of his country and served in the United States Army?

"When we went into the service, we matured in a hurry," Tibbets said. "The transition period was very short. During World War II, if you didn't mature fast, you were dead.

"It wasn't a choice we made—it just happened, because of where we were. In most societies, the maturing process takes place over a period of years. We didn't have that. I went from a twenty-three-year-old kid to a person who felt like a forty-year-old service-man in a big hurry.

"So of course it was hard for your dad to stay mad at Presley after Presley was in the Army. Presley was being put into the same situation that your dad and I were in—although Presley didn't have a war to fight. But by going in, he was growing up. And any man who has done it understands that."

And was that why—when my father and Tibbets and all those men came back from the war—they seemed so solid? Was that why their music was the music of adults, and all that followed seemed designed for the ears of children and adolescents?

"Let me put it to you this way," Tibbets said. "Where we were—during the years that we were serving—there was not much time for levity. You grew up so fast precisely because you weren't given any time to grow up.

"We came to maturity quickly. We didn't do it because we had sat down and made the choice. We did it because our lives depended on it."

* * *

And their lives had depended on one another—both in matters that could kill them if someone did something wrong, or matters that would merely inconvenience them if someone declined to do a little thing right.

It's something else I had been thinking about when moments from my father's life came back to me. And I decided to tell Tibbets one small story, from a Christmas Eve long ago.

"We were in the house," I said. "All of us were still little kids. And there was this huge sound from the garage, like an explosion or something, and then the sound of water gushing.

"It was freezing outside. We opened this side door that led into the garage—and a water pipe had burst. It must have been a pipe that extended across the ceiling of the garage, because the water was just pouring onto my father's and my mother's cars. I mean, more water than you've ever seen come out of a pipe.

"And you could tell that it was very hot water—it was really steaming as it came out of the ceiling of the garage. And we stood there—I can see my father looking at it—and what were we supposed to do? It was Christmas Eve—late in the evening on Christmas Eve, if I'm remembering right. Who are you going to find on Christmas Eve to come fix a burst water pipe?"

"What did your father do?" Tibbets asked.

"Well, I remember him going to the phone in the back hallway, and calling all these plumbing services," I said. "But of course, no one was there. So he looked up the home numbers of some plumbers who lived near us, and he told them what had happened. But they didn't want to go out on Christmas Eve. I couldn't blame them—but the water was just gushing into our garage.

"I guess what I think about when I think about that is: In the Army, you always must have had all these people to do every job with you. You had been asked to save the world—but even on the little things, there were millions of you, always doing everything together. However tedious it might have been, however hurry-up-and-wait it might have been, at least you were all there. You know that old line: 'Yeah? You and what army?' You had the answer, back then. You and what army? The United States Army."

"So what's that have to do with the garage on Christmas Eve?" Tibbets said.

"If he'd been back in the Army, there would have been hundreds of guys around to fix the pipe," I said. "Hundreds of pairs of hands. And I remember him standing there with his family, with all the water pouring out . . . and I think about whether life got so much harder for all of you once you got home, and there was no army with you. The pipe blows, the furnace breaks . . . and it's not you and what army anymore. It's just you."

"It's still you and the Army," Tibbets said.

"What do you mean?" I said.

"That's one of the things that the war did for us," he said. "It's an old saying, but it's a true one: There is nothing like American ingenuity. For the GIs during the war, it was a question of coming upon new problems to solve every day. Problems that none of us had ever anticipated before—and we had to figure out ways to solve them every day of the war.

"Yes, we did it together—but I don't think that made it harder once we got home. I think it made it easier. Because we had all those months and years of coming up with solutions when there was no choice but to find a solution. So your friends might not be with you once you got home and were faced with problems—but the experiences you had gone through were with you."

"So you don't think a lot of men didn't know what to do once they didn't have the Army at their side?" I said.

"I think a guy's lost if he feels that way," Tibbets said. "And I don't think a lot of us came home feeling lost. We had our experiences inside of us. That was as good as having our friends from the Army next to us. Or almost as good."

"I don't know," I said. "I keep thinking about the expression on my father's face that Christmas Eve."

"Let me ask you something," Tibbets said. "What finally happened?"

"What do you mean?" I said.

"What happened with the burst water pipe in the garage?" he said. "Did it just keep pouring the water out all night long?"

"No," I said. "He got it shut off."

"I'm not surprised," Tibbets said. "Did a plumber come over?"

"No," I said.

"Then how did he fix the pipe?" Tibbets asked.

"I don't know," I said. "I don't remember what he did."

"He did something," Tibbets said. "And whatever he did, it worked."

"It must have," I said.

"That's my point," Tibbets said.

In the last days of my father's life, the tree trimmers were next door.

It's a sound I will never forget. He had lost the battle; he was going to die.

And there it was, just out the bedroom window: the sound of power saws revving up, the high whine of the motorized blades cutting into wood, the throaty rumble as the teeth did their job—and then that whine again, louder, sharper, a dentist's drill amplified a thousand times.

And my father in his bed. Outside our house, no one knew; it wasn't a question of a neighbor being rude or unfeeling. This was the tree trimmers' day to come to this neighborhood. They had their job to do.

And he lay in his bed, and there was no silence. Only noise, as his life slipped away.

I told Tibbets. And I told him about how quiet the street where I grew up had always been—so quiet that even something as mild as teenagers yelling at each other from their cars late at night was a big event. Even noise like that seldom happened—it was enough to make us all wake up. What's wrong? we would think in those first moments of wakefulness. What's that noise?

Teenagers calling out to each other. That broke the peace and the quiet.

I asked Tibbets about the noise of war—what it had been like to leave a country where there was usually quiet, and enter a world where the sounds were like nothing they had ever heard before.

"That's something that no one ever thinks about," he said to me. "The sounds of war. I haven't even thought about it for a long time.

"But it was a big part of it. The war was not quiet. We were all raised to respect our neighbors' privacy—to keep things quiet in the neighborhoods where we grew up.

"And then we went to the war, and the noise wasn't like anything else we ever experienced before, or like anything we would ever experience again.

"There was no mistaking it. The gunfire, and the tank noises, and the sirens and the aircraft overhead all the time. It never really stopped. It became part of the background of our lives—sometimes it was louder than other times, but it never completely went away. We even got used to it. That war sound."

I asked him if it was difficult adjusting to the quiet once the soldiers came home to the United States.

"No," he said. "It was a pretty easy adjustment. We liked the silence of home. It meant something to us."

"What did it mean?" I asked.

"The silence?" Tibbets said. "It meant that we weren't going to get killed the next minute.

"Think about it," he said. "What does silence indicate?

"Tranquility."

NINETEEN

I don't know if my father even heard the power saws cutting into those trees. His face was filled with sporadic flashes of pain, but that had been happening for a while; the noise may have contributed to his discomfort or it may not have, but in any event we finally went out to speak to the neighbors and to the tree crew, and they were kind enough to give my father some quiet.

Even if he was aware of the noise, though, it couldn't have been anything close to the level to which he had once had to train himself to become accustomed. The tranquility of which Tibbets had spoken was homefront tranquility—it was the tranquility that awaited those men once they returned to the American towns they had left.

The places to where their country had sent them were a different matter entirely. My father's voice:

. . . The Bay of Naples was something that I shall never forget as long as I live. The harbor was absolutely jammed with the wreckage of all kinds of Italian warships, French warships, and it had been practically impossible to thread our way into the bay. But it was accomplished. We had to pick our way over the decks of these sunken ships. . . .

. . . . I was all pumped up with the glory needle and everything, and I thought, this was it. If ever I was going to be a hero it was going to be right now, because we were closing in on the Germans who were retreating very, very rapidly, but we were proceeding rapidly, right on their tail.

They made good use of their 88s—they were called 88 howitzers, and they actually used them to pick off trucks and even individual soldiers. One night we were bivouacked at a little place called Piombino. And it was in this little village that we got our first taste of an air raid and an attitudinal change.

During the night, as was really necessary, we slept beneath the trucks because we didn't know when we would be hit by incoming artillery or what. To our great surprise and horror we received an air raid that night, and the shell fragments were flying all around, injuring and killing more guys. And I can only imagine what the front line troops were receiving. . . .

One day toward the end when I was visiting him in Columbus, and my mother, my sister and I were in the bedroom with him, I walked out to get something in the kitchen.

As I left the room, my mom and my sister shifted chairs, so that he could see them from the bed.

I could hear him say to them:

"You girls stay here, now."

And then:

"Don't leave me."

Two simple declarative sentences. Yet the plaintiveness of them. . . .

I don't think I had ever heard him ask for something that directly before—at least not ask for something that important.

I stopped where I was, and looked back into the room.

"We're not going anywhere," my mother said, holding his hand.

"We're not leaving," my sister said, with the smile I was seeing on her face so often during those months—a smile that didn't match the wetness of her eyes. The smile was for him to see; I think she was hoping he didn't notice the tears.

Don't leave me. I knew that those were words he never would have said out loud during the years when he was younger and stronger. Would he have thought them to himself? I didn't really know. There was no way for anyone but him to know the answer to that.

But as my mother and sister sat with him that day, I asked myself a question that I knew I would never ask my mother:

If the circumstances had been reversed—if my mother had been the one whose health and life were slipping away, and my father had been the one who was still vital—would he have been this good with her?

Would he have had the fortitude and the patience and the singlemindedness to do for her what she, over all these months, was doing for him?

I knew one thing: No one could ever do this better.

"We're not going anywhere," she said, moving her chair closer to the bed. "We're right here."

His voice, telling about the sunrise after the German howitzer attack:

. . . The next morning we saddled up as if nothing had happened and proceeded northward. We finally learned that our goal was to go through Florence, which was right across the Arno River, and occupy the slopes to the north of the city.

This was really a beautiful part. . . . we went through Tuscany and saw all the beautiful old Italian towns, and it was an experience that no one will ever forget—and it was very peaceful at that time. . . . We went across the Arno River on pontoon bridges and saw the most beautiful city you can ever imagine.

Florence was declared an open city, which meant that while the bridges would be bombed and taken out, none of the city was to be touched. This was an arrangement that had been made by the Axis and the Allies, so it was really something to see.

We went through the city very, very fast. Oh, I meant to tell you that the only remaining bridge was the Ponte Vecchio, which was a bridge that was made up of small shops, silversmiths, jewelers and everything like that—a beautiful bridge.

Up we came to the slopes to the north of the city, and there we bivouacked to wait the next phase. . . .

There was a drive-in on East Main Street where he always used to take us for hamburgers and milkshakes. The Eastmoor, it was called—car hops and cruising convertibles and warm summer nights. The men who had come home from the war would bring their young families out for burgers and fries and Cokes—the Eastmoor felt like fun and freedom, it felt like the kind of place they must have dreamed of during those months and years in Europe and the Pacific.

Come to think of it, the Eastmoor wasn't all that far from the Top. If the men home from the war would take their wives to the Top for adult nights out—steaks and martinis—then the Eastmoor was the place where the children were welcome. Both a part of Main Street; both a part of what, in central Ohio, made the post-war years feel as good as they did.

Once, I remember, we ate inside at the Eastmoor—we were headed somewhere on a car trip (maybe to see his parents in Akron), and we stopped off at the Eastmoor and went to a booth. There was loud music playing in the restaurant—not jukebox music, just music coming out of the ceiling.

He called the waitress over and asked her to turn it down.

"We can't turn it down," she said. "It comes from downtown."

I thought his eyes were going to turn to icicles and steam was going to come puffing out of his ears. "The music comes from downtown," he said, each word an accusation.

"It does," she said.

"*Where* downtown?" my father said.

"I don't know," the waitress said. "It just comes from downtown."

My guess is that it was Muzak; my guess is that this is what she meant. And even with Muzak, or so I assume, there must be a way for an individual place of business to control the volume. If there's not, then there should be.

Which is what my father seemed to believe, too. "You're telling me that we have to sit here and have this music blast into our ears because someone downtown is controlling the volume?" he said.

I wanted to sink into the cushion. He was probably right; why should he have to eat his meal with high-volume music blaring right over his head? But when you're a kid, you don't want to be around any public confrontation in which your parents are involved. It doesn't matter who's right or who's wrong; you just want things to go along on a smooth path.

"Do your *hamburgers* come from downtown?" he said. "Because if they do, maybe you can tell the person who brings them to turn the music down on his way."

I was telling my brother that story as we looked for the medical supply store. It was on East Main Street, too; it probably had been there for years—maybe going back to the early years of the Eastmoor and the Top—but we'd never seen it. At least we'd never noticed it.

You don't see places like that until you need them. A sickroom supply store—that's what it was. As he lay dying, there were all kinds of things that suddenly became necessary. Things you don't have around your house until your life turns downward.

Items needed for the basic functions of daily living when you can't get out of your bed—items that, by their existence, speak of the new unpleasantness of your mornings and nights. Products and devices designed to help you accomplish those functions you never had to even think about needing help with before.

"I think it's that place, right there," my brother said, and we turned into the parking lot.

And so we went shopping. The place wasn't glitzy or inviting; this was not some Wal-Mart designed to lure its customers into impulse purchases. The people who came in here to shop knew what they wanted before they walked through the door, and in most cases they weren't shopping for their own needs. They were doing it for someone who couldn't come here himself or herself. Anyone who could come in here himself probably wouldn't.

So we went through the aisles like kids in an old 5-and-10, looking for articles to buy. Except no one would enter this particular version of a 5-and-10 unless they had to. We found some of the things our mother had said that our father needed, and the ones we couldn't find we asked the man at the counter, and he bagged everything up for us—all the things made of plastic, all the things made of glass, all the things made of cloth—and as we left he said, "Have a good weekend."

"Those words have a different sound, in there," I said to my brother as we got back into the car.

"What, 'Have a good weekend?' " he said.

"Yeah," I said. "That's not exactly a good-weekend kind of place."

"It's Saturday," he said. "He's just being nice."

"And he probably knows that he'll see us again next week," I said.

"Until we stop coming," my brother said.

I didn't have to ask what he meant.

We drove onto Main Street, on our way back to our father.

"Where was the Eastmoor Drive-In?" I asked my brother.

"One of these blocks," he said. "It's been gone for years."

Main Street must have seemed like such a blithe piece of roadway to him, after where he had been:

. . . *We sat on the northern hills of Florence for a few days or maybe a week or so, and then the order came to saddle up and get going up Highway 65.*

You kids have heard me talk about Highway 65 many, many times, and are probably sick of it, but as I am recounting my experiences now, it really flashes back very clearly. What we knew, and what was rumored, didn't sound very good. As we were going up Highway 65, you must remember that it was barely sixty or sixty-five miles from where we left, to Bologna, which was to be our phase line and our goal.

This ordinarily could have been done in a couple of hours, but believe it or not it took us over six months to get up that sixty or sixty-five miles of road to accomplish our objective. . . .

When I was in high school I'd had some summer jobs—including some in the factory of the company where he worked—but things changed the summer I got a job as a copyboy at the *Columbus Citizen-Journal.*

I was seventeen; it was a morning paper. I would ride the bus downtown and start my shift at noon, or sometimes at two o'clock in the afternoon. I'd get off at nine, or at eleven.

This was different from anything with which he had ever been familiar. Factory work, he knew; cutting lawns and painting street addresses on curbs, he could understand. I'd done those things, without taking much of an interest in them. They were what you were supposed to do: work during the summer to make a little money.

The job at the newspaper seemed to interest him, in the sense that for the first time I was doing something that had absolutely no connection with anything that he had been involved with in his lifetime. It's not that he asked a lot of questions about it. He didn't.

But there was something in the tone of his voice, and in the way he would look at me on weekend mornings. Our lives suddenly had fewer intersections—I would still be asleep when he left for his office in the morning, and in the evening the family would have dinner without me, and by the time I got home from the *Citizen-Journal* often everyone would be in bed. So there were weekend mornings when several whole days had passed since I had seen him.

And he would look at me as if he knew I was doing something special. Not just the fact that it was newspaper work—the look on his face had more to do with me finding something that I liked, not something that he liked or that my mother liked or that any of my friends liked, but that I liked, on my own, and then going out and pursuing it. Without very many words being exchanged, it was clear to me that he thought this was good.

There was something else in the air, too, something beyond the fact of my discovering at a young age a kind of work that I was falling in love with. There was the parallel idea that our lives were beginning to diverge—that by finding this kind of work, and devoting myself to it, I was setting a course that would send us off in different directions forevermore. It was not that he minded this; I think that he kind of liked it. It was just that, as a father, he was seeing something for the first time—his child, his oldest child, becoming a different person than the boy from all those thousands of dinner table evenings.

I would ride the bus downtown in the off-hours, hours when few other people were commuting to work, and I would do my job in the city room. There wasn't much grandeur to it—running copy and filling pastepots and going to Paoletti's restaurant next door to get coffee and sandwiches for the editorial staff—but the world in that city room was a world he had never seen, never been a part of. Everything else in my life, up to that point, had been in the context of our family. This was mine alone.

There were nights when he and my mom would drive downtown to pick me up. Most nights I took the bus home, but if I was working late, or if they had been out with friends, they might offer to give me a ride.

So at nine o'clock or eleven o'clock, I would grab an early copy of the morning paper from the first press run—a seven-cent newspaper that we who worked there got for free—and I would take the stairs down to the newspaper building's front entrance on Third Street, and they'd be waiting in the car, he behind the wheel, my mother next to him.

I'd show him the paper—this was all done very casually, we didn't make a ceremony out of it or act as if it really mattered, I'd just hand it to him, with tomorrow morning's headlines on it—and he'd glance at it, seeing on the night before what all his friends wouldn't see until breakfast. And he'd always say the same thing to me:

"How was work, Scoop?"

It was a joke, of course; by then newspapermen weren't called Scoop anymore, he was making fun in the gentlest of ways. But joking or not, that word—*Scoop*—meant a lot. It was shorthand for: You're doing something on your own. You're doing something exciting. You're doing something that I think is all right.

And at seventeen, it was exciting—to be a young man starting off in a line of work that seemed like so much fun. I look back on those nights now, and it seems most generous of him, to be so quietly happy to see his son doing something like this. I often ask myself now whether he ever wished that as a young man he had been able to lead a life like that one.

Because through no fault of his own the nights of his young manhood had turned into something very different.

. . . It started to get cold and it started to rain and the hills began to get steeper, and lo and behold they turned into mountains, which were the Apennines. And up and up we went, and in the far distance we could hear artillery fire, and we knew that the Germans were just waiting for us to come around a bend.

But still we kept going, making a few miles a day and then bivouacking in any place that seemed good. In the meantime the front line troops up a few miles ahead of us were engaging the Germans and we started to take many, many casualties, and this is where I first got a real taste of seeing dead soldiers, both American and German.

It was a very, very pitiful sight, because the grave registration people would gather these bodies up, put them in white mattress covers, and stack them neatly, if you will, at a road junction. . . .

The white mattress covers, of course, had turned color, and that color was red blood, and the stench was something that one would never forget. But that was part of the cost of that awful war, and still we continued going up and up, maybe a few yards at a time.

The day before he was supposed to be buried there was a telephone call at my mother's house. It was from a woman at the cemetery.

The house was full of people making condolence calls. The woman from the cemetery asked to whom she was speaking, and said, "Honey, I think there may be a problem with the burial plot."

She asked to speak with my mother. I said no. I said to tell me what she meant.

She said, "Honey, I'm confused about which plot your family thinks your father is supposed to be buried in. I think we may have it reserved for someone else."

My mother, having heard the phone ring, came into the room where I was talking. She asked me what the call was.

I said it was nothing.

After she had left the room, I told the woman that I was quite certain she was wrong about there being any misunderstanding. My parents were very precise in all of their dealings, I said, right up to getting the arrangements for their burials taken care of years in advance.

And I told her that I could not believe she was making this phone call on this day.

She said, "Sweetheart, I know it's hard."

My brother came into the room. I put my hand over the

receiver and told him what was going on. I thought his face was going to turn purple.

I asked for the woman's name and I told her I would call her back in five minutes.

My brother and I made an excuse to have my mother let us take a look at the paperwork from the cemetery—the paperwork she and my father had taken pains to have completed years before. As I expected, everything was in order, in a file folder, with no detail unrecorded or left to chance. They wouldn't have let it be any other way.

With my parents' friends and loved ones all over our house, I called back the cemetery. I was told that the woman was unavailable—she was involved in a sales meeting with other prospective clients. Could she call me back?

I said no. I said to get her.

Five minutes passed. I was told that she was still in her sales meeting.

I said to get her.

She came to the phone. I read to her from the paperwork that the cemetery had given to my parents.

"All right, sweetheart," she said. "Then the burial plot is your father's."

My father always had quite a temper. I have always tried to keep mine in check.

On this day, I thought a combination of the two might be in order.

In a voice so soft that I could barely hear it myself, I asked her for the name of the director of the cemetery. She told me.

I said, "First of all, you and I have never met. I am not honey. I am not sweetheart."

There was a silence. "I'm sorry," she said.

"Second of all, I'd like you to find [the director of the cemetery] right now. As soon as we get off the phone. Can you do that?"

She said that she could.

"I want you to tell him exactly what our conversations have been about," I said. "I want you to tell him that you have made this call to my mother as she is getting ready to bury her husband.

"And then I want you to tell him that I don't want to see either of your faces tomorrow at the cemetery. I don't ever want to hear your voice again.

"And please tell him that if there are any complications like this at the cemetery tomorrow—any complications at all, anything my mother is asked to deal with—then he should make plans for two more funerals, too."

"Why two more funerals?" she said.

"Because both of you are going to wish that you were dead," I said.

I looked across the room, where he used to sit at his desk. That one was for you, I thought. They may not have been able to turn down the music over your head at the Eastmoor Drive-In, but they're going to get your burial right. Hope you thought I did OK.

A few minutes later, when I was back with the people in the house, my mother said, "What was that call all about?"

"Just someone making sure that you have everything you need for tomorrow," I said.

TWENTY

That day went smoothly—and later, when I told Tibbets about what had happened, I had a question for him:

Because my father had always been so careful to have every detail buttoned up and taken care of, because he always planned everything out in advance, I had long half-assumed that this was a quality of all men with his background: all men who had served in the armed forces and who had come of age imbued with military discipline.

Thus, when something happened where someone was sloppy, where someone was not attentive to detail, I often found myself writing it off to the person not being part of the same generation of Americans he and Tibbets were a part of. But was I right?

Or even in the Army had there been people who were just plain bad at what they did? Even in the victorious American Army of World War II, had there been guys who were total screwups?

I think I knew the answer before I asked the question—which is why I asked it. And when Tibbets started laughing before he talked, I had a good idea of what he was going to say.

"Were there guys who were no good?" he said. "Hell, yes. They were all over the place."

"And what happened to them?" I said.

"Most of them made out all right," he said. "Listen, we were surrounded in our own units with some of the worst fuckups in the world. It's just the way mankind is."

"Your unit?" I said. "In Wendover? And on Tinian?"

"Well, that unit was a little different from most," he said. "As

I have explained to you. But we had our guys who could never quite get with the program, and who were always messing up. If you're thinking that your dad's close attention to detail was because of the Army, give him a little more credit than that. There were a lot of guys in the Army who never got anything right."

"And they didn't end up being tossed out?" I said.

"No," Tibbets said. "But whenever there was something difficult or important that needed doing, you knew where you could find them. Showing up at sick call, running to the infirmary."

"So the people who screw everything up today are nothing new?" I said.

"They don't wear uniforms," Tibbets said. "Our fuckups did."

Maybe that was why the rank of major meant so much to my father—maybe that was why, even though it was a joke with his friends, they often good-naturedly used that rank when they spoke to him. The more I thought about it—the "Is-the-major-home?" kidding that went on for so many years—the more I wanted to understand its significance to him.

"He and his friends may have joked about it, but there are a lot of things you can joke about," Tibbets said. "The idea that they picked 'major' out, all those years after he came home from the war—of course the rank meant a lot to him. And it should have."

"But why all that time later?" I said. "Fifty years had passed since he had left the Army, and the 'major' references were still there from his friends."

"He was entitled to be called 'major,' " Tibbets said. "The rank of major was not taken away from him. Look—I know that you tell me he kidded about it, I know he must have made fun of himself about it, but there are certain things that a man can't wash out of his mind.

"Military service will change the personalities of most people who serve. If they're lucky, they will change for the better. You *think* differently when you come out of the military. If you're lucky, you come out changed for the good.

"So if you come out as a major . . . it's like I told you before. Certain decisions have been made about the kind of man you are. The decisions may be made when you're a young soldier—but even when you grow old, the fact that those decisions were made means something to you. And it ought to."

"And yet he wasn't a member of the VFW," I said. "There were no VFW magazines around the house, no American Legion magazines. He must have had the chance to join—and he didn't."

"Neither did I," Tibbets said. "It's quite understandable."

"Why?" I said.

"For me, I guess more than anything else, I didn't want to be a has-been," Tibbets said. "I'm not knocking those who did join. But I stayed in the military for a long while after the war, and when I finally did get out I made the decision not to join the VFW and not to join the American Legion." [He later was made an honorary life member of both organizations.]

"Did you have something against them?" I asked.

"No," he said. "I'm just not a joiner. I never joined the Boy Scouts when I was a kid. So joining the American Legion or the VFW would have been very much against the way I have always been.

"That's not a comment on their members—it's a comment on me, on how I feel about joining up. To go down to the American Legion hall, in my opinion, is too often an excuse to go in and get stinking drunk and talk about the good old days.

"They weren't so good, a lot of those days—they were days of warfare. So, yes, I can understand why your father was proud of what he did, but why he also chose not to join any of the organizations. It makes perfect sense to me."

* * *

And there was that lingering thought I could not escape—the thought of how my father, as he grew older, viewed so much of the world with increasing disdain. As he looked upon the things he didn't like—the carelessness of contemporary society, the lack of respect for institutions, the every-man-for-himself mentality that made millionaires and cultural heroes of go-for-broke financial flim-flam artists, and consigned people who played by the old rules and followed the chain of command to lives of modest means and subdued anonymity—I could tell that there were days when he questioned what he and his fellow soldiers had fought and won the war for. If this was the country that resulted from the victory, then what was all the bloodshed and heartache for?

At least that was what I had for many years read into his outlook. Maybe I was wrong.

"You're not wrong," Tibbets said. "I'm not saying that your father and I were right for feeling that way—but you're not wrong in the accuracy of your observation. Yes, there are a lot of times that I feel that way—so I can understand why your father would feel that way too."

"What is that like?" I said. "To have that anger toward the way things are in the country you fought for?"

"Oh, it comes and goes," Tibbets said. "It's not an all-the-time thing. But you see little things—how undignified people purposely are in their conduct and mannerisms, how people's behavior when they are in public shows a complete lack of a proper upbringing—and you find yourself asking yourself: Why did I do it all? Was it just for this?"

"So it's not politics?" I said.

"Politics has nothing to do with it," Tibbets said. "It's just . . . you know, what really bothers me, and I'm not even sure why, is how many loudmouths there are walking around, not caring who they are offending, not caring when they use certain words in front of ladies and their elders. It's disgusting.

"And the reason they can get away with it is that we have

freedom of speech in this country. Which is as it should be. But you know, someone fought to preserve that freedom for them. And it's like they never stop to think about that—as they're walking through a store using language that you should never use in public, at the top of their voices, they never stop to think that some of the older people they are offending are the people who fought as hard as human beings can fight to save those rights for future generations.

"Is it an old man's viewpoint?" Tibbets said. "Is this how old men think? Maybe it is. But you know something? That doesn't make it wrong."

There was a moment—when Tibbets was trying to explain something to me—when I failed to understand what he meant at first.

He ended up raising his voice. The matter at hand was that important.

I had told him that I was struggling with the question of why my father—and, apparently, so many men his age—thought that on some level the war was the best experience of their lives.

Not that it was fun; not that it was enjoyable. But as terrible as the war was, there was nothing else in my dad's entire life that meant quite as much to him. Nothing that came before, nothing that came after, ever seemed to contain the same power.

And although I understood some of the reasons for this, I didn't understand them all. I asked Tibbets if he did.

"It was because your father was a man among men," he said.

That sentence stopped me. Tibbets had never known my dad—the two had never met. I thought, just for a second, that Tibbets might be patronizing me—might be saying something he knew would please me by praising my father to an extent that was not possible from someone who had never set eyes on him. I thought that he was calling my dad a man's man—giving him a macho, dagger-between-the-teeth, pistol-swinging-from-the-belt stature.

And I said so: "How do you know that he was a man among men? It's a very nice thing for you to say—but my dad was just another soldier."

That's when Tibbets' voice got louder.

"I don't mean it that way!" he said. "What I mean is that the war was the one time in a man's life that he got to be a man surrounded by men, all of them working for the same thing, no one better than the person next to him, regardless of rank.

"A time like that comes along only once in a lifetime—if that. You are literally risking your life every day, and you're doing it with the men who are next to you. You form friendships during days and nights like those that nothing and no one in your entire life will ever match.

"Please pay attention: The reason those years mean so much to so many of us is that it is the one time in your life that you are absolutely proud of what you are doing, and you are absolutely proud of your friends and what they are doing. It's a relationship of man to man.

"It is your ass and his—your ass and the guy next to you and the guy next to him. And the people back home can't see you, and they don't know what you're doing, and they don't know who you're doing it with. These men are your friends, and you are depending on them to live.

"Men among men! Men among men! And when you come back home after the war, it is never the same. You faced odds, and you made it back, and you faced down your worst fears. And all of a sudden you're back in a country where things are quieter, things are safer, and the people around you on the streets are not all working for the same goal.

"And you go on, and the war is over, and you become the person you will be for the rest of your life. But inside of you, the time when you were men among men will never go away. That's all I was trying to tell you.

"You had asked me a question. Why it all meant so much to your dad. I was trying to explain. It's no big secret. I think it was probably the same for all of us. We would be fools to think that anything that ever came along later in our lives could affect us like the war did. The best experience of our lives? 'Best' is a funny word. But there is nothing we could ever do that could ever measure up to what we found in each other's company when our country sent us off to do what we did."

One day when I was with Tibbets I saw the most unexpected, most moving thing:

A yearbook.

It looked like a high school yearbook, the kind that come out each spring. More specifically, it looked like a high school yearbook from the middle of the Twentieth Century—blue cover made out of that hard-yet-slightly-soft material all school annuals seemed to use back then, gold lettering meant to set off a vibrant contrast, pages and pages of group pictures inside, the feel of young people doing something together that is short in duration but will create memories to last forever. . . .

Yet this wasn't a yearbook from a high school, and the young people whose photos were inside were not living an Archie-comic-books existence.

It was the yearbook of the 509th Composite Group—a school annual for young men who were not in school, a volume of personal memories that also were history that changed the world.

It's easy to forget that a lot of these soldiers were little more than kids. Of course it would make sense that they had a yearbook—if the planet had not been at war they might have been the recipients of yearbooks from their high schools, or colleges. Instead there was this.

Pictures with captions identifying the "service club dance." The "base bowling alley." The "base swimming pool."

Pictures taken in Wendover. Pictures taken on Tinian Island.

Photos of the 509th's musical combo—one young soldier/musician identified only as Shad, one identified as Flip, one identified as Bill.

Lots of shy, youthful expressions throughout: guys smiling stiffly for the yearbook photographer.

There were only a few hints that this was a yearbook unlike the ones most Americans grew up with.

The photo of a group of young men gathered around a radio, for example—obviously, from the looks on their faces, listening for news of something of great moment.

And before-and-after photos of a city: Hiroshima.

Headlines in the back of the yearbook—newspaper headlines describing the result of the mission that the 509th had worked toward.

There was a letter in the book—a letter of the kind that high school principals write in yearbooks, summing up the school year just past.

There was no principal for the 509th.

The yearbook letter was written by Paul Tibbets.

It was as direct as the man himself.

"On August 6th we dropped our first atomic bomb. Three days later we dropped our second.

"Two days later Japan asked for peace, and three days later she got it.

"That is the significance of the 509th Composite Group."

I don't think I ever saw my father in uniform, except in pictures.

Perhaps, when he was just returned from the war, he would wear his uniform out to dinner, out on the town; perhaps not. But by the time I was old enough that any of my memories stay with me, there was no uniform. Not on him—and, as best as I can recall, not in the house.

I asked Tibbets what the routine was on this. Didn't men, in the years immediately after 1945, wear their uniforms on the streets and in the restaurants of their hometowns? It would be difficult to imagine that they didn't—the country was in love with the soldiers who had won the victory, the soldiers who were rejoining civilian life had to have been a little heady about all the adulation . . . it would only make sense for them to wear their uniforms, even after leaving the service.

"There was some of that," Tibbets said. "It still went on—guys would have left the service, but when they went out with their wives or their girlfriends, they would put on the uniform. It didn't last all that long."

"What happened?" I asked.

"Oh, I suppose they wanted to live with their glory for a while, before they put it away," he said. "Hard to blame them. As fast as I could, I got my uniform off—but it was a matter of personal choice. I can understand that when we came home, a lot of men liked what it felt like to walk the streets of America in their uniforms."

"Did the women have a lot to do with it?" I asked.

Tibbets laughed. "What do you think?" he said.

"Well, I would imagine that a lot of women liked the idea of being out with men in uniform," I said. "They always have—and you had just won the war."

"Yes, of course," he said. "Don't forget—during the war it was very common to see men in uniform on the streets. You saw it everywhere. So when the war ended, it wasn't like men in uniform taking women out to dinner was something new. It had been going on for a long time.

"It was just the fact that now the war was over, and the uniforms meant something different."

"So tell me what the women had to do with it," I said.

"There are women who marry men to present a certain image of themselves in the eyes of society," he said. "At that time, being out with a man in uniform presented a very favorable image for the women who were with the men. Yes, the women liked the uniforms.

"But for some of the men—and I was one of them—it was a feeling that you wanted to relax now that the war was over. You didn't want to have to have that uniform looking spotless every time you got dressed. But sometimes the women got their way—and anyway, the uniforms were the cause of a lot of trouble between men and women."

"What do you mean?" I said.

"There were a lot of women who fell in love with men in uniform, and married men in uniform," he said. "They never knew their men any other way—the men were soldiers when they met, soldiers when they became engaged, soldiers when they got married.

"And then the men came home from the war, and eventually the men started dressing in regular street clothes. The uniform was put away. There was no longer a need for it.

"And in the minds of some of the women—some of the wives—their men became different people."

"Just because they weren't in uniform," I said.

"Yes," Tibbets said. "Because they weren't in uniform. The wife would look at the husband, or the girlfriend would look at the boyfriend, and without the uniform something was missing. In the woman's mind, the man had become something other than what she was used to."

"Not very fair, right?" I said.

"Well . . . maybe not fair," Tibbets said. "But also not entirely inaccurate. In reality, a lot of guys *were* different once they left the service. It wasn't the clothing itself, of course—but a lot of men were one way in the service, and a different way once the war was over. Whatever it was that they were in the Army—whatever they were inside the uniform—out of uniform, it was gone. Happened a lot."

My father, in his last years, walked very slowly. I never said anything to him about it.

But in restaurants—when he would be arriving for a family

dinner, when he would be leaving after dessert—his pace was so slow that there were times when it felt as if he was hardly moving at all.

It's not that people stared—there are a lot of older people who go out, and they don't move quickly, and it's part of the landscape—but for my dad it was new, and I didn't know how aware of it he was. Whether he knew just how deliberately he was walking.

I had seen Tibbets the same way.

There wasn't any question about it: He sometimes moved slowly. Not as laboriously as my father had, but in the same category.

I asked him: Were men aware of this when it happened to them? Did they know they were walking so slowly, or did it just seem to them that the rest of the world was too fast?

He smiled.

"Oh, believe me," he said. "We know."

I asked him if he could guess what was going on inside of my dad's head on those occasions when he was leaving public places and taking so much time to get to the door.

"He's hoping he can keep you fooled," Tibbets said. "He's thinking that he doesn't want anyone feeling sorry for him, and hoping that you don't see just how bad he's feeling. I can tell you that this is the way he was thinking—because I've gone through it myself."

Tibbets said that he had been ill recently: "I was shuffling. Did I feel bad that people noticed? Yeah. But what am I going to do about it?

"I was tired, I was making myself move my feet one after another, and that was hard—just doing that was hard. I was walking like an old man and I knew it.

"I felt like, in sports, like a boxer—when someone hits you and you're unsteady on your feet. I felt like I didn't dare even sneeze or I would lose my balance.

"You get older and your muscles aren't as springy. They're not as capable of carrying the load. So you just tell yourself that there's no hurry. It depends where you are, of course. Everyone wants to be twenty-one, and you don't want to make it so obvious how slow you have become."

I told him some more about walking out of a certain restaurant with my father—about how I had slowed down to walk with him, and he had told me to go on ahead: He didn't want me helping him, and he didn't want me seeing just how difficult this had become for him.

And I hadn't known—not then—that he was aware of it. Or at least to what extent.

"He wasn't walking slow just to walk slow," Tibbets said. "He didn't want to fall on his face.

"That's what is going on in your head—I can tell you that because I know. You watch your footsteps, and you go slow for a reason. You don't want to fall down. If you fall, you know that you will not be able to catch yourself. That's why you walk so slowly. It's not that you can't go any faster—you could if you wanted to. But you're afraid you might fall down and embarrass everyone."

"He never said anything like that," I said.

"Of course you don't say what's in your head," Tibbets said. "Say how afraid you are of falling? Of course you never talk about it."

The science-fiction movies of the 1950s—the films that made their money by scaring the children of the men and women of the World War II generation, children who were delighted to be scared—usually centered on a generic plot device: Monster attacks Earth. Heroes emerge to save the world.

A case can be made that, in a very real sense, the Allied soldiers of World War II really did save the world. But did they see it that way as they were in the midst of doing it—did they see themselves in grand, heroic terms? Or did they, at the time, see their service just as something difficult that their country had asked them to carry out?

"Those sons of bitches—the German leaders, the Japanese leaders—upset my whole life," Tibbets said. "They infuriated me. That's how I thought about it—that they disrupted my damn life.

"That's what it came down to. Not politics—the politics of Germany and Japan had nothing to do with me directly. What did affect me directly was that I was trying to live my life, and because of what their leaders decided, my life changed forever.

"And I was just one of millions and millions of young American men who that was done to. It happened to millions of young American women, too—the lives they had thought they were going to lead became something different, because the men were sent to fight the war. So young wives and mothers and girlfriends said goodbye to their men, and the women went to work in factories for the war effort.

"Our lives were not supposed to be that way. Our lives became what they became because of what the Germans and the Japanese decided to do. We who fought the war were not trying to 'defeat the enemy's way of life.' It wasn't anything like that. We were trying to kill the sons of bitches. That's the level where we were—we were put into a position of basing our every waking moment on trying to kill the other guy.

"We did it for each other. We did it because if we didn't, we knew the other side would be just as serious about killing us. So, no, we weren't trying to save the world. We were trying to kill people, because that is the position we were put into. It doesn't sound very nice, but it's true, and it's not a decision that any of us made. It was made for us."

It seemed that, in so many ways, their boyhoods were stolen from them. They never had a chance to be very young. Was that how Tibbets saw it? Was something irreplaceable—their youth—taken from them? Or was it a question of something better—solid adulthood—being given to them under the hardest possible circumstances?

"My father put me in military school when I was thirteen years old," Tibbets said. "So in a way, I think my boyhood was taken from me then. I was in military school for five years. When I got out my boyhood was over.

"Was military school good for me? Probably. Would I do it again, if the decision were mine to make? I would not do it again.

"But I look back on my young life, and on going into the war, and I think that I am glad that I did grow up quickly. There's something to be said for growing up in a hurry. So many temptations are out there in the world to get you in trouble. I became cautious very young. And I'm glad I've been cautious."

"So you don't think that any part of your life has been stolen from you?" I said.

"If it has, it probably doesn't matter," he said.

One day he had left his car in the parking lot of the Park Towers, the apartment building where his friend Gerry Newhouse had his office.

We'd had lunch. Tibbets was going to go home.

It was an extremely cold and windy afternoon, with ice on the ground; people were bent over against the gusts, trying to keep their balance.

A woman was getting out of her car in the little driveway in front of the main entrance to the building. She must have been twenty years younger than Tibbets, but she was having trouble in the weather, so he stood by her car as she stepped out and he helped her to the front door.

Then he walked off toward his own car.

I was in the lobby talking to Jesse Harrell—the doorman who had been there all those years, the young man I had first met when I was just a teenager and he was not all that much older. Now, at sixty, he as usual was at his post.

Security cameras had been installed in the building and in the parking lots in the years since I was a boy; Jesse had a television monitor in front of him, and a console to control the camera selections and angles.

After Tibbets had walked off, I asked Jesse, "Where's his car?"

"It's in the side lot," Jesse said.

"The outdoor lot?" I said.

"Yes," Jesse said.

The lot was west of the building—a hundred feet or more from the door, down a sloping sidewalk.

"Is he OK getting there?" I said. "In this weather?"

"He hates people trying to help him," Jesse said. "He likes to take care of himself."

"But you see how windy it is," I said.

"He would hate it if either of us came after him to help him out," Jesse said. "It would make him angry."

Jesse hit a button on his security console. We could see a grainy black-and-white picture of the parking lot.

An elderly man was leaning forward against the wind.

"There he is," Jesse said.

"That's him?" I said.

Jesse hit another button and the camera showed a closer shot. It was Tibbets, all right. He had his hands on top of the roof of a car, steadying himself.

"Is that his car?" I said.

"No," Jesse said. "It's the next one. He'll be there in a second."

Tibbets was the only person in the parking lot. The man who brought World War II to an end.

"There he goes," Jesse said.

The figure on the screen opened the door to a car, and got inside. We watched on the screen as the car pulled away.

"He's fine," Jesse said, and then we lost sight of the automobile.

TWENTY-ONE

Tibbets wasn't the only one who seemed almost constitutionally incapable of accepting help from anyone.

When it became apparent that my father's dying was not going to be quick—that it was going to transpire painfully over a period of months, if not longer—we hired someone to assist my mom with the things she simply could not do.

Lifting my father from the bed, getting him into the shower (before even that became impossible), helping him across the room into a chair during the weeks when he was still able to sit . . . my mother did not have the strength.

So Andre Frazier entered my father's life.

My father hated the idea of anyone having to carry him, to bathe him, to shave him. Andre—physically strong, full of vitality, an African-American man who had grown up in Columbus—was a daily reminder to my father of everything that he had lost. Here would arrive this stranger to assist my father with the tasks he had never had to think twice about. It made him despondent. It made him fully understand that things would never be the same.

And Andre overcame that. He made his relationship with my father work.

Because in the months when my father could do virtually nothing for himself, Andre made sure that he still knew he was a man. "Good morning, Mr. Greene," he would say in a bright, upbeat voice every day as he arrived. And then—small gesture—he would extend his hand for my father to shake.

I'm not sure if Andre had any idea what an enormous effect

that daily handshake had on my father's self-regard. My dad was in bed, he could hardly move, yet Andre would approach him—in the minutes before he would begin assisting my dad with the most private and potentially humiliating bodily necessities—and would greet him like one businessman greeting another. "Good morning, Mr. Greene"—that sound, those words, were so reassuring. He was being treated with respect. He was being treated as a full person.

There was an almost military precision to Andre's routine. My dad liked that—he liked the cut of Andre's jib. When Andre sensed that my mother and father wanted to be alone, just the two of them together, he would quietly disappear from the bedroom and give them their time. When the moments came that he would have to lift my father to take him into the bathroom, he would approach it with great decorum and an unwavering sense of the humanity of all of this, allowing my father his dignity.

And they would talk. Andre was studying to try to get a degree that would help him do well in the world; he would explain to my father what he was aspiring to, and my father would talk to him about his own start in business, but much of the time my father would tell Andre about the Army. He would—in the last months of his life—explain to Andre about his time in the war.

Andre would ask him questions—about the people my father had known back then, about the places he had gone—and it was a gift, those questions that Andre asked him. They were two men who might have been thought to have almost nothing in common, but in Andre's curiosity about my father's life my father found a kind of confirmation that he still mattered. Someone was interested.

Who would have thought it—these two men, separated by so many years, and by two lifetimes of utterly different experiences, yet the connection that they established was one of the most precious things to help my father keep his sense of who he was. Two men, talking.

One day—this was at the very end—Andre helped my father into a wheelchair and took him from the bedroom to the front door of the house. It was the first such trip out of the bedroom my dad had taken in days. My mother, and Andre, wanted my dad to see the street on which he lived.

So they went to the front door and opened it to the winter's cold, and my dad looked out. The vistas of a man's life—after all the places he had traveled, all the roads he had walked, it had come to this: this one view.

My father's voice, telling of that long journey with the 91st Infantry up into Italy:

Finally we reached the Futa Pass, which was a pass through the mountain peaks. And then we were going to approach the north side with the road going downward.

Well, it was going downward for a while, but then it would go up some. In the meantime, more cold, more rain, more deaths and more fear. We lived with fear all the time on that terrible trip up Highway 65. . . .

One of the things about which he became confused concerned his father's death.

His father had been dead for well over thirty years, but during my father's dying there were days when he seemed to believe that it was his own father who was departing the Earth. He would talk to my mother and my sister about a memorial service for his father; he would ask, "Are the people from Cleveland here yet? Have they arrived for Dad's memorial service?"

I remember when his father really was dying. I was a boy, my sister and brother and I were growing up in Columbus, and in Akron my father's father was slowly nearing the end. My dad would drive up to Akron to sit with him, then, the next day, drive back to Columbus to be with us.

It must have been a very solitary time for him—those long

hours on the road, back and forth between his two families. Once when he came back at the end of a weekend—weariness all over his face—I asked him what he and my grandfather had done.

"We listened to a baseball game," he said. "We listened to the Indians game."

"Who won?" I said, really wanting to know—I had no idea just how bad off my grandfather was, I suppose I sort of liked the picture of the two of them listening to a ballgame on the radio, so I asked him who had won.

"The Indians," he said distractedly.

Later I went to the sports page and I looked. There had been a game the day before, all right. The Indians had lost.

And I pointed it out to him. I was that young—I told my father that he had said the Indians won, when in fact the Indians had lost.

To his great credit, he did not blow up. On some level he understood that I did not know what he and his father were going through, that I could not comprehend that as the radio played neither man was hearing a word.

He didn't get angry. He merely said that he had been mistaken. No, he said, I was right—the Indians had not won.

Now—on one Saturday afternoon during his own dying—I sat with him, and there was an Ohio State football game on the television set in front of his bed. A game in the stadium in whose stands he had sat with my mother on every football Saturday for more than fifty years. His eyes barely saw the screen, and he never asked the score, and I could not tell you—then, or now—who won the game. If someone were to have asked me, I would not have known. Not on a day like this, in this room with my dad.

Once when he kept asking about the memorial service for his father—when he continually wanted to know, from my mother and my sister, the only other people in the house at that time, whether the guests from Cleveland had arrived yet for the service—they did one of the kindest things I have ever heard. They said that the service was just about ready to begin.

They got out three prayer books. One for each of them, and one for him.

And through their tears my mother and my sister held a memorial service. For his father. Afterward, he told them that it was beautiful.

On Highway 65 in Italy, his voice on the tape said, things had become momentarily, and deceptively, calm. It was an illusion.

. . . We were merrily, if you could use the word, on our way to Bologna when something terrible happened.

Unbeknownst to us, the Germans had dug in on a huge mountain called Monte Adone, which straddled Highway 65. And we came up around a curve in a line of trucks when all hell broke loose and the German artillery was being poured down on us.

It was at this point when all forward movement was halted and all the line troops were dispersed laterally to the east and west astride Highway 65, and there we stayed for six months. Beyond a certain point there were no lights at all allowed, so trucks had to move in blackout because the Germans were dug in and had zeroed in every possible road crossing and could hit everything that moved.

All movement, all truck travel, all everything was done at night. In the meantime the poor dogfaces were digging in the best they could along this line with the Germans looking down their throats. . . .

Andre's presence in the house gave my father something he seemed desperately to need: an audience.

With my mother, my brother, my sister and me, the talk was often of the details of his illness, the parameters of his pain. We weren't really an audience; we were his family.

He had always enjoyed getting laughs out of strangers—it

always seemed to please him more to evoke an appreciative reaction from people who did not live under his roof.

So when Andre was around, his presence provided a surprising kind of spark in my dad. Andre was someone he could play to.

One afternoon my Uncle Al—my mom's brother—was visiting. He, my mom, my sister and I were talking quietly in the living room.

My dad had allowed none of his friends to see him. He was embarrassed about how he looked, he instinctively knew that if they were to come into his room they would know that he was a dying man. He didn't want it; he gave my mother strict instructions: Keep everyone away.

I knew that his friends wanted to say goodbye. But there was no arguing.

On this day he called out from the bedroom, and in the living room I said to my mom, my sister and my uncle, "I'll go in."

He was sitting with Andre. He said, "Where's Mother?"

"She's in the living room," I said. "Al's over."

"Al's here?" my father said.

"He's with Mom," I said.

"Tell them to come in," he said.

I was shocked.

"Both of them?" I said. "Or just Mom?"

And—out of nowhere—there was this flash of the old cutting, sarcastic, I'll-tell-the-jokes-around-here him.

"What do *you* think?" he said. It was like fifteen years had just dropped away.

"I don't know," I said. And I didn't—if I were to bring Al into the room and it turned out that my father didn't want him there, it could be a very bad moment.

"You don't know," he said. "You don't know." There was no confusion here—he was sharp, he was parrying, he was in charge.

"I don't know," I said. "Do you want just Mom, or do you want Mom and Al?"

And—here was the key moment, here was the reason he was being like this—he turned to Andre. His audience.

My father motioned at me with his thumb and said to Andre, "What the hell is wrong with him?"

Andre started to laugh. "I don't know," he said to my dad.

My father looked at me and said, "It never changes, does it?" And then he looked back at Andre, motioned in my direction again, and said to Andre: "It never changes. My son, the village idiot."

Andre laughed out loud, and my father started to laugh, too, and I was so grateful for that moment. "Yes, *Bob,*" my father said, emphasizing the word to make sure Andre understood that the village idiot had a name, "I'd like to see Al, too."

And he meant it. I went to get them—my mother and my sister were startled, they could hardly believe that he was willing to see someone—and Al, who had known my father since the 1930s, when Al's big sister, my mom, first started dating this guy from Akron, came into the bedroom.

He tried to put up a cheery front, but this was too much, seeing my dad this far gone, and he began to cry and said to my father, "You've had a hell of a run." And my father, from his bed, said, "I really have, haven't I?"

Tibbets may have had that high-school-yearbook-that-wasn't: the 509th's words-and-photo history. My dad, it turned out, had a book like that, too.

It was a scrapbook, of a kind that by all appearances had been manufactured in large numbers for sale to soldiers and their families. What set it apart from other dime-store scrapbooks was the embossed title on its cover:

HIS SERVICE RECORD

That such books existed makes sense; the sixteen million Americans who served in the armed forces during World War II could have been expected to keep some written and photographic memories of their time in uniform, so there was a ready market for scrapbooks like this. The pages gave helpful tips—on this page, fill in the details of basic training; on this page, fill in the names and places that were a part of going overseas. . . .

The first thing in the scrapbook was the Pledge of Allegiance—pre-printed by the manufacturer. "I pledge allegiance to the flag of the United States of America. . . ."

My dad's scrapbook was completely filled out—in my mother's handwriting. She had done this for him—for them. Every step of his time in the military she vigilantly had kept track of; he was fighting the war, she was making sure his scrapbook was up to date.

Little things: Near the front of the book was a page on which the birthdates of the father and mother of the soldier were to be filled in. This book said—in my mother's blue fountain pen—that my father's father was born on October 18, 1878; my father's mother was born on April 5, 1888. The sight of those years on a page: 1878, 1888 . . . it had the look and feel of once upon a time.

So painstakingly, my mother recorded it all. Training? "Infantry, Camp Shelby, Mississippi, January 28, 1941. Three months Louisiana maneuvers, 1941."

She was writing down what the man she was in love with was doing. "Left country April 1, 2, 1944. Arrived April 20, North Africa, near Oran, Algiers. June 21, approximately, moved to Italy. July 21 in Naples. May, June, 1945—occupied Trieste."

The idea of it—of "moving to Italy," as if this was a business transfer; of occupying Trieste—of this young man coming from Akron, Ohio, to occupy a city in Europe . . .

And there was this, in her careful penmanship:

"June 24, 1945. Bronze Star at Cormons, Italy."

Hers were not the only words in the scrapbook. There was, pasted onto a page, a copy of a letter that apparently had been handed out to the fighting men in Europe on one of the proudest days of their lives, and in the life of their country:

From the headquarters of the Fifteenth Army Group to the soldiers of the Fifteenth Army Group:

With a full and grateful heart I hail and congratulate you in this hour of complete victory over the German enemy and join with you in thanks to Almighty God.

Yours has been a long, hard fight, the longest in this war of any Allied troops fighting on the continent of Europe.

(from) Mark W. Clark, General, U.S.A., Commanding

I had found the scrapbook in a back closet of my parents' house. The events in the scrapbook were getting ahead of what my father's voice was telling me on the tape. Victory hadn't come yet, in the words he was saying; he and his fellow infantrymen were still slogging their way up Highway 65:

. . . In basic training we really had gone out of our way to make ourselves miserable—that's what we were training for. But in actual combat we did every possible thing to try to make ourselves comfortable, because there was no other way to live unless you did it that way.

So there were a lot of well dug-in dugouts, which were protected by sandbags and every other possible thing that would deflect incoming ammunition. And as the days and weeks and months dragged on, we actually did get a little more comfortable, which is not very good in combat. It is one of the things that cuts down on the momentum of an infantry division. You get too comfortable and you don't move forward.

Well, that's what happened. Every division that was on the front lines in the Fifth Army was sitting ducks for air raids, all kinds of artillery fire, for weeks on end. . . .

The phrase "television war" was often used to describe Vietnam, but that was before cable, before all-news channels had the air-time available to show endless unedited hours of war coverage, live. And at the beginning of the 1990s, when the Gulf War—

"Operation Desert Storm"—was telecast live on CNN, my father seemed more interested in that than in any television show any of the networks had broadcast in years.

I think it was Norman Schwarzkopf—at least that was part of it. Here, again and at last, was a general who got to be admired for being a general. The last time the nation had—with no sarcasm, with no irony—paid respectful attention to a general was . . .

When? William Westmoreland? Not really—he had been at the center of so much controversy that the chaos around him overrode everything else. Probably there hadn't been a time since Eisenhower's day when a general of the armed forces, and the country he represented, looked each other directly in the eye and admitted how much they were counting on each other.

So my father watched General Schwarzkopf with considerable approval—this was a man he could understand, this was a man, or so I sensed, that my father felt would understand *him* if they were ever to meet.

But the telecast of the Gulf War had confused him in ways he could not quite elucidate. There was no sprawl, no distance—you could see everything all at once, it was packaged with great expertise for the home viewer. It was warfare neatly delivered into your house, with no feeling of anyone being lost or stranded or confused or scared or alone. General Schwarzkopf seemed at times more like a genial master of ceremonies, your friendly host, here in your living room right on schedule to guide you through the evening's proceedings.

My dad had watched every night and when the war ended he found something to watch on another channel.

His voice, telling what happened to the infantry on Highway 65:

. . . *The problem was, in back of us there was a battery of 90-*

millimeter anti-aircraft guns, which fired constantly and were being used as artillery against the Germans.

This meant that while it was fairly peaceful during the day, you couldn't sleep at night because of this constant din of those 90-millimeter shells streaking overhead.

The Germans didn't seem to react to this until one terrible morning when they made a direct hit on us, killing several people and wounding some of my best men. And there but for the grace of God . . . I was not wounded that day, which was a lucky day for me, believe me, one of many, many that I had during my Army career. . . .

Many times toward the end, when my father was sleeping, or my mother wanted to be in the bedroom alone with him, Andre would pick up a book he found around the house to pass the time until he was needed.

I had written a couple of books based upon time I spent with Michael Jordan, and my parents had those books in their home, and often Andre would read a chapter or two from them while he waited for my father to wake up. When I would come to town he would ask me questions about the books: what Jordan was like, what Scottie Pippen was like, what it was like to be in all of those NBA arenas.

The context of this was so discordant. Here Andre was—doing work that was, to me, more vital and moving than anything I could imagine, helping my father die with decency, with a sense of still being a man, and he would ask me about Jordan's and Pippen's and Dennis Rodman's food preferences and training routines, as if even those famous athletes' most mundane activities were worthy of notice and praise, endlessly compelling.

I understood, of course—a lot of people found those things compelling, and I was happy to talk with Andre about them, but every time I did so I asked myself whether he fully understood just what a magnificent thing he was doing—whether he knew what an unforgettable gift he was giving to our family, to take such tender care, to pay such close attention, to our father. "He has five or six of them, if I'm remembering right," I said, answering a question about Jordan's cars, thinking the whole while: Thank you so much for being here with my parents every day.

On the day of my father's funeral Andre came to the services, and then came back to the house to help out when the people arrived to pay their final condolences. He waited until the last visitors had left, helped straighten up, and then told my mother that unless she needed anything else he guessed he would be going home.

This would be it—his time in our house was over. Had my father hung on for a little longer, Andre would have had this job a little longer; my dad was dead and so this particular employment was ended. Soon enough, if someone called, he would be in the home of another man or woman nearing the end of life. This is how he made his living: helping families help their loved ones die gently.

I walked him to his car. It was a cold December afternoon; it was just the two of us out there, and he said to me, "You know, I could tell that your dad was tough on you sometimes, but he really loved you."

It was not what I had expected to hear.

"He was very proud of you," Andre said. "He would tell me that, when you weren't there. When you were around, he was always making fun of you—I think he was trying to get a laugh out of me. But he told me how proud he was of you when you weren't there to hear."

I just nodded my head in thanks. Andre opened the door of his car, and I said:

"I have to tell you something."

He stopped.

"You know that I've written some books about people who are the best in the world at their jobs," I said.

"Mr. Jordan," Andre said.

"Right," I said. "But I want you to know something. I have never in my life met anyone who is better at what they do than you are."

We stood there together for a few moments and then Andre said, "I'd like to ask you one favor."

"What is it?" I said.

"If you ever write anything about your father's life, and about his death, I'd appreciate it if you would put something in there," he said.

"What would you like me to say?" I said.

"I'd like you to put that your father and I became very good friends," he said.

Back at the house, I could see that my mother was standing in the front doorway, looking to see where I'd gone. Andre and I stood there together for a little bit longer and then I watched his car head down the block and around the corner and disappear from view.

TWENTY-TWO

"Sometimes when I was a kid, I'd make those model airplanes," I said to Tibbets. "The ones that were made out of plastic, and you'd glue them together."

"I know what kind you're talking about," he said.

"You'd have to dip the decals into warm water," I said. "And the water would soak the paper the decals were attached to, and when the paper got wet enough you'd slip the decals off, and put them on the airplane."

"I never put one of those things together," he said. "I'd see them in stores, but I never worked on one."

"That's what I was going to ask you about," I said. "The way I remember it, those model airplanes weren't all American planes. Some of them were German Messerschmitts. Some of them were Japanese Zeros. And we—all of us kids, all of the sons of the men who came home from World War II—were putting them together like toys. We were having fun doing it. And this was less than ten years after the war was over."

"So what's your question?" Tibbets said.

"Well, I remember my dad coming into my room a few times when I was putting the planes together," I said. "And I'd be working on this Nazi plane, or this Japanese plane, and he'd stand there and look at what I was doing, but he wouldn't say anything. I don't know what was going on in his mind while I put together the planes that all of you had just risked your lives against."

"He was probably just glad that you were having a good time," Tibbets said.

"But what must he have thought when he saw the planes?" I said.

"If he saw a Nazi plane or a Japanese plane, most likely he was thinking that plane was no toy," Tibbets said. "That was a real thing, in his experience. That was an enemy. If you ever saw one with your own eyes, you never for the rest of your life forgot that that thing was up there to hurt you."

The more questions, in the months after my father's death, that Tibbets answered for me, the more questions I seemed to come up with. About what those men had been through, and what they came home to, and what they thought when they saw things that their sons and daughters grew up taking for granted.

The Army fatigues that young people used to wear in the Sixties and Seventies, for example—the surplus military uniforms that became fashionable for young male and female civilians to walk around in on the streets of the United States. The fatigues certainly hadn't been worn in an attempt to honor the military—the intent, it had often seemed, was the opposite.

My father, when he would see young people walking down the sidewalks in the faded, torn fatigues, would usually stare for a second, then turn his gaze somewhere else. Clearly the sight bothered him. I asked Tibbets if he knew what I was referring to.

"Of course," he said. "Sure, it bothers you. You see some kid in Army fatigues and combat boots, slouching around, and you know for damn sure that he's never seen a shot fired, that he has never bled for his country, never had sore feet from marching. And you look at him and you can tell that he's making a joke out of the idea of wearing military clothing.

"I suppose the people who did it wanted to attract attention," he said. "They wore the combat clothes so that it would have just the effect that it did—to make people look at them."

"My dad never said anything when he saw people in the fatigues," I said.

"Of course not," Tibbets said. "I never did either. I'd take two looks at them, and then look away. What they were doing was a disgrace to the uniform, yes—but what were we supposed to do? Make a scene?

"You couldn't fight it, so you just kept your mouth shut. Thinking back on it, do you think it would have done your dad any good to create a scene? The best thing to do was just keep walking."

"He did," I said. "But I remember the expression on his face so well. Like he'd bitten down on something that had a terrible taste. This complete disdain. Like, 'Is this what we fought the war for?' "

"I do that same thing," Tibbets said. "I know I probably shouldn't, and I know that we've talked about this before—but so often you see the way that people choose to conduct themselves, their total lack of manners and courtesy toward others, and you do find yourself thinking: 'Why did I do all that I did, and risk all that I risked?'

"We came home from the war, and somehow the way that our parents brought us up—where your parents' word was a command—all changed. And we must have been the ones to make things change—we must have decided to raise our families differently than our parents raised us.

"Like I say, you just see it, and you walk on. It's a fight you can never win. Not anymore."

Listening to Tibbets say something like that—remembering my father's growing disenchantment for some of the everyday aspects of the America he saw around him—I kept coming back to *The Best Years of Our Lives,* and to that movie's message that the greatest years for the men and women of World War II were supposed to be the years right after their homecoming, as they rejoined the way of life for which they had fought all those battles, and spent all those months and years away.

The movie notwithstanding, there were many times when I asked myself again the question that had been so much on my mind lately: whether the real best years of my dad's life were the war years themselves. I couldn't shake it.

"Could be," Tibbets said. "He was very satisfied with what he was doing. He told himself that he was in the war for his family and for his country, and he was surrounded by men who were telling themselves the same thing. It wasn't comfortable and it wasn't fun, but there was never a day when you thought that what you were doing didn't matter."

"Was that how it was for you?" I said.

"This was so *different* for me," Tibbets said. "From what my life would have been like otherwise. Being in the service—being in the war—gave me some experiences to build on that I couldn't have gotten any other way."

"I keep coming back to that, too," I said. "The idea of all you boys who grew up during the Depression, and you thought you had no prospects of going anywhere. And then you ended up going places that you had only read about, or seen on a map of the world. Do you think you ever in your life would have seen those places, if there hadn't been a war?"

"Unlikely," he said. "The places that I ended up going . . . they were, literally, a world away. Africa? It was just a word that people talked about, a shape on someone's globe. What were the people like there? What went on there? What was the climate like? It never even occurred to me. And then I was there.

"Germany and France would probably have always remained for me what they were when I was a boy—places that were portrayed certain ways in the movies, places I would never have a perception or knowledge of myself. Certainly places I would never be."

"And then there was Japan," I said.

"I can't remember even thinking about Japan when I was a boy," Tibbets said. "Japan? What ever would I possibly go there for?"

* * *

Whenever I came to see Tibbets and our meeting place was the Park Towers, I couldn't help but notice something as I said hello to Jesse Harrell, manning the front door:

Jesse kept a baseball bat next to his chair.

It was for protection, I assumed; it was for him to put up a defense if some criminal came bursting into the lobby. Older man, baseball bat that is not meant for baseball—I had seen it somewhere else:

At my father's house.

He had kept a baseball bat in the bedroom. After my sister and my brother and I had moved out of the house—after it was just my mom and my dad, alone—he had begun to keep that ball bat in the room. For the same reason Jesse did: to give himself at least the illusion of being ready for anything. My father didn't like guns, but he lived in a world where many people did. His answer was the baseball bat.

It was such a melancholy sight that I never brought it up. But after I had noticed Jesse's ball bat once again, I pointed it out to Tibbets. I asked him—one more older man in central Ohio—if he kept a baseball bat in his house, too.

"I don't have a baseball bat," he said. "I have a 12-gauge shotgun."

"So you can . . ." I began.

"I have a 12-gauge shotgun," he said again.

It shouldn't have surprised me. He once armed himself with the atomic bomb; it shouldn't have come as startling information that now he kept a gun in his home.

"My father raised me around guns," he said. "One night—our family was living in Des Moines at the time—my dad heard someone fiddling around with our front door. My dad came to the stairs with a .45 in his hand."

"You were there?" I said.

"Yes," Tibbets said. "I was five or six years old. My dad stood on the stairs and the person kept fiddling outside our front door, and my dad took aim and put seven bullets through the front door."

"Come on," I said.

"Yes, he did," Tibbets said. "He had me sit still and he shot the front door seven times."

"What happened?" I asked.

"The person must have gotten away, but he got hit," Tibbets said. "There was blood on the bricks outside our door."

"But what if it was someone you knew?" I said.

"It wasn't," Tibbets said. "This was at midnight, one A.M. No one we knew—or at least no one we wanted to know—would have been fiddling with our front door at that time of the night."

"What did you think, that young, looking at the blood from where your father had shot the person through the door?" I said.

"I felt glad that my dad had the gun," he said. "There was nothing but wood and glass between whoever was trying to get in, and our family."

"So that's why you have a gun in your house?" I said.

"I had a nephew living with us once," he said. "I told him, make noise when you come in the house at night. Make noise to let me know it's you. Because if I hear someone coming in the house late at night, I'll shoot."

"No baseball bat at all in your house," I said.

"I couldn't swing a baseball bat," Tibbets said. "Not in my house, not so that it would do any good. There's not enough room downstairs in my house. Not enough room to swing it. It would be the same as having nothing."

Just when I thought that he had told me everything there was to tell—just when I thought there was no more for me to learn about him—it happened.

I had been thinking about my dad's last months—about how unbearable some of those days had been, about how he had been alive but less than alive, in a living state that seemed worse than death. I knew that, given the choice, he would rather have been gone. But he didn't have that choice; his body would not give out, not completely.

I told Tibbets a little about that, and I said to him: "How long do you want to live? If it comes to something like that, how long do you want to be here?"

"As soon as I lose the mobility that I've got, as soon as I lose the energy that I have left now—or as soon as my mind goes—then I'm going," he said.

"But what if you don't?" I said. "What if you don't want to be here, but you are?" I said.

"I just told you," he said. "I'm going."

He stopped for a moment, as if deciding whether to tell me something. And then he did.

"My old man had cancer of the throat," he said. "I saw him after he was declared 'cured.' He would start to cough, and he would be choking on whatever was in there, and he would have to stick his finger into his throat.

"And he would pull out this long string of stuff, and that was the only way he could stop coughing.

"He told me, 'I will not go through the radiation again. If they say that I need it, I will not do it.' I asked him what he meant, and he said, 'I will commit suicide before I go through that again.' "

"Did you believe him?" I said.

Tibbets stared at me. "Of course," he said. "And he did it."

"Did what?" I said.

"He killed himself," Tibbets said. "He shot himself right through the center of his heart."

I had this momentary half-feeling that Tibbets was pulling some bizarre joke on me, saying something just to shock me. But it was no joke.

"I was in business at the time," he said. "I was over in Switzerland. I got a telephone call at one or two in the morning—it was my brother-in-law. He said that my old man had just shot himself."

"What did you do?" I said.

"I got ready to come back to the United States," he said.

"Were you beside yourself with grief that he had done it?" I said.

"No," Tibbets said. "I didn't feel sorry for him at all. That's what he wanted, and that's what he did. What I was trying to tell you was that I hope I would do the same thing."

"Kill yourself," I said.

"I hope I would have the courage," he said. "I wouldn't want any of my kids to go through seeing me the way I saw my dad. I wouldn't want any of them to go through seeing me the way you say you saw your dad.

"I wouldn't want to be a burden on anybody, and I don't intend to."

"And what do you think your family would think after you did it?" I said.

"I want to be cremated as fast as the law allows it," he said. "No services. No announcement."

"What do you mean, no announcement?" I said.

"I don't want anyone telling people that I'm dead," he said. "I don't want my friends fretting over me. Memorial services are to pacify the survivors. I don't need to pacify anyone. They can think nice things about me if they want. They don't need a guy in a cloak standing there."

"You've got to have a funeral service," I said.

"No, I don't," he said. "I've listened to too many of them. They're upsetting to me. That weeping wailing attitude."

"People cry at funerals for a reason," I said. "They cry because they're going to miss the person who has died."

"Not for me," he said. "I won't have one."

"Well, you know there's going to be an announcement," I

said. "You're not a person who's going to die without anyone noticing it."

"I've had enough notice during my lifetime as it is," he said. "I've had enough hoorah, and enough of the opposite."

"So what do you want to happen?" I said.

"Cremate me and take my ashes out over the North Atlantic before anyone finds out that I'm gone," Tibbets said. "Dump the ashes into the ocean."

"Why the North Atlantic?" I said.

"Because that's where I've had some of the most peaceful moments of my life," he said. "Flying in a plane alone, over the North Atlantic. That's where I want to finish up. With no one knowing."

If what he had told me stopped me cold, what happened next was just as unanticipated, but in a different way.

It had started simply enough. I had asked him how many members of the crew of the *Enola Gay* were still alive, and if he still kept in touch with them.

"We're almost all gone," he said. "I've gone to reunions of our crew over the years, seen certain people, and at the next one they're dead."

His two closest colleagues on the flight—navigator Theodore "Dutch" Van Kirk and bombardier Tom Ferebee—were still living and in good health, he said; the only other survivor from the flight, radio operator Dick Nelson, was in such poor medical shape that the others virtually never saw him.

"It was a close group," he said. "It really was. The ones of us who are left don't talk about who's going to be the last, and we don't talk about the others who have gone."

Trying to change the subject to something lighter—and not realizing at the time where this would lead—I made a little meaningless conversation, and then, in an attempt to steer his mind elsewhere, asked him what made him laugh.

"All kinds of things strike my funny bone," he said. "I like Bob Hope's humor. But what's funny now is not funny to me. It's the separation of generations. I don't understand why people think some things are funny."

"Were you ever a fan of *Saturday Night Live*?" I asked.

"No," he said.

"Leno?" I said.

"No," he said. "Don't get me wrong—I don't think I'm necessarily a complete sourpuss. But there's all this *innuendo*. I hate that. *Alluding* to something. That kind of thing doesn't appeal to me at all. Don't allude. I like a straight pitch."

"Give me an example," I said.

"Well," Tibbets said, with genuine delight in his voice and on his face, "last year Dutch and Tom and I went to Branson, Missouri. . . ."

"Dutch Van Kirk and Tom Ferebee?" I said, trying to imagine the three of them on the town.

"Yes," Tibbets said. "And we went to see the Andy Williams show—he has his own theater there—and he had this acrobat act as part of his show. They were acrobats, and they were comedians too. They had me laughing out loud."

It occurred to me, as he told me about the acrobats, that the humor was probably mostly visual. With his hearing as close to gone as it was, Tibbets didn't have to strain to understand the acrobats—he could see the humor.

I still didn't know what was coming. I told him that when my father used to go out to have a good time—whether just for the evening with my mother, or on a vacation with my sister, my brother and me—he had done it with the same military-style planning that had defined his life. If we were supposed to leave the house at 7:30, that didn't mean 7:25 and it didn't mean 7:35. If he had planned to have us home by 11, then no matter how good a time we were having, 11 it was going to be. It was just a part of who he was.

"I sometimes think about whether that's such a good idea," I said to Tibbets. "If all that planning—even making a timetable for having fun—takes away the happiness. If you're so devoted to your timetable that the timetable replaces the fun."

"It does not," Tibbets said.

"How can you be certain?" I said.

"Your father was organized," he said. "So am I. That doesn't mean that you miss anything."

"It just seems that it might rob you of the joy," I said.

"You don't rob yourself of anything by making a plan," he said. "You don't rob yourself of any joy."

And then he said it:

"Dutch and Tom and I are going back to Branson over Memorial Day. You're welcome to come with us."

I looked at him. He was looking straight back.

"I could come?" I said. "With you and your crew?"

"Those acrobats are the funniest thing you've ever seen," he said.

"Are you sure you'd want me?" I said. "It sounds like it's supposed to be your reunion."

"We've known each other since before you were born," he said. "We've said just about everything to each other that there is to say. If you'd like to come, I'd like you to meet them."

TWENTY-THREE

My father's best friends—the men with whom he had been closest for all of his adult life, friends he had made as a young man, men who, with their wives, had remained the people he and my mother saw constantly during the half-century after the war—sensed increasingly, in his final months, how badly he was doing, and wanted very much to visit him.

He continued to resist it. My mother would tell him that they had called; he would say "maybe in a few days," but it was clear to us that he had made the decision: He did not want their final memories of him to be of a weakened, disoriented man. If they were to come into his bedroom—or so he seemed to fear—then forever their impression of him would be the impression of how he looked and sounded as death approached.

But forever would not be all that long, at least for them; they were old men too, they would almost certainly be in a bed like this one before very much more time had passed. A former FBI agent, a leading merchant of the town—these were men who were exactly his age, and I found myself wishing that he felt differently about this, because not only would it be good for him to look them in the eyes one last time, but it would be good for them to be able to look back and say goodbye. He didn't want it.

When he and my mother were a young married couple, they had a name they called their group of friends: the Saturday Night Crowd. Each weekend one couple would serve as host and hostess, and everyone would gather for cocktails and a light dinner and conversation. The Saturday Night Crowd—men and women celebrating Saturday nights, celebrating friendships and a seemingly cloudless peacetime future in the years after the war.

On Saturday nights now, the only crowd with my father was us: my mother, my sister, my brother or me when we could get to town. My father's parents were long dead, as was his only brother; he had never had a sister. So we were it, on Saturday nights that had become no more special than any other night of the week. If he knew it was Saturday, it made no difference to him. The scenery was the same as it was every day and every night—his bedroom and the trees outside his windows—and the crowd was small.

I found myself hoping against hope that he would relent and let his friends in. On Saturday night, or Tuesday afternoon, or Sunday morning—any time. But they would bring cookies, or books for him to read (they didn't know that he wasn't reading), and he would ask my mother not to allow them to come past the front hallway.

In the winter of his dying I thought about another lonely winter of his, far away from here, when he had counted on the nearness of friends.

Winter came and the snow started piling up. It was at least thirty to thirty-six inches deep in some places, and nothing moved, nothing at all.

Try to imagine the troops in the front line enduring the bitter cold and all this snow, with very little relief in sight.

Finally Christmas came, and Bill Ehrman and another guy and I were in our quarters, and it became midnight, and all of a sudden, along the whole perimeter of the front, the Germans started shooting tracer bullets straight up into the sky.

If it wasn't such a horrible thing, it would have been a beautiful sight. I shall never forget this as long as I live. The curtain of bright points of light lasted about three minutes, which was just about a minute and a half before the stroke of midnight and a minute and a half afterwards. The tracers suddenly ceased and it was all quiet on the Italian front.

Several months after my father died, my mother said—almost in a panic—that his friend Bill Ehrman had been scheduled to have surgery on his back, and that she had forgotten to call and see how he was doing. It was almost as if she had neglected to take care of some vitally important, the-world-is-counting-on-this, task.

But Bill Ehrman didn't live in our town, or even in the continental United States. He lived in Hawaii. I had never met him. He was not a part of our lives; he had been a part of my father's.

So many years before, they had stood together in the first minutes of Christmas, and watched as the German tracers flared in the wartime sky of Europe. Now—with my father so recently gone, with my mother having so many new things on her mind—she could have been excused for not remembering that this man was going to have an operation. And excused for not getting in touch even if she had remembered—he was somewhere off in the Pacific Ocean.

"Daddy would have called," she said. "He always called his friends at times like this."

And so she went to the phone. And did what he would have done.

His voice, from a time when he was able to take care of all his responsibilities himself:

. . . About this time the Battle of the Bulge was taking place in the Ardennes Forest in Germany, and the whole Italian front was demoralized because rumor had it that the paratroopers were going to drop on us, and we weren't prepared for it.

So the whole division was alerted to repel the paratroopers that never came. All the cooks and bakers and truck drivers, armed to the teeth and put on red alert, awaiting the paratroop drop which, thank God, never came.

December ended, January arrived, February, March, and all this time we were stuck below Bologna. We knew that very shortly, things would start happening that would permit all the divisions on this Italian line to go forward, and that day came—I believe it was April nineteenth—when our division got the go-ahead to jump off and start attacking up Highway 65. . . .

One winter day, not long after his death, I had to travel through southern Illinois and beyond for my job, and a blizzard hit Chicago, closing O'Hare International Airport.

I got to Union Station as quickly as I could to try to get a seat on the only train that might get me to my destination on time. I just made it; I found myself sitting next to a woman who also was on her way southward—she was going to St. Louis.

She seemed a little distracted, a little unsure of herself; she was about my mother's age, maybe a year or two younger, and I could sense something in her demeanor: that she wasn't used to doing this.

The conductor came to collect our tickets, and when he asked her for hers she hesitated a second before reaching into her purse. She gave her ticket to him, and after we were a good way down the tracks she told me that she was on her way to grandparents' day at her daughter's children's school.

"My husband and I never missed a grandparents' day, and I decided that I'm not going to start now," she said. "But this is hard."

Her husband, she said, had died five months before. They had been married for forty-eight years. This was her first trip out of town since his death.

"We would always drive down to St. Louis," she said. "We liked the long drive, just talking on the way."

Outside our window, to the right of the train, was a highway. She asked me if it was Interstate 55. I said it was.

"I thought it was," she said. "We used to drive I-55 on the way to St. Louis—well, he did the driving—and we would look at the trains as they went by."

From the train window she looked at the cars. She didn't say anything for a few miles.

She was wearing a pair of shoes she said she had bought to make walking easier during her trip; she read a hardback novel and put it down every so often to stare back out at the highway where she had ridden with her husband not so long ago.

In her face I saw my mother's face; in her face I saw the faces of all the women who have to learn this so late in their lives: how to be alone.

"I'm really looking forward to this trip," she said. "My daughter says it will be good for me."

The blizzard was whipping the winds around the train and blowing snow up past our window, and there were entire minutes when you could not see the highway and when the whole world seemed to be inside this railroad car.

On that trip up Highway 65 in Italy, my father's voice said, there were sights for which his young life up to that point had not prepared him.

. . . We rolled northward, rolled through Bologna before you knew it, debouched into the Po River Valley and turned eastward toward Yugoslavia. At last we were out of those horrible Apennine Mountains, and we could just smell victory coming. We knew we had them on the run.

And sure enough, after several days we saw columns of hundreds of trucks bringing German prisoners back from the front so that they could be put in prison camps, which were merely big fields surrounded by barbed wire.

We knew that the war in Italy was going to draw to a close. . . .

* * *

His place in the world was measured by his place in the hearts and the memories of the people he knew—both those who knew him the best, and those who knew him only a little. And, in small moments, I kept being reminded of that.

Early in the spring after he died, I was in Florida and I ran into Bud Collins, the NBC television tennis commentator and writer for the *Boston Globe.* Bud and I have known each other for years, and there had been occasions when—out to dinner with my parents—I had seen him and all of us had talked. Bud is one of the friendliest and most gregarious men you could every be lucky enough to meet, and he always went out of his way to be welcoming to my mom and dad, both when I was with them and when he occasionally encountered them by themselves.

So he didn't know my father well at all—but he knew him. And that spring after my father's death, when I saw Bud I told him the news.

"Oh, I'm so sorry," he said. "Your dad was such a lively guy."

When I spoke with my mother on the phone the next day, I told her that—told her what Bud had said. She was pleased to hear it.

Then—a day later, when I was speaking with her on the telephone again—she said to me:

"That word that Bud Collins used to describe Daddy—what word did you say it was?"

" 'Lively,' " I said.

"That's it," she said. "I was trying to think of it all last night. 'Lively.' He got it right—Daddy really was lively, wasn't he?"

And I thought to myself: There is love. There is love that lasts a lifetime and more. Her husband is gone, he's not there to hear the compliment, but it means enough to her—he means enough to her, in death as in life—that she stays up at night trying to recall the word that had been used to compliment him. She hadn't been present when the person had said the word—but even getting it secondhand, it was important to her to want to remember it correctly. As if she wanted to pass it on to him, because she knew it would please him.

Love?

Sometimes you can hear it in a question.

What word did you say it was?

There were days when he surprised me, even after his death.

One afternoon I received a letter with a Columbus postmark, and a return address not far from the house where I had grown up.

The letter was from a man named David Hathaway. He wrote:

> A few years ago your dad telephoned me after he had received a membership list of the 91st Infantry Division Association. He said he didn't recognize any names on the list, but noticed that I lived just a block from where he used to live in Bexley.
>
> We had a long chat about the 91st in Italy. Later a mutual friend (Walter Kropp, a local retired banker who served with the 4th Infantry at Anzio and later in the invasion of southern France) got us together for an afternoon of reminiscing. . . .

Mr. Hathaway said that the three of them—he, Mr. Kropp and my father—had spent at least three hours at lunch that day, talking about their days with the Army in Italy, drawing word pictures over all the years, of friends and commanders and colleagues from a war that was at the same time global in its span, and achingly personal in the tiny, yet eternal, memories it left in those who were there.

I never knew—not only never knew that he'd had that lunch on that particular day, but never knew that he did such things. That he was moved to pick up the phone—a man in his early eighties—

and say to a person, a stranger whose name he had read on a list inside a newsletter:

"I see that you were with the 91st Infantry in Italy. I was in the 91st, too. . . ."

I don't know how I missed it.

I had been listening to those tapes—the tapes of his voice telling our family about the war—and I must have heard the one passage three or four times and I never understood what it was telling me.

But then I played it again.

Now I knew Tibbets—now I knew the whole story of what he and his crew had done, and why they had done it, and what happened because of their flight.

Perhaps that was it—because I had come to know Tibbets, my father's words on the tape were telling me something completely different than what I had heard in them before.

But there it was—unmistakable.

My father's voice, talking about what was happening as the victory in Europe was finally won:

After a very hot summer we started to retrain, because we knew that the war in Japan was continuing, and we were earmarked to transship to Japan.

When that day came, we all saddled up again—the whole 91st Division—and headed southward down the same route we came. We were bound for Naples and I was a convoy commander leading a huge convoy of trucks down through Florence, through Rome, and south of Rome into Naples. . . .

He had been bound for Japan. The land invasion of Japan—the invasion that was beyond question going to cost so very many American lives, the final push of the war that was going to be paid for in death on a scale like nothing that had been previously seen in the fighting—was ready to be mounted. And he had been scheduled to be on his way.

He was traveling southward through Italy, he and the men who were with him were traveling on a route that would send them eventually to Japan, to shores where the Japanese army would be waiting for their arrival.

I went through that wartime scrapbook again—the one my mother had put together for him.

There was a second letter from General Mark Clark—not the one congratulating and thanking the infantry troops for the victory over Germany, but a different one, with a different tone. This one had been written to the soldiers in May of 1945:

> Men of the Fifteenth Army Group, I know you will face the task ahead with the same magnificent, generous and indomitable spirit you have shown in this long campaign. Forward, to final victory. God bless you all.

They were being sent to Japan.

His voice on the tape:

. . . I believe it was just south of Rome that we were in a bivouac area when somebody brought the news of a brand new weapon that had been used in Japan. This was the first atomic bomb that had been dropped on Hiroshima, and we had no idea what it was, but from all rumors and intelligence that filtered down to us, we knew it had to be the end of the war because the destruction was so complete. . . .

We got to Naples and there were a lot of ships there, just waiting to take us on. The transshipment of us to Japan was still a field order—and evidently in mid-ocean the plans were changed, because Japan had surrendered.

We were on this huge ocean liner, which was traveling without escort, because the seas had been cleared of submarines and mines, and there were no attacking airplanes. When we finally steamed into Newport News and saw all those welcome banners and bunting and bands playing and people waving and screaming and welcoming us, it was a never-to-be-forgotten sight, and there were lumps in many throats as we finally saw our country, a sight that many of us had really thought we would never see again.

They were home. Tibbets and his crew had flown the *Enola Gay* to Hiroshima, and then the second atomic bomb had been dropped on Nagasaki, and the Japanese government had surrendered. The ship that my father and his fellow soldiers had boarded in Naples had gone straight from Italy to the United States. The war was over. They were home.

He was home.

To rejoin his young wife in an America at peace, to make plans for a future together—a life, a family.

Two years later, I was born; then came my sister, then came my brother.

What would have happened if that ship had sped, either directly or after further training exercises, toward Japan? What would have happened had my father been delivered not to Newport News, Virginia, but to a very different shoreline in the distant Pacific Ocean?

Would he and my mother have had a life? And if they had not . . .

I played the tape one more time.

. . . We knew that the war in Japan was continuing, and we were earmarked to transship. . . .

I reread General Clark's letter to the troops.

God bless you all. . . .

* * *

And now it was Memorial Day weekend—the first Memorial Day since my father's death.

I was on my way to meet up with three men—Tibbets, Van Kirk, Ferebee. The men who dropped the bomb—the men who ended the war.

TWENTY-FOUR

I flew from Chicago to St. Louis, where I would get a connecting flight to Springfield, Missouri. From there we would drive to Branson.

I was using a pay phone on the TWA concourse in St. Louis, checking in with my office, when, twenty feet away, walking slowly as if looking for the right gate, came Tibbets.

He too had flown to St. Louis en route to Springfield, and I was tempted to call out to him, but I knew that he would not be able to hear me. And besides, I wanted to see this—I wanted to watch the reaction to him in the airport.

There was none, of course. He was an eighty-four-year-old man being brushed past by younger people in a hurry. I followed him with my eyes as he made his way down the noisy hallway, and then I finished my call and followed him in person. He had stopped to greet a big fellow in a baseball cap, and the two were laughing, lighting up in each other's presence.

I approached them. "I wondered whether you'd be here yet!" Tibbets said to me, full of the enthusiasm of a boy. "I've got someone I want you to meet!"

He took my arm and nudged me toward the man with whom he had been speaking.

"Bob, this is Tom Ferebee," Tibbets said.

Ferebee, the bombardier on the *Enola Gay,* was eighty. We shook hands, and in a molasses-Southern voice he said, "This is my wife, Mary Ann." She seemed shy as we said hello to each other.

"I was just telling Paul that I don't know if they'll let me back into Branson," Ferebee said. "Last time we were there, we were at dinner at this restaurant, and I got up from the table to go to the rest room, and I walked right into the ladies' room.

"All the women who were in there turned around, and there I was, standing in front of them. . . ."

Tibbets was laughing out loud. "They've probably got your picture posted all over town," he said to Ferebee. "They're on the lookout for you."

Behind us, two small voices called out: "There she is! There she is!"

A boy and a girl had spotted their grandmother coming off an arriving flight; they had been waiting for her. They excitedly ran to her and she hugged them, a joyful family gathering for the weekend leading up to America's day of memorial for its war dead.

There were tears in the grandmother's eyes as she knelt to embrace the children. Just a few feet away, Paul Tibbets was saying:

"Yeah, Tom walks right into the *ladies'* room, and Dutch and I are cracking up, waiting to see what happens next. . . ."

Dutch Van Kirk would be meeting Tibbets and Ferebee in Branson; he and his wife were driving to Missouri from their home in California for this reunion of the crew. Tibbets' friend Gerry Newhouse and his wife Judy had flown to St. Louis from Columbus. Newhouse had arranged all the logistics for the trip; he had lined up a public appearance for Tibbets, Ferebee and Van Kirk during the weekend in Branson, where the three men would be available to greet and talk with veterans.

Branson was the ideal place for them to do this; renowned as a wholesome entertainment center, the small southwestern Missouri town liked to picture itself as Las Vegas without the gambling or the risque shows. Whatever the phrase "middle America" was supposed to mean, Branson aspired to be its capital; the average age of the people who came to Branson in search of good times was much higher than in virtually any similar venue in the country—this was a place for grandparents looking for staid, safe fun.

So if there was anywhere in the land where the crew of the *Enola Gay* was likely to be remembered and treated as celebrities, Branson was it. Tibbets, Ferebee and Van Kirk knew that on this weekend, they probably would be made to feel that they were among their own.

First, though, there was the matter of getting something to eat. A vote was taken; the idea of lunch in Springfield, before the one-hour drive to Branson, won. A second vote was taken on where exactly to go.

Bob Evans.

Of course.

Can I have that menu, hon?"

Tom Ferebee had been in the middle of a sentence, telling me—matter-of-factly, with no evidence of rancor—that as far as he was concerned, most people still had no real understanding of why the men of the *Enola Gay* crew were asked to do what they did, or what effect their mission had on hastening the end of World War II—when the waitress interrupted him.

He stopped what he was saying to turn in the direction of her voice.

"You're all done ordering, right?" she said to him.

He handed the shiny Bob Evans menu to her.

"I've always thought that these things are a work of art," I said to him.

"What?" he said.

"Bob Evans menus," I said. "Look at the pictures of the food. How can you look at these things and not want to order everything?"

Ferebee—who had a laconic, there's-a-joke-hidden-behind-every-moment-in-life-if-you-look-hard-enough-but-I'm-not-going-to-tell-you-where-it-is-until-you-find-it-yourself manner I have seen in very few people, one being the sportswriter and novelist Dan Jenkins, whom Ferebee reminded me of the minute I met him—looked at the now-departing waitress.

"So you want to put the menu in a frame?" he said.

We had waited a while for our table to be set up; it was clear as soon as we walked in that this place was accustomed to tour buses full of senior citizens on vacation, and Tibbets and Mr. and Mrs. Ferebee fit the bill. There had been no real sense of urgency in getting their table prepared—these were people, the staff seemed to assume, who were used to waiting, and would not complain—and indeed as the minutes had passed Tibbets and Ferebee had showed no annoyance, even though the restaurant was far from full and other tables were sitting empty.

Tibbets—whose wife had not come on the trip—leaned over to Ferebee and said:

"If you have to go to the rest room, you better double-check to see which one it is."

He leaned back in his chair and laughed at Ferebee's shaking-of-the-head reaction, and in all the time I had spent with Tibbets, this was the most relaxed and happy I had ever seen him.

David Bean said to wait by the front door of the restaurant, and he would bring the van.

Bean, an earnest young man with a deep admiration for veterans of World War II, was shepherding the crew around during the trip. He was an employee of an Arkansas-based company known as Cooper Communities; he had met the *Enola Gay* crew during their previous visit to Branson, had taken an immediate liking to them, and had arranged for them to stay at a Cooper time-share property called StoneBridge Village, just outside the Branson city limits. He and his wife Rita had been waiting at the Springfield airport when we had arrived.

So on a hot afternoon he pulled the van closer to the entrance of the Bob Evans, and we climbed in, and he started on the drive over to Branson. We passed car dealerships and antique stores and cafeterias, and we crossed a bridge that spanned a small river, and I saw Tibbets just looking out the window at his country, saying nothing.

There was a billboard for a Branson theater, featuring a likeness of an Elvis Presley imitator and the slogan YOU WILL BELIEVE; there was another, promoting a different Branson attraction, with the words FORGET YOUR TROUBLES, COME ON, GET HAPPY. Rocks were being blasted on either side of the road as part of a project to widen the highway; Tibbets gazed at another billboard, this one advertising a show by the Osmond family, and said, "There's something about that name that sounds familiar."

"Marie and Donny," Mary Ann Ferebee said to him.

He nodded, maybe understanding the reference, maybe not.

David Bean called back from the driver's seat:

"Dutch called me the other day and asked, 'What's the best way to get to the village?' I told him that the best way was to wait a day, and I'd send him a map." The navigator—the man who had gotten the *Enola Gay* to Japan and back—had been phoning for directions.

Bulldozers were everywhere as we continued toward Branson; Bean said that the highway improvement program was in high gear in an effort to speed the day when an expressway would stretch all the way into the town. We passed a meandering creek, and Ferebee put his hand on Tibbets' shoulder to get his attention, and when Tibbets turned to him Ferebee said: "Look at that. Good trout water."

Tibbets craned his neck to get a look at the creek, and when he turned back around, a contented expression on his face, he said to me—he was suddenly like an eager, unguarded and giddily energized teenager promoting a New Year's Eve party he's trying to put together—"Once you get home after a weekend with Tom and Dutch and me, you'll never be the same."

I looked at him and then at the creek and then back at him again.

Dutch Van Kirk—"the baby of the group," he told me (he was seventy-eight)—was waiting for us at the condominium complex.

His wife Jean had suffered a stroke several years before, and Van Kirk said he and she found travel easier by car. This was going to be an extended trip for them; after the crew's reunion weekend, they were going to continue east to spend some time with friends.

I told him I was happy to meet him, and he said, "Yes, but you won't say that once you know me." He smiled and put an arm over my shoulder—his line had been the kind of harmless-old-guy humor you tend to hear a lot around men of his generation (it had reminded me of the jokes my dad's friends used to make).

The condos were low-slung, in a straight line cut out of a piece of the Ozarks, surrounded by rugged forest. David Bean had organized everything, but Tibbets, once the three-man crew was fully assembled, almost imperceptibly took charge. "Now you'll give us all our room assignments," Tibbets said to Bean, and the younger man, as if following an order, handed out photocopied sheets telling us which units were ours.

I have traveled with sports teams and with rock-music groups, where such lists are a part of the daily logistics, but there was something different about this. The names were all neatly typed—Paul Tibbets, Dutch Van Kirk, Tom Ferebee, Gerry Newhouse, David Bean, myself—and the unit numbers and individual phone numbers were placed next to each one. Yet there was something else on the list, that took me a moment to comprehend: a notation to the right of each name, under the category STEPS.

It was the number of stair-steps required to get to the front door of each unit from the parking lot. For the men and their wives who had the most trouble getting around, David Bean had made certain that there were no steps to climb—there was a zero in the "Steps" column.

I thought of these three men climbing into the *Enola Gay* for the night flight over the Pacific to Japan to end the world's war. "I'll see you at dinner," Van Kirk said, and I headed with my bag toward Unit 174B; my unit mates Tom and Mary Ann Ferebee, in 174A, were already inside and unpacking. I could hear their television set through the wall.

Hey, Dutch—want to ride a roller coaster?"

Tibbets—still in the highest of spirits—was in David Bean's van; we were on our way to dinner, and we passed a little amusement park in Branson that offered a roller coaster ride for children.

Van Kirk, instead of answering, started to tell Tibbets a story about a jelly bean factory in California—a factory that offered tours of its production facilities. Apparently Dutch and Jean Van Kirk had visited the facility, or were planning to.

Mrs. Van Kirk had walked with some difficulty to the van; Dutch had helped her in. The stroke she had suffered had affected her severely, and now, riding next to her husband, she was silent on our way to the restaurant. Tibbets, having abandoned the roller coaster idea, was talking about how, in the late 1950s, an Air Force flight surgeon had given him a choice: Quit smoking, or stop flying.

"You?" I said. "They were going to ground *you*?"

"Damn right," Tibbets said. "I took my physical, and he said it was up to me—smoke or fly."

"How many cigarettes were you smoking a day?" I asked.

"How many hours was I up?" he said.

"So did you stop as soon as he told you to?" I asked.

"I had to," he said. "For a while there, it was so hard that I wanted to bite my hands off."

David Bean pulled into the lot of a restaurant called Shorty

Small's—a big, raucous barbecue-and-burgers place. Evidently Bean had called ahead; the sign in front of the place had letters that said:

WELCOME TO ENOLA GAY CREW

"Look at that," Mary Ann Ferebee said.

"Yeah," Van Kirk said. "And look what it says underneath."

In the same size lettering, the sign said:

NOW HIRING

Bean put the van into "Park" and came around to open the side door and put a stool on the ground. Dutch Van Kirk got out first and extended both arms to his wife.

"Come on, honey," the navigator said. "Big step."

Mrs. Van Kirk, doing the best she could, moved toward her husband's arms, and he eased her way to the pavement and made sure she was steady on her feet before releasing his grip.

David Bean went inside to see if a table had been saved as he had requested. A family pulled into the parking lot, and the driver called out his window to Van Kirk: "Do you know how long the wait is here?"

Van Kirk—having no idea at all—said to the man: "You won't have to wait more than twenty-five minutes."

Ferebee shook his head. Van Kirk—who had the look of a retired high school biology teacher, and the voice and demeanor of a 1950s situation-comedy dad, his feigned befuddlement and gentle pranksterism mixed equally with good intentions—said to Ferebee, "Well, it *could* be twenty-five minutes."

Out the door of Shorty Small's came an older lady with some young children by her side. We were waiting for David Bean to come out and tell us what to do; the woman, encountering our group, said, "Grandma's tired."

"Well, then sit out here with us," Van Kirk said.

She declined the invitation and moved on. Van Kirk began to tell me a story that I could see Tibbets and Ferebee were long familiar with. He mentioned the name of a minister; he said that the minister had inquired of him, "What are Paul's plans for passing on?"

"I asked the guy, 'What do you mean?' " Van Kirk said. "And the guy asked me again: What were Paul Tibbets' plans for passing on?

"I said, 'He doesn't have any plans for passing on.'

"And this minister said, 'Everyone dies sooner or later.'

"I said, 'Paul will take later.'

"It turned out that what he was leading up to was that he was offering to do free eulogies for the crew."

"Come on," I said.

"It's true," Van Kirk said. "He wanted to be the guy who did the funerals for the crew of the *Enola Gay.* He told me that he'd do all of our eulogies on the house."

"What did you tell him?" I asked.

"I told him to practice on Tom and Paul first," Van Kirk said. The three men erupted into laughter, and David Bean came out of the restaurant and said our table was ready, and in we all went.

I never drove through rain like the rain we saw yesterday," Van Kirk said. We were at a long table in the loud, boisterous restaurant; Branson may draw a predominantly older crowd, but there were plenty of younger people here tonight, and most of the waiters and waitresses appeared to be of college age. If the crew had been hoping for something sedate, this wasn't going to be it.

On our way in, some people in their twenties had been leaving the restaurant in a hurry, and had stopped to move aside to let Tibbets, Van Kirk, Ferebee and the women pass by. I heard one of the young people say to another, "It seems like we're in Florida." As far as they were concerned, the crew of the *Enola Gay* was here for the Early Bird Special.

And now Van Kirk was telling about the downpour on his drive to Branson.

"All the way from the border of Colorado to Wichita," he said. "The rain never let up, even for a minute."

A waiter of about twenty-three approached the table and slapped Tibbets on the back without looking at him.

"Good evening, guys, how you doin'?" he said. "Shannon will be coming over in a minute; we'll be taking care of you guys tonight." He handed a menu to Ferebee. "Here you go, buddy," he said to the eighty-year-old bombardier.

Tibbets—who had told a long story during the afternoon about getting drunk on moonshine as a young man—said to me now that it had made him so sick that he still can't stand even the smell of hard liquor. As we were discussing this, the voice of a young restaurant hostess came over the loudspeaker. She obviously was reading from something that either Gerry Newhouse or David Bean had handed her; she said that the crew of the *Enola Gay* was having dinner in the restaurant—she stopped when she got to the name of the airplane, hesitated, then pronounced it "Enolya"—and some of the customers stopped eating to applaud.

"What's going on?" Tibbets asked me. "What are they clapping for?"

I told him about the announcement that had just been made.

"I can't hear, doesn't make a damn bit of difference," he said.

We studied our menus, and the waiter and waitress took our drink orders, and Van Kirk, sitting close to Tibbets and Ferebee, said to them:

"You know that trip when we took Eisenhower down to Gibraltar? . . ."

And of course Tibbets had not been alone on that flight; his friends had been there with him. Now they were in Branson, together more than fifty years later, and Van Kirk went on with his story, as if he were describing a cab ride they had once shared.

"Paul, I remember when you were making up your mind whether to take off," Van Kirk said, and as I sat with them and listened I thought about what my father would have made of this scene, and this meal, and how much he would have loved to be here this weekend with these men.

TWENTY-FIVE

"As much as I washed my hands, I couldn't get that smell out of them."

Van Kirk was talking to Ferebee; they were standing outside the row of condominium units, early in the morning, just the two of them. This was on Thursday; we had arrived for the long Memorial Day weekend on Wednesday, and I had awakened early the next morning and had decided to go out for a walk.

I had been alone on the walk, in the hours just after dawn in this isolated part of southwestern Missouri; I had wandered the roads for about an hour and a half, and when I returned the two of them were standing in the early sun talking. Evidently everyone else was still asleep inside their units.

"It was like roast beef," Ferebee said to Van Kirk.

"Oh, I know it," Van Kirk said. "It is a smell I will never forget."

I asked them what they were referring to.

"We were in Algiers," Van Kirk said. "In 1942. We were at the airfield in Maison Blanche, and during the night a German dive bomber had hit one of our planes that had been getting ready to take off—a B-17."

"Every man in that plane was crushed and burned," Ferebee said.

There were birds singing all around us on this beautiful Ozarks morning, and the sound of a dog barking somewhere in the woods behind us.

"Dutch and I were just talking about what it was like to drag those men out of there," Ferebee said.

"You were the ones who had to do it?" I asked.

"Someone had to do it," Ferebee said.

"Who told you?" I said.

"Nobody told us," Ferebee said. "The sun came up the next morning, and there was the wreckage of the plane, and somebody had to get the remains out of there. I think there were only six crews at the base at the time—somebody had to do it. We just went into the plane and did it."

"It was like burned roast beef," Van Kirk said, looking away for a second. "That's what the smell was like."

"It got under your nails," Ferebee said. "You couldn't get the smell of it out of your hands . . . I think it was days before I was finally able to wash away that smell."

A minute or so passed and Van Kirk said:

"We probably ought to go see if the girls are up yet."

They went into their condo units.

I took a shower and when I came out I could hear the Ferebees' television through our common wall.

A news channel was on; the anchorman was talking about a nuclear testing dispute between India and Pakistan.

The anchorman, finishing the story, continued: "And a different kind of bomb is expected to be dropped by the World Court today. . . ."

Someone in Ferebee's room hit the zapper and changed the television to another channel.

We gathered for a late breakfast in Tibbets' unit.

The men were talking about the series of raids that American-led forces had recently been flying over the former Yugoslavia.

"We brief the whole world every day, telling them exactly what we're going to do," Ferebee said. "We announce our flight plans on television."

The others shook their heads. Tibbets passed the toast.

Around noontime a young visitor burst through the doorway: Paul Tibbets IV, Tibbets' grandson.

"Well!" Tibbets called out, his face lighting up. He got off the couch to embrace the younger man.

Paul IV—"P4," he was called by everyone in the room who knew him—was thirty-two years old, an Air Force captain assigned to fly the B-2 bomber. He had that Tom Cruise, I can-do-anything look to him; he wore a pair of shorts and a casual shirt, and he had driven to Branson with his wife Angele to spend the weekend with his grandfather and his grandfather's friends.

Angele, a friendly, model-pretty woman who wore a short skirt and a pair of sandals, hurried over to Tibbets to give him a welcoming hug.

Van Kirk, sitting on a couch, said to Ferebee: "Oh, to be young like that."

"I'm not sure we were ever that young," Ferebee said.

Tibbets was in the midst of a story about going fishing when he was a teenager:

". . . I'm telling you, I caught a four-hundred-pound grouper."

"Four hundred pounds," I said, disbelieving.

"Yes," Tibbets said.

"What kind of bait do you use to catch a four-hundred-pound fish?" I said, certain he was putting us all on.

"Well, it's not a worm," he said.

"Then what?" I said.

"You use thirty-five or forty pounds of dead cow or horse," he said.

"Why would you even want to catch a four-hundred-pound fish?" I said.

"To sell," he said. "To get money to buy gas to take girls out."

"And the hook?" I said.

"Iron hook," Tibbets said. "Big iron hook."

But it wasn't a story about catching fish that I was interested in hearing from Tibbets. I had something else I had been wanting to ask him about.

"What happened on that flight your mother took?" I asked.

"Which one?" he said.

"When she was coming to Wendover to visit you," I said.

"Oh," he said, as if dismissing it. "That flight."

I had heard bits and pieces of the story from people who knew him. Tibbets always seemed to pride himself on his lack of emotions, his ability to put his feelings on hold. The trip to Wendover his mother had taken during the war, though . . .

The way I had heard it, he had invited her to come to Wendover in the months he was preparing the 509th for the atomic-bombing mission. She had flown on a commercial airline from her home in Florida to Utah.

And Tibbets—this was the story—had flown a fighter plane alongside the commercial flight. He had been her escort—getting her safely across the country.

"So?" he said.

"So, that was a pretty nice thing to do," I said.

"Well, we were both going to the same place," he said, trying to change the subject.

"There are other ways to get to the same place than flying escort for a commercial plane," I said.

"I had been in Washington," he said.

The way he told it, his mother had been booked on a United Airlines flight that was scheduled to take her from Chicago to Des

Moines, and then to Omaha, to Cheyenne, Wyoming, and into Salt Lake City. This was in March of 1945.

And Tibbets decided to fly alongside the flight—to fly off to the side of his mother's plane as it crossed the United States. It struck me as a pretty impressive show of love and concern.

"They could see me from the plane," Tibbets said, as if that was what I was asking him. "The passengers could see me—it wasn't like I was going to scare them. I was talking on the radio to the pilot, so everyone on the plane knew that nothing was wrong."

"I didn't think that anyone thought anything was wrong," I said. "I just think that was an awfully nice thing for a son to do for his mother."

"What was nice about it?" Tibbets said.

"That you flew that whole flight next to her plane, to look out for her."

"I didn't do it to look out for her," he said. "I told you—we were just heading for the same place."

"Well, I think you were looking out for her," I said.

"OK, you do," he said.

A presentation to the crew—the key to the city of Branson, by the mayor—had been scheduled at the clubhouse of the condominium complex in the afternoon, so we all got into David Bean's van to go over.

The building felt like a country club—it was located on a golf course—and once we arrived, I talked with Paul Tibbets IV about his relationship with his grandfather.

"We've really become good friends," he said. I knew about the emotional distance that Tibbets had felt with his own sons. Apparently it had taken a generation, but now there seemed to be a genuine closeness in the family—between Tibbets and P4.

"My grandfather and I never really had any conversations about me becoming a flier," the younger man said. "But there's a picture of the two of us when I was three or four years old. And there's a model of a B-29 in the picture.

"He didn't tell me that I should be a flier, but he's the reason that I'm a flier."

Tibbets saw us talking and came over to join us. I asked his grandson how many crew members flew the B-2 with him.

"Just one other guy," he said. "That's the whole point of it—it's so technologically advanced that two pilots can fly it. The two of us *are* the crew—we can fly that plane from the United States to a war zone in Europe, if need be, deploy the bombs ourselves, and fly it back to our base in the U.S. without landing anywhere."

I looked over at Van Kirk and Ferebee, sitting together against the wall across the room. The *Enola Gay* crew had been twelve men; I thought of that crew, and then thought of Captain Paul Tibbets IV flying a bomber with just one other man aboard, and the older Tibbets seemed to be having the same thoughts.

"He won't have the camaraderie that I did," Tibbets said.

"Well, things are different," his grandson said.

"All of us in our crew knew each other as well as you can know a person," Tibbets said. He nodded in the direction of Van Kirk and Ferebee. "I trust those guys with my back turned."

"I know," his grandson said. "But in the B-2, we really don't need a navigator."

"All the money the government spent to build that plane," I said to him. "It's just such an odd thought—two guys having control of the whole mission. . ."

"That's the whole idea," Paul IV said.

"Is your plane much bigger than the plane your grandfather flew to Japan?" I asked.

"The B-2 is all wing," he said.

"The B-29 we flew was actually longer than the plane P4 flies," Tibbets said.

"Is that why you had to use every inch of the runway when you took off from Tinian?" I asked.

"No, no," Tibbets said. He and his grandson looked at each other as if to say: What's the use trying to explain this to a non-pilot.

"Lookit," Tibbets said. "We did not have the thrust back then. We were not flying jets. I needed that whole runway because I needed to have the thrust to get it off the ground."

"Our plane can do a lot more things," his grandson said.

"That may be true, but I grew up fast in the B-17 and the B-29," Tibbets said. "When you get shot at, you mature pretty fast."

"I know you did," the younger man said.

"We had to fly low to the ground," Tibbets said. "You don't. Hell, when I was flying the B-17, they shot at us with *rifles.*"

"Big rifles," his grandson said.

"They were just rifles," Tibbets said.

From across the room, someone called to say that the presentation of the key to the city was ready to begin.

Gerry Newhouse pulled Tibbets aside and said that Wayne Newton had wanted to be present for this, but that he was not in town.

"So this is the mayor?" Tibbets said.

"The mayor had to be somewhere," Newhouse said. "You're going to get the key from the head alderman."

Tibbets, Van Kirk and Ferebee lined up and were handed a key that also could be used as a bottle opener, and then we returned to David Bean's van to go back to the condos. On the radio, an announcer was reading a commercial for a Memorial Day weekend sale.

"Memorial Day," Tibbets said. "People drink beer, people play golf."

"Does that bother you?" I said.

"Not at all," he said. "I don't know if 'memorial' is even the right word. War's a mess."

I waited to see if he was going to expand on that.

But he just looked out the window and said, "War is a mess."

* * *

"You'd have to be a damn idiot not to be able to get to Japan from Tinian."

Van Kirk was talking; it was dinnertime, and we were all back in the van, on our way to a Landry's seafood restaurant in Branson. I had asked him about the difficulty in navigating the *Enola Gay* from the minute Pacific island to the target city in Japan, and he was answering that it was no big deal—to fail, one would have had to be an "idiot."

"You would?" I said.

"Yeah," he said. "You had all kinds of barrier reefs to guide you—once you got to Iwo, it was easy."

He was talking as if the flight had been a stroll in the park—maybe. For I was finding that with Van Kirk, as with all three of them, there was a constant deprecation of the skill the mission had required, but a deprecation cloaked in confidence, almost as a challenge: Yes, it was easy for us. But could *you* do it?

We got to the restaurant and were given a table in a back room, against a window; we were in a hurry tonight, because we had tickets to a show later at the Lawrence Welk Theater. We were looking at the menus, getting ready to order, and a waiter came in and said: "Is one of you named Tibbets?"

"Who wants to know?" Ferebee said.

"There's a man out in the main restaurant who said he heard the crew of the *Enola Gay* was here tonight," the waiter said. If he had any idea what the *Enola Gay* was, it was not obvious. "He wanted to know if a Mr. Tibbets was here, and if he was, which one was he?"

Van Kirk, staring at his menu, said, without looking up: "Tell him it's Tibbets and a bunch of bums."

I had seen a flash of this at dinner the night before, when a woman had approached our table because she wanted an autograph from Tibbets. She had gone up to Ferebee—the biggest of the men—guessing that it might be him, and when she had asked, he'd had to say that, no, Paul Tibbets was the fellow across the table. I had observed this kind of thing before, in a different context: with the Chicago Bulls on the road during the championship years, when people would come up to Scottie Pippen . . . and ask him if he could get them Michael Jordan's autograph.

So tonight the waiter, a little confused, went back to the diner in the other room with the answer that, yes, he *thought* Mr. Tibbets was in there. We continued our conversation at the table; I told Ferebee how Tibbets, the first day we met, had described the jolt of the plane once the bomb had dropped out—"The seat slapped me on the ass"—and asked if that had been his observation, too. Had the plane's sudden motion felt like a slap, a kick?

"Depends who's kicking," Ferebee said. "We'd felt things before."

Meaning that the atomic bomb was hardly the first bomb that Ferebee had dropped out of a Tibbets-piloted plane during World War II. We talked about it for a minute, and Van Kirk joined in, and I guided the conversation to a more mundane aspect of the flight: It had been such a long one—had they eaten? The history of the world might have been hanging in the balance—but did bomber crews take food along with them?

"He always fed us real well," Van Kirk said, gesturing at Tibbets and rolling his eyes, as if to say: Don't even ask.

Then: "Maybe an apple. Maybe with Paul, we got an apple on the flight."

"Come on," Ferebee said. "That's not true. Paul always fed us halfway through a flight."

They were making fun of the question. They were saying: This was not a businessman's flight from Chicago to New York. We were trying to win a war. We weren't concerned with having lunch.

Van Kirk said he had heard or read somewhere that a famous New York auction house was going to be selling the "original log" of the *Enola Gay* to the highest bidder.

"I called them up," he said. "I said to them, 'I understand you have the original log from the *Enola Gay*?' And the man said yes. And I said, 'Well, that's very interesting. Because I'm the navigator of the *Enola Gay.* And I have the original log up in my attic.' "

"What did the guy say?" I asked.

"He took whatever it was he had off the auction block," Van Kirk said.

"Do you really have the original log?" I asked.

"Oh, yes," he said. "With my own handwriting."

"What does it say?" I asked.

Van Kirk—trying to get a rise out of Ferebee—said: "I wrote in the log just before we got to Hiroshima: 'Woke Tom up.' "

Ferebee, who had heard it before, said: "Yeah—that's why I missed."

Behind the banter seemed to be two things—a stolid acceptance of the horror and death that followed what they did, and a quiet, enormous pride about the mission and the victory that ensued.

"What did you really write in the log?" I asked Van Kirk.

"At that moment?" he said.

"Yes," I said.

"I wrote 'Bomb away,' " he said. "That's all."

We rushed through our dinner so that we could make it to the show at the Welk Theater; in David Bean's van on the way to the performance it seemed as if we might be lost for a moment, and Ferebee tried to remember directions from the last time the crew had been in Branson.

"Don't listen to him," his wife said to Bean. Then, to me: "Tom still doesn't even know how to fold and unfold a map."

Ferebee—continuing the conversation about the purported flight log at the auction house—said he had heard somewhere that the bombsight from the *Enola Gay* was for sale.

"I called up the Smithsonian," he said. "I told the person who answered the phone who I was, and I said, 'Is my bombsight there?' "

He sounded like a man looking for a lost dog.

"Was it?" I asked.

"Yep," he said. "The man said, 'It's here.' So the bombsight that someone was trying to sell was a phony."

A block of seats had been saved for us at the theater—a big, ornate place—and an usher was waiting in the lobby to take us in. He wanted to ascertain that we were the right party, so he looked at a piece of paper in his hand and said: "Are you the *Enola Gay* group?"

Van Kirk said, "You ever hear of us?"

The usher said, "Of course." Then: "Who flew the plane?"

"Who flew the plane," Van Kirk said softly, more to himself than to the usher. Then, nodding in the direction of Tibbets: "That, over there."

The usher led us in. Well over half of the seats in the theater were empty; this was a weeknight, and there were yawning sections of upholstered chairs with not a soul in them. We were taken to a row near the front; on stage, the master of ceremonies was beginning the show, but he could not stop coughing. It wasn't a put-on—he was hacking away, and he was unable to do anything about it.

Another usher hurried to him with a glass of water. The MC apologized; he said this was his first night back with the show after being sick for six days. His coughing resumed, even worse. "Talk among yourselves," he said, embarrassed, and the audience, understanding and polite, waited until he could compose himself.

"Did I ever tell you about Andy Williams' dressing room?" Tibbets whispered to me. "It was more beautiful than most homes I've ever seen."

The show was billed as "The Welk Resort Center and the Champagne Theater Present This Wonderful Century of American Music." It commenced with a marching band parading down two aisles, playing rousing marches—"You're a Grand Old Flag" was performed while an enormous American flag was displayed in the background.

The entertainment centered on re-creations of events from U.S. history, to the accompaniment of songs from each era. Over the public address system, Franklin D. Roosevelt's voice on tape boomed out the "date which will live in infamy" speech; on the stage, the cast re-enacted the Lawrence Welk television show, circa 1955.

During a pause in the theatrical tapestry of moments and music, the master of ceremonies read a list of announcements about people in the audience. "Mr. and Mrs. Paul Sommerville are celebrating their fifty-sixth anniversary. Mr. and Mrs. Glenn Moore are celebrating their fifty-seventh anniversary." There was enthusiastic applause for each anniversary couple; this crowd, for the most part, was composed of contemporaries of the couples.

But when the MC then announced that the crew of the *Enola Gay* was in attendance—and when Tibbets, followed by the other two men, stood up to wave to the crowd—there were a few moments of uncertainty.

"Is that really them?" I heard a man behind me quietly ask his wife. Some in the audience clearly felt this must be one more re-enactment; after all, the Sousa-style band had marched right through the audience, so were these men part of the performance, too? Were they cast members pretending to be the men who had won the war?

Tibbets applauded the crowd—he held his hands up and clapped in their direction—and within seconds they were applauding the crew in return. Most seemed eventually to believe that, yes, these men were combat fliers, not entertainers.

After the long show, ushers approached our group and invited us to come backstage and meet the cast. I walked with Tibbets—he told me he just wanted to go back to the condos—and after we had spent a few minutes with the singers and musicians, David Bean said he would bring the van around.

Jean Van Kirk—who had appeared filled with delight to meet the actors and actresses—was moving with great difficulty, the effects of her stroke the most evident they had been on the trip.

"That's OK," I heard Dutch say to her as he helped her. "If they're going too fast for us, we'll just let them walk past us." And he got her to the van and eased her into a seat near the front.

It was after 11 P.M. as we began the drive down unlighted roads to the condominium complex, back in the woods. There wasn't much conversation; a few of the people appeared to be sleeping.

I looked at Tibbets, I looked at Van Kirk, I looked at Ferebee. The strains of the old-time music were still ringing in my ears from the performance we had just seen, but it was another song that I was hearing—a song from a much more recent era.

It had been playing on the background tape at the seafood restaurant during dinner. I had been struck by it then—it's a famous song, written and performed by Bob Seger—and now, in the silence of our ride home, I looked at the men and I heard Seger's words anew:

My hands were steady,
My eyes were clear and bright.
My walk had purpose,
My steps were quick and light.
And I held firmly
To what I felt was right
Like a rock.

I thought again of a man who wasn't with us tonight, and I wanted to tell someone about it, but no one was speaking, so I remained quiet.

Like a rock,
I was strong as I could be,
Like a rock,
Nothing ever got to me. . . .

We rode through the darkness, at times the only vehicle on the two-lane roads.

TWENTY-SIX

Friday morning was the time that had been set for the public appearance Gerry Newhouse had arranged for the crew; they were scheduled to go back to the same theater where we had watched the Welk show the night before, and to sit at a table in the lobby to greet people who wished to meet them.

The way the table was set up, Van Kirk sat on the left, with Ferebee next to him and Tibbets on the right. But the line of people who had come to see the crew—it wasn't long, but it was respectable—was forming on the right wall of the lobby. So the first man they encountered at the table was Tibbets.

"Thank you for what you did," a woman said.

"Good morning," Tibbets said.

"I just want to shake his hand," a man said to me, as if permission were needed. Tibbets seemed slightly uncomfortable today—later he would tell me that the acoustics in the lobby were making it very difficult for him to understand what the people were saying—and when the man did extend his hand to Tibbets, Tibbets took it and the man asked a question about the war.

"Good morning," Tibbets said.

Gerry Newhouse and Paul IV were at another table about twenty feet away, where they had unpacked from boxes items available for purchase, for the crew to autograph. There were photographs of the crew from World War II, there were lithographs, there were copies of a career-retrospective book that Tibbets had first had privately printed some thirty years before, and that Newhouse kept updated and in stock at his office back in Ohio. Throughout the year, on occasions when Tibbets visited military bases and air shows around the country, Newhouse would accompany him and arrange signing sessions such as this one; sometimes there would be good crowds, sometimes it would be less than successful, but this visit to Branson was the only time that Tibbets' crew would join him to meet the public.

"Good morning, General, sir." "Such an honor to meet you." Some men and women who had come to the Welk theater to purchase advance tickets for the stage show, or to buy Branson souvenirs in the gift shop, or to have lunch in the restaurant, appeared puzzled by the sight of the three elderly men at the table, but those who did know who Tibbets, Van Kirk and Ferebee were seemed genuinely thrilled to be able to have a few words with them.

In the line, I saw a man in a wheelchair, accompanied by his wife. I introduced myself to them; he was Howard Casle, seventy-seven, she was Lilli Casle, seventy-four. Mrs. Casle nodded toward Tibbets and said to me: "He's still a looker, isn't he?"

I glanced over at Tibbets. "Are you talking about General Tibbets?" I said.

"Yum yum," Mrs. Casle said.

She told me that her husband had cried when he heard that Tibbets was going to be in Branson.

"He was an MP with the 509th in Wendover and on Tinian," she said. "You have no idea what these men mean to him."

Mr. Casle held something in his hands; I could see that it was a 509th yearbook—the same kind that Tibbets had shown me in Columbus.

When it was Mr. Casle's turn to speak to Tibbets his eyes teared up, and he said, "They said that what we did was going to end all wars. They lied to us. We worked so hard . . ."

Tibbets, instinctively recoiling from any outpouring of sentiment, said a few words to Casle and then introduced him to Ferebee. Ferebee seemed almost amused at this setup—the three of them sitting shoulder-to-shoulder, as if in a receiving line—and he knew that Van Kirk was the gregarious one of the bunch, that Van Kirk would be the one to spend the time and listen to the stories.

Which he did.

"You were an MP with the 509th, were you?" Van Kirk said to Casle. "Well, then you must have arrested Ferebee. . . ." Within seconds he had Casle smiling and then laughing; he asked Casle if he knew about the reunions that the 509th held from time to time, and when Casle said he didn't Van Kirk wrote down an address and handed it to him. "You ought to come," he said. "We have a lot of fun."

I stood with Mrs. Casle and asked her what was tougher duty for her husband—serving with the 509th during the war, or getting around in a wheelchair today.

"He was twenty-three," she said. "Nothing was tough duty for him back then."

The morning passed and the pattern did not change. Sometimes the line was steady, sometimes it winnowed down to nothing, always the people were almost awestruck to have their few moments with Tibbets, were uncertain how to deal with Ferebee's taciturn, if pleasant, demeanor, and were warmed by Van Kirk's chamber-of-commerce-style openness. "These your children?" Van Kirk would say. "Great, great, now tell me what their names are. . . ."

One man got to the front of the line and said to Tibbets: "You ever know a bombardier named O.K. Graves?"

Tibbets nodded toward Ferebee and said, present tense, "He's the bombardier. He'd know."

To Van Kirk, a man said, "So you're the fellow who found the way across the blue Pacific." To which Van Kirk responded by launching into a detailed discussion of the coral reefs he could see from the plane en route to Japan.

I saw a man put his three-year-old daughter up on the table so that she was sitting right in front of Tibbets' chair; the father snapped a picture. He was Jimmy Dolan, thirty-two, of Sherwood, Arkansas; he said that he had brought his little girl Abbie to the theater lobby today because "I know my history. I had a grandfather in World War II. Not enough attention is paid."

Another man with a child—Lamar Steiger was the father, his nine-year-old son was Eli—told me that they had driven to Branson from Bentonville, Arkansas. "These three men helped to save my father's life," Steiger said. "Once Eli heard they were going to be here, he wanted to come."

Steiger's own father, Don, had been stationed with the Army in California toward the end of World War II, he said. "They were practicing hitting beaches in California. They were going to be sent to Japan for the land invasion."

The little boy came back from the table, where he had said something to Tibbets.

"What did you tell him?" Steiger said.

"I thanked him for saving Daddy Don's life," the child said.

There was a show going on inside the theater; I walked in, to find even fewer people in attendance than had seen the Welk production the night before. This daytime performance featured the Lennon Brothers (the Lennon Sisters were saved for prime time, in the evenings); I stood in the back for a few minutes and watched a skit based on old-time college football weekends.

When I returned to the lobby, Tibbets was being approached by a man named Fred Jones, who was seventy-four. With him was his wife, Marilyn.

"Sir, you saved my life," he said to Tibbets.

"Well, we thought that might happen," Tibbets said.

After Jones had spoken with Tibbets and had said hello to the other men, I asked him what he had meant.

"I was a paratrooper in Europe," he said. "We knew we were

on our way to Japan. I had a friend in high school who went to the South Pacific. He died within six weeks."

He said that he had grown up in Oakley, Kansas, a town with a population of approximately 1,500. His father owned a farm on which he raised wheat and milo. "Dad died when I was seven," he said. "He was only forty-three years old. My mom managed to keep the farm—I don't know how she did it. I went off to the war.

"I got to come home because of those three men who are sitting there. I still live in Oakley—I still work that farm. My wife and I have been married for fifty-two years. And I know in my heart why I have had the chance to do it. Because of what those men did. That's why I came here today. I just wanted to thank Paul Tibbets for letting me live my life."

Things slowed down, and the crew said that they thought they'd break early for lunch. I went back to where we were staying, and walked around the area for a few hours; afterward I walked over to Tibbets' unit, and he was sitting in the living room.

Something had been on my mind since the night before—and it had only been reenforced by what I had seen on stage at the Lennon Brothers' performance this morning.

The G-rated nature of the entertainment—it was what older people are expected to enjoy, I supposed, but when you thought about it, it didn't necessarily make sense. These men had seen things during warfare that no person should ever have to see—the carnage they witnessed on a daily basis had to be indelibly branded on their psyches.

But they were part of a generation that grew up seeing no nudity in movies, hearing no foul language and seeing no explicit violence in their popular entertainment—yes, they were the target audience for the Lennon Sisters and the Lennon Brothers, they had been raised in an American society where forbidden things were just that: forbidden. Their children and grandchildren came of age in a culture that laughed at the concept of the forbidden, that did not understand or honor the idea of anything being out-of-bounds.

And that's what I wanted to know. Did my father, and Tibbets, and the men and women of their generation, go through their adult lives feeling that they had been unnecessarily sheltered because there were so many things they had not been permitted to see? And did it all ring false with them—having been eyewitnesses to the death and bloodshed of warfare in their young adult lives, did it now feel faintly ridiculous that the entertainment they were allowed to see when they were young had been cleaned up, sanitized?

"If your dad and I had grown up with the nudity and the language and the violence that young people see on TV and in the movies now, I don't think it would have had an effect on us one way or the other," he said.

"You really don't think so?" I said. "You don't think it would have changed you—to grow up seeing the things that people see in entertainment today?"

"I think it would have certainly been better for the country, if the violence and the nudity and the foul language hadn't taken over," he said. "But you asked about us—about your father, about me. And I don't think we would have been any different as men, even if we had seen all those things when we were growing up."

"Why not?" I said.

"Because it's not like we didn't know it was out there," he said. "Sex was all hush-hush—you couldn't see it everywhere like you see it on cable TV today. But it was there—the world just didn't serve it up to us on a silver platter. The entertainment when we were boys was based on the thought that sex was a sin—but no matter what we weren't allowed to see, we knew about it."

"I was sitting with you at that show last night," I said, "and I was thinking about how wholesome the performance was, and then I thought of all the killing and gore that you got used to when you were a young man. . . ."

"So what?" Tibbets said. "We were better served, being protected from the kinds of things that kids see now as they're growing up. By the time we got to the war, we were ready to look the hard side of life right in the face—and if we weren't ready, we got ready, real quick. I do not feel deprived that when I was a boy the entertainment was clean and happy."

"Would you have said so at the time?" I asked.

"I don't know," Tibbets said. "I was a boy. But if you're asking me to look back and guess how I would have felt about having sex and violence all around me in entertainment when I was young . . .

"I suppose I feel that seeing all of that would have put a pretty heavy burden on me when I was a kid. Having to pretend that I understood it all. I suppose I'm glad that it was kept away from me, that I was allowed to wait a while before I saw some of those things."

"And you enjoyed the show last night?" I said.

"It was fine," he said. "I'm just sorry Andy Williams isn't in town, so I could show you those funny acrobats."

I went back to my place and Ferebee's door was open. His wife was in the bedroom; he said he thought she might be taking a nap. He waved me inside; I was pleased, because I had been hoping to get some time alone with him and with Van Kirk.

"So I take it they were kidding last night when they said they had to wake you up when you got to Hiroshima," I said.

"Yes, but the fact was, there wasn't a lot for me to do until we got there," he said. "You look at your film in advance to pick out the target area—you decide what the best aiming point will be. In Hiroshima, it was pretty clear to me that it had to be the T-shaped bridge.

"And then you talk about whether you want to come in upwind or downwind. I wanted to approach upwind—I would be more sure that I would hit the target. Downwind would have given us the chance for a faster getaway. But I wanted to hit the target, that's all, and Tibbets agreed."

"The bombardier flies the plane in the last minutes?" I said.

"Yes," Ferebee said. "But it's not the way you're probably thinking—the bombardier doesn't climb into the pilot's seat. The pilot turns it over to the bombardier, so that the plane is being controlled mechanically through the bombsight. You're steering the plane toward your target."

"When Tibbets turned the *Enola Gay* over to you, did you tense up?" I asked.

"No," he said. "The only thing I was nervous about was that I didn't want the bomb hanging up in there—I wanted to make sure it left the plane.

"I could see the bridge from more than sixty miles away—it wasn't a case of having to find it visually at the last moment."

"And when you released the atomic bomb?"

"I knew I didn't screw up," he said.

Tibbets took the controls back as soon as the bomb was released, Ferebee said: "I couldn't see the bomb anymore after he started turning. But then, as we flew away . . . it was like something I'd never seen before. Parts of *buildings* were coming up the stem of the bomb—you could tell that something strange was going on, because you could see parts of the city, pieces of the buildings, like they were being sucked up toward us.

"I had forgotten to put my goggles on. It was the brightest thing you've ever seen, underneath us."

And when the *Enola Gay* landed back on Tinian?

"I was just thankful that it worked," he said. "It was just another mission, and it was over."

A preposterous notion, of course—"just another mission"—but I was beginning to understand that this was Ferebee's style: low key, understated, not overly interested in explaining a lot. He was born in Mocksville, North Carolina, in 1918; he had stayed in the Air Force until 1970. His forearms were enormous, like a lumberjack's, or a professional arm wrestler's; of the three men, he was the one who, even at his age, had the look of a person who could intimidate strangers if he was of a mind to. He wore a baseball cap most of the time, and his drawl was so thick that there were moments when it was difficult to understand every word.

I asked him if he recalled the first time he had met Paul Tibbets.

"I was reporting to Sarasota in April of 1942," he said. "I was walking down this dirt road to the tents. I was supposed to be picking up a .45, for some reason, and I ran into this guy. Tibbets.

"You could tell right away that he was a real competent person. We weren't buddies—not then. We were just in the service together."

And now?

"I know him like a book and he knows me like a book. He is one of the most *loyal* men in the world . . ."

His voice kind of trailed off, and I asked the question: What's it going to be like when there are not three of them, but two? When the first of the three goes?

"It'll hurt bad," he said. "If Dutch or me goes first, it'll hurt Paul, but he'll keep it inside. He won't show it."

"And if he or Dutch are the first to go?" I asked.

"I'll try to do it like Paul would," Ferebee said. "I'll try to keep it inside. But I don't know if I'll be able to."

I asked him his thoughts about the people beneath his bomb—the people who lived in the houses and the buildings that he saw being sucked up the bomb's stem toward the plane.

"I would hate to think about someone in my family being down there," Ferebee said. "But it's just a part of war. If you let those kinds of thoughts get to you . . . This is a war. If you let yourselves think those kinds of thoughts, you might end up going nuts."

"Is that how you got through it?" I asked. "Not just the Hiroshima flight, but the whole war up to that point? By trying not to think about it?"

"I always told myself, never get close to anyone," he said. "Never get close to anyone, because you might lose them."

"But you did lose them," I said. "In Europe, you lost people in your unit all the time. People you knew really well."

"I told myself, when you lose someone, treat it like they've gone on vacation," he said. "Tell yourself that they're on vacation, and they're not back yet."

I was afraid that our talking might be disturbing his wife in the next room, but Ferebee said that she, like Tibbets, had significant hearing loss—hers was just in her right ear—and that there was no way, with the door closed, that she could hear us. I asked him if he was really as matter-of-fact about the Hiroshima flight as he seemed. Not only about the death—but about what he seemed to feel was the routine nature of it.

"It was just another flight," he said. "Another mission in that war. We'd flown a lot of them together."

"But this . . ." I began.

"Paul tells me it was a boring flight," he said. "I know what he means. At least on a B-17 flight, there was a little shooting going on. This was just like a cross-country flight in an airplane. Basically uneventful, except for what happened when we got there. You're trying to win a war."

"And you did," I said. "Is that what you dreamed about when you were a kid—being a soldier and winning a war for your country?"

"I wanted to play baseball," he said. "That was my dream. I went down to Florida with the St. Louis Cardinals for spring training in 1939. That's the dream I was after."

"What happened?" I asked.

"I wasn't good enough yet," he said. "And then the war came."

"Well, you helped to win it," I said.

"I would rather have helped the Cardinals win a World Series," he said. "That's all I ever wanted."

Tibbets seemed in a somewhat pensive mood as we got ready to go out to dinner—when I had come to visit him in his unit I had picked up from a table a piece of historical literature about World War II that he had been reading, and I noticed he had left it open to a passage that listed the number of casualties among bomber crewmen from the Eighth Air Force in Europe during the war: 44,786. Whether that was on his mind, or if it was something else, I wasn't certain. But he was quiet this evening.

When some people who were joining us for dinner were late showing up at David Bean's van, Tibbets said to me, "If they had been on my crew, I would have taken off without them. Left them behind." We had reservations at a restaurant called the Outback—not part of the national chain, but a hometown steakhouse of the same name in Branson—and when we arrived we found that a table for twenty-one had been set up in a private room.

Some owners of the restaurant were joining us, and some executives of the company that ran the condominium complex, and some Branson civic leaders—this seemed to catch Tibbets by surprise. He said nothing—just looked at the long table, then chose a chair on one side near the end.

The noise level was high, and he didn't seem eager to join in the conversations all around him. A young man stood behind him and said to some of the people at the dinner table, "I fly some—I don't have a pilot's license, but I do some flying anyway." To Tibbets it seemed to be part of a great wash of noise; Mary Ann Ferebee said to me, "This is difficult for me, and I only have bad hearing in one ear. It must be so hard for Paul—you feel so isolated in a setting like this, and you have to work so hard to try to hear what everyone is saying. It's just . . . tiring."

Dutch Van Kirk was expressing some opinions—"Well, if you

can't get a job now, in *this* economy, then you can probably never get a job"—and Ferebee was telling some war stories, perhaps apocryphal, perhaps real: "I offered to sell one of our planes to some Arabs for twelve eggs. . . ." Van Kirk and Ferebee were exchanging reminiscences about an old gunner they referred to as Horizontal Hague, and waiters were passing big platters of appetizers, and Tibbets turned to me and said:

"This will be the last big blowout for me."

I wasn't certain what he meant, but he looked up and down the long table.

"No more of having all these people at dinner this trip," he said. "I don't like it. It's just too damn noisy."

Wanting to remind him of the small lunches that he, Gerry Newhouse and I had eaten at his favorite hangout in Columbus, I said, "For me, a table for three at B.J. Young's is the maximum size."

"I know it," Tibbets said.

A few minutes passed, and he seemed lost in thought, and I could see something in his eyes. He got up in a big hurry, and started off for the rest room alone.

The conversation at the table was loud and lively, and no one appeared aware of his absence. I looked into the main restaurant—jammed, high-decibel, with ramps leading from one level to the next, and music playing, and a surprisingly young crowd standing shoulder to shoulder, waiting for tables to open up—and I stood and followed him.

He seemed a little confused in the midst of all the people. "You don't have to do this," he said when he saw me next to him. "Go back and have your dinner."

"That's OK," I said.

I asked someone for directions to the men's room, and I got us there, and walked in with him. "Something just hit me in the belly, Bob," he said. "I'm not feeling so hot."

"Well, I've got to use the rest room, too, so we can just walk back together when you're finished," I said.

I did not, in fact, have to use the rest room, but I waited until he had gone into a stall before I went back outside for a moment. I was going to wait for him and pretend that I had just finished up, too, so that I could make sure he got back to the table all right. I stood there outside the rest room, and I thought about this being the first Memorial Day since my dad had been gone, and I picked up the receiver of a pay telephone and I called my mom.

She was at home tonight. "Where are you?" she said. "It sounds like you're at a party."

"No, I'm just out to dinner," I said. I didn't tell her where; I didn't say that I was in Branson, or who I was with.

"You're having dinner in a bar, from the sounds of it," she said.

Sort of, I told her; the place was sort of a bar.

We talked for a few minutes, and she seemed as if she was doing all right, and two young guys talking at high volume, with beer bottles in their hands, came past me and into the men's room, and after a while Tibbets came out by himself.

I told my mom goodbye; I told her I'd be coming to see her soon.

"You must have finished before I did," Tibbets said, and I said, yes, I had. I asked him if he was ready to go back to the table.

"I suppose," he said. "You know . . . one of the things I've lost is my taste for things. I just don't have the same taste for food that I used to."

I put my hand on one of his arms, as softly as I could so that he would not realize that I was guiding him, and we walked onto one of the wooden ramps that would take us back to the others. When we got there everyone was in full conversation and no one seemed to have noticed that he had been gone.

TWENTY-SEVEN

On my walk the next morning I found myself in a part of the complex that was just being constructed; a man and a woman were being shown a model unit, and as they were coming out they saw me and called hello.

I didn't recognize them; at first I thought they might be greeting someone else. But they walked over and said that they were in Branson for the weekend from their home in Iowa, and that they had seen me in the lobby of the Welk Theater the day before with Tibbets and the crew.

"We were really surprised at how few people were there to say hello to those men," the woman, a second-grade teacher, said.

Her husband said, "I was a senior in high school when the bomb was dropped. I went into the Navy after I graduated, and I served Stateside. I've always thought that if Colonel Tibbets and his crew hadn't flown their mission, I probably would have been on my way to Japan."

I asked the couple if they had overheard anything that the other people in the theater lobby—not the ones in line to meet the crew, but the people who were just passing through—were saying about Tibbets, Van Kirk and Ferebee.

"Nothing much," the husband said. "To tell you the truth, there was a lot of confusion. No one really knew who the three guys were."

When I got back to the development where we were staying I thought I saw that Tibbets' door was ajar, so I walked up to find out. I knocked; I heard him say "Come in," and I stepped inside. . . .

To find him sitting in a pair of boxer shorts and a T-shirt, working on something as he sat at a table. I was embarrassed to be walking in on him like this: He was all but undressed. I apologized and began to leave.

"No, no," Tibbets said. He motioned for me to come in. "That's all right—this is how I am around the house in the morning." I saw what he was doing: trying to load new batteries into his hearing aids.

"This may help," he said. "I was having a lot of trouble last night."

We talked for a while, and I told him that I had heard a few people during our trip—not many, but some—discussing him and the crew in disparaging terms. Saying that when they flew the mission in 1945, the war was going to end soon anyway—that had the crew, and the country, been patient, the flight of the *Enola Gay* would have been rendered unnecessary.

He finished inserting the batteries. Then—looking, at the same moment, all of his eighty-four years and like a seventeen-year-old kid gearing up for a street fight—he turned to face me.

"Those people never had their balls on that cold, hard anvil," he said. "They can say anything they want."

I asked him the same thing I had asked Ferebee the day before—I asked him whether he ever thought about a trip like this when there would be only two of them, instead of three. And of how he would feel once that one of them was gone.

"If I'm the one to go first, I hope to hell that the other two don't shed any tears over me," he said. "Because I'm not going to shed any over them."

I was stunned.

"Why do you say that?" I asked.

"Because I don't shed tears," Tibbets said.

"Come on," I said.

"What good do tears do?" he said.

"Even in private?" I said. "Even for these two men? I don't believe you."

"Maybe I'll wipe my nose," he said, and grinned at me, meaning: Change the subject.

I ran into Ferebee a little later. He asked me what I had been talking to Tibbets about, and I hesitated for a few seconds and then I repeated what he had told me.

"It's probably the truth," Ferebee said. "Paul probably won't shed a single tear. It's just his way."

Van Kirk had invited me to come by sometime during the day, and I had been looking forward to it. Wry, constantly observant, seemingly filled with a full sense of life's dark absurdities, and of blessings disguised as disappointments, he appeared to me to be both of the crew and outside it—he, more than Tibbets or Ferebee, had the air of looking at the three of them, including himself, from a certain remove.

When I arrived at his place, he told me that he was in no hurry—that he had all afternoon to talk. I looked at him—this pleasant-faced man who had been born in Northumberland, Pennsylvania, in 1921, who had navigated the *Enola Gay* to Japan at the age of twenty-four, who had earned a degree in chemical engineering from Bucknell University and who had gone on to work for DuPont for thirty-six years, finishing his career as a district manager on the West Coast—and I tried to envision him on that August midnight in 1945. What must have been going through his mind—being in charge of getting that plane to a place no one on board had ever flown before?

"We took off from Tinian at 2:45 A.M.," he said. "Total darkness, of course—we knew it was going to be about two and a half hours to Iwo Jima."

"Where were you physically?" I said.

"In the B-29, when you're the navigator you sit up in the end of a tunnel across the top of the bomb bays," he said. "So you're sitting there alone, and you look around, and you've pretty much already made up your mind about which stars you're going to use to set your course."

"And it was all done by hand back then?" I asked.

"A hand-held bubble sextant," Van Kirk said. "You select your star, and you get it in the middle of the bubble . . ."

There were books on board, he said—a series of them—to translate the positioning of the aircraft in relation to the stars: to let the navigator know whether his airplane was on course.

"How many times back then—not just on that flight, but on your B-17 flights in Europe—did you ask yourself, 'What am I doing here? How did I get here?' " I asked him.

"You know, I don't think I ever asked myself that question," he said. "Not then."

The dawn, he said, was lovely to behold.

"That morning was just a beautiful sunrise morning," he said. "The colors . . . The sun came up just before we got to Iwo."

And once he had daylight, getting the airplane to Japan on schedule was no problem. The *Enola Gay* arrived on time, Tibbets turned the controls over to Ferebee, Ferebee guided it through his bombsight . . .

And then?

"What I probably saw was kind of a flash in the airplane," Van Kirk said. "Sort of like a photographer's bulb. And the sound . . . the best way I can describe it to you is that it sounded like a piece of sheet metal rolling. That *snapping* sound.

"At first I thought that they were shooting at us from the

ground. But it was the shock waves. With the shock waves and that rolling metal sound from the bomb, it felt and sounded very much like a bunch of flak used to sound when we were flying the B-17s over Europe. And there was that white cloud."

"Do you recall being able to put any thoughts together?" I said.

"A sense of relief," he said. "You've been training for this for six or seven months—all of the training for this one flight—and you've carried it out, and there was just this sense of relief. It had happened.

"It had happened, and even though you were still up there in the air and no one else in the world knew what had happened, you just sort of had a sense that the war was over, or would be soon. And that you could go home."

"You all knew that?" I asked.

"I think so," he said. "I think we knew."

"Did you show it?" I said.

"Do you mean celebrate?" Van Kirk said. "No. There was no celebration. You were trained not to do something like that. I don't think that people back then were as demonstrative as they are today—and we certainly were trained not to be that way on our missions. Think about the era we grew up in. Babe Ruth would hit a home run and he would run around the bases and that would be it.

"You didn't show much. You took pride in being disciplined."

I asked him if, when he had first met Tibbets, he had sensed that they would end up as lifelong friends.

"Well . . ." Van Kirk said. "I think, number one, he was a captain and I was a brand-new second lieutenant. I regarded him as very exacting and capable—but as a friend? Not at first. He was twenty-seven when I met him, but if you'd asked me at the time, I would have thought he was sixty years old.

"The way he carried himself, the experience he had . . . compared to other squadron commanders, Paul Tibbets was so consistently no-nonsense. . . .

"For a long time, our relationship was one where he was our commanding officer, which was really not the same thing as being our friend. We flew with him—and it's hard to even explain to you just what an excellent pilot Paul was. He could do things with an airplane that I never saw anyone do in my life.

"I've looked at Paul over the years, and I've listened to him talk to other pilots. I think he just understands the dynamics of an airplane, how they fly, more than other people. I'm not even sure if *he* is aware of how far above other people's feel for airplanes his feel is.

"But you were asking about when the real friendship started. I think that we started getting closer to each other on a flight when we took Mark Clark to Gibraltar, and then when we took Eisenhower to Gibraltar. You're together so much, you're washing your clothes together, you become friends.

"But it wasn't until after I'd left the service that I called him 'Paul.' "

"You didn't call him by his first name?" I said.

"Oh, no," Van Kirk said. "Never in the service, and not for years after I was out of the service. Even when I had been out for a while, and I would see him, I would address him by his rank."

"And would he do the same with you?" I asked.

"No," he said. "I was always 'Dutch' to him."

"What about on the airplane?" I said. "What would you call him on a mission, when you were on the intercom?"

"It was always 'Navigator to pilot,' " Van Kirk said. "That's who we were, on that airplane."

Tibbets, it seemed to me, always operated under the assumption that the world did not really understand what he and his crew had done on the Hiroshima mission, and why they had done it; Ferebee seemed almost not to care what the world thought.

And Van Kirk?

"I think that if people take the time to research it, and think about it, then they do understand the mission," he said. "The majority of the world will not do that—but the people who do look into the history of it, I think, will at least have some understanding of what we were trying to do, and why we were sent to do it.

"Paul says he has had some pretty bad reactions from people over the years, but I personally have never had any venomous phone calls or anything like that. Oh, you'll get questions—one girl one time asked me, 'Don't you feel bad?,' and that pretty much sums up what is on people's minds who disagree with the mission. And yes, if you were a resident of Hiroshima, you would have a very different feeling about the mission than if you were a member of the family of a person whose life we saved by hastening the end of the war."

"So you don't resent people who have doubts about what you and the crew did?" I asked.

"Of course not," Van Kirk said. "It's reasonable to have doubts about what we did. There are pros and cons to what we did—and I don't think anyone, in good conscience, can say that it's wrong to have doubts."

"How about you?" I asked.

"Do I have doubts?" he said.

"Yes," I said.

"I don't," he said. "I never have. It's never bothered me any. I really think it was a necessary act."

"The most violent act in the history of the world," I said.

"But I don't think we were violent people," he said. "I was twenty-four when I flew the mission, and to the best of my memory, I had never had a fistfight in my life.

"You can ask yourself, 'Gee, why did this happen, gee, why did that happen?' I've asked myself that. And I always come up with the same answer: that what we did was for the overall good."

* * *

I asked him—as I knew I would—the question I had asked Ferebee and Tibbets. The question about what he envisioned it would be like when there would no longer be three of them.

"When the first of us dies?" he said. "That'll hit me pretty hard. I've lost a fair number of friends. Some in the last few years. That's what happens when you get to be our age.

"But if it's Paul or Tom? I like to think that I handle things pretty well."

I told him what Tibbets had said. I told him that Tibbets had vowed that he would not shed a tear.

"I'm sure he did say that," Van Kirk said. "Paul will never let on. That doesn't mean that it won't be doing the same thing inside to him that it would do to Tom or me. It just means that he'll never let on. He's telling you the truth."

"And you?" I said.

"I'll feel it a lot," he said. "I won't be able to hide it, but then, I won't want to hide it. That's how Paul and I are different. For whatever reason, he'll choose to hide it."

Before I left Van Kirk's room, I asked him if he ever thought about how he and the crew would be remembered two hundred or three hundred years from now.

"You tell me how the world's going to be at that period of time," he said. "And I'll tell you how the people will think of us."

"What do you mean?" I said.

"I hope the world two hundred years from now is a peaceful world," he said. "If it is, then I think people will look back at the atomic bomb and think of it as something that helped the world evolve toward a lasting peace."

"And if the world isn't peaceful?" I said.

"If it isn't," he said, "people will be tossing atomic bombs around like they're going out of style."

Just before we sat down to dinner that night in the clubhouse of the condo development, I saw Gerry Newhouse and David Bean whispering to one of the waiters.

I walked over. Bean was saying, in the softest of voices, "Please clear his plate as soon as he finishes his food. Right away."

I asked him what was going on. "General Tibbets is a real stickler about dirty plates," he said. "He doesn't want the plate in front of him once he's done with what's on it."

Newhouse said that at one restaurant on one trip, "The waiter was slow coming around to clear the plates, so Paul got up and cleared the table himself. Every plate—he removed them from the table and walked them over to a tray."

I found myself smiling, and thinking about my father in restaurants—how sensitive he was to what he perceived as even the slightest inattentiveness or lack of diligence in service. Organize, delegate, supervise, check—and, in Tibbets' case, if, when you checked, everything didn't check out just right, the next step was to bus the dirty plates yourself.

Dinner was quieter tonight—the group was smaller, even with the inclusion of the Lennon Brothers, who had accepted an invitation to join us (the Lennon Sisters were said to be working and unavailable). And after the meal, there was to be a presentation of sorts.

Tibbets—for the edification of the Lennon Brothers—was going to speak about the *Enola Gay* mission. Gerry Newhouse had brought along a videotape—an educational documentary about the flight—and Tibbets had asked him to show it following dinner. He would answer questions afterward.

So we went to a small meeting room, and Tibbets—appearing

a little keyed up—entered first, and said with some concern to Newhouse: "Where's the projector?"

Newhouse explained that a VCR was hooked up to a television set in the room; no movie projector would be necessary.

"We'll take a count," Tibbets said, meaning that Newhouse was not to start the videotape until everyone from dinner was present and accounted for.

There weren't many of us—beside the crew and their wives, there was Paul IV and Angele, there were some relatives of Angele, there was an aunt of Gerry Newhouse's wife, there were a few executives from the development company that owned the condos. And there were the Lennon Brothers.

Tibbets made sure that everyone was in the room and seated, and then—to an audience of fifteen—began to explain the end of World War II.

"We're not quite as bad as some people have depicted us," he said, standing at the front. "In fact, we think that we're pretty good citizens."

Van Kirk and Ferebee looked as if they might be here under duress—not only had they seen this video before, but they had been on the flight of the *Enola Gay,* this wasn't exactly new to them—yet they did not stir from their chairs; Tibbets was the commanding officer, and this was a command performance. The video played, and then the lights came up, and Tibbets said he was available to answer questions.

Someone asked him if he had ever had any doubt that the mission would succeed. He cleared his throat; even though he had been with these people all through dinner, and with some of them all through the weekend, he had assigned himself the role of orator tonight, and spoke formally.

"I was so confident," he said. "There was no question, it would be done. I can fly an airplane from Point A to Point B."

Had he ever given any thought to entering politics?

"They wanted me to run for governor of Florida after I came

back from the war," he said. "But I said no. I wanted to fly airplanes."

He was briefing—briefing these fifteen people, briefing the Lennon Brothers. Someone asked him what he thought of Paul IV as a pilot, and Tibbets said, "My grandson knows more than I ever knew or will ever know about the operation of airplanes. But I'll tell you one thing: He'll never have as much fun flying an airplane as I did."

There weren't many questions, and within a few minutes we headed back to our units. I ended the evening in Van Kirk's room; someone had brought a bottle of wine, and Ferebee was trying to get it open, but couldn't quite figure the cork out. Fifteen minutes into trying, the bottle still stayed shut tight, and there they were, on a warm Missouri night fifty years and more after their war, and I saw Van Kirk shoot an amused look at Ferebee, and Ferebee shake his head in frustration as he kept twisting at the bottle's neck.

TWENTY-EIGHT

For our last day in Branson, Tibbets had planned a cookout lunch with hamburgers, hot dogs and cold soda pop, but it rained in the morning, so we gathered in his living room and had cold cuts inside. This would be it for the trip; the three men would be going their separate ways at the end of the weekend.

That Thing You Do!, the Tom Hanks–directed movie about a one-hit rock band in 1964, played silently on a cable channel on the television set against one wall, while the men fixed themselves sandwiches and talked of an even earlier time. Ferebee was telling the others about an occasion just after the Bay of Pigs—he was still in the service then—when he had met President John F. Kennedy at an air base. I asked him if there had been the feeling of electricity around Kennedy that we have read and heard about for so long—that special quality that people still analyze and reminisce over.

"No," Ferebee said. "He looked sick. When you saw his face up close, he looked like a sick person who had been under a sun lamp."

There was nothing much planned for the day, and the weather was unpromising. After lunch everyone drifted off on their own, with plans to get together early in the evening for the one event that had been scheduled: The Shoji Tabuchi Show.

Shoji Tabuchi had become the entertainment phenomenon of Branson. Born in the Japanese city of Daishoji, raised in Osaka, he had begun taking violin lessons at the age of seven. When

Tabuchi was in college in Osaka, American country-and-western musician Roy Acuff, famed for his appearances on *The Grand Ole Opry,* was visiting Japan, and performed in a show that Tabuchi attended. The young man was mesmerized, especially by the song "Listen to the Mockingbird."

He told his parents that he wanted to become a country-and-western musician. He moved to the United States, got a job as a waiter in Japanese restaurants and worked part-time polishing cars. He eventually was hired to play fiddle in a country band at the Starlite Club in Riverside, Missouri, and in 1968 ran into Roy Acuff again. He told Acuff about the time he had seen him perform in Japan; Acuff invited him to come to Nashville and look him up, and Tabuchi did just that. Acuff arranged for Tabuchi to perform a song on stage at the old Ryman Auditorium, home of the Opry, where audience members greeted him warmly.

He moved to Kansas, where during the days he worked in a hospital's X-ray laboratory and at night played in a country music club. By the mid-1970s he was touring as a backup musician for a country singer, and eventually ended up in Branson. He set a goal for himself: to become so popular in the town that he could some day be the featured performer in his own theater. The tourists who came to Branson fell in love with the Japanese violinist who put on the country show, and in 1990 he built his 2,000-seat Shoji Tabuchi Theatre.

It became the hottest ticket in Branson; the word-of-mouth was like nothing anyone in the city of 3,700 had ever encountered, and soon enough Tabuchi was selling out almost 400 shows a year. People would return to their hometowns and would give their neighbors a two-word piece of advice about what to do when they took their own trips to Branson: "See Shoji."

The recommendation had gotten to Tibbets, Ferebee and Van Kirk: No visit to Branson would be complete unless they saw the Shoji show.

And so they had made their plans for the evening: dinner at a steakhouse, followed by Shoji Tabuchi's performance.

* * *

We ate hurriedly, and then David Bean drove his van to the front of the Shoji Tabuchi Theatre—where staff members were waiting outside to greet Tibbets and the crew, to guide Bean's van to a special roped-off area of the pavement within steps of the theater entrance, to escort us to a private room where we could wait before going into the auditorium itself. Three steps into the theater building and we all knew that this was a different Branson than anything we had seen before.

The lobby was breathtaking, elegant, like a new version of one of the movie palaces of the 1930s—a place designed to make its customers feel like royalty for a few hours. There was a hush; the men and women who were finding their way to their seats spoke softly, reverentially, as if by instinct. Women were telling their husbands to please wait for just a minute—they wanted to get a look at the famous rest rooms (word around town was that each rest room, men's and women's, had been decorated at a cost of $250,000, although a Tabuchi Theatre staff member told us that figure was low). The capacity crowd that was arriving was treating the edifice as if it were an art museum.

Which seemed to be the point—the people who were running this place clearly understood that separating the Tabuchi Theatre, and the Shoji show, from everything else in Branson could only be good for business. We were taken to the private waiting area, so that we could go to our seats inside the theater at the very last minute; chairs had been reserved for Tibbets, Van Kirk and Ferebee so they would not have to stand. Tibbets sat down, and a woman—she appeared to be a relative of a theater staff member, and, like everyone we had seen so far, was not Japanese or Japanese-American—approached him and said she would be honored if he would hold her baby.

She handed the baby to Tibbets. Tibbets looked the baby in the face; the baby looked Tibbets in the face.

Lights blinked in the lobby, and we were told that it was time for us to go to our seats.

A staff member said to me that the management of the Tabuchi Theatre would be grateful if Tibbets, Van Kirk and Ferebee could sit together, right next to each other.

I told this to Ferebee as we were walking down the aisle toward our row.

"Why?" he said to me. "So they can shoot us?"

The show was . . .

Well, it was Las Vegas minus the drinks and sex and dirty jokes, but it was more than that. There were lasers, there was smoke and mist, there were fireworks and dancers and computer-timed stagecraft. There were musicians all over the place—the theater, we were told, employs two hundred people—and above all there was a sense of unending bigness. And into this—the lights, the colors, the pyrotechnics, the coming-at-you-from-every-corner sound—strode Shoji Tabuchi.

He was a tall man dressed in combination Elvis/Liberace; before he was two feet onto the stage the crowd was standing and shouting. He carried his violin in one hand, he wore a broad smile that registered even in the back rows of the cavernous theater, and his first words—heavily accented, much more so than you would expect from a man who had been living in the United States for so many years—were:

"How many people are first time in this theater?"

He waited for the show of hands.

"Whoa!" he called out. "Where you been?"

And lifted the violin to his shoulder and began to sing a spirited rendition of the old Louisiana-Texas rouser "Jambalaya."

Hank Williams and Bob Wills by way of Osaka, and at one point balloons and confetti came drifting down from the ceiling—there was never a second during the Shoji show when something wasn't going on—and I looked over at the crew, and their eyes were riveted on the stage, and it was much too loud for me to say anything to them.

There was everything—show tunes, classical, bluegrass, Cajun, rock and roll, gospel, polka—and the show barely stopped to exhale. During a section of the performance devoted to nostalgia for the 1950s there was a big replica of an I LIKE IKE button on the wall, and before one part of the show in which Japanese music was played, Shoji said to the cheering audience, "We thought you'd like to see a little different culture."

Then: "And now we'll take you to Hawaii. I wonder how many of you folks have been to Hawaii?"

Dutch Van Kirk raised his hand.

He had told me before of visiting the memorial at Pearl Harbor, but I had no idea whether that was what was on his mind at this moment, or if he was merely responding to the I-ask-it-every-night question of the show's star.

As I looked around at the people in the audience, there was no escaping what was going on here: In a contemporary American culture built on the new concepts of "edge" and "attitude" and "in-your-face," a culture that seemed to constantly devalue the literal in favor of the jabbingly off-angle, here, in Branson, Shoji Tabuchi had discovered, and was prospering from, something quite basic:

There was a huge, largely uncatered-to American audience—many of them from the World War II generation—who were starving for an old form of entertainment: welcoming, courteous, based on the assumption that the people in the seats were ladies and gentlemen. Earlier in the day I had spoken with my mother on the phone; she had said that she and a friend were planning to go to a movie in Columbus this night, and that she was trying to select "a nice one—not upsetting."

I understood. And so, clearly, although he had never met her, did Shoji Tabuchi. He treated his audience with unending respect—not just during the performance, but from the moment they walked into his building. Much of the rest of American society these days—everything from MTV to crudely suggestive situation comedies to the sardonic, dizzying, rapid-cut nature of many television commercials—might have seemed foreign to many members of this audience, but Tabuchi's stage show felt like home. Like a place with which they had somehow lost touch, a place they missed.

"Are you having a good time tonight?" Shoji called from the stage.

They answered with applause.

"Good!" he called, beaming, and picked up his violin to give them more.

At intermission I went out to see the rest room.

It was everything I had heard. In the men's room there was a pool table, there were leather armchairs, there was a spectator section in case anyone wanted to watch the pool players. There was marble everywhere, and fresh flowers, and a long line outside—not because there was a paucity of facilities inside for the guests to use, but because once the men arrived, they tended to stay a while to absorb it all, as if at an exhibit of some sort. Many men talked animatedly to friends about the lavishness of the room; some were taking snapshots.

When I left—intending to walk over to observe the line in front of the ladies' room—I noticed someone midway back in the long line waiting to get into the Shoji Tabuchi men's room:

Tibbets.

He was by himself, and remained so as the line moved slowly forward.

* * *

Following intermission the pace of the Shoji show intensified—there was one part in which gigantic Japanese ceremonial Taiko drums were played, one of them weighing a ton and having been purchased at a cost of more than $200,000—and then Tabuchi himself stepped to the front of the stage and the music stopped.

"Thank you," he said to the audience. "We have some very, very special guests here with us in the theater tonight."

The customers in their seats looked around, as did the musicians with Tabuchi on the stage, not knowing to whom he was referring.

"They are the original flight crew of the *Enola Gay,*" Tabuchi said.

There was applause, tentative at first—as if the audience was surprised—and then building in volume and in duration.

"They have been in town for the last several days," Tabuchi said, "and we are very honored to have them here tonight."

He gestured from the stage to the row in which we were sitting.

"Would you mind standing up, please?" he said.

The three crewmen did; this is why the theater personnel had wanted them to sit together.

"Brigadier General Paul Tibbets," Tabuchi said, with great flourish, into the microphone. "General Tibbets served our country for twenty-nine years in the military. . . ."

And it was, indeed, "our country" for Tabuchi. He had become a United States citizen in recent years; when Tibbets and the crew had dropped the atomic bomb on Hiroshima, Tabuchi had been a child in Japan, but now he was an American.

"Major Dutch Van Kirk. . . ." Tabuchi said.

As he read the names, staff members of the theater came up the aisle with gifts and flowers for the crew and the women in the party.

"Also, Colonel Tom Ferebee. . . ." Tabuchi announced.

The crewmen were on their feet, accepting the presents and letting the applause wash over them.

"These men have served our country with great loyalty and honor," Tabuchi told his audience. And then, directly to the three crewmen:

"We are so glad to have you here."

There was one more sustained ovation, and then the show continued. At the end, Tabuchi said to the packed house:

"America will always be the place where every one of your dreams can come true. Thank you for being with us tonight."

He raised his violin and began to play "The Impossible Dream," as the audience stood and cheered him.

We had been invited to meet Tabuchi after the show. Ushers came to our row and led us to a flight of stairs, which we climbed until we were in a lounge area near his dressing room.

There were snacks and beverages and a cake; Tabuchi was taking a few minutes to rest after his performance, so for a while it was just us in the room, standing around, not quite sure what was expected. There was some small talk between the crew and the theater staff, and then Shoji entered and walked from person to person, shaking hands.

We had been sitting far enough back in the theater that I wasn't sure whether Tabuchi, on stage with the spotlights in his eyes, had been able to see the faces of the men he was introducing to the audience; now, as he circulated through the room, he seemed to be trying to determine who was who. He approached Tom Ferebee, who extended his hand and said to Tabuchi:

"I'm one of 'em."

The two men spoke briefly, and then a theater employee took Tabuchi over to meet Tibbets. "This is my grandson, Paul," Tibbets said. "He flies the B-2."

"Glad to meet you," Tabuchi said to the young aviator.

There was a small silence, and Tabuchi said to Tibbets, "How long will you be in town for?"

"I apologize for my hearing," Tibbets said.

In this low-ceilinged room he was having trouble making out words, so the pilot of the *Enola Gay* was saying he was sorry to his Japan-born host—sorry for not being able to understand him.

A photographer from the theater staff said that he would like to take a picture of the three crewmen with Tabuchi. As he prepared his camera, he said, "I need for you all to turn around."

Van Kirk, joking with him, said: "The proper word is 'About face.' "

As the four men posed, Van Kirk said to Tabuchi, "You put on a great show."

"Thank you," Tabuchi said, and began to discuss with the crew the traditional foods of Louisiana.

When the photographer was finished, Tabuchi and Tibbets went to a part of the room where Tibbets might be able to hear a little better. Tabuchi spoke of war—of how countries down through history have always fought, and how sometimes the fighting even breaks out within.

"Inside the country," Tabuchi said, referring to the Civil War, "the United States, North and South, fight . . ."

"I understand, " Tibbets said. "We know that."

"My mom and dad," Tabuchi said, "they are from—where they were born—was the prefecture right next to Hiroshima. And my mom, after the bomb, they were told to move. Because of the cloud. They did not know what kind of bomb . . ."

This, Tibbets was hearing. He was staring straight into Tabuchi's eyes.

"Actually," Tabuchi said, talking of the days after the bomb fell, "my mom carried me on her shoulder, and my brother in a . . ."

He stopped, not able to come up with the right English word.

"In a . . ." he said.

"Carriage?" Tibbets said.

"Yes," Tabuchi said. "Carriage."

"OK," Tibbets said.

". . . to go into the mountainside, to get away," Tabuchi said.

He told Tibbets his father had said that had the war continued, "all would have died"; that his father had said the end of the war spared the lives of "men, women, children" all over Japan.

Tibbets said, "In 1959, I was fortunate enough to have as a guest in my house the man who led the airplanes on the attack on Pearl Harbor. Mitsuo Fuchida."

Tabuchi nodded.

"He was a fine man," Tibbets said. "As warriors, we understood each other."

"I am very, very honored to have you here," Tabuchi said.

"I've enjoyed every moment of it, and to make your acquaintance was very nice," Tibbets said. "I hope our paths will cross again."

It was late when we got back to where we were staying. Mrs. Van Kirk was not feeling well; the evening had been long, there had been a lot of walking and climbing, and the consequences of her stroke were more distinct than usual. David Bean drove his van close to the unit where the Van Kirks were staying, and Dutch helped his wife inside and told the rest of us that they were just going to turn in.

The Ferebees said that they were tired, too; we all made our goodnights. Paul IV stood and talked to his grandfather in the parking lot for a few minutes, but then they, too, went to their separate rooms.

I had trouble falling asleep, and when I woke up in the middle of the night I realized that Sunday had turned to Monday. I was going to be leaving before the rest of them; a car was supposed to pick me up right after dawn to take me to the airport in Springfield for the first leg of the trip back to Chicago.

When the alarm radio went off I got dressed, and then walked outside. It was still dark. I knew they'd all be sleeping; I knew that I would not be seeing them before I left.

I walked to each of their doors; I just stood there for a second. No lights inside any of the three places; not a sound to be heard. I was the only person up and about, my footsteps echoed on the little sidewalk that connected the condominiums, and I wasn't sure why I was doing this. But I stood in front of each of the three doors, and on this Memorial Day morning I thought about the men on the other side, and I knew that this would have to serve as my farewell.

The car arrived right on time, and as the sun came up I departed.

TWENTY-NINE

My father's voice, on the tape he gave to us, describing the day of his return from the war:

We disembarked from our troop ship and got on trucks for that glorious ride back to Camp Patrick Henry, where the welcoming flags were waving and the girls were blowing kisses and people were throwing flowers. . . .

We went through a few requirements when we got back there, and they gave us a huge steak dinner, and I had fresh milk for the first time in eighteen months—which made me deathly sick! But I got well enough to get on a troop train for that long, sooty railroad ride to somewhere in Indiana. The name of the camp in Indiana, or the fort, where we were to be mustered out escapes me at this moment, but I had gotten word to your mother to meet me there, where I would be for only twenty-four to forty-eight hours, and then, by God, it was over.

So that train ride was, I think, the longest that I've experienced in my life. Finally we got to this camp and the train slowly wound around until we stopped and got off, and marched to our quarters and started the first of a few hours of being debriefed and demobilized. Phyllis had driven the same blue/gray Pontiac all the way from Columbus to the camp to pick me up, and that reunion was something that happens to a man only once in a lifetime, and I shall never forget it as long as I live. All the months of mud . . .

He and she headed for home; they wanted to stop off and see his parents.

* * *

We drove her Pontiac, and I was relishing all the scenery of Ohio, because it had been in my mind for all of those long months. Of course the first thing we did was drive to Akron to see my mother and father. They were ecstatic, and believe me, we all said a lot of prayers.

I think we stayed there a day or so. . . . I tried to make a deal with the Ford people from whom I had bought the flying omelette lo those many five years before, and had had to give it up because there was no way for me to pay for it. And it so happens that I was very hung over and was shaking like a leaf when we went into that Ford agency, and the salesman was kind of rough, and Dad, bless him, came through. He said, "Do you know what this boy has been through? Just look at him."

Of course my hands were shaking and I was shaking but it was not because of what I went through, it was because I had a terrible hangover. But the guy gave me a car—didn't give it to me, but permitted me to buy one—and that's the situation as it was in the early fall of 1945.

He went back to work for the company that had hired him before he entered the Army; he would end up staying with that company for his entire career, becoming its president before his retirement. My brother, my sister and I would be born; he and my mother would remain a couple until the night he died.

All of that would come later, though. Right now, the war had just been won, and he was home.

His voice on the tape:

I think it's about time to wind this up, but before doing so I think that I ought to speak about goals. I really never was goal-oriented, one of my many faults was and is my habit, if you will, to ad lib my way through life, being lucky most of the time to get away with it.

However, as a kid I did have certain dreams, among which were to be happily married to an understanding, tolerant, intelligent, beautiful and loving woman, to be blessed with happy children, to be a good son to my parents, to be as successful as possible in all of my endeavors, to realize my ambitions, some modest, some a little more ambitious, such as being a good provider for my family. . . .

To live a good, long, full life, to be respected by my peers, to keep what sense of humor I had. . . .

And here were his very last words on the tape—in which he recalled what his earliest hopes had been when, as a child, he had looked out the schoolroom window and had wished for the grandest that life could ever offer:

. . . to serve my country, and to realize a little boy's dream of walking up that diagonal path at King School, after a war, in full uniform, with the love of my life, your mother, on my arm.

ACKNOWLEDGMENTS

There were many people who helped me along the way in the writing of this book, and I'd like to thank them here.

At Morrow/Avon, the professionalism under intense deadline pressure of Tom Dupree and his assistant, Kelly Notaras, made my job much easier. My special gratitude goes to Hamilton Cain and Lou Aronica, whose early support and enthusiasm were indispensable to this project.

At Janklow & Nesbit, Eric Simonoff's unfailing advice, counsel and creativity, as well as his friendship, were and are a constant source of value and enjoyment to me. To Mort Janklow, as always, go my thanks, friendship and great appreciation.

At the *Chicago Tribune,* the men and women with whom I work made the dual tasks of writing a daily newspaper column while writing this book possible. My thanks to Howard Tyner, Ann Marie Lipinski, Gerould Kern, Janet Franz, Joe Leonard, Geoff Brown, Tim Bannon, Kaarin Tisue, Jeff Lyon, Linda Bergstrom, Chris Rauser, Marjorie David, Nadia Cowen, Jim Musser, Tom Hinz, Marsha Peters, Stacy Deibler and Ben Estes. Off the newsroom floors, my continuing thanks go to John Madigan, Jack Fuller, Scott Smith, Owen Youngman and David Williams. My special gratitude goes to two young women who worked with me at the *Tribune* during the period of my writing this book and who, through their diligence and attention to detail, helped me in large ways and small in getting my work done: Kim Miller and Aimee Nieves. Bill Hageman, who worked closely with me during the editing of the newspaper series that resulted from my first conversations with Paul Tibbets, is as fine an editor as any reporter can ever hope for.

At *Life* magazine, Isolde Motley and Marilyn Johnson have been a constant pleasure to work with.

The staff of the United States Air Force Museum, and the officers, enlisted men and women, and staff of Wright-Patterson Air Force Base were courteous and extremely helpful. To the surviving members of the Doolittle Raiders, and to their families, go not only my thanks, but my deepest admiration.

Gerry Newhouse, his wife Judy and their children could not have treated me with any more thoughtfulness and generosity had I been a member of their family. The military career retrospective that General Tibbets had privately printed some thirty years ago, and that Gerry Newhouse, who himself served as a Marine corporal during the Vietnam war, has kept updated and privately in print, was an invaluable source of research material; for any reader who has enjoyed this book, I highly recommend it. For information on *Flight of the Enola Gay* (later retitled as *Return of the Enola Gay*), as well as information about lithographs and photographs pertaining to the flight, readers may contact Mr. Newhouse in care of his office at 1620 E. Broad Street, Room 106, Columbus, Ohio 43203.

To help me in writing with as much factual precision as possible about events that took place during my father's time in Africa and Italy more than fifty years ago, surviving soldiers from that era were exceedingly generous with their time and recollections. I would like to give special mention and thanks to two men in particular, both members of the 91st Infantry Division during World War II: Roy Livengood, who in 1943, at the age of eighteen, joined the Army out of his hometown of Concordia, Kansas, and who was awarded a Purple Heart for injuries sustained during combat in Italy; and David Hathaway who also joined the Army in 1943 at the age of eighteen out of his hometown of Grantsville, West Virginia, and who, like Mr. Livengood, was awarded a Purple Heart. Any time I had a question about a date, a place or an incident that occurred overseas during the 91st's time there, they were tireless in their willingness to go over their own records and memories in an effort to come up with the answers.

To Paul Tibbets, Dutch Van Kirk, Tom Ferebee and their families, any words I might attempt to use here to express the depth of my thanks would be insufficient. So I will just say that I will never forget a moment of the time I have spent with them, and that I hope this book has conveyed that time in a way they will find fair and accurate.

About the Author

Bob Greene is a syndicated columnist for the *Chicago Tribune* and columnist for *Life* magazine. His reports and commentary appear in more than two hundred newspapers in the United States, Canada and Japan, and can be read daily at www.chicagotribune.com/go/greene. As a broadcast journalist he has served as contributing correspondent for *ABC News Nightline.*

His bestselling books include *Be True to Your School; Hang Time: Days and Dreams with Michael Jordan; Good Morning, Merry Sunshine;* and, with his sister, D. G. Fulford, *To Our Children's Children: Preserving Family Histories for Generations to Come.*

His first novel, *All Summer Long,* was published in a new paperback edition this spring; his latest collection of journalism, *Chevrolet Summers, Dairy Queen Nights,* will be published in paperback by HarperCollins early next year.

Grand Opening

OTHER BOOKS BY JON HASSLER

A Green Journey
The Love Hunter
Simon's Night
Staggerford

Grand Opening

Jon Hassler

WILLIAM MORROW AND COMPANY, INC.
NEW YORK

A portion of this novel appeared originally in *Twin Cities* as a short story entitled "Dodger's Return."

Library of Congress
Cataloging-in-Publication Data

Hassler, Jon.
Grand opening.

I. Title.
PS3558.A726G65 1987
812′.54 86-28654
ISBN 0-688-06649-6

Printed in the United States of America

2 3 4 5 6 7 8 9 10

BOOK DESIGN BY SUSAN HOOD

For Betsy

The author is grateful for the fellowship awarded him by the Minnesota State Arts Board from funds provided by the Minnesota Legislature.

Autumn

1

As they followed the Mississippi out of the Twin Cities on U.S. 61, Brendan wondered why his parents and his grandfather seemed not to share his dread. Year after year he had listened apprehensively to his mother and father talk about moving to a small town and going into business for themselves, and now it was happening. Tomorrow he would begin the school year among strangers in a village he had never seen. The lawn mower was strapped to the roof of the car and his bike rode the front bumper. The moving van was some miles ahead. It was Labor Day. A light rain was falling.

His parents sat in front, his father gripping the wheel tightly, fighting the car's tendency to wobble into the left lane, and his mother reading *For Whom the Bell Tolls,* which she had promised to return to the city library by mail. The book was causing her to gasp repeatedly as she read the final pages. Grandfather and Brendan sat in back, separated by a pile of coats and coathangers. Brendan was twelve, born the year Roosevelt defeated Hoover; Grandfather was nearly eighty, a baby when Lincoln was shot. The car, a 1928 De Soto (black, square and noisy), was propelled quite literally by the river, for the engine leaked coolant, and every thirty miles or so Hank had to pull off the highway and divert a gallon of the Mississippi through the coils of the steaming radiator.

"Hank, look at these hills, how awful," exclaimed his mother the instant his father switched off the ignition. She had closed the book on her lap, marking her page with both thumbs, and was shrinking back from the forested bluffs rising on her right. Brendan opened his door, handed his father the pail at his feet and watched him carry it

down a long path to the wide, slaty river. The path was muddy. The rain was dwindling.

"Plum has hills around it, but they're gentle, rolling hills." She turned in her seat to reassure her son and her father. "They don't rise up and slap you in the face the way these do."

Brendan was sorry to hear it. These bluffs looked like fun.

"There!" shouted Grandfather, startling her, clutching the back of her seat, pulling himself forward and peering past her through the windshield. "Look there, the *Hiawatha*!" At the base of the bluffs, a green train came snaking north beside the highway. "Seven passenger cars," he said. He reached across the coats to nudge Brendan. "See how smooth she rides, lad? You know who laid that track, don't you, level as water?"

Brendan nodded. He counted the passenger coaches going by, pleased to see eight, not seven. Adult error was reassuring. Small error, that is. Large error, of course was frightening. For weeks it had been his secret prayer that uprooting themselves from the city was not the large error he felt it to be.

Don't think of the move as scary, his mother had told him. If we're a little lonesome at first, remember we've got each other.

Kids make friends fast, his father had said.

"*I* was the one," said Grandfather, easing himself back into his seat, sighing, feeling behind him for the wooden hanger poking him in the spine. The train slipped around a curve and out of sight, leaving behind a stream of soot slanting down with the raindrops. "I laid that track."

It was true. Not this selfsame track, of course, but the original track on this roadbed had been spiked down by Grandfather and Grandfather's father, two of the construction hands of the 1880's who led the railroads west. Brendan had heard all about it.

His mother said, "These are as close to mountains as anything I hope to lay eyes on." In her past—a railroader's daughter after the tracks had grown out of the deep river valleys—were the flat fields and rolling swells of western Minnesota and the Dakotas. She loved flat earth. She abhorred restricted vision.

Grandfather said, "When I was sixteen they made my father foreman of a section crew and right away he let me quit school and go with him." His hand trembled as he felt his pockets—suitcoat, vest, shirt—for his pipe and tobacco pouch. "That was the spring of 'eighty. We were laying track to Aberdeen when Aberdeen was nothing but a city of tents."

Only by an act of will could Brendan stand to hear the rest of the story, the part about ice cream. He'd heard it, along with the rest of Grandfather's stories, a hundred thousand times.

"We headquartered in Aberdeen that summer and I thought I'd die for lack of ice cream. You couldn't buy yourself even a spoon of ice cream anywhere in South Dakota . . ." His voice drifted off with his memory. His eyes narrowed as a glimmer of sunlight filled the car, highlighting his silky white hair and his pale, blue-veined temples. On his chin were the purple wounds of a shaky shave with a new blade. He murmured, "Holy smut, how I loved ice cream in 1881."

Brendan saw sunlight flashing here and there along the valley as the wind opened the low sky and folded it shut again. Down at the water's edge, his father's white shirt was momentarily agleam.

"How far now?" he asked.

"It can't be much further to Uncle Herman's farm, and Plum is about forty miles beyond that." His mother looked at her watch. "Eleven thirty? Is that all? It seems like we've been on the road forever."

Grandfather asked, "Where did you say we were going?"

"Plum!" they answered together, their voices, their impatience in tune. She added, "We're stopping to say hello to Uncle Herman on the way."

"I never heard of a town named Plum," Grandfather insisted, aware that he was on the verge of being scolded by his daughter, a sensation he rather enjoyed. He packed his pipe expectantly, scattering tobacco across the coats and coathangers. He added, asking for it, "I've laid track in three states of the union and a province of Canada and I've never once heard of a place named Plum."

"There *is* a Plum," she said precisely, peevishly, "and our house is on the west edge of town. Upstairs you and Brendan will have the two bedrooms at the back, and Hank and I will have the bedroom at the front. And there *are* railroad tracks, just half a block from the house, I've told you a dozen times."

Closer to two dozen, but it hadn't sunk in, Grandfather having aged to the point where change was unimaginable. Though briefed at every stage of this move, he had never truly believed moving day would ever dawn. He had said fifty or sixty times during August, "There's not a mile of rail I haven't ridden in the state of Minnesota, and I've never heard of a place named Plum," and it was only at seven o'clock this morning when two strangers backed a truck up to the house and came in and took apart his bed that he agreed to pack

his grip. "I'll tell you one thing sure," he had muttered to the movers as he gathered up his hairbrush and handmirror from his bureau, "there can't be a railroad running through it, or I'd know about it."

Hank came up the path carrying the pail in one hand and flowers in the other—daisies bunched around a frond of wild fern. Brendan jumped out to take the bouquet and act as his father's emissary. His parents were linked by a love as direct and mute as a beam of light, and very few of Brendan's joys equalled that of coming between them and feeling himself pierced by that beam. He opened the driver's door and handed the bouquet across to his mother. She chuckled.

"Catherine, will you start the engine?" Hank asked. He stood at the front bumper, removing the radiator cap. She slid over behind the wheel and stepped on the starter. As the pistons idled busily, Hank poured slowly, mixing the cool water with what remained of the warm. "It's a wonder the way this old clunk putts along, overloaded like she is. I expected at least two flat tires by now."

"But we've got only one spare."

"One'll do. The way it works you can usually get the first one patched before the second one goes flat."

"But what if you can't?"

"It's a chance you take."

Hank, the eldest son in a family of nine, was accustomed to taking chances. He had quit school at twelve and gone to work for a drayman, delivering ice in summer, coal in winter. Now he had a son of twelve, and during the intervening years he had held at least a dozen jobs, each one an improvement over the last by a dollar or so per week. From his most recent work as a streetcar motorman, he had saved enough money for a down payment on what was surely the least promising grocery business ever offered for sale in the classified ads of the *Minneapolis Star Journal.* A month ago Hank and Catherine had gone twice to Plum, the first time to see the trashy store behind the attractive newspaper ad, and the second time—after the price had dropped—to sign the papers that would make them grocers and to find a house to rent. Both times they were gone a full day, and old Aunt Nancy was brought to the house to watch over Brendan and Grandfather, particularly Grandfather, who sometimes wandered away and got lost.

This morning they had left Minneapolis by way of St. Paul in order to say goodbye to Aunt Nancy, who lived in an overheated

apartment on Grand Avenue. She had delayed them by insisting they stay for tea and muffins and then by accompanying them slowly and arthritically down the steps and out to the curb, where there was a ceremony of kisses under umbrellas. Aunt Nancy's age was a guess—ninety-one probably. She was Grandfather's aunt. She was stronger of mind than Grandfather, but she was fearfully shriveled and frail. Every time she made a move Brendan held his breath, expecting one of her bones to snap. "Remember this," she called in her weak, reedy voice, watching them get into the car, sensing their uneasiness, "I've lived enough of life to know it works."

"What works?" asked Catherine.

"Life works. Now be sure to give these to Herman and tell him he owes me a letter." She handed Catherine a small bag of muffins tied shut with a red ribbon.

Hank tipped the last drops into the radiator and handed Brendan the can. They got into the car, clouded now with the eye-smarting fumes of Grandfather's pipe. Hank sat poised with his hand on the ignition and waited for Catherine to finish talking. She was telling Grandfather that their house in Plum needed paint but there was no chance of painting it before winter set in, what with all that needed to be done at the store.

"The old dame will need convincing about the paint," said Hank, referring to their landlady-to-be, a woman named Ottmann who lived with her retarded son in a small house facing theirs across Corn Street.

"Yes, I know what you mean," said Catherine. "She has that nasty way of pursing her lips whenever you bring up money."

Hank nodded, switched on the ignition and stomped with both feet on the starter and the accelerator. The engine clattered, the exhaust pipes thundered like guns and the car moved off down the highway.

It had been Aunt Nancy's idea, seconded by Catherine, to stop and see Uncle Herman, who years ago had become attached to the family by marriage, but not very securely. They assumed that Grandfather and Uncle Herman would enjoy renewing their neglected relationship as brothers-in-law. Turning in at his driveway near the town of Flensboro, they saw rusty machinery scattered across his yard, they saw the crumbling foundation and swayback roofline of his unpainted house, they saw Uncle Herman himself standing in

the barnyard to receive them. He wore a shiny black suit, an uncertain smile, and a pair of glasses with a diagonal crack across the right lens. He was an earth-colored man, his complexion and eyelashes the color of sand, his hands, neck and ears burned a permanent bronze, his eyes green as agates. He was about fifty-five and handsome in a weatherbeaten way. Being shy, he avoided looking through the windshield as the DeSoto came toward him; he kept his eyes on the radiator cap. When the car came to a halt, he opened Catherine's door and said without preamble, "Could we drive into town? I'd like to buy you all the dollar dinner at the St. Charles Hotel."

"We weren't expecting a meal, Uncle Herman. We're only stopping to say hello—it's our moving day."

"So Aunt Nancy wrote." He took two steps backward and looked meekly at his feet. "I don't want to delay you, but I can't take you into my house—it's a mess. The neighbor lady says I'd be better off trading places with my pigs."

"We'll take him up on the meal," said Grandfather from the back seat. "We went pretty light on breakfast."

"Please get in," said Catherine, making room for him in front.

He did as he was told, pulled the door shut and pointed through the windshield at his barnyard of puddles. "You could make a U-turn there by the chicken coop and head into town. The St. Charles gives you a dandy meal for a dollar on Sundays and holidays."

They had to raise their voices above the noise of shifting gears and clashing pistons:

"The neighbor lady says she'd have had us over for dinner, but she's got company from Iowa."

"Uncle Herman, this is my husband, Hank Foster. I wasn't married when I saw you last."

He shot a quick glance at Hank, then looked out his side window. "How you been, Hank?"

"Just fine. Pleased to meet you." Hank turned onto the highway and picked up speed.

"And that's our son Brendan in back."

Herman didn't look around; he kept his eyes on the ditch going by. "How you been, Brendan?"

"Fine."

"And did you see who else is back there?"

Herman nodded without turning to see. "How you been, Michael?"

"Fit as two fiddles, Herman. How about yourself?"

"Can't complain."

Sitting at a round table in the busy, noisy dining room of the St. Charles Hotel, they ate hamburger steak, fried potatoes, mashed carrots, and pie. Throughout the meal Herman and Grandfather exchanged the memories they held in common, happy and sad. Grandfather's style of reminiscing was exuberant, full of moans of regret and sighs and laughter. Herman's was restrained. Happy, he emitted a whispery chuckle. Sad, he lowered his head and shook it. They brought up names Brendan had heard over and over at family get-togethers in Aunt Nancy's apartment, names printed on the funeral cards the family used as bookmarks in their missals, names mythical to Brendan because he had never seen the flesh they stood for. Margaret was one such name. In 1919 Herman had married Grandfather's youngest sister Margaret, and they had settled down on the farm at the edge of Flensboro. Margaret died of cancer in 1928. Herman, childless, remained alone on the farm, working only hard enough to support himself from harvest to harvest, allowing his yard to become more cluttered by the year, his buildings to become more dilapidated. Except for a field of oats and a field of corn, he had let most of his acreage revert to brush. His livestock, besides chickens, consisted of four or five cows and a family of pigs.

By the time they finished dinner the sky had cleared. The bluffs wore a mantle of sunlight. Leaving Flensboro, Uncle Herman pointed to what might have been the campus of a small college and said it was the State Home School for Boys. "It's bad what goes on there," he told them at the top of his voice. "They try to hush it up, but it gets out anyhow. The guards are rough on the boys. Break their arms sometimes."

"What boys?" Brendan asked. Above the hedge running along the highway, he saw the upper half of the buildings—yellowish brick, tall windows, red-tiled roofs.

"Criminal boys not old enough for the reformatory in St. Cloud," Herman told him. "Eleven to sixteen, they say."

Through a gateway in the hedge Brendan caught a glimpse of the grounds—yellowing elms standing like enormous umbrellas over well-kept lawns, flowers growing beside the doorstep of each building.

"Some years ago there was a killing. I never heard the details—just a killing is all anybody'd say."

Farther along, through a gap of dead hedge, Brendan saw a group of boys working in a garden, supervised by a guard. The boys wore

brown caps and brown shirts. He saw the guard raise a stick as if to strike one of the boys on the head, and he saw the boy throw his arms up to protect himself, then the hedge closed off his view.

"Now this next place coming up is where the lady lives I told you about." This being the third mention of the neighbor lady, Brendan was reminded of the way boys sometimes dropped the names of girls they had crushes on.

"She's got eighty acres in corn and another sixty in barley."

It was a more prosperous farm by far than Herman's. The outbuildings were squared up and freshly painted. The large, pale-green house stood on a knoll commanding a view of the river and the town. Two large horses grazed in a pasture.

Letting Herman out in his yard, they all thanked him for the meal. Catherine said, "Come and see us in Plum."

"Might do."

"You'll find us in the grocery store on the south side of Main Street," Hank told him.

"Why Plum? . . . I have to ask. You're city people."

"That's what I'd like to know," said Grandfather, rolling down his window. "Did you ever hear of the place before?"

"Yeah, heard of it."

"Small town property's a lot cheaper," Hank explained.

"Makes sense. Funny name for a town, I always thought."

2

The village had been named for a grove of wild plum trees which were said to have borne a biennial crop of delectable sweetness, but by the time Brendan and his family arrived the grove was long dead and so were most of the people it had warmed when it was chopped into firewood. The streets were now lined with enormous elms shading the houses of at least fifteen hundred people Brendan and his father didn't know as they stepped outdoors at sunrise on the morning after Labor Day. They slipped out quietly, so as not to waken Catherine and Grandfather. Hank and Catherine had been up until three, arranging furniture and pacifying Grandfather, who kept coming down from his bedroom to ask where he was. Hank hadn't slept at all. He had lain awake worrying about the house; there were salamanders in the dirt cellar, the loose window casements let in flies and drafts and the roof leaked. He worried about the store, which hadn't been properly cleaned for years; trade was down to nothing. He worried about his family; small towns, he'd heard, were hard for city people to fit into.

Brendan, too, was worried. This was the opening day of school and he was leaving the house earlier than necessary in order to walk with his father, afraid that on his own he might get lost.

They stepped down off the front porch. Hank stopped and cocked his ear. "Listen."

Brendan listened. "What?"

"Silence."

After a few seconds they heard the faint barking of a farm dog. A few seconds more and a little breeze came along and rattled the cornstalks in the garden next door.

Hank gave the sky a long, suspicious look. It was much bluer and a lot broader than the sky over Minneapolis. "So this is the famous peace and quiet you hear so much about."

They looked at the small white house across the street where their landlady Mrs. Ottmann lived. They looked up and down the street at the white frame houses with wide gaps of high weeds between them. "It's quiet all right," said Hank, "but what's peaceful about it? It makes me nervous as hell."

Brendan understood. In Minneapolis, where he had been unacquainted with a quarter of a million people, he had never felt so unknown.

Across the street a path led through a vacant lot and up to a railroad embankment that ran behind the Ottmann house and curved off toward the center of town.

Heading for the embankment, they saw a large, bony face smiling out through the Ottmanns' front window. Brendan recoiled, for it resembled monster faces he had seen in movies, the eyebrows wiry and wild over hollow-looking eye sockets, the smile a great gaping mouthful of whatever the monster was having for breakfast.

"That's Rufus," said Hank. "He lives there with his mother."

Brendan shuddered and ran ahead a few steps. Passing through the vacant lot, he saw Mrs. Ottmann watching him from her kitchen doorway. Mother and son had the same dark, deep-set eyes, but only the mother's eyes appeared connected to a brain. Hank waved at her. She flourished a dish towel.

They climbed the embankment and set off along the cinder-buried crossties between the rusty tracks. Raised above the back yards on their left and right, they noticed themselves being noticed by several people breakfasting in their kitchens. Who were these strangers, Brendan imagined them saying, this man moving along at such a swift, tipped-forward pace and wearing a white shirt and red tie, and this boy hurrying to keep up, both of them squinting into the rising red sun?

The tracks ended behind Plum Feed and Seed. They walked around the building and came out on Main Street. Hank pointed to Plum School (two stories, twelve grades) down the street on their left. They turned right, walked past a row of houses where the lawns were groomed more neatly than those on Corn Street, and came to Plum's two-block stretch of storefronts. They stopped and regarded their store from across the street. It stood between the Plum Theater

and Gordy's Pool Hall. The mustard-colored letters—KERMIT'S GROCERY—had partially flaked from the glass.

"Kermit said he'd leave the keys under the mat on the doorstep," Hank said as they crossed over. There was no mat on the doorstep. They went through the narrow passage between the store and the theater and found no mat at the back door either. They returned to the front, and while Hank pondered his next move, Brendan read the decals on the glass of the door. USE RED STAR YEAST. BUY WAR BONDS. CHEW COPENHAGEN. Brendan tried the door. It was unlocked.

They stepped into the rank smell of old meat and festering fruit. Following him through the building, Brendan watched his father confront each disappointment with a nervous nod, as if he had foreseen the worms in the sugar, the rat drinking from the toilet in the basement (the rat and Brendan jumped back at the same instant) and the man sleeping on a bed of flour sacks in the back room.

"Who are you?" Hank touched the man's shoulder. He lay face-up, snoring. He wore a green shirt, black suspenders, a black beard.

"Out!" said Hank.

The man opened his eyes. He brought his hands to his face, buried the tips of his fingers in his beard and slowly scratched. "I work here. I come with the store."

"No, I'm sorry, I won't be hiring help."

He sat up, lazily. "Well . . ." He yawned. He was young, about twenty-five. He had gaunt eyes and a long nose. He wore blue socks with red arrows at the anklebones. No shoes. His black hair was clipped shorter than his beard. "I was Kermit's clerk for eight years and I know the ropes. I don't need much pay. I live with my mother, and we live very frugally." (Hank would tell Catherine later that he had never heard the word "frugally" spoken before.) "I'd never say a word against Kermit, he was a likable boss, but let's face it, he was a failure. Somebody with a thirst like his will never be anything but a failure. Kermit inherited this place from his father ten years ago, and his first day on the job was the high-water mark of his interest in groceries."

Brendan thought it remarkable the way this young man never paused to form his thoughts or choose his words. His voice was melodious, fluid. "In the ten years it took Kermit to bring his trade to a standstill, he taught himself to appreciate cheaper and cheaper booze. He drank Cutty Sark as recently as 1937, but he dropped

down to a medium-priced rum after that, and last week he was guzzling white wine without a label the day he sent you that postcard saying the keys would be under the doormat."

He reached into his pocket and displayed two keys on a loop of dirty string. He put them back in his pocket. "He's gone off somewhere for the cure, and I wish him luck, but I'm not hopeful. Somewhere in Wisconsin, I guess. A sanitorium where they dry you out for a hundred dollars, he told me."

He stood and glanced about for his shoes. He was shorter than Hank by two or three inches. The back of his shirt was flour white.

"Here." Hank handed him a shoe. "Don't you have a bed at home?"

"Sure, but I wanted to be here when you came in." He yawned. "Isn't it awfully early? Kermit never had me open up till eight." He found his other shoe.

"It's seven thirty. I'm sorry, but there's no work for you here anymore."

"Well . . ." He sat down and put on his shoes. He stood and tucked in his shirt. "The last year or so I've been practically running the place. I'm a steady worker. I've been here since high school. I hardly ever drink. Saturday was the first time in months. We locked up at noon, seeing it was Kermit's last day, and we went out and tied one on together. It's not good for me to drink, the doctor says. My epilepsy." He shook Hank's hand. "My name is Wallace Flint."

Hank had trouble being stern. "I'm strapped, Wallace. I cashed in my life insurance to make this move. My wife will be all the help I need, she's coming in later to help me clean. So let me have the keys."

Wallace ran his thumbs under his suspenders, untwisting them. "What about deliveries? I could at least deliver."

"My boy will deliver. This is Brendan. He has a bike."

Wallace didn't offer his hand, but gave Brendan a searching look, his dark eyes glistening. Under his intent gaze, Brendan wanted to squirm.

"What grade?" Wallace asked.

"Seventh."

"Mmmm, seventh. Your homeroom teacher is Mrs. Roberts, a crabby old bag."

Hank led them out of the back room to the front of the store,

where they found a girl and boy standing near the cash register looking over the meager display of candy. They were older than Brendan. The boy wore a gold sweater with a maroon "P" stitched on the front and a maroon "45" stitched on the arm. The girl wore a green dress and a green ribbon in her hair. They chose a pack of licorice and handed Wallace a nickel. They left, holding hands.

Hank deftly crowded Wallace toward the door, explaining again how penniless he was.

Wallace gave up. He handed over the nickel, then the two keys on the string. "Ask around if you need me. I'm not hard to find." He opened the door, but before going out he turned for a last look at the interior. He reminded Brendan of the haggard and dying exiles of eastern Europe he had seen in newsreels and *Life.* Backing out, but still leaning in, Wallace put his fingertips delicately to his brow and said, "I don't have fits very often, if that's what's worrying you. As long as I get lots of rest I'm fine." He backed slowly outside, and a moment before the door went shut his eyes fell again on Brendan. They were watery eyes. Not tears, Brendan felt sure, nor the bleariness of fatigue or boredom such as he had often seen in Grandfather's eyes. This was a feverish gleam, suggesting illness.

They watched him go to the curb and look up and down Main Street, saw him wave at someone in a passing car, saw him tip his head to the sky, saw him return to the doorway and sit on the concrete step. Brendan wondered if his father sensed in Wallace the overdramatic manner of an actor.

"You'd better be off to school, Brendan."

No, his father never speculated on people's expressions or mannerisms. He took people for what they said and did and never mind the subtleties. Brendan wished his mother had been here to meet Wallace; she would certainly have had something to say about his stagy movements and his spooky eyes.

Hank turned from the window and gazed at the discouraging interior. After a sleepless night he felt crushed by the toil ahead. Sunlight was falling in the window now, defining more clearly the cobwebs sagging from the ceiling, the dust fuzzing the cereal boxes, the dirt underfoot.

Brendan stepped outside and his father followed, bringing a second nickel out of his pocket and asking Wallace, "Where can we get ourselves a cup of coffee?"

Wallace sprang to his feet. "Next door."

Hank locked the door and said, “Come on.”

On his way to school Brendan looked back to see a very large man unlocking Gordy’s Pool Hall from inside, pushing the door open, leaning forward for a moment as Wallace made the introductions, then shaking Hank’s hand and ushering them in.

3

The moment he set foot in home room, Brendan was offered a stick of gum by a shifty-eyed boy named Dodger Hicks, who had been lying in wait for a friend. Among the twenty-four boys and girls of the seventh grade, Dodger had not even one friend, the parents of Plum having warned their children away from him because his father was a convict, his mother drank, and Dodger himself stole things from stores—crayons, comic books, candy.

Dodger was older and taller than the rest of the seventh grade, having taken nine years of school to get there. A poor reader, he was taunted for what his classmates assumed was stupidity and had spent every recess and noon hour of his life lingering at the edge of a game. His face was dark, his cheekbones prominent. He had the habit of nodding his head when he spoke, and of squinting and showing his long teeth when he listened. His dark hair, which hung unevenly about his ears, he trimmed himself, using a pair of small shears pilfered from art class. As he gave Brendan a stick of grape gum (the off-brand, crumbly gum of wartime) he said he had stolen it that very morning from Kermit's Grocery, the door being unlocked and no one inside.

"That's our store," said Brendan. "My mother and dad bought it."

"No kidding?" asked Dodger. He gave Brendan the rest of the pack.

Mrs. Roberts was a large, white-haired woman with a voice like a rasp and a propensity for threatening and shaming. The students' twenty-four names grated on their ears as she called them out and pointed to their alphabetical places in the room. A girl named Lor-

raine Graham took her place between Brendan Foster and Dodger Hicks.

It was a novelty to change rooms with each class. The day began with arithmetic, which was followed by art, current events, geography and health. At noon Brendan went home to eat with his mother and grandfather. He told them he had a new friend named Dodger. He asked if he could bring him home after school. Catherine said, "Yes, that's fine, but don't wake Grandfather if he's napping."

"Let's see your toys," Dodger said, arriving at Brendan's house after school, and he wasn't satisfied until he had examined every last gameboard and tin soldier. From a large box in a closet he drew out a boomerang—a beautifully curved piece of laminated wood, thick at the middle and tapered at both ends. It had been a Christmas gift from Brendan's Aunt Mae and Uncle Howard and had never interested Brendan because it returned only to throwers with stronger arms than his. Dodger had never seen a boomerang. "What is it?" He hefted it, turning it over delicately in his hands, obviously pleased by its smooth lines. His fingers were long and sensitive.

"A boomerang. You grab it by one end and throw. It's supposed to come back."

Dodger nodded eagerly. "Let's try it."

"Some other time, when my dad's home. He has to throw it."

"Let me throw it."

"No, you need lots of room."

Dodger pointed out the window. "More room than that?"

Brendan had momentarily forgotten that behind this house lay whole counties of open land. In the city his father had had to take him to a football field to show him how it worked.

"All right, see for yourself." They went downstairs and out the back door.

The field behind the house had undergone its fall plowing. Dodger carried the boomerang to the edge of the furrows, drew back his right arm, kicked up his left foot and accomplished a magnificent throw—all by sheer instinct apparently, for Brendan's only instruction had been to demonstrate the proper grip. The boomerang sailed up and away, spinning as it climbed, and at its apogee—incredibly high and small—it tilted almost vertical as it wheeled around and began its return flight, picking up speed and spinning faster and faster and heading straight for their heads and passing over them as they threw themselves flat and crashing through the

kitchen window. At the sound of breaking glass, Dodger was up and running. He never glanced back or said goodbye.

The noise woke Grandfather, who called from his window upstairs, "Where are we, lad, and what was that noise like a china closet tipping over on its face?" This being Grandfather's second awakening in this unfamiliar house, he was of the opinion—as he had been for a while this morning—that he and his wife and two daughters were lodging in a tourist home en route West, retracing a trip he had made in 1921 to visit relatives. At breakfast it had taken three cups of coffee and a stern word from Catherine to convince him this wasn't a stopover in Billings.

"We live here," Brendan shouted up at him. Then softer: "And my friend broke a window."

"We live here?"

"Plum! Remember?"

Grandfather backed away from the window, smartly rapping his skull with a knuckle—usually a sign that a surge of fresh blood was making a swing through his brain and carrying off his delusions.

While Brendan swept up the glass in the kitchen, Grandfather dressed for dinner. He put on his green necktie and the darker of his two suitcoats. Then he picked his silver hairbrush and handmirror off the dresser and stroked over and over the tuft above his right ear that would never lie flat. Brushing, he thought of his wife. The brush and mirror were her gift to him on their twenty-fifth anniversary. The last year of the Great War, he thought, holding the mirror at several angles—1918. So if she had lived, this past summer would have been their fiftieth—and another great war going on. Their wedding day was June seventh. Or seventeenth, he could never recall. Where did you get money enough for a silver brush and mirror set, Sade?—I've admired this set in the window of Hudson Jewelry and I know it cost a fortune and a half. Her smile was her only answer. But later, after she died, he learned that she had earned the money by sewing and baking for the neighbors when he was out on his railroad runs. His daughter Catherine told him.

Their thirtieth anniversary was their last, 1923. One day that summer he came home from his run to Duluth (he was a brakeman by that time, no more pick-and-shovel work for a man nearly sixty) and Doc Hays was sitting on the front porch of their house on Clinton Avenue. It was hot. Doc was smoking a cigar. He said, "Morning, Mike." "Morning, Doc, don't tell me Sade's heart is fluttering

again." Doc nodded, leaning forward and flicking a big ash over the porch rail. "She's dead, Mike. Died out back in the garden this morning. A neighbor saw her drop." Late June of 1923. Doc said that scattered around her were the radishes and green onions she had picked. Grandfather ran into the house and knelt at the sofa where she lay. She was covered to her shoulders by a blanket. Her face had dark spots. "Father Cullen!" He shouted back toward the front porch. "Call Father Cullen!" Doc came into the room: "He's been here and gone, Mike, I called him first thing. Said he'd be back later to see you."

She was cold. He couldn't get over how cold she was, and this during a heatwave, a stifling, sweaty morning. He backed away from the sofa and flopped into a deep chair. Doc fussed with the body, staightened the hair on her brow, adjusted the blanket. "You want the Moriarity brothers to make the arrangements, Mike?" Grandfather nodded, staring at the body, remembering he still had on his cap, taking it off, his visored brakeman's cap. Doc said, "I'll call Moriaritys," and while he was in the kitchen phoning, Catherine came across the porch and into the living room. Doc had called her before he called the priest, called her at Dayton's, where she clerked in the book department. She had to wait a long time for a streetcar. She and her father embraced. Then Mae, his other daughter, came in from playing somewhere. More embracing. They went and stood by the sofa, weeping freely.

Thirty years married and twenty a widower—Grandfather stroked and stroked his hair. Thirty years building railroad lines, then nearly twenty years as a brakeman. In those years a brakeman was exactly what his title implied. Besides throwing switches in the railyards and keeping tally of the boxcars dropped off and picked up, a brakeman scurried along the tops of the cars, often while they were in motion, to turn the wheels that set the brakes. Treacherous work. He had seen a brakeman killed one icy afternoon in the St. Paul yards. His own freight was pulling out, heading west; he was standing on the rear platform of the caboose and looking off to his left at another freight pulling in. He saw a brakeman standing on a cattle car of the inbound freight. The man wore a long black coat and black mittens. He noticed Grandfather and waved, and then as he turned and was about to leap the gap between cars he slipped. Down he went, striking his head on the coupling and then dropping to the track, and the wheels of the cattle car passed over his legs, or

rather passed through them, for they were cut clean off just below the hip. Grandfather, riding away, signaled his engineer to stop and he jumped from his caboose and ran through the sleet to the other train, which continued to move, wheel after steel wheel rolling over the bloodsoaked pants and coattails. Grandfather pulled the man away. He was out cold, had been knocked out before he hit the ground, thank God. Grandfather waved and shouted but the train continued to crawl through the yard, and when the caboose finally rumbled by, there on the back platform stood the second brakeman looking down in disbelief at his dying partner, whose loss of blood was so lavish it spouted like a fountain from his stumps and he lost his life before he came to.

Ah, the damn trains. The wonderful damn trains.

In this strange house in this strange town named Plum, Grandfather, brushing his hair, heard the whistle of a locomotive. Short toots: crossing ahead, although on Grandfather's trains short toots sometimes meant the baked potatoes were ready. Hauling potatoes out of the Red River Valley, he and his crew always had themselves a baked potato feast. Delicious, huge, tender-skinned russets. He himself would buy the pound of butter in Fargo before they set out, giving half to the engineer and fireman in the locomotive and keeping the other half for himself and his partner in the caboose. The fireman was in charge of the baking; he would set the four potatoes in a covered pan next to the firebox, and when they were ready to eat—somewhere in the hills of Douglas County—the engineer would give five short toots to stop the train and the fireman would get down and set the pan beside the track—having removed two of the potatoes—and then the train would pull slowly ahead and stop again when the caboose reached the pan. Grandfather and his partner would pick it up, roll their potatoes out onto their tin plates, cut them open with their jackknives and cover them with salt and pepper and a quarter pound of butter apiece. Ah, what potatoes. To this day, short toots made Grandfather think of potatoes.

Another toot, this time accompanied by a bell. Grandfather stopped brushing. He heard the chuffing of steam. Noisy locomotives often moved through that part of Grandfather's life that was pure memory, but hardly ever this loud. He put down his brush and mirror and went to his window. Nothing there but farmland, no train. He went down the hallway to the front bedroom, Hank and Catherine's room. He looked down on the small Ottmann house. He

saw an alley behind the house. Or no, not an alley but an embankment. Holy smut, a railroad. And there, drifting slowly into town from the north, emerging from a cornfield where the stalks stood nearly as tall as the letters SOO LINE on the caboose—drifting into town *backward,* of all things—was a train, by God. Caboose, three cars, coal tender, steamer. Another toot. More dinging. Chuff, chuff.

Grandfather took the stairs as fast as he dared and got to the front door in time to see the engineer leaning from his window before the locomotive disappeared behind the Ottmann house. Setting off at a hobbled run, Grandfather tried to recall the names of engineers he had met on the Soo Line; he might know this man. He angled through the Ottmanns' yard and through the vacant lot beside it, thistles and sharp-bladed grass nicking his ankles because he wore slippers and no socks and didn't notice the beaten path. He passed under some trees and came to the embankment. The headlight of the locomotive was moving slowly away from him now, rocking as the train rounded a curve. So Plum had a train after all. Where did it come from and where was it going? And why backwards for God's sake? He climbed the embankment. It was only ten or twelve feet higher than the thistly lot, but the slope was steep and when he reached the top and stood between the rails he felt his heart pounding in his temples and in the hollows above his elbows. He wiped his brow with the heel of his shaky hand.

He heard someone call, "Yoo-hoo." He turned. When Mrs. Ottmann saw him hurry past her kitchen door and scramble up the embankment wearing his suit, tie and slippers, she wondered if the old guy was dotty or in trouble. Now, waving a dish towel, she stood outside, calling like a loon. "Yoo-hoo, be careful of the train." She wore a black dress down to her black shoetops.

Grandfather turned to her and bowed from the waist, and then, straightening up, he put both forefingers to his brow in a double salute—the best he could offer since he had no hatbrim to touch. All his life, women inspired this sort of gallantry in Grandfather. He called to her, "Have no fear, my good woman, I laid track as a boy, and I have been around trains since 1881, when Aberdeen, South Dakota, was nothing but a city of tents. I was brakeman on freights much bigger than this puny puddle-jumper." He gestured down the empty track, the locomotive having backed around the curve and disappeared. "Now if you'll please excuse me, I wish to speak to the crew."

Grandfather was hot. He took off his suitcoat, hung it over his arm, turned and waved again at Mrs. Ottmann, his baggy shirt-sleeve fluttering. He hurried along the oily cinders of the roadbed thinking, Imagine telling me to be careful of trains, as if I didn't know the dangers of walking in the right-of-way. He remembered 1925 and being on the train that struck a man around two o'clock in the morning and carried him on the cowcatcher, dead as a stovebolt, till dawn. That was on the run from Minneapolis to Brookings. At dawn a depot agent in South Dakota saw the body as the train sped by and he telegraphed the crew. The train stopped on a hilltop and a sheriff and a coroner showed up. From his stiffness and the address in his wallet they figured the dead man, who was dressed like a farmer, had been riding the ledge under the headlight for five hours, and was 160 miles from home. He belonged back in Carver County, Minnesota.

Some months later when Grandfather was laying over in Carver County he inquired about the dead man, met one of the dead man's cousins in a saloon, in fact, and learned that the man had been out on the tracks that night searching for a stray bull, that he had died a week short of his sixtieth birthday and that as a dead man he had traveled nearly five times as far as he had while alive. He had once been to St. Paul, according to the cousin, and he often spoke of crossing a state line some day just to see what it felt like, but he never did. The cousin said it took some of the edge off everybody's sadness to think that if he hadn't crossed a state line before he died at least he crossed one before he was cold. The cousin insisted that Grandfather meet the widow and took him out to the farm. The widow was a husky, friendly woman with a grown son to help her carry on. She served her visitors a meal. She, too, spoke of the solace of knowing her husband had crossed a state line, and Grandfather wondered if the whole family was a little bit cracked. "Actually, he crossed *two* state lines," Grandfather told her, "because that run we were on cuts through a corner of North Dakota before it gets into South Dakota." Leaving with the cousin after the meal, he bowed out the door with a flourish, kissing the widow's hand and feeling gallant and false. It wasn't true that the line cut through a corner of North Dakota, and he wouldn't have said it if it didn't seem to mean a lot to the family.

Panting, pulling at his tight necktie, Grandfather hurried along the embankment and came to an intersection where cars were cross-

ing. He stopped traffic by raising his hands palm-flat to the drivers. Somebody honked. Somebody said, "Watch it, Pop, you could get flattened that way," and another voice, because he looked so bedraggled in the heat, called out, "Sir, are you all right?" This being a woman's voice, he turned in the direction of her car and without slowing down but with a grand sweep of his arm threw her a kiss.

Rounding the curve, he came face to face with the standing locomotive. It seemed to float on the hissing clouds of steam billowing out from its underbelly and obscuring the wheels. He passed through the steam, squinting and covering his ears. Gripping the handrail, he struggled up the steps to the cab. He grabbed the startled engineer by the shoulder and shook him. "Michael McMahon," he shouted, "brakeman on the Milwaukee Road through the teens and most of the twenties. Charter member of the Brotherhood of Railroad Trainmen."

The racket from the boiler was deafening and he couldn't hear what the red-faced engineer replied, but it must have been a warning or a curse, judging by his scowl.

Grandfather turned to the fireman, who looked friendlier. "Michael McMahon, brakeman on the Milwaukee Road. Why did you come to town backward?"

The fireman, smiling, took off his sooty glove and laid a brotherly hand on Grandfather's shoulder. He gently turned him around and guided him down the steps.

"Where does this spur lead to?" Grandfather spoke into the fireman's ear.

"It stops here in Plum." The fireman helped him off the last high step and pointed to where the track ended—a pile of ties serving as a buffer a few yards beyond the caboose.

Grandfather shook his head in disapproval: "No through train? I knew this was a no-account village. Where do you come from?"

"Winona."

"You live in Winona?"

The fireman nodded. He lifted his cap and drew his sleeve across his hot brow.

"And the engineer? Does he live in Winona?"

"Right."

"And both brakemen?"

"We make this run with just one brakeman. Yeah, he lives in Winona."

"Why backward?"

The man pointed again at the buffer of ties. "No turntable in Plum, no siding. If we come to town backward we can go home frontward. Sometimes we do it the other way around—leave Winona frontward and go home backward."

"Christ almighty, frontward, one day, backward the next—a hell of a way to run a railroad." He looked at the boxcar, the grain car, the empty cattle car. "What's your freight?"

"That there." The fireman pointed to the boxcar. "That's half a carload of feed."

"What's in the grain car?"

"We picked up a carload of oats in Pinburg." He gripped the handrail and swung himself up to the bottom step.

"Pinburg?" called Grandfather.

"Pinburg's about six miles down the track."

"You coming back tomorrow?"

"No, just once a week. Tuesdays." The fireman returned to his fire.

Taking out his handkerchief and wiping his throat, Grandfather walked past the open door of the boxcar and saw a man unloading it from the other side, wheeling large bags of something down a ramp and into the back door of Plum Feed and Seed. He passed the grain car and the empty cattle car and came to the caboose. He climbed aboard the front platform. Both doors were open and he could see through the caboose and out the other end. "Coming aboard," he called as he stepped inside so as not to startle the brakeman the way he had startled the engineer. The brakeman wasn't in the caboose. Grandfather hung his suitcoat on a peg and inspected the brakeman's tools—lanterns, oil cans, pry-bars. He looked at the papers on the brakeman's desk—timetables, bills of lading. He climbed up to the brakeman's high seat in the dusty window bay and sank into the dusty cushions. He took three dusty breaths and fell asleep.

Twenty minutes later, at the blast of the whistle, Grandfather began the strenuous work, for the third time that day, of collecting his wits. He had collected only a very few when the train began to move, bell ringing, whistle tooting, caboose rocking. He let himself down from the high seat and saw that he was alone (the brakeman was riding home in the locomotive), and although the caboose was unfamiliar and he couldn't remember which run he was making, he did recognize his coat hanging from a peg, so he assumed he was where he belonged.

Bracing himself left and right against the tilt, he made his way

onto the rear platform, where the back yards of Plum passed slowly under his gaze. He waved at the motorists at the intersection. He waved at a man in coveralls who was kneeling in a garden pulling carrots. He waved at two women standing near the embankment, and both of them waved back—frantically, for they were Catherine and Mrs. Ottmann. Catherine, on her way home from the store to prepare dinner, had been detained by Mrs. Ottmann, who had barely begun tattling on Grandfather when they saw him go by on the outbound freight, his silky hair awry in the sun. He wore a grin of blissful mischief, and as he disappeared around a curve in the tall corn he threw Catherine a kiss.

In bed that night Catherine asked, "What will we do with him, Hank? How will we keep him out of trouble while we're at the store?" In the DeSoto she had raced the train to Pinburg, where she and the crew removed Grandfather from the caboose.

An enormous yawn from Hank, then: "Maybe we should bring him to work with us. Find him a comfortable chair."

"But he couldn't sit there all day. Where would he take his nap?"

"You could take him home in the afternoon. There's sure not enough to keep us both busy once we get the place cleaned up. I think we bought a tomb."

"Don't say that, Hank. It won't be long before we'll need all the help we can get. I can feel it."

Silence.

"You feel it too, don't you? The business we'll have?"

Hank snored softly.

Catherine lay awake for a long time. She heard the beginning of a soft drizzle of rain, and then she heard the beginning of a puddle on the bedroom floor. She got up and looked in at the other bedrooms. Brendan slept silently. Grandfather slept noisily, his nose whistling, his chest rumbling. She went downstairs for the dishpan, which she took to the bedroom to catch the water. She went downstairs again and put the kettle on for tea. She sat at the chipped enameled table at the center of the enormous yellow kitchen (she had not yet unpacked her tablecloths), and as she waited for the water to boil she thought about Wallace Flint.

One look at his quick, dark eyes and you knew he was a man of intelligence and humor. And something else besides. Something painful, like sorrow or desperation. Working together, Catherine and Wallace had laughed a great deal, excited by one another's wit.

She told Hank at supper that it was a stroke of luck, Wallace volunteering to work for nothing more than a meager supply of groceries until they could afford to pay him a wage. Hank's agreement was less than wholehearted. He said Wallace would never be a grocer. She argued in Wallace's behalf: he would help them get acquainted with the villagers. He knew every last person in town, everything about them. Seeing a car go by, he could tell you where it was going and who was driving. Smelling a funny smell, he knew where it came from.

"That's silage," he had explained to her when she inquired about the odor drifting over Main Street. She and Wallace were removing stock from the shelves in preparation for scrubbing and painting.

"What's silage?" she had asked.

"Rotting vegetation—cornstalks and pea vines, for instance. A lot of farmers keep a pile in their yard for feed."

"Feed?"

"Cattle feed."

"It's putrid. It's worse than smelling smoke in the city."

"I agree," Wallace exclaimed. "I'd love to be smelling smoke instead of this rot." He faced out the front window with his hands on his hips. "I despise this town!"

His vehemence cast a temporary cloud over Catherine's hopes. Of all days to be told that Plum was despicable! Coaldust covered everything in the store including the cobwebs. There were rats in the basement. Hank was finding empty wine bottles in the drawers of his desk. Their customers for the day numbered twelve. Their proceeds amounted to $4.36. And as though defying fate, they had gone into debt for new stock, placing an enormous order with a wholesaler named Bob Donaldson from Minneapolis. He had pulled up in front of the store in a 'forty-two Ford, the newest car on Main Street, had spent half an hour in Legget's Grocery and then crossed over to Kermit's. He was a freckled man of about forty-five who smelled of the samples he carried on the road, primarily sage. He was effusive in his greeting. He said he had always believed Plum to be a two-market village waiting for its second good market. He explained that for an order of four hundred dollars or more he would allow Hank and Catherine to delay payment until after their Grand Opening. Hank looked at Catherine, they looked about them at the mess and they decided to shoot the works, sending Bob Donaldson away with a thousand-dollar order.

4

On the second day of school Dodger was distant. Brendan passed him a note by way of Lorraine Graham. The note said, "Boomerang after school?"

Dodger read it and crumpled it. He didn't look in Brendan's direction. Brendan was grieved. He spent arithmetic period (fractions) totalling up the friends he had left behind in the city. They came to seven. During current events (a new death in Belgium, a new Gold Star Mother in Plum) he tried memorizing the names of his classmates as the teacher called on them. He noticed which ones responded with indifference to his uncertain smile, which ones with a sneer of disdain, and which ones—there were two or three—with smiles of their own.

During noon hour as the others hunched against the misty wind and chose teams for softball, he followed Dodger across the wet sand to the swings and told him there was nothing to fear from the broken window. His father had already replaced the glass.

"No kidding?" Dodger squinted, lifting his lip on his unclean teeth. "Didn't you catch heck or nothing?" He looked doubtful. His own errors had always led to punishment, never pardon.

"My dad just said to throw it from out in the field farther. Come back this afternoon and we'll throw it some more." He almost said please.

Dodger examined his face for deceit. Was this a trap? "My dad would have strapped me for breaking that window." Then he added, with relief: "My dad's in prison for taking money from a plumber he used to work for." Then, fearfully: "He had a leather

strap he used to use on me." He gazed far off, scowling thoughtfully, and Brendan respectfully gave him a few moments with his memories before asking:

"Will you come over after school?"

Dodger spoke decisively. "Yep, but we'll go to my house first. I've got something for you."

After school they walked along the alley of puddles behind Main Street. "See that door?" said Brendan, pointing. "That's the back room of our store. And this is our car. We drove this morning because it was raining." The boys saw Wallace Flint standing in the doorway, watching them. Brendan waved, but Wallace did not.

"You know Wallace?"

Dodger nodded.

"Doesn't he give you the creeps?"

Dodger shrugged and changed the subject. "See that door over there? That's the back door of Gordy's Pool Hall. And see that door there? That's the fire exit from the theater. Sometimes it's not shut tight and you can get in and see a free movie."

In the next block Dodger said, "Let's look in here," and led Brendan through the back door of a furniture store. The place was gloomy and smelled of cigars. There seemed to be no one minding the store. They zigzagged through the disorderly display of chairs, tables, lamps, and bedsteads and went out the front door. "Sometimes there's a dead body to look at, but not today."

Brendan was horrified. "In there?"

"Yeah, in a coffin."

Brendan read the sign over the door: KIMBALL'S FURNITURE AND FUNERAL HOME.

They walked several blocks and came to the wide, sagging rooming house on Hay Street where Dodger lived with his mother. Its ash-gray paint was peeling. In the entryway were five mailboxes and the smell of fried onions. "Ma?" he called as they climbed the stairs, but his mother wasn't home. He led Brendan into number six and showed him around the three-room apartment. Brendan saw a hot plate and a toilet but no sink or refrigerator or bathtub. He asked where they took baths, where they kept their food cold. They washed in a basin, Dodger explained, and kept their milk on a windowsill overlooking the blacksmith shop across the alley.

In the sitting room, Dodger opened a drawer of the dresser that stood beside his cot and took out a cap gun fresh from the five and dime, a snub-nosed pistol of heavy steel, a wartime rarity. He said

Brendan could have it. Brendan took it and admired it. The silvery barrel was untarnished, the crosshatching of the grip pleasingly rough to the palm, the trigger stiff. He had outgrown cap guns, but he said thanks.

Dodger nodded, leaning over him, his hand on his shoulder, admiring it himself. "I'll get you some caps for it tomorrow."

Then they went to Brendan's house and took the boomerang out into the plowed field, where Dodger perfected his delivery. Moving about the classroom and schoolyard, Dodger's insecurity made him ungainly and hesitant, but here in the open his movements were swift and certain, and at least three times out of four he sent the boomerang sailing farther than he had yesterday. "Unnnnn," he sighed each time it left his hand. "Yeaaah," he whispered as it curved into its wide arc and started back. Its return was erratic because of the wind, and as they ran this way and that to retrieve it, the heavy soil built up on their shoes and they had to pause every few minutes to pare it away, using the edge of the boomerang as a blade.

Brendan studied Dodger's style. He was throwing it sidearm, with a vigorous snap of his wrist. Brendan tried that method but was only half successful. Although it sailed a good long way, it didn't come back; at the point where it should have made its midair turn it was already falling to earth.

"Maybe you should try it like a discus," said Dodger, demonstrating how a discus thrower uncoils like a spring before letting go. "You get more power that way."

Good advice. Brendan's next throw climbed high into the wind, turned and came back like a shot and stabbed itself into a hummock of wet earth.

"Who taught you to throw a discus?"

Dodger squinted, trying to remember.

"Your dad?"

It came to him: "No, I saw a guy throw one once in a newsreel."

They threw till their arms ached, and they kept on throwing. They couldn't seem to get enough of watching the boomerang turn in the air. By what miracle did something you cast away come back to you? Fire off anything else in life—a bullet, a tantrum, an insult—and there was no hope of retrieving it; you let it go and hoped it did or didn't hurt somebody. But time after time this crooked stick steered itself around to its starting point and gave Brendan a curious sense of consolation, suggesting that not every law of the universe was immutable, that you *could* rethink your impulses. He chose this

afternoon to tell Dodger about certain regrets from his city life, words and actions he wished could be undone. The time he took incense from church and packed it in Grandfather's pipe, causing him to be very sick when he smoked it. The time he went to a friend's birthday party bearing as a gift a tiny toy motorcycle so wonderfully mechanical that he couldn't stand to give it up and stole it back when the party was over and took it home and hid it in his room. The time he bawled and carried on, fearing the move to Plum.

Dodger got the drift. Out and back the boomerang flew as he told Brendan about the day his mother took him to the Winona County Jail to see his father before he was shipped off to prison. "He told me he was being sent up for five years, but he'd be out on parole in less than two, and I said, 'I hope not.' And he wasn't even being mean that day. He was acting pretty nice." Out and back the boomerang flew. "It was that leather strap I was thinking about."

At dusk Catherine drove home from the store with Grandfather, who was now under close surveillance. Hank followed later on foot. Brendan was called in to supper. Dodger accompanied him up onto the back porch, and when Brendan slipped off his muddy shoes so did Dodger.

"Don't you have to go home?"

Dodger said he didn't. He went into the kitchen and said hello to Brendan's mother and was already sitting down at the table when she invited him to eat with them.

Brendan went to wash his hands and face.

"Are you sure you wouldn't like to wash up before you eat?" she asked Dodger.

He said he was sure he wouldn't. He poked a knife into the honey pot and lifted out a gob.

Hank and Grandfather came to the table. "This is Dodger, Brendan's new friend," she told them.

"Are you one of the Brooklyn Dodgers?" asked Grandfather, taking his place at Dodger's right hand and playfully jabbing him in the ribs.

"No," said Dodger, ticklish, squirming, twirling his knife to sever the trailing string of honey.

Hank sat on Dodger's left and said, "Maybe he's the Artful Dodger from—what was that book, Catherine? You aren't a pickpocket, are you, Dodger?"

Dodger's eyes narrowed. How did this man know?

* * *

After the dishes were washed—Grandfather and Brendan drying, Dodger looking on—the Fosters groomed themselves for the priest. That Brendan should wash his face and hands a second time within an hour and change his shirt and comb his hair struck Dodger as ridiculous. Lying on Brendan's bed, he asked, "How come you're going to church at night?"

"We're not. We're just going to the priest's house to register." He took his sixth grade blazer from the closet, hoping Dodger would be impressed with the brass buttons. On the breast pocket was the crest of St. Bonaventure's, where he had been schooled by nuns for six years.

"Register for what?"

"Just register, so the priest knows we're Catholic."

"How come you're Catholic?"

He considered the easy answer—we were born Catholic—but settled on the scholarly one: "The church is one, holy and apostolic." At St. Bonaventure's he had advanced to Book Four of the Catechism.

"It is?"

"Yep."

"Is it true you pray with beads?"

"Yep."

"And tell your sins to a father?"

"Yep."

"And what else?"

"We dip our fingers in holy water." Buttoning his three brass buttons, he led Dodger downstairs.

"I heard you don't eat meat on Friday."

"We don't."

It was a moonless night. Dodger walked with them for a block or so, then angled off toward home. Watching him go, Brendan felt suddenly very grateful for the boomerang instruction. But all he could think to offer Dodger in return was more religious instruction. "And we don't get divorced either," he called after him.

Under a distant streetlight, Dodger turned and considered this for a moment, relieved that his parents hadn't been Catholic and forced to stay together. Then he went on.

"And we don't join the Masons," Brendan shouted.

Approaching the church grounds, the four of them checked their buttons and shifted into a churchly frame of mind, which didn't

mean quite the same thing to any two of them. No one was so taken with the outward forms of Catholicism as Brendan was—the rituals, the candles, the Latin. The nuns had put him through a rigorous course of worship. Processions. Chants. Long silent vigils on his knees before the Blessed Sacrament. But what portion of Brendan's piety was devoted to God? Not very much, he realized, and it was God's fault entirely. God was so evasive, so hard to know. Brendan planned to get better acquainted with God when he was older.

Brendan's religion at twelve was strangely ascetic compared to Grandfather's at eighty. Brendan's was meditative. Grandfather's was social. At Mass Grandfather carried on a kind of restrained dialogue with those around him; he smiled, nodded, winked and whispered. Bored with prayers, he might turn and pick lint off the clothes of strangers. He rose to his feet while others were kneeling. One time at the Consecration he had struck a match to light his pipe.

Church for Brendan's mother was a place to evaluate actions—hers, Brendan's, everybody's. Life was a contest between good and evil, the Church was umpire, and Catherine helped God keep score. In a typical week she acquired a full load of moral questions to ask her confessor: Was I wrong in doing this? Was my family right in thinking that? Like her father, she had a long memory, and if there was nothing close at hand to make judgments about, she would reconstruct a problem from the past. Was Cousin Fred justified in leaving his old and irascible parents alone on the farm and going into the Navy even though he had been declared exempt from the draft? Such were the puzzles she presented to the priest, and to her family later at supper, together with the priest's response. Fred, it turned out, *was* justified, given the Navy's need, if not Fred's.

Hank's faith resided in the marrow of his bones. He never spoke of doctrine or morality. He simply accepted whatever the Church asked him to, and he went about his life accordingly. If he was expected at Mass on August 15 every year to commemorate the Blessed Virgin's disappearance from earth, then he would be there dressed up and on time. He believed, of course, being a practical man, that much of what he believed was unbelievable, but this caused him no misgivings because another of his beliefs was that there was more to life than he could understand, more ways of looking at things than the one afforded him by his human and therefore limited sight. Avoid meat on Ember Days and Fridays, decreed his

Church, and so he did. Register with the priest when you move, and that's why he was leading his family up the dark sidewalk to the front door of Holy Angels Rectory.

The house was dark. Hank, having phoned ahead, rang the doorbell. They waited a long time. They turned and looked across the wide lawn at the church. Behind him, Brendan heard Grandfather's breathing moistly through his wet pipe. There was a sound beyond the door. An inner door opening. A light coming on under the eaves. A key rattling in a lock. The outer door opening. A dark human shape behind the screen.

Hank said, "We're the Fosters."

"Except me," put in Grandfather. "I'm Michael McMahon."

The priest's Roman collar caught the light as he unlatched the screen and held it open, but his face remained in shadow.

Catherine was first to step into the glassed-in porch, which despite the dank weather was oppressively warm and smelled of stale sunshine. The priest led them single file across the inner threshhold and down a dim hallway to his office, which was lit by a glaring light in the ceiling.

"Be seated," he said, standing behind his desk. He was old; the creases around his mouth and eyes were as deep as Grandfather's. He was tall—well over six feet—and nearly bald. His collar was tight to his throat and its square of white moved with his Adam's apple when he spoke. "I'll need your names." From a bookcase he drew out an enormous record book with metal corners. He opened it on his desk. He sat. He dipped his pen and looked at them.

Grandfather said, "I'm Michael McMahon, what's your name?"

"Father O'Day."

"*Father* O'Day? Don't you have a first name?"

The priest closed his eyes. Such impertinence. Opening them, he picked a pair of wire-rimmed glasses off the desk. He ran them up and down his shirt-front, cleaning them. He hooked them over his ears. His ears and nose were freckled. His thin fringe of hair, apparently red in his prime, had faded to an ivory-rose. There was aggression in the jut of his jaw. There was ice in his blue eyes.

"Foster, you say?"

Hank said yes.

"It's a rare thing, moving to Plum, bringing your family. I haven't registered five new families since I came here. The parish grows, but the growth is mainly brides from somewhere else marrying our farm-

ers' sons and then having babies." His voice was husky. It didn't rise and fall but scraped along at the same dull pitch. "How does it happen you're not in the war, Foster?"

"I'm too old by a year and a half."

"Were you in the first one?"

"I was too young."

The priest smoothed the open page with a freckled, sinewy hand. "And your first name?"

"Hank."

"You mean Henry?"

"Yes."

The priest clenched his teeth as he wrote.

"Middle name?"

"Richard."

"Where were you born?"

"Minneapolis."

"What do you mean *Henry*?" said Grandfather. "You mean to say your name is Henry?"

"It was to start with."

"You knew that," said Catherine. She was sitting near the priest on the chair drawn up to the side of the desk. The others were on the couch.

"If I did, I forgot, probably on purpose," said her father. "I never cared for that name. I once had a neighbor named Henry, an unfriendly chap. He kept bees. They always came zinging across the yard like they meant to sting you. Sometimes they did."

"Minneapolis," said the priest, writing it. "What's your business in Plum?"

"I bought Kermit's Grocery."

"Where do you live?"

"We're renting from Mrs. Ottmann, her big house."

The priest nodded. "Good woman, Mrs. Ottmann. Hard to say what will become of her son when she dies. He's feeble-minded, you know."

"Yes."

Grandfather cleared his throat. "My uncle Albert's daughter was feeble-minded." He emptied his pipe into an ashtray. "But then, so was his wife." He opened his tobacco pouch. "And so was Uncle Albert, come to think of it."

The priest's stern eyes came to rest on Grandfather, and the look

the two old men exchanged reminded Brendan of the classroom diversion known as the staredown. But this was more intensely inquiring, like the look between long-lost enemies, one old Irishman measuring himself against another. Measuring what? Facial erosion? Lifespan? Depth of soul? Father O'Day lowered his eyes; Grandfather won.

"And you, Mrs. Foster."

"I'm Catherine."

"With a 'C,' I assume."

"Yes."

" 'K' is an affectation. Middle name?"

"Lynn."

"That's not a saint's name."

"Oh?"

He didn't write it. "Maiden name?"

"McMahon."

He wrote that. "Where were you born?"

"Minneapolis."

This filled the heavy page, which trembled noisily as he turned it.

"When did you get married to Mr. Foster, what year?"

"Nineteen thirty-one."

The priest wrote this, pressing the page flat.

"What's your boy's name?"

Brendan piped up confidently, certain that both his names had belonged to saints: "Brendan Richard, and I was born in Minneapolis."

The pen scratched jerkily across the paper; the characters were sharp and illegible. Upside down the line looked to Brendan like a stem of thorns.

"Does he serve Mass?" Father O'Day asked this of Hank, a twelve-year-old being too insignificant to consult.

"No."

"I'm short of servers. Send him to me for early Mass on Sunday."

Brendan, shy of the limelight, had been afraid of this. An altar was like a stage.

The priest turned to Grandfather. "What's your name?"

"Michael McMahon. Born in November of 'sixty-four, went with the railroad the spring of 'eighty, married Sadie Crocker June of 'ninety-three, had two daughters, Catherine here and Mae. Mae went into hats, but left the hat business when she married a Navy

flier. She lives in Florida and has no children, so the lad here's my only grandchild. His mother had female trouble a few years ago, had the sort of operation that puts a stop to babies."

Catherine blushed.

"I rose as high as conductor once, but I lost that job and went back to brakeman. It might interest you how I lost it."

The priest clapped the book shut, and they all stood.

"Give as much as you can every Sunday," he said, leading them out of the office. "Sunday Masses at eight and ten. Send me the boy at eight. Confessions between two and four on Saturday."

In the hot porch Catherine said, "We're told the Catholics in Plum are at odds with the Protestants." Wallace Flint had said so.

"I've been told that myself. The priest here before me said so."

"Do you find it's true?"

Father O'Day cupped his chin in his hand, meditating. "Mmmmmm, no."

"You're friendly with the Lutheran minister?"

"No, I haven't met him."

"He's new here?"

"No, he was here when I came."

"You're new here?"

"Yes, I've been here only seven years. Go home now, it's late." He unlatched the screen door for them.

Outside, Grandfather turned to speak through the screen. "To make a long story short, I lost my job as conductor because I let my friends ride free. I could have lost all my rights and seniority, but they let me go back to being brakeman. I'm just too damn likable to be treated harshly, is what it amounts to. But I never got the good runs anymore. No way-freights. No passenger runs. Only spurs. Twin Cities to Wells. Twin Cities to River Falls. All the godforsaken places."

The priest latched the screen. "At least your fault was on the side of charity, Mr. McMahon." He switched off the light.

5

Early the next morning, working with Wallace Flint at the produce display, Hank told him about Dodger's visit. Wallace's initial reaction was amusement. "How incongruous," he said, chuckling, imagining the no-good, dimwitted son of a jailbird being the Fosters' first dinner guest.

But when Hank went into the back room and left him alone to pick through the apples, checking for bruises and rot, Wallace quit chuckling and began to smolder, jealous that Dodger should be present where he himself wished to be. For two days now Wallace had been trying with all his might to attach himself to this family from the city. Picturing himself as Hank and Catherine's indispensable confidant and advisor, he had been waiting for an invitation to their house. Hank and Catherine, he sensed, were bleeding hearts, suckers for anyone needy.

In a few minutes the front door opened and Brendan, on his way to school, stepped in to pick up a pack of gum. Unwrapping a stick, he said hello to Wallace, who had found a bad apple and was holding it daintily by the stem.

"I have some advice for you," said Wallace, smirking, dropping the apple into the box at his feet. His glistening eyes were penetrating.

"Yeah?" Brendan stood in the open doorway, ready to run. The school bell was ringing, and he had three minutes to be present in his homeroom desk.

"If you know what's good for you, you'll quit hanging around with Dodger Hicks."

Brendan bristled, sensing that Wallace seldom had an idea that wasn't self-serving.

"If you want to fit into the seventh grade, you can't start out by having Dodger Hicks over to dinner. Hang around with Hicks and nobody else will come near you."

Brendan replied defiantly, "What do you know about it?" and he ran off to school. Being uncivil to Wallace made him feel good. Wallace asked for it with his superior tone, his smug expression. What did Wallace know?

Perhaps quite a lot, he decided later in the morning as he studied the cliques of the seventh grade. The more thought he gave it, the clearer it became that in order to be accepted by his more glamorous classmates he would have to put distance between himself and Dodger.

During noon hour Brendan and Dodger sat suspended on adjacent swings watching a softball game. Sam Romberg punched a single into centerfield, Philip Crowley scored from third and Pearl Peterson and Lorraine Graham jumped up and down and cheered, Pearl holding her carefully curled hair in place. These four made up the inner circle of the seventh grade. Pearl Peterson used lipstick and got nothing but A's. Lorraine Graham carried cigarettes in her purse and had what the music teacher called perfect pitch. Philip Crowley was said by the girls to be cute; his father owned the movie theater. Sam Romberg wore a self-confident expression beyond his years, he excelled at athletics. Brendan sensed that these four, while holding him at bay, were keeping an eye on him, watching to see if he could somehow unlock their trust.

The key, it occurred to him, was his boomerang. Having fascinated Dodger, wouldn't it fascinate others as well? Maybe not Pearl and Lorraine, but surely Philip and Sam? With twenty minutes remaining of the noon hour he ran home for the second time and returned with the boomerang. He carried it across the softball diamond, interrupting the game and for the first time in his life purposely drawing attention to himself. He ran down the long grassy slope to the high school football field. Dodger left the swings and came loping after him. Brendan paused under the goalpost and made sure Sam and Philip and the rest of the boys were watching, and then he unleashed what he hoped would be his mightiest throw. Alas, it was one of his worst. In his eagerness he had forgotten to snap his wrist as Dodger had taught him and the boomerang flew scarcely forty yards before falling to the ground like a stick of firewood. He ran to retrieve it, but was outrun by Dodger, who in a sin-

gle motion of great beauty, like a dancer's, snatched the boomerang off the grass and sent it flying sixty yards at least; sent it out over the far goalpost, out over the edge of the hayfield beyond, and then—a magic moment—he stretched forth his arms and beckoned and the boomerang turned and came back and glided to rest at his feet. A multitude came rushing down the slope. They scuffled for turns. Dodger and Brendan stood aside, watching them experiment with various deliveries. Although the boomerang did now and then return, no one's throw was nearly so grand as Dodger's. The next best throw was Brendan's when he finally stepped in and threw it forty yards out and forty yards back. Everyone cheered. They devised a system for taking turns, Dodger excluded, and they followed the boomerang off the football field and through the standing hay and by the time the schoolbell rang they were clustered in a field of oat-stubble.

Brendan returned to the schoolyard surrounded by new friends. They made a chant of his name. They clapped him on the back. They asked him where he came from and why. From Minneapolis, he said, and that was impressive. Kermit's Grocery, he said, and they made faces. No brothers or sisters, he said, and they thought that very odd. An uncle in the war, he said, and that made up for a lot. He caught glimpses of Dodger at the edge of this crowd, slouching along with a faint smile on his lips, thinking perhaps that by his skill with the boomerang he had won acceptance along with his only friend; but of course he had won nothing of the kind, and Brendan knew it if Dodger didn't.

The extent of Brendan's treachery wasn't clear to Dodger until after school when he began to follow Brendan home and was turned back. Standing under the elm near the swings, Brendan said, "We can't be friends any more."

"We can't? Why not?"

"Because." He chose not to accuse him of being a weight on his rising fortunes. "Just because."

"Because why?" The "why" was drawn out, a whine.

"Because my folks said so." Brendan averted his eyes, avoiding Dodger's squint. Brendan wasn't good at lying.

But good enough, apparently, to convince Dodger, for whom this rejection was nothing new. "Who cares?" he said, walking away from the swings and out of Brendan's life with the same surprising swiftness and grace with which he had mastered the boomerang.

6

With paint and soap and the help of Wallace Flint, Hank and Catherine gradually overcame the grime and gloom of Kermit's Grocery. They scoured and oiled the wooden floor and improved the lighting. They whitewashed and stocked the shelves and above the shelving they painted the walls tan and the high ceiling white. They acquired two cats, a gray and a yellow, to hunt in the basement. With a razor blade Hank peeled Kermit's name from the front window and hired a signpainter to letter his own: HANK'S MARKET.

A round, bald man named Stan Kimball, who came in every day to buy six cigars, became the Fosters' self-appointed mentor. Stan Kimball was Plum's undertaker and furniture merchant. Averaging only two funerals a month, he spent his days popping in and out of stores, inquiring into each proprietor's personal life as well as his business methods. He left his furniture display room unattended for hours at a time; if you wanted to buy furniture you tracked him down. It was usually late morning when he showed up at the market, lit a cigar, and let flow a stream of gossip and economic advice.

"You'll want to put on a big Grand Opening sale," he insisted. "You'll want to flood this town with circulars offering prices these tightwads can't resist. Ask your wholesaler to try and get you a shipment of something there's a shortage of—candy or coffee or detergent—and hold a drawing every hour and give it away like dirt. You'll have customers coming in here like pigs to a trough."

Although Stan Kimball had a few unclean habits which kept Catherine from being as fond of him as Hank was (his talk was peppered

with vulgarities and he drooled juice from his spongy, malodorous cigars), she found his frankness disarming:

"This town will support your store just fine, once you get established, don't worry about that, but if you've got social aspirations, don't get your hopes up. There's two kinds of people living in Plum, the newcomers and the native born. My wife and I have been here seventeen years and we're still outsiders—except my wife's one close friend happens to be the mayor's wife, which makes Plum heaven on earth in my wife's opinion, never mind that the mayor's wife is a baboon."

Catherine was the first to sense that Stan Kimball did not care for Wallace Flint. She saw his eyes grow wary whenever they fell on Wallace. Before long she realized that Wallace was about the only person in town that Kimball didn't talk about behind his back. Only once did he bring up Wallace when Wallace wasn't present; Grand Opening was drawing near and Kimball was conducting an inspection tour:

"Your produce looks a little shopworn, Hank. Don't you refrigerate it overnight?"

"I can only cram so much in the compartments under the meat cooler."

"Then you'll have to build a walk-in cooler. There's space for one in the back room."

Hank nodded. "Someday, I suppose."

"Not someday. Do it soon. You'll get a jump on your competition across the street. Legget's never been known for good produce."

"Where would I get the money?"

"You could get rid of your clerk and save his wages."

"Wouldn't help much. Wallace works for next to nothing."

"That's more than he's worth."

One of Wallace's favorite topics was religion, especially Catherine's, which he teased her about. "You Christians have this ridiculous system of putting everything in categories. The Ten Commandments. The Seven Deadly Sins."

"Categories make sense out of things," Catherine replied.

"The Six Corporal Works of Mercy," he said. "Or is it five?"

Brendan was present for this exchange. Coming from school, he had found his parents and Wallace in the back room, Catherine brewing coffee on a hotplate, Hank sorting through window posters

he had found in the basement, most of them still tightly curled in their mailing tubes, bargains from Kermit's Grand Opening of several years before and never displayed by Kermit.

"I've seen the Catholic Catechism." Wallace went on. " 'Who made me? God made me.' 'What are the two kinds of ignorance? The two kinds of ignorance are vincible and invincible.' " His smile was crooked and supercilious, and Brendan hated him for it. "You can't say there are two kinds of ignorance, Catherine, like two kinds of sugar—white and brown."

"Of course you can," she said brightly, pleased to have found a villager with a philosophical turn of mind. She handed him a cup of coffee. "Think of it like the night sky, Wallace. The Big Dipper. It's nothing but a few unrelated stars until somebody sees the pattern and gives it a name. Seeing the pattern in stars is like seeing the pattern in human actions."

She looked to Hank for corroboration, but Hank only smiled, content to let her handle faith and morals because she did it so well, leaving him free for other things.

"When you group stars and give them names, they're easier to understand," she continued. "Does anybody in this town even look at the stars?"

"I do," said Wallace.

"I do," said Brendan, competing.

"And your categories of life after death, Catherine. Hell and limbo and purgatory and heaven. They're straight out of fairy tales."

She turned her back on him, pouring coffee for Hank.

"Do Lutherans go to heaven, Catherine?" Wallace asked.

"I don't know who's in heaven and who isn't. God knows."

"But you must have a theory about it. You've got a theory about everything else. Hank, what do you think?"

"About what?" Hank was rerolling posters, taking out the curl.

"Can a Lutheran go to heaven?"

"It's fine with me."

They fell silent for a few moments. Catherine sat down on an apple box and blew on her coffee. She had spent most of the day peeling old paint from the wall behind the meat case. She wore an old blue smock, patched and faded. On her head she had tied a blue kerchief. In her forlock Brendan noticed for the first time a glint of gray.

"And what about atheists like me, Catherine? I suppose my goose is already cooked."

"Nobody knows who's in hell Wallace. God knows."

"What does God know? Does God know there's so much religious hate in this town that nobody deserves to be saved? Holy Angels Catholic and Emmanual Lutheran—they compete for places on the village council and the school board and they bury their dead on opposite sides of the cemetery."

Another silence. His expression changed from sardonic to sour to hostile. "I'll tell you who's in hell, Catherine. We all are. Because Plum is hell."

7

"Did you notice, lad, that poor wretch has done nothing since Labor Day but stare out the window of that crackerbox of a house over there?"

It was a scorching afternoon. Grandfather and Brendan had moved out onto the front porch for a breath of air. Brendan, sitting on the steps, was applying postage stamps to a stack of Grand Opening circulars, which would go out tomorrow on the rural-delivery routes. Stacked in the kitchen were four hundred additional circulars to be distributed door to door through the village. Brendan and Wallace would do that tomorrow after school. The three-day Grand Opening was to begin the following day.

"Hell of a way to spend your life, staring out a window like that."

Grandfather, just up from his nap, sat in his shirt and tie, smoking, perspiring and concentrating on the face across the street. He felt a strong need for diversion. Ever since boarding the train for Pinburg, he had been forbidden to leave the house on his own. Most days after his nap, Catherine accompanied him downtown, where he gave the market a brief inspection and then went next door to Gordy's Pool Hall and sat through the late afternoon under Gordy's watchful eye, nursing a beer and visiting with the other idlers; but today Catherine was too busy to pick him up and Brendan had come straight home from school to make sure he didn't wander. Sickening, thought Grandfather, to be a prisoner in your own house. Depressing to be put in the care of a twelve-year-old. No fault of the lad, of course. He was a fine young lad and the only grandchild but he never had much to say. Too much like his father in that regard—a listener, not a talker. And no great shakes as a listener, come to

think of it. Ah, well, just so the war ended before the lad came of age and he grew up happy and healthy and found himself a pretty lass to carry on the good Irish line and didn't get her with child before the wedding.

"What did you tell me is the matter with that poor wretch?"

Brendan, tearing a sheet of stamps into strips, explained, "He's a moron."

"How do you know?"

"Everybody says so. Father O'Day says so."

"Father O'Day, now there is a case for you. A man off in his own world somewhere. The only time he speaks to you is from the pulpit, and then it's endless sermons you can't make head or tail of. How would a man like that know a moron from a motorcycle?"

"You've seen Rufus in the store, haven't you, standing there like a moron?"

In order to go about her shopping unencumbered by Rufus, who couldn't turn a corner without being steered, Mrs. Ottmann sometimes deposited him in Gordy's Pool Hall or in Hank's Market. She would look in at the pool hall first because there Rufus could sit on one of the chairs near the card table, as Grandfather did, but if her card-playing son Orville was not there she would lead Rufus next door to the grocery store and place him in the care of Hank and Catherine.

Not that Rufus needed care. He was content to stand endlessly at the full-length window of the front door, looking out as though enchanted, his hands clasped behind him, his eyes directed vaguely at the people who passed on the street, his face locked in its customary grin. When someone entered or left the store, Rufus shuffled backward and allowed himself to be pressed for a moment between the plate glass in front of him and the glassine doors of the cookie display behind him. Then as the door went shut he shuffled forward, keeping his nose about six inches from the glass. Brendan noticed that most of the customers ignored Rufus as they entered the store—perhaps in a village as small as Plum the ordinary population didn't outnumber the odd by enough to make the latter seem rare—while a few gave him a fleeting smile.

Brendan wished he could do one or the other, ignore Rufus or smile at him, but he could do neither. When as an exercise in good will he tried smiling at Rufus through the plate glass, he found that he couldn't force himself to look upon the horrible hollowness of those eyes for more than a split second; and conversely when he tried

to put Rufus out of his mind, he couldn't shake the haunting sense of his presence until Mrs. Ottmann came and took him away. Movies set in the desert or on the polar icecap triggered a similar vague terror in Brendan, a fear of any vast emptiness.

A week ago his aversion to Rufus had led Brendan to commit what the nuns at St. Bonaventure's would have called a shameful sin of omission. It had been very warm, like today. Brendan had propped open the front door of the market for a breath of air and Rufus, apparently thinking it was his sign to leave, went walking off down the street. Brendan saw his duty, but he couldn't do it. The very thought of running after Rufus and taking his hand and bringing him back made Brendan shudder. So he continued stocking shelves, assuring himself that when you were only twelve you weren't expected to be your brother's keeper, particularly if your brother was an imbecile going on forty. After a half hour of trying not to imagine Rufus stepping in front of a speeding car, he decided he'd better tell his father, nonchalantly, that he noticed Rufus was gone. But before he said anything, Stan Kimball showed up leading Rufus by the hand. Stan had found him sleeping on a mattress in his display window.

"You can never be sure about morons," said Grandfather, perspiring on the porch. "Some of them play the dolt for money. I've known of cases."

Brendan paused in his work, holding a strip of stamps over the moist sponge in the saucer. He had stamped two hundred circulars, and had a hundred to go. "What do you mean?"

"I mean they aren't always as dumb as they look." Grandfather pressed his thumb on the hot coals of his pipe, a habit which had long ago burned the pad of his thumb nerveless. "I'd like to take the measure of that boy's thickness. He might be playing the dolt for money. My cousin Albert was a case like that. Albert was no great shakes as a thinker but he was nowhere near as dense as the woman he married. Flo was her name. Flo was so dumb she didn't know if Christ was crucified or shot by the Indians. They had a daughter. Flo was the daughter's name, too. She was dumber than her father and mother put together, and she had to be taken away and put in an asylum for the feeble-minded."

An old story. Brendan went back to his circulars.

"Well, it so happened that Albert and his wife would go and visit their daughter at the asylum and eat a meal with her now and then, and they couldn't get over how good the food was. So pretty soon

Flo the mother started to get dumber and dumber, if such a thing was possible, until she herself was put in the asylum. I knew, if nobody else did, that she was aiming to be taken care of by the State so she could get in on all that good food. See, lad, she was playing the dolt for money. Then wouldn't you know, when she and her daughter had been living in the asylum for a while, Albert himself went sort of mental. One day in December he started up his tractor and tried planting himself ten acres of corn in a field covered with snow. And you know why?"

"He wanted to live in the asylum, too."

"Right you are, lad, right as rain. But he wasn't playing the dolt for money, you see. Poor Albert was playing the dolt for companionship—he was lonesome as hell. But it didn't pan out the way he wanted. The State never took him in. He lived out his life on that farm, getting by."

Grandfather was silent for a long time, then he stood up, laid aside his pipe and straightened his tie. "Come along, we'll go over there and take the measure of that boy's thickness. Bring one of your handbills."

Brendan shuddered at the thought of being enclosed with Rufus in his tiny house.

"I can't, I've got all these stacks to do before supper."

"Then I'll go myself." He picked up an unstamped circular. "I'll be back shortly."

Rufus Ottmann, seeing Grandfather approach the house, broadened his grin. Grandfather nodded at him curtly as he passed in front of the window and stepped up to the screen door, which was latched. He stood back and made beckoning motions with the circular, but Rufus remained in his chair by the window, grinning. Grandfather went over to the window and said through the glass, "Get your mother," but Rufus stayed put. Grandfather pressed his face to the glass, trying to see deeper into the house, and he rapped on the window frame. At this, Rufus rose from his chair and pressed his face to the inside of the glass, centering his nose on Grandfather's. His smile was gay and toothless, his nostrils cavernous and hairy. As Grandfather moved from side to side to see around him, he could hear Rufus's throaty noises of delight as he, too, moved from side to side to block the view.

Mrs. Ottmann appeared behind her son, looking pleased, as though she and Rufus had been hoping for just such a playmate

as Grandfather. She unlocked the screen and stood in the doorway with a dust mop in her hand. "What is it, Mr. McMahon?"

"It's the Grand Opening of Hank and Catherine's store, my dear woman, and they've got more bargains than this one-horse town deserves. Here, see for yourself if they aren't giving you a ring of bologna for nineteen cents, two cents below cost."

She reached for the circular, but he withheld it. It was his ticket indoors.

"Do you mind if I come in out of the heat for a minute? I've been wanting to meet your son."

Now she looked skeptical instead of pleased. Her face didn't say welcome. She was thinking of the old gentleman's train ride of three weeks ago, how quirky he could be.

"Coarse ground or fine, take your pick, nineteen cents a ring. This handbill is full of bargains and nobody else in town has seen it yet. You're the first."

A frugal woman, she couldn't resist a man whose talk was so full of reasonable bologna. "Come in." She held open the door. "You can have a snack with Rufus."

In the tiny front room she directed him to sit on a chair facing Rufus across a little table. Rufus resumed his accustomed place, a rocker with high wooden arms and a leather seat and back. On her way to the kitchen, Mrs. Ottmann said, "Will you take a cracker with your milk?"

"I will indeed," said Grandfather, "and thank you so very much."

In a minute she was back with a tray, which she set on the table. Rufus's milk was in a heavy unspillable mug, Grandfather's in a small glass, half-filled. On a plate were four saltine crackers.

"Mr. McMahon, what's your Christian name, if I may ask?" She stood beside Rufus's rocker.

"Indeed, why shouldn't you ask? My Christian name is Michael, after the archangel who protects us against the malice and snares of the devil."

"Rufus, this is Michael."

Arduously gumming a small bite of cracker, Rufus moved his wide jaw like a horse, his cheek muscles bulging, his eyes clamped on Grandfather, who had been so much fun at the window. Grandfather could see the family resemblance. The old woman had the wide nostrils and deep eyes of her son, but not his coarseness. She looked refined. She had once been pretty.

He felt the Ottmanns waiting for him to speak. He said, "I can see he's a true idiot."

She was outraged: "I beg your pardon!"

"No playacting in that boy, he's dense as a rock."

"He's not dense, Mr. McMahon."

"Not?"

"No."

"The priest says."

"Never mind the priest, Rufus is not dense."

"What is he then?"

"Happy."

Grandfather leaned forward. "How long has he been happy like this?"

"He was born happy."

"Does he talk?"

"Of course. Rufus, say hello to Michael."

There was a quick shift in Rufus's eyes as though a thought had flickered behind them and vanished. The smile remained.

"How old is he?"

"Five."

"Go on."

"He's been five for over thirty years. It's what he wants. He's decided he's very happy to be five."

Grandfather nibbled his cracker. He said, "Do you have any ice cream?"

"No."

"Vanilla's sixteen cents a pint at Hank's Market." He opened the circular to show her. He read on: fruit, cereal, spices, flour. He folded the circular and handed it to Mrs. Ottmann. He stood up and said, "Thank you very much for your hospitality."

"You haven't finished your milk."

He patted her hand. "The cracker was very filling, thank you indeed."

"Will you come again and be company for Rufus?"

"Well . . ." Grandfather was rarely stumped for an answer.

"Do you like celery soup? I'm making celery soup today."

"I can smell it."

"Do you like celery soup?"

"When it's creamy. Is it creamy?"

"I can make it creamy."

"Make it creamy, Mrs. Ottman, and I'll come and have a bowl."

"Rufus would be pleased." She followed him to the door. "He has no playmates, you see. Five-year-olds are ideal but they grow to be six and seven and then they make fun of him. And most of the old men at the poor farm are no better. We take cookies out to the poor farm, where we once found an old man slipping back to the age of five and Rufus struck up a great friendship with him, but the next time we went out they didn't get along at all because the old man couldn't stay five. Old men keep slipping back to four and three and set bad examples for Rufus. When they're four and three they sometimes muss themselves."

"Goodbye, Mrs. Ottmann, thanks a million for the snack."

As he crossed the street, it flashed into Grandfather's mind that the more circulars he could snitch from Brendan the more households he might investigate in this odd little town. He climbed the steps onto the porch and sank into his chair. He slowly filled his pipe, lit it and puffed.

"Well?" said Brendan.

"Hundred percent."

8

After school the next day, Brendan went out with Wallace Flint to cover the village with circulars.

"That's the McDowell house you've just been to," Wallace called from his side of the street. "Next is the Newlanders'. Over here I've got the Lingles coming up next, and then the Underwoods." Thus Brendan learned to associate the surnames of Plum not with faces, but with front doors, front porches, and dogs. Youngren, Simpson, Howell—screen door, glass door, blistered wooden door. Sandberg, O'Brien—poodle, collie.

At several houses they were met by women tending their doorways like sentries, expecting the paperboy with the *Rochester Post-Bulletin* and surprised that they should be handed a red and black circular:

GRAND OPENING
HANK'S MARKET
FORMERLY KERMIT'S GROCERY
THURSDAY, FRIDAY, SATURDAY
ALL FRESH STOCK
DRAWING EACH HOUR FOR FREE MERCHANDISE

Wallace was struck by the great interest these housewives showed in the bargains. Having worked nearly three weeks with Catherine and Hank, Wallace shared their pride in the refurbished store, but he never for a minute believed that their Grand Opening would be anything but a flop. In Wallace's experience, aspiration came to

nothing. Success, on those rare occasions when it seemed to exist, was merely a prelude to failure. Hadn't Wallace's own success as a straight-A student in high school led to his dead-end life as a grocery clerk? Hadn't his teenage dreams of living in a city and moving in a circle of smart, sardonic friends vanished at graduation? Now at twenty-five he still half-regretted not enrolling in the state college in Winona when he'd had the chance. His high school teachers, speaking of scholarships, had encouraged him to do so, but he was terrified at the prospect of having seizures among strangers and was relieved when his mother had stepped in and made plain to the teachers (as for years she had made plain to Wallace) that for an epileptic there was no place like home.

Hank's Market, then, would fail because hopes were invariably dashed, and it would fail for other, more practical reasons. Hank's inexperience was appalling. Hank had never so much as candled an egg until Wallace showed him how. Hank didn't know debits from credits until Stan Kimball the undertaker spent an entire afternoon with him, setting up his books. Catherine's flaw was her city background. Talk to her five minutes and you knew she'd never last in Plum. As a misfit she would eventually implore her husband to move away, and with the store floundering they would have no reason to stay.

Brendan, approaching the gray rooming house on Hay Street, was tempted to leave a handful of circulars inside the front door rather than risk meeting Dodger in the doorway of his apartment. For nearly three weeks he had been avoiding Dodger in school, taking care that they shouldn't come face to face. While Dodger never approached him, he glanced at him a hundred times a day. Even looking the other way, Brendan felt the glances, and they made his face prickle with shame.

He pushed open the door. Cooking smells mingled in the entryway. He looked up the stairs. Seeing the door to number six closed, he decided he'd be safe dropping a circular at each doormat, four downstairs, four up. When he reached number six at the head of the stairs the door opened and Dodger, smiling, said, "Hi, did you come for your caps?"

"No, I'm delivering these." He handed Dodger a circular.

"The dime store's out of caps. A shortage because of the war."

"That's okay, I can wait." He hurried down the steps.

"Is there other stuff I can get you instead?"

"No, that's okay, Dodger. So long."

"How about marbles? I seen you guys playing marbles in the lumber yard."

"No, thanks."

Brendan slipped out the door. Caps. Marbles. Was it Dodger's purpose to pile more shame on him than he already felt?

Wallace stood out in front, having crossed the street while Brendan was inside. "It's time for us to change sides again," he told him.

"How come we're always changing," Brendan asked, obediently heading for the other side.

"Because the sun isn't good for my skin. This side's got more shade."

Wallace, whose dark, bearded face was unaffected by sunlight, was setting Brendan up for dogs. Until this afternoon Wallace had not realized how intensely he despised Brendan. He felt a thrill of satisfaction each time Brendan was set upon, particularly by the larger dogs that nearly knocked him to the ground. It was a hatred born of jealousy. Brendan had everything that Wallace at that age had been denied. Perfect health. A living, breathing father. A witty, attractive mother. In the next block, on Brendan's side, lived an irritable black Lab and a slobbering Saint Bernard.

Meanwhile the market stood ready. After three weeks of toil there was little to do but wait for the Opening tomorrow. Catherine, staring out the front window, sensed Hank's anxiety. All day he had been busying himself with small, unnecessary chores while speaking scarcely a word. At this moment, he was kneeling behind the meat case, tinkering with the refrigeration motor, trying to make it run more quietly. Catherine was annoyed by his reticence. She needed to talk. To dissipate her nervous energy, she had spent the afternoon dusting shelves—or rather interrupting her dusting to run errands. She had gone home and driven Grandfather downtown, she had gone to the post office for the afternoon mail, she had gone to the drugstore to buy a birthday card for her sister Mae. Now it was four thirty, the dusting was done, all errands were run, and very little of her energy was expended. As she gazed at the storefronts across the street, she felt an acute longing for her sister.

They had not been especially fond of one another as girls—Mae was eight years younger than Catherine—but as adults they had become great friends. Their afternoons together in downtown Minne-

apolis became a weekly ritual; after shopping and seeing a movie they squandered an hour or more over ice cream at Cellini's on Hennepin Avenue. That was before Mae married Howard and went with him to Pensacola, Florida, where she now remained, clerking in the PX at the naval air station while awaiting his return from the North Atlantic. Catherine recalled their last afternoon together and how they had splurged. Mae needed a skirt and blouse for traveling; Catherine was looking for a scarf and shoes. When Mae found the skirt and blouse she wanted, Catherine bought a skirt and blouse just like it; then Catherine bought tan, open-toed shoes and a paisley scarf, and so—impulsively—did Mae. The sisters had never before worn identical outfits, but they did so on the day of Mae and Howard's departure; and walking along the platform beside the train, they shed identical tears.

It occurred to Catherine as she stood in the store window fidgeting with the buttons of the blouse that matched Mae's, that throughout her life she had had two friends at a time, never more, never fewer. Through high school and beyond, her two close friends had been Loretta and Patsy. When Loretta got married in her mid-twenties and moved away, Mae took her place in Catherine's heart. Patsy in due course was displaced by Hank. Who would replace Mae? For a long time Catherine had supposed that her sister would return at war's end and fill the void she had left, but now she didn't think so. The move to Plum wasn't the only reason. They had been separated for two years and their letters were growing lifeless, perfunctory. Although they continued to write often, they couldn't get down on paper anything like the happy, headlong discussions they used to have over ice cream at Cellini's. Furthermore, there was a sour tone in Mae's recent writing that Catherine didn't care for, a veiled resentment that Hank, who, being too old for the draft by a little more than a year, hadn't enlisted anyhow.

She picked up her feather duster and made another circuit of the store without finding a particle of dust on any shelf or can. She hung the duster on its nail in the back room and said to Hank, "I'll be back in a few minutes."

"Where to now?" he asked, his head in the meat case.

"The public library."

"Fine. Take your time."

She stepped out the front door into the warm, hazy sunshine of late September. Plum's main street was perfectly silent, perfectly

still. Three old men sat on the bench in front of the post office. Two were staring at her. The other was asleep. Above them the Stars and Stripes hung limp.

Passing the pool hall, she glanced inside, expecting to see her father sitting under his column of pipe smoke, but he was gone from his customary chair. She went in and stood at the bar, waiting for Gordy to come out from the enclosure that served as his short-order kitchen. Looking out of the corner of her eye at the cardplayers, she saw them directing guarded glances her way, heard them muttering. She and Hank had been coming in here for coffee almost daily, and as the only woman among Gordy's clientele she never entered the door that the men didn't fall silent and scowl. They regarded her as a desecration, she knew. There were certain words you couldn't utter with a woman in the place. Certain directions you couldn't spit.

Gordy, however, made her feel welcome. Turning from his fry table and peering over his swinging doors, he said, "Just a sec, Mrs. Foster." Gordy was a large, soft man, gentle, passive, maybe a little simple-minded. He had a dimpled face and bushy eyebrows. He said things to Catherine he couldn't say to men. He had told her one day that when he attended Emmanuel Lutheran and heard Pastor Dimmitburg read from scripture about the lion and lamb lying down together, he got a warm feeling and thought of his pool hall because this was one of the few places in town where Protestants and Catholics mixed with each other. Catherine's reply to this had become their private joke: "The Peaceable Kingdom Pool Hall," she would say, and Gordy would quiver with laughter.

He stepped out of the kitchen wearing a long, soiled apron tied high under the armpits. "What'll it be, Mrs. Foster? Anything with your coffee?"

"No coffee, thanks. Has my father gone out?"

"Gone to the toilet."

"You're sure?"

"I saw him go in." Gordy pointed to a door at the back of the room, beyond the pool tables. He was a little hurt that she should suspect him of negligence.

"I thought he might have gone out. He sometimes wanders, you know."

"Look, Mrs. Foster, settle your mind about that. I keep watch. And so what if he wanders? It's a small town."

"But he'll go from place to place and forget how he got there. In the city we used to get phone calls from bus drivers and policemen."

"That's because the city's got too many places." Gordy's laugh, like a child's, had a gurgle in it. "Here, the whole town is only one place."

She left the pool hall and continued along the street toward the village hall, in which the public library was situated. More than once Wallace, with a smirk, had urged Catherine to visit the library. "Why are you giving me that look?" she had asked him, but he ignored the question, insisting that if she loved books as much as she claimed she must get herself a library card without delay and take advantage of the holdings. "After Grand Opening I'll have more time," she told him, concealing her main reason for putting it off, which was her need to believe that somewhere in this village a pleasant discovery awaited her. All her life she'd found pleasure in books, not only in reading them but also in their physical presence. She had clerked in books at Dayton's. She had loved smelling them, handling them and regulating the heat and humidity for them. She was counting on Plum's library to help dispel her longing for Minneapolis, which was growing more intense by the day. She yearned for the sound of streetcars in the night, the clink of milk bottles on the stoop at dawn. Most of all, she missed the anonymity of the city. Step into the Plum Five and Dime and the clerks turned and looked at you like a freak. Try to strike up a conversation with the druggist or the postmaster and all they wanted to talk about were the weather and crops. Was she doomed for the rest of her life to dwell on bushels per acre and rain by the inch? What in the world was alfalfa? Paging through a magazine at the drugstore this afternoon, she had come across a series of photos of an abandoned movie set, street scenes shot from behind the flimsy facades, and with every page her heart had grown heavier. It was a stunning display of nullity and it stood, in her heart, for Plum.

Passing the barbershop, she would have collided with Stan Kimball as he came out of the door if he hadn't nimbly sidestepped her; for a squat, heavy man he was quick on his feet. He smiled and said, "Excuse me, Mrs. Foster."

"My fault entirely, I was a thousand miles away."

"More likely a hundred." He was well aware that Catherine's heart had not followed her to Plum. There were very few secrets in this town that Stan Kimball didn't know. "Where are you going? I'll walk with you if you don't mind."

"To the library. Please do."

Before they proceeded, Kimball took a cigar from his breast pocket, unwrapped it, licked it and lit it, sucking and puffing so deeply that Catherine had to move upwind from the smoke cloud. As they walked, he repeatedly ran a hand over his scalp, front to back, as though smoothing hair he didn't have. His baldness was not the gleaming sort; his scalp was bumpy, with discolored splotches.

"My wife and the mayor's wife like to take credit for our public library. They make up two thirds of the board. Between you and me it's a very rotten library."

She laughed. "What's rotten about it?"

"I'll let you see for yourself. Fortunately, from now on you won't have time for reading books. Tomorrow you're going to be swamped with shoppers."

"Could you be wrong? I'm almost afraid for tomorrow to come."

"Nonsense. It's been years since this town has been hit with a good, big grocery promotion. Already I hear people talking about your ad in the *Alert.* There's been a shortage of detergent and Jell-O and coffee ever since the war started, and they can't believe you have all that stuff in stock, much less at sale prices."

"Hank is hoping to average three hundred dollars a day for the three days."

"That's peanuts! A thousand a day is more like it."

"You're dreaming, surely."

"Wait and see."

They came to the village hall, a cube of brown brick set between the bank and the Standard station. Stan Kimball sprang onto the step and held the door open for her. "I'd accompany you further, Mrs. Foster, but it would destroy my image as Plum's leading illiterate. As I tell my wife, I haven't read a book since the Bible I burned as a teenager. Goodbye, and be prepared for a land-office business tomorrow." He shut her inside.

Despite the summery weather the furnace in the basement was producing heat; she felt waves of forced air rushing up from the vents along the dark hallway. On her right was a door with "Constable" lettered on the frosted glass. This, according to Wallace, was Constable Heffernand, a disabled veteran from World War One who spent most of his on-duty hours putting together model airplanes because he had little else to do—crime was unheard of in Plum. The village ordinance assigned only one official task to the constable: the stopping of traffic to let funeral processions go by.

On Catherine's left, a door marked "Mayor" stood ajar. Inside she saw a man in his shirtsleeves studying a ledger. This would be Harlan Brask, whose illegal conflict of interest (said Wallace) was both well-known and condoned. Wallace claimed that besides his municipal duties Mayor Brask carried on his private insurance business from this desk, seeing to it that all village property was overinsured—the road grader, the dump truck, the sewage plant, the village hall, the lives and health of all village employees, the drums and horns of a village band long defunct—and thus his most lucrative premiums came from the village treasury.

Facing her at the end of the hallway was a third door.

LIBRARY
Wipe Your Feet

It was locked. She retraced her steps and put her head in at the mayor's office.

"Excuse me."

The mayor, a gray-haired, gray-faced man in a starched shirt, raised his head from his bookwork, removed his glasses, and peered at her with ice-blue eyes.

"Will the library be open this afternoon?"

He shook his head.

"Tomorrow?"

"Saturday," he said, putting on his glasses and lowering his nose to his ledger.

As she backed into the hallway, chilled, the constable's door opened behind her and a tall, middle-aged man leaned out with a smile. "Hello, I'm the constable. Can I help you?" His back was severely bent—injury to the spine in World War One, according to Wallace. Offering Catherine his hand (knobby, arthritic knuckles, razor-nicked fingers) he said, "I'm Charles Heffernand, and you're the grocer's wife. My sister Melva pointed you out in church."

"Catherine Foster. And I'm also the grocer's partner."

"Are you interested in aeroplanes? Step in and take a gander at my Japanese Zero."

She went in. The upper half of his high-ceilinged office was thick with model airplanes hanging on strings. A long table was covered with blueprints and planes in various stages of construction. Taped to the walls were newspaper photos of planes and their pilots. On his

desk she saw tiny bits of wood he had been shaving with a razor blade.

"Ever since Pearl Harbor I've been building Jap and German aeroplanes and setting them afire. Bombers, transports, fighters. It gives home-front morale a big boost. Here's my Zero. There's this rubber band attached to the propeller so it actually flies—see it here? When it's finished I'll put a notice in the paper and at the appointed time I'll take her up on the roof of the village hall and turn the propeller tight and set a match to the wing and let her go. She'll zip out over the street trailing smoke and flames and crash like the planes in the newsreels. You'll want to see it, Mrs. Foster. There's always a good crowd. I do it during noon hour so the school children don't have to miss it. Jack Sims from the *Plum Alert* always comes with his camera and puts the picture on the front page of the next issue. Last year a reporter came from Rochester and covered it for the *Post-Bulletin*."

Catherine made several appreciative remarks, then asked about the library.

"The library? You want to see the library? Here, I can let you in this way." He opened a door at the far end of his office. "Library's open only on Saturday from one till four, but I can let you have a look-see. Watch your step."

The library was a small, stuffy room with one window. Its holdings were a hundred books, a buffalo head, and a collection of janitorial supplies—brooms, dustpans, buckets of paint and detergent. A few books were laid out on a table beneath the buffalo head; the rest stood in two small bookcases flanking the window. Catherine recognized none of the titles on the table. The two she picked up, *The Blind Jurist* and *The One-Armed Apothecary*, were written by someone named Edward Hodge Fleet.

"Oh, oh," said the constable, hurrying to the window and pulling down the dark brown shade, "the janitor must have raised the shade. My sister Melva says books hate the sun."

"They hate dryness too," Catherine told him, imagining all the cracked spines in this airless room. "Why do you open only on Saturdays?"

"My sister Melva's librarian, and during the week she's telephone central. I take over the switchboard for her on Saturdays so she can open up the library, and on Sundays so she can sing in church. We've got the switchboard in our living room. It was our father who

brought the telephone system to Plum back in the teens, and we've kept it in the family."

Crossing to the small bookcases beside the window, Catherine recalled the solo voice that emanated from the choir loft during High Mass, an off-key quaver which together with the croaks of the old priest made for an unholy mixture of sour sounds. Now that she thought about it, it was the same voice that said "Number please" when you picked up the phone. She asked, without much interest in the answer, "Who takes over as constable while you take over the switchboard?"

"Nobody. No need for it. Nothing much happening on weekends around here, or any other day either. Stray dog now and again. Or maybe somebody having a stroke and needing a ride to the Mayo Clinic."

She examined the titles in the bookcase on the left. The few she recognized were insipid romances of ten or fifteen years ago. The shelves on the right held the collected works of Edward Hodge Fleet. She drew out a volume and turned it over in her hands. "Who *is* this?"

"Ah, our pride and joy. We're one of the few libraries in Minnesota with a complete set of Edward Hodge Fleet. When we bought the twenty-fifth book his publisher awarded us that plaque." He pointed to a small copper plate hanging on the wall. "And this special bookcase to hold his books. He's an inspiration."

"I've never heard of him."

"That's because he's only now becoming known west of the Mississippi. Culture comes from the East, my sister Melva says, and it was Mayor Brask and his wife who brought the first Fleet books with them when they moved here from Chicago."

She examined the book. The embossed binding was elegant. The paper was cheap, the print coarse. She looked at the front matter. The Tisdale Press, Chicago. Dozens of titles by the same author, all suggesting physical impairment.

"A new volume is sent to us every three months and the Christmas volume is free. Last Christmas it was *The Hobbling Cobbler.* It's a particular favorite of the mayor's. Come with me, you'll want to meet the mayor."

"I think I've met him."

"He's a literary man, come with me."

She returned to the bookcase on the left, searching desperately for a name she knew—Hawthorne, Cather, Galsworthy—but there was

none. She felt a little dizzy. The heat in the room was oppressive. She called to mind Wallace's smirk, which she now understood. Dropping the Fleet book on the table, she followed the constable out of the room.

The mayor, as before, raised his eyes reluctantly from his ledger and removed his glasses. He seemed no more pleased than last time. It occurred to Catherine that getting acquainted in Plum was like learning your way through a zoo—an odd new specimen at every turn, vertebrates like yourself but not the kind you can communicate with.

"Mrs. Foster, Mayor Brask," said the constable. "Mayor Brask, the new woman in town."

The mayor stood up from his padded leather chair. He was chunky, solidly packed, shorter than the constable by six or eight inches. "Will you be attending one of our fine churches?" were the first words out of his mouth. He was quite sure of her answer, but he liked to verify hearsay.

"Yes, we're Catholic."

Rotten luck, his expression seemed to say. He cleaned his glasses on his necktie. "How many others in your family, Mrs. Foster?"

"My husband, my son, and my father."

He was relieved when she stopped after three. Not quite enough to tip Plum's religious balance. Now the risky issue:

"Is your husband politically inclined, Mrs. Foster?"

"Not at all."

He nodded approvingly as he returned his glasses to his face, using both hands to hook the bows carefully over his ears.

"But I am," she added.

The mayor turned away, frowning. The constable, a peace-loving man, wished she had not said that. The mayor, he knew, was upset by the very idea of political-minded women. Whiling away long afternoons in the village hall, the mayor had often told the constable about his running for the school board in Chicago and being defeated by a woman. Political women were dangerous, and it was schools they usually tampered with. Besides being mayor, Harlan Brask was chairman, ex officio, of the five-member Plum school board, on which there were two Lutherans besides himself—a majority nearly offset by the influence of the superintendent, who was Catholic.

"The Fosters have taken over Kermit's Grocery," said the constable.

The mayor said, "I see," not admitting that on recent afternoons he had stood in Legget's Grocery across the street from Hank's Market and watched the Fosters at work. His friend Louie Legget, always one to put the worst face on things, cursed whatever fate had brought him this ambitious competitor, who was sure to drain off all the Catholic trade Legget had gained through Kermit's decline.

Because this too was obviously an unhappy topic, the constable shifted to books. "She's a reader, Harlan. I showed her our Fleet collection."

The mayor brightened, looking her over. "Pain is gripping, don't you think?"

"Gripping? Pain?"

"In books, I mean. Don't you like reading about pain?"

"No, not as a rule."

"Edward Hodge Fleet is a master of pain. There's pain in all his work. Sometimes even mutilation and dismemberment. And it's always followed by happiness."

"Yes," said the constable, "my sister Melva says Fleet's got the sequence correct. Pain comes first and happiness follows."

"Inspiring," said the mayor.

"You bet," said the constable. "His books have done wonders for the war effort nationwide."

There were noises from both men, upper respiratory noises of satisfaction as they recalled passages of pain and the happiness that followed.

Catherine excused herself, claiming to be needed at the store. The mayor said goodbye, and the constable accompanied her down the hall to the front door.

"Tell the men in your family that most likely I'll burn my Zero two weeks from Monday."

As she returned slowly to the store, her shoulders drooping in discouragement, Catherine advised herself to forget about finding friends and books in this outpost and concentrate instead on caring for her family and building up the market. She would be satisfied with Plum, she vowed, as long as her men were satisfied, and as long as Plum bought their groceries.

Passing the pool hall, she looked in. Grandfather's chair was still empty. She went in and said to Gordy, "Don't tell me he's still in the restroom."

Gordy said, "Oh, dear," and went to look. He returned. "I'm sorry, Mrs. Foster, I should have been more watchful, but I'm sure there's nothing to worry about."

In the market, Hank said the same: "Don't worry. It's Tuesday—no train."

"I'm going to look for him." She went out the back door, started the DeSoto and roared off down the alley.

Gouth said, "[illegible] and [illegible] in [illegible] [illegible] [illegible] him [illegible] I should have [illegible] [illegible] [illegible] nothing [illegible] about."

In the [illegible] and the [illegible] [illegible] [illegible] —[illegible]

"I'm going to [illegible] [illegible] [illegible] and [illegible] Lescio and [illegible] everything [illegible]

9

Meanwhile Grandfather found the house he was looking for. The other evening he had been in the car when Hank and Catherine gave Wallace a ride home in the rain, and he was struck by how closely the Flint house resembled his own boyhood home in Prairie du Chien, Wisconsin. It was an old two-story house, not very large, with latticework under the eaves and a dormer window facing the street. In Prairie du Chien that dormer had stood out from the room he shared with his brothers. For old time's sake he was determined to go upstairs in this house and stand at that window and look out.

Crossing the brown lawn, he saw that unlike the house of his boyhood the Flint house leaned slightly forward as if to get a jump on its neighbors. Its green paint was flaking off. It had a sheer face; the front doorsill was three feet off the ground and there were no steps. Taking a circular of bargains from his pocket, he went around to the side, stepped up onto the low, slanting porch, and rapped on the screen door, calling, "Anybody home here?"

A woman came through the kitchen from another room. She was short, fat and unkempt. She had gray hair and intelligent-looking eyes.

"See here," said Grandfather, unfolding a circular. "These wonderful prices on groceries. Lettuce at fifteen cents a head. I saw it come off the truck, great whopping heads packed in ice." He guessed the woman's hair hadn't been combed today. He guessed she weighed two hundred pounds.

Through the screen the woman said, "I'm well aware of all that stuff. My son brought home one of those fliers day before yesterday."

She was aware, too, of the old man's identity. Wallace had described him.

"He's a son to be proud of, madam. A steady-working young man, I've heard Hank and Catherine say it more than once. Though why he should be wearing all that hair on his face is beyond me. When I was with the railroad, beards were against regulations. It's too easy for a bearded man to go seedy."

She laughed and pushed open the flimsy screen door. "Would you like to come in? You look hot."

"Delighted."

It had been a long time since Mrs. Flint had invited anyone into her house, but here was a case where kindness might not go unrewarded. For Wallace's sake the good will of the Fosters was all-important.

Grandfather came to a stop in the middle of the kitchen and turned in a circle, studying the cupboards, the icebox with its two oak doors, the black cast-iron range standing on its six chrome legs.

"Sit down and take a load off your feet," said the woman. "How about a drink of something cold?"

Grandfather had no intention of sitting down. He was here to look for his boyhood. He glanced again at her alert, knowing eyes. In Grandfather's experience, women with eyes like that required very little cajoling, so he got right down to business, pushing open the pantry door. "Ah, just as I thought. My brothers and I grew up in a house like this, and it was here in this pantry when our mother wasn't looking that we ate jam out of jars."

Mrs. Flint opened the upper door of the icebox and chipped a few shards of ice into a very small glass.

"And when we were a little older we got into the wine. My father was a great one for brewing wine in vats which he kept in the pantry. I remember sitting right back there in that corner, twelve years old and tight as a tick."

She opened the lower door and took out a pitcher of lemonade.

Grandfather strode into the dining room, where he looked disapprovingly at the furnishings—a couch, two easy chairs, a radio, books all over the place. "Where's your dining room table?"

"We don't use that as our dining room."

"But it's your dining room."

"No, we use it as our living room. We eat in the kitchen."

"Then what's your living room for?" He passed through an arch-

way into the sparsely-furnished room facing the street. The shades were drawn; the room smelled like dust.

She followed him, handed him the glass. "We don't use this room, it's too cold in the winter."

"But it's summer."

"It's easier not to be changing rooms with the seasons."

"We had drafty rooms in Prairie du Chien, but the living room wasn't one of them. It was the bedrooms where we froze our follicles. My guess is that you have two bedrooms upstairs."

"Yes." Mrs. Flint lit a cigarette and waved the match out forcefully. "Won't you come sit in the kitchen?"

"One bedroom facing the street and the other facing the back."

"Yes." She shifted her weight from one leg to the other as she waited for him to finish examining the room.

He pointed to a ridge of stained glass running along the top of the front window. "We didn't have that in our house."

She observed that although the man's suitcoat was worn with age, it was made of a sturdy, expensive material. She was impressed with his necktie as well; it had the narrow diagonal stripes the men of Roosevelt's cabinet wore in the newsreels. These newcomers were people of substance, and Wallace's boss had obviously been lying about being short of money. The boss's wife was decked out, too, whenever you saw her on the street. Yesterday on her daily trip to the post office, Mrs. Flint had seen the boss's wife wearing a pair of open-toed shoes of a style not available in Plum. How lucky that Wallace was attaching himself to this family. He liked them and admired them. Maybe now he would quit threatening to leave home.

Grandfather downed the lemonade in three swallows and smacked his lips. "Delicious," he said, handing her the glass, "and now, if you don't mind, I'll dash up to the front bedroom and have myself a look out the window."

She didn't object.

He climbed, pausing on every third step to catch his breath. Halfway up, he looked down on the woman and thought, My God, she looks exactly like a rubber ball from this angle, no taller than she is wide. "If this is an inconvenient day for me to be doing this," he said, proceeding up, "just say the word."

She waved him onward and started up herself. It wasn't only his clothes, it was his way of speaking. Why had Wallace failed to tell her of the old man's charm?

At the top of the stairs she was close behind him, making sure he didn't turn left toward Wallace's bedroom. Not that he could get in if he tried, the door was locked. Not even she herself was allowed in to clean or change the sheets. Wallace did that himself.

The front room was hers. She remained in the doorway, smoking, as the old man crossed to one of the windows.

"You should have more shade trees in your front yard," he said, looking out. "But I don't recommend cottonwoods."

She felt suddenly sad at the sound of a man's voice in her room, at the sight of a man's silhouette against the afternoon sun. She hadn't shared this room with a man since her husband had died nearly twenty-four years ago.

"We had cottonwoods in our front yard and they shed like cats, dropping their twigs every time a breeze came off the river. Across the street was a woods. Hardwoods mostly. Wonderful trees for climbing, especially the oaks."

Mrs. Flint paid no attention to his words, but listened to the rising and falling of his voice as though it were music. It made her husband's death fresh in her memory. Luckily, the grief was no longer fresh. The memory of grief was not the grief itself, thank God. The grief itself had been unbearable. It had lasted for years. It was Wallace, of course, who had pulled her through. Wallace was two when his father died. By the time Wallace was six she was nearly herself again and had quit punishing him in physical ways. She stopped hitting him and biting his fingers. It was the most marvelous thing to watch him grow up. He was so full of determination, so smart in school. Teachers kept telling her he was quicker in class than anyone else.

"If you climbed high enough in the oaks you could see out over the other trees to the river," Grandfather droned, half to himself. "You could see trains chugging across to Iowa on the floating bridge."

Wallace never climbed trees as a boy. She had urged him to. Go out and climb a tree, she used to say when he was owly. Go out and play darts. Go out and make something out of all that old lumber behind the shed; make a fort. On his ninth birthday she had nailed up a dartboard for him at the back of the house, but he never threw a single dart, not even when she threw a few to demonstrate. Maybe *because* she threw a few to demonstrate. He was always negative when she suggested something, even though none of her suggestions

entailed playing with other children, which she knew he hated to do. He liked doing things indoors—reading, drawing, listening to the radio, splashing paint on the walls of his room. The summer he was sixteen he actually plastered his room, learning how from a book. He did it piecemeal, applying paint to the plaster before it dried, and ended up with what he called frescoes. She never saw them, for that was the summer he declared his room off limits and began locking the door.

Looking down from the window, Grandfather stopped speaking and watched the DeSoto pass slowly along the street, an elbow out the window on the driver's side. Catherine's elbow. She must be looking for him. He watched the car until it was out of sight; then he turned to Mrs. Flint and thought how various were the shapes women developed into. At the very least this one was two axhandles broad in the beam. Good eyes though. Brains behind the eyes, you could tell. Doubtless a woman you could talk to about trains.

"Did you ever take the *Hiawatha* to Chicago between 1918 and 1926?"

She nodded, guessing the correct answer was yes.

"Ahhhhh." He stepped forward and took her hand. She let him kiss it. The kiss was firm and moist. He stepped back and said, "I punched your ticket."

She smiled at him.

Without speaking they went downstairs and through the rooms to the back porch, where Grandfather asked, "I wonder, could you tell me the name of the Lutheran pastor and where he lives?"

"Reverend Dimmitburg. He lives in the white house next to the church."

"And where would that be?"

She pointed. "On the other side of town. Eight or ten blocks."

"Will this street take me there?"

"No, the church is one street over. Do you have to go? Will you have more lemonade?"

"I'm sorry, I must go."

"All right, I'll show you." She stepped off the porch and went with him to the front walk. "See that steeple?"

"So that's it. Is the Reverend the sort of man you can talk to about the verities?"

"The what?"

"The verities. The meaning of life. The good old days. Trains."

"I don't know, I'm not Lutheran."

"What are you then?"

"I'm whatever's on the radio Sunday mornings."

Gazing at the steeple, Grandfather realized that it was going to be nip and tuck covering that distance with Catherine out patrolling in the car, but he felt the need of a companion outside the pool hall. All they talked about in the pool hall was farming, and all they knew of railroads was that miserable puddle-jumper that backed up from Winona. The minister might have a broad view of life, might have had years of experience riding trains.

He regarded the houses across the street, saw an alley behind them.

"Does that alley run as far as the church?"

"Yes, it will take you to the back door of the parsonage." She watched him hurry across the street. "Good-bye," she called, but he didn't hear.

He had gone only three blocks down the alley when he heard the DeSoto drawing near, so he stepped into the nearest doorway. It happened to be an outdoor privy, unoccupied, which he made use of as long as he was there. With the clatter of the engine fading, he set off again, but slower now, for he was tired.

Again the DeSoto sounded in a nearby street, and he ducked into the doorway of a garage, where he found a young woman standing over a bushel basket shucking corn. She was facing away from the doorway and was startled to hear Grandfather say, rather close to her ear, "I beg your pardon." She spun around and stepped back from him. She was dressed in a two-piece sun-bathing suit, and Grandfather admired her shapeliness, her bronzeness, her honey-colored hair. In her blue eyes he detected uneasiness, which he attempted to relieve by saying, "I'm on my way to church. I only stepped in for a moment to get out of the sun." From his pocket he drew the circular intended for the Lutheran pastor, unfolded it and held it by its top corners as if displaying a bath towel. "Do you like Iced Aunt Sallys?"

Seeing Hank's Market printed on the circular, she recalled her husband's saying that the new grocer's family included an old man. She said, "My husband likes them."

"And doesn't everybody! That gingery taste. I eat four at a sitting sometimes."

"Actually all that icing is a little much for my taste."

"I know what you mean. I've thought so myself. I like candy well enough but not when I'm eating cookies."

The woman giggled and resumed her work, bending over and picking an ear of corn out of a wooden box. Grandfather admired the curve of her haunch.

"And speaking of candy, let me tell you a secret. It's a lean time for candy as we all know, Hitler and Tojo having seen to that, but in the back room of Hank's Market is a box of Hershey bars, one of which I'd be honored to set aside for you."

She giggled again, wrenching the shucks from the ear of corn and dropping them into the basket.

"I'll put it in a sack with your name on it and leave it with Catherine at the counter. What is your name?"

She said her name was Phyllis Clay, but Grandfather didn't hear her; he was listening instead to the DeSoto drawing near. It was coming down this very alley. He backed into a corner of the garage where he couldn't be seen, and when the car had passed he came forward.

"How far is the Lutheran church from here?"

"It's in the next block."

"Will I find the pastor at home, do you know?"

"I have no idea. I thought you people were Catholic." Her husband, a crabby bigot twenty-five years older than she was, had complained about the influx of fish-eaters: today the grocer, tomorrow the Pope.

"I'm Catholic to my bones, but I'm looking for companionship among the educated class. I've given up on the priest. To see eye to eye with the priest in this town you have to get down on your knees. If the minister's no better, I'll go to the schoolhouse and meet the teachers. What about your husband, is he fond of talking about the verities?"

"The what?"

"The verities. Love and death and railroads."

"No, all he knows is turkeys." There was bitterness in her expression, hardness in her voice. "He's a turkey-grower. He's got turkeys on four different farms around here. He's rich." Until recently she had considered him too rich to divorce, but now she poured out to Grandfather what she had told her chiropractor in Rochester the other day. "I met him at a turkey-growers' convention in Omaha. I was the entertainment for their stag party. He came back to Omaha

three times to see me. He'd get drunk and ask me to marry him. The third time I agreed. He was a lot friendlier drunk than he turned out to be sober. I married him because he was rich and because I had this idea that small-town life was cute and happy, like in the *Saturday Evening Post,* and he said he was one of the leading citizens of this town and we'd live like royalty." She picked up another ear and tore at it roughly, all the more angry now that she realized that this old codger with the grocery circular was making her feel more like a woman than her husband did. "What does he mean, royalty? We never go anywhere. We never see anybody. I'm more like a slave than a wife. All he wants me for is cleaning his house and shucking his corn and feeding him pot roast five times a week."

Grandfather gave her problem a few moments of thought and decided not to concern himself with it. He felt like a nap. He stepped over to the workbench and smoothed the circular flat, leaving it for her to read at her leisure. He would go and see the minister another time. He was dizzy with fatigue—he shouldn't have skipped his nap. He staggered backward and braced his shoulders between two studs of the wall.

"What's wrong?" cried Mrs. Clay, drawing the wooden box toward him and turning it on its side for him to sit on, the silky ears of corn sliding like fish across the concrete.

He sat heavily, his forearms on his knees, his narrow shoulders hunched beside his ears, his head bowed.

"Can I get you anything? Water?"

With effort he smiled sadly up at her and said, "Yes, a bit of water." As she hurried away, he added, "If you please."

She went to the phone in the kitchen and reported to Central that the old man belonging to Hank's Market was having a breakdown in her garage. Miss Heffernand, sitting at the switchboard in the front window of her house on Bean Street, said she had seen the man's daughter driving around in her black car. She would ring a few houses and ask that she be hailed.

It was Mrs. Brask, the mayor's large, officious wife, who stopped Catherine by standing in the middle of Bean Street and holding her arms straight out from her sides and moving her small hands up and down like fins. She wore an ankle-length, flowered dressing gown that billowed as she stepped up to Catherine's window and said, "Your father is over there." She pointed between two houses, indicating a garage.

"Oh, thank you. I've been looking and looking."

"He's had a collapse."

"Oh, no!" Catherine let out the clutch and began to move.

"Just a second, I'm not finished."

Catherine stepped on the brake.

"I am Cora Brask."

"I'm pleased to meet you. I'm Catherine Foster."

"My husband is the mayor."

"Oh, yes, I've met the mayor."

"Perhaps he mentioned that we don't encourage noisy vehicles on Bean Street."

What a perfect wife for Mayor Brask, thought Catherine. She gunned the engine and roared off. She screeched around the corner and sped down the alley.

She found her father sitting on a box and conversing with a leggy woman without much on. The woman introduced herself as Phyllis Clay. In one hand Grandfather held an empty water tumbler and in the other an empty shot glass. He was feeling much better.

"I had a grandmother with spells," said Mrs. Clay. "Her doctor recommended a shot of brandy. It always seemed to help."

Catherine had never heard a twang quite like Phyllis Clay's. She would have been interested to know how long Mrs. Clay had lived in Plum and how she liked it, but this was hardly the time to inquire.

"Brandy cures many an ill," said Grandfather as they helped him to the car. He got in and immediately began to doze.

"I hope you'll be all right," Mrs. Clay told him through his window.

He raised a hand and weakly wiggled his fingers.

Catherine thanked Mrs. Clay and started the engine. As they moved along the alley, Grandfather leaned into the breeze coming in his window. It was very refreshing.

Catherine kept glancing at him. The brandy was bringing his color back. He looked well enough for a reprimand.

"You lied to Gordy," she said.

His eyes widened. "Now wait a minute, Catherine, I never lie to anyone."

"You told him you were going to the toilet."

"And so I did." He pointed to the outhouse they were passing. "Right there."

* * *

Brendan and Wallace distributed circulars for three and a half hours, and when they finished, Brendan was hungry, weak in the knees and lost. He was also proud of having accomplished the first job in his life for pay. Walking beside Wallace, who showed him the way home, he hoped there would be more special sales with circulars. Next time he would carry a stick from the start. From the moment he picked up a stick today, the dogs had kept their distance. He had never seen so many dogs in his life—growlers, snappers, waggers, leapers and lickers. Only one biter, fortunately, and that, by coincidence, was the only dog to which Brendan was formally introduced. "Don't mind Georgie," said a wan, gray-haired woman drawn outside by the strident yap of her ugly little mutt. "Georgie loves little boys and never bites." Georgie didn't love Brendan and tore his sock.

The streets were pitch dark under the massive elms. Hanging on a post at each intersection was a solitary lightbulb casting a glow so feeble it was absorbed by the night before it fell to the ground. Brendan found Wallace slightly less creepy in the dark than in daylight. In the dark you couldn't see his eyes, which held too many expressions in quick succession, hardly any of which seemed to wish you well. Next time there was a sale, Brendan resolved to ask his father to hire Philip Crowley or Sam Romberg as his partner. Working with Wallace, you got too little sense of doing a man's job. What you got instead, for some reason, was a sense of Wallace doing a boy's job.

Turning down a dark alley, Wallace pointed and said, "Cut between these two buildings and you'll be on Main Street. You'll know the way home from there."

Brendan saw a glimmer of light on Main Street and knew where he was. Wordlessly he left Wallace and walked through the shadowy space between the village hall on his left and the gas station on his right. He came to a scattering of tires and tripped and fell. He got up and moved forward more slowly, shuffling his feet, feeling his way toward the light. The ground opened up under his right foot and he drew back from a hole six feet deep—a grease pit for servicing the undersides of cars. As he walked carefully around it and continued on his way, it occurred to him that Wallace might have steered him toward the hole on purpose. By the time he reached home he was convinced of it, and he said so to his mother as he sat

down to the supper she had been keeping warm for him. She made a few consoling remarks, none of which indicated that she believed him, and he resented her lack of faith in his word, her loyalty to Wallace.

Stepping into his dark kitchen, Wallace called, "What's for supper? I'm starved."

"Stew," said his mother from the next room. "It's on the range."

He struck a match, removed the glass chimney from the lamp and lit the wick. He went to the range and lifted the lid of a small pot. "It's cold."

"That's because you're late."

"How come you let it get cold?"

"It's been a hot day, Wallace. The whole house was heating up from that one little pot of stew."

"Couldn't you have waited and eaten with me?"

"You know I can't put off my meals, Wallace."

He removed the pot and lifted the stove lid. He stuffed crumpled newspaper down the hole and dropped in a few sticks of kindling. He lit the paper, waited for it to flare, then replaced the lid and the pot.

"There's mail on the table," his mother said. There was no home delivery in Plum, and because Wallace had been known to destroy his mother's letters, the postmaster held the Flint mail for her to pick up at the window each day.

He looked at the brown envelope standing between the salt and pepper shakers and knew that it contained his third draft notice in three years. He felt none of the fear that had swept over him the first time. When the first notice arrived shortly after Pearl Harbor, he and his mother had ridden the mail truck to Pinburg and showed the letter to old Doctor Rowan, who had been seeing Wallace once or twice a year since his first seizure at the age of eleven. Doctor Rowan had lost most of his practice along with most of his eyesight. His office was the tiny back room of a barber shop. Wallace recalled how his mother's hand trembled as she handed the letter to him. He remembered the doctor bending low over his desk, straining to read, and then finally explaining to them that draft boards put epileptics into the same category as invalids and idiots; they didn't even have to show up for the physical examination if a doctor verified their condition in writing. Which Doctor Rowan did. The second letter

arrived a year later. Again mother and son traveled to Pinburg in a state of nerves, believing that the Allied setback in the Mediterranean might have made epileptics draftable, but Doctor Rowan assured them that it was normal for the selective service to repeat their summons every so often in order to verify a man's disability. He told them to go home and quit worrying—he'd write to the draft board—and when the next notice arrived to forward it to him through the mail.

Waiting for his stew to heat up, Wallace slit the envelope with a paring knife. *Greetings.* He had thirty days to put his affairs in order. He would report to the Federal Building in Minneapolis for his pre-induction physical examination at 1:00 P.M. on October 22, 1944. Enclosed for his convenience was a Greyhound bus pass and a time-table. At 9:20 A.M. the bus to the Twin Cities would stop at the junction of Highway 61 and the road to Plum.

He slipped the letter back into its envelope and carefully sealed it with adhesive tape. He crossed out his name and address and wrote Doctor Rowan's and "Please Forward."

He went into the dining room and sank into the couch, his head low, his feet up on the arm.

"What kept you?" his mother asked. She was reading *Screen Romance.* A cigarette burned in the ashtray beside her mug of warm lemonade.

"Covered the whole town with circulars, the kid and I. Didn't have one minute to rest. I'm going to tell Hank I need more pay for work like that. At least in the store you get to sit down every so often."

"Wallace, you'll never guess who came calling today."

He turned his head to look at her. "Came calling?" Their last callers had been a pair of young Mormons in suits and ties whom Wallace had tried to provoke with his atheistic views. "Who was it this time, Jehovah's Witnesses?"

"Guess again." She took up her cigarette and inhaled, looking coy.

He couldn't guess. Callers were unimaginable.

"Your boss's old gent."

"Catherine's father?"

She nodded, smiling through her smoke.

"What did he want?"

"He said the view from my bedroom reminded him of his boyhood home."

"You let him upstairs?" He raised his head off the couch and glared at her.

"He's a nice old gent. I told him to come again."

"He probably will. He's a pest."

She put down her smoke and sipped her drink. "I hope he does. It's important to your career that we treat him nice."

"Since when does stocking shelves qualify as a career?"

"Since the Fosters took over. They're up and coming, Wallace. You've got a future in that job."

Wallace laughed. "We're taking in ten dollars a day. They'll be bankrupt by Christmas."

He got up and went into the kitchen, imagining the pleasure of watching the business go belly-up. Failure was always so much more dramatic than success. The only bad part would be losing Catherine, the first kindred spirit of his life. He sat at the table with his bowl of stew and a spoon.

"Lux Radio Theater's on in five minutes," said his mother. He heard the creak of her rocking chair as she leaned forward to turn on the radio. "Claudette Colbert and Dana Andrews."

"I can't stand Claudette Colbert." He chewed with his eyes on the ceiling as he calculated how long the Fosters would last. Bankrupt by Christmas might be pushing it. They were a persistent pair, more stubborn than was good for them. They'd stick it out far too long and leave town under heavy debts. Next spring, probably.

When he finished eating he said, "I'm going upstairs to read."

"Read here. I'll fix you some cocoa."

"I can't read with the radio going."

"Yes, you can. You do it all the time. Come and sit down." Her tone was the one he despised the most, tender and coaxing.

He went upstairs to his bedroom and slammed the door.

10

Stepping into the market after school the next day, Brendan found his parents and Wallace scurrying among a swarm of shoppers. His father put him immediately to work, sending him to the basement (ratless now, the cats on patrol) to bring up potatoes.

At closing time he was sent next door to retrieve Grandfather. Hank pressed the *Total* button on the cash register and lifted the lid to read the tape. He turned to Catherine and Wallace, who stood nearby removing their aprons, and said, "Guess."

Catherine wanted to guess five hundred dollars, but said four hundred to be safe.

Wallace said, "Three seventy-five."

He tore off the tape and showed it to them: $683.43.

Catherine said, "Oh, my God."

Wallace shook his head in wonder, recalling that Kermit, even years ago on his best day, had never hit six hundred dollars.

They still had deliveries to make to a few people who had called in their orders. Brendan and Grandfather rode in back with the groceries. Wallace, sitting between Catherine and Hank, pointed the way down the twilit alleyways. Brendan carried the bags to the various kitchen doors accompanied by his mother, who made change from a drawstring bag and apologized for not showing up before suppertime. Their last delivery was Wallace himself, who had been excused from carrying bags because his feet hurt and his head ached.

"See you in the morning," said Hank, as Wallace got out.

"Get a good rest," Catherine told him. "Tomorrow may be even busier."

Wallace nodded and said goodnight. He stood on the curb and watched the De Soto disappear down the street. Mingled with his fatigue was an odd sense of buoyancy such as he had not felt since his high school days when he was the class brain and imagined a bright future for himself. It was exciting to think that the Fosters might prosper in Plum. Until yesterday he would have bet his life's savings—all two hundred dollars of it—on the failure of Hank's Market, but now it seemed possible that they might remain in Plum indefinitely. They might go on and on, Wallace and Catherine, reminding one another of their superiority to this village, helping one another resist its downward pull.

Trade was even brisker on Friday. This was the day that convinced Wallace that the Grand Opening had transcended religious barriers. One after another as they left the store, he named for Hank and Catherine the Lutherans they had just waited on. Again Brendan worked after school, Wallace got sore feet and a headache, and there were deliveries to make at twilight. The proceeds for Friday were $804.20.

Brendan was in and out of the store all day Saturday, balancing the demands of his parents with the demands of his friends Sam Romberg and Philip Crowley. He managed an hour of marbles and boomerang-throwing in the morning, and got away again later for the Gene Autry matinee.

After the movie, he was replenishing the bin of oranges when he overheard the observations of two women who had come into the store not to shop but to inspect. One was tall and square; she wore a circle of foxtails draped around her shoulders. Her companion was much smaller; she had a long neck, narrow shoulders and the overall shape of a bowling pin. They stood in front of the canned soup, like wallflowers at a dance.

"She seems very businesslike," said Small.

"Being businesslike never becomes a woman," Large declared. "Why isn't she home tending to her family?"

Catherine darted up to Brendan, whispered, "The one with the furs is the mayor's wife," and darted away again.

"She has only one," said Large.

"One? And she's Catholic?"

When they both turned to look Brendan over, he realized he was the one.

After a few moments Large added, "I spoke to her in that awful car she drives. It was the day her father turned up in Webster Clay's garage."

"Stanley says her father is in the pool hall nearly every day talking about trains."

Could Small, Brendan wondered, be Stan Kimball's wife?

They left the soup and strolled along the produce rack, checking prices.

"Look at Wallace Flint spruced up," said Small. "He's trimmed his beard."

"Yes, he looks downright useful."

"And handsome."

Just then, Wallace wore out. Having never worked so hard in his life, he went suddenly very pale and had to be helped into the back room, where Hank sat him down on his desk chair and Catherine gave him coffee and felt his forehead. Wallace said he'd be fine as long as he rested. Hank returned to his customers. Catherine felt his forehead once more, then left him alone. After a while Brendan, hurrying through the back room to fill a vinegar jug, noticed that Wallace seemed not to be resting but was sitting upright and tense, his eyes wide and distracted.

"Are you okay?" he asked him.

"Fine!" Wallace shot back resentfully, curling his lip.

"Just take it easy," said Brendan, repeating his father's instruction to Wallace. "Just sit and rest."

"Never mind!" Wallace snapped.

Returning with the gallon of vinegar, Brendan found his father and mother standing at the cash register reading the tape. "We did it!" his mother said gleefully.

Hank explained to Brendan, "Our income so far equals what we paid for stock and overhead. From now on it's all profit."

Brendan turned and saw his mother running through the store to tell Wallace. He ran after her, magnetized by her high spirits, but by the time he reached the doorway to the back room it was closed off by the two women who had been standing in front of the soup. Now they stood shoulder to shoulder peering into the back room. Brendan came to a stop behind them and looked over the smaller woman's shoulder. He saw his mother acting silly, chirping, "Good news, good news," as she flew toward Wallace with her arms flapping. He saw Wallace spring up from his chair and take Catherine

tightly in his arms and at the same time make a curious growling noise in his throat. Catherine, laughing, gave him a peck on the forehead. Wallace, his arms locked tightly around her neck, began jerking along the entire length of his body. Catherine cried, "Wallace!" and broke free.

The two women turned away, looking as though they had witnessed the vilest sort of degradation and were outraged but not surprised. Setting off at a quick strut toward the front door, they missed seeing Wallace topple to the floor and roll onto his back, mucus oozing from his mouth and nose, his half-closed eyes showing all white.

Catherine's scream and Brendan's were a single note.

Customers came running. A man in overalls shouted, "Stuff something in his mouth or he'll bite off his tongue." Another man lifted Catherine's feather duster off its hook and tried to insert the wooden handle between Wallace's grinding teeth.

"No, not that," said the man in overalls. "You'll break his teeth."

Then Hank was suddenly there, holding a ring of bologna in his hand. He bent over Wallace, waiting for him to open his mouth.

Two dozen people stood entranced, watching Wallace writhe, froth and shoot his arms and legs about.

"I thought he was getting better," said a largely pregnant woman holding two toddlers by the hand. "He hasn't had one in public for a long time."

"Not since the basketball tournament last spring," said her companion, a woman with her arms full of a baby in blue blankets.

"Were you there for it?"

"No, but I heard about it. They had to stop the game because he sprawled out onto the floor."

Three times Wallace snapped his mouth open and shut, and the third time Hank made his move and Wallace sank his teeth into the bologna. He lay rigid for a minute or more before his muscles began to relax. He whimpered unconsciously for a while, and then went limp. Hank gently removed the meat from his mouth. Sweat, saliva and tears came flowing out of Wallace. He shuddered. Catherine covered him with her coat, Hank's jacket and several empty potato sacks.

"He's all right now," said the man in overalls. "He'll sleep it off."

One by one the shoppers went back to their shopping. Catherine sat at the desk and kept watch. In a few minutes Wallace woke up. She looked down at his eyes and saw them gradually fill with the

knowledge of what had happened. She saw shame and then anger. He turned his eyes away. His voice was a weak whisper: "Home."

She called to Hank, who carried him out the back door to the car unaided. Comparing him to hundred-pound sugar sacks, Hank guessed his weight to be about 130.

Hank drove him home, carried him up onto the side porch and kicked at the door. Mrs. Flint opened it and cried, "Oh, my poor Wallace. Oh, Mr. Foster, thank you, thank you."

So this is Wallace's mother, thought Hank. He had seen her short, heavy figure moving along Main Street toward the post office each day about the time the afternoon mail was distributed. It occurred to Hank that she was the only person who passed the store without being singled out and identified by Wallace.

"Please put him in there." She pointed to the room beyond the kitchen.

Hank laid Wallace carefully on the couch in the dining room as Mrs. Flint turned down, but not off, the fiddle music on the radio.

"Thank you ever so much, Mr. Foster. He'll be just fine by Monday. He'll be at work bright and early. You wouldn't fire him for this, would you?"

"Of course not." No such thing had occurred to him.

"Will you stay for a cool drink? I have lemonade."

"Thanks, I have to get back." He returned through the kitchen to the door.

"A hot drink?" she asked, following him. "I have coffee."

"No, thanks, we're very busy and my wife and boy are alone."

"Oh, that's wonderful—I knew you'd be busy. I said so to Wallace. He doubted it, but I said, 'Mark my words, these new people will make the business go.' Did you know your father-in-law came and paid me a call on Wednesday?"

"No, I didn't."

"A very gentlemanly old gent. I gave him a glass of lemonade."

There was a moan from the other room. Mrs. Flint went to the doorway and looked in. "Just a minute, Wallace, I'm seeing Mr. Foster off."

He moaned again, and his mother stepped in and covered him with an afghan.

Glancing around the kitchen, Hank saw that the appliances were a generation behind the times; in the late thirties, before the war made them scarce, most people had acquired electric refrigerators

and gas or electric stoves, but not the Flints. Noticing the kerosene lamp on the kitchen table, he realized they were without electricity. He glanced again at the radio in the room beyond; it was cordless, battery-powered.

Mrs. Flint followed him out onto the porch, thanking him again and again.

"Call us if there's anything you need," he told her. "Medicine or anything." Having said this, he realized they probably had no phone.

"No, you're very kind, all he needs is rest. He'll sleep tonight and Sunday and be as good as new on Monday morning. He likes his job, Mr. Foster, he likes working for you and your wife, he told me so."

Hank found Catherine and Brendan swamped, and the market grew even busier after supper when the farm population came to town after the day's fieldwork. The last customer left the store shortly after 10:00 P.M. The proceeds for Saturday were $1,460.96.

11

Expecting the high tide of Grand Opening to flood over into the following week, Hank was at the market before sunrise on Monday to take stock of his diminished grocery supply. He filled out a lengthy order form provided by Bob Donaldson and took it to the post office before eight o'clock so that it would go out on the morning mail truck and delivery of the stock would be assured before next weekend.

Wallace came to work at eight thirty, looking restored if slightly bleary-eyed. Catherine showed up at nine. They worked quickly in preparation for the day's trade, Catherine sweeping and dusting, Wallace replenishing the shelves with the last of the storeroom reserves, Hank taking down the posters in the front window and washing it inside and out. The day darkened and a light rain began to fall. By ten o'clock Catherine and Hank were avoiding each other's eyes, not wanting to acknowledge that half the morning had passed without a penny of income.

The first customer came in at ten fifteen to buy a pack of cigarettes. He was followed by a woman needing a small can of floor wax. The woman was followed by no one. At eleven Catherine cried desperately, "Where is everybody?"

"Mondays are always dead," Wallace told her. "Haven't you noticed?—not even Legget is busy on Monday."

As it happened, they turned their eyes across the street just as three shoppers were filing into Legget's Grocery and two were coming out.

"I see what you mean." Her tone was ironic.

"Well, it's been dead over there until just now."

Catherine recognized one of the women coming out as the mayor's wife. "Who's the woman with Mrs. Brask?"

"Mrs. Kimball."

"Stan's wife?"

Wallace nodded. "You hardly ever see one of those women without the other. They live on Bean Street, two doors apart. Mrs. Kimball is mousy. She listens devoutly to everything Mrs. Brask tells her."

"They're looking this way. Maybe they're coming over to shop."

"No, they'd never do that. They belong to Legget. Always have."

"They were in here on Saturday."

"No."

Catherine nodded. "In the afternoon, while you were resting in back."

"I bet they didn't buy anything."

"I don't remember."

They had bought nothing. They had come into the market on Saturday merely out of curiosity, and they had hurried away with the most stupendous gossip of their lives. They had gone straight to the village hall and told the mayor and the constable that Mrs. Foster hugged and kissed Wallace Flint in the back room of the market when Mr. Foster wasn't looking. Constable Heffernand, not much affected by the news, went on assembling the tail section of his Japanese Zero. The mayor, however, was agog. He locked up his office, said goodnight to the constable, and drove his wife and Mrs. Kimball home, muttering along the way that it was no surprise to him that a woman who had no time for the right-thinking books of Edward Hodge Fleet went in for hugging and kissing the help. Getting out of the car in front of her house, Mrs. Kimball was advised by the Brasks to point out to her husband how ill-advised his friendship with the Fosters was, how shortsighted he had been to associate with them without verifying their moral character beforehand. "I will," Mrs. Kimball said obediently. She went into her house and spoke baby talk to her dog, a white, high-strung pup with pointed ears and hair hanging in its eyes. Then she went into the living room and announced to her husband that Mrs. Foster had hugged and kissed Wallace Flint in the back room of the market when Mr. Foster wasn't looking. Stan Kimball sat in his easy chair with only the bumpy top of his bald head and a cloud of cigar smoke visible be-

hind the *Post-Bulletin.* "Cora and I saw it with our own eyes," she told him as the dog barked and danced, catching at her coat and stockings with its claws. "They held each other tight, and Cora and Harlan wonder if you'll be thinking twice before associating with them in the future."

"What I'm thinking is, Cora and Harlan ought to mind their own business." He turned a page. "Can't you get that mutt to shut up?"

Two doors away Cora Brask phoned the Lutheran parsonage to tell Mrs. Dimmitburg the news, and Mrs. Dimmitburg agreed that the pastor must be told immediately, for it was a scandal with theological overtones, proving beyond a doubt that the union of Catholicism and atheism led to depravity. Wallace was known as Plum's lone atheist.

A block and a half away Melva Heffernand, a slender, aging woman whose short, dyed hair resembled a black helmet, sat at her switchboard and listened to the conversation between the minister's wife and the mayor's wife. When it was over, she watched dusk gather under the elms of Bean Street and pondered the ethics of her profession. It was her policy not to use the facilities of Plum Telephone for broadcasting gossip except to her closest friends, and then only if the gossip consisted of verifiable fact. That Mrs. Brask had witnessed the hugging and kissing was verification enough, she decided. That she numbered over three dozen women as her closest friends accounted, in part, for the great number of curiosity-seekers who crowded into the market on Saturday evening.

Although the Webster Clays lived on Bean, across from the Brasks and the Kimballs, word of the affair did not reach Phyllis Clay until her husband came home for his noon meal on Monday. "I hear the new grocer's wife is carrying on with Wallace Flint," Webster Clay muttered around his mouthful of rump roast and potato. "People seen them smooching in the back room of the grocery store." Rump roast, boiled potatoes, turnips and cake made up the noon meal of Webster Clay five days a week, after which he napped for an hour and then returned to his turkey farms. "I heard it from Skeffington in the bank and Downie at the gas station."

Phyllis Clay was elated to learn of another adventuresome woman in town. Since arriving here a year ago as Webster Clay's bride and discovering very quickly that he had nothing to recommend him but his wealth, Mrs. Clay had had a couple of flings of her own. The first one, with Fred Butz, the high school shop teacher, hadn't lasted

long. After two weeks the affair somehow came to the attention of the school board, and Fred Butz was threatened with the loss of his job if he didn't stop seeing her. Currently she was seeing a chiropractor in Rochester once a week for treatment of her lower spine and for dalliance as well.

After her husband finished eating and went upstairs to lie down, she picked up the phone and asked Central for Hank's Market. She asked Wallace for Mrs. Foster.

When Catherine said hello, she asked, "Does Hank's deliver?"

Catherine recognized the voice. "Yes, Mrs. Clay. Around three every afternoon."

"Oh, good, I need a few things. I need powdered sugar and ten pounds of potatoes."

Catherine wrote this down.

"My husband comes home from his farms with filthy overalls. Which soap is best for that?"

"I've always had good luck with Rinso."

"Then give me a big box of Rinso. And how is your father, Mrs. Foster?"

"He's fine. He had a good rest and is feeling himself again."

"I'm so glad. I was worried."

"Thank you for asking."

"Mrs. Foster, I get the feeling we've got a lot in common." She giggled briefly. "You and I."

Catherine tried to think what it might be. All she remembered of Mrs. Clay were her youth, her accent, and the scanty clothes she wore.

Another giggle came over the phone, followed by the rest of the list for delivery.

Putting the order together with Wallace's help, Catherine asked, "What do you know about Phyllis Clay?"

"She married Webster Clay for his money. He's the sourest man on Bean Street, and that's saying quite a lot considering Mayor Brask lives on Bean."

"She says she and I have a lot in common."

"Oh, really? What?"

"I'm asking you."

Wallace scratched his beard and smiled. "She used to come in and make suggestive remarks to Kermit."

"She's a flirt?"

"And then some."

By three o'clock there were two deliveries to make, and Wallace went out in the DeSoto. It was raining rather hard. His progress was jerky, for despite several driving lessons from Hank, his clutch-coordination was clumsy. Though his history of epilepsy made him ineligible for a driver's license, he had assured Hank and Catherine that he was to be trusted at the wheel because he could feel his seizures coming well beforehand.

The car coughed and shuddered as he brought it to a halt in front of the rooming house on Hay Street. He carried in a bag of groceries for Mrs. Lansky in number seven. At the top of the stairs he looked through the open doorway of number six and saw Dodger Hicks emptying clothes from a dresser drawer into a cardboard box.

"Dodger, how come you're not in school?"

Dodger turned and smiled. Two mismatched socks hung from his hands. "I quit."

Wallace stepped into the room. "You can't quit. You're not sixteen."

"I quit," he said again, because the words gave him such pleasure. Since grade one, nothing in Dodger's education had been quite so satisfying as quitting.

"They'll make you go back. Just wait and see."

"Not here they won't. We're moving to Winona."

"You are? Why?"

Dodger shrugged as he dropped the socks into the carton. "My ma wants to. We got a nicer place to live there." It was a worse place, actually—two rooms instead of three—but Wallace didn't need to know that. Nor did he need to be told that a number of roomers here had been complaining about the night noises in number six whenever one of his mother's men friends drove up from Winona to see her. A couple of them got a little wild when they drank. They hollered and smashed beer bottles and made his mother angry. The loudest noises of all came from his mother when she was angry.

Wallace said, "You'll have to go to school in Winona."

Dodger's smile weakened. "I suppose." It brightened. "If I lay low they might not know I'm there."

"Who is it?" called his mother from the next room.

"Wallace Flint."

"What's he want?"

"Nothing."

Mrs. Hicks emerged from the other room. She was tall, thin and round-shouldered. Her face was long like Dodger's, her hair the same light brown as his. Her features, however, were not large and open like her son's; they were small and pinched. She frowned. "You want something?"

"I was just taking groceries to Mrs. Lansky."

"You got the wrong apartment."

"I know it. I was just wondering why Dodger wasn't in school."

"So now you know." She returned to the other room.

The door to number seven opened into the kitchen. Mrs. Lansky, an old woman in bedroom slippers, was stirring something on the stove. She told Wallace to set the bag on the counter and asked how much she owed him.

"A dollar and eighty cents."

"Heavens." She put down her wooden spoon and dug through the bag, examining the price of each item. "How come crackers are twenty-five? I thought they were nineteen."

"That was just during Grand Opening."

"Take them back."

Wallace substracted twenty-five cents from her slip and she paid him, carefully counting coins out of her purse.

Picking up the crackers, he said, "You're losing your neighbors."

The old woman looked suddenly sad. "Poor Dodger."

"Why poor Dodger?"

She said nothing. Shaking her head, she turned to the stove and resumed her stirring.

When he heard Mrs. Clay call, "Come in," Wallace opened her kitchen door and found her sitting at the table, her face heavily made up, a magazine open in front of her, an amber drink in her hand. Her blouse, thought Wallace, had too many buttons open to be modest.

"You can set them on the drainboard," she told him, smiling.

He put down the bags and handed her the sales slip.

"I'll have to pay you next time, Wallace; I don't have any money."

Wallace told her that was fine.

"How about having a drink with me?"

"No, no," he said. This woman had been making Wallace uneasy ever since she started coming into the store and batting her eyes at Kermit. It had been embarrassing to witness Kermit trying to look

roguish while turning to jelly. As far as Wallace knew, there had been nothing between them beyond eye-batting and giggling.

"Why not have a drink? Webster buys Old Crow by the case and never keeps track. He has no idea how much I drink or give to my friends—just so his pot roast is ready at twelve and his supper at six."

Wallace folded the slip and tucked it into his shirt pocket. "I'll put this on your account," he said, staring at her as he edged toward the door. Uneasy as she made him, he couldn't take his eyes from her.

She put her glass to her lips, took a sip and licked the rim. "Wallace, would you tell me something if I promise not to spread it around?"

"What?"

She looked him over, smiling, thinking he was handsome enough in a miniature sort of way, but feeling her seductive manner wasted on him. "I hear you and the boss's wife are really hitting it off." She giggled.

"What do you mean?"

"Lovey-dovey stuff." She rolled her eyes. "Is it true?"

"Where did you hear that?"

"Everybody's saying so. Webster heard it from two different parties this morning. I called up and told Central and she said she knew it already."

There was a touch of hysteria in Wallace's laugh. "That's ridiculous."

"Central said she heard it on Saturday. Is it true?"

He told her there was nothing to it, but he spoke weakly and she assumed he was guilty and ashamed. She giggled when he said goodbye.

On his way back to the store, Wallace stopped at the post office and asked for the Hickses' forwarding address in Winona.

"What do you want it for?" inquired the postmaster from under his green eyeshade.

"We're billing them for groceries."

"I thought Mrs. Hicks shopped at Legget's."

"She did, mostly, but Dodger ran up a bill for candy."

The postmaster, referring to a note tacked to the wall, read off the address and Wallace copied it down.

Entering the store, Wallace laughed and called out, "I found out

what Mrs. Clay meant on the phone." He saw that Catherine was dusting, Hank was working at the produce display, and they had been joined by Rufus Ottmann, who stood at the front door staring out. Wallace told the Fosters of the rumor in terms he intended as amusing, but they weren't amused.

"Is she crazy?" cried Catherine. "Is everybody crazy?" She picked up a jar of preserves, swiped at it with her feather duster and plunked it down angrily. "Are there nothing but lunatics in this village?" She closed her eyes and seethed.

Hank, checking grapes for decay, said, "Catherine, don't take it so seriously."

"Don't tell me how to take it," she flared. "It's our lives these gossips are playing loose with. How did we happen to choose the town with the highest percentage of lunatics, bigots, gossips, and . . ." She would have added "idiots" if Rufus Ottmann at that moment hadn't turned his magnanimous, empty smile upon her.

Hank took the feather duster from her and handed it to Wallace. "We need a good, long coffee break. Wallace, mind the store."

Left in charge, Wallace leaned on the cash register, his arms folded across its top, his eyes on the children passing along the wet street from the direction of the school. Rain fell in sprinkles. He felt strangely elated at having been accused of illicit love. It was a damaging rumor, for it worked against Catherine's adjustment to Plum, but it was delightfully bizarre. He was reminded of the rumors that had accompanied his graduation from high school. Somehow it started going around that he would attend the University of Minnesota on a full scholarship. Others said Winona State. A few had heard the University of Chicago. The rumors stayed alive for a year or more, while only Wallace knew he was going nowhere.

Brendan came angling across the street, having promised his parents he'd look in to see if he was needed before going off to play. He hoped he wouldn't be needed. Philip Crowley was waiting for him in the covered shed of the lumber yard, where they had dug nine small holes in the dirt floor and devised a rainy-day game combining the principles of marbles and golf. Loser paid winner a marble per hole, each marble being redeemable for a cigarette at such time as the loser came into possession of cigarettes.

Nearing the market, he saw Wallace and Rufus looking out at him. The faces put him in mind of the puzzle page of *Boys' Life*. For ten points, which face is the idiot? Which is the heartless villain?

Stepping through the door and cringing under Rufus's smile, he said to Wallace, looking him in the eye as though he neither hated nor feared him, "Not very busy, huh?"

"Dead all day. Only the gossips are busy."

"What gossips?"

"All the gossips in town. They're saying your mother and I are having a love affair."

Brendan's eyes widened in wonder, then went shut as he laughed. "Boy, that's rich."

Wallace, having expected him not to take it so lightly, found his glee offensive and changed the subject:

"Have you heard about Dodger Hicks?"

"What about him?"

"He's moving away."

Brendan's expression turned serious. His betrayal of Dodger continued to nag him. After three weeks of turning it over in his mind, he had decided on Saturday that the betrayal was a sin, and following the Gene Autry movie he had gone to church and told Father O'Day about it in the confessional. The old priest hadn't seemed the least interested. He had assigned him a perfunctory penance of three Hail Marys, and his murmur of absolution had been followed by a yawn.

"Where's he moving to?"

"Winona, where he came from." A change came over Wallace's face as he spoke. His tone of contempt was such that Rufus momentarily lost his smile and shifted his eyes, and Brendan feared that Wallace was on the brink of another fit. But he wasn't. Immediately he eased up on his clenched look.

Brendan went off to marbles.

Wallace, gazing out the window, yawned.

Rufus, gazing out the door, did the same.

Catherine and Hank inhaled the odors of beer, smoke and hamburger grease as they stepped into Gordy's and slid into their customary booth along the wall opposite the bar. Gordy brought them two mugs of coffee and commented on the continued warm weather, but sensing Catherine's agitation, he did not linger to chat.

Hank ventured a consoling remark: "It's only gossip, Catherine, that's all."

"That's all?" she seethed. "It's people lying through their teeth.

Whoever saw Wallace have that seizure saw the way he clung to me and they made it into a love affair."

"I know it's a lie and I'm sorry. We have to ignore it."

Catherine rolled her eyes at the ceiling and let them fall on her cup. She sipped in silence for a minute or more, then stated in a subdued tone, "Hank, I don't have any friends here."

"Give it time. We've only been here three and a half weeks."

"But I don't have any *hope* of friends."

He spoke softly, carefully: "Who were your friends in the city, Catherine? After Mae went to Florida, who did you have?"

"The city was different. In the city I had . . . the city."

"Well, here at least you've got Wallace."

She was startled. "What are you saying?" Her voice rose. "You believe that lie?"

"No, of course not. I'm saying you and Wallace get along. You seem to have fun at work."

"Hank, Wallace is our charity case."

"You don't think of him as a friend?"

"In a way a friend, but don't you see, it's a sign of how impossible this town is that my only friend outside the family is a man years younger than I am, with such a cynical view of life that I sometimes find myself taking on his bitter ways and hating myself for it."

"Ways like nicknaming our customers?"

She broke out in a laugh. "I have to take the whole blame there. Wallace didn't start that, I did." Her laugh quickly died.

"Catherine, it's very bad for business, those nicknames. When Mr. and Mrs. Dombrowski were in the store Saturday, I saw you and Wallace snickering behind their backs, and I think they noticed it too."

"I couldn't help it." She smiled, remembering. "They're so stodgy and serious looking, so Victorian, and Wallace came up to me and said, 'Will you wait on Marx and Engels, or will I?' "

Hank sat back, studying her. "I don't get it."

"See, their real names are Max and Enga."

He observed her atttempt to quit smiling. He said, "I still don't see the humor."

She sat forward and lowered her head, cupping her face in her hands and staring down at her mug of coffee. Her shoulders were shaking with giggles.

But they weren't giggles; he saw this a few moments later when

she raised her head. The tears she wiped away were not tears of amusement.

"I'm sorry," she said. "For being such a misfit."

He placed his hand over hers. "Catherine, there were times on Friday and Saturday when I felt like I'd never felt before. We had more customers than we could keep up with, and I felt a thrill almost like the day you said you'd marry me."

She gazed at him.

"Like we were having a kind of Grand Opening inside ourselves." He paused. "Like we finally got where we were meant to be in life."

He saw renewed tears in her eyes. He said, "But then I felt a letdown yesterday morning in church. I was thanking God for all those customers when I realized that no matter how well the store goes, it's no good if you're not happy here."

"I'll be all right. I'm sorry."

"Don't apologize. It could have been Brendan who had trouble moving. It could have been your father. It could have been me. I'm just saying it never occurred to me before we moved that there was more than one way for us to fail. I thought everything depended on how many groceries we sold."

"Give me time," she said. "I'll be all right."

"But I want you to be more than all right. I want you to feel what I felt on Friday and Saturday."

She nodded, smiling weakly.

"Because I can't feel it if you don't."

12

After supper Wallace took a long nap in his room. When he awoke he lit the kerosene lamp on the table beside his bed, and as the flame grew brighter he watched the purple faces materialize on the ceiling and walls. They numbered thirty-two. They were crude faces, applied with a wide brush, but with enough detail to be distinguishable one from another. He gazed at Emily Dickinson above the dresser. Her features were guesswork, for he had had no picture to go by, only her poems, which had gone unpublished until after her death. Next to her was Vincent van Gogh. Eyes slightly aslant, an ear missing. One painting sold in his lifetime. Above them was John Keats. Curly hair, jutting jaw. By the time he was Wallace's age, John Keats was dead. The faces consoled Wallace, belonging as they did to people whose genius had not been acknowledged in their lifetimes.

He read for a time, then went downstairs, where he found his mother listening to the ten-o'clock news and snacking on Spam. He stood in the doorway for a minute as H. V. Kaltenborn set forth his nightly analysis: "The final blow at Germany is of course inevitable. Only two things might delay it: a new German weapon of unforeseen effectiveness or an unbridgeable rift in the Allied Coalition. The victory over Japan appears to impose greater problems. Measured in total size of forces alone, the task ahead is stupendous. Add to it the vast areas that must be conquered and it tries the imagination."

"I'm going for a walk," he told his mother.

"But it's raining."

"No it isn't." He took his jacket from the coat stand next to the kitchen door and stepped out into the sprinkling rain.

No teacher or janitor ever stayed in school beyond 10:00 P.M., but to be safe Wallace walked the dark streets until 10:30; then he crossed the playground to the back of the school. The faulty latch was on the third window from the left, an opaque window at ground level, opening into the boys' physical education area. He made his way through the darkness to the coaches' office, his refuge whenever he couldn't stand one more minute under the same roof with his mother, an ideal place for night work, being an inner room with no windows to show the light. He closed the door, switched on the overhead light, and settled himself at Mr. Torborg's desk.

Wallace had never met Mr. Torborg, but he knew him by reputation and recognized him on the street. A wounded veteran of the Pacific campaign, Mr. Torborg had joined the teaching staff only a year ago. According to the *Plum Alert,* he had been awarded medals for heroism. He taught math and coached basketball and track. Watching a basketball game last winter, Wallace had perceived him as a kindly, patient young man, well liked by his students. He had a small blond moustache, which he habitually groomed with the thumb and forefinger of his right hand. His paralyzed left hand, hanging useless at his side, was the badge of his heroics in the Philippines, and more than once Wallace wished that he had come by his own disability in such a glorious way.

Wallace opened the drawer in which Mr. Torborg kept his school stationery. He found an envelope, rolled it into the typewriter and addressed it to the superintendent of schools in Winona. Next he rolled in a sheet of paper.

> Dear Sir:
>
> I wish to alert you to the fact that a student of ours, aged 15, is moving with his mother to 321 Broad Street in Winona. Being a reluctant student and the son of negligent parents, he might well pose a truancy problem. His name is Dodger Hicks.

Wallace was about to forge the name of Thomas Reinhart, the principal, when it occurred to him that administrators often ran across one another at meetings and this letter might come up in conversation. Instead, he closed the letter with an imaginary name and title:

> Jeannette Horvath
> Assistant to the Principal

He sealed the letter and cursed under his breath because he had forgotten to bring along a postage stamp. He wanted it to go out on the morning mail truck so that Dodger would be confronted by the authorities the moment he got to Winona. Searching through the desk, he found, along with stamps, an envelope containing three snapshots from Mr. Torborg's time in the service. In one he wore a dress uniform and looked very young; he was probably just out of basic training. In the second he stood with several buddies in fatigues under a palm tree; he was holding a water canteen in his left hand and laughing. The third picture showed him wearing white pajamas and sitting in a wheelchair; an officer stood at his side with his hand on his shoulder, and there was a nurse in the background.

Wallace placed the snapshots side by side on the desk and studied them for a long while, feeling envy for this man no older than himself who had gone halfway around the world and made friends and done heroic things and come home with medals. Serving in the military was amounting to a lot more than Wallace had foreseen when he had sought deferment early in the war. Papers and movies were full of stories in which the common sailor, infantryman or pilot did glorious things. By now, Wallace thought, were it not for his medical disqualification he might be wearing medals of his own. At this very moment he might be involved in a valorous act at the front, dying a valorous death. Dead or alive, he'd be shipped home to acclaim. Dead, he'd be given a hero's burial. Alive, he'd be given a parade down Main Street, after which he'd leave town and never come back.

He replaced the pictures in the drawer, sadly aware of how little he was affecting the course of world events. He switched off the light and left the office.

The next morning, waiting for the school bell to call them across the street, Brendan, Sam and Philip played marbles in the lumber yard. They were between the seventh and eighth holes when Brendan saw a pickup stop in the alley at the far end of the shed and a figure enter the wide doorway and come slouching toward them. Against the sunlight flooding the doorway Brendan thought at first it was an employee coming to work carrying a lunchpail, but as the figure drew nearer he saw, with a tinge of shame, that it was Dodger Hicks carrying a brand new bag of marbles.

"Hi, Dodger," said Brendan, getting down on one knee, ready to shoot.

"Hi." Dodger stepped boldly into the path the marble would take, and in a voice oddly authoritative he told Brendan to stand up and hold his pockets open.

Brendan stood and smirked at Sam and Philip, trying to make clear to them without words that this intruder was no friend of his. He held open his right pants pocket and Dodger poured marbles out of his bag until the pocket overflowed. Then he filled the left pocket. Brendan had been playing with a meager capital of about ten marbles, losing half a dozen a day, winning them back the next. Now suddenly he had this wealth of glassies, five or six dozen gems of swirling, brilliant design—amber, violet, crimson, green. What did they mean? Were they Brendan's reward for having eased Dodger's loneliness during the first two days of school? Or were they meant to deepen his shame?

Dodger didn't explain. He simply nodded when Brendan said thanks, and he turned and left the shed, his stride long-legged and lazy, his wrists dangling far out of his shirtcuffs, the back of his head carelessly barbered. Out in the sunlight he climbed into the cab of the pickup, in which a man and a woman sat waiting. As the truck moved past the doorway, Brendan saw that it carried a load of furniture.

"What was that all about?" Philip wanted to know.

"Beats me," said Brendan nonchalantly, getting down on one knee and feeling enormously relieved to have seen the last of Dodger Hicks.

13

"Look at these books, Hank. You've been in business two months, and you've had only one week when it was worthwhile to unlock your front door." Stan Kimball, undertaker, sat on an orange crate beside Hank's desk. Having just come from a funeral, he wore a large white carnation in the lapel of his dark suit. A short, spongy cigar smoldered in the corner of his mouth. "Turn back to that other page and let's have a look at your weekly totals."

The ledger told them that whereas weekly income avaraged $48 before Grand Opening, it averaged $165 thereafter.

"It's an improvement," said Hank, concealing his fear that the market would never produce a living for himself and his family. After overhead, his net profit was very small. Now in the chill of late October he was burning coal like paper, particularly at home, where the walls lacked insulation.

"It's peanuts! You've got to hit these people with more sales. Your Grand Opening got you a hell of a flock of customers, but when it was over they mostly went back to Legget. You've got to hit them with one sale after another until they get the habit of coming in here even when there is no sale."

"But here it says you can put on too many sales." Hank handed him the latest issue of *Independent Grocer.* "People get so they ignore sales."

Kimball riffled the pages. "Where does this come from?"

"Chicago."

"What the hell does anybody in Chicago know about Plum? Your Grand Opening was the first grocery sale this town has seen in this

millennium. Kermit never put on a sale, and therefore Legget never had to. Hit these people with a sale a month and pretty soon you'll have this store so goddamn full of customers you'll have to double your staff."

Hank took the magazine back. "It says the best way to build trade is to be dependable day to day." During a sale his profit margin decreased.

"Dependable to who—Mrs. Ottmann and her idiot child? Listen, Hank, haven't I told you about the economics of groceries as compared to the economics of death?" Kimball held his handkerchief to his chin and dribbled brown cigar juice into it and returned it to his pocket. "I average twenty-four funerals a year in this town and there's no way short of murder I can change that number. If I offered a hot price on caskets, how many people would die to save a few bucks? Now you, on the other hand, you can mount a sale as often as you feel like it, and people will flock to your groceries like cows to a saltlick. You're in complete control of your business, Hank. My business is run by the angel of death."

They heard the DeSoto come to a stop at the back door, heard the engine die, cough three times and die again.

"Tell that to Catherine," Hank said.

"I will. Excuse me, I've got to take a leak." Kimball went into the basement.

Entering the back door, Catherine sniffed, smiled and said, "I smell Stan's cigar."

Hank nodded. "He's downstairs. Catherine, it's time to talk seriously about our next sale."

"Haven't we talked it to death?"

Indeed, they had gone so far as to name it Hank's Harvest Sale and to lay out the circular, but they had not carried through for fear of failure. Grand Opening, while a triumph in itself, had brought them very few permanent customers. If it was novelty and low prices that had made Grand Opening a success, could a second sale possibly succeed on low prices alone? Day after discouraging day in October, they had felt their hopes become stunted, their courage disappear.

Catherine hung up her coat and slipped the loop of a fresh apron over her head, tied the strings behind her. She saw Stan Kimball mounting the steps.

"Hi, Stan, how's your dog?" It was her standard greeting to him, for he had a complaint a day to get off his chest.

"Hello, Catherine. She's all mouth and digestive tract. If she isn't eating, she's eliminating, usually on the living room carpet."

"She? I thought it was a he."

"Maybe it is. You'd have to ask my wife."

"What a lovely flower you're wearing."

"Like it? I picked it fresh off a graveside bouquet. Catherine, I'm trying to convince your husband to mount another sale."

"We've talked about it."

"Do it. Call it a Halloween Sale and give away pumpkins."

"There isn't time before Halloween," said Hank.

"Then call it an Election Sale. Have a mock election where each customer gets to cast a ballot, and on Saturday night count them up and see if Dewey can take Roosevelt."

Seeing that Catherine looked interested, Hank cautioned, "I don't think we should mix politics with business."

"Well, how about an Armistice Day Sale? As long as we have to fight this goddamn war, we might as well take advantage of it. Advertise a big drawing for eleven o'clock on the eleventh of November—give away a lifetime supply of grapefruit or Brillo pads or some such thing."

"Lifetime?" laughed Catherine. "That could be seventy years."

"All right, birdseed for the life of some bird, but the main thing is to get yourself a gimmick and offer prices like you did the first time and print up a red, white and blue circular and you'll have shoppers crowding in here like you've never seen. What do you say?"

She looked at Hank. "Should we do it?"

Before he could answer Wallace appeared in the doorway and said, "Catherine, I'm starving." He pointed to his wristwatch.

"Go ahead, Wallace, I'll take over." She went to the mirror and straightened her hair.

Stan Kimball said, "Wait a minute, Catherine, there's something else I want to say to both of you."

Wallace remained in the doorway listening.

"The house next door to mine on Bean Street is going on the market next month. The name is DeRoche. He delivers auto parts and his company is moving him to Wisconsin. I think you ought to buy the place."

"With what?" said Catherine.

"With your profits on Hank's Armistice Sale and all the sales after that. DeRoche is asking less than four thousand. The bank will give you twenty years. There's not a doubt in my mind this town will

support two grocery stores and support them damn well. Your house is an old ark on the wrong end of town and you're paying Old Lady Ottmann twice what it's worth. Get yourselves a place of your own on Bean Street before the war ends and prices go up. Don't you agree, Wallace?"

It made no difference to Kimball what Wallace thought, but he was careful never to ignore him entirely, sensing that to ignore Wallace was to turn your back on a poisonous snake.

Wallace, leaning against the doorframe with his hands in his pockets, did not reply. Kimball pressed him:

"What do you say for yourself, Wallace?"

"How's your dog?" In this as in many other things Wallace followed Catherine's example. "Is it trained yet?"

"People do not train dogs. They train themselves to accommodate dogs. My wife and I have trained ourselves to predict within one minute when this dog of ours will go to the bathroom."

"Well, that's progress."

"Yes. It's the minute after we bring her indoors."

He removed his cigar and examined the ash. "Catherine, maybe you're thinking you'd prefer a house with more amiable neighbors, and I can understand that. It's not the happiest prospect having my dog on one side of you and the mayor's commander-in-chief on the other. But apart from the neighbors you'll love the house. Three bedrooms, all on the ground floor—no need for your father to climb stairs. DeRoche gave it a fresh coat of paint last summer. The yard is big and full of shade trees."

He put on his coat and made for the door. "Come on, Wallace, it's lunch time. I'll give you a ride home."

The red, white and blue circulars were delivered by Brendan and Philip Crowley on a cold afternoon. Sam Romberg had declined, saying he had to work for his father (Plum Bottlegas was the Romberg enterprise), which probably meant that Sam was out delivering cylinders of gas with his brother Andy in the family pickup. Brendan couldn't call Sam his best friend, but he wished it were so. As a companion Sam was unfaithful. He had time for Brendan and Philip only when his other friends weren't available, older friends mostly, whom he had come to know through his brother Andy, who was sixteen. Andy's friends were Plum's fast crowd. They knew girls as far away as Pinburg. They sometimes drank beer.

Philip Crowley had red hair, freckles and large teeth. He was

taller than Brendan, but he seemed younger, given as he was to hijinks, giggles and whiny moods. The hijinks and giggles were fine with Brendan, but the whiny moods were not. Brendan distrusted moods, his own included. He considered the moodlessness of his father ideal behavior. He wanted to be like that himself, and not like his mother, who in recent weeks had become very peevish. This was a side of his mother he had never seen before. She was all right in the market, where she had her work and Wallace to divert her, but around home she was temperamental, and at the suppertable her talk was peppered with the word "disgusting." The smell of silage was disgusting, and so were the idlers who spat tobacco juice all over the sidewalk in front of the post office, and so were the school board members who had voted to double expenditures in the athletic department without adding a dime for badly needed facilities in music, home ec, and business education. "Twenty stenography students are taking turns on five typewriters," she would announce over dessert, and Brendan would try to knit his brow and show concern the way his father did, feeling quite certain that his father's concern, like his own, was caused by his mother's discontent rather than by the shortage of typewriters. Part of her trouble, he knew, was the nonsense going around about her being in love with Wallace. He had heard it first from Wallace, and then from Pearl Peterson in school. More than once he had overheard his parents discussing it in low tones as they did dishes together after supper. He wanted to speak up and assure his mother that he, for one, knew it was nonsense, but he was wary of his mother these days and he kept silent.

Distributing circulars along Bean Street, Brendan came to the houses of the mayor and the undertaker and the house in between that was for sale. It was painted creamy-yellow. It had two porches and a lot of bushes and trees around it. At the undertaker's urging, his parents had made an appointment to look at it. Brendan hoped with all his heart they'd buy it, for it stood directly across the alley from Sam Romberg's house.

Further along, he came to the Heffernand house. Here lived the lady who played the organ in the choir loft and sang through her nose. She lived with her brother, the constable. A few days ago Brendan had joined the crowd in the street in front of the village hall and watched the constable fling a burning airplane off the roof, and although he cheered with the others when it crashed in flames against the plate glass window of Plum Hardware and fell to the

ground a cinder, he did not feel cheerful in the least. He felt instead a sense of war's ruination of all things fine and human, for he had put together enough model planes of his own to know how much intricate work they required. He felt, too, that the constable might be a little crazy.

The wind being cold on his hands and face, Brendan was relieved to enter the rooming house on Hay Street. He left circulars at the various doors and smelled the various suppers cooking. Upstairs the door to number seven stood open, and Brendan saw old Mrs. Lansky tending two pots on the stove. He stepped in and handed her a circular.

"Is it Hank's again? Are they having that good price on crackers?"

"I'll look." He unfolded the sheet and they examined it together, finding not crackers but three or four other items the woman was interested in.

She thanked him, and as he turned to leave, she said, "What grade are you in?"

"Seventh."

"Then you knew Dodger Hicks. Have you heard about poor Dodger?"

"No."

"Mrs. Slocum downstairs heard it from her sister-in-law in Winona. Dodger robbed a gas station and was caught and sent to the Home School for Boys in Flensboro. Think of it, not sixteen and already a convict."

The news stung Brendan. He pictured the red-tiled roofs of the Home School, the flower beds, the boys working on the grounds, the guard raising his stick to a boy. It was Labor Day in this picture; they had just eaten a restaurant meal with Uncle Herman. "Poor Dodger," Mrs. Lansky said again. This was the first tender word Brendan had ever heard ascribed to Dodger. Her saying it made him feel sad. Slowly descending the stairs, he realized that it had been easier to be indifferent toward Dodger when everyone else was indifferent.

Making his way across town by way of the alleys, Grandfather turned up the collar of his long black coat and pulled his gray fedora down tight to his ears. He wished he had worn gloves. The cold wind stung his fingers and made his eyes water. He patted his coat pocket, making sure it contained the red, white and blue circular intended for the Lutheran minister. He recalled that the original Armistice

Day in 1918 had been warmer than this. News of the Armistice had reached Minneapolis just as his train was pulling in from Chicago. Crowds poured out onto the streets and he had some difficulty making his way from the depot to the carline on Hennepin, for along with his grip he carried a large box containing a flowered pitcher and bowl for Sade's birthday. He boarded the Bryant-Johnson streetcar and looked down on the people moving deliriously along the street. It was stop and go for several blocks until they reached the Basilica of St. Mary, where the way was completely blocked. Caught up in the rejoicing, everyone on the streetcar including the motorman and conductor pushed his way out onto the street. Grandfather would have joined them had it not been for his grip and his box. Looking toward the Basilica, he saw Monsignor Murphy in his cassock and biretta standing in the portico and motioning with his arms for the people to come and thank God for peace. Grandfather leaned out the window and shouted, "Go and thank God for peace!" to those milling around below him. He repeated it several times, pointing to the priest, and soon the mass of people began moving out of the street and up the steps of the church. With the tracks more or less cleared, Grandfather sat down at the controls and confirmed what he had suspected after years of watching motormen at work, that compared to a train driving a streetcar was easy as pie. He moved it along as far as Hennepin and Lake, where he encountered not only another mob but also a confusing junction of tracks. This being only eight blocks from home, he picked up his grip and his box and walked. He found the house empty. Sade and the girls, he learned later, were over at the neighbors, toasting the Armistice with apple juice. He changed out of his uniform and hurried to his favorite saloon on Lyndale and drank and sang songs till midnight.

Windchimes tingled pleasantly over Grandfather's right ear as he let himself into the enclosed back porch of the parsonage, slamming the door behind him and taking out his handkerchief to wipe his eyes. Almost immediately the inner door was opened by a very tall young man in his twenties who scowled and blinked as though he found daylight painful. He wore thick glasses and clothes so dark Grandfather took them for clericals.

"Are you the minister?"

"No, that's my father," said the young man in a soft, deep voice. "Can I help you?"

"I was hoping to talk to the minister himself."

"He's out, probably until this evening, but I can give him your message. Are you a parishioner?"

"Yes."

The young man put out his hand and Grandfather shook it, adding, "But not of this parish. Michael McMahon, section hand, brakeman and conductor with the Milwaukee Road for forty years."

"Paul Dimmitburg," said the young man.

"Paul's a fine name. If we'd had a son, my wife and I, we'd have named him Paul. With our second daughter we were expecting a boy and Paul was the name we'd chosen. Paul McMahon, now there's a name for you. I see a man with a name like that coming in off the road after a few years and taking an office job. I see him directing the railroad's affairs from behind a desk in St. Paul and going home to a house on Summit Avenue in the same block as James J. Hill's, a house with a stone fireplace in every room." From his coat pocket he took out the circular. "I want the minister and his lady to see these wonderful prices on groceries." He unfolded it shakily, turned it right side up. "See here, fresh carrots, Lava soap—all of it under cost at Hank's Market in honor of Armistice Day."

The young man's face registered no interest. It was the sort of face you couldn't open without a key, thought Grandfather, the sort of face you ran into all over this town. What the hell was on the minds of all these farmers and villagers that they should be so hard-shelled and unforthcoming? Aside from Gordy there was scarcely a soul in the pool hall with an amiable manner about him. They all had a way of hooding their eyes and speaking in monosyllables. Cold. Hot. Rain. Snow. Yup. Nope. Well, at least the pool hall was warmer than this porch, and this tall young man with glasses obviously wasn't going to invite him in.

"I'd be much obliged if you'd give this to your father." He handed him the circular. "Tell him I stopped by." Opening the outer door, he paused. "Perhaps you can tell me. Does your father enjoy talking about the verities?"

"Of course, it's his vocation."

Grandfather laughed happily. "In the words of the great MacArthur, I shall return."

Paul Dimmitburg returned to the kitchen, where he had been sipping tea and reading. When the temperature fell below freezing, the kitchen was the warmest room in the parsonage. He dropped the circular next to the two books open on the table, a volume of Kier-

kegaard and a carpentry manual. He turned the heat on under the teakettle, and as he waited for the water to boil he stood at the window with his arms crossed, watching the old man walk away with his head cocked against the wind and relishing the stillness pervading the house. He was enjoying his first day of solitude since arriving home from the seminary a week ago. Not that he wasn't fond of his parents and his brother John, but they had been paying him altogether too much attention, his mother acting as if his problem were a physical malady and treatable with enormous helpings of food, both during and between meals; his father pretending he had no problem and treating him as if he were a colleague, drawing him into conversations about his parishioners and asking advice about next Sunday's sermon; John proudly bringing home troops of his high school friends to meet Plum's all-time high-scoring basketball player. Today his parents had driven to Red Wing on church business and John was occupied after school by the first basketball practice of the season.

Paul Dimmitburg went to the stove and held out his hands, warming them over the spout of the teakettle. Having progressed six weeks into his third year of post-graduate training, he had suffered a nervous collapse in late October from an overdose of moral theology. In Paul's case, fear of the Lord was not the beginning of wisdom, as Scripture claimed, but of neurosis. His professors diagnosed his problem as overscrupulosity. The very thought of God's majesty and man's sinfulness filled him with trepidation. Falling so hopelessly short of God's perfection, the human race would have been better off if God had not made His covenant with them, but had instead left them to grovel in their iniquity. When Kierkegaard suggested, perhaps in jest, that all of Christianity ought to carry their Holy Bibles to a mountaintop and plead with God to take them back and relieve humanity of its terrifying responsibility, Paul Dimmitburg murmured to himself, Yes, dear Lord, yes, turn to your angels, make them your chosen people, for we mortals are too weak to offer you anything but disappointment. His fear of God's punishment was at its most acute on Sundays. Sitting in church and listening to the preacher call down God's blessing, he cowered, aware that when you asked for blessings you sometimes got curses, much the way when you prayed for rain you sometimes got hail.

And so, late last week, on the advice of his professors, he had packed up and left St. Louis. They had advised him to go home and

look for a job that would not tax his moral sensibilities and maybe next fall he could resume his studies. They told him that if he could learn not to be quite so hard on himself and on the rest of humanity, if he could learn to relax, then he would be free to develop into one of the most brilliant ministers that the seminary had yet produced. They said they'd pray for him.

With his fresh cup of tea, Paul Dimmitburg sat down at the table and resumed reading, alternating every fifteen or twenty minutes between his two books. He had trained himself to study this way, to interrupt his heavier reading with a few pages of something unrelated. It helped his mind stay sharp. In fact, theology and woodworking, his two favorite subjects, weren't as unrelated as they seemed, Christ having grown up in his father's carpentry shop. Paul picked up a pencil and underlined:

> Sermons as we know them today constitute a form of communication in complete disaccord with Christianity. Christianity can be communicated only by witnesses, i.e., by men who existentially express what they proclaim, realize it in their lives.

A few minutes later he underlined again:

> The wooden spline, inserted in a saw kerf, is a sure and simple way to strengthen miter and butt joints. A spline's width should be slightly less than the combined depth of the kerfs, allowing for a layer of glue.

After a while, leaning back and stretching, Paul let his eye fall upon the red, white and blue circular, and it came to him that Hank's Market must be Kermit's Grocery under new management. In searching unsuccessfully for work this week, he had avoided Kermit's Grocery, assuming it to be the same squalid operation it had always been. He had applied to several Lutherans for work (Louie Legget, Mayor Brask, Len Downie at the Standard Station, Russell Romberg of Plum Bottlegas) and against his mother's wishes he had even gone to a couple of Catholics (B. L. Skeffington in the bank and Ben Crowley at the movie theater) but he had found nothing.

He looked at the clock on the kitchen wall. Hank's Market would be closed. He would apply first thing in the morning.

Walking door to door with circulars was the hardest work Philip Crowley had ever done in his pampered life, and when he came near

his own house he crossed to Brendan's side of the street, handed him his sack of circulars and said he had to go in.

"You can't go in. We're not done."

"I've got an earache and a stomachache."

"But we've got all of Clover Street and Corn Street to do yet. And that bunch of houses out by the poor farm. You're getting paid for this."

"When my ear feels like this I have to lie on a heating pad so I don't get mastoiditis."

"What's mastoiditis?"

"And when my stomach feels like this, it might be appendicitis, and I think I've got a blister on my foot. I get infections from blisters."

He limped across the street and into his house.

Alone, crisscrossing streets, the job took three times as long. Nearly an hour later, crossing Clover Street in the dark, Brendan ran to avoid a pair of headlights bearing down on him. It was the Romberg Bottlegas pickup, which, after passing him, screeched to a halt and backed up. Sam Romberg called, "Hey, Bren, want a ride?"

Looking into the cab, Brendan saw five faces reflecting the dim lights from the dash. He saw the red glow of at least three cigarettes. Pearl Peterson sat on Sam's lap. Against the far door Andy Romberg was at the wheel, and next to him was Norma Nash, a blonde from the junior class who, it was said, went all the way with boys. Squeezed in the middle was Lorraine Graham, who said, "Hi, Bren, what are you doing in this end of town?"

"Delivering circulars."

"Aren't you done yet?" asked Sam. "You've been at it since school let out."

"I'd be done if Philip didn't get sick."

"What was it this time? Appendicitis?"

"I guess so."

"He always quits games when he's on the losing side. It's usually appendicitis."

"Why don't you get in and ride with us?" said Lorraine.

"Yeah, get in," said Andy. "We're taking a tank of bottlegas out to the poor farm."

"He'd have to ride in back," said Pearl sourly. "It's too crowded in here."

"No," said Lorraine, "it's too cold in back."

"You just wish you had a lap to sit on," Pearl told her. "You're always begging some boy to hold you on his lap."

"I am not. You're the one who's always pushing yourself on boys."

Norma Nash said, "Let him in and close the window, it's cold in here." She raised a bottle of beer from between her legs. "Want a swig of beer, Bren? Warm you up?"

"I've got to finish Clover Street and then do the houses out by the poor farm."

"Hell, we'll do those houses for you," said Andy. "Give us a bunch of them bills."

Lorraine said, "Why not do Clover Street too? Come on, let's get out and help him."

Sam threw open his door. "Pick us up at the end of the street, Andy." He slipped out from under Pearl and hopped to the ground.

"Wait," said Pearl, "I'm not delivering any old bills."

"Don't be such a crumb," said Lorraine. "Let me out."

"Let me out too," said Norma Nash. "I've got to pee."

The girls pushed Pearl out the door and got out themselves.

"You're all horrid," said Pearl, climbing back in and slamming the door.

Brendan and Lorraine took one side, and Norma Nash, after pausing behind a bush, joined Sam on the other. They finished Clover Street in ten minutes and packed themselves into the truck, Brendan next to the door with Lorraine on his lap.

Andy gave the bottle to Norma and reached into the tangle of legs to shift gears.

"You drank it all," said Norma.

"There's a swallow left."

"Here, Bren, you get to drain it."

He took it from her and gulped it down. It was warm and fizzy. As the truck bounced over a rut he belched loudly in Lorraine's ear. Lorraine laughed wildly and so did Brendan. He brimmed with happiness. What could be better than fitting tightly into the Romberg pickup with a girl on your lap and fizz in your nose? In abandoning him to this, Philip had done him a great favor.

"Should I open the other bottle?" asked Norma Nash, feeling under the seat.

"Why not," said Andy, picking an opener off the dash and handing it to her. "How come nobody's smoking?"

They all helped themselves from a pack on the dash.

Dragging cautiously on his cigarette, Brendan watched Norma Nash open the bottle. "Where do you guys get beer?"

Norma said, "We always keep a bottle or two under the seat, don't we, Andy?"

"Yep, always. Ever since yesterday."

"They only started going together yesterday," Lorraine explained to Brendan. Her voice was birdlike, twittery with giggles. Her hair brushed his forehead.

"My dad drinks beer by the case," said Norma, "and Andy's dad smokes like a chimney, so that's why we decided to go together. I snitch a bottle or two and Andy supplies the smokes. Right, Andy?" She gave Andy a loud kiss on the cheek and passed the bottle around.

Brendan, seeing Pearl and Lorraine decline, asked, "How come you aren't drinking?"

Lorraine said, "We've got to go home for supper pretty soon."

Pearl said, "Our parents would smell it."

"Don't your parents care?" he asked Sam, who was guzzling.

"Dad's not home tonight."

"How about your mother?"

"My mother can't control us."

Andy laughed. "We jolly Ma up with a few jokes and then we get away with murder."

Brendan could picture it, for although he didn't know their mother he knew Andy to be the clown of the Romberg household. Sam was the serious one. They had a little brother called Larry-the-Twitch, a nervous wreck.

Speeding out to the west end of Main Street, they rolled down the windows for oxygen and shivered in the wind.

Brendan and the girls waited in the truck while Andy and Sam attached a full cylinder of gas to the fittings under the kitchen window of the poor farm. Through an adjacent window they saw heads of white hair bent over a meal in a dimly-lit dining room: institutional living at its gloomiest. The sight put Brendan in mind of Dodger.

"Guess what I heard about Dodger."

"Who's Dodger?" asked Norma Nash.

"A classmate of ours who got F's all the time," Pearl told her.

"He got caught robbing a gas station, and they sentenced him to a year in the home school."

"What's the home school?"

"A prison for boys in Flensboro."

Lorraine sighed, "Poor Dodger." Mrs. Lansky's very words. Though they caused Brendan to grieve for Dodger, he loved Lorraine for saying them.

The dozen houses in the neighborhood of the poor farm stood well back from the road. Andy roared up each driveway in a low, grinding gear and turned the truck around while Brendan ran to the door with a circular.

"Can't you guys hurry up?" Pearl kept asking. "I'm late for supper."

"Me too," said Lorraine. "I was supposed to be home ages ago."

Andy took this as a challenge. He cut corners, driving across lawns and flowerbeds. Careening up the drive to the house of the banker, B. L. Skeffington, he nearly ran over a cat. Lorraine screamed, Norma Nash laughed hysterically and Pearl Peterson ordered him to slow down. On his way out he clipped several boughs off a spruce tree and sideswiped a stone pillar. They sped back to the center of town.

At home Brendan's mother told him he smelled like Gordy's Pool Hall, and he said he had spent some time there warming up.

Business was booming the next morning when Paul Dimmitburg found Hank behind the meat counter. He introduced himself and asked for a job. Hank, looking up from the wedge of cheese he was cutting, replied, "Don't you realize I'm known as the Catholic grocer in this town? Won't your father's parishioners say you've sold out?"

Paul Dimmitburg's smile was world-weary. "Please don't think I'm bound by the bigoted ways of this village, Mr. Foster. I'll give you a full day's work for a full day's wages, and religion won't enter into it."

Hank looked him over. Six foot three. Hunched shoulders. Dark, serious eyes behind thick glasses. Hank would need another clerk if this trade held up throughout the sale, particularly if Wallace continued to work at half speed, afraid of dropping in a fit if he exerted himself. Further, mightn't the minister's son attract Lutheran shoppers? "Okay," he said, "if you'd like to try me out as a boss during the sale, I'll try you out as a clerk. Get yourself a fresh apron from the shelf in the back room and I'll show you the ropes."

While learning the ropes of the grocery business, Paul Dimmit-

burg also came to understand the ties connecting Wallace to the Fosters. He had been in school with Wallace and knew he required special handling, not only because of his seizures but also because of his smug, disdainful behavior calculated to fend off friendship. The smugness and disdain were still in force, he observed—Paul himself was the target of Wallace's most withering look—but the force was modified in the presence of Hank and Catherine. That Wallace should respect Hank and work with him in a grudging sort of harmony did not surprise Paul; Hank was the father Wallace never had. What surprised him was the closeness between Wallace and Catherine. It was a brother-sister sort of closeness turned up a few degrees. Their habit of nicknaming shoppers struck him as reckless. He thought it in bad taste for them to refer to the round-shouldered Charles Heffernand as Quasimodo. Worse, one day he heard them call Mrs. Brask and Mrs. Kimball, who were passing by with a jittery little dog on a leash, "sounding Brask and tinkling Kimball," blaspheming St. Paul in his letter to the Corinthians. Regarding Brendan, Paul observed that whenever the boy turned up in the store Wallace drew back in haughty repugnance. Wallace's remarks to the boy were designed to cut and wound, as though the boy were a foe in possession of some fearful power. Paul sensed that if Wallace would deign to speak to him it would be in this same manner, and he resolved to react, if need be, in the same way Brendan did, by paying Wallace only enough attention to keep him from feeling ignored. Paul rather liked Brendan. The boy gave you a level look that made him seem older than twelve, his eyes settling on you and lingering, observing. His disposition reminded Paul of his own at that age, quiet and generally serious.

During the three days of the Armistice Sale, Catherine and Hank were impressed by Paul. He was a dependable worker, not speedy but steady and untiring. They liked his way with customers; he was more accommodating than Wallace, less brusque. His dark, heavy-browed eyes were thoughtful, sincere, without guile. His speech was soft, devoid of all sharpness, including wit. Catherine wondered if he ever laughed. There was nothing spontaneous in his strange little chuckle; it sounded like a subdued form of throat-clearing. She wondered, too, why he addressed all his questions about the store to Hank, never to her. Didn't he realize she was a full partner in this enterprise? Or was he one of those men who didn't take women seriously?

"What are you majoring in?" she asked during a Friday-morning lull, her first opportunity to chat with him.

"Philosophy was my undergraduate major," he said, looking somberly down at her and straightening his tie as though for inspection. "My master's will be in theology."

"You'll be a minister like your father?"

"Yes." He waited in silence for additional questions.

She thought his formality odd, and assumed it was due to shyness, but in fact it was due to Wallace's presence not six feet away. Shut up, you flunky, said Wallace's hate-filled eyes.

She approached Paul again when Wallace had gone to lunch. "What's it like coming home to Plum after St. Louis? Isn't it horribly dull?"

He blinked a few times and replied ominously, "Plum is in danger of losing its soul, Mrs. Foster. I have never seen such sectarian bigotry. If I were God I'd be so sick of the prideful ways of the Catholics and Lutherans in this village I'd vomit them out of my mouth." He went on to describe his father, who, though virtuous in all ways and unbigoted, had so far been unable to erase the prejudice of his parishioners. It was Paul's ambition to devote his life to the cause of unity among Christians.

Catherine was intrigued. His speech was absolutely flat, and by the end of his sentences his voice faded to a whisper, as though he were losing strength. Here was a thinker after her own heart, a young man who would go out in the world and make a difference. His mind was bent to a purpose. Wallace's, by comparison, was haywire.

After returning from lunch Wallace Flint realized that he had been deposed in Catherine's heart. Through the afternoon he fumed and pouted and snapped at customers. He hated Catherine for being captivated by a gawky basketball player whose grades in high school were inferior to his own, a humorless stuffed shirt who planned to waste his life in the service of a nonexistent God.

When Catherine came to work on Saturday morning and went straight to Paul and said, "I had a dream about you last night," Wallace was outraged. He didn't hang around to hear about the dream, nor did he attend to any of the several customers who were waiting for help. He went out the back door and touched a match to the pile of cardboard boxes and waste paper in the incinerator. Warming himself at the flames, he came to the bitter realization

that as far as he knew Catherine had never dreamed about him. He had had dozens of dreams about her. Most recently she had been his mother and taken him for ice cream at that place with an Italian name she was always talking about in Minneapolis.

Hank put his head out the back door and said, "Don't bother with the trash now, Wallace. We're too busy up front."

Wallace came away from the fire reluctantly. He loved watching fire. He stomped indoors with his eyes cast down and his mind made up to join the army. Removing his apron and putting on his jacket, he told Hank he was going home. "If I keep working I'll have a fit. I don't feel good."

Hank believed him. "Do you need a ride?"

"No, just rest. I'll see you Monday."

At home his mother asked him what was wrong and he told her to shut up. He climbed the stairs to his room and searched through his jumble of books for military biographies. He lay down on his bed with the lives of Lee, Pershing and Genghis Khan.

In the late afternoon he pulled his ironing board up to his bed and wrote a letter to his draft board, volunteering for induction. Until today he had dreaded serving in the military, but his jealousy of Paul Dimmitburg had jarred him out of his cowardice. Soldiering seemed the opportunity of a lifetime. The army was his ticket out of Plum, launching him into the larger world. The army took care of its own, had doctors and nurses to help you through your seizures. Certainly it was a better life than living anonymously in some city where if you had a fit they'd just stand there and let you bite off your tongue.

After dark, carrying the letter to the post office, he saw that Legget's was not as busy as Hank's. The moment he dropped the letter into the slot, he was relieved of his resentment of Paul Dimmitburg. By the time Wallace came home on leave, in uniform, Paul would either be ordained a cowardly, draft-dodging preacher or be still selling groceries for eighty cents an hour. Wallace returned to the market and said he was feeling much better. He put on an apron and worked until closing time.

Income for the Armistice Sale came to $3,155, ten percent more than Grand Opening.

Winter

14

In late November Catherine was amazed to open a letter from a woman who announced that she was Uncle Herman's bride. She said she was looking forward to meeting Herman's relatives and asked if the Fosters and Grandfather would come to Flensboro on the following Sunday afternoon and stay for supper. "We're living not on Herman's farm but on mine, which is adjacent to his and easy to find if you stay on Highway 61 through town and turn left just beyond the Home School for Boys. We're inviting relatives from the Twin Cities as well, and they will bring Nancy Clancy along if she feels up to it. I want this to be what has been lacking in Herman's life for too many years—a good old family reunion." She signed her name *Virginia.*

Catherine passed the letter around at supper.

Grandfather chuckled. "Funny to think of Herman as a ladies' man. Why didn't he tell us about her when we stopped to see him."

"He did, in his way," Catherine told him. "He kept talking about the woman on the next farm."

"But he didn't mention romance."

"Can we go?" she asked Hank. "Can we get there and back?" The DeSoto had developed a serious cough, accompanied by a lurch, and the radiator, which had had its holes soldered shut several times, was becoming porous with rust.

"Let's see," Hank calculated. "Flensboro's forty miles. I could clean the spark plugs once more and see how she runs. We'll have to take six or eight gallons of water in the trunk."

After supper he and Brendan carried tools and a flashlight out to

the back yard and, as they removed the plugs, reset the gaps and cleaned the points, Hank taught Brendan how pistons worked. "Hold the light steady," he said more than once. It was a chilly night, and the light wavered as Brendan shivered.

When they were nearly done, Brendan brought up what was troubling him. "Dodger Hicks is in the Home School in Flensboro."

"I know."

"Mom says I should visit him."

"Do you want to?"

"I suppose I should." His voice trembled with cold. "It's one of the corporal works of mercy, visiting prisoners."

Catherine's very words—Hank was vaguely irritated to hear them from his son. He wished his son were less fretful, a little less pious. "Hand me the smaller wrench, and try to hold the light still."

Watching his father wipe the last spark plug with an oily rag, Brendan recalled how often in the past weeks he had heard Dodger's name brought up around town, recalled the pang of guilt he felt each time, as though by rejecting Dodger's friendship he had somehow caused Dodger's trouble. It surprised him how much attention the arrest was commanding in Plum. It seemed as though after four years of discussing heroism, everybody found it refreshing to concentrate on vice for a change. The war was dragging on and valor was becoming old hat. Every hamlet had turned out its share of soldiers and sailors (Pinburg had produced an army colonel, no less) but how many towns could boast of a father-son team of convicts? In the pool hall Brendan had heard the men recounting the crimes of Dodger's father—embezzlement, extortion—and predicting what lay ahead for Dodger—armed robbery, murder. In the store, Wallace Flint went on about Dodger like a man obsessed, instructing shoppers that Dodger's downfall could be traced to three causes other than his father's criminal example; namely Dodger's inability to read and thus his humiliation in school, his mother's promiscuity and thus his feeling of rootlessness, and (here Wallace threw a meaningful look at Brendan) the insincerity of his so-called friends.

Replacing the spark plug, Hank said softly, "What do you feel like doing? Seeing him or not seeing him?"

Brendan steadied the flashlight on the fender. "I feel like not seeing him."

"Then don't see him."

A long pause.

"But I should see him."

"Then see him."

They arrived at the farm in the late afternoon. It was immediately evident that by marrying his neighbor, Uncle Herman had risen in the world. Virginia's farmhouse stood on a knoll commanding a view of the river, the fields and the town of Flensboro. There were a dozen cars parked in the drive. As Hank steered the rattling DeSoto around to the back of the house and parked near the stoop, so as to be handy to water, Brendan saw eight or ten children's faces looking out the hayloft door and other apertures of the barn.

The newlyweds came out onto the back stoop to welcome them. Married only a few days, his bride had already done a lot for Uncle Herman's appearance. He wore a new suit and a carnation in his lapel. There was no sign of the hair that used to grow out of his ears or the crack that ran across the right lens of his glasses. But she hadn't cured Herman of his shyness; he stood behind her, smiling off in another direction, while his bride introduced herself. "I'm Virginia, and I've been dying to meet you." She pumped their hands energetically. She was about Herman's age, maybe a year or two older, a broad-faced woman with a broad smile and broad shoulders. She wore a rose blouse and a figured apron over a full black skirt. "How wonderful to know you," she said to Grandfather as he bowed deeply and kissed her hand.

The house was jammed with strangers. Though Virginia had called it a reunion, it was actually a wedding reception, and she had invited her family and friends as well as Herman's. Grandfather plunged in, giving each woman in his path his brightest smile and a courtly bow. As though by instinct, he found his way to the place in the living room, where the ancient and diminutive Nancy Clancy was tucked into the corner of a very large chair. She had a translucent look, the flesh of her face paper thin, paper pale. Her dress was burgundy, tied at the throat with an enormous white bow, giving her the aspect of a small jewel wrapped as a gift. The instant her piercing black eyes fell upon Grandfather she rose weightlessly to her feet and held both of his hands to her breast. "Michael, why don't you ever come to see me?"

Hank, Catherine and Brendan gathered around and bent over her. Catherine apologized for their neglect, explaining about their untrustworthy car. She asked how Nancy was feeling.

"I feel just fine for ninety-three, but I simply must see you people more often. When you're as old as I am, you feel like you're coming unmoored from the human race unless your dear ones stay in touch. Do you realize, Catherine—my, this boy of yours is shooting up like a weed—do you realize, Catherine, that your father is the last of his generation, and I'm his *aunt*? You know what that means? It means he's my last link with your generation. He's my bridge." She lowered her voice. "Tell me frankly, Catherine, how has your father been getting along?"

"None of that," Grandfather broke in. "You're the same today as you were when I was a boy, asking about me as if I wasn't old enough to answer for myself. I'm fit as a fiddle, thank you." He did two steps of a jig to prove it.

"But don't you miss the city, Michael? How do you occupy yourself in that little burg?"

"I'll tell you how I occupy myself. Mornings I sleep late. Afternoons I take a nap, and after my nap I visit the pool hall. Evenings"—he laughed, pinching her elbow—"evenings are given over to the digestion of my supper."

Nancy Clancy said to Catherine, "Your cousin Marge is here, did you see her? She picked me up and drove me here. If you haven't seen her daughter Julie in recent years you're in for a delight. She's fourteen and a vision of loveliness."

Brendan brightened at this; he had expected to find no one his age at this affair. He remembered his cousin Julie from family get-togethers in the city. She had been a gawky nine or ten when he saw her last, and very likable for a girl.

Nancy Clancy laid a feathery hand on Brendan's arm. "You must make friends with her, my boy. Cousins must not grow apart."

Brendan searched the rooms of the farmhouse but didn't find Julie. He was about to go outside and look for her when she came in looking for him. She planted herself in front of him with her fists on her hips and said, "Hi, you're twelve this year, I've been keeping track. Come on outside and see the horses."

She was an inch taller than Brendan. She had black hair, dark gray eyes and freckles. She wore a rich-looking gray dress with a single red flower on the skirt. She had breasts.

They made their way through the chattering crowd and out the back door.

"So do you think seventh grade is harder than sixth, Brendan? I

think eighth is easier than seventh. It's nice being in junior high, isn't it, moving around to different classrooms instead of sitting in the same old desk all day. In my school we got to take home ec in the seventh grade, do you get to take shop? Are you out for sports?"

She made him feel important. Who else considered all these areas of his life interesting enough to ask about? Walking down to the pasture behind the barn where a team of workhorses were grazing, she asked him how many friends he had. He said he had three close ones; their names were Sam, Philip, and (fibbing to test her reaction) Pearl. She said she had twelve, none of them boys at the present time. Laughing, she twirled around so that her dress swirled at her knees. "Would you want to be my boyfriend if we weren't cousins?" He shrugged and blushed a little, thinking yes.

The horses were gigantic and old, their brown hide beginning to grow woolly for winter, their tails busily brushing flies. A number of younger children, their Sunday shoes soiled with manure, emerged from the barn where they had been tormenting the piglets, and joined them in the pasture. They hopped about picking grass and handing it to Julie, who held it out to the horses. "Here, Julie, take mine." "No, take mine." The horses chewed slowly, blinking and twitching their ears. Each time one of them dipped for another bite, wetting Julie's palm with its muzzle, she giggled.

Eventually the children grew bored and went off to play hide and seek among the outbuildings. As Julie wiped her hands on the neck of one of the horses, Brendan gazed across the pasture, searching his mind for something to say that would impress her. Her eyes fell upon the Home School for Boys at the edge of Flensboro.

"You know what this place is, those buildings?"

She said she didn't.

"It's a reformatory for criminals under the age of eighteen."

"Really? Is it a prison?"

"Sort of, I guess." He paused for effect. "I've got a friend in this one."

"You do?" She covered her mouth in trepidation. Her eyes, searching his, were wide. "A prisoner? What did he do?"

"He robbed a gas station in Winona."

"All those trees. It looks so pretty. It's scary to think it's a prison."

"Want to go and look it over?"

"You mean actually go inside?"

"Yeah. We'd say we're visiting Dodger."

She looked back at the farmhouse. "Should we tell our folks?"

"Let's go before the little kids follow us."

They ran across the pasture.

Inside the entrance, an archway of stone, they came upon a man sitting in a black pickup. He poked his head out the window and said, "Who you seeing?" He had small eyes and a crooked nose. He wore a khaki shirt with a small badge pinned to the collar. Beyond the pickup was a high hedge of lilac with its leaves turning brown. The hedge was full of sparrows, chirping and fluttering.

"Dodger Hicks," said Brendan. "Is he here?"

The man looked them over. "Where's your adults? Kids aren't allowed in without adults."

"Oh? We didn't know that." Brendan was relieved. Though he feigned disappointment, he thought it a great stroke of luck to have impressed Julie and tried to carry out a corporal work of mercy without actually having to see Dodger. What could he and Dodger possibly say to each other?

"Come on, we better go," he said to Julie.

She didn't respond. She was looking through the opening in the hedge at the main building. Five people stood on the front steps, visiting. Two adults and three teenage boys. One of the boys was bald.

"But it's okay this once," said the man in the pickup. "Hicks ain't had a visitor since he got there. Sign your names." He handed a clipboard out the window.

Brendan backed away. "No, that's all right. Dodger probably wouldn't remember me anyway."

But Julie was already signing her name.

"I seen Hicks on the grounds a few minutes ago, just look around. If he's not outside, ask at the desk in that first building."

Brendan signed his name.

As they came to the main building and turned left to skirt it on a pathway of sand, Julie whispered, "Look, he hasn't got any hair."

The bald boy, slouched in a posture of boredom and ignoring his visitors, was looking down at Brendan and Julie from the steps. Julie waved and said, "Hi," but the boy turned away.

Behind the main building they came to a fork in the path and stopped. They stood looking at the people scattered on the lawns. They saw a pack of boys in the distance playing leapfrog; their heads were all shaved. They saw a pair of hairless boys sitting under a tree

reading a comic book. Another bald boy came toward them on the path surrounded by a crowd of visitors—parents, grandparents, brothers, sisters, babies. They saw a young couple in love, embracing as they strolled, the bald boy burying his hand in the girl's thick red hair.

They took the path leading off to the right and came upon a skinny, dark-skinned boy sitting on a glider that hung from a large wooden frame. He, too, was bald. His pants were too short for his long legs; his short-sleeved shirt was old and faded. His eyes kept darting toward Brendan and Julie and then shifting away. As they passed him, he got to his feet and fell into step beside Julie. Fearful, she leaned into Brendan, taking his arm. The boy was tall. He spoke, looking straight ahead:

"Say, did I ever give you caps for that gun? I don't think I did."

"Dodger!" Brendan gaped at him. He hadn't recognized him without hair.

Without breaking stride, Dodger said, "I'll bring you some caps first chance I get. You still live in the same house?"

"Yes." Brendan, holding Julie's hand, kept his eyes riveted on Dodger. Hairless, he looked much older than the boy who threw the boomerang, but he was Dodger all right—long teeth exposed when he pulled back his lip in that self-conscious smile, head hanging forward on that long neck, eyes shifting away when you tried to engage them.

"Or can I drop off the caps at the store? Your ma and dad still got that store?"

"Yep."

Dodger nodded approvingly. Some things, at least, were permanent.

Julie whispered, "Introduce me."

They stopped walking. "Dodger, this is my cousin Julie."

"Hi." He didn't look at her. "Brendan's an old friend of mine."

"Yes, he told me."

"How's your boomerang? Jeez, wasn't that fun?" Dodger's eyes lit up as he put out his hand and slowly traced the boomerang's arc through the air. "Damn if it didn't come back like it had a leash on it." He laughed with delight. "Damn if I ever saw another one. You still got it?"

"Yep, I have."

"You still throw it?"

"No, the ends got splintered and it doesn't fly so good." Brendan noticed tiny round scars and scabs on Dodger's forearms, a similar scab on his throat.

"Damn if this wouldn't be a good place for a boomerang." Dodger indicated the lawns and the fields beyond. "Damn if I wouldn't like to have a boomerang here—show these guys."

"Maybe we could find you one," said Julie. Brendan saw that she was entranced by Dodger. Her eyes were sad and serious. "Brendan, let's try to get a boomerang for Dodger."

"Okay."

The three of them walked on.

She asked, "How long will you be here, Dodger?"

He shrugged. "I guess I could get out any time."

"Then why don't you?"

"Well, see, I'd have to go live with my ma. My dad's still doing time in Stillwater, and my ma she's living with this guy in Winona and they only got two little rooms, and I'm not crazy about the guy, he's crabby. So this here's my home for now." His eyes fell on Brendan, shifted away, came back. "Maybe I could live in your house? Your folks could be my guardians."

To be so utterly homeless and needy—it took Brendan's breath away. He wished he hadn't come. Having no sooner bragged to Julie that this loser was his friend, he was now being asked to prove it.

"I don't know, Dodger, we've got my grandfather at the house, and he's pretty hard to live with. Gets up at night and talks out loud." A very lame excuse, as Dodger implied:

"Yeah, it gets sort of noisy here nights, too, sixteen of us to a room."

A bell sounded. Dodger stopped and said, "That's supper. Hey, how about if you eat with me? Visitors get to stay for supper on Sundays."

Boys ran past them on the path, heading for the door of the dining hall.

"No," said Brendan, "we've got to get back. We're having a family reunion over there at that farm."

Dodger looked where Brendan pointed. "Whose farm is that?"

"Relatives'."

"Boy, that's a big house. How many people live there?"

"Two. My Uncle Herman and his wife."

Dodger gawked at the farm for a few moments, his head hanging

forward; then he sucked in his saliva and said, "Would you ask them if I could live there?"

Julie and Brendan exchanged a pained glance, and Dodger, seeing it, gracefully withdrew his suggestion by laughing as though he hadn't meant it. This was the Dodger of old, all right; at the first sign of rejection he backed off with something of apology in his manner. Sorry for needing you, he seemed to say.

The family they had seen on the front steps came around the corner of the building and went into the dining hall. They were followed by the boy with the large delegation of visitors. Last, slowly, came the two lovers.

They walked Dodger as far as the doorway, where Brendan said, "We'll be seeing you, Dodger."

"Can't you stay and eat?"

"We've got to get back."

"Okay, I'll go to the gate with you."

"Don't you have to go in and eat?"

"I ain't very hungry."

As they retraced their way along the path, Dodger scanned the grounds for someone to notice that he had visitors—he was feeling very proud—but everyone had gone in to supper.

Passing through the opening in the bird-filled hedge, Julie said, "How long will you be here if you don't go and live with your mom?"

"I don't know, till next summer, I guess. Or if my dad gets paroled I might go and live with him." He turned to Brendan. "Don't worry, I'll bring you some caps for that gun as soon as I get out."

"It's okay, Dodger. I can get caps at the dime store." Didn't Dodger realize that cap guns were for children?

"Yeah, but a guy always needs more caps than he thinks he does. I'll bring you a few rolls."

They said good-bye and Dodger left them.

As Brendan took the clipboard from the man in the pickup, Julie gripped his arm. "You've got to eat supper with him."

"I do?"

"Look at him."

Dodger was moving away with the same loose-jointed shuffle Brendan remembered from the lumber yard the day he filled his pockets with marbles.

"You're his only friend in the world."

He shook his head. "No, I was kidding about being his friend."

She scolded, "You told me you were his friend."

"Yeah, but that was a long time ago, and it was only for about three days."

"That's good enough for Dodger."

He gave her an impassive look, concealing his unease. Appalling, the magnitude of Dodger's need.

"He wants to eat with you, Brendan."

"What good would that do?"

"He wants people to know he's got a friend, don't you see?"

He turned away, stirred by jealousy that she should have so much room in her heart for Dodger. He was stirred by admiration for her as well.

"Please?" she said. It was a drawn-out, wheedling please.

"Will you eat, too?"

"Sure." She smiled.

He handed back the clipboard. "Hey, Dodger, wait up."

A burly man wearing a white apron stood inside the door of the dining hall. He had a flat, scarred face and cold eyes. He said, "You're late, Hicks."

Dodger nodded agreeably.

"Who's your visitors?"

"Brendan and Julie." Dodger grinned crookedly.

"Sir!" the man in the apron demanded.

"Brendan and Julie, sir."

"They relatives?"

"Old friends, sir."

The man put out his hand. "Friends pay." Two of his fingers were half gone.

"I thought it was free for visitors on Sundays."

"Relatives eat free, but friends pay the fifty cents."

Brendan and Julie were without money. As they stood awkwardly in the entryway looking at each other, the man hooked his thumbs in his apron straps and drummed his fingers on his chest, the whole fingers and the fractions. "You sure they ain't related, Hicks?"

It was Julie who recognized the opening he offered. She said to him, "We're cousins."

"Yeah, cousins, sir," beamed Dodger, delighted at the thought of having cousins.

The man looked at Brendan, who echoed, "Cousins, sir." It was true of two of them at least.

The man growled, "Hurry up then, before the food's gone."

The dining hall doubled as a small gymnasium. Trestle tables were set up on the basketball floor. Dodger led them to a hole in the wall where three trays of food were handed out to them from the kitchen. The main dish was a slice of meatloaf and a boiled potato; the other dish was melting ice cream. They found places to sit at the end of a table where a dozen bald boys were chattering loudly and throwing their shoulders into one another as they ate. The presence of Julie quieted them for a minute—there was something reverent in the looks they stole at her—and then it inspired them to greater horseplay than before. They punched one another in the ribs and belly; they cried out in pain, shouting insults. Watching them bounce on their benches, Brendan thought of the rising and falling of pistons in the DeSoto, energy pressing against confinement; compression and combustion. The burly man in the apron came across the room and restored quiet by roughly knocking six or eight shaved heads together. For several minutes thereafter the heads were bent low and silent over the table, the boys trying to conceal the tears of pain brimming in their eyes. Julie and Brendan ate very little—the meatloaf was cold, the ice cream warm—but Dodger ate swiftly and hungrily and went back to the hole in the wall and asked for more. He returned with a small, wrinkled potato.

A buzzer sounded and a small, important-looking man wearing a suit and tie came into the room and drew a paper from his vest pocket. He wore a fussy little moustache and goatee. He walked up and down between the tables until everyone was silent, then he read the day's announcements. His voice was shrill. Softball equipment would no longer be provided during free hour (a groan sounded along the tables) until it was discovered who had been stealing balls. Study would be extended by one half hour tonight (another groan) because of the mid-term exams beginning tomorrow. There was to be a lyceum program tomorrow at three o'clock; a penmanship expert would demonstrate how beautifully he could write with his right hand and left, frontward and backward; and his wife would show slides of historical houses in Massachusetts. But if the boys behaved as they had at the last lyceum program (the man's voice rose in anger), if they couldn't learn to shut up and sit still (the man glared so hard his face turned red), and if they had no more manners

than monkeys and jackals (his anger silenced him for a moment), then there would be no more lyceum programs (a brief cheer), *and* no more Saturday night movies (a groan). He gave his emotions a few seconds to subside, and then he ran through the last few items, concluding with this, delivered with a chilling smile:

"It would seem there is no end to the consequences of the fight that occurred last week in the lavatory on the second floor of Building C. Whoever it was that struck Jerry Ludbeck in the face and broke his glasses, will no doubt be happy to know that at eight o'clock tomorrow morning a doctor in Rochester is going to remove Jerry Ludbeck's right eye."

An intense hush.

"All right, dismissed."

Everyone stood. Watched over closely by the man in the apron, they all lined up at the kitchen window to dispose of their trays; then they hurried outdoors.

"I'd show you around some more," said Dodger, "but it's the end of visiting hours now. When you coming back?"

"I don't know," said Brendan, hurrying them along to the front gate.

"If you come back again, I'll look in my trunk for something to give you."

The man in the pickup handed them the clipboard and they signed out.

Julie said, "Thanks a lot for supper, Dodger."

"Sure." He stood in the stone archway facing them, blocking their exit, one hand in his pocket, the other rubbing the top of his smooth head. "One thing I got in the trunk I could give you right now is a *Superman* comic. You like *Superman*? I could run and get it."

"No, that's okay," said Brendan, "we've got to be going."

For the first time since they were introduced, Dodger looked fully into Julie's eyes. "You like Superman?"

"He's okay, I'm not crazy about comics."

He thought. "Or I could give you *Blondie.* You like *Blondie*?"

She nodded, aware that accepting his gift was a gift. "I do like *Blondie.*"

"Wait here." Dodger loped off up the path.

"Hicks ain't a bad kid," said the man in the pickup. "It's a shame the way he's picked on, but you know how kids are, they need to find

one amongst them that won't fight back so they can pick and pick and pick to their heart's content." The man waited for them to ask for the brutal details, but they wished not to hear them. Which made him all the more eager to tell: "They come at him in his sleep and burn him with their cigarettes. If I was Hicks I'd wait for them sons of bitches to go to sleep themselves, and I'd take a knife and castrate them."

The sparrows in the bushes sang and sang. The family of five came down the path. The parents and two of the boys signed out; the other boy hurried back to the main building. The separation appeared a relief on both sides.

The lovers came down the path. The girl signed out, then held the boy's bald head on her shoulder. The man in the pickup said, "Scram now, and remember what I told you. Next time bring an adult or you don't get in."

The girl stamped her foot angrily. "I *am* an adult. We're both adults." There were tears in her eyes as she ran out the gate.

Soon Dodger was back with a tattered comic book.

"Thanks," said Julie, taking it from him.

"Yeah, it's okay."

"And I hope you get good grades on your exams."

Dodger laughed. "I never do. I always flunk everything. They say if I'm still here next term they're maybe going to take me out of school and put me in one of the shops."

"The shops ain't so bad," said the man in the pickup.

"I hope it's woodworking," said Dodger. "I hope it ain't the foundry. But maybe I won't be still here next term."

"So long," said Brendan, his eyes on the scab at Dodger's throat. "Be seeing you."

"Good-bye," said Julie. "Thanks again for everything."

They walked out through the gateway and across the road, and as they were about to step into the pasture, they looked back and saw him standing in the gateway, his bald head gleaming in the slanting sunlight. He called, "When you coming back?"

"We'll see," said Brendan.

The shiny head bobbed, nodding.

The sun set as they crossed the field in silence. Brendan, trying to rid his mind of the scars, wished he could relive the afternoon, leaving Dodger out of it.

Nearly everyone in the farmhouse had eaten, and some of the

guests had left. Brendan's parents came up to him as he stood at the buffet filling his plate with ham and corn and scalloped potatoes. "Where have you been?" his father asked. "We've been waiting to start home."

"Julie and I went to see Dodger."

"Oh, good," exclaimed Catherine.

In his mother's eyes Brendan saw a sparkle he remembered from their days in the city. The afternoon away from Plum had obviously been good for her. "He must have been glad to see you," she said.

"I guess he was."

"What's it like there? How's he getting along?"

"It's okay. He's doing okay."

Because Julie was sitting at the dining room table, he took his plate to the kitchen. He didn't want Julie to overhear his false account of Dodger in the Home School, nor did he want his mother to know the truth. His mother's cheer must be maintained as long as possible.

"How long will he be there, did he say?" Catherine sat across from him at the kitchen table.

"He'll be there a year, unless he decides to go where his mother lives. He can get out any time if he does that."

His mother must have detected a false note, for the sparkle in her eyes was replaced by concern, like Julie's. "Are you sure he's all right? Virginia says it's a dreadful place. Boys get injured in fights."

"No, he's fine." He glanced through the doorway, making sure Julie couldn't hear him. "He's doing fine."

His mother looked skeptical. "Really and truly?"

He nodded emphatically, his mouth full of corn.

15

Boys with records of good behavior and homes to go to were released from the Home School for ten days at Christmas. Dodger was one of them. On the afternoon of Christmas Eve, two days after the other boys had left, he stood on the porch of the main building and watched for Mr. Cranshaw's car to turn in at the gate. In a cardboard box at his feet were a change of underwear and socks, a clean shirt, and several comic books. It was Mr. Cranshaw, his Winona County case worker, who had delivered Dodger to the Home School in October. He was a sharp-faced little man with a brusque manner and not much to say, but with a certain amount of compassion in his eyes. Dodger had been grateful when, after sentencing, Mr. Cranshaw assured the judge and the sheriff that Dodger did not require an armed guard on his way up the river.

The clouds of Christmas Eve were darkening to gunmetal blue and threatening to unload a heavy snowfall into the Mississippi Valley. Dodger wore no cap; his bald head was numb with cold. His jacket was a thin flannel shirt he had appropriated for himself in the laundry room, where he had been working half days since being declared uneducable by the teaching staff. On his feet were warm, sturdy work boots lent him by the barber who came out from Flensboro every second Thursday and shaved 109 heads. "Are those raggedy old things the only shoes you've got?" the barber asked him, "you can't go home for Christmas looking like a bum." The barber, whose name was Johnson, took a special interest in Dodger, more than once having spoken to the warden about the two cigarette burns near Dodger's hairline that were slow to heal. The warden fi-

nally relented and allowed Dodger to see the doctor during his weekly visit to the school. The doctor gave Dodger a tube of ointment for his burns and he gave the warden a piece of his mind for allowing physical abuse in the dormitories. "If you don't take action," the doctor threatened, "I'll report it to the governor and the state board of health." The warden's only action was to warn Johnson to quit meddling in the affairs of the Home School or else lose his barbering contract with the state.

In an office at the front of the main building, the warden looked up from his desk and saw Cranshaw's car turn in at the gate. He clapped a hat on his head and scurried out to the porch. "Come on, Hicks, we can't keep your man waiting." Dodger picked up his box and descended the steps with the warden. One of the few things Dodger had in common with the other boys was his dislike of the warden, whose eyes were angry and whose tiny moustache and pointed goatee reminded Dodger of drawings he had seen of the devil.

Dodger went around the car and got in on the passenger side while Mr. Cranshaw rolled down his window and greeted the warden.

"About time you got here," piped the warden.

"I told you I was tied up till today." Mr. Cranshaw handed him a document.

"It wasn't in our budget to feed the kid for two extra days. How come his mother didn't come for him?"

"She has no car."

The warden glanced at the signatures at the bottom of the document and said, "All right, take him away, and be sure he's back here by suppertime on New Year's Day. And while you're at it, give him a talking to about laziness. He makes no effort in his classes and he makes no effort in the laundry. He's well on his way to being a bum."

Mr. Cranshaw rolled his window shut before the warden finished. He shifted gears and the car moved down the sloping drive.

"Well, how have you been, Dodger?"

"Not so bad." Dodger smiled. He sat holding his box on his lap.

"You sound like you've got a cold."

"Yeah. It's real hot in the laundry, and then I go outside and my nose runs."

"Haven't you got a cap? You'll freeze your head."

"Yeah, I've got a cap but I keep forgetting it. It's hard to keep wearing a cap when you never did."

Driving out through the gate, Cranshaw felt a sense of freedom almost as great as Dodger's. Over the years he had seen enough of the Home School to despise it. His work took him to prisons, hospitals, orphanages, insane asylums and schools for the blind and deaf, none of which made his skin crawl the way this institution did. The guards were thugs and the warden was a martinet with a treacherous look in his eye.

"Dodger, your mother isn't home. I called her last week to make sure she'd sign your release form. She said she'd sign it, but when I went to the apartment this morning the landlady said she'd been gone for a week or more. But she expects her home for Christmas."

Dodger shrugged and nodded and shrugged again.

"I'm not supposed to take you home, Dodger, without your mother being there."

Dodger said nothing.

"But I'm taking you anyhow. I forged your mother's name."

Dodger chuckled.

They rode in silence for twenty miles. The highway was a narrow, winding shelf at the base of the bluffs. Below them the blue-black river was dotted with small ice floes. As they sped past the sideroad leading up over the bluffs and beyond, Dodger asked, "Have we got time to swing through Plum? I've got a friend there."

"Afraid not. I'm late getting home as it is. Maybe on our way back on New Year's."

It was dark when they reached Winona. Snow was dropping in large, watery flakes. Cranshaw drew up in front of a house facing the highway and said, "Okay, Dodger, I'm sticking my neck out for you, so return the favor by staying out of trouble, will you?"

"Sure."

"Starting the day after tomorrow I want you to call me up every day or drop in at my office. It's just like being on parole—you've got to keep checking in."

"Sure."

"You remember where my office is?"

"Sure."

"Your landlady said to tell you she wouldn't be home tonight but she's left your apartment unlocked."

"Okay."

"Merry Christmas, Dodger."

"Merry Christmas."

Snowflakes melted and ran down the dome of his scalp as Dodger

carried his box into the tiny front hallway and climbed the stairs. He wished the landlady, Mrs. Wrobleski, were home. She had been nice to him during the short time he lived here, offering him a cookie or a cupcake every so often and letting him look at her stereopticon. He opened the door at the head of the stairs and entered the apartment. He switched on the light. His mother's bed in the living room was unmade. Standing on the table and the two windowsills were a number of empty beer bottles. He went into the kitchen and saw that his mother had been using his cot as a catch-all for clothes and groceries. He added his cardboard box to the clutter on the cot and went to the refrigerator for something to drink. Mr. Cranshaw's heater fan had been going high speed the whole trip and dried out Dodger's throat and nose. He uncapped a bottle of milk and took a big swallow before he realized it was sour. He went into the tiny bathroom, spat into the sink and drank a glass of water. He returned to the living room and pulled a chair up to the window. He watched the headlights moving along the highway below him. He savored his solitude. After two months in the Home School, this was pure peace. There was no one to taunt you or hurt you or put you to work. He was glad his mother was gone. Christmases without his father were hard on his mother. She drank and got weepy, then drank some more and got angry, and then drank some more and slept. With his father present, come to think of it, her behavior wasn't all that much different, except the weepy part was shorter and the angry part was longer. "For them that can be merry," she'd say when anyone wished her "Merry Christmas." Wherever she was tonight, Dodger hoped she was with a man she liked, someone thoughtful enough to give her a present.

It dawned on Dodger that he had no present for her. He went to the closet and found a cap he hadn't seen before, a black watch cap probably left behind by a riverboat man. He pulled the cap down over his ears and left the house. Snow slanted into his face as he hurried along the highway toward the lighted sign of the Conoco Station. He feared it might close early because it was Christmas Eve, but he got there in time. He stopped in the shadows beyond the gas pumps and saw only one attendant on duty, luckily not the same man that had caught him stealing money from the till. The attendant was giving change to the driver of a pickup, and there were two cars waiting for service. Dodger unbuttoned the cuffs of his flannel shirt, then went up to the man and asked if he could use the toilet.

The man said sure. Dodger went into the grimy, brightly lit station and looked around, making his choices, his heart beating wildly as it always did in the act of stealing. Keeping his eye on the man pumping gas, he slipped a Zippo lighter into the pocket of his flannel shirt and a candy bar up his left sleeve. He went into the restroom while the attendant came in and rang up a sale and went out again. He emerged from the restroom and studied a standing display of windshield-wiper blades. He put a blade up his right sleeve and opened the door and left, the thrill of success washing over him, his heart beating faster and faster. Stealing was wrong, he knew, and most people were dead-set against it, but how could you resist doing the one thing in life you were good at?

He walked through the deepening snow, buttoning his shirtcuffs and taking pleasure in the warmth of his feet in the barber's thick-soled boots. He walked to the neighborhood store where his mother bought groceries. A bell tinkled over the door as he opened it. The old woman proprietor came out from her sitting room at the back and said, "Merry Christmas" before she saw who it was. She replaced her smile with a stony glare. He saw at once that there would be no stealing from this woman. He asked for a bottle of pop, a sack of potato chips, and a tin of shoe polish the color of the barber's boots.

As she took his money, made change and put his purchases in a bag, he noticed balloons and jacks and other toys on a shelf behind her.

"Have you got caps?" he asked.

"This is a grocery store, not a clothing store."

"I mean caps for a cap gun."

"No."

He went home and put the Zippo, his mother's gift, on the dresser. When Mrs. Wrobleski came home he would ask her for a scrap of wrapping paper. As he ate his candy bar and drank his pop, he examined the windshield-wiper blade, disappointed in himself for having stolen it simply because it was available. He had no use for it. It was Dodger's policy to steal only out of necessity and never—or seldom—at random.

When he finished eating he put the wiper blade in his cardboard box and took out a clean handkerchief. He opened the tin of shoe polish and went to work on Mr. Johnson's boots, applying three coats of polish with his fingers and buffing them with his handker-

chief. When he finished they gleamed like new. He resolved to pick up a new pair of bootlaces before he returned them to Mr. Johnson.

Then he sat by the window and watched the Christmas Eve traffic diminish to almost nothing. Snow fell thickly, like feathers, and he grew very sleepy watching it. He moved to his mother's bed and fell immediately into a deep sleep. Sometime after midnight he awoke with a cry, having dreamed that he was about to be burned with a cigarette. He lay with his eyes open for a minute, savoring the stillness and peace of the empty house; then he turned over and went back to sleep.

The falling snow enveloped Holy Angels like fog, piling itself high on the roof and window ledges and quickly filling the mass of footprints leading up the front steps to the wide oak door. Inside, Father O'Day slowly led his flock through Midnight Mass, periodically losing his place in the altar missal and finding it again, losing his place in the sermon and not finding it again. The ceremony was punctuated by his cries of *"Dominus Vobiscum,"* to which Melva Heffernand responded nasally from the choir loft, *"Et cum spiritu tuo,"* accompanying herself on the organ and adding an extra trill because it was Christmas.

During Communion, Brendan and Philip, vested in red and white, sat on adjacent stools in the sanctuary and gazed at the faces coming forward to receive the Sacrament. Ordinarily Brendan and Philip would have tossed a coin before Mass for the privilege of holding the paten under the chin of each communicant and watching their heads go back and their eyes flutter as Father O'Day placed the Host on their tongues, but tonight Deacon Gilbertson, a seminarian home on vacation, got to do all the glamorous things. Throughout the mass Deacon Gilbertson had carried the missal and rung the Consecration bell and lit the incense, while Brendan and Philip shared the merely decorative role of kneeling and standing on cue while looking devout.

The church was packed and Communion took a long time. Philip, growing impatient, leaned close to Brendan's ear and whispered, "How many presents did you get?"

"We don't open our presents till morning."

"I got eight."

Brendan saw Lorraine Graham kneeling at the rail with her two brothers and her parents. Lorraine wore a new coat of a nubby,

dark-green material and a new dark beret tilted over her ear. She glanced at Brendan and immediately lowered her eyes and looked solemn. She was pretty, thought Brendan with surprise. Funny how you never looked twice at Lorraine Graham when she was hanging around Pearl Peterson, which was ninety percent of the time. Pearl's mouthiness and pushiness was the sort that contaminated everyone who came near. Seeing Lorraine by herself, though, you had to admire the blond hair and the small round face with the blue eyes.

"I got a football from my grandma and grandpa," whispered Philip. "I got a bunch of games and some clothes from my ma and dad."

Brendan saw Lester Higgins lining up at the rail with his wife and his scads of children. Once a week Mr. and Mrs. Higgins came in from their farm and bought more groceries from Hank than anyone else. It was the Higgins barn that stood beside the road three miles east of town with an ad for spark plugs painted on the wall. It was the Higgins pickup Hank would borrow next Sunday for the move to Bean Street. Higgins had offered himself as well, but Hank said no thanks; he had Wallace Flint and Paul Dimmitburg to help him with the heavy things, and Brendan and Sam and Philip would carry the lighter pieces. For Brendan the excitement of Christmas this year was far surpassed by the excitement of moving. On Bean he would be living about a block from Philip's house and across the alley from Sam's.

"I got a dumb book from my sister," Philip muttered. "It's never any fun opening my sister's presents. It's always a dumb book."

Among the next rank of communicants were Hank, Catherine and Grandfather. The hour being so late, Grandfather was fuzzy-minded and had to be steered to his place at the rail. Settled there on their knees, the three of them gave Brendan a glance—Hank winked—and then lowered their eyes as the priest approached them. He saw that his mother was wearing her severe look. It had nothing to do with her hairstyle or makeup; it was all in the tightness of the muscles around her eyes and the way she held her mouth. It was a look she had never worn in the city, but now he saw it almost every day. Brendan's heart had nearly stopped the other evening when she told Hank in the kitchen that instead of moving to Bean Street she wanted to move back to the city, that in Plum she felt like a prisoner banished to Siberia. "We can't move back to the city!" Brendan had cried, rushing into the kitchen and breaking in on the talk they had

assumed was secret. "Not now," he added, on the verge of tears. Not now that he had friends in Plum. Not now that he had become accustomed to Plum school. Not now that basketball season was underway and he was out for the junior high squad. No, his father assured him; if they ever moved back to the city it couldn't be now, with all their money tied up in the market. His mother got hold of herself and said she had been kidding.

"I wish I didn't get a football from my grandma and grandpa," said Philip. "I've already got a football. What I need is a basketball."

Among the communicants Brendan saw Rufus Ottmann drifting sideways along the middle aisle like a rudderless boat in a stream. He had come unmoored from his mother, who knelt at the rail, and was turning left and right and casting his grin over the congregation. Philip Crowley's father left his pew and took Rufus by the hand and led him back to his place. As usual, the sight left Brendan full of questions. Why did the idiot's idiocy make Brendan fearful? What did Rufus have in his head instead of brains? Sam Romberg said straw. His brother Andy's guess was cold oatmeal. How, if the Catechism was correct in defining the human soul as understanding combined with free will, could Rufus be human? Where else but in Plum would Rufus be so well taken care of? Wasn't this village, despite the religious bigotry Paul Dimmitburg complained of, a kind of peaceable kingdom after all? By making a place for misfits weren't the villagers carrying out Christ's command to love one another? But why, Brendan wondered, hadn't Plum made a place for his mother?

Melva Heffernand began a fugue on the organ, and Brendan looked at his watch. It was one fifteen. Philip went on about presents; the clothes he got from his parents were no more satisfactory than the football and the book; as for the games, they were all right, but not really the ones he wanted. The church had grown extremely warm, the air stale. Fighting sleep, Brendan turned his mind to the house on Bean Street and imagined how his room would be arranged. He asked God to speed up the time between now and Sunday. He thanked God for making the market a success. He asked God to make his mother happy.

Catherine, returning to her place after Communion, asked God to ease her mind concerning Bean Street. Hank had insisted that the property was a bargain and the interest rate of three percent was not

unreasonable, but a house mortgage on top of a store mortgage struck her as an awful encumbrance. If the store failed, they'd lose both. Hank said it couldn't fail. He showed her the figures and said it was clear that their hard work was paying off. Weekly trade had doubled after the Armistice Sale, doubled again after the Thanksgiving Sale, and the Christmas Sale set a record for three-day income. He was so happy explaining this to her that she tried not to let her anxiety show. "We're established now," he said, "and there's nothing ahead but steady growth." She fought believing it because she was afraid to believe it. With a market thriving on Main and a comfortable house on Bean, she was afraid of being planted in Plum forever.

Hank's prayer, as he took his place beside her in the pew, was a prayer of thanksgiving for the many permanent customers he had won away from Legget. Bob Donaldson of Minneapolis Jobbing had been right; Plum had been a two-market town waiting for its second market. The only unfortunate thing was that all of Hank's new customers, except during sales, were the same people he saw returning tonight from the communion rail. He had thought that the combination of bargains and Paul Dimmitburg might have won him a few Lutherans, but it hadn't happened. Stan Kimball said it would never happen, no matter how superior to Legget's the market became. Kimball claimed that these villagers were never so happy as when they were at odds for the love of God, and when Hank came to town he restored to them their long-lost divisiveness in the area of groceries. But Hank wasn't convinced. If he and Paul and Wallace and Catherine remained steadfast in serving the public and absolutely noncommittal in matters of religion and politics, he foresaw the market becoming as neutral as Gordy's Pool Hall, patronized by one and all. Please let it happen, O Lord. And to this prayer he added the words he had addressed to heaven a thousand times in the past several weeks: Above all else, please help Catherine cheer up.

All his life it had been Grandfather's policy not to burden God with complexities, and tonight his prayer was as simple as usual: With all due respect, God, could you prevail upon your priest to move this along a little faster? I'm dying for my pipe.

In the alley between Hay and Bean Streets, Larry-the-Twitch Romberg turned his small face up to the thickly falling snow, shut his eyes, opened his mouth and screamed "Assholes" at the top of his

lungs. Larry-the-Twitch and his brothers had been given a pair of skis by their parents, and now at one fifteen on Christmas morning Andy and Sam were gliding down the sloping alley in the dark and ignoring their little brother's demand for a turn of his own. Mrs. Romberg opened the back door and called into the swirling snowflakes, "You boys get in here this instant, you'll wake up the neighbors. We're going to early service in the morning, and you'll be dead on your feet."

"Fart-blossoms," screamed the nine-year-old. "Piss-ants."

At the base of the slope Andy and Sam, who had just come to a stop in tandem, on one ski apiece, laughed until they couldn't stand up. They fell into the snow and shook with silent laughter, listening to their mother's futile calls interspersed with Larry's obscenities. Their laughter increased to the point of pain when they heard their father burst onto the scene, heard him chase Larry across the alley, heard his roars of anger alternating with Larry's piping pleas for mercy. Hidden in the dark, they laughed themselves breathless, confident that if they lay low long enough they would return to the house and find Larry-the-Twitch asleep and their father relieved of his anger and ready to laugh himself at the words the little twerp had shouted into the snowy peace of Christmas. "Oh, you men," their mother would say, trying to sound disgusted, but failing to conceal entirely her own amusement.

Henrietta Kimball turned over in bed and said, "I hear a ruckus, Stanley."

"I hear it too," replied the undertaker in the dark. "It's Russell Romberg chasing his kids."

The pup lying under the bed heard it as well and began to bark.

"Are you sure the doors are locked?" Mrs. Kimball asked.

"Yes, the doors are locked." Stan Kimball covered his ears and added, "I swear to God we're going to get a muzzle for that mutt."

"No, Stanley, Otto is our good little watchdog."

Otto continued to bark and Stan Kimball buried his head under his pillow.

"Hush," said his wife, reaching under the bed to calm the dog. "Hush, Otto dear."

Stan Kimball spoke through his pillow. "Either that or we'll have his voice box removed."

* * *

Two doors away Cora Brask, awakened by the voices of the man and the boy under her window, said to her husband, "The neighborhood goes down, Harlan."

The mayor, who had been listening to the Romberg noises for several minutes, agreed. "Families like that ought to be restricted to the other end of town, by the tracks." After a few moments he added, "You can always tell the riffraff—they're underinsured." He was thinking of the old pickup the Rombergs used for delivering bottlegas, and the careless way the oldest boy drove it, sometimes so loaded with youngsters the wheels rubbed the fenders.

"And to think the Fosters are moving in next door," said his wife.

"Yes. That rattletrap of a car they drive."

"She's nothing but a common grocery clerk. How can they afford a house with their store no busier than it is?"

"It's getting busier."

"Worse luck," she said.

They heard a shout and a howl as Mr. Romberg nabbed Larry-the-Twitch and dragged him home. They heard the Rombergs' back door slam shut. They lay in silence for several minutes, before Mrs. Brask said, "Must we go to early service, Harlan? We'll be short of sleep."

"You suit yourself, but I'm going. The boy is preaching."

"I can't respect a boy like that, dropping out of the seminary and going to work for a Catholic."

"It has nothing to do with respect. I want to hear firsthand what his ideas are. If he's a freethinker, he'll have to be nipped in the bud."

The Reverend Dimmitburg worked on the sermon he would deliver at the late service until one thirty in the morning; then he switched off the light in his study and stood at the window in his pajamas and robe, watching the snow come piling down under the streetlight in front of the church. Whatever ailed his son in October was a thing of the past, he was sure of that. Perhaps Paul's mistake had been taking a job on campus and staying there all through the summer, allowing himself no time for refreshment between school years. He came home in October looking like a cadaver. His job in Hank's Market was a godsend. Got his mind off his troubles. Allowing the unordained to preach was highly unorthodox, but the Reverend Dimmitburg was eager to help his boy find his legs and send him back

to the seminary with his confidence restored. Once back, he'd sail quickly through to ordination, no doubt about it. A peerless candidate for the ministry, so his professors said.

The minister left his study and went upstairs. Seeing a light under Paul's door, he rapped gently and said, "Put your sermon aside, Paul, and get your rest."

"Okay, Dad."

"Good night, son."

"Good night."

Paul's sermon, which Kierkegaard would have abhorred, had been dashed off hours ago. It was fifteen minutes of innocuous thoughts on the Nativity, for Paul had no desire to inflame people like Harlan Brask, whose ears would be cocked for heresy; he had no desire to stand his father's parish on its ear. He was lying in bed reading the four issues of *Independent Grocer* Hank had given him. As he studied the monthly article on store design, a new Hank's Market, vastly remodeled, began to take shape in his mind.

Long after Wallace had gone to bed, Mrs. Flint sat beside her radio and grieved, holding in her lap the letter Wallace had presented her as his Christmas gift. It was his draft notice. He had told her that instead of seeking deferment this time, he would answer his country's call. Seeing tears in her eyes, he had added, "I thought all mothers wanted their sons to be heroes. I thought this would make you happy." Of course he had thought nothing of the kind. And she knew it.

Constable Heffernand, minding the switchboard while his sister Melva attended Midnight Mass, was not able to connect Phyllis Clay with her party in Rochester.

"Nobody answers, Mrs. Clay."

She sobbed in his ear.

"I'm sorry, Mrs. Clay, shall we try again in the morning?"

"Morning will be too late, Mr. Heffernand. It's now I need to talk to him. It's Christmas Eve and Webster's been asleep on the davenport since eight thirty. No kiss, no hug, not even a smile for Christmas. I've got nobody to talk to."

"Well," said the Constable, feeling pity for her.

"He went straight from his supper to the davenport and he's been snoring ever since."

"I'm sorry."

Another sob. A burp. He supposed she was drunk.

"I have this friend in Rochester. He's my chiropractor. I've got lower back pain. If I could talk to him for a minute I wouldn't feel so blue."

"For what it's worth, Mrs. Clay, let me say Merry Christmas."

"Oh, thank you, Mr. Heffernand. I suppose it's a happy season for you and your sister. It seems like everybody's got somebody, but all I've got is Webster. At home we always used to have mistletoe and my uncle would give us girls a kiss under it, and I've said ever since that a kiss means more at Christmas than any other time."

A long silence.

"Webster's"—a hiccup—"not a kisser."

The constable kindly held the connection open.

"Don't you agree, Mr. Heffernand? A kiss means a whole, whole lot at Christmas?"

"Yes, I suppose it does." He tried to remember the last woman he had kissed at Christmas. Or at any other time.

"Mr. Heffernand, would it be all right if you didn't cut me off quite yet? It's nice talking to you."

"I tell you what, Mrs. Clay. Could you step outside your house for just a minute?"

"Outside? It's snowing like hell."

"Just for a minute, I mean. There's something I'd like to give you for Christmas." He couldn't believe he was saying this. He never did romantic, spontaneous things. He was Plum's dependable drudge whose idea of fun was igniting model airplanes. He spoke fast now, afraid that his voice, already shaky, would fail him at any syllable. "If you came up the street toward my house, I'd meet you halfway."

He was trembling as he put on his coat. His heart was pounding. He hurried through the deep snow in the street and saw the bewildered Mrs. Clay materialize in the amber glow of the snow-shrouded streetlight. Whether from drink or from slippery footing she was staggering. Her fur coat was open. When he saw the large snowflakes glistening in her hair and eyelashes, something dormant for decades fluttered to life in his breast. He took her in his arms rather awkwardly, for his trembling had grown to a kind of shudder, and he kissed her hard on the lips. As he tried to raise his head to say Merry Christmas, her mouth remained clamped on his; she held him tightly around the neck and didn't release him for several seconds.

Then he blurted, "Merry Christmas, I have to get back to the switchboard."

"You're an angel," she sighed.

"See, there's lots of long-distance calling on Christmas Eve, and my sister'd be mad as a hornet if she knew I was away from the switchboard." Overcome with shyness now, he was backpeddling as he spoke, and Mrs. Clay was becoming an indistinct form in the amber night, her arm raised in good-bye, her voice muffled by the snow as she called, "You're an absolute angel."

16

The morning after their move to Bean Street, Brendan went out to clear the porches and sidewalk of the snow that had fallen overnight. He began with the back porch, which his mother called a veranda. It overlooked the spacious back yard, and his mother said it would be pleasant having their meals there on warm summer days. Brendan was heartened by the effect of the move on his mother. From the moment they carried in the first piece of furniture yesterday, the lines of strain had vanished from around her eyes. She had gone through the house exclaiming over her favorite features. The veranda was one of many. She loved the living-room fireplace, the built-in buffet in the dining room, the breakfast nook in the kitchen. She said that as soon as they could afford one they would buy a piano and put it in the sunroom. Asked what he liked best, Hank named the automatic stoker attached to the coal-burning furnace and operated by a thermostat. No more days of eight trips to the basement to fuel the fire by hand. No more fires going out when no one was home to tend them.

For Grandfather, this move proved easier than the last, though until the final piece was carried in and the help went home he was stirred up and confused, pacing from room to room and muttering, "Who lives here and why aren't they home?" Hank soon cured his disorientation by arranging a corner of the living room in exact imitation of their previous living room, placing the standing ashtray on the left side of Grandfather's armchair and the console radio on the right, with his rack of pipes on top of the radio. Grandfather sat down, fiddled with the radio, and was quickly pacified by the voices of Amos and Andy.

Shoveling snow from the steps of the veranda, Brendan saw the Rombergs' battered brown pickup come bouncing down the alley, Andy Romberg at the wheel. According to Sam, Andy was spending his Christmas vacation working for his father, and whenever he went out in the pickup to deliver tanks of gas he took Norma Nash along for the ride. If Norma was unavailable he took Sam.

The pickup came to stop in the Rombergs' back yard. The horn blared. Two seconds later the back door opened and Sam leaped out of the house with one arm in the sleeve of his jacket. He climbed into the pickup and slammed the door. Larry-the-Twitch came running after him in his stocking feet, carrying a half-eaten banana. He tried to get in as well, but his brothers turned him back with good-natured insults. Sam said, "Stay home, garbage gut. If you don't get your twitchy little hands off the doorhandle," laughed Andy, "we'll drag you to Pinburg." Larry-the-Twitch was enraged. He threw down his banana and turned purple screaming "Shitheads!" as the pickup backed out of the yard, its wheels spinning in the snow.

Brendan, shoveling, wished that Sam had noticed him and asked him to ride along. Not that he could have gone. In a short time he would be due at the market, where he was working two hours a day during vacation.

Finishing the steps, Brendan went around to the front of the house, and as he began to work on the sidewalk he saw Mrs. Brask step out of her house next door. She wore her circlet of red foxtails over a coat of black fur. She approached Brendan and said, "How do you do. I am Mrs. Brask."

"Hello," said Brendan. "We're your new neighbors."

"Yes, I know. Would you please go in and tell your mother that Mrs. Kimball and I are coming to call on her? She's not at the store, is she?"

"No, she's home."

"That's what I thought. I didn't see her leave the house." Mrs. Brask continued along the sidewalk toward the Kimball house.

"You're coming today?"

"Yes, in ten minutes."

Ten minutes gave Catherine scarcely time to set a pot of coffee percolating and, with Brendan's help, to clear the empty cartons from the living room. She was in a high state of nerves. "Are they out of their minds? Do they think we're settled and ready for visitors overnight?"

From his corner by the radio, Grandfather said, "This will not be a formal visit." He was getting out of his chair and brushing the tobacco from his shirtfront in preparation for being charming. "This will be only a moment's call to say we're welcome in the neighborhood."

When the bell sounded, Grandfather opened the door. "How do you do," he said, beaming with pleasure, for he thought the young woman before him exceptionally pretty. She had dark hair and large, lively eyes. In her hand she held a plate covered with wax paper. "I understand you're the mayor's wife."

"No, you silly man, I'm Phyllis Clay, don't you remember? I gave you a shot of brandy in my garage."

He remembered, and was doubly pleased. "And what a timely drink that was. I've been meaning to come by and thank you ever since. Please come in."

"No, heavens, you're not settled. I'll come back some other day. I only wanted to say welcome to Bean Street and give you these cookies."

He took the plate and lifted the wax paper. "Oatmeal with raisin?"

"Yes," she giggled. "Now don't be naughty and eat them all. Promise you'll share them with your family."

"I make no such promise."

By the time Brendan and Catherine came to the door from the kitchen, she was already hurrying away. Catherine called, "Thank you." Mrs. Clay turned and waved cheerily, making room on the sidewalk for Mrs. Brask and Mrs. Kimball, who were advancing in single file.

Lumbering up across the porch and into the house, Mrs. Brask declared, "We're here only for a minute, Mrs. Foster, and we won't even sit down. I know what moving day is like. I remember the day we moved here from Chicago." Saying this, she removed her foxtails and coat, handing them to Brendan as though he were a butler. "We met the day you were looking for your father." She nodded politely at Grandfather. "But you may not remember. I'm Cora Brask and this is Henrietta Kimball."

"Of course, I remember," said Catherine.

Mrs. Kimball came stooping through the doorway so as not to snap off the enormous feather standing up from her hat. She did not remove her coat, but clutched it tightly as if fearing she might be

forcibly disrobed. She said, "How do you do" to Catherine, to Brendan, to Grandfather, smiling kindly to each in turn.

Catherine was fascinated by her first close-up view of Stan Kimball's wife, her innocent expression, her tentative gestures, her meek eyes.

"Do sit down," said Catherine. "I'm making coffee."

Mrs. Kimball looked at her large friend for a decision, which turned out to be affirmative, Mrs. Brask lowering herself onto the couch and patting the cushion beside her to indicate Mrs. Kimball's place. Catherine went to the kitchen, and Brendan hung the heavy coat and the foxtails in the closet and went outside to finish his work. Grandfather pulled a chair up facing the ladies and asked the mayor's wife, "When you lived in Chicago, did you take the Milwaukee Road to Minnesota?"

Yes, she had done so, a time or two.

"In that case I may have been your conductor."

"I see. Well, if you're acquainted with Chicago you know the streets of large houses near the university. My husband and I lived in one of those houses. A perfectly lovely street. Wide boulevards. Elms." She withheld the fact that they had lived in a third-floor apartment of such a house while her husband tried and failed to establish himself selling life insurance to graduating seniors, who proved less gullible than he had been led to expect by his supervisor. Nor did she mention that their moving to Plum was actually a return home, both she and her husband having grown to adulthood here.

"I've never been to Chicago," said Mrs. Kimball timidly.

"Oh, how we miss Chicago," Mrs. Brask rhapsodized. "The hub of the nation."

"Yes, Stanley's embalming fluid comes from there."

Catherine came in with coffee, and Mrs. Brask addressed her: "Melva Heffernand says her brother showed you around the library. We're all so pleased that you're interested in books. What sort of books do you like?"

"I read *A Farewell to Arms* three months ago, and I haven't gotten over it yet."

"Yes, Shakespeare is wonderful, but we know someone better, don't we, Henrietta? Will you tell her the good news, or shall I?"

Mrs. Kimball asked shyly, "About the new book?"

"Yes."

Mrs. Kimball turned to Catherine. "Henry Hodge Fleet's new book has arrived."

"*Edward* Hodge Fleet, Henrietta."

"Yes, Edward Hodge Fleet. It's called *Heart Throbs.*"

"No, Henrietta, *Pangs of the Heart.* I'm halfway through it, and I can assure you it's simply wonderful. It's chock-full of tragedy, three heart attacks so far, but with Edward Hodge Fleet you know the sun will come shining through. Would you like to borrow it when I finish?"

Catherine did not say no. She said, "Well . . ."

Mrs. Brask concealed her disappointment at this tepid response and changed the subject: "Will you continue to work in your husband's store, now that you're living on Bean Street?"

"Oh, yes, we're in partnership, Hank and I."

Instead of stating outright that working wives were not approved of on Bean Street, that implicit in a Bean address was a certain elevation above the more sordid aspects of getting and spending, Mrs. Brask told Catherine a story. "Your predecessors in this house, the DeRoches, were lovely, lovely neighbors, Mrs. Foster, and so it always tugged at our hearts whenever we saw Mrs. DeRoche go out and help her husband on his auto-parts route. He traveled for a firm in Rochester, and sometimes when he stayed home to do his bookwork, she would take the truck out alone, delivering parts hither and yon."

"And what was the problem with that?" Catherine inquired.

"Well, you have to wonder, don't you, when you see a wife out in the working world, how she can properly care for her children and keep house and put wholesome meals on the table? The DeRoches never kept their yard up properly, as you'll discover this spring when the snow melts."

Catherine was firm. "I help at the store, and my husband helps at home."

"Well, of course it's entirely your business and Henrietta and I would be the last ones to advise people how to live their lives. Goodness, we've watched Mrs. Clay drink like a fish ever since Webster brought her home from Omaha and we haven't said a word to her about it. And speaking of drinking, we don't talk about it because they are two of the most respected residents on Bean, but there is a history of moonshine in the Heffernand family. Unavoidable perhaps, their being Catholic. And Charles and Melva have certainly

overcome the shame. They've restored honor to the family name. A pity that the family will end when they die. When he was just out of high school in 1911 Charles Heffernand became engaged to a classmate named Mary Boyle, but she died of TB before the wedding. Their grandfather, Herman Heffernand, was the first mayor of Plum. He farmed what is now the west end of town. Their father, Hector Heffernand, established Plum Telephone Incorporated, along with bootlegging his homemade whiskey. Poor Melva, she suffers from psoriasis. The Woodruffs live just beyond the Heffernands. Who would have thought even ten years ago that Abraham Woodruff would be living on Bean, much less serving on the school board with Harlan? Ten years ago Abraham Woodruff mowed lawns and changed storm windows for whoever needed odd jobs done, and he and his wife and children went around in rags. Clean rags, of course—they've always had a good, healthy Protestant sense of cleanliness about them—but rags all the same. They used to receive food baskets from the church at Christmas. Then his brother in St. Paul somehow got him the postmaster's job, and he's been on easy street ever since. His wife's raisin pie is all the rage when we have our church bazaar in the fall. It seems like only yesterday Abraham came and asked Harlan to lend him money to pay his bill at Legget's. Harlan was left a nice little sum when his mother died, you see, and Abraham had the nerve to ask him outright for a loan. Poverty makes people so shameless. Abraham has a glandular disorder that makes him a little pop-eyed."

There was no stopping Mrs. Brask once she got up her momentum. Not that Catherine wanted to; these thumbnail sketches were fascinating. Although they were conceived with a Lutheran bias, there was a perverse generosity in the way she delivered them, as though she were opening doors for Catherine and inviting her into all these lives.

"Do you know Mr. and Mrs. Philip Crowley? They have a son named Philip about the age of your boy. Mr. Crowley owns the movie theater and Mrs. Crowley is a Catholic of the most militant, disgusting kind. I hate to say it, but the whole family is a little bit loose in the area of morals. Mr. and Mrs. take separate vacations, their daughter who lives in Minneapolis was said to have borne a baby out of wedlock last year and Mr. Crowley one time brought a movie to town in which Henry Fonda used the name of the Lord in vain. The Peterson girl is also your son's age, is she not? The Peter-

sons became well-to-do by selling Chevrolets and Buicks before the war, and they contribute generously to Emmanuel Lutheran. Mr. Peterson moved here as a young man to work in his uncle's gas station, and it was here he met his wife, a farmer's daughter. Besides Pearl they have two other children, a son in the navy and a daughter in nurses' training in Rochester. Mrs. Peterson is afflicted with bursitis. The Dimmitburgs are without a doubt the nicest people I have ever met, so kind, so intelligent, so well-dressed. It's regrettable that as a Catholic you will never hear the Reverend Dimmitburg preach. His voice is beautiful, his message always such a consolation. Mrs. Dimmitburg brought the money to that marriage. Her father was a contractor in St. Louis. How long can little old Emmanuel Lutheran hope to hang on to them? The smallest house and the largest family on Bean belongs to the Nicholis. Mr. Nicholi is the barber and his wife does sewing for hire. They have seven children—so Catholic—grown up and moved away. One of their daughters started college on scholarships and never quit, one degree after another. Her field is nutrition. She looks a fright when she comes home for the holidays, bags under her eyes and skinny as a rail. Mrs. Nicholi is burdened with an invalid sister who came to visit five years ago and never left. She's paralyzed in her limbs and her eyes don't shut. Well, Henrietta, don't you think we should leave Mrs. Foster to her housework? My, I like the upholstery on that chair over there. Next time we call we won't know the place, I'm sure. You'll have made this house your home. What will you hang over the fireplace? The DeRoches had a Biblical picture there, Geronimo battling the Philistines or some such thing, it was all reds and yellows and too active, I thought, for a living room."

Grandfather helped Mrs. Brask on with her coat while Mrs. Kimball made her first attempt at conversation:

"Stanley and I have a dog named Otto. I named him after my doctor."

"I've seen him," said Catherine. "He's a handsome little thing."

Grandfather opened the door and Mrs. Brask lumbered out, saying "If there's anything we can do to help you get settled, just say the word."

"Thank you so much, do come again," said Catherine. Then she called past them, "Brendan, dear, it's nearly time."

For his stint of work at the store, she meant. He whisked away a little more snow, then stood aside to let the two women pass.

Mrs. Brask said, going by, "I suppose you'll grow up to take over your father's market, young man."

His policy with adults was unswerving agreement. He said, "Yes, I'll be a grocer." Actually he had no such intention. He would be a brakeman, maybe. Or a priest.

"Or perhaps you'll join the navy," said Mrs. Kimball. "I have a nephew who's very fond of the navy."

"Yes, that could be, too."

Catherine held the door open for Brendan, and for the woman who came hurrying along behind him. She was a small redhead with green eyes and freckles. She bounded onto the porch and said, "You're Catherine Foster, so happy to know you, I'm Bea Crowley. So sorry not to have been buying your groceries, but my brother is the grocer in Pinburg and we do all our shopping there. The ties of blood, you know. Now don't let me take you away from your work. I just wanted to say welcome to Bean Street and I'm so happy you're Catholic. The DeRoches were Catholic too, and when they moved away I was afraid we'd lose ground. This would be Brendan. My Philip talks on and on about Brendan, they're the best of friends."

"And this is my father," said Catherine, leading her into the living room.

"How do you do, I'm so happy to meet you." Removing her glove, she thrust her hand at Grandfather, who took it in both of his own and thought, Now this is more like it, neighbors in and out, a wise move leaving the Ottmann house at the lonesome edge of town, where the only neighbors were idiots and cows.

"I was saying to Philip yesterday when we saw you moving—Philip my husband, not Philip my son—that it's a shame we're in the middle of remodeling because we'd love to have a party and get you acquainted. We're doing over our whole ground floor, taking out partitions and brightening up the dark, old woodwork. Ordinarily one's parish church is the ideal place to get acquainted, but Holy Angels has done nothing but go downhill since Father O'Day took over. He discourages potluck dinners and teas and social occasions of all kinds. Philip and the rest of the Men's Club are planning a trip to the bishop to petition him to replace Father O'Day. He's old and forgetful and he lives in that rectory like a hermit. He ought to be retired. What did Mrs. Brask say about me? She's an awful gossip."

"Let's see, we talked mostly about whether I plan to go on working in the store. She doesn't approve."

"Oh, that woman. Just ignore her, if you can. I'm so glad she's not next door to me. I can't believe she didn't bring up my name."

"She only mentioned the theater. She said your husband showed a movie one time with swearing on the sound track."

"How would she know? She never goes to movies, she says they're immoral. Well, I'll tell you what's immoral, her trashy taste in books."

"Oh, I'm so happy to hear you say that. I thought I was the only one who felt that way. Have you read *A Farewell to Arms*? I can't get over how sad it is."

"That's Hemingway. Philip and I don't read Hemingway, his philosophy's wrong. We read Catholic writers. Bernanos and Mauriac and people like that. I'll bring you some of their work."

"I think I've read most of Bernanos and Mauriac."

"And don't you agree, their philosophy's right?"

"Yes, I do, but then I don't read only for philosophy. I read to be moved."

"You don't find Bernanos and Mauriac moving?"

"Very. But I like variety. When I get our books unpacked you'll have to come and see if there's anything you'd like to read. I thought Wallace Flint was the only real reader in town."

Mrs. Crowley's eyes became suddenly clouded. She peered at Catherine darkly. "That awful man. We all wondered how long he would last with you. Philip didn't think he'd last a week."

"Actually, he's been a great help in getting us started. He's a walking Who's Who of Plum."

"But people despise him, you know."

"No, I don't think they do. Our customers deal with him just fine."

Mrs. Crowley shrugged. The lift of her eyebrows said, Wait and see. She took her leave, promising to have the Fosters over as soon as her house was presentable.

Catherine went straight to the phone and asked Central to ring the market. When Hank said, "Hank's," she told him, "I've just had four neighbors drop in to wish me well, Hank. Count them, four."

"Good for you. Good for them."

"Let's have a housewarming, Hank. Let's invite all our new neighbors and sort through them for kindred spirits."

"A good idea."

"And invite Wallace and his mother and the Dimmitburgs. We

did nothing for our help at Christmas. Let's do it on New Year's afternoon."

"That's when the Rose Bowl's on."

"Those who want can listen."

"We can be ready by New Year's?"

"It will be very informal."

"I'm all for it."

"How's business this morning?"

"Humming right along. Send Brendan down. It's delivery time."

"He's on his way."

"How's unpacking?"

"I'm through in the kitchen."

"Don't overdo."

"No, I'm stopping now. I'm going to jot down our guest list."

Wallace poured a mixture of water and antifreeze into the radiator while Brendan carried bags of groceries out the back door and lined them up across the back seat. Then they got in and Wallace, starting the engine, said, "I've got something to show you." He reached inside his jacket and drew a brown envelope from his shirt pocket. "Read it and weep."

Brendan read it as they chugged along the snow-packed alley. It was a draft notice. It ordered Wallace to report for his induction physical in Minneapolis on January 16.

"I thought you always got deferred."

"Not anymore. I believe in taking up arms against Fascism."

"What have you been reading, *Joe Palooka*?"

"Don't take that tone with me, Brendan, dear."

"Don Winslow Helps the Marines?"

They came to their first stop, and Brendan ran in with the groceries. Hopping back into the car, he said, "But there's basic training."

"What do you mean, there's basic training? Of course there is."

"I can't see you crawling on your elbows and knees under a crossfire of live ammunition."

"I'll do what I'm asked."

Brendan imagined Wallace as a buck private. "The first time you're given an order you'll probably say, 'How horribly arch of you, sergeant.' " More than once he had heard Wallace accuse his mother of being horribly arch.

Wallace saw no humor in this. "When I'm given an order, I'll say, 'Yes, sir.' "

"You might get shot," Brendan pointed out.

"I might get shot and I might not." Wallace's voice rose. "I might come home a hero and I might not." His eyes shone zealously. "But at least I will have stood up and been counted when it counted."

17

The guests, all four of them, stood visiting at the dining room table, which was covered with sweets. Catherine opened the front door and welcomed Paul Dimmitburg.

"Happy New Year, Paul."

"And a blessed New Year to you," he said gravely, stepping in out of the failing gray light of mid-afternoon. "Sorry to be so late." He was followed by a heavy-faced man of great girth and a lean, angular woman. The man wore a smile, the woman a severe expression.

"I'd like you to meet my parents."

"How nice to know you."

"Our pleasure," said the minister. "Paul speaks highly of you and your husband."

His wife mumbled something unintelligible. She was tall and dark-eyed like her son.

"You must be pleased to have Paul home," said Catherine. "He's a great help to us in the store."

"We were hoping he would return to school for spring semester," said Mrs. Dimmitburg resentfully. "We are sorry he's waiting till fall."

Paul directed his impassive gaze over his parents' heads, and when they had taken off their coats and gone into the dining room he said, "Please forgive my mother. She can't understand why God didn't create all of humanity Lutheran." He helped hang up their coats. "Have you given any more thought to my plan?"

"Yes, Hank is all for it."

"And you?"

"If we can afford it."

"It won't cost much. I'll do all the carpentry." With his ambition to transform the world temporarily thwarted, Paul was determined to transform Hank's Market; he had presented them with detailed drawings.

"I'm sure we'll go ahead," she told him. "The question is when."

Paul looked into the dining room. "My, a guest list of Lutherans. Isn't that Mrs. Peterson?"

"Yes, mother of Pearl."

"And her husband and the Kimballs."

"The Kimballs are only half Lutheran."

"Where are the Brasks?"

"Mrs. Brask said her husband devotes New Year's to his bookwork." Catherine said nothing to Paul about the poor turnout. The Dimmitburgs made seven. She had invited thirty-two. Bea Crowley had extended her regrets when she heard that Protestants had been invited. The Nicholis were entertaining family. Mrs. Clay was visiting a friend in Rochester. None of the other absentees had bothered replying to the invitation.

In the dining room, the Reverend and Mrs. Dimmitburg, declining Hank's offer of wine, greeted Mrs. Kimball, who thrust a photo of her dog at them. "Look at him, chewing on one of Stanley's shoes. Isn't he the most precious thing?"

"Perky-looking all right," said the minister, passing the photo to his wife.

"My doctor prescribed the dog to relax me."

"I'll bet he doesn't relax Stanley."

"What kind of dog is it?" asked Mrs. Dimmitburg.

"I can never remember. He's like a scottie, only white. His name is Otto."

The Dimmitburgs approached the table and greeted the Petersons, Stan Kimball, and Hank.

"Looks like more snow," said the minister.

"Too much snow," said George Peterson of Plum Chevrolet-Buick. He stifled a yawn.

"Saw your dog's picture," he said to Stan Kimball.

"Vicious little cur," said the undertaker, whose badly-chewed cigar hung from his mouth unlit. "Teeth like razors. Nips at my ankles all the time. I have to read with my feet up."

"Doctor's orders, I understand."

"The doctor's a quack."

"What kind of dog is it?" asked Mrs. Dimmitburg.

"The incontinent kind."

There followed an awkward pause while the group searched their minds for more to say about snow or dogs. Finding nothing, they turned to cars, the minister asking George Peterson, "How long after the war ends will General Motors start sending you cars?"

"My guess is six months, but there'll be a shortage for a long time. I expect to have a waiting list for at least two years."

Stan Kimball said, "Put Hank at the top of your list, would you? His car's got a death rattle if I ever heard one."

"The kickoff!" Grandfather announced, emerging from the bathroom and lifting the men instantly out of their tea-party torpor. Hank led them to the radio, where they pulled up chairs and stools and agreed that Tennessee would be too much for Southern California. Grandfather was delayed in joining them, stopping to apologize to the three female guests—"You'll forgive me, please, for listening to football, I have fifty cents riding on Tennessee."

When Catherine opened the door to Wallace Flint, it took her a moment to recognize him. He wore a crew cut, waxed and standing up straight. His beard was gone. His smile was a new one for Wallace—broad and guileless.

"Wallace, what have you done to yourself?"

"Government issue." He bounced his hand off his springy flattop.

"And your beard. Do you realize I've never before seen your entire face?"

He gave her his profile. "How do you like it?"

"Exquisite," she told him, though she thought his weak chin quite unattractive. Beardless and all but hairless, he put her in mind of the featherless baby bird she had found on the lawn last spring after a windstorm. Unformed. Vulnerable. "But why?"

"No beards in the military."

"Oh, Wallace." Her voice was plaintive, her expression tender. He'd never make a soldier. He'd wash out and come home depressed. Yesterday Mrs. Flint had come into Hank's Market for the first time ever and begged Hank to use his considerable influence on Wallace. She was near tears, Hank reported later to Catherine. Wallace was sure to meet with disaster, she said. His epilepsy would worsen. Her own heart would break. Hank had then tried to dissuade Wallace, had urged him to ask his doctor in Pinburg for an-

other deferment, and Catherine did the same when she came to work, but Wallace was adamant. He was a changed man. In gearing himself up for induction, his mental machinery seemed to have slipped a cog. His military aspirations, begun in spite, were now apparently in earnest. Yesterday in the store he had talked about nothing but Robert E. Lee.

"They're staring at me, Catherine." His eyes were on the two groups of guests, women in the dining room, men at the radio end of the living room.

Indeed, all eyes were on him. Catherine saw her guests turning to one another with "It's Wallace Flint" forming on their lips.

He stayed a very short time. Outside, he drew a stocking cap from the pocket of his jacket and pulled it down over his ears, regretting what it would do to his waxed flattop. With longer hair he had never worn a cap, but the flattop provided no insulation. He didn't want to go to his physical exam with a cold; he must be in perfect health.

He walked with what he guessed was a military bearing—eyes ahead, back straight, arms swinging, It was mid-afternoon and daylight was already dying. A few grainy snowflakes were zipping about on the cold breeze. Turning into Main Street, he saw a car parked in front of the market, its lights on, its motor running. He saw a man behind the wheel. He saw a second figure get out and stand at the door of the market, peering through the glass. He approached the figure quietly from behind and said, "What do you want?"

The figure turned abruptly from the door. It was Dodger Hicks. "Ain't this the Fosters' store any more?"

"Of course it's the Fosters' store. Why wouldn't it be?"

"I been to their house and it looked empty."

"They moved."

"Yeah? Where to?"

"Bean Street."

"Yeah? Which house?"

"What do you want to know for?"

Dodger shivered. "I got something for Brendan."

The driver, a man in a gray overcoat and a black hat, got out of the car and spoke across the hood. "We're looking for the Foster family."

"They're out of town for the holiday," said Wallace. "Won't be back till tomorrow."

"All right, Dodger, let's run along." The man returned to his place behind the wheel.

Dodger took from his pocket a tiny parcel and handed it to Wallace. "Give this to Brendan, would you?"

Wallace nodded, taking it. It was a two-inch cube wrapped in Christmas paper.

"Tell him it's from me. It's for Christmas."

"Okay."

Dodger got into the car and it moved off through the flying snowflakes.

Wallace peeled the paper from the gift. It was a box containing five rolls of caps for a cap gun. He dropped the paper in the snow and started across the street toward home. Halfway across he saw a pickup approaching from his left. He stopped to let it go by. He tossed the caps into the pickup as it passed.

18

Included in Wallace's dream of leaving Plum was the pleasure of watching the village recede behind him as he rode away. Though Plum was eleven miles from the nearest passenger train and bus route, the conveyance in the dream was sometimes a train, sometimes a bus, the time of departure was a brilliant spring morning, and the village was quickly lost in a fold of green hills. On the morning of January 16, in fact, his conveyance was the morning mail truck, which left town before first light. It was eight below zero and all was blackness except the frozen gravel in the beam of the headlights.

"I was in the first war," said the driver, a chain-smoking man whose route began in Rochester each morning at five. "That's how I got this job. Veteran's preference. Going to war's better than going to college. It's something they can't ever take away from you. It gives you first crack at government jobs. What branch you going into?"

"I haven't been told yet," said Wallace. "Probably the Army."

"How come you got no suitcase?"

"We're not called to camp until a week or so after the physical."

"They changed it then. In the first war we had our physical and left for camp on the same day. They sent me to a camp in Georgia. Cured me for life of ever wanting to live in a hot climate. Sweated off ten pounds the first four days. About died."

"Is basic training difficult?" Not being equal to the rigors of military life was Wallace's primary fear.

"Difficult!" The man laughed. "I about died."

Nine miles out of Plum the road tipped downward, beginning its

descent through the densely wooded bluffs. In the dim gray dawn Wallace caught glimpses, between the bare trees, of the ice-covered Mississippi. The mail truck coasted down to river level and came to a stop at the intersection of Highway 61.

"You got quite a wait. The bus ain't through here till nine thirty."

"I know." Wallace shut the door and the truck growled away. He crossed the highway to the gas station which served as the bus stop.

"Where to?" the attendant asked as Wallace stepped through the door. A layer of oily grime covered everything in the station including the attendant's jacket and eyeglasses.

"Minneapolis."

"Two fifty, round trip."

"I've got a pass."

"Going for your physical, I suppose."

"Yes."

A car pulled in for gas. The attendant, going out the door, repeated the mail carrier's words, "You've got quite a wait."

With his handkerchief Wallace wiped off the top of a carton of oil and sat down. He might have avoided this two-hour wait if the Fosters had been more cooperative. Instead of consenting immediately when he had asked Catherine to deliver him to Highway 61, she had consulted Hank, who said it was doubtful that the car would start—it never started on subzero mornings. Rather than risk missing the bus, he ought to ride the morning mail truck. Hank said he would drive to the junction in the evening to pick him up—by afternoon the temperature invariably climbed above zero and the car came to life. At this point in the conversation, Paul Dimmitburg had stepped forward and offered to ask his father for the family car, but Wallace had declined with a wordless sneer. He hated Paul for having insinuated himself into Hank and Catherine's good graces. Especially Catherine's.

The attendant reentered the station and offered Wallace the morning *Tribune* to pass the time. Reading the war news, Wallace decided he'd rather be assigned to Patton in Europe than MacArthur in the Pacific. Patton was getting more press. *Events of the past two days in the Battle of the Bulge point to an eventual victory for the Allies. After exactly one month of the fiercest fighting yet in the European theater, Patton's Third Army is beginning to turn back what military analysts in Washington are calling the last German offensive of the war.*

Shortly before bus time a truck pulled into the station and let out

a young man who held in his hand a pass like Wallace's. He had sandy hair, buck teeth and a crooked nose. He violated Wallace's concept of the military. Service personnel portrayed on billboards and in magazines were handsome, and it hadn't crossed Wallace's mind that he would be expected to serve side by side with homely people. The young man came into the station and said "Howdy" to Wallace, and when the bus arrived, the young man took the seat next to him. If he had tried to strike up a conversation Wallace would have changed seats, but the young man was shy and said nothing all the way to the city.

Among the people boarding the bus at each stop were two or three men of draftable age who handed the driver their government pass. Most of them looked to Wallace like stupid farm boys. Wallace himself was feeling very snappy. He kept bouncing his hand off his springy crew cut as he took in the sights he had heard of but never seen. Lake Pepin with clusters of fishhouses here and there on the ice. The pottery plant in Red Wing, and near it the factory where Red Wing Shoes were made. The Home School for Boys at the edge of Flensboro. The spiral bridge in Hastings.

By the time they disembarked in Minneapolis a dozen or more recruits at the back of the bus had become friends, and they stood in the depot discussing what they would do until their one o'clock appointment at the federal building. They asked Wallace if he would like to go with them to find something to eat.

"No," he said sharply.

The buck-toothed boy seemed reluctant to leave Wallace's side. "Go eat with them," Wallace snapped, and the boy obeyed, following the group out the door.

Wallace left by another door, and, referring to the map in his brown envelope, he made his way toward the federal building. To be on his own among city people made his heart beat fast. He saw a lot of important-looking men in expensive-looking coats. He saw men and women in military uniform. He saw a policeman. He saw Negroes. He saw a Negro policeman. He saw a blind man selling pencils. He saw a midget. He was nearly pushed off the sidewalk by a swarm of young women emerging from the Minnesota School of Business. He was asked for money by a woman with *Salvation Army* stitched on her coat. His picture was taken by a man who handed him a card explaining how he might receive the picture in the mail. The city is my true home, he told himself as he stood at the corner of

Seventh and Hennepin waiting for the light to change. These are all my people. Except the midget, he thought a moment later. Midgets aren't my people.

He stopped before a display window of Dayton's Department Store: imitation people lying on imitation sand with imitation drinks in their hands and umbrellas overhead. He went in and found his way to the book department, a quiet, dark-paneled alcove where a middle-aged woman with a pencil in her hair was taking books down from a shelf in the history section and showing them to her only customer, a small, white-haired man with a cane. "This covers the Civil War and after," he heard the woman say. "It's the 'after' that I'm particularly interested in," the man replied. "The presidency of Grant."

No wonder Catherine longed to be back in the city, thought Wallace. Who wouldn't feel dislocated having to give up this lovely room of books and intelligent customers and be surrounded by pickles and potatoes? He browsed in the drama and poetry sections until the woman came over and asked if she could help him.

"Do you remember a woman by the name of Catherine Foster?"

"Oh my, yes. She and her husband moved away. They went into the grocery business."

"They're friends of mine. I worked for them until yesterday."

"Well, how interesting. How are they getting along?"

"All right. Nothing sensational, but all right."

"Catherine was the most knowledgeable bookseller we had. She knew titles and authors like nobody else. Please tell her we miss her."

"I will."

"Is there something I could help you find?"

Wallace, in a moment of inspiration, saw an opportunity for vengeance. "The Fosters would be doing better if they weren't involved in a scandal. Catherine's been seeing another man, and you know how small towns are. You can't get away with a thing like that."

"No, not Catherine Foster."

"A thing like that affects your business."

"No," said the woman with certainty. "We can't be talking about the same woman."

"Are you calling me a liar?" he shouted angrily.

There was alarm in the woman's eyes as she turned away from him and went back to the elderly man with the cane, who had selected the book he wanted. Writing out the sales slip, she kept an eye

on Wallace as he browsed, or pretended to browse, making his way to the hallway and then hurrying away.

"What do you make of that, Mr. Samuelson? Did you notice how distraught he was?"

The elderly man did not look up from the check he was writing. "Crazy as a coot."

Wallace, his anger cooling, was pleased by the classical lines of the federal building. He climbed the wide, granite steps, passed between two enormous pillars and entered the building through tall, heavy doors. It struck him as a fitting portal for a man about to take up arms against the forces of evil. Inside he found several recruits standing in a circle eating candy bars. He stood apart from them and looked out a window at the cars and trucks and streetcars going by. He regretted speaking angrily to the woman in the book department. What if she were the manager? What if she remembered his angry tone when he returned there after the war to apply for a job? He should have told her instead about the interest he and Catherine shared in books. But speaking ill of her gave him such pleasure.

A soldier wearing olive drab ordered the recruits down a hallway. The soldier's haircut, Wallace observed with satisfaction, was identical to his own. In a narrow room smelling of overshoes the recruits were ordered to take off their shirts and pants and shoes and socks and to proceed into the next room in their underwear. They made a comic procession in their shorts and union suits and Wallace, euphoric once again, laughed out loud. Then he was silenced by a shocking sight at the far end of the examination room. A grossly overweight doctor sitting in a chair with a cigarette hanging from his lips was probing and squeezing so roughly—it was the hernia and rectal exam—that the recruit standing before him cried out in pain. The recruits waiting in that line looked on in terror. Wallace broke out in a sweat. He couldn't stand anyone touching him there. He went from station to station—the hearing exam, the throat exam, the lung X ray—fighting off panic. He reminded himself that there were worse atrocities awaiting him in the military than having his groin poked at by a sadistic slob in a white coat. There were suicide planes in the Pacific. There was the story in the morning paper about the infantryman in Belgium whose stomach was blown open by a land mine and who staggered into the medic's tent carrying his intestines in his hands. Thinking these things made Wallace woozy. He stepped up to the eye chart and found the large black letters il-

legible. They moved fuzzily up and down. He heard himself utter a moan he hadn't intended to make, and then an animal sound like a growl. The last thing he remembered was throwing his arms out and tipping over backwards.

He awoke in the narrow room that smelled of overshoes. He lay on the floor with a blanket over him. He was wet. He lay in a pool of urine. The buck-toothed young man with the crooked nose got up from a bench and came over to him. Then a medic in a white coat appeared and the two of them raised Wallace to a bench and began to dress him. It took a long time. He was limp and shaky and he couldn't control his fingers and feet. With his suspenders twisted and his shirt buttoned wrong and a copy of his 4-F classification stuffed in his pocket, he was carried out the high, heavy doors and down the wide granite steps to a cab. The buck-toothed boy sat beside him on the way to the bus depot, patting him gently on the shoulder in an attempt to quiet his moaning.

The pool hall was crowded with farmers idling the winter away, the large front window opaque with frost. From the jukebox came Vaughn Monroe's furry rendition of "Racing with the Moon." Gordy, serving coffee to the Fosters, said, "Vern at the lumber yard says you folks've got a big remodeling job coming up."

"We start tomorrow." Hank took a folded sheet of paper from his shirt pocket and showed Gordy the sketch he and Catherine and Paul had been working on.

Catherine explained, "This is the new trend in grocery stores. We're going to open up the entire stock to the shoppers and they'll go around with baskets, serving themselves. The lumber's going into new shelving."

Gordy studied the sketch. "I was in a store like this in Rochester. They call it a supermarket. You going to change your name to Hank's Supermarket?"

Catherine said, "Let's."

Hank looked dubious. "Supermarket sounds like boasting."

Gordy handed back the sketch. "I told Louie Legget about the Rochester store. He says it's an idea that'll never catch on."

Hank smiled at this, pleased to know his competitor lacked foresight.

"Customers come into a store to be waited on, Legget says. They'll never take to serving themselves."

"Legget obviously doesn't read the trade magazines," Catherine

said. "This new plan not only frees the help to do other work, it sells more groceries."

"It does?"

"It's been proven that people buy twenty percent more when they serve themselves."

Hank nudged her knee with his, and after Gordy left she asked, "Did I say something wrong?"

"Everything we tell Gordy, Gordy tells Legget. They're both trustees of the Lutheran church."

"But it's no secret we're remodeling."

"The secret's the twenty-percent increase. The longer it takes Legget to modernize the better off we'll be."

Hank recognized her gesture of frustration—casting her eyes at the ceiling while letting out a long, slow breath. He waited for the words he knew were coming:

"That's exactly what I can't stand about this town, Hank. Everything takes premeditation." She drilled him with her blue eyes. "Before I state a simple fact to Gordy, I have to stop and think what church Gordy goes to and what effect it will have on our income. Before I get dressed in the morning I have to think what effect my clothes will have on Mrs. Brask. Yesterday I saw a dress in the Sears catalogue that I felt like ordering, but skirts are going to be short this spring, and I decided I'm not up to being the first woman on Bean Street to be wearing a short skirt, not after all the nasty things Mrs. Brask says about Phyllis Clay's flashy clothes. It's no wonder Phyllis Clay sits home drinking herself silly. It isn't her husband she can't stand, it's the old biddies living all around her." She put her finger to her mouth, silencing herself. She had determined some days ago to try to spare Hank further complaining about her loneliness, about her dashed hopes for happiness on Bean Street. The New Year's tea had been the final straw. Two dozen people staying away without acknowledging their invitations. Soon after, as a palliative, she had accepted an invitation from Bea Crowley to go shopping in Rochester, hoping that in Bea, a reader of books, she would find a kindred spirit; but the woman's religious fanaticism proved insufferable. She blamed Luther and Lutherans for every ill including World War Two and her major purchase in Rochester was a set of soap dishes depicting saints of the Near East.

"Give me the pencil, Hank. I'll show you where the produce section ought to go."

He withheld the pencil. "I know it's not a happy time for you

Catherine, but remember, it's Plum that's given us a house of our own, and the store we always wanted."

She made a helpless movement with her hands.

"And think how happy we are as a family." This was all part of Hank's formula response, repeated so often that he faulted himself for not being more original. "And remember," he added, "you've got me, and I've got you."

She nodded. Original or not, it always seemed to help. She took the pencil, smoothed the paper in front of her and began to draw. He reached under the table and gave her knee a tight squeeze.

They were on their second mug of coffee when the door opened and a man stepped into the pool hall brushing snow from his overcoat. Because he was a stranger, everyone turned to examine him, Hank and Catherine included.

The man stepped up to the bar and spoke to Gordy, who pointed to the Fosters' booth. The man walked swiftly over to them and put out his hand to Hank.

"How do you do, Mr. Foster, Mrs. Foster. Your man in the store said I'd find you here. My name is Cranshaw, I'm with the welfare office in Winona." He took off his overcoat and hung it on a peg. He wore a heavy green sweater under his tight suitcoat. "I'm sorry to bother you. My business might strike you as very odd, or it might not, depending on how much truth there is in what I've been told about you. May I?"

Hank made room for him to sit.

"So far, the roads aren't drifted shut, but I want to get home in daylight, they say there's worse weather coming." He rubbed his cold hands together—small, hairless hands, Catherine noticed—and he called to Gordy for coffee. Then he smiled shrewdly across the table at her; small teeth, she noticed. He had a foxlike face, a sharp nose, a thin smile. "What does the name Dodger Hicks mean to you, Mrs. Foster?"

"Dodger? Is he in trouble again?"

Ignoring her inquiry, he turned his smile on Hank. "And you, Mr. Foster?"

"Why do you ask?"

"I'll explain in a minute. I just want to know what the name Dodger Hicks means to the two of you. To your wife it obviously means trouble. What does it mean to you?"

Hank nodded. "Sure, trouble. He's in the Home School, isn't he?"

Cranshaw smiled up at Gordy, who brought him his coffee. He thanked him and held the mug in both hands for warmth. "Now my next question is this, Mr. Foster. Do you *like* Dodger Hicks?"

"Like him? I hardly know him."

"Hicks tells me you and your family are friends of his, Mr. Foster."

"That's laying it on pretty thick, considering we saw him probably twice in our lives."

"And you, Mrs. Foster? Do you like Dodger Hicks?"

"Pity him is more like it."

Hank tapped the man's sleeve impatiently. "Mr. Cranshaw, what's this all about?"

"I've just come from the Home School, where I've had a talk with Hicks and the warden—if you can call it a talk, the warden kept being called away, and Hicks is a boy of few words—but here's what it comes down to. The boy's serving a one-year term, which won't be over till next November, but they'd like to release him early and they're asking me to find him a temporary home till he goes to live with his father."

Catherine said, "I thought his father was in prison."

"So he is, but he's getting out in April. His parole board is convinced he's rehabilitated." He smiled cunningly at the Fosters. "It's been my observation that parole boards are wrong in their judgments exactly two times out of three, but here's a case where they might be right. In less than two years he's worked his way up to assistant foreman of the prison twine plant. He's told the parole board that he's set two goals for himself when he gets out. He wants to make an honest living, and he wants to make a home for his son."

"Would that be good for Dodger?" she asked. "I've heard he used to beat Dodger."

"His father's a better prospect than his mother these days. His mother has a number of men she lives with, one after another, and they all come from the bottom of the barrel. Besides that, Dodger's bigger than his father now. Hard to imagine him standing for any roughhouse. His father's puny."

"Dodger's willing to live with him?"

"Says he wants to live with him. Not hard to see why, compared to life at the Home School. They pick on him a lot."

Hank asked, "Where will they live?"

"Winona. I've lined Mr. Hicks up with a job at the box factory

there, starting in the middle of April." His eyes darted from Catherine to Hank and back again. "Will you take Dodger till then?"

"Take him?" Hank drew back. "You mean to live with us?"

Cranshaw nodded.

"Why us?"

"He says you're his only friends. Wasn't it your son who went to visit him last fall?"

Catherine looked sad. "His *only* friends?"

"There have been ten visiting days since he entered the home school, and your son has been his only visitor. If you take him in, Winona County will pay you three dollars a day."

Catherine asked, "What do you mean, he gets picked on?"

"Has things done to him. He's a meek sort of kid, as you probably know. He needs to learn to stand up for himself, and he'll never learn it there. The place is a hell-hole. The warden's under a lot of pressure to stop physical injuries ever since one of the boys lost an eye in a fight. In Dodger's case the solution is simply to release him to custody. The judge who sentenced him agrees."

Hank said, "I thought welfare boards had families lined up to take in wards of the county."

"We do, but we're filled up. Besides, nobody wants to take in a fifteen-year-old with a record."

"So why do you expect us to do it?"

"Because you know what Hicks is like. He's not the criminal type."

"Exactly what is being done to him?" Catherine demanded.

Cranshaw looked at his watch. He looked at the wall. He looked at Catherine. "He has forty-some scars on his body from cigarette burns."

She shuddered and closed her eyes. "Hank," she breathed, turning it over to him.

"All right, Mr. Cranshaw, we'll have to see Dodger about this. You can't expect us to take a kid with a criminal record without making sure he'll live by the rules of our house."

Cranshaw nodded. "Why not go and see him during visiting hours on Sunday? My office will pay your mileage."

"I don't trust our car that far. They're predicting twenty below on Sunday."

"Okay, how about this? I've got tomorrow morning free. I can come and pick one or both of you up and take you to Flensboro, you

can have your conference with Hicks, then I can bring you home. After that, if everything works out, I can deliver Hicks to your house on whatever day you designate."

"I'm tied up tomorrow. We're remodeling the store."

"I'll go," said Catherine. "What time in the morning?"

Cranshaw suggested nine thirty.

"I'll bring our son along. After all, it's Brendan's life more than ours that Dodger will be sharing."

"Very good." Cranshaw sprang up and put on his overcoat. "I'll see you in the morning."

"You can pick us up at the market."

With a satisfied smile Cranshaw shook their hands. "It's a pleasure to know you both."

They watched him cross to the door and step outside, turning up his collar against the falling snow.

Catherine spoke, her eyes lingering on the door. "We really don't have a choice, do we, Hank?"

He said nothing.

"I mean, poor Dodger. How could we say no?"

"We couldn't, of course." He drained his mug.

She faced him, her eyes lively. "It's high time we made our mark in this town by doing something large-hearted. Paul says the Christians in this town, for all their talk, hardly ever *act* like Christians, and he's absolutely right. Dodger may just be what this town needs to save its soul."

She seldom spoke in such an inflated way, and Hank, folding the sheet of sketches and slipping it into his shirt pocket, was a little alarmed that she should pin impossible hopes on the likes of Dodger Hicks. Yet he realized, taking her hand as they left the booth, that she was never more appealing to him than when her eyes shone with purpose, never prettier.

Fortunately the wind diminished after dark, and so the snowfall wasn't blinding as Hank made his way across the farmland and down the winding road between the bluffs. At the gas station on Highway 61 he added a mixture of water and antifreeze to the radiator; then he and the attendant stood warming themselves at the oil stove as they watched the snow build up on the lighted apron surrounding the gas pumps. Soon a truck pulled in and a man in his sixties came inside and stood with them. His clothes smelled of a cow

barn. "I've got a son due back from his induction physical," he said to Hank. "You here for the same reason?"

"One of my employees."

"If they keep this up there won't be an able-bodied man left in the United States of America," said the farmer. "They already got my two older boys, one in France and the other in the Solomon Islands, and who knows if they're alive or dead?"

"Hitler can't last much longer," Hank assured him. "Then we'll throw everything we've got at Japan."

"I got a younger one at home yet. He's seventeen. When he's drafted who's going to help me with the cows?" The farmer turned to the attendant, who looked about thirty. "How did you get out of it?"

"My left leg's shorter than my right one."

"See what I mean? The home front's nothing but women and children and cripples and old guys like me." He looked more closely at Hank. "What's your excuse?"

"Too old for the draft."

"You could have enlisted."

So Catherine's sister had been implying in her letters. He nodded at the farmer, offering no defense.

"Not that I fault you for it."

The attendant spoke up. "I'd damsite sooner go to war than have a short leg."

Trailing a cloud of snow, the bus turned off the highway and came to a stop in the circle of light. The driver descended from his seat and asked, "Anybody here to pick up a guy named Flint?"

"Me," said Hank.

"He's pretty sick. You better pull your car up close."

As Hank brought the DeSoto around, Wallace was helped off the bus by the driver and the farmer's buck-toothed son. Hank opened the passenger door for them.

Wallace, shivering, his eyes fluttering, mumbled, "Back seat. Want to lie down."

"It's cold back there, Wallace. You'd better sit in front."

As they lifted him into the front seat and shut the door, the young man explained, "He was standing right in front of me at the eye chart when he threw a fit. Scared the bejesus out of me. He fell down and shook the way a hog does when you knock it in the head. The doctor said he'd be all right, but they hadn't no use for him. He's

4-F." The young man turned to his father. "I'm 1-A and I'm off to camp next Tuesday."

The farmer nodded sadly. "Come on, we'll go help Willie and your ma with the milking."

Driving home, Hank had all he could do to hold the car between the ditches, for the snow in the headlights dazed him—it was like driving through gauze.

"Hank," said Wallace, not loud enough to be heard over the roaring engine and rattling exhaust pipes. "Hank," he said again.

"Yes?"

"I can't go back to work, Hank. I can't go back to the store."

"No, you can take as long as you need to rest up."

"I mean ever, Hank. I can't ever go back." His voice broke.

"Why?" Hank searched the darkness beside him for the young man's face. He saw only the gleam of watery eyes.

"Because." This ended the conversation.

Driving, Hank kept seeing Wallace being helped off the bus and half-carried to the car. That very picture had appeared last week in the *Post-Bulletin*—a wounded G.I. supported by two of his buddies as he moved between a tank and an ambulance. It was the Battle of the Bulge and it was snowing. Wallace, too, was coming home from war. Never mind that Wallace's wound came not from a clash of armies but from an unfortunate mix of genes, he had volunteered for the service, which was more than Hank had done. Hank could imagine the incredible courage Wallace must have called up to overcome his unwarlike sensibilities. He experimented with one hand on the steering wheel, and when he found that he was able to hold the car between the ditches, he put his other arm around Wallace, who immediately began to weep, snuggling up to him like a little boy.

19

The sun on the fresh snow was blinding as Brendan and his mother stepped out the front door of the market and got into the large gray car belonging to Mr. Cranshaw.

"Good morning, Mrs. Foster." He sat very low behind the wheel. Threads were unraveling from the brim of his black hat.

"Good morning. This is our son Brendan."

Cranshaw turned and offered his wily smile to Brendan in the back seat. "No school today, young fellow?"

"I'm excused."

"And not sorry about it either, I'll bet."

"Glad about it." In January the school year became eternal.

As the car pulled away from the curb, Catherine waved to Hank in the window. Hank waved his crowbar. Between customers, he and Paul were beginning to tear out the old shelving.

Three miles east of town the road took them up over a rise known as Higgins Hill, from which the view was unobstructed in all directions. Rolling fields deep in snow. Leafless trees a lifeless gray. Here beside the road was the red barn of Lester Higgins with an advertisement for spark plugs painted on its side. Horses and cows stood in a pen breathing steam. Ordinarily Catherine enjoyed the long vistas offered by high ground, but here, looking back at Plum huddled in a snowy hollow so remote that God Himself might overlook it, she shuddered, thinking of the twenty-five neighbors who had declined or ignored her New Year's invitation.

As the car descended Higgins Hill, cutting off the view, she took a piece of paper and a pencil from her purse and began making a list.

"I think we can be ready for Dodger in two days," she told Cranshaw. "I've asked Hank to bring the rollaway down from the attic and put it in Brendan's room, and I'll empty out one side of the wardrobe in the hallway and assign it to Dodger." She knew, of course, that these household details were of no interest to Cranshaw, but she was elated by her mission and needed to talk. "Tomorrow I'll see about enrolling Dodger in school. That's something I'll have to bring up with him today—he'll have to agree to regular school attendance. And we'll have to come to an agreement about bedtimes and household chores."

Brendan, listening, wished his own preparations for Dodger were simple enough to put into a list. His preparations consisted mostly of suppressing his resentment. Dodger the ex-con was certain to be an even greater embarrassment than Dodger the mere outcast had been. Dodger was so tall and gawky and unhealthy-looking that everybody would stare at him—and at Brendan because Dodger would be at his side every moment of the day. Last night at supper when his parents proposed taking Dodger in, Brendan was shocked. He had turned to Grandfather and asked if he wasn't upset to think that a stranger was moving into the house, but Grandfather said no, he wouldn't mind another lad underfoot, the more the merrier. Before Brendan had a chance to register his dread, his father brought up Dodger's cigarette burns and said it would be heartless to turn their back on him, and his mother said there was more to Christian duty than the example set by Father O'Day; more important than prayer was doing good for others, and Dodger was their God-sent opportunity. How did you counter an argument like that without sounding selfish? Brendan kept his mouth shut.

By the time they reached Flensboro, Catherine's list covered both sides of the paper. "And I was thinking," she said to Cranshaw as he turned in through the gate of the Home School, "it will be good for Dodger to help out in the store on Saturdays—teach him the satisfaction of holding a job."

"There he is," Brendan said from the back seat.

Dodger stood smiling down at them from the steps of the main building, his baldness gleaming in the sun, his breath steamy. At his feet were two cardboard boxes.

Catherine said, "Does he think he's leaving with us? Mr. Cranshaw, didn't you tell him we were coming here only to talk?"

Cranshaw looked pained. "That's exactly what I told him, and

that's exactly what I told the warden. Don't worry, I'll straighten this out."

He stopped the car at the foot of the steps, and they got out. Dodger came down to them.

"I've got a bunch of comics for you, Brendan." The pink scar on his throat was pale and barely noticeable. There were two new, bright red scars under his ear.

"This isn't the day you leave," said Cranshaw.

Dodger ignored him. "I've got a new *Superman,* Brendan. You said you like *Superman.*" He set his boxes on the snow near the trunk of the car.

Cranshaw muttered angrily to himself as he climbed the steps and went inside.

Brendan explained, "You aren't supposed to come home with us today, Dodger. We're here to talk it over, is all."

Dodger laughed softly and politely, as though at an unsuccessful joke.

Catherine took Dodger's hand. "Remember me? I'm Brendan's mother."

"Sure." He averted his eyes.

"We're not taking you home with us today, Dodger, I'm sorry."

Again he laughed quietly, looking at the ground to conceal his desperation. He'd been told at breakfast that the Fosters were coming to discuss the possibility of taking him home, and from that moment forward he knew that no power on earth could force him to endure one more night in the dormitory.

She continued: "We've come to tell you what it would be like to live with us, Dodger, and we want you to have a day or two to think it over." She opened her purse and took out her list, but she didn't look at it. She couldn't take her eyes off Dodger. His face had matured since last September—his eyes deep-set under ledge-like brows, his jawline long and bony. She tried to engage his eyes, but he wouldn't let her. They were fascinating eyes, shifty not out of furtiveness (she wanted to believe) but out of shyness. His smile, too, was fascinating. It came easily to his face and gave him a soft, kindly look. Catherine's heart, already full of pity, brimmed over with love.

Cranshaw came out onto the porch and down the steps, followed by the warden. Both men spoke at once, angrily, Cranshaw angry at the warden and the warden angry at Dodger.

"I went ahead and did the impossible, I found a place for this kid nobody wants, and you let him foul up my plans."

"I'll take care of this," seethed the warden. "I'll put him in solitary for a week." Brendan recognized his piping voice and his fussy goatee. He was the man who had come into the dining hall and made announcements on that Sunday last November. Though smaller than Dodger, the warden gripped him roughly by the arm and turned him so that he faced his two cardboard boxes. "Pick up your belongings, Hicks, and get back inside."

Chuckling softly, Dodger removed the man's grip, finger by finger, and climbed into the back seat of the car and shut the door.

Cranshaw railed at the warden, "You put him up to this to save the State money. You weren't supposed to unload him on us till we gave the word."

The warden looked through the window at Dodger, who sat staring straight ahead, smiling. "Give me a minute to find a guard, and Hicks will regret this to his dying day." The warden was livid. He turned abruptly and went up the steps and inside, slamming the door.

Brendan and Catherine had backed away from this encounter, alarmed by the ferocity of these two small men. Now Catherine stepped forward and said, "If you haven't any other business here, Mr. Cranshaw, let's start back. We'll take Dodger along." She motioned for Brendan to climb into the back seat.

"You're serious?" asked Cranshaw. "What about your list of conditions?"

"We'll talk them over on the way." She got into the front seat and shut the door.

Cranshaw loaded the boxes into the trunk; then he got in behind the wheel. "You're sure?"

She nodded.

"Just a word of warning before we leave the grounds, Mrs. Foster. It can be disastrous to let a type like Hicks win the first round. You could find yourself spending the next twelve weeks on the defensive."

"Dodger does not belong to a type, Mr. Cranshaw." She turned and gave Dodger a reassuring smile, and Brendan, seeing it, was jolted—a motherly smile directed elsewhere.

The door above them opened and the warden stepped out onto the porch with the eight-fingered guard from the dining hall. As they came down the steps, Dodger locked his door.

The guard rapped on Dodger's window and said, "Get out of there, Hicks."

Catherine said, "Please, Mr. Cranshaw, let's go."

Cranshaw started the car, and as it began to move, Dodger rolled his window open two inches and said, beaming up at the guard, "Go piss up a rope."

20

The next day being Friday, a busy day at the store, Catherine hoped that Dodger might be enrolled in school immediately, but the principal was out of town and she was asked to bring Dodger in on Monday. She stayed home through the morning, therefore, and assigned Dodger chores, the first of which was shoveling coal. For this, she took him down to the basement and demonstrated how to fill the stoker; she left him to finish the job on his own, instructing him next to go out and sweep from the sidewalk the dusting of snow that had fallen overnight.

Alone in the basement, Dodger—dazed by happiness—worked very slowly. Lifting small scoops out of the coalbin and dribbling them into the stoker, he went over in his mind yesterday's wonderful liberation, beginning with the dazzling drive through the snowy countryside from Flensboro to Plum. His first sight of Plum from Higgins Hill had filled him with joy. When they arrived at the house on Bean Street, Brendan had helped him carry in his boxes and showed him the room they would share. It was a strange house to live in. You were assigned a certain towel in the bathroom. You spoke to God before meals. You hung your clothes on hangers. There was an old man who sat in the living room and listened to the radio all the time. Yesterday when Dodger was introduced to him, the old man shook his hand and said, "Welcome aboard, lad," and when he took his hand away Dodger found a fifty-cent piece in his palm. Then the old man ran his hand over Dodger's bald scalp and laughed, and Dodger laughed too. Later, Brendan's father came home from work and gave Dodger a handshake as firm as Grandfa-

ther's (but without the fifty cents) and a hardy pat on the back, as one man to another. By the time they sat down to supper, Dodger felt such a wonderful sense of well-being that when they paused after grace to be silently mindful of personal favors they wanted from God, Dodger was stumped. Supper was chicken, beans, potatoes, and gravy, as much as you wanted and all of it hot. For dessert Brendan's mother served a cake with "Welcome Dodger" written in the frosting. After that, there were dishes to wipe (Dodger dropped and broke two saucers; no one punished him) and then there were three of Brendan's favorite radio programs, one of them exciting ("The FBI in Peace and War") and two of them sort of dull. After that, Brendan brought out a game played with dice and squares on a board. As the two of them played the game, Brendan talked a lot about Sam and Philip, boys for whom Dodger felt an immediate affection, not because he remembered them clearly but because Brendan was obviously so fond of them. Then it was bedtime. Both boys fell asleep quickly, but Dodger awoke with a start several times, expecting the searing pain of a cigarette burn.

Finishing in the basement, Dodger closed the lid of the stoker and slipped upstairs to the living room, where Grandfather sat in a deep chair between his pipe stand and the console radio. Dodger stretched out on the carpet in front of him and they listened to Don McNeil's "Breakfast Club" together. In a few minutes Catherine came into the room and reminded Dodger about clearing the sidewalk.

Looking out from her house next door, Mrs. Brask saw the tall young stranger lazily sweeping the Fosters' sidewalk. He was wearing the same red stockingcap she had seen on the Foster boy, and a jacket sometimes worn by Mr. Foster. She put on her boots, her hat and her fox tail and went outside to investigate.

"Are you hired help?" she asked, strutting toward Dodger in a manner he found vaguely frightening. He didn't reply. He leaned on his broom and gave the sky a tentative smile.

"Who are you?" she inquired, shaking him by his broomstick. "Where do you come from? What is your name? What is your business in Plum? Are you a transient?"

He sorted through her questions for the one he could answer. He said, "Hicks."

"Hicks? Not the hoodlum Hicks! What are you doing here?"

He showed her his broom. "Sweeping," he answered.

"Don't talk smart to me, young man. Why are you sweeping this particular sidewalk is my question."

"Because it snowed last night."

She studied his face for insolence, but saw none. Perhaps he was retarded. "Are you Fosters' hired help then?"

He shook his head. "No, I'm just living here."

"You're living with the Fosters? I don't believe it."

He could hardly believe it himself. "For now," he added.

"When did you arrive? What can the Fosters be thinking?"

Dodger stood with his head politely bowed as she fired off eight or ten more questions. When she fell silent and waited for answers, he said nothing. She put Dodger in mind of the many schoolteachers who by scolding him for wrong answers had taught him not to open his mouth.

"Explain yourself," she ordered, but he raised his eyes to the overcast sky and kept them there.

She snorted, imagining the speedy decline and fall of Bean Street now that it was open to hoodlums. She gave up and went home.

When he finished sweeping, Dodger went back to the living room, lay down again near Grandfather's chair and listened to "Ma Perkins." At the funny parts, Grandfather laughed and slapped his knee and asked, "Did you hear that, lad?" Dodger nodded, chuckling contentedly and running his hand over his whiskery scalp.

Meanwhile Mrs. Brask phoned Mrs. Kimball and asked if she knew that a hoodlum was living next door. Mrs. Kimball gasped and went around the house locking her doors and windows and instructing her pup to be watchful; then she returned to the phone and called her husband at the funeral home. He told her not to be alarmed; Dodger Hicks was harmless. She then called Mrs. Brask and conveyed her husband's judgment. "He's a disgrace to the neighborhood," declared Mrs. Brask, "and I'll never speak another word to the Fosters as long as they harbor him in their house."

Catherine made ham sandwiches and called Dodger and Grandfather to the table. Hank was lunching at the pool hall, Brendan at school. Sitting across the table from Dodger, Grandfather decided to try him out as a listener. He told him two or three railroad stories and then, catching sight of snowflakes spiraling down past the dining room window, he called to mind a blizzard story he seldom told because no one believed it.

"When I was seven years old and living in Prairie du Chien, Wis-

consin, a railroad town on the Mississippi, we had the blizzard of the century—the nineteenth century, that is—and the blizzard caused something to happen at our house that was too strange to be anything but a miracle."

They were finished eating now, and Catherine had left the table. Puffing and puffing as he lit his pipe, Grandfather rested his eyes first on Dodger and then—unfocused—on that day in 1870 when the sky grew heavy at sundown. "We lived in a house at the edge of town facing a hardwood forest, and shortly after supper a young deer came out of the woods and put its front hoofs up on the kitchen windowsill and looked in at my mother washing dishes. After she got over her shock and took a closer look, she saw in its eyes that it was afraid of something. She called us into the kitchen, and as soon as we all gathered at the window it got down on all fours and stood by the door. 'He wants to come in,' my oldest brother said. My father was off in Iowa with his section crew. He weathered the blizzard in a bunkhouse car sitting on a Great Northern siding near Dubuque. My brother opened the door and, believe it or not, the deer came indoors. It went straight through the house to a bedroom closet, where it curled up on the floor.

"Well, sir, we all stood looking into the closet, not believing our eyes. My mother told us it was a sign. She was always saying that about things, always on the lookout for signs, my mother. Signs of what, she never said. She said something was a sign and left us to figure out what it was a sign of. Do you understand my meaning, lad?"

Dodger nodded, enchanted by the tale of the deer indoors. So soothing was Grandfather's voice and so honored was Dodger to be the recipient of Grandfather's stories that his eyes stopped flitting and came to rest on Grandfather's face. With his head thrust forward, his mouth open, Dodger hung on Grandfather's every word. He had no memory of anyone taking thc trouble to tell him a story.

Grandfather, for his part, was so pleased to have found an attentive listener that when Catherine prepared to go off to the store, he insisted that she let Dodger stay home. She phoned Hank and they weighed the alternatives. Bring Dodger to work with her? Leave him and Grandfather in charge of each other? They decided to risk the latter and she went to work alone.

Lingering at the table, Grandfather spun out the rest of the tale. "Not an hour after the deer came into our house it began to snow

and blow," he said. "Never has a blizzard begun so suddenly. It took everybody by surprise and killed hundreds of people in the Mississippi valley all the way from Minnesota to Missouri. It caught farmers out in their fields and froze them to death. It trapped hunters in their duck blinds and buried them alive in snowdrifts with an icy crust. It stopped all trains. It raged on for two nights and the one full day in between, and all that time the young deer never budged from that bedroom closet. Three of us boys slept in that room, and now and then in the night we could hear it stand up and step around and find itself a more comfortable position, but that was all it did. We set a pan of milk and a pan of oats nearby, but it never ate or drank. For two nights and the day in between it stayed in the closet and never once ate or drank or peed or moved its bowels, now tell me if that's not a miracle. And then on the morning of the second day when it stopped snowing and the sun came out, the deer came out of the closet and went into the kitchen. My mother let it outside, and we never saw it again. We told our father when he got home and he didn't believe it. As long as he lived—and it was a long, long time he lived, the McMahons being a family of old, old men—he called it malarky. Now you'll excuse me, lad, it's time for my nap." He left the table and went to the couch in the living room.

Though he hadn't been directed to do so, Dodger went to Brendan's room and lay down on the rollaway in order to experience again the pleasure of falling asleep undisturbed by cigarette burns.

Arriving at work, Catherine was surprised to see Wallace Flint's mother carrying on what appeared to be an urgent conversation with Hank. The two of them stood at the back of the store—she short and squat and looking up at Hank with a supplicating expression, Hank staring at the wall and feeling the back of his head with the palm of his hand, as was his habit whenever he was nervous or perplexed—while at the front of the store Paul Dimmitburg worked as speedily as he could to keep up with the trade.

"Catherine, this is Wallace's mother."

"Hello, Mrs. Flint. I've seen you going to and from the post office."

"I'm so pleased to meet you, Catherine." She truly was—the Fosters could see it in her beaming smile. "I'm calling you Catherine the way Wallace does, I hope you don't mind."

"Not at all."

"My name is Margaret."

"Is Wallace feeling better? We miss him in the store."

"He'll come around."

Did Catherine really miss him? Hank wondered. Though he felt a certain new tenderness toward Wallace since their drive home in the snow, he didn't miss him. He said to Catherine, "Mrs. Flint says he refuses to come out of his room."

"Of course he's done this before," his mother explained. "He'll lock himself in his room a day or two at a time and tell me to go away when I try to get him to eat. I hear him go down to the kitchen in the middle of the night. Wallace can be *so* temperamental."

All this, Catherine noticed, was delivered with a placid smile; she might have been describing the night habits of a newborn baby. Catherine had never seen this woman up close before. Given Wallace's age, she had to be in her mid or late forties, yet she looked younger. Her round face was remarkably free of creases and wrinkles; her eyes were lively. She was obese; her tentlike coat of green and black plaid was stretched tight around her middle.

"But this time he's saying wilder things than usual." Her expression changed, grew serious again. "He's saying he's seen the last of the inside of this store. He's through working, he's saying, for life. He's saying it's my turn to go out and earn the money. I'm sure he doesn't mean it about never working again, but as I was telling your husband, if it's going to take Wallace a few more days to recover—his seizure in Minneapolis must have been one of his worst—then why shouldn't I go out and try to bring in some money? I'm not helpless. I know what work is. I used to wait on tables before I was married. I quit because my husband was against working wives. Then after he died he had two brothers who supported us until Wallace was eighteen, so I got used to the easy life." She laughed nervously. "I got spoiled and I got fat." Her laugh died. "Is there any chance you could give me a job?"

Catherine and Hank exchanged a look. Though unspoken, their thoughts, they knew, were identical. Without Wallace they were shorthanded, and if his absence continued into next week they had resolved to hire someone else, most likely a woman because of the wartime manpower shortage—but how much work would this overweight, flaccid woman be capable of?

"Could you come back?" Hank asked. "Say in an hour?"

"After we've talked it over," Catherine added.

"Sure," she piped cheerily.

But she wasn't feeling cheery. Walking the length of the store, she felt embarrassed and frightened and hopeless. She feared the Fosters were watching her ridiculous way of walking, the rolling, strenuous motion of great bulk set upon short legs. She feared she couldn't work at a job requiring her to be on her feet all day; at home she sank into a chair every so often to let her energy build. She feared this was no two-day snit Wallace was going through; she had never seen such fierce anger in his eyes as when, last night, when she rapped on his door with food on a tray, he burst out of his room and called her a repulsive sow and smacked the tray out of her hands. She would never erase from her mind the glimpse she caught of all those horrible faces. How could he stand to be in that room hour after hour, day after day, with all those bug-eyed, bruise-colored people staring down at him?

When Grandfather awoke at two thirty, he went into Brendan's room and shook Dodger awake. "Come on, lad, we'll go to the pool hall and I'll buy you a soda pop."

Dodger sprang up and slipped into Hank's jacket and drew Brendan's stockingcap down over his ears. He waited by the front door while Grandfather slowly put on his vest, his suitcoat, his muffler, his overcoat, his rubbers, and his hat.

"Winters are milder than they used to be," he told Dodger as they stepped out into a chilly breeze. It had stopped snowing. The sun was low in the southwest, the shadows on the snow were deep blue. Gripping Dodger by the arm whenever they came to a stretch of snow-packed sidewalk, Grandfather rambled on. "We had a number of winters back in the thirties when it was below zero more noons than it was above, and I can remember one February when the cold spell broke and it snowed for a month. Why, the drifts were so deep on the prairie west of Fargo that my train ran three days late, creeping along behind the plow an inch at a time. Wind-driven snow can block your tracks like a wall of stone. Many's the time a sudden blizzard didn't give the ranchers time to bring their cattle in off the range, and we hitched a flatcar of hay behind our passenger train and threw off bales wherever we saw cattle along the tracks. I've seen it in the spring where the snow melts off a pasture and uncovers dozens of steers lying dead, their carcasses bloated like balloons."

In the pool hall Grandfather introduced Dodger as a friend of the family, and although the cardplayers and everyone else in the place knew he was the outlaw son of an outlaw father they refrained from staring at him too openly and restricted their hostile remarks to mumbles Dodger and Grandfather couldn't hear.

Dodger watched a card game he didn't understand while he savored the bottle of cream soda Grandfather bought him. Though his head was hot, he kept his itchy wool cap on to hide his baldness.

The moment he finished his bottle, Grandfather bought him another. Sipping, he let his mind wander. He tried to remember when he had last drunk a bottle of pop, since it was either milk or water at the Home School, never pop. He tried to remember when he last had a companion as generous as Grandfather. Never.

He finished his second bottle and Grandfather bought him a third, which made him sick. He said to Grandfather, "Save my place," and went out through the back room of the pool hall and vomited into the snow. Returning to his place at the cardtable, he found a fourth bottle of cream soda waiting for him. He made this one last until five thirty, when he and Grandfather left the pool hall and went next door to ride home with Hank.

They drove home by way of the Flint house. Hank, pulling up in front, said to Catherine, "Come with me please." To Grandfather and Dodger in back, Catherine said, "We'll be just a minute."

They stepped onto the side porch and knocked. The door was opened by Mrs. Flint. Behind her the kitchen was dimly lit by a low flame in the kerosene lamp. There was no sign of Wallace.

"Why didn't you come back to the store?" asked Catherine.

"Well, I got to thinking I'm not sure I could be on my feet that much. And I figured you didn't want me anyway."

"But we do. We'd like you to work for a few days and see how it goes." She explained their plan. Mrs. Flint would work short periods at first, learning the trade, then possibly full time when the market was remodeled and they'd need a cashier at the checkout counter. They would devise a way for her to sit.

"Could you give us a few days?" asked Mrs. Flint, speaking for herself and her son. "Maybe in a few days Wallace will want to go back to work."

"We can give you till midweek," said Hank.

Catherine added, "We'll definitely need to know before next weekend because I've got more work at home these days and we'll

need to hire somebody. We've taken in Dodger Hicks to live with us."

"Dodger Hicks!" cried Wallace, stepping around from behind the door. "Dodger Hicks in your house?" He laughed wildly. He was a ghost of himself, short-haired, beardless, emaciated.

Hank took Catherine's hand as they recoiled. They descended the steps.

"Catherine," called Wallace, leaning out into the moonlight. "I went to Dayton's where you used to work and talked to a gray-haired woman who wore her glasses on a ribbon around her neck and had a mole beside her nose."

"Marjorie Smith," Catherine said, halting and looking up from the snowy yard.

"I told her I knew you, but your name didn't register with her."

"Please, Wallace, that's not true." She set off with Hank toward the car.

"She said she works with so many clerks she has trouble keeping track of them all."

He was left standing on the cold porch feeling triumphant. He had never before tried to injure Catherine. It raised his spirits immeasurably.

After supper Brendan took Dodger to the Friday night movie, purposely arriving late so they could enter the dark theater unnoticed. Judy Canova played a hillbilly singer who traveled the Ozarks with a string band and outsmarted and brought to justice a pair of gangsters hiding in the hills. Brendan was bored by the singing, amused by the jokes, and excited by the railroad chase along a twisting track. Dodger, he noticed, was engrossed from beginning to end. He sat perfectly still with his head thrust forward and his lip lifted in half a smile. He emitted soft chuckles throughout. Only once did he break his concentration and turn to see Brendan's reaction and that was at the end of the railroad chase. Nudging Brendan with his elbow, he said, "We should have brought Grandpa."

After the movie, as Brendan feared, they ran into Sam and Philip outside under the marquee. To Brendan's surprise, the boys spoke to Dodger as though they cared for him.

"Hey, Dodge, how you been?"

"What's it like at the Home School, Dodge? Is it true they put you in solitary if you smart off?"

Dodger smiled at them and said, "I never smarted off."

Philip asked, "What's it like to be in jail, Dodge? We heard you were in jail."

"Yeah, the night I got arrested."

"What's it like?"

"Pretty nice, you get your own bed and your own toilet."

Sam asked, "Is it true all the guards at the Home School are ex-cons?"

Dodger, basking in their attention, said, "Naw."

Philip said, "I heard you're starting school on Monday, Dodge. Does that mean you know how to read?"

"Naw."

"What grade'll you be in?"

"I don't know, I was in tenth for a while this year. Then they put me in eighth. He laughed, "Then they put me in the laundry."

"How about coming out for basketball?" said Sam. "We could use some height."

"Think I should?"

"Yeah, you should. How tall are you?"

A shrug. "Five or six feet, I guess."

"You're close to six," Sam estimated. "If they put you in eighth grade you can be on our junior-high team. If they put you in ninth or tenth you get to play for the high school."

"I'd like to play with you guys."

The group left the theater and walked along the street, Philip dribbling an imaginary basketball, Sam miming hook shots over Dodger's head, and Brendan feeling elated, proud to be Dodger's host and to oversee his social debut.

But his pride was abruptly dashed. When they came to the pool hall, where Brendan and his friends customarily bought Fudgesicles after the Friday night movie, his friends ran inside and slammed the door, leaving Brendan and Dodger standing in the cold.

Dodger, hunched over, hands in pockets, waited for Brendan to make the next move.

"Want a Fudgesicle?" Brendan asked. He dug in his pocket for change.

"Sure."

"I've only got a nickel left. Can you pay for your own?"

Dodger showed him his fifty-cent piece.

They went in and stood at the end of the bar next to the peanut display, waiting for Gordy to serve them. Brendan saw his friends

scurrying out the back door, ditching him, and he was considering running after them and assuring them that he was their friend, not Dodger's, when Gordy said, "What'll it be, the usual?"

Brendan nodded.

"How about you, Hicks?"

"Yeah."

"Boy, you sure got tall since last summer, Hicks. When you came in here this afternoon I didn't hardly know you."

Dodger said, "I'm close to six feet, Sam Romberg told me."

"How are you at basketball?"

"Never played it."

"How about other sports?"

"Never played them either."

They watched a pool game until their Fudgesicles were gone and Brendan said, "Let's go."

They walked in silence, Dodger now and again leaping and turning in the air, imitating Sam's hook shot, Brendan hanging his head and assuming, sadly, that it was his lot for the next three months to be ditched night and day by his friends.

At the corner of Main and Bean, Dodger said, "How about some peanuts?" He reached into his pocket and gave Brendan one of the small bags he had stolen when Gordy wasn't looking.

They were salty and delicious.

"You've got to quit stealing stuff," said Brendan, chewing. "You'll end up back in the Home School."

"Yeah, I know it."

"If you know it, how come you took these peanuts?"

"I thought you might like some."

"But you didn't need to steal them. You've got money."

"Oh yeah, I forgot."

21

As a proponent of diagnostic testing, Mr. Reinhart, principal of Plum Junior and Senior High School, gave Dodger a written exam followed by an interview. His findings were these: while Dodger read like a second grader, his acne and dark whiskers looked like a senior's; therefore he split the difference and placed him in the seventh grade. As a proponent of remedial education, Mr. Reinhart gave him two study halls instead of one.

Brendan was dismayed to find Dodger in four of his classes—English, math, physical education, and choir. Brendan observed that while Dodger was not as thoroughly ignored by his classmates as he had been last fall, he was still nobody's friend. By robbing a gas station and getting caught, he had made himself interesting, but the curiosity he aroused was morbid and momentary. Again and again on the way to school or between classes, Brendan and Dodger found themselves drawn into an encounter like that which followed the Judy Canova movie—"Did they handcuff you, Dodger?" "Do you suppose someday you'll go big time and kill somebody?" It took only a minute or two to satisfy the questioner, who then hurried away.

Brendan wished he had the nerve to tell Dodger to quit hanging around. In September he had given Dodger the brush-off with ease but that had resulted in a serious case of guilt. Now he tried to ditch him by subtler means. He tried leaving for school earlier than usual, but Dodger was wonderfully adaptable. If Brendan got up an hour early, so did Dodger. If he skipped breakfast, if he set off for school at a run, if he lingered at the store and arrived nearly late for first

period, so did Dodger. One morning Brendan said he felt sick and Catherine sent Dodger off to school while keeping Brendan home, but later when Brendan threw off his feigned illness and left for school he found Dodger at the corner of Bean and Main, where he had been standing for an hour, waiting. Brendan gave up then, reconciled to Dodger's constant presence. He thought of him as a kind of freakish appendage, like a third arm. Ten weeks and three days, he told himself, counting down. Nine weeks and four days. Eight weeks even.

For the first time in his life Dodger made headway as a student. That is, he maintained a D average in math. He achieved this with the help of Brendan and the math teacher, Mr. Torborg. Being an athletic coach as well as a wounded veteran, Mr. Torborg was enormously respected in the classroom. He deserved to be. He was a kindly, patient young man who took time to explain things to Dodger. So did Brendan. Each night they did their homework together, Brendan reading the story problems out of the math book and nudging Dodger toward the correct answers. This wasn't easy, because Dodger invariably became engrossed in the story and forgot about the numbers. Never mind the gas tank capacity of their cars, what was wrong with Mr. A's engine that he should run out of gas halfway between his house and his office while his next door neighbor Mr. B, who was driving the same distance, ran out at the three-quarter mark? Or, more to the point, what was wrong with the men themselves that they should forget to fill their tanks? And why, if a bushel of tangerines cost so much more than a bushel of oranges, did Mrs. X insist on buying tangerines? Didn't she like oranges as much as Dodger did?

Dodger got F's in English. No matter how Brendan tried, he couldn't get Dodger to understand the function of the preposition or to memorize "The Charge of the Light Brigade." Near the end of the six-week marking period, Catherine advised Dodger to ask his English teacher Miss Dale for extra help, and he did, but Miss Dale ignored him. Miss Dale was a dense, sentimental and slightly unbalanced young woman who thought of her junior high girls as a garden of lovely little blossoms and her junior high boys as noxious weeds. She particularly despised Dodger for being so tall and mature and lazy. She had assigned him a desk in the back row of her classroom, where the sun falling through the high windows made him happily drowsy, a condition she was unwilling to disturb.

In choir Dodger's fate was sealed the first time he opened his mouth. Plum's music teacher, Mr. Paulson, was a temperamental perfectionist. Whereas another teacher might send a student to the principal for misbehavior, Mr. Paulson did so for singing off key. Mr. Paulson had spent the fall and winter winnowing the frog-throats, monotones, and other repellent voices from his choir and banishing them to study hall, and he felt certain that he would bring home the trophy from the spring music festival in Rochester. This was before Dodger showed up. Heretofore "America, God shed His grace on thee" had sounded to Mr. Paulson like the ringing of small, clear bells, but with the addition of Dodger's growl it sounded like a dirge. He sent Dodger to Mr. Reinhart's office for assignment elsewhere. Catherine, hearing of this, was firm with Mr. Reinhart on the phone. Did choir class exist for the purpose of training students or for satisfying the enormous ego of Mr. Paulson? She had a mind to run for the school board (she told Mr. Reinhart) and look into any number of questionable practices in the Plum school system. The boys' and girls' toilets were not properly cleaned, she'd been told, and Miss Dale in English was positively batty. Mr. Reinhart, a proponent of harmony in the community, told her he'd speak to Mr. Paulson in Dodger's behalf, and he did, but he had uttered only a few words when Mr. Paulson drove him from the music room screaming, "His voice is disgusting!" and so Mr. Reinhart, a proponent of harmony among his faculty, withdrew Dodger from choir and assigned him to manual training.

Because of Dodger's height, Mr. Torborg urged him to come out for basketball. There were no junior high teams as such, but boys of that age were allowed to share the gym and put themselves through calisthenics and scrimmages similar to the high school team's. Thus Brendan, who had been out for basketball all winter, found himself allied to Dodger during the two hours of the twenty-four when he had expected to be free of him. For a few days Mr. Torborg stole time from his high school team to work with Dodger, and he observed that while Dodger picked up the individual skills of basketball very quickly, he was helpless when it came to teamwork. Give him a lot of room on the court and Dodger learned to dribble with either hand and to go in for layups with smooth footwork, but put him in a scrimmage and he fell over the lines painted on the floor. Mr. Torborg also observed that whenever he put Brendan in at guard instead of Sam Romberg (who was somewhat better at the

position) Dodger settled down and made fewer mistakes. Not few enough, however, and Mr. Torborg finally gave up on him. Thus Dodger, sitting out of scrimmages but continuing to show up at practice because Brendan was there, lapsed into his customary role as a misfit.

In manual training Dodger became adept at sandpapering. He avoided the power tools (the scream of the band saw made his ears ache) and he was awkward with hand tools (it took him five minutes to drive a nail) but he never grew tired of standing at his workstation and sanding the rolling pin he was making for Catherine. When he took it home and gave it to her for her birthday in mid-February, her pleasure was everything he had hoped for. It had a curious shape for a rolling pin—oval rather than round—but it was smooth as a tube of glass and she hugged him and told him she loved it.

His birthday gift for Hank, in March, was a socket wrench for removing spark plugs. While assisting Hank in tuning up the DeSoto, he had watched him skin his knuckles on the engine block each time the pliers slipped off a plug, so he filched a socket wrench from the tool room at school, scrubbed off the grime and gave it to Hank. Later Brendan told his father where it came from; he recognized the identifying dab of red paint on the grip. Whereupon Hank invited Dodger into the kitchen, shut the door and sat facing him in the breakfast nook.

"Dodger." He laid the wrench before him on the table. "This belongs to the school."

Dodger studied the wrench and nodded, half smiling.

"You stole it, didn't you."

He nodded again, without hesitation.

"Don't you know that's bad? Wrong? A crime?"

Dodger pondered this for a while. "It didn't seem wrong at the time. They've got a whole lot of these wrenches."

"But now, when you think about it, doesn't it seem wrong?"

"I guess so."

"You have to quit stealing. You don't need to steal. We're giving you an allowance."

Dodger, nodding happily, agreed.

"I want to help you quit stealing. Will you let me help you?"

"Sure."

"All right, Catherine and I have a plan. But first, promise you'll take this back to school tomorrow."

"Sure."

"And you'll apologize to Mr. Butz."

Dodger scowled.

"Tell him you took it and you're bringing it back and you're sorry."

"Can't I just put it back and not say that?"

"No, you have to tell Mr. Butz. You have to make sure he understands that you're sorry and you'll never steal again."

Dodger sighed. Mr. Butz didn't like him very much.

"Will you do that?"

"Okay." He looked worried.

Hank patted his arm. "Good, now here's the plan. We're going to get you used to handling other people's property in an honest way." He leaned out of the nook, pushed open the door and called to Brendan in the living room.

"Boys," he said when they were both seated across from him, "we have decided you're both old enough to start taking on more responsibility at the store. We're going to put you in charge of the overnight change from the till." Leaning out again, he opened the silverware drawer and drew out a green drawstring bag. Coins clinked as he dropped it on the table before them. "Every evening after Paul checks out the till he puts forty dollars in this bag—a ten, three fives, ten ones, and the rest silver—and he gives it to me. I hide it overnight and put it back in the till in the morning. From now on Paul will give the bag to one of you instead of me. You'll take turns being responsible for it between closing time at night and opening time in the morning. You'll put the currency and coins back in their compartments every morning."

"Where do we hide it?" Brendan asked.

"That's up to you. I hide it in various places. Behind canned goods on a shelf. Sometimes down in the cellar in a potato bag. Sometimes I bring it home, like tonight."

"You mean we've got to be there every night when you lock up?"

"Yes, both of you. And while you're there I want you to sweep the floor and put the produce away in the cooler under the meat counter. It'll take you twenty minutes or so."

"And every morning when you open up?"

"Right. And get the produce out of the cooler."

"Geez, Dad, guys our age? Isn't Saturday morning enough? I mean, we've got school and everything."

"When I was your age I had to quit school to work ten hours a day."

"Yeah, but it's different now."

"Not so different. The Higgins kids spend an hour and a quarter milking cows before school every morning."

"Yeah, we smell cows on their clothes."

This irritated Hank—was his son a snob?—but he let it pass. "And they spend another hour and a quarter milking every night, and they're younger than you. I'll raise your allowance, both of you, to a dollar and a half a week."

Brendan looked mollified, Dodger pleased.

"Now remember, take turns with the bag. Change off every day or every week or however you decide. If you don't assign yourselves particular days, you'll get mixed up and maybe neither one of you will take care of it." He pushed the wrench toward Dodger. "Here, don't forget this in the morning." He pushed the bag toward Brendan. "We open at eight."

The next morning Mr. Butz saw the wrench protruding from Dodger's back pocket as he came to class. He accused him of theft, which Dodger did not deny. "I'm putting it back in the tool room. I'm through stealing stuff."

"A likely story," said Mr. Butz. He reported Dodger by memo to the principal and by phone to all five members of the school board. His motive was less to bring Dodger to justice than to improve his own reputation as an alert and discerning teacher. His reputation, because of his glum disposition and his dalliance with Mrs. Clay, was badly in need of enhancing.

At the next meeting of the board Chairman Brask moved that Dodger be expelled. He said that his wife was acquainted with scores of mothers who wished to see the young criminal banished from school before he contaminated their children, and the socket-wrench incident gave them just cause. Webster Clay agreed, muttering that if they didn't act fast crime and criminals would infiltrate American education the way pip ran through his turkeys. Abraham Woodruff, the postmaster, was undecided. The two Catholic members of the board, Nicholi the barber and Crowley of the movies, argued for leniency; their reason for defending Dodger was to ingratiate themselves with Hank, who they were hoping would file for the school board election and replace Webster Clay, whose term was nearly up. Thus the vote was split two to two, with Woodruff abstaining.

The next morning when the Fosters heard about Dodger's near-expulsion, it wasn't Hank who filed for the board, it was Catherine.

Spring

22

Wallace Flint, resting from his labors, his hands and clothes spattered with green paint, lay on the couch reading the *Plum Alert* and fuming with hate. He could scarcely turn a page of the paper without seeing reference to the Fosters. The lead article on page one was devoted to the market's new design, with most of the credit going to Paul Dimmitburg. It was continued on page two, where Hank was quoted as thanking his employees by name for their part in the market's success. Wallace's name was not among them. Who had done more than Wallace to get their precious market off the ground? Who had scrubbed and painted and lifted and carried and been nice to people when he hadn't felt like it? Who had been Hank's right-hand man through thick and thin and cheered Catherine up when she lost hope? Who but Wallace? And now he was cast out like a leper. When he had asked for his job back in March, the Fosters had had the gall to turn him down, claiming they were fully staffed. But they were growing busier, he had argued; spring and summer were always busier; they'd need more help. No, they said, in addition to his mother they had hired Mrs. Pelzer, a young woman whose husband had recently died in the Pacific. They were selfish turncoats, and the simmering hatred he felt for them was growing more delicious by the day. They had usurped his place in Plum. From the time he was sixteen he had overseen the goings and comings of the villagers from the window of the grocery store; Plum had been his princedom, and now he was overthrown and banished to the horrifying boredom of his mother's house. But he was not banished forever. Sooner or later, he vowed, he would reclaim his rightful place in the store.

The ad for the sale, which was getting underway this morning, took up all of page three.

GRAND OPENING
HANK'S *NEW* MARKET
Completely remodeled.
New self-serve shopping.
New expanded produce department.
New shopping carts.
New low prices.

HOURLY DRAWINGS FOR FREE MERCHANDISE
FREE CUT-GLASS TUMBLER WITH $5 PURCHASE
FREE COFFEE AND COOKIES
Thurs., Fri., Sat.: April 12, 13, 14

Wallace had been told by his mother, who worked part-time at the packaging counter, that he wouldn't know the place. Swank was her word for it. New shelving. A new cash register and check-out counter. A new red awning out front. New red aprons for all the help with their names stitched in white on the bib.

On page four were a number of boxed ads from merchants who had profited from the remodeling. Best wishes from Romberg Appliance and Bottlegas, suppliers of the refrigeration unit for the walk-in cooler. Congratulations from Bob Donaldson of Minneapolis Jobbing. Good luck from Plum Lumber.

Wallace hooted when he turned to page seven and saw the photo of Hank and Catherine and their staff standing outside under the new awning. His mother, who only ten minutes ago had come dragging home from work with the flu, bringing the *Alert* with her, called down from her bedroom, "What's so funny, Wallace?" but he didn't respond. He folded the paper and studied the picture closely. What a collection of misfits, his mother the biggest misfit among them. She stood in the middle of the group with Dodger on her left and Brendan on her right and peered shyly out over the shoulders of Catherine and Mrs. Pelzer, who stood in front. Under their aprons Brendan and Dodger wore white shirts and black bow ties, as did Hank and Paul, who stood behind them. Wallace was incensed to think of a dunce like Dodger on the payroll. At Catherine's behest,

Dodger was released from his late morning study hall each day for an hour of work at the store (vocational education was Catherine's term for it), and he spent most of that hour with Wallace's mother at the packaging counter. He wasn't a bad kid, she reported to Wallace. She enjoyed working with him. "That's because you're two of a kind," Wallace pointed out to her.

Peering more closely at the grainy photo, he saw that his mother was giving the camera her public look, her smile small and tentative, her eyebrows raised expectantly. That she had taken the job and stuck with it was a surprise to Wallace. For somebody who had spent over twenty years sitting by the radio reading magazines and smoking, she sure as hell got ambitious when the money ran out. They had been down to a few soda crackers and a Hubbard squash that day in January when she went back to the Fosters and accepted their offer. She'd been working fifteen to twenty hours a week ever since. She'd had a phone installed in the house so Wallace could call her home whenever he felt a fit coming on. She was in charge of the packaging counter, which formed an L with the meat case at the back of the store; she weighed and bagged merchandise as it arrived in bulk lots from Minneapolis Jobbing and other wholesalers. The perfect job, she reported to Wallace. She got to sit on a bench as she worked, and was not required to face the public. Wallace guessed it was a long-dormant social-climbing instinct that accounted for his mother's fondness for the market. She got a kick out of rubbing shoulders with the Fosters. She came home chattering like a schoolgirl about what Catherine said and what Hank said and what Brendan said and what Grandfather said until it made Wallace want to throw up.

After his army physical, Wallace had spent sixty days in a fog. He never left the house. He didn't so much as raise the shades and look out. He looked in the mirror instead, watching his beard grow back, and tried to imagine how he had ever mustered the energy to go to Minneapolis. He read very little; the printed word required mental exertion beyond his means. During those sixty days he never turned the radio off; fragments of programs wound in and out of his consciousness. Though he spent endless hours in bed and on the couch, sleep didn't come easily. He thought about things in a dazed sort of way. One of the things he thought about was suicide.

His depression lifted in March. He felt his energy gradually rising like liquid in a tank, felt his mind stretch itself and grow active. He

wanted to talk. He wanted to see people. He wanted to resume his job at the market. He ordered his mother to stay home from work and let him go in her place.

She said no.

The shouting match that ensued was like nothing so far in their lives. It went on for a long time, his mother refusing, for once, to capitulate. She told him to find a job somewhere else. She said she was behaving like a normal human being after twenty years of avoiding people and she wasn't about to give up her job for anybody, not even Wallace. The battle ended in a draw, both of them stomping into their rooms and slamming their doors, their ears ringing, their throats hoarse.

The next morning he began painting the faces of seven Axis leaders on the walls of his mother's bedroom. These were to be murals, not frescoes, for he could find no plaster amid the clutter in the basement. The only paint he could find was half a can of the green enamel his mother had used years ago to paint the kitchen table and chairs. Tulip green it was called. At first he was dissatisfied to be working with such a fresh, happy hue, but after finishing Hitler and Tojo he was quite pleased with its effect against the background wallpaper of dark puce. It thrust the faces forward out of the wall.

Since he had only seven in mind, these were much larger faces—nearly four feet from ear to ear—than those in his bedroom. On the long wall opposite the window were Mussolini and Himmler and Hess.

"Get me back in the store," he told his mother when she put up a fuss. Her fuss took the form of shouting. The anger she'd been holding back for two decades came spewing forth every time she returned home from work and found a new green face. "Stay out of my room!" she screamed. But what could she do? She was gone from the house four mornings a week and her bedroom door had no lock, nor did it fit its frame snugly enough for a lock to be installed. "Get me back in the store and I'll stay out of your room," he replied with a smile as he went serenely forward with his next portrait. He enjoyed his mother's screaming fits. It was a much less boring household since she started blowing her top.

When Hank delivered her home sick this morning, Wallace was up on the stepladder, for the balloon face of Hermann Goering was going on the ceiling, looking down at his mother's bed. "A mate for you," he said. She was too sick to shout. She stood there looking de-

jected and feverish. "All right, go to bed," he relented, taking the *Alert* from her and leaving the room. "You look like death warmed over."

It took twenty minutes to read every word in the *Alert* from front to back. On the last page he saw Catherine's campaign ad.

Vote
For a New Voice
On the Plum School Board
CATHERINE FOSTER

In smaller print she set forth her intentions. She would redirect the flow of money for facilities, upgrading the business and home economics departments. She would promote periodic meetings between parents and teachers. Wallace was reading this list of promises when he heard footsteps on the porch. He got up and went to the door, pushing it open only an inch and peering out.

"Hello, Wallace."

It was Catherine. Her face, her voice, caused a surprising hitch in his heartbeat, a shudder such as a man might feel for a lover he hadn't seen for a long time. Or an enemy. He opened the door a little wider and looked her over. Her pale face was framed by her dark hair and the turned-up collar of a jacket he hadn't seen before. He thought her beautiful. He wanted to paint her portrait.

"Can I come in a minute?" she asked.

He made room for her to enter. He closed the door behind her. He didn't ask her to sit.

"We need help," she said, standing on the small rag rug by the door. "It's our Grand Opening and we've got scads of packaging to do."

His wish come true. But he hid his eagerness. He shrugged and turned partially away, hoping he looked aggrieved.

"Just while your mother is sick," she added.

"Why me?"

"Because you don't need to be trained. If we hire somebody else, by the time they get the hang of things the sale will be over."

"When would I start?"

"Now. As soon as you clean up. Is that paint all over your hands and shirt?"

He nodded. "I'm painting my mother's bedroom."

"That's nice." She smiled. "Will you come to work?"

"I'll be there in half an hour."

She thanked him and hurried away.

Stepping out onto the porch to watch the car drive off, he took his first breath of outdoor air in three months. He noticed it was spring.

Spring was unusually far advanced for mid-April. All across town songbirds were nesting in the budding elms. On the athletic field thirty junior-high boys in gym shorts responded to the whistle of Mr. McWhirter, who had been putting them through a series of track and field events, and followed him up the slope to the showers. Dodger brought up the rear, stalling, hoping to be too late for a shower. He hated showering with others. He was always asked about the scars on his arms and legs and neck and back. He wished he could go straight from the field to his hour of work at the market, but of course his clothes were in the locker room.

After the others entered the back door of the school, Dodger remained at the top of the slope, looking down at the football field surrounded by the oval grass track and thinking of the day he had sent the boomerang sailing so far and high that everyone came running from the playground and took turns. Never before or since had he done anything that attracted such admiration. He drew back his arm and brought it forward in slow motion, releasing an imaginary boomerang, aiming it at the high, warm sun.

His reverie was interrupted by Mr. Torborg, who came hurrying toward him, calling his name. He wore a blue suit and red tie and carried a math book in his good hand. "Dodger," he said, "you're a born runner."

"I am?"

"I've been watching you from up there." He pointed to his classroom windows on the second floor. "You've got long legs and a natural stride. You ought to be out for track. The Rochester Relays are having junior-high events this year, and I think you could win yourself a ribbon or two."

"A ribbon?" Dodger imagined the ribbons girls wore in their hair. "Shucks," he said, pretending more disappointment than he felt, "I'm moving to Winona. I'm going to live with my dad."

"So I've heard."

"Mr. Cranshaw's got it all set."

"Who's Mr. Cranshaw?"

"My case worker. He's got my dad a job at the Bemis Box Factory." This was a matter of pride with Dodger. Working at Hank's, he saw the Bemis trademark on many crates and cartons. "Me and my dad are going to live in the Hogan Hotel."

This didn't sound like a promising arrangement to Mr. Torborg, who knew the Hogan to be scarcely more than a flophouse. "When are you moving?"

"Monday."

"Well, at least you can run in the Rochester Relays. They're Saturday." No less than his interest in helping Dodger to a modicum of self-esteem was his interest in being well thought of by Catherine in case she became his superior on the school board, for along with his wound and his medals, Mr. Torborg had brought home from military service a strong respect for chain-of-command.

"Saturday morning?"

"Saturday all day."

"I work Saturday morning."

"I'm sure Mr. Foster would let you off."

"Think so? It's Grand Opening, starting today. It's busy."

"I could talk to him. I'm sure he and Mrs. Foster would be proud to have you on the team."

Dodger squinted. He could see that.

"There are other junior-high boys out for track. Philip Crowley's out, and the Holderbach twins."

Dodger nodded without enthusiasm. He didn't care for Philip. The Holderbach twins he scarcely knew; they were eighth-graders. He wished Brendan were out for track. Brendan, following Sam's lead, had gone out for baseball. Dodger had tried going out for baseball, but the owly coach, Mr. Butz, knowing he wouldn't be around to finish the season, had told him to forget it.

"What do you say, Dodger?"

He pictured himself in a PHS track uniform. It was gold. On the back of the shirt was a number, on the front a winged foot. He pictured Brendan in the uniform, standing beside him. "Do you think Brendan could come with me?"

"Brendan's out for baseball."

"Yeah, I know, but I mean just to Rochester."

"I don't see why not."

"You'd have to fix it with Mr. Foster for both of us."

"I'll fix it."

* * *

Phyllis Clay was washing her hair when the news came over the radio. She burst immediately into tears. She drew a towel over her head like a cowl, pulled on her bathrobe over her slip, and ran out the front door and across the street to the Fosters' house. She pounded on the door with both fists. It took Grandfather a minute to work his way out of his afternoon nap. He opened his eyes, rose up on his elbows and repeated the formula that usually helped him wake up: I am living in Hank and Catherine's house in the village of Plum and I have not been employed by the railroad since 1929. He got to his feet and opened the door.

"Oh, Mr. McMahon, the most awful thing has happened," sobbed Mrs. Clay on the threshold. "President Roosevelt is dead. It happened this afternoon. He was at his vacation place in Warm Springs, Georgia, and he slumped over dead in a chair. I just heard it on the radio." She covered her eyes and shook with grief.

Grandfather's heart grew suddenly heavy, his expression grave. He put his hand tenderly on her shoulder and led her into the living room and over to the couch, where she sat with her legs curled under her. Drying her tears, she asked if he would turn on the radio. "Webster's gone to his turkeys, and I can't bear to listen all by myself."

Her toenails, he saw, were painted red. He switched on the radio, and as they waited for it to warm up he asked if she cared for something to drink, some tea or coffee or whiskey.

"Oh, whiskey would be just the thing," she told him, smiling fondly.

In the kitchen Grandfather put the bottle of Southern Comfort to his lips and took a swallow, fortifying himself against the malaise that inevitably overtook him at the death of someone dear. For twelve years Roosevelt, by means of his Fireside Chats, had taken Grandfather into his confidence. Together they had eased unemployment, improved pensions, brought electricity to rural areas, insured bank deposits and put the Axis armies on the run. What would America do without FDR? God was great, but His timing was off. Ever since that summer morning when Sade fell dead in the garden, Grandfather was aware of God's terrible habit of taking people when they were needed most. The Germans were as good as licked, but the Japs vowed never to surrender, and how would the great MacArthur manage without his commander in chief? Grand-

father had no confidence in the haberdasher from Missouri who would now move into the White House.

Returning to the living room, he found Mrs. Clay briskly drying her hair with her towel. He set the bottle on the endtable and pulled a chair up close so he could reach it too. He handed her a glass.

"You're so kind," she said. "And I'm so silly to come here crying like this over a man I've never met dying a thousand miles away, but the second I heard the news I thought of my granddaddy and how he died without telling me how much he loved me. Of the three girls in my family it was me my granddaddy loved most, even though it was my two older sisters that got all his attention. We never knew our daddy and it was our granddaddy we were with all the time, because he and Grandma lived on the next farm over from ours on the road running north out of Fayetteville. When he was plowing with his team and we took his lunch to him out in the field, he'd let my two sisters ride the horses a ways before he sat down to eat. When he took us to town on Saturday afternoons, my two sisters asked him for candy and soda pop and combs for their hair, and they were such pests about it that they got everything they asked for, but I knew he loved me best for not asking for anything. I hardly ever asked for anything and he hardly ever gave me anything, but I knew the reason was that if he gave me things I'd be no better than my sisters, and he knew I didn't want to be in the same class with them. I was away living in Omaha when he died. I wrote and asked my mama if he said anything about me before he died and she said not that she knew of. I cried for a week or more. I just couldn't get ahold of myself. I went around spouting tears like a pump, thinking how he didn't get it off his chest how much he loved me. My granddaddy didn't look anything like you, Mr. McMahon, he was short and wiry and hardly any bigger than a boy, but it's your hair that's the same. His hair was white like yours and he combed it straight back like you do. I can't explain it, but the second I heard President Roosevelt was dead I thought of my granddaddy and then I thought of you. This is very good whiskey, Mr. McMahon. I'm feeling much better."

They listened to a radio voice say that a cerebral hemorrhage was the cause of death. A funeral train was being assembled to carry the body to Washington. They sipped whiskey until the news report was replaced by somber music; then Mrs. Clay got up to go. They both

spoke at once, she apologizing for breaking in on him and he saying reassuring things about her granddaddy's love. She said she had to go downtown and buy a ribbon for her hat. He said he was going downtown himself—would she do him the honor of walking with him?

"Oh yes, I'd love to. I'll go home and dress and be right back. It's a lovely day for a walk."

Grandfather dressed as well, putting on a fresh shirt and a new tie and his Sunday shoes. He stepped out the front door just as Phyllis Clay was stepping out hers. She wore a short pink dress with puffy sleeves and carried a wide-brimmed hat of blue straw. She flew to his side emitting an intoxicated giggle, which she stifled by burying her face in his shoulder. Doing this, she dropped her hat.

"Your hat, Mrs. Clay, allow me." He bent over and picked it up. "A very pretty hat. I'm fond of a straw hat on a woman."

"Isn't it posh? Montgomery Ward. In the catalogue it was pictured with a ribbon attached, so I planned to wear it hanging down my back, but it came without the ribbon."

"Yes, I can see the eyelets where the ribbon would go."

They set off, Grandfather strutting, proud to have a pretty young woman on his arm, Mrs. Clay swinging her hat in rhythm with her flouncy walk. They met Mrs. Kimball and Mrs. Brask.

"Don't forget to vote next Tuesday," Grandfather said, lifting his hat. "A new voice is needed on the school board, and Catherine is the one to provide it." It was his practice these days to plead Catherine's cause to everyone he met on the street.

Mrs. Kimball said, "I'm sorry, Mr. McMahon, but I've promised my vote to Harlan Brask."

"Harlan Brask isn't running."

"He's not?" She frowned and turned to Mrs. Brask. "Didn't you tell me to vote for Harlan?"

"No, Harlan is board chairman ex officio by virtue of his being mayor," crowed Mrs. Brask, adjusting her foxes. "I said we must write in the name of someone who will cooperate with him."

"And who would that be?" asked Grandfather.

The mayor's wife appeared not to hear the question. She was looking contemptuously at the knees of Phyllis Clay.

"There are wrongs in our school that need righting, ladies. The toilets aren't clean and several windows are broken. Miss Dale in junior-high English is a dunderhead." There were a dozen other

wrongs he had heard Catherine speak of, but he couldn't remember them at the moment.

Mrs. Brask said, "Come, Henrietta," and walked away. Her friend followed obediently.

"You must be proud of Catherine," said Phyllis Clay. "Webster says she just might win."

"She's always been one to set things right. Can we count on your vote?"

"You bet. Webster says I shouldn't vote for her, but you know what I say to that, don't you? I say to hell with Webster." They resumed their walk. "You want to know the real reason Webster's not running for re-election? He's afraid to be gone from the house nights. He's afraid I'll go out and find myself another man." Her laugh was throaty. "But I'll tell you a secret—the nights are the least of his worries."

Downtown Grandfather steered Mrs. Clay into the Plum Five and Dime, where he bought her a length of ribbon for her hat. They decided on pink, to match her dress. As the clerk slipped it through the eyelets and knotted the ends, Mrs. Clay's eyes filled with tears. "My granddaddy would have bought me things like this if my two older sisters hadn't been such pigs." She hugged Grandfather's arm. "You're just like my granddaddy, only nicer."

They continued along Main Street to the school. "Look at all those cute boys." She was pointing at the athletic field and the two dozen members of the track team. She led him across the playground and halfway down the grassy slope.

"Do you like my hat on my head or back on my shoulders?" she asked as she went ahead a few steps with the hat on her head. Then she stopped and dropped it down her back. She turned for his judgment.

"When it's on your head I can't see your pretty hair."

"Oh, you're so sweet." She leaped to his side and hugged his arm again, causing him to tip over. She uttered a cry as she watched him go down very slowly and end up on his back, his head uphill. She knelt over him. "Are you hurt? Could you just kill me for being so rough?"

He sat up and waited for his head to clear.

"I'll kill myself if you're hurt, Mr. McMahon."

He wasn't hurt, but his pipe was broken. He fished it from the pocket of his suitcoat and tried fitting the stem to the bowl.

"Oh, look what I did. I'll buy you a new one. We'll go straight to the drugstore and I'll buy you a new pipe."

"Never mind, this doesn't happen to be my favorite. It's always been a little on the sour side."

So pleasant was the sun on the fresh-smelling grass, so heart-warming the sight of boys cavorting below them, so restful the view of farmland in the distance, that neither of them felt like moving. They sat for a time with their legs straight out in front of them. Mrs. Clay pulled her skirt up a bit, to sun her knees.

Grandfather, looking away, cleared his throat and said, "You have very pretty legs, Mrs. Clay."

Her laugh was melodious. "Shame on you, Mr. McMahon, at your age."

He chuckled contentedly.

23

Hank's new office, built high off the floor at the back of the market, was designed so that by turning in his chair and looking out over the soap display he could see at a glance who his shoppers were and what his help was up to. Catherine called it his crow's nest; Stan Kimball, his poop deck. On this second morning of the sale—Friday—he was pleased to see all his shopping carts in use. The wheeled shopping cart was a new phenomenon in Plum and he was already planning to double the size of his fleet. Thursday's proceeds had vastly exceeded his hopes, and it appeared certain that the sale as a whole would bring in over twice as much income as the first Grand Opening last September.

As shoppers passed below him he overheard their conversations, most of which had to do with the President's death.

The bell of the new cash register rang and Hank cast his eyes upon Mrs. Pelzer at the checkout counter. The bell was shrill and the drawer sprang open with such force that she had to step backward to avoid injury to her ribs. The Fosters were more than satisfied with Mrs. Pelzer. She was too tiny to lift much, but she was quick on the adding machine and offered customers a line of sprightly chatter. She had applied for work in January after her husband, a sailor on his way back to the States to be discharged, had drowned while swimming off a reef in Hawaii. Mrs. Pelzer had confided to Catherine that she was grieved as much by her childlessness as by her widowhood; yet Hank, watching her carry on happily at the checkout counter, would never have guessed she was grieved. "Your change is two dollars, Mrs. Scott," he heard her say. "Thank

you so much. Paul, will you carry Mrs. Scott's groceries out to her car?"

Hank watched Paul Dimmitburg rise from the low shelf where he was setting out cans of pork and beans and hurry to the counter. He bowed politely to Mrs. Scott as he took her groceries in his arms. Following her outside, he nodded politely at Rufus Ottmann, who had been standing in place for nearly an hour, backing up and coming forward as the door opened and closed. Seeing this, Hank was struck by the curious mix of people he had brought together under his roof. How peculiar that a scholarly would-be preacher should greet the village idiot. Or that Dodger Hicks should be working side by side with Wallace Flint.

"Listen, Dodger, how many times do I have to tell you to put fewer cookies in the bag to start with. Then when the bag's on the scale you can add what you need to make a pound."

"Yeah, that's what I been doing."

Both yesterday and this morning during Dodger's hour on duty, Hank had been forced to listen to Wallace Flint's relentless, fussy instructions at the packaging counter, which stood at the foot of the office steps. Never again, he promised himself, would he ask Wallace to work. Wallace had undergone a change since last fall. It was clear to Hank, and Catherine agreed, that the lighter side of his personality—the laughter, the joking—had vanished, and what remained was bitterness in its dark, pure form. He soured the atmosphere.

"If you've done what I told you, then why did I just see you taking cookies out of that last bag?"

"Because I had more than a pound in there." Dodger's voice was quietly adenoidal.

"But you just said you've been doing what I said to do."

"Yeah, I have been. But sometimes not."

"Now listen to me once and for all, Dodger. If you can't train yourself to be exact, train yourself to put less in each bag rather than more, and your work will go faster. It's easier to drop another cookie into a bag on the scale than it is to take a cookie out."

"Okay."

"You're as slow as molasses."

"I am?"

"It's not good for business, being as slow as you are."

"Why not?"

"Because time is money."

"It is?"

Hank's phone rang. It was Catherine.

"Is it busy, Hank? Should I come down early?"

"No, twelve will be fine."

"But you wanted to go out for a haircut."

"I'll go anyway. If you get here by the time Mrs. Pelzer goes to lunch, that will be fine. We're keeping up."

"Hank, I've been snubbed again by Cora Brask."

"Oh, my." He turned in his chair and faced the opening that had been cut in the wall to give him a view of the back room. Stock was piled against three walls. Against the fourth stood the enormous new walk-in cooler.

"It started raining and we both happened to be out bringing in wash at the same time and I spoke to her and she pretended not to hear me."

Hank said nothing.

"Isn't it a wonder the way the Brasks found each other, Hank—the world's most unenlightened man marrying the world's most priggish woman? I can still hear her saying, 'The neighborhood goes down, Mrs. Foster.' Wait till I'm on the board, her husband's lordly days will be over."

As Catherine paused to sigh and let her anger cool, Hank wondered if there had been a single day in the past two weeks when he hadn't heard his wife's imitation of Mrs. Brask's breathy falsetto: "The neighborhood goes down." She had said this to Catherine in reference to Dodger's theft of the socket wrench and his continued presence on Bean Street.

"How are you coming along with Dodger's things?" Hank asked.

"His clothes are all clean and ready to pack. Mr. Cranshaw just phoned. He said Dodger's father is going to phone here tonight from prison. He wants to talk over last-minute details with his son."

"What time?"

"Around seven."

"I'll tell Dodger."

"How are he and Wallace getting along?"

"Not so well." Hank lowered his voice so the two of them wouldn't hear. "They can't work together five minutes without Wallace getting his dander up."

"Then maybe they shouldn't work together. Why don't you have Dodger work with Paul?"

"Because packaging is where we need him. Paul's almost caught up."

"But isn't there something else he can do? Go out and wash the front window?"

"Not in the rain. Maybe I should have Wallace and Paul exchange jobs until Dodger's hour is up."

"Oh, Wallace would die," she said. "He's above stocking shelves."

Hank swallowed his irritation. "Why did we ask him back? He's impossible."

"Well, it's only for one more day. And tomorrow Dodger will be gone to the track meet."

"One more day of Wallace Flint will be my limit. Never again, Catherine."

"Whatever you say. I'll see you at twelve."

"Right." He hung up and turned to his bookkeeping, but was again distracted:

"Dodger, did I just see you put a cookie in your mouth?"

A masticating reply: "Yump."

"Listen, Dodger, you can't be eating what the customer's paying for."

"Hank said it's okay to eat a cookie once in a while."

"But you can't eat it out of a bag you've already weighed."

"I didn't."

"Yes, you did. I saw you."

"No, I didn't. I took it from the box."

"Like hell you did. I saw you take it out of that last bag you weighed."

"No, I took it from the box."

Wallace raised his voice: "Weigh that sack, Dodger, and see if it isn't a cookie short."

"You fellows pipe down!" Hank yelled.

"Damn him, Hank, he's eating cookies."

"Don't argue with me, Wallace, and quit being such an old hen!" Hank descended the steps. "I'll be back in a little while. I'm going for a haircut."

The moment Hank left the store Wallace left the packaging counter and went into the back room, where he lay down on the flour sacks. He savored his growing hatred for Dodger, for Hank, for Catherine, for everyone who had had a hand in changing this grocery store

from the quiet, comfortable place it had been into a noisy, crowded shrine to the almighty dollar. How was a person supposed to keep his equilibrium with all this business going on, all this food to be weighed and packaged, all these stupid people cluttering the aisles with their ridiculous carts and lining up at the checkout counter where the parrotlike Mrs. Pelzer took their money and every so often had the nerve to call on Wallace to carry out groceries? With no lulls in the day, when could a person rest? When could a person talk to Catherine? Not that Catherine was worth talking to any more. Between mothering Dodger and taking up lofty thoughts with Paul Dimmitburg and spouting off to all the customers about tax levies and curriculum and teacher preparation, she had no time for the banter of their early days together.

But all in all, the rigor of grocery work was better than the boredom of staying home, and Wallace was determined to remain on the job. Come Monday at least Dodger Hicks would be gone to Winona. That nonentity. It was the ultimate humiliation to work side by side with an illiterate, thieving child who stood around with his mouth open and didn't know how to add. What's more, the child was on the payroll, earning nearly as much per hour as Wallace with his nine years' experience, and he was in charge of the overnight change bag. But Dodger had one attractive quality, and that was his vulnerability. This morning after Dodger emptied the change into the till and before Mrs. Pelzer came to work, Wallace had bought himself a pack of gum, ringing up a five-cent sale and filching a five-dollar bill. Unfortunately Mrs. Pelzer didn't notice that she was starting the day with two fives instead of three, didn't set off the investigation Wallace had imagined. Well, he had one more chance. Tomorrow he'd take a ten.

Hank peered in the window of Nicholi's barbershop and saw Stan Kimball lying flat in the chair with lather on his face. Stan Kimball spent a great deal of his idle time being barbered and shaved and watching others being barbered and shaved. Hank saw Phil Crowley sitting at the back of the shop, a newspaper in his lap. He put his head in at the door and said, "How about calling me when your chair is open?"

"Come in and sit down," ordered the barber. "We've been talking about you."

"No, I've got to get back. We're busy."

Nicholi beckoned with his shaving brush. "Stop bragging and come in and sit down. We've got something to ask you." The barber was a bald, wiry man who sent everyone away with the same haircut—clipped high on the sides and smelling of eye-smarting hair tonic. He kept a messy shop—wet towels hanging everywhere, the mirror smudged, clipped hair gritty underfoot.

Hank walked to the back of the shop and greeted Phil Crowley, whose jacket smelled of last night's theater popcorn. Above Crowley's head hung a calendar, a Navy Spitfire featured for April. Hank sat down and said, "What's up?"

The barber spoke across Stan Kimball's large stomach. "Tell him, Phil."

Crowley unfolded the *Plum Alert* and showed him Catherine's two-column ad.

"I've seen it," Hank said flatly, concealing his pride.

Crowley said, "A bunch of us men from Holy Angels have been trying for years to get another Catholic seat on the board and tip the balance." Crowley was a tall, unruffled man whose words came out smooth and unhurried. "When Webster Clay decided not to run for another term we figured this was our chance, and we figured on you as our candidate."

"My wife's your candidate."

"That's just the trouble."

"Trouble?"

"A woman can't win."

"Oh?"

"Nobody will vote for a woman. You're our only chance, Hank. We don't know how you do it, but you've got Lutherans buying your groceries and you just might get Lutherans to vote you onto the board."

Hank frowned. "What's religion got to do with a public school?"

Nicholi answered, his razor poised over Kimball's lathered face: "I'm on the board three terms and Phil's on two, and we can both tell you religion makes a hell of a difference when certain issues come up to vote."

"What issues?"

"Issues like whether to sell our old desks to the Lutherans for their school."

"What school? The Lutherans don't have a school."

"Then you haven't heard," said the barber. "If you'd poke your nose out of your store once in a while, you'd know what's going on in

this town. Emmanuel Lutheran's got the idea of starting a grade school of their own next fall, and they're shopping around for a building and fixtures. We've got sixty old desks in Plum Elementary we're replacing, and unless we come up with one more Catholic voice on the board they'll go to the Lutherans."

"And if you get one more voice, where will they go?"

Nicholi waved his razor, slashing the air. "Into the furnace, out to the dump, who gives a damn as long as they don't go to the Lutherans, am I right, Phil?"

"Right."

Hank stood up. He paced quickly to the front window, saying, "None of this makes sense to me."

"Me neither," erupted Stan Kimball from his flat position. "Listen to these guys talk you'd think it was the Inquisition."

"None of your business," the excited barber told him, drawing the razor along Kimball's cheek, exposing a swath of florid flesh. "Just because you've got no beliefs of your own, Kimball, you can't understand people who do."

Kimball waited until the razor was safely lifted before he replied. "Is it your belief that Lutheran children shouldn't sit in desks?"

Nicholi silenced him by pinching his nose shut and shaving close around it. "Don't listen to this atheist, Hank."

Kimball gripped the barber's wrist and freed his nose. "How could anybody function as an undertaker in this town if he wasn't an atheist? The only reason I'm welcome in both churches is because I don't belong to either one."

Hank gazed out at the wet cars passing along the wet street and wished he could flee this small-minded carping; yet he felt obliged to stay and convince these men that even if Catherine couldn't win she was justified in running. Not that he was entirely convinced himself. It struck him as unwise of her to try to find her place in the community by seeking a place *above* the community. He had warned her that running for office might be asking for another, more damaging, sort of rejection; but of course there had been no dissuading her. She was caught up in this election the way she'd been caught up in the grocery business last fall, her energies poured into a cause the village deemed hopeless. What bothered Hank most was his suspicion that Catherine was striving for more than a seat on the school board, that all her disappointments in this village had come together in her drive for public office, and that defeat would leave her terribly embittered.

He spoke at the window, his back to the men. "Tell me this. Filings have been open a month, and my wife's the only one filed. If there's a religious war going on, why aren't the Lutherans running anybody to take Webster Clay's place?"

"Just wait," said the barber. "We figure they're going to run Len Downie."

"I'd be surprised," said Hank. "Len Downie's not the type."

"He's popular with the farmers."

Hank had played an occasional game of pool with Len Downie, proprietor of the Standard station. He was a man of mild opinions and few words, a man to Hank's liking. "He's not a leader. He's more of a follower."

"A faction only needs one leader, and that's Harlan Brask on the Lutheran side," said the barber. He slapped lotion and powder on Kimball's face and raised him to a sitting position. "You're next, Hank." He gave his barber cloth a vigorous shake, raising hair off the floor.

Kimball stepped to the mirror to examine his looks, then sat down next to Crowley and speculated aloud on who his next corpse might be. "There's an old codger named Foss at the poor farm who's got lung trouble and sinking fast. Father O'Day's nothing but skin and bones, but then he's always been nothing but skin and bones. The color isn't coming back into Mrs. Ottmann's face this spring the way it used to in years gone by. Did you know her big house is up for sale? She and her family are unloading it now, to avoid probate when she dies."

"Who'd buy that place?" said Hank, settling into the chair. "I lived in that house. It leaks heat like a tent."

There was silence for a time—the snip of scissors, the squeak of the rotating chair—and then Phil Crowley said in a slow, lazy tone, as if he weren't scheming, "Hank, you know about Harlan Brask trying to get your Dodger Hicks kicked out of school."

"Of course, it's one of the reasons my wife's running. Tell Brask the boy's transferring to Winona on Monday. That ought to make him happy."

"Well, that's not all there is to it. Did you know he's trying to get him sent back to the Home School?"

Swinging his head to look at Crowley, Hank was nearly speared in the ear. "What's the matter with him? Is he crazy?"

Nicholi and Crowley exchanged a satisfied look in the mirror. Arousing Hank Foster wasn't easy.

"Don't tell me it's the socket wrench. The socket wrench is back where it belongs. It was only gone overnight."

"But all the same, Brask has a point. When Hicks took the wrench he broke his parole."

"Who says?"

"The law says. Brask checked into it. If charges are pressed, Hicks automatically goes back to the Home School."

"And Brask will press charges?"

"He's thinking about it."

Hank understood then why Mrs. Brask had avoided speaking to Catherine this morning, and why Harlan Brask had avoided speaking to Hank last night when they both stepped out their back doors at the same moment. Brask had turned his back and pretended not to see him. Not that Hank minded. He had given up trying to be neighborly with the Brasks.

The barber took his turn. "There's lots of pressure to get the kid sent back."

"Pressure from who?"

"There's people living in fear."

"Nonsense."

"Mrs. Kimball is one of them, right, Stan?"

"You can't go by what my wife's afraid of." Stan Kimball was sitting low in his chair, picking hairs off his lapels. "My wife runs indoors when airplanes go over."

The barber continued, "But I think Phil and I could talk him out of pressing charges if we put our minds to it."

"Then put your minds to it," said Hank indignantly.

"If we went to the trouble of talking him out of it, would you do us the favor of running for the board? You can file till five o'clock this afternoon."

"My wife's already filed, remember?"

"Can't you get her to unfile?"

"No, damn it!"

The topic was dropped.

Later, his hair trimmed, Hank left the shop with Stan Kimball. They walked into arrows of wind-driven rain.

"We'll appreciate your vote, Stan. You and your wife's."

"Catherine's got my vote, but my wife will no doubt follow Cora Brask's advice and vote for the opposition."

"There is no opposition."

"There will be." As they drew near the market, Kimball added,

"I hate to say it, Hank, but Catherine getting mixed up in politics is the worst thing that could happen to you. She's bound to alienate one faction or the other and your business is bound to suffer."

"I thought you knew her better than that. Do you think she's running for the board to take the Catholic side of things?"

"No, I don't think that."

"Do you think she'd vote to burn those desks?"

"Of course not. But what I think is that the more she keeps her opinions to herself the more groceries you'll sell. Say she votes to sell the desks—that makes the Catholics mad. Another issue comes along and she votes the Catholic side—that makes the Lutherans mad. As long as she's not a bigot you stand to lose *all* your customers, not just one side or the other. Come on, let's shoot a game of pool."

"Are you kidding? Look . . ." Hank pointed proudly through the window of the market. The aisles were crowded; a line of shoppers waited at the checkout counter.

"That's a pretty sight, Hank. Come election day, I'm going to hate to vote against it."

Hank assisted Mrs. Pelzer at the checkout counter until trade diminished as noon hour approached; then he went back to his office. Sitting over his ledgers, he tried hard not to believe that Catherine's emergence as a candidate for office—and worse, a woman of opinions—might be their downfall as grocers. He didn't have time to fully reject this depressing notion before he heard someone on the steps behind him. "Hi," he said without turning, assuming it was Catherine.

A man's voice said, "Hank, can we talk?"

It was Phil Crowley. Behind him on a lower step, was B. L. Skeffington, the banker. Skeffington was an emaciated man in his sixties wearing high-heeled boots and a loud sportscoat. Currently he was president of the Holy Angels Men's Club, an organization that met twice a month in the basement of the church. Hank paid his dues but never attended, having little interest in the two primary activities of the club—political scheming and cardplaying—and being too fond of his evenings at home.

Both men crowded up into Hank's crow's nest. Phil Crowley sat on the edge of the desk. B. L. Skeffington sat on the safe and looked out over the soap. He said, "Hank, you've got yourself a little gold

mine here. When you first came to town last summer and took over from Kermit, I thought you must be the biggest sucker in the world, but, by Christ, look what you've done."

Skeffington's unctuousness made Hank uneasy. He turned to Crowley and said, "I'm not running for office, if that's what you want."

"No, no, we're here to talk property. B.L. is handling Mrs. Ottmann's big house and the Holy Angels Men's Club has decided to buy it. I'd have told you about it in the barbershop, but Kimball would have blabbed it all over town. B.L., give him the figures."

It took Skeffington a few moments to quit staring down at the market from this interesting angle. He turned, crossed his arms, crossed his boots, and said, "Mrs. Ottmann's letting the big house go for three thousand."

"I lived in that house," said Hank. "It's cold. It's got a wet basement and no insulation."

"But it's big and roomy and the framework is good and solid," said the banker. "Insulate it and seal the foundation and make some other improvements and we'll have ourselves a mighty fine piece of property. It's a steal at three thousand."

"I don't get it. Don't we have enough expense keeping up the church and the rectory without taking on a run-down house?"

"It's a money-making deal," said Skeffington. "The Men's Club buys it, refurbishes it, and then sells it for six thousand."

"Sells it to who? In this town a refurbished house for six will be a bigger white elephant than a run-down house for three."

Skeffington's voice was powerful: "There's a postwar boom right around the corner, Hank. It's going to be a seller's market in real estate."

"But six thousand for a house in this town? My own house was the most expensive on the market last year, and I bought it for four."

"You bought it just in time. Demographers say Plum's going to double in size. Our dear old farming village stands a good chance of becoming a bedroom community."

"What's that?" It sounded vaguely sinful to Hank.

"It's a town people live in who work in a city."

"But we're a hundred miles from Minneapolis."

"And only twenty from Rochester. Rochester's going to get real big."

"Twenty miles is a hell of a long drive to work."

"Not after the war, Hank. New cars. Paved roads."

Crowley unfolded a sheet of paper and gave it to Hank. "Here's what we've collected so far. We're asking each Catholic businessman for fifty dollars toward the down payment. When the house is sold you get your fifty dollars back and Holy Angels gets the profit and we use it for a new roof on the church and repairs to the rectory."

Hank scanned the list. Skeffington was down for fifty. So was Nicholi. Crowley was down for twenty-five.

"How come only twenty-five?"

"Are you kidding? On forty-cent movie tickets?"

Hank opened and closed his checkbook, looking at his balance. "Does Father O'Day know about this?" Hank distrusted the laity in church affairs.

"Yeah," said Crowley. "We went to see him about it."

"Does he approve?"

"I guess so, he said something holy."

The men turned politely away as Hank opened his checkbook again, intending to make out a check for twenty-five, fifty being too steep for such a dubious scheme. But as he wrote *April 13, 1945,* he saw in his mind's eye how attractive the Ottmann property might look with a fresh coat of paint and the yard trimmed. Standing empty this spring, it was becoming an eyesore, weeds standing high as the windowsills, rain gutters loosened by the wind. Perhaps he should contribute fifty after all, and help upgrade that end of town. Then, as he wrote *Holy Angels Men's Club,* he felt a sudden compulsion to atone for his absence from meetings and decided that seventy-five dollars would buy the good will of the Catholic men and keep them and their wives as steady customers. And then he thought of something else to atone for—his wife selling desks to the Lutherans. He wrote the check for one hundred.

24

Dodger sat in the breakfast nook ready to pick up the phone when it rang. Brendan had gone to the movie with Sam and Philip. Hank, Catherine and Grandfather were in the living room listening to a somber voice from Washington, where the train carrying the President's body was pulling into the station. It was a warm, cloudy evening. The rain had stopped. Through the open windows came the chirp of robins and the smell of wet earth.

Waiting, Dodger called to mind the Hogan Hotel, where he and his father would live. Mr. Cranshaw had arranged for them to have two rooms with a connecting door. The Hogan stood in the shadow of the big bridge across the Mississippi—a good location, Dodger thought. If his parents had to be in the same town at least they'd be twenty blocks apart.

In the Home School Dodger hadn't thought much about his parents, but since moving in with the Fosters he thought about them all the time. Sometimes he thought that if he could be more like Brendan, then his mother would be more like Catherine and his father would be more like Hank. His mother would quit swearing at him and getting drunk, and his father would quit being sneaky and having mean spells. But then common sense would break in and he'd realize this was too much to hope for. He could never be like Brendan. Brendan was smart and good-looking and had lots of friends. Dodger had overheard girls in school say that Brendan's dark eyes and dark hair were adorable and they loved his dimples when he smiled. What he'd overheard about himself wasn't so great. It was funny (he'd heard a girl say) the way Dodger's mouth hung open all the time and his ears stuck out.

But if he couldn't look like Brendan, why couldn't he at least *act* like Brendan? Brendan was better at everything. Work, for instance. After three hours of work on Saturday mornings, Brendan was never worn out the way Dodger was. To be a good worker, a good student, a friend to lots of people (Dodger concluded), you probably had to start early in life. To be like Brendan your parents probably had to be Catherine and Hank Foster.

The phone rang. His father's voice was faint over the wire: "How you been, son?"

"Okay, Dad, how *you* been?"

"Swell." There was a long pause. "Is it raining in Plum?"

"No. It was, a little."

"Yeah, it was raining a little here, too."

"Hey, Dad, are you and Ma thinking about getting back together?" It was his only serious worry and he held his breath. Hank and Catherine, too, held their breath in the living room as they tried but failed to concentrate on the President. To prevent eavesdropping, Catherine had turned up the volume on the radio, but there were long silent spells between the commentator's observations.

"No," said Mr. Hicks. "What ever gave you a crazy idea like that?"

"I thought maybe that's why you decided we should live in Winona. I mean, when we lived there when I was little, you never liked it."

"No, that's a crazy idea. The only thing me and your ma ever agreed on was splitting up. See, the reason I'm going back to Winona is because the county you go to prison from is the county you're supposed to go back to. It's where your parole officer is. You got a parole officer, Dodger?"

"Yeah. Mr. Cranshaw."

"Yeah, he's mine too. Kind of a sissy-looking guy, isn't he."

"So you're going to like Winona okay this time?"

"It'll be swell, son. Bemis Box will be swell. It's a big enough operation so a guy can work his way up. See, when I was with Pierce Plumbing I couldn't go nowhere with my life. They had me in the back room all the time taking toilets out of packing crates. Speaking of jobs, Dodger, Cranshaw tells me you've been working at a job."

"In Hank's Market."

"That's swell. Are you going to have any money when you get to Winona?"

"Yeah, I might."

"See, because when I get out of Stillwater all I'll have is a twenty-dollar bill from the warden, which isn't much considering even if I go back to work the very next day there's no telling when my first paycheck'll come through—I don't know how Bemis Box works their payroll."

Dodger said, "I'll have a little money."

His father told him to speak up, this was a poor connection.

He said it again, louder. Hank and Catherine exchanged a look.

"Swell," said Mr. Hicks.

"Hey, Dad, how come we're staying in a hotel, Mrs. Foster wants to know. How come we're not getting an apartment?"

"We are. The Hogan's not really a hotel. They call it a hotel, but people live there like it was apartments."

"You mean we got a kitchen and everything?"

"No, but there's a sink in the bathroom down the hall. Who needs a kitchen? Do you cook?"

"No, I don't cook."

"Neither do I. I like eating out, and there's a lunch counter next door. Don't you like eating out?"

"Sure."

"By the way, son, how do you like the Fosters?"

"Like them fine."

"Yeah, Cranshaw says they're real nice. Got a lot of money, have they?"

"Yeah, I guess they've got money. They own a store."

"And a nice house, I suppose."

"A real nice house."

A long pause.

"Well, good-bye son. I'll see you Monday."

"Good-bye, Dad."

As soon as Dodger hung up, Hank took him outside. He handed him a screwdriver and asked him to take off the inside panel of the driver's door—the window roller needed fixing. It was brighter now, the western sky clearing, the sun going down in a blaze of orange. As Dodger turned the screws, Hank cleared his throat and said, "Are there going to be any problems, do you think, when you go and live with your dad?"

Dodger recognized this as the sort of question Hank wouldn't ask unless Catherine put him up to it. Hank always asked easy questions, like what are you working on in shop these days?

"No problems that I know of."

"No problems about money or anything like that?" Catherine had indeed put him up to it. Dodger's reference to money on the phone had aroused her fear that his father would lead him back into thievery.

"No, nothing like that."

Hank lifted the hood and checked the oil. He whistled a tune. He closed the hood and said, "We're going to miss you around here, you know that?"

Dodger stopped working and stared at Hank. "You are?"

"Yep."

Hank was held by Dodger's eyes, which were no longer so shifty and evasive. They were intensely hungry eyes. Three months with the Fosters had given Dodger an appetite for kindness. He stared hard at Hank, hoping to hear more.

"Yep, we will," Hank repeated. Now he saw more than hunger in the boy's eyes. He saw starvation, and he felt very sad. He turned away, lifted the hood again, and checked the hoses and belts. He whistled another tune as he closed the hood. He said, "What have you been working on in shop these days?"

"I can't tell you, it's a surprise." Dodger removed the panel from the door, exposing the window roller.

"A present?"

Dodger nodded. "For the house. I'm getting each of you something else besides, but this is a present for the house." He had shown it to Brendan. On a slab of wood designed to hang over the front door, he had chiseled *THE FOSTER'S.* Brendan would bring it home next week when the varnish was dry. Dodger had argued against the apostrophe in order to leave ample room for the *S,* but Mr. Butz was a purist albeit an unlettered one, and the *S* ended up very thin.

"Catherine's rolling pin was sure nice," Hank said.

Dodger smiled at him with bald-faced love.

Returning from the movie at nine, Brendan said good-bye to Philip and Sam and stood for a few minutes in the dark. Through the kitchen window he saw his father and mother playing rummy with Dodger in the breakfast nook, and the sight filled him with a surge of ill will such as he seldom felt any more. Since January he had gradually overcome his resentment of Dodger. Yesterday and today on the track he had actually been proud to be Dodger's teammate;

in the 220 and the quarter-mile Dodger ran like the wind and left everyone behind. Brendan could hardly wait until tomorrow's track meet, where he and Dodger would represent Plum in the quarter-mile. Coach Torborg had explained that only Dodger would run in the 220 tomorrow because each runner was assigned a lane and entries were limited, but the quarter-mile would be open to all, including Brendan. Yet now, watching Dodger absorb his parents' attention as he picked a card off the deck and pondered his discard, Brendan felt the old resentment. Dodger was a very large pain in the neck. Not that he asked for any favors. He asked for practically nothing, but he needed everything. His very presence was an enormous demand. He needed food and clothes and a bed. He needed help with his homework and he needed to be told that he needed it. Worst of all, there wasn't a moment in the day when he didn't need companionship. Brendan had come to resent how soft his mother was on Dodger. She kept saying how touching it was that Dodger and Grandfather should be such great friends, Dodger asking again and again for stories, particularly the story of the deer that came indoors during the blizzard of 1871. Okay, so it was touching; Brendan could see that. More than touching it was a relief to have help in listening to Grandfather's stories. With Dodger tuning in, Brendan could tune out. But if Dodger and Grandfather were such pals, why didn't they room together? It was tiresome having Dodger in your bedroom night after night, breathing around his adenoids. It was downright depressing waking up every morning to the sight of that face looking at you from the rollaway and knowing that this guy you didn't have anything in common with wasn't going to let you out of his sight for the rest of the day. Catherine praised Brendan for his patience with Dodger, speaking of it in religious terms—Christian charity. She was right, of course—the nuns at St. Bonnie's had explained about Christian charity—but was there no limit to the things God expected you to do for others? Didn't God ever let you off the hook? Didn't God realize that while helping Dodger learn to be normal Brendan was in danger of becoming an outcast?

Last Sunday Pearl Peterson had organized a picnic at Pebble Creek, which Brendan didn't hear about until Monday morning in school. Everybody had been there—Sam, Philip, and Lorraine from the seventh grade, as well as Andy and his girlfriend and some other high-school students. Sam took along his fishing rod and caught a big sucker. They roasted marshmallows and drank pop. Brendan

accosted Pearl in math class the next day. "Pearl, how come you never told me about it?"

"Because you take your shadow wherever you go."

"What do you mean, my shadow?" He knew what she meant.

"I mean Dodger."

"So what? He just hangs around. He never bothers anybody."

"Listen, Bren, nobody wants to go to anything Dodger's at. He's so . . . You know, he's so . . ."

As Pearl scanned the ceiling of the classroom for the precise word, Brendan felt as if his heart were being crowded by a hard growth in his breast. It was his resentment of Dodger, and it felt like a coconut.

Pearl smiled her prim smile, having found the word. "Dodger's such a goon."

25

On Saturday morning Dodger withdrew the money bag from the hiding place he had chosen behind the dog food, and because they were pressed for time he gave it to Brendan, who was much quicker at distributing the coins and bills into their proper compartments. He then wheeled the produce from the walk-in cooler to the display rack, and together they made short work of setting out the lettuce and celery and other perishables. They called goodbye to Hank and Paul and dashed out into the sunshine. On their way to school they met Wallace Flint trudging to work looking bilious and sleepy. They exchanged no greeting with him. In the locker room they slipped into their track uniforms and their maroon and gold warmup suits and followed the rest of the team out to the bus. Crossing the schoolyard, they met Mrs. Pelzer on her way to work. She wished them luck.

They were on the road an hour. Stepping through the gate of Soldier Field, Brendan beheld four hundred boys warming up for the Rochester Relays. The track was cinders, black and smooth. The football field it circled was lush and green. The sun was high. A stiff breeze made the new flag over the pressbox stand out straight. A few runners were practicing their starts, dashing short distances along the track; others did calisthenics on the grass; most stood idly in groups, waiting. Brendan picked out the ice-blue uniforms of the Pinburg team, the orange and black of Clarkville, the red and blue of Lewiston, the green of Haymarket. These colors seemed holy to Brendan and caused something like worship to stir in his soul, as if the feats he and these four hundred boys would perform today—the

pole vault, the shotput, the quarter-mile—were the rites of a new and saving covenant.

Mr. Torborg blew his whistle, and his athletes gathered around to hear their instructions. The junior events, said the coach, would take place intermittently throughout the meet. He read aloud the day's schedule from his clipboard, and each time he came to one of Dodger's events he raised his eyes to Brendan, as if Dodger were his responsibility. At eleven o'clock Dodger would throw the discus. At one thirty Dodger would run in the 220. At three Dodger and Brendan together would run the quarter-mile.

When he finished reading, Mr. Torborg tucked his clipboard under his arm and said, "It looks to me like Clarkville and Lewiston are the junior teams to beat. Each one of them's got about ten boys suited up to our five."

"Just so we beat Pinburg," piped Philip.

The coach turned to his senior team. "As for you guys on the varsity, if you end up anywhere in the top twenty you'll be doing good. Last year Plum came in twenty-fifth."

"If you guys come in behind Pinburg, I'll puke," Philip said to the older boys, who ignored him.

The public-address system came to life with a ten-count, a cough and a message of welcome from the Rochester High School athletic director. Then everyone on the field—athletes, coaches, bus drivers—stood at attention while a recording of the national anthem blared from speakers, and currents of wind swirled through the stadium carrying the melody off in one direction and returning it from another. When the music ended and the first events of the day were announced, Dodger said to Brendan, "Let's go up in the seats."

"What for?" The vast seating, which curved around three sides of the field, held a scattering of about thirty people.

Dodger shrugged. "So we can sit."

"Who wants to sit?" It was Brendan's intention to spend the day darting from one event to the next, learning all the skills of track and field.

"Just for a while, I mean." Dodger was pointing to the top row of seats. "Just see what it looks like from up there."

"Okay," said Brendan, for he had resolved to devote these final two days entirely to Dodger. He hoped that by resisting all of his anti-Dodger impulses, not once ditching him or ignoring him, he might forestall any twinges of guilt when it came time to say goodbye on Monday.

Standing on the top row of seats where the wind blew strong, Brendan regarded the spectacle from above. The cinder-black track with its bright white lines looked like the college tracks in newsreels. That he himself would run on it seemed a miracle. Perhaps he'd be faster on cinders. He regretted being something of a hindrance to Dodger during their two practice sessions in Plum. Running a quarter mile with him, Brendan simply wasn't fast enough to keep up, and Dodger couldn't seem to resist turning his head to see how Brendan was doing. "Don't look back!" Coach Torborg shouted again and again, but Dodger kept doing it. "Promise me in Rochester you won't look back," pleaded the coach last night after practice. "You lose half a stride every time you turn your head." Dodger promised.

"Hey, Dodge, does running in a real track make you nervous?" Brendan asked.

Dodger didn't hear the question. He had moved away from Brendan and was looking out over the parapet of the stadium toward downtown Rochester, trying to spot a Woolworth store. He had certain presents in mind to give the Fosters and Grandfather before he left Plum, more expensive gifts than he could pay for, and he was partial to Woolworth stores because the Woolworth's in Winona had always been a pushover. And as long as he was at it, he'd pick up a greeting card for his mother, whose birthday, he guessed, was a week or so ago. He saw no Woolworth store from where he stood; trees obscured the west side of Broadway. He returned to Brendan and said, "I'm going downtown."

"What for?"

"Shopping."

"We aren't here to go shopping, Dodge, we're here to win ribbons."

"Yeah, I know, but we got all this time to kill."

"No, we haven't. You're throwing the discus at eleven."

"That's almost an hour, isn't it? I need to get my ma a birthday card."

Brendan looked at his watch. "It's not an hour, it's a half-hour. There's birthday cards in Plum."

Dodger didn't reply. It was impossible to pick things up in Plum. The storekeepers were laying for him.

The junior qualifying heats for the hundred-yard dash were announced. "Hey, look, Philip's getting ready to run—come on!" Brendan hurried down to ground level and reached the finish line of

the hundred-yard dash in time to see Philip come in last. Philip had more talent as an actor than as a runner. Coming off the track he draped his arms around Brendan and another teammate and hung limp between them, his knees buckling, his tongue hanging out. Brendan knew he had picked this up from the recent movie about Jesse Owens and the 1936 Olympics: athlete winded. A moment later Philip broke away and ran vigorously in place, his knees nearly as high as his chin: athlete rejuvenated. He stopped running and said to Brendan:

"It's not fair having us run on cinders, Bren. Running feels funny on cinders. Wait till you try it. If we run on grass at home, how come we can't run on grass here? I would have won on grass."

"Cinders are supposed to make you run faster."

"They don't though." Philip dropped to the ground and lay on his back with his eyes shut: athlete spent. "I'm faster on grass than anybody. Cinders feel funny. I didn't come in last, did I? Wasn't there other guys behind me?"

"One or two," Brendan lied, knowing how annoyed Philip got when the truth went against him.

Coach Torborg, hearing this, looked down at Philip and said, "There was nobody behind you."

Philip rolled over and buried his face in the grass. "Oh, no."

"But don't feel bad," the coach added, "you were up against older runners."

Philip spoke into the sod: "I hate cinders."

Brendan watched a few qualifying heats of the hundred-yard dash and then wandered over to the sawdust pit and watched the pole vaulters. From there he went to the high jump. After a few minutes at the high jump he felt a hand on his shoulder. It was Coach Torborg. "It's time for the discus, Brendan. Where's Dodger?"

Dodger was shopping. Four blocks from the stadium Dodger had found a drugstore that carried watches, but they were kept under glass and so he left the store after picking up only a birthday card for his mother and a small tin of Union Leader for Grandfather and slipping them up under the front of his sweatshirt. Where else, besides a jewelry store, might he find watches? Catherine's watch was in need of repair and he wanted to get her a new one. Jewelry stores were tough to crack.

Further along Broadway he came to an auto-parts store. He went

in and looked over the displays of tires and mufflers and other things in the showroom until a man came out from the maze of shelving behind the long counter and said, "What'll it be, Bud?"

"Have you got a gas cap for a DeSoto?"

"What year?"

"Twenty-eight."

"Nobody carries parts that old."

Which Dodger knew.

"Only place you'll find parts that old is a junkyard." The man returned to his maze.

Dodger opened and closed the door and remained inside. He continued to browse among the auto parts. He came upon a fan belt which he judged would fit the DeSoto. He slipped it under his sweatshirt and hurried away.

Across the street he stopped to tuck the waist of his sweatshirt into his warm-up pants. He walked down the street with his arms crossed, holding his loot in place against his chest. He came to a Woolworth's. He went in and walked the aisles. Passing combs, he picked out a small black one—Catherine had been urging him to carry a comb—and slipped it up his sleeve. He found watches. The more expensive ones were inside a display case, but the cheaper ones were on top, each one lying on a bed of cotton in its small, open box. He bent over and examined them closely. One looked nice enough for Catherine. It had a white face with small black Roman numerals and a black leather band. He took it, box and all, and slipped it up his sleeve.

He continued to walk the aisles until he decided that comic books would be Brendan's gift. On the comic book rack he saw at least three of Brendan's favorites (*Captain Marvel, Archie, The Katzenjammer Kids*) but the clerk facing him across the cosmetics counter—an elderly woman with a sour face—gave him no opportunity. He went outside, where he took the comb and the watch from his sleeve and slipped them down the collar of his sweatshirt. He tucked the waist more tightly into his pants, adjusted his load, and held it in place again by crossing his arms.

Passing a window of the Zumbro Hotel, he looked into the lobby and saw a newsstand. He went in. An idle bellhop, a registration clerk and an old man sleeping in a deep chair were the only people in sight. The clerk and the bellhop glanced at him without interest. He scanned the magazine rack and saw the new issue of Hank's fa-

vorite, *Popular Mechanics.* He considered picking it up, but decided that two gifts for Hank would be unfair to the others. He looked over the comics and found the same three he had wanted for Brendan at Woolworth's. He stood for several minutes waiting for his chance, and when it came—the registration clerk on the phone, the bellhop gone—he slipped his shirttail out of his pants and tucked *Captain Marvel, Archie,* and *The Katzenjammer Kids* up and under his armpit. As he did so, the fan belt fell out. He stiffened with the same jolt of fear he had felt last fall in the Winona gas station when the attendant came in and caught him robbing the till: cops, handcuffs, jail, Home School. But this time the jolt was a false alarm. No one was looking. The bellhop wasn't back and the clerk was still on the phone and the old man snored softly. Dodger gave himself ten seconds to relax and regain his lightfingered touch, then he picked up *Popular Mechanics* and tucked it under his shirt with the comics. He sauntered away, leaving the fan belt on the floor. Chances were it was the wrong size anyhow.

Out on the street, sensing that it was nearly time for the discus, he looked for a clock. In a jewelry window he saw a number of clocks and watches, but they all said different times. He set off toward the stadium, walking as fast as his shirtful of merchandise permitted and planning how he would wrap it all in his warm-up suit and hide it under his seat on the bus. He came to a clock over the entrance to a bank. Eleven thirty already? How could it be eleven thirty? It only proved what Grandfather always said at the end of the afternoon when Gordy reminded him it was time to go home: "My, how time flies when you're having fun." For this had been great fun. Stealing was his talent and his calling and it gave him a wonderful sense of accomplishment. It was wrong, of course, but when you walked into a store, how could you help casing it for clerks and floorwalkers and settling on the thing you wanted most and waiting for the right moment and then snatching it up and stashing it in your clothes in a single, natural, unhurried motion and walking out of the place in a casual way that hid your excitement? It was the best feeling in the world—ten times better than winning a footrace—and it felt especially wonderful when the thing you took was a gift for a friend.

In the parking area beside the stadium, all the buses looked alike and it took Dodger several minutes to find the right one. He found it locked. He stood for a minute with his arms crossed, looking left and right down the aisle between buses, wondering what to do next. He couldn't very well enter the stadium with all this stuff under his

shirt. He decided to hide it under the bus. As he was taking off his warmup pants, he heard the public address system announcing the winner and runner-up in the discus competition. He told himself that this was probably the senior competition; the junior event was yet to come. He tied one of the pantlegs shut at the ankle and filled the leg with his loot. He was about to push it under the bus when he heard Brendan calling to him:

"Hey, Dodger, where you been?" Brendan came running toward him between the buses. Behind him were the rest of the Pirates, senior and junior. It was noon and their sack lunches were on the bus.

"You missed the discus!" Brendan took Dodger's arm and gave him a shake. "You could have won, Dodger. Nobody came close to a hundred and twenty feet."

Philip came running, whining, "Hey, Dodge, what happened to you? Some guy won the discus that only threw it a hundred and ten. Boy, are you going to catch it from Mr. Torborg."

Dodger clutched his bundled-up pants to his breast and smiled warily at Mr. Torborg, who looked less annoyed than Philip, less disappointed than Brendan.

"We waited and waited for you, Dodger." The coach spoke softly. "I got them to hold up the meet while we all went around looking for you."

Dodger's eyes began to grow shifty. "I got sick."

"You did?"

"I threw up." Dodger pointed behind him. "Back over there, in the bushes."

"You don't look sick," said the coach.

"I'm okay again."

Brendan noticed how awkwardly Dodger was clutching his pants to his chest, and he realized where Dodger had been, what he'd been doing. Fearing that Coach Torborg, too, would understand, he stepped over to the bus and said, "Coach, could you unlock the door? I'm starving."

As Mr. Torborg drew out his keyring and unlocked the bus, he said, "He's your responsibility, Brendan. Promise you won't let him out of your sight this afternoon."

"I promise."

When the junior-high 220 was announced, Brendan accompanied Dodger to the starting line. Removing his gold sweatshirt, Dodger took his place in the third lane from the inside. He and the runner in

the fourth lane, a redhead from Pinburg, were a head taller than the other boys. Standing nearby, Mr. Torborg turned to the Pinburg coach and Brendan heard him ask, "Who's the redhead?"

"Transfer student from Iowa." The Pinburg coach was a small, round man.

"What grade's he in?" asked Torborg.

"Eighth. Name's Jerry Franzen."

"Big for his age, isn't he."

"Yeah, about like that runner of yours. How old is he?"

"Fifteen."

"Is he the ex-con I've been hearing about?"

Torborg looked pained. "That's a little strong. It was only the Home School."

"What else you got him entered in besides the 220?"

"Quarter-mile."

"I've got Franzen in the quarter-mile too. Ought to be interesting."

The starter, wearing a jacket of vertical black and white stripes, shouted "On your mark!" and the eight runners got down on their hands and knees. Studying Jerry Franzen, Brendan was reminded of the athletes pictured in magazines. He was somehow more colorful than real life. He had short hair, a tan complexion and shoulders already muscular at fifteen. His brow was knit in concentration, his eyes riveted on the track ahead. Dodger, by comparision, looked limp. His head was hanging down, his eyes on the cinders. His shoulders were scrawny and his ears stuck out. "Get set," said the starter and the eight boys tensed, rising to their toes. At the gun Franzen leaped off to a quick start and was two strides ahead of Dodger at the turn. Brendan and the others ran across the grass to the finish line and saw them come out of the turn neck and neck, well ahead of the other six runners. He saw that despite Franzen's athletic appearance and fast start, Dodger was the better runner. Franzen had a jerky way of pumping his arms and his head, while Dodger galloped like a stallion and broke the tape two strides in the lead.

Brendan leaped to his side and slapped him proudly on the back, shouting, "Way to go! Dodge, way to go!"

A Plum runner from the senior high shook his hand and said, "At least we'll take home one blue ribbon today." There was great satisfaction in Coach Torborg's smile, which was interrupted by Philip pulling at his arm and insisting, "I think the 220's my race, Coach. Next year I want to run the 220."

Franzen, recovering his wind, sidled up to Dodger and hissed, "You haven't seen the last of me."

"Swell," said Dodger, assuming that Franzen was proposing a friendship.

"I won four blue ribbons already this spring."

"You did?"

"In Iowa."

"Gee, that's swell."

"Just wait till the quarter-mile."

The afternoon grew warm and beautiful. The wind had gone down.The sky was cloudless. What breezes wafted through the stadium from the prairie south of town carried with them the smell of freshly-turned earth. A growing number of fans were trickling into the stadium and milling among the athletes on the field.

Among these fans, to Brendan's surprise, were Pearl Peterson and Lorraine Graham. Lorraine was wearing pink lipstick and a fluffy new sweater the color of her fluffy blond hair. Brendan went up to her and said, "Hi," proud to present himself in his maroon and gold warm-up suit. He greeted Pearl as well. Too long he had cultivated the image of the scholar. Though he didn't care much for Pearl, she was a girl nevertheless, and girls were impressed by athletes.

She looked him over. "Aren't your pants a little big?"

"They're supposed to be. They're warm-up pants."

"Have you won any races?" asked Lorraine.

"I haven't run in any yet. Dodger just won the 220."

The mention of Dodger caused Pearl's nose to wrinkle.

"You should have seen it. He beat that big guy from Pinburg."

Pearl looked where Brendan pointed. "Wow, you mean him with the cute haircut?"

"His name's Jerry Franzen. He's a crumb."

"Gee, is he handsome! Look at his shoulders, Lorraine. Don't you love track uniforms on boys? Those little straps over the shoulders?"

Jerry Franzen, pretending not to be listening, preened.

"He's a crumb," repeated Brendan, removing his sweatshirt. "He doesn't know the first thing about sportsmanship. He said he was going to get back at Dodger for beating him."

"I would too, if Dodger beat me. Dodger's the crumb."

"Oh, don't be so mean," Lorraine said to Pearl.

Brendan saw Dodger coming and changed the subject. "Who did you come with?"

"There's a bunch of us. Lorraine and me and Andy Romberg and

Norma Nash and Sam. Bren, would you introduce me to Jerry Franzen?"

"I never met him myself."

As Dodger came up and stood at Brendan's right shoulder, Pearl stepped over to Franzen, smiled up into his blue eyes and said, "A bunch of us from Plum are having a party at the creek tomorrow."

Franzen gave her a squinty, appraising look. "Yeah, what creek?"

"Pebble Creek. My name's Pearl." Brendan watched her put her whole face—lashes, lips, dimples—into a look that Franzen could not mistake for anything but adoration.

"Where's Pebble Creek?" asked Franzen.

"It's between Pinburg and Plum." There was a kind of music in her voice that Brendan had never heard before. "You leave Pinburg and go till you get to a big barn with a sign painted on it, and that's where you turn and go down the hill through the woods and there's the creek."

"Yeah? What time?"

"Two."

"Will there be beer?"

"Who knows?"

"How do you get there? You walk?"

"Some walk, some ride their bikes. A few of us have friends with cars. The sign on the barn is for spark plugs."

Brendan was annoyed by her refusal to see what an egomaniac Franzen was. But more than that, he was annoyed at being annoyed. Why couldn't he ignore Pearl and her party plans? Why did he feel that if he wasn't invited he would die of humiliation? What power did girls possess that by merely showing up with lipstick and curled hair they could set up this jealous competition in the otherwise pure hearts of boys?

Franzen told Pearl he might possibly show up at the creek, and he went jogging off to join his teammates.

Brendan moved over to her and said, "Don't tell me you're falling for him." Dodger moved with him.

"He's like a movie star," she said. "Lorraine, did you notice he's got whiskers and chest hair already? I'd love to see him run."

"He runs like a chicken." Brendan gave her a brief imitation of Franzen's jerky movements.

Dodger, to be of help, put in, "He runs at three o'clock. Me and Brendan run against him in the quarter-mile."

Brendan cringed, fearing he would cross the finish line far behind Franzen, far behind everybody, a sight Pearl and Lorraine shouldn't see.

Pearl said, "Come on, Lorraine, let's watch the hurdlers," and they set off across the field.

Brendan called, urgently, "Pearl, aren't you inviting me to the creek tomorrow?"

Pearl stopped and turned around. Dodger looked the other way, aware of what was coming.

"Consider yourself invited, Bren, if you come alone."

"Thanks," said Brendan with sarcasm.

For the quarter-mile there were no assigned lanes. It took the starter several minutes to arrange the twenty runners in three ranks. Dodger was in the second rank, with Brendan on his left and Jerry Franzen on his right. When the starter shouted, "Once around the track, boys," and added, "On your mark," snickering broke out as Dodger got down on all fours, having forgotten that in this race everyone started from a standing position. He got to his feet and nudged Franzen with his elbow to show he understood his mistake and could laugh at it, but Franzen wasn't wasting any energy on laughter. Franzen was biting his lip and looking nervous. It occurred to Brendan, witnessing this, that Franzen and Pearl Peterson were perfectly suited to each other, both of them so humorless. "Get set," the starter yelped, and the boys hunched forward, leaning from the waist.

The crack of the gun was followed by the scuffling noise of eighty shoes on cinders and a few grunts and curses as the aggressive runners fought for position by bumping the timid. Going into the first turn, Dodger moved ahead of Brendan and kept pace with Jerry Franzen in the lead.

"Go, Dodger, go!" Mr. Torborg shouted from trackside.

Brendan glimpsed Philip standing with Pearl and Lorraine. Philip hollered, "Step on it, Bren."

Coming out of the first turn Brendan was about halfway back. Ahead he saw Dodger lose a stride on Franzen as he turned his head to look back at Brendan. "Don't look back!" Brendan shouted to him, the words burning in his throat. The string grew longer on the straightaway, and though he gave it everything he had, Brendan fell farther behind. Jerry Franzen continued in the lead with Dodger

losing ground. As they came out of the final turn the Pinburg coach shouted, "Start your sprint!" and this was where Jerry Franzen—his sprint full of wasted, jerky effort—would have lost the race to Dodger if Dodger hadn't cut his speed in half in order to let Brendan catch up.

Jerry Franzen, the winner, was cheered and clapped on the back until he pleaded, "Air, give me air!" and he moved off the track and strutted back and forth on the grass. Pearl Peterson stood at a worshipful distance watching him breathe.

At the finish line, meanwhile, Coach Torborg watched Brendan and Dodger finish side by side and gave his clipboard a despairing toss in the air. "Dodger," he said, "what the hell was that all about?"

Dodger ignored him. With his half smile directed at his long shadow on the grass, he went walking off across the infield. He ignored Lorraine, who asked why he slowed down. He ignored Philip Crowley, who told him that he and Brendan had tied for sixteenth place. He ignored Brendan who asked if he was feeling all right. What he was feeling was an enormous sense of relief at having remembered, in the nick of time, his mistake with the boomerang. In front of everyone in the schoolyard, he had picked up the boomerang and thrown it twice as far as Brendan had thrown it, and he had almost lost Brendan for life.

26

Brendan, true to his vow to be Dodger's ally all weekend, pushed open the door, and when he saw that the coast was clear he motioned Dodger to follow him into the back room. Dodger had wanted to take his warm-up pants full of loot straight home, but Brendan reminded him that they were expected to help out at the market as soon as they got back to town. It was already after sundown. While Brendan took off his jacket and tied on an apron, Dodger went down to the basement and stuffed his bundle into an empty potato sack and left it in a dark corner. Then he climbed the stairs, put on an apron and helped Brendan replenish the apple and grapefruit bins. Business was brisk: Mrs. Pelzer rang up sales while Catherine bagged groceries and Paul carried them out to cars. Hank worked the aisles, helping shoppers find what they were looking for. Wallace, looking tired and speaking to no one, toiled away at packaging. At the first lull, Hank and Catherine approached the boys and asked about the track meet. Dodger pulled his blue ribbon from his pocket and handed it to them. Catherine said it was wonderful and Hank said, "Congratulations," but neither of them looked happy. They looked heavy-hearted and a little angry.

"Dodger, was this your week with the money bag?" Hank asked.

"Yep."

"Come up to the office. We have to have a talk."

Brendan followed, thinking he was included in the "we," but his father turned him back at the office steps, ordering him into the basement to fetch a supply of paper bags for the checkout counter.

Downstairs, curious to know what Dodger had brought home

from Rochester, he looked for the warm-up pants and found them in the potato sack against the back wall. He examined the watch, the magazines, and the tobacco. He guessed they were gifts for himself and his parents and Grandfather and he wondered if he, in Dodger's place, would have been so thoughtful.

As he started up the steps into the back room, his arms full of paper bags, he heard his father's voice coming through the opening in the wall high above him. "How much money do you have on you?"

"I guess about a quarter," Dodger replied.

"And how much at home?"

"I guess about two quarters."

Brendan laid his bundles on the step above him and stood with his ear cocked upward.

"Go through your pockets for us, would you?"

There was half a minute of silence before Catherine said, "Is that all?"

"Yep."

Hank spoke harshly: "We were five dollars short when we checked out last night and the cash register was another ten dollars short this morning when Mrs. Pelzer rang up her first sale. The five dollars could have been a mistake, I suppose, but when it happens two days in a row with you in charge of the money bag, it looks suspicious."

Brendan listened for Dodger to point out that he had not put the money in the till this morning—Brendan had done it—but he heard Dodger say only, "I never took it."

"Then how else could ten dollars disappear before a single sale is rung up?"

"And not only that," added Catherine, "didn't we hear you tell your father on the phone that you would bring him money?"

"Did I say that?"

"Yes."

"I don't think I said that. He asked me did I have any money and all I said was I did."

A long pause. If Dodger wasn't going to save his own skin, Brendan decided he'd better do it for him. He distinctly recalled putting the ten-spot in the till. It had to have disappeared after the two of them left for school. He was about to climb up to the office and explain this to his parents when he heard his father say, "You'll be staying in the house all day tomorrow, Dodger. No movie, no bike-riding until you level with us about the money."

At this, Brendan changed his mind. He picked up the paper bags and carried them to the front of the store. If Dodger was determined to cook his own goose, who was Brendan to interfere? With Dodger housebound tomorrow, Brendan would be free to go to Pebble Creek. After the party would be soon enough to clear Dodger's name. Unless, of course, Dodger or his parents spoke to him about the theft. Then he'd have to tell what he knew.

As the evening passed, it became obvious that his parents, as he expected, were discreetly keeping the theft a secret betweem themselves and Dodger. What surprised him was that Dodger, too, was keeping it under his hat—perhaps upon their advice. So Brendan allowed himself the luxury of imagining the fun he'd have at the creek.

During the next lull Brendan learned from Paul and Mrs. Pelzer, who were speaking in low tones at the checkout counter, that Dodger wasn't the sole cause of the trouble in the air. Wallace Flint, they said, had been acting moody and defiant. Ordinarily the packaging process was closed down on Saturday evenings, but Wallace, against Hank's wishes, had continued working.

Mrs. Pelzer told Brendan, "Your dad tried to give him his pay and send him home at suppertime, but he wouldn't go."

"He just kept weighing bags," Paul added, "and ignoring your dad."

"Look at him." Mrs. Pelzer nodded toward the back of the store, where Wallace was scooping something from a large bag into a smaller one. His movements were slow and mechanical, his eyes cast down. "He acts like he's in a trance."

Paul said, "Your dad told him he was caught up and not to open any more boxes or sacks of anything, but he's been opening them anyway."

"We're wondering how long before your dad blows up."

Wallace worked without interference until closing time; then he tidied up the packaging area and washed his hands. He wiped them on his apron as he strode up to the checkout counter, where Hank was counting the proceeds. "You can pay me what I was getting last winter," he said, "but eventually I'll want a raise."

"I'm sorry," said Hank, handing him his wages. "We've got all the help we need."

To Brendan, who was sweeping nearby, Wallace looked ghostly. His face was gaunt and white, his eyes hooded.

"Does this include tonight?" asked Wallace, counting the money in his hand.

"Yes, plus a tip for helping us out in a pinch." Hank turned back to the cash register. "Good night."

Wallace set his jaw, stood his ground. "What time on Monday?"

Hank spoke with his back to him: "Listen, Wallace, I can't hire help I don't need. Now please . . ."

"My mother might not come back to work."

Hank finished counting a handful of coins before replying, "We're expecting her back."

"She's not getting better. I might have to take her place."

Wheeling around, Hank raised his voice: "I do the hiring here! Don't plan on taking anybody's place!"

Brendan paused in his sweeping and stared, so rare was his father's anger. His mother, he noticed, was looking on from a distance. So were a couple of last-minute customers as well as Stan Kimball, who had dropped in to judge the success of the sale.

Wallace, untying his apron, said, "I'll come back in the middle of the week—give you a chance to change your mind."

"Don't come back, Wallace. Ever."

For several moments Wallace remained at the counter, watching Hank count quarters; then he turned and saw the several eyes upon him. A leering smile spread over his face as he took off his apron, dropped it on the floor and wiped his shoes on it. Still smiling, he walked out into the night.

Riding home with the Fosters in the DeSoto, Dodger had had no choice but to leave his bundle of gifts in the basement of the store, and now, lying in bed, he thought it just as well. He had not intended to present them in person anyhow. In order to avoid questions about where they came from, he wanted the gifts to be discovered after he'd left for Winona on Monday morning, and the store was as good a place as any. But he'd somehow have to bring them up out of the basement and put them on Hank's desk with a note explaining who got which gift. And he'd have to do it tomorrow. Getting a key was no problem; he'd take Catherine's key out of her purse. And sneaking away from the house might not be a problem either, if Hank and Grandfather took their usual long Sunday naps and Catherine spent the afternoon out in the back yard working on the shrubbery, as she had done last Sunday.

He turned and looked at Brendan in the adjacent bed. He was covered by moonlight and breathing softly, obviously asleep. Dodger was sorry to think that his time with the Fosters was ending on a sour note, but he simply couldn't squeal on Brendan. Brendan always had good reasons for what he did, and he must have had a good reason for taking the ten dollars. Besides, Brendan wanted to go to the creek tomorrow and he didn't want to go with Dodger. He hadn't said so, but Dodger knew it. A lucky thing, my being forced to stay home, thought Dodger. Now he can go without me and not feel guilty.

Brendan, feigning sleep so that Dodger wouldn't interrupt his thoughts, lay awake for a long time puzzling over the money. Having put the ten-spot and the rest of the change into the till, he had shut the drawer, which could be opened only by ringing up a sale. There had been no sales before he and Dodger left for the track meet. They had met Mrs. Pelzer on her way to work and they had met Wallace. Or was it the other way around? Yes, Wallace first. He would have arrived at the store five minutes or so before Mrs. Pelzer. On Friday morning Wallace had bought a pack of gum before Mrs. Pelzer showed up; Brendan had seen him ring up the five-cent sale and drop a nickel into the drawer. Had he taken out a five-dollar bill before closing it? This morning had he bought another pack of gum and taken out a ten—not only to line his own pockets but to get Dodger in trouble? Yes, of course. It was exactly what you'd expect of Wallace Flint. What a relief to be rid of him once and for all.

27

There was a hitch in Catherine's voice as she called her family to the table for Sunday dinner. After grace, which they all said in unison, Catherine added, "And we thank you, Lord, for giving us Dodger." Immediately her eyes filled with tears. She left her place and stepped into the kitchen, where she wept in silence. Tomorrow Dodger would resume his directionless life in Winona; if under strict supervision he couldn't resist stealing from the money bag, how could he be honest on his own? She fought back her tears and returned to her place at the table. Hank and Brendan kept glancing at her with curiosity. To divert their attention she scolded Grandfather for the fresh tobacco stains on his new shirt.

Grandfather, ignoring her, turned to Dodger and asked if he would join the track team in Winona.

"No," he said. "Track's too hard."

"But you should," said Catherine. "Track is what you excel at." She pointed to the wall over the buffet, where Dodger's ribbon hung from a pin.

"Yeah, I guess you're right. I guess I should." Though it was sometimes difficult to conform to Catherine's expectations, it was more difficult not to. But he wouldn't join. It wasn't easy being on a team. Everybody expected you to be a standout. Dodger had spent too much of his life standing out—or standing off to the side. What he wanted most in life was what he had attained with the Fosters—the chance to blend in.

"I remember my schooldays with loathing," said Grandfather, startling everyone with his vehemence. "Aren't you glad it's nearly summer?"

"I sure am," Dodger replied. He was happier than he could say, for very little remained of his education. He would turn sixteen in August, and then he could legally quit.

After dinner, after dishes, Hank went to sleep on the couch while Grandfather studied the section of the Sunday paper devoted to Roosevelt's life and death. Brendan followed his mother out into the sunny back yard and asked if he might bicycle with Sam and Philip to Pebble Creek, where Pearl and Lorraine were hosting a marshmallow roast. Catherine, pruning a bush, said yes, and he rode away on his bike.

The Sunday matinee was *Wonder Man,* starring Danny Kaye and Virginia Mayo. Standing in line at the box office, Wallace Flint studied the posters and was disappointed to see dancers. What he liked in a movie was a tense, grim story without dancing or singing. *Wonder Man* looked insufferably airy.

Down the street the Romberg pickup was parked at the curb and Wallace saw a number of youngsters pile out of it—Andy and Sam Romberg, Norma Nash, Pearl Peterson, Lorraine Graham—and go into Gordy's Pool Hall.

Wallace bought a ticket, stepped through the doorway and handed it to Philip Crowley, Sr., who tore it in half. He lingered in the lobby until the show began; then he walked down the aisle to the fire exit. Stepping outside, he saw Brendan jump off his bike and enter the back door of the pool hall. Waiting a minute in case Brendan reappeared, he heard the engine of the pickup come to life. He hurried through the passageway between the buildings and watched the pickup pull away from the curb with Brendan, among others, riding in back. He returned to the alley and let himself into the back room of the market, using a key he had stolen years ago from Kermit.

The two cats had been dozing in a pile of excelsior beside the walk-in cooler. During the sale Hank had given away six dozen cut-glass tumblers, which had been shipped to Plum in boxes filled with this excelsior. The gray cat rubbed against Wallace's leg; the yellow one remained at a distance and yawned.

He gathered up an armful of excelsior and went into the basement. He switched on the light and dumped the excelsior on the floor next to the rear wall. He looked at the four large hooks above him in the ceiling, from which stalks of bananas were sometimes

hung, and judged them to be almost directly beneath the walk-in cooler—exactly where he had seen them in his mind's eye as he lay in bed this morning planning the fire. Sifting through the embers and tracing the fire to its starting point, the firemen would blame it on faulty wiring in the cooler.

He went upstairs and brought down another armload of excelsior, then looked around for empty potato bags. He found three. He stuffed them with excelsior and hung them from three of the hooks. Searching for a fourth bag, he picked up the one containing the comic books, the watch, the can of tobacco, the birthday card and the current issue of *Popular Mechanics*. Such an odd collection, Wallace realized, could be only one thing, a cache of Dodger's stolen goods; therefore it gave him special pleasure to add excelsior to the bag and hang it from the fourth hook. He touched a match to the bags. The dry burlap crackled like kindling and the excelsior burned with a blinding, white-hot flame. Retreating to the steps, he paused to watch the flames cup the ceiling joists and lick at the floor above; then he hurried upstairs with the cats at his heels. He slid the remaining excelsior across the floor so it covered the wisps of smoke coming up between the floorboards next to the cooler. Then he went to the back door and opened it a crack. He cursed. Two men were pulling up to the rear of the pool hall in an old gray car. They were engrossed in a conversation that delayed their getting out. Wallace waited. The gray cat stood beside him, making hissing noises; the yellow cat paced the room, its tail twitching. When the excelsior beside the cooler suddenly went up in flames, ignited from below, the gray cat stood on its hind legs and planted its claws in Wallace's thighs. Stooping to smack the cat, he saw that his pants and shirt were covered with bits of excelsior. He brushed frantically, but the bits clung like lint. As the pile of excelsior turned quickly to ash, he saw that the wide floorboards beneath it were no longer so wide; gaps of flame were opening up between them. The smoke was thickening. The room was growing hot. The cats, he noticed, had vanished. Again he peered outside. The two men were gone. He slipped out and locked the door.

The cats, sensing someone at the front door, had streaked through the market, and the moment Dodger pushed the door open they shot outside to safety. Dodger shut the door and looked out the window to see if he'd been noticed. He had hoped to enter by the back door, but the only key in Catherine's purse was this one. Apparently no

one had seen him. He turned around, sniffing, and assumed that the stoker in the basement was emitting smoke, as sometimes happened when it ran empty of coal. But why was the stoker running on such a warm day? Then he heard the crackle of burning wood. He ran to the threshold of the back room and saw flames opening a hole in the floor. He started down the basement steps, but stopped, realizing that retrieving his bag of gifts was less important than putting out the fire. At the sink he filled a basin with water and threw it on the flames—to no effect but a thicker billow of smoke. Again he started down the steps and again he changed his mind: first he'd better phone for help. He rushed up to Hank's crow's nest and picked up the phone. There were ten or fifteen seconds of silence on the line, during which he watched the fire through the opening in the wall. The smoke at this level made it hard to breathe.

"Number?" said Constable Heffernand.

"Hank's Market's on fire!"

He dropped the phone and descended into the basement. He had to pass through a shower of fiery ash to reach the point along the back wall where he had left his bag of loot. The bag wasn't there. He was turning in a circle, looking for it, when the walk-in cooler leaned sideways into the disintegrating floor, tore itself loose from its wiring and crashed into the basement.

From his switchboard Constable Heffernand activated the fire siren atop the village hall. When Catherine heard it, she went indoors and woke up Hank, who had joined the volunteer fire department last October, recruited by Stan Kimball. He tied his shoes and hurried out to his car. Stan Kimball came over from next door and climbed into the front seat with him. Russell Romberg crossed the alley and got in the back.

"Where is it?" asked Hank, driving out of the yard.

"We'll find out when we get to the fire hall," said Russell Romberg.

"Where's the fire hall?" Since October there had been no fires.

Kimball directed him to a small, clapboard garage, where they found Len Downie already sitting behind the high steering wheel of the red truck, racing the engine, and Woodruff the postmaster and Legget the grocer climbing aboard. They wore helmets and rubber coats. Nicholi the barber was on the phone.

"Hank, it's your store," said Nicholi, hanging up and hopping onto the back step of the truck as it began to move.

The DeSoto followed the truck to the alley behind the market. When Hank unlocked and threw open the back door, a cloud of white and black smoke came pouring out. Next door the theater was being evacuated, moviegoers spilling through the fire exit into the alley. They were joined by the pool hall crowd, led by Gordy, who as a member of the department helped Nicholi pull the hose off the spool and tug it through the passageway to the hydrant on Main Street. Russell Romberg buckled climbing spikes onto his legs and ascended a power pole to cut off electricity to the store. Legget went around breaking windows with a small hatchet—more windows than necessary, thought Kimball, who told him to stop. Hank peered through the smoke and located the flames. They were climbing the wall where the cooler had stood. They were licking the ceiling. He backed out, making room for Woodruff and Downie, who braced themselves in the doorway and trained the water on the fire.

In ten minutes the flames began to diminish. In thirty the fire was out. Russell Romberg set up a large fan in the doorway, running the cord next door to the pool hall. When the smoke had cleared enough to breathe, Hank went inside. He stood at the edge of the hole in the floor and looked at the hole in the ceiling. He felt raped.

Constable Heffernand conferred on the stoop with Len Downie; then the two of them explained to Hank that unless the cause of the fire was obvious the deputy state fire marshal in Rochester had to be notified. It was Downie's theory, given the location, that the fire was caused by faulty wiring in the new cooler.

"The hell it was," said Russell Romberg. "I did that wiring myself and it was all up to code. Look at the floor—the size of that hole. Fire doesn't burn down, it burns up. It had to start in the basement."

They went downstairs with a flashlight and sloshed through the two inches of water standing on the concrete floor. It was the constable who first saw the arm and leg protruding from underneath the walk-in cooler.

"God almighty," Hank whispered, "it's Dodger." He recognized the checkered shirtsleeve and the tennis shoe. "It's Dodger," he said again as he tried to move the cooler off the boy, but it weighed at least half a ton and it took all four of them to tip it on its side. Hank knelt in the water and rolled Dodger over on his back. He felt splintered ribs through the bloody shirt. Lifting Dodger's head, he felt the spine bend in the middle as though hinged. Dodger was dead.

Downie called up through the hole, "Send Kimball down here."

Constable Heffernand climbed to Hank's office, where he found the phone off the hook. He told his sister to call the fire marshal in Rochester and the sheriff in Winona.

Hank went out to his car and drove home.

Catherine looked up smiling from the Sunday paper as he came into the room, his light Sunday pants begrimed, his eyes inflamed. "I was worried. I wish you hadn't agreed to fight fires." Then, reading his grim expression, she asked, "What is it?"

"The fire was in the store."

She put her hand to her mouth. The paper slithered to the floor.

"It burned the back room. We got it out before it spread to the front."

Grandfather turned off the radio—an account of this morning's burial at Hyde Park.

"But there's something worse," Hank said.

Catherine, seized by fear, grimaced and asked, "Dodger?" All day she'd entertained a series of fears about Dodger. They'd grown more insistent after she'd come in from the back yard and discovered that Dodger had sneaked away.

"We found him in the basement."

When Hank turned silently away, she sprang out of her chair. "You mean he's burned?"

He faced her. "He's dead."

"Dead?"

He nodded.

"Dodger's dead?" Her eyes shone with terror.

"The lad?" asked Grandfather, getting to his feet.

"The walk-in cooler fell through the floor into the basement. It landed on top of him." Hank moved to embrace his wife, but she stepped back.

"What was he doing there?"

"I don't know. I have to get back and meet with the sheriff and the fire marshal. Will you come?"

She nodded and strode through the house and out to the car.

"I'll come too," said Grandfather. On his way out he paused in the kitchen for a swig of bourbon.

Riding to Main Street, Catherine sat touching shoulders with Hank and trembling as she stared through the windshield.

"I'm not crazy about the way the Lord is running things," muttered Grandfather from the back seat.

Hank parked in front. They found the front door unlocked, Catherine's key in the keyhole. They stepped inside. Smoke hung from the ceiling like a layer of cirrus. None of the stock on the shelves had been burned or sprayed with water, but the stench of smoke and wet ash was pervasive. "I believe I'll go next door for a beer," said Grandfather, taking his leave.

"He's in the basement," Hank said to Catherine. "Do you want to come down?"

"Yes," she said. Then, "No."

"I'd better go down."

She nodded.

He found Stan Kimball alone with the body. He was standing on a wooden crate to keep his feet dry. His shoulders were hunched, his hands in his pockets, his gaze absent. Dodger, covered with a sheet, lay on a stretcher.

"Shall we carry him up?" asked Hank.

It took Kimball several seconds to gather his thoughts. He turned to Hank and said, "No, the sheriff will want everything as is. But I had to at least get him out of the water."

Reliving this Sunday in months to come, Hank would remember this picture: the man on the box, the boy under the sheet, smoky light filtering down through the hole in the ceiling, the floor of water below, the walls of stone.

"How's Catherine taking it?"

"It's hard to tell."

Catherine, crossing the back room, avoided looking down the hole. Kimball's black hearse, open and empty, was parked at the stoop with two dozen people clustered around it. The movie had resumed, but some of the moviegoers, preferring real-life drama, remained outdoors waiting for the sheriff and the fire marshal to arrive. Gordy, standing in the sun, nervously wiped his hands on his dirty apron as he watched Catherine approach.

"Terrible for you," he said, giving her elbow a consoling squeeze. She was stiff to the touch. Her eyes were dry.

Constable Heffernand said, "He wasn't a bad kid, was he, Mrs. Foster? There's some that couldn't say a good word for Dodger, but I wasn't one of them. Nor my sister either. We always said, Where would any of us be if we started life out with parents like Dodger's?"

Catherine pinched the bridge of her nose and stared at the hearse.

"I can't remember what Dodger's voice was like," said the Constable. "Did he sound like he had a cold?"

Catherine didn't answer.

"I'm trying to place the voice that called in the fire. It sounded like a teenager, and it sounded like his nose was plugged."

Catherine nodded. "Adenoids."

Legget the grocer, a sallow man with big ears, joined them and said, "I'm sorry about Dodger and I'm sorry about the fire damage."

She thanked him without moving her eyes from the hearse.

"I was changing my window display and I saw Dodger let himself into your store. It wasn't a minute later the whistle blew. If you want to bring your perishables across the street, I've got more refrigeration than I need."

She thanked him again, shifting her gaze from the hearse to a gray car that was pulling up beside it. It had an emblem on the door. Two men got out. Constable Heffernand shook the driver's hand and called him "Sheriff." He was an overweight, elderly man wearing a black suit and cowboy boots. He introduced his passenger, a red-haired man in shirtsleeves, as Doctor Burke, the county coroner. The constable led them inside.

The crowd of spectators increased. They waited for the body to come out, their voices subdued, their eyes on the doorway. The two cats showed up. The gray one purred at Catherine's feet. The yellow one kept its distance, sitting on Gordy's back step and looking distrustful. Paul Dimmitburg came walking down the alley. He went directly to Catherine and looked solicitously into her eyes as he listened to Gordy's account of what happened. He made some consoling remarks, to which Catherine responded with a mechanical smile. Her gaze had returned to the hearse.

In a few minutes Stan Kimball appeared on the stoop lighting a cigar. He was followed by Hank and Dr. Burke carrying the stretcher, which they slid into the hearse. Kimball got in behind the wheel and the doctor got in beside him. The hearse glided off down the alley, raising a thin trail of dust, as a red car pulled into the alley and parked in its place. This was the deputy fire marshal, a pudgy young man in a baseball uniform. He had been called away from a game. The crowd watched him confer in the doorway with the constable, then follow him inside. He limped. His number was twelve.

Stepping over to Catherine's side and taking her hand, Hank felt

shock setting in. He felt giddy and cold. "Are you all right?" he asked.

"I'm all right." It was true. She felt strong in a wooden sort of way. She felt, to her surprise, that if she allowed herself to shed tears there might be no tears to shed.

"How did it start?" asked Paul.

"The excelsior must have caught fire. There's a hole in the floor where we piled it, next to the cooler."

"What was Dodger doing in there?"

"God knows. Maybe hiding things. We found a watch in the basement, and a can of tobacco."

"Damn shame," said Legget. He repeated his offer of refrigeration.

"Thanks," said Hank. "We'll see what's worth saving when we open the cooler."

"Lucky the front end wasn't touched," added Legget.

Hank's "Lucky all right" was barely audible. Standing in the sun, he was shaking with cold.

Minutes passed. Grandfather came out and sat next to the yellow cat on the back step of the empty pool hall, sipping a beer he had drawn for himself. A procession of cars crept through the alley. A few moviegoers returned to the theater by way of the fire exit. Philip Crowley, Sr., remained outside, helping Nicholi and Woodruff feed the hose onto its spool. Russell Romberg taped up the severed cooler wires and restored electricity to the building.

The sheriff led the marshal and the constable out onto the stoop and asked the crowd, now numbering about forty, to gather close around. "Whatever you folks might know about this fire, I want to hear about it." He held a small, tattered notebook and a stubby pencil, ready to write.

Constable Heffernand spoke first. "I was tending the telephone switchboard. It was a boy's voice calling in the fire."

"Dodger Hicks," said Legget. "I saw him let himself into Hank's front door. I was working on my window display."

The sheriff, writing, asked Heffernand, "What did he say—his exact words?"

"Hank's Market's on fire."

"And he's the boy you found dead?"

The firemen nodded. Gordy added, "He's a ward of the Fosters."

The men stole glances at Catherine, whose eyes were far off.

"So Dodger didn't start it," Gordy continued. "I mean he'd hardly report a fire he started."

"Unless he started it by accident," said Russell Romberg.

"Wouldn't have been time," said Legget. "He went in the door and right away the whistle started blowing."

The fire marshal spoke up: "It doesn't look like an accident to me."

"Foster," said the sheriff, "what business did the boy have in your store on a Sunday afternoon?"

The constable answered for him: "We figure he was hiding stolen goods. He was a petty thief from the time he was a tyke."

"He had a key?"

"He took my wife's key," said Hank.

As the sheriff made notes, Catherine suddenly lost her distracted look and scowled sharply at the man in the baseball uniform. "Why did you say it wasn't an accident?"

"I said it doesn't *look* like an accident. There's the remains of burned excelsior in the basement. Somebody could have touched it off. That stuff goes up like gasoline."

Paul Dimmitburg said, "It must have fallen through the floor. We left a pile of it in the back room when we locked up last night."

"But that isn't all. There's a trail of it leading down the steps. Did you carry any of it into the basement?"

Paul looked at Hank, at Catherine. "No."

The sheriff turned a page in his notebook. "Now let's talk about keys, Foster. Who else has keys to this place?"

"Paul here. Myself. That's all."

"I doubt if that's all," said a voice from behind them. Everyone turned. It was Stan Kimball, who had left the body and the coroner in his embalming room and returned to the market on foot. "I'd be surprised if Wallace Flint didn't have a key from Kermit's time."

When Wallace left the kitchen and hurried through the dining room saying, "We've got company," Mrs. Flint imagined Grandfather dropping in.

"Will you see who it is?" she asked, straightening the pillows on the couch, but Wallace was already climbing the stairs. Then she heard a rapid pounding on the door that could hardly be Grandfather's; it was too loud, too impolite. She sensed trouble before she opened the door.

"Sheriff," announced the large, white-haired man who stepped inside without being invited. He was followed by three others, and she shrank back as they advanced. The fourth man, she saw to her relief, was Hank. The other two were Constable Heffernand and a stranger dressed in a baseball suit. Standing in the kitchen, they craned their necks to see into the rooms beyond while the sheriff asked her questions. Was Wallace home? Had Wallace been out earlier? How long ago had he returned? Would she go get him so they could talk to him? Answering, she thought it odd that Hank said nothing to put her at ease.

She went into the living room and called upstairs to Wallace, who said he'd be down in a minute. The men moved into the dining room. As she answered more questions, she wondered why on earth the baseball player was examining the pillows on her couch, the seat of her chair, the rug. Wallace had been to the movie, she told them. He always went to the movie on Sunday afternoon. No, he hadn't told her about any fire. No, he didn't have a key to the market. Nor did she. No (she lied, growing wary) she hadn't noticed any white particles on his clothing. She kept her composure until Wallace came down, then she retreated to her chair by the radio and sat facing partly away from the men so they wouldn't see her distress. Wallace, stepping boldly into the room, asked Hank, "Who are these men?" But Hank appeared not inclined to talk to him. It was the constable who answered:

"The law, Wallace. They've got some questions to ask you about the fire."

His mother, trembling, listened to enough of the interrogation to understand why her son had come home only a half hour after the movie began and why he had stood so long in the kitchen picking white crumbs off his clothes and dropping them into the range. As Wallace delivered his answers without the slightest trace of defiance or uneasiness, she turned and studied the faces of the four men and saw with great relief that they appeared to believe every word. Yes, said Wallace, he had gone to the movie. Yes, he had stood for a time in the alley with the rest of the moviegoers and watched the firemen at work, then he had gone home—the movie was too insipid. No, he had not told his mother about the fire for fear of aggravating her illness, for it looked to him as though most of the back-room stock was destroyed, which would put her out of work.

Because his setting the market afire was too horrible to think

about, Mrs. Flint shut out the men's voices and let her mind slip back to that other Sunday afternoon when outsiders invaded this room and a confrontation ensued. It was twenty years ago. Her dead husband's two brothers and their wives drove over from Wisconsin to visit. Wallace was whining and making a fuss during dinner (he was four) and without thinking she bent over and bit his hand. Her in-laws were shocked and angry. They talked of nothing else for the rest of the meal. They looked him over and found other bite marks. Since these in-laws were her means of support, she half believed them when they told her they had the legal right to take Wallace away from her. Leaving, they said they would report her to the authorities and return often to check the boy for signs of abuse. Later, she doubted if they told anybody, and it was nearly a year before their next visit, but they succeeded in scaring her. From that day forward she stopped biting him. She doted on him instead. She discovered that impatience and anger were much less gratifying than the remorse and love that replaced them.

"Look here!" sang out the man in the baseball suit. Startled, she turned and saw him holding up a curlicue of excelsior he had picked off the floor. As the men handed it from one to another, she despaired. She saw her son imprisoned for arson. Having made him so dependent upon her all these years, was she to blame for his terrible frustration? Should she have given in to his pleading and allowed him to join the high school debate team and go off to other towns and have his fits among strangers? Should she have permitted him to accept those scholarships and go off to Winona State and bite off his tongue in a dormitory room?

But her despair was unfounded. Wallace explained to the four men in a steady, relaxed voice that he had come home both Friday and Saturday with excelsior on his clothes, having unpacked the tumblers Hank had given away as Grand Opening gifts.

Brendan, sitting on a rock beside the water, was starting on his third beer. So was Jerry Franzen, the track star from Pinburg, who was sitting beside him and proving more amiable than he had been in Rochester. Both he and Brendan, as it happened, had read *Gone with the Wind,* and they were comparing their favorite parts, agreeing that for great writing it was hard to beat the leg amputation performed in a field hospital with a crosscut saw and no anesthetic.

Sam had waded upstream alone, carrying his cane pole, a can of worms and a bottle of beer. Philip, halfway up a pine tree, was

making noises like Tarzan. Lorraine and Pearl were gathering sticks to build a fire. Norma Nash and Andy Romberg stood in the creek holding hands and laughing at how funny their feet looked underwater. It was Norma who had supplied the beer, having been snitching from her father's supply for weeks in preparation for this party.

Though Brendan was where he had longed to be, he wasn't altogether happy. Besides the queasiness caused by the beer, he was feeling acute pangs of guilt over what he had done to Dodger. Or not done. He shouldn't have left him home unjustly punished. He should have come clean about the moneybag and brought him along to the creek. Sam, in fact, had asked on the way out from town, "How come you didn't bring Dodger?"

The noises in Philip's tree changed to groans, then to retching. "I'm sick," he cried faintly. Philip, too, was full of beer. He was hidden by pine boughs but his vomit began to be visible, seeping down through the needles. Philip himself came down next, dropping in stages, and when he let go of the bottom branch and fell to earth, his face was smeared with pine tar and tears. He lay in a ball with his eyes closed, moaning. Brendan turned away, somewhat nauseous himself, and was astonished to see his father advancing toward him through the bushes.

Everyone froze, caught holding beer. But Hank appeared not to notice. He fastened his eyes on Brendan and said, "Come with me." Brendan smiled a weak, puzzled smile at his friends and departed, following his father through the brush. Halfway to the road Hank halted and said, "There's been a fire at the store, Brendan." His eyes were inflamed, his lips thin and taut. "Dodger is dead."

He turned and resumed walking. Brendan, almost too stunned to move, followed slowly. They climbed up out of the bushes to the gravel road, where the DeSoto, leaning into the soft sand of the shoulder, was parked behind the pickup. His mother got out and threw her arms around him. Grandfather sat in back, wearing no expression behind the smoke of his pipe.

"Where's your bike?" asked Hank. "We'll put it in the pickup and let your friends bring it home."

"It's in town. We all came out in the truck."

Hank's reaction was a flash of anger. "I don't want you riding in that pickup. Ever." His biting tone frightened Brendan. "Andy's a reckless driver."

Brendan got in with Grandfather. Hank started the car, turned it

around and climbed up out of the ravine in second gear. When they stopped at the hilltop intersection, Brendan asked, "You mean Dodger burned to death?"

They sat with the engine idling, facing the giant spark plug on the barn across the road, while Hank told him what he knew of the facts. He said the fire marshal suspected arson, and Stan Kimball suspected Wallace, but there was no way to prove it.

"Do you think they're right?" asked Brendan.

"I don't know what to think."

"Mom, what about you?"

Catherine shook her head slowly, inscrutably.

"Have you any idea what Dodger was doing in the store?" His father was looking at him through the rear-view mirror.

"He brought home some things from Rochester and was hiding them in the basement."

"Hiding them because they were stolen?"

"Because they were presents, I think. Going-away presents for us."

Catherine, turning her gaze out her side window, saw Plum tucked into its fold of hills three miles away, two steeples, a grain elevator, and a water tower protruding above the elms. She said, "I can't believe we live in that town. It's like having a nightmare and never waking up."

Brendan, along with Grandfather, was dropped off at home, and his parents continued on to Kimball's Furniture and Funeral Home. Grandfather fell asleep on the couch. Brendan went out and sat under a tree in the back yard, waiting for the pickup to return from the creek; he was frightened—if Dodger could die then Brendan could die—and he wanted friends to divert him. He heard a snapping of twigs and looked nervously about him, sensing death's presence nearby. His eyes fell on the large brushpile his mother was adding to week by week as she pruned the shrubbery. He imagined death taking up residence there. The brushpile was a short leap to any house in the neighborhood. Whose house was next? Would death strike Brendan's house twice in a row? He felt a powerful urge to run indoors and see if Grandfather still breathed, but he was paralyzed by a renewed snapping of twigs. The brushpile seemed to be moving. After a moment of terror he saw Larry-the-Twitch come crawling out from the midst of it. He hopped toward Brendan on one foot and threw himself on the ground. He scratched his chest and ankles and head and picked at the grass. "Dodger got killed."

"I know it."

Larry gave him a disgusted look. He had the sort of pinched face that comes from amounting to nothing in the eyes of older brothers. For once he knew something before his brothers knew it, but his brothers weren't home to tell and it wasn't news to anybody else.

"My dad says you'll probably keep Dodger in your house because it's expensive to keep a body at Kimball's."

Brendan was horrified. Death in the house?

"My dad says he'll be okay to look at. His ribs are mashed but his head is okay."

"Your dad saw him?"

"My dad's a fireman. He put out the fire. If it wasn't for my dad the fire would have burned down your store and the movie house and the pool hall. It might have burned down the whole town." He rolled over on his back and probed his nose with a twig. "What's it feel like to get killed?"

Brendan went indoors. He lay on the floor of the living room, paging through the Sunday paper while keeping an eye on his sleeping grandfather and listening to him breathe. When Grandfather awoke, he told him what he was afraid to tell his parents:

"They think Dodger stole money from the store. Dodger didn't steal it. I think Wallace stole it."

Grandfather, drawing on his pipe, opened and closed his hand in a beckoning way, as if asking to hear more.

Brendan told him that he had wanted his parents to think Dodger stole the money so he could go to the creek without him. He said that if he had come out with the truth right away Dodger might be alive. They might have gone to the creek together no matter what Pearl Peterson said. Who cared what Pearl Peterson said? Did she own Pebble Creek? Saying these things, Brendan realized that never in his life had he felt so close to Grandfather. Never before had he opened his heart to Grandfather in exchange for the five hundred stories Grandfather had told him. Listening to Grandfather over the years, Brendan had always been aware of the man's great age, but now, their roles reversed, the six decades between them fell away to nothing.

"No, it can't be tomorrow," said Stan Kimball, sitting behind a walnut desk at the rear of his furniture display room. "The grave won't be dug."

"Then Tuesday," said Catherine. She and Hank were facing the

undertaker on dining room chairs with orange price tags dangling from their ladder backs. The chairs were $48 apiece, the walnut desk was $179. "At Holy Angels," she added.

Kimball searched his pocket for a cigar. "You know as well as I do, Catherine, that a non-Catholic can't be buried from a Catholic church."

"Dodger went to Mass with us every Sunday." The memory of him beside her in the pew brought tears to her eyes.

"But he wasn't a Catholic."

"Not yet. We didn't want to press him. It would have come about."

"I'm sorry, Catherine." He lit his cigar. "You'll have to have the funeral here."

She turned in her chair, scanning the display room, the furniture standing in crooked rows, the upholstery smelling of cigars, framed prints of flowers and windmills hanging on the walls, everything adorned with an orange price tag.

"I'll talk to Father O'Day."

"He of all people, Catherine. In seven years I've never known him to bend a rule."

"I'll talk to him."

While Hank went into the basement with Stan Kimball to select a coffin, Catherine used the phone on the desk. Waiting for the priest to answer, she looked at her watch. They had spent nearly an hour on these arrangements. It had taken the Winona police most of that time to locate Mr. Cranshaw, who was away on a family outing, and when he returned Kimball's call it was too late to reach Dodger's mother, who according to her landlady had gone out for the evening. Cranshaw next phoned Stillwater and broke the news to Dodger's father, who crumbled, making sighing and sniffing noises over the phone and saying "No, no, no," when asked if he wanted to be consulted about funeral arrangements. Cranshaw, phoning Plum for the second time, advised the Fosters to make the decisions and he would try to round up Mr. and Mrs. Hicks for the funeral.

"Hello. Holy Angels."

"Father, this is Catherine Foster. The boy who has been living with us was killed this afternoon."

"What's his name?"

"Dodger Hicks."

"Are you calling for the last sacraments?"

"No, it's too late for that. I'm calling to ask if you'll have the funeral at Holy Angels."

"What did you say his name was?"

"Dodger Hicks."

"He belongs to the parish, does he?"

"No, but he came to Mass with us every Sunday.

"Catholic, is he?"

"No."

"Then you can't have the funeral here."

"But my husband and I are Catholics, and we're his guardians."

"Nobody's Catholic by association. Every soul is separate in the sight of God."

"Father." She swallowed her rising indignation and tried to sound less fiery than she felt. "I'm appealing to you as my fellow Christian."

"What did you say your name was?"

"Catherine Foster."

"You're new in town?"

"We moved here last September."

"Then why haven't you registered?"

"Father, don't you remember us? We have the store. Hank's Market."

"The precepts of the Church are very clear on this. It's your duty to register with the priest as soon as you move into a parish."

Catherine hung up and set about rearranging Kimball's furniture for the funeral.

28

On Monday evening the four of them took their places in the DeSoto and drove to Kimball's for Dodger's hour of visitation. They wended their way through the furniture to the back of the store, where Stan Kimball was switching on a few floor lamps and table lamps and Dodger lay in creamy satin. Brendan had not expected Dodger dead to look so much like Dodger alive. Yesterday morning Brendan had awakened and seen him exactly like this, lying on his back on the rollaway, snoring lightly. Catherine wept and Grandfather turned away. Brendan wandered up and down the rows of furniture, death riding his shoulder and whispering into his ear about people going into the ground in sealed boxes. He heard his father and Kimball reciting a litany of groceries. Flour. Cereal. Cookies. Butter. Meat. The day after tomorrow the market would reopen for a week-long fire sale, and they were enumerating products that might have absorbed a smoky smell and should be sold well below cost. Sugar. Cheese. Dried fruit. Bread and rolls.

Visitation brought only three visitors. Mrs. Lansky of the rooming house patted everyone on the arm and moaned, "Poor Dodger, poor Dodger." Paul Dimmitburg stayed the whole hour, saying little. Coach Torborg endeared himself to Catherine and Hank by offering to bring members of his varsity track team to the funeral to act as pall bearers. Leaving, he said to Catherine, "Good luck at the polls tomorrow," and it was a moment before she remembered that she was running for the school board. When the hour was up, Kimball switched off his table lamps and floor lamps and locked the door, leaving Dodger alone among the dining room sets.

At home Grandfather went straight to the radio, turned on *Doctor IQ*, picked up a section of the evening paper and divided his attention between the quiz show and the news from the Pacific. Hank, too, was silent, sitting across the room from Grandfather and opening another section of the paper. On an inside page he found a short article about the fire: arson was ruled out after a suspect, unnamed, had been questioned but not arrested. Catherine, her eyes moist, settled into the couch and asked her father for the page with the daily recipe and dress pattern, both of which she studied at length. Sometimes even the roomiest house lacked enough partitions for family living, Brendan observed, and on such occasions in this house the *Rochester Post-Bulletin* became a folding wall. He asked his father for the sports page.

The next morning Catherine and Hank went driving in search of blossoms for the funeral. A mile or so beyond Higgins Hill they spied a crabapple thicket at the far end of a grassy meadow. Hand in hand they crossed the meadow. They broke off armfuls of sweet-smelling, white blossoms. On the way back to the car Catherine said, "I have to leave town, Hank."

He walked beside her with his head bowed, waiting for more. He was not surprised. He had feared this very thing.

"I want to go and stay in St. Paul with Aunt Nancy."

They came to the road and stood in front of the car. He did not look at her. He looked at a bird perched overhead on the power line. He listened to frogs croaking in the wet ditch. He was afraid to ask how long she would be gone.

"You see why, don't you Hank? Ever since the first time I stepped into the store and saw the mess Kermit left behind, I've wanted to run away. I wanted to run away when the rumor went around about Wallace being my lover. In the winter when we moved to Bean Street and Mrs. Brask began instructing me on how to behave and hardly anybody came to our New Year's tea, I wanted to leave and never come back. There hasn't been a day in the past seven months that I haven't wanted to go back to the city. And now this."

"Not one day?" He swept his eyes over a field of new grain, a field of new corn, a pasture. Did she intend to leave forever? If so, he must follow. He felt like weeping.

"Not one," she said with conviction.

In the fields each stem of grain was a small blade of grass, each corn sprout the size of a tulip. In the pasture stood a herd of brown

and white steers. Never before had he been so deeply impressed by the rich look of this farmland. He saw prosperous years ahead, the war ending, young men returning to the farms, price ceilings no longer imposed by Washington, Hank's Market reaping greater profits. "Not even the day we moved into our new house?" he asked.

She didn't answer.

"Think what we have here, Catherine." He faced her. "The house and the market. The way your father and Brendan have taken to the place."

"It's not enough, Hank. Nothing's enough now." Her cheeks were pale as bone. Her eyes were slits. "Dodger meant something different to me than he did to you."

The bird overhead warbled a long, arduous melody. The steers in the pasture faced the road with their ears perked, as though listening to Hank plead, "How can you say that, Catherine? You have another boy besides Dodger."

At this she dropped her blossoms and threw herself at Hank, sobbing, "He won't die, will he, Hank?" She shuddered in his arms.

"Of course not."

"If Brendan died, I couldn't go on living."

He patted her on the back.

"And you won't die, will you, Hank?"

"I'm healthy as an ox."

"I have this feeling everyone is going to die." She shook with loud, choking sobs.

After a long embrace, he picked up the blossoms and they got into the car. After they drove away the steers continued to stare at the place where they had stood. The bird on the wire fell silent. The frogs in the ditch croaked on and on.

Entering Kimball's twenty minutes before the funeral, they found no one present but the undertaker, no names in the visitors' book since last night. Grandfather chose a soft chair and sat down while Brendan and his parents stood at the coffin—briefly this time, the sting of death blunted now, the shock gone, nothing more to be learned by gazing down into Dodger's face, which was taking on the look of a museum artifact, waxy and ancient. Brendan drifted to the front of the store and looked out the window while Stan Kimball helped his parents arrange the apple blossoms in vases at Dodger's head and feet.

Next to arrive was Mrs. Lansky. She spent a minute at the coffin,

then she took a seat next to Grandfather and said to him, "Poor Dodger."

"Yes, quite the good lad," he replied, and considered going on at length about Dodger, how agreeable the lad was to live with, but he lacked the gumption. He was feeling low. He had felt this way when Roosevelt died. When Sade died. Whenever one of his fellow trainmen died. When relatives and friends died. Oh, was there no end to it? His spirits rose when he saw Mrs. Clay come in wearing her wide straw hat and her pink dress. She plopped into the chair on his right and patted his arm. He picked up her hand and gave it a kiss.

Paul Dimmitburg arrived carrying a Bible. He conferred with Catherine and Stan Kimball about the service he would conduct.

An old car louder than Hank's pulled up to the curb and backfired as the engine died. The driver, a man wearing a soiled Stetson and a baggy blue suit, got out and went around to the passenger door, which required all his strength to pull open. A tall, long-faced woman got out. Mrs. Lansky, turning in her chair, identified her as she came through the door: "Dodger's mother, poor thing."

Dodger's mother was drunk. She lurched up to the coffin, where she uttered a searing, bone-chilling shriek that quickly softened into a whimper. Her escort, too, had been drinking, as was apparent in his studied manner of walking; he picked up his feet and put them down as though trudging through snow. Coming to a stop at the coffin, he removed his large hat and held it over his stomach, and when Mrs. Hicks turned to him and said, "Christ almighty, my Dodger!" he led her to a matching set of dining room chairs. Catherine and Hank went over to her and said how sorry they were, which caused her to wail anew. "Here," her companion said, handing her a small flask. She took a swig and was consoled. She looked up at Hank and said, "Who do we sue?" Hank froze. The possibility of a lawsuit had not entered his mind. Stan Kimball stepped between them and told Mrs. Hicks that whatever litigation might ensue, this was neither the time nor place to bring it up. As he patted her on the shoulder she clutched his arm and wiped her eyes on his pinstriped sleeve. Then she took another swig from the flask and said, "Where's the preacher? Let's get on with it."

Coach Torborg and his runners came in and sat on two sofas. It was time for the service to begin, but Catherine, expecting a larger turnout, asked Paul to wait a minute or two. Brendan, still at the window, doubted if anyone else was coming. There were many cars

parked along Main Street, many shoppers crossing from store to store, and no one was heading for Kimball's. Plum wasn't pausing to mark Dodger's passing.

Stan Kimball closed the coffin. Hank stepped up and placed Dodger's blue ribbon on the lid. Brendan took a seat between his parents. Paul solemnly cleared his throat and said, "Dear friends." He was interrupted by the arrival of Mr. Cranshaw and Dodger's father, a pale, wizened man who looked nothing like his son except for his long teeth and his way of exposing them as he smiled apologetically. He took a seat behind the Fosters. Cranshaw sat in a distant armchair.

It was then, as Paul began reading from Luke, that Brendan achieved his breakthrough to God. Dear God, he thought, let people live! They were his most earnest words to God, ever. Until now he had mustered this sort of urgent feeling only for certain saints—Mary, Bonaventure, Brendan—but this was high-intensity prayer straight through to God Himself. He was certain God was listening—he could feel the current. In a flash everything he'd been taught by the nuns seemed confirmed: every human voice, though a whisper, though a silent thought, had reverberations in a world apart from this one. God, he pleaded again, his eyes on the dark gray coffin, let people live.

Paul put down his Bible and stated, to the amazement of most of the mourners, that Dodger had been a lot like Jesus Christ, and with this he embarked on the daring sort of sermon he couldn't get away with in church, his father's parishioners being (in his view) too hidebound and smug to understand Christianity's challenge to love one another. "Dodger's ways were not our ways, and our ways were not Dodger's ways," he said, his voice low and resonant, his eyes roving the faces before him. "Like Christ, Dodger passed through the world wanting next to nothing for himself. All he asked was to be accepted." (Here Brendan lowered his head, afraid that Paul's accusing eyes would fasten on him.) "For all we know, God might have sent Dodger on the same mission as His Son—to put us to the test, to bring us the message about loving one another to see how we reacted to it. True, Dodger was a thief, but he did not steal to accumulate the goods of this world. He stole out of need and he stole out of generosity. He stole in order to keep his body and soul together and he gave away the rest. His heart was larger than most, and he deserved better than he got from us. If the people of Plum, including myself,

had been more open-hearted with Dodger, his life, though short, would have been happier and we would feel much less guilty today as we carry him to his grave. Take at least one thing home from Dodger's funeral: my assurance that each time we fail to care for one another we carry out, one more time, the act of crucifixion."

Paul picked up the Bible and read a psalm. Then he asked everyone to recite with him the Lord's Prayer. They got to their feet and did so. As he concluded by calling down God's blessing on everyone present, Dodger's mother wailed anew.

Stan Kimball asked Mr. Hicks if he'd like the coffin opened so he could look at his son. "No thanks," he said, smiling in a dazed, bleary way. Having been released only yesterday from Stillwater, he had not yet fully comprehended his freedom, much less his son's death. He wore a dark suit that had evidently belonged to somebody else, somebody shorter and heavier. When Hank and Catherine introduced themselves and offered their condolences, they were amazed by his gracious response. "You people deserve the condolences," he said. "You were better parents to Dodger than I ever was."

Dodger's grave stood open and waiting on the non-Catholic side of the cemetery. Nearby was a fragrant lilac hedge full of chattering sparrows. Mr. Torborg and his athletes settled the coffin on the taut straps over the grave and Paul, in the briefest of terms, commended the body to the earth and the soul to God. Paul was undemonstrative by nature, but because one of his professors in St. Louis had recommended the graveside embrace, he turned to Dodger's father and gave him a hug. Dodger's father wept for a moment in his arms. Then Paul turned to embrace Dodger's mother, but she fended him off by swinging her purse and shouting, "Keep your hands off me, Buster." Mrs. Clay stepped in and served as her substitute, slipping her arm around Paul's middle and laying her cheek on his chest.

The polls were open from four to eight. On her way to the school with Hank and Grandfather, Catherine tried to picture herself on the board and couldn't do it. She couldn't imagine living in Plum long enough to serve out her term. Or even begin her term. The woman who had filed for election was someone else, someone capable of sitting through biweekly meetings with the likes of Mayor Brask and maintaining her optimism about the village school system. About the village. About herself as a villager. So why was she

voting? For Hank's sake? Yes. She wasn't ready to tell Hank that she'd given up on Plum forever.

The polling place was the school gymnasium, and the election officials were the principal's secretary and Constable Heffernand. They sat behind a trestle table at midcourt and handed out ballots with Catherine's name printed above a space for a write-in candidate.

"How's the turnout?" Hank asked.

The constable tipped back his chair and put his feet on the table. "Pretty slow. It's going to be a long four hours."

The secretary consulted her tally marks. "Your three votes make eighteen so far. We've only been open half an hour."

They marked their ballots and dropped them into a scoured lard bucket with a slot in the cover.

In order to appear indifferent toward the election, and thus inspire indifference in the Catholic electorate, the mass of Lutheran voters waited, by prearrangement, until seven thirty to begin crowding into the school and writing Leonard Downie's name on the ballot, and when the results were announced shortly after eight o'clock, Catherine was defeated by nearly two hundred votes.

Stan Kimball carried the news to the Fosters. He was surprised by how little it seemed to matter to Catherine, who smiled in a mysterious way and thanked him for his vote and his concern. Leaving the house by the back door, he drew Hank outside and said to him on the veranda, "You're a babe in the woods, Hank. You're too innocent for life in this town."

"What are you talking about?"

"You put up money for buying Mrs. Ottmann's big house."

"Part of the money. A hundred dollars."

"And you have no idea why the Catholic Men's Club bought that house, do you?"

"To raise money for church repair. We're going to fix up the house and sell it at a profit."

"You had no idea, did you, that the Lutherans intended to buy Mrs. Ottmann's house and convert it into a parochial school?"

"No."

"As soon as your Men's Club got wind of the Lutheran school, they put together enough money to take the house off the market. And that's why the Lutherans ganged up on your wife today." Kimball went home.

Hank stood at the railing for a few minutes, looking out over the dark lawn, then he went in to break the news to Catherine. He found her ironing a dress for her trip to St. Paul. He told her about the hundred-dollar check he had given B. L. Skeffington and Philip Crowley and about their ostensible reason for wanting it as opposed to their real reason. He said he had helped bring about her defeat. He said he felt awful.

She shrugged. "Don't feel awful, Hank. It makes no difference." And when he saw in her face that this was the truth, he felt worse.

29

Catherine was gone a week when she sent home a breezy account of her progress through Aunt Nancy's four-bedroom apartment—cleaning, papering, painting. She said she had gone to Dayton's and had a long, happy chat with her former co-workers. Also she had spent a day with her cousin Ann and Ann's daughter Julie, who asked about Brendan. She said Uncle Howard was on his way home from the North Atlantic and after a ten-day leave, which he and Mae would spend in St. Paul, he was to take up a new assignment in the Pacific. Howard was in touch with Northwest Airlines in Minneapolis about a postwar job as a pilot. Catherine would remain in the city a while longer in order to see her sister. How was Brendan? How was Grandfather? How was Hank? How was business? How was the repair work coming along? Was she missed?

Brendan, caught up in the novelty of bachelor life, didn't miss her very much. Weeknights he and his father took turns preparing supper, and on weekends they went with Grandfather to Gordy's and ate the evening special, usually hamburger steak and fried potatoes. Brendan had remained on the track team and participated in another meet, winning no ribbons but at least outrunning Philip in the hundred-yard dash. A senior-high teammate was tutoring Brendan in the discus.

Grandfather was slow to emerge from the malaise that had begun on the afternoon of the President's death. Day after day he stayed home from the pool hall and listened to the radio news, as though Roosevelt had left him (along with Eisenhower) in charge of the European front. His grief was somewhat mollified near the end of April

when Mussolini was captured, shot, dragged to a public square in Milan and strung up feet first to the beams of a gutted gas station. His spirit quickened in the first week of May when, after a seven-week siege, Berlin fell to the Russians. A few days later when he heard that Germany had surrendered and Hitler was dead, he put on his light spring coat and resumed his daily trips downtown. Japan he would leave to MacArthur.

Hank missed his wife day and night. He spent all his waking hours at work, trying not to speculate about her intentions. "Awhile longer," her letter said—that meant she was coming home, but for how long? While Mrs. Pelzer and Mrs. Flint cleaned the smoky residue from the shelves and stocked them with fresh merchandise, Hank worked with Paul Dimmitburg and Russell Romberg, repairing the back room and installing a new refrigeration unit. His few minutes of leisure each day were spent over a cup of coffee in the pool hall, and that was where it became apparent to him that while the authorities had not seen fit to arrest Wallace and charge him with arson, the village at large had convicted him and passed sentence. There wasn't a merchant along Main Street who hadn't been convinced by Stan Kimball that Wallace had started the fire. Never as long as he lived, they vowed, would Wallace find employment in Plum.

Hank was more perplexed by this than gratified, for he was far from certain of Wallace's guilt. Lacking clear evidence, he found it hard to imagine Wallace capable of a crime so grave. Further, he found it conducive to his peace of mind to blame the fire on the wiring. "Do you fellows know something I don't?" he asked Stan Kimball. "How can you be sure it was Wallace?"

"What you're seeing here is small-town justice," Kimball explained. "Oftentimes a town as remote as Plum gets overlooked by the law, and the citizens have to be their own judge and jury. The sheriff decides there's not enough clues to make a case against Wallace, but the people who've known Wallace all his life find more than enough clues in their hearts. For the rest of his life Wallace Flint is going to be known in this town as the man who set fire to Hank's Market, and everywhere he looks he's going to see accusing eyes and he's going to live out his days in a kind of solitary confinement. Tell that to Catherine when you see her. Maybe it will help."

Catherine was gone for three weeks. On a Friday afternoon in mid-May, Hank drove to Highway 61 to meet her bus, and when he

saw that she had only one suitcase (she had left with two) his dread was confirmed: his days in Plum were numbered. On the drive home she was full of city news. Howard had come home from the Atlantic and left for the Pacific. Mae and Catherine were staying together at Aunt Nancy's. There was a terrific housing shortage and Catherine felt obliged to return to the city and help Mae find an apartment, for Howard would surely be discharged within six months; it was everybody's opinion that Japan couldn't last longer than that. Coming up over Higgins Hill, she glanced ahead at the village without the slightest interruption in her talk. There was a lilt in her voice such as Hank hadn't heard for a long time, an excitement in her eyes, a radiance in her smile. This was not the Catherine of the past winter and spring. This was the Catherine he had married. This Catherine would never be a villager. And thus neither would he.

Grandfather and Brendan were overjoyed to have her back where she belonged. Bachelor life had very quickly grown stale; the house without its heart had grown lifeless.

The next day, Saturday, Catherine helped at the market. Paul Dimmitburg's greeting was as warm as his grave manner would allow. "How are you?" he asked, sincerely wanting to know. "Never better," she told him. "The city is my tonic." She was greeted cheerily by Mrs. Flint and Mrs. Pelzer, who had become the closest of friends. When asked about Wallace, Mrs. Flint spoke of him in a light, dismissive manner, saying that a house could accommodate only one recluse at a time and Wallace had taken over where she left off. His hobby, she added, was painting portraits of movie stars.

Neither Paul nor the two women got much of Catherine's attention while she was in the store. What time she stole from clerking she devoted to Hank, engaging him in hushed, urgent conversation in his office. Their manner together made Brendan uneasy. He recalled their talking like this last summer, before their decision to move to Plum.

Because Father O'Day was gone on vacation, the priest celebrating Mass the next morning was a stranger. He was a large, handsome man scarcely thirty years old, and he opened his sermon with a joke. The Crowleys were instantly crazy about him, as Bea reported to Catherine on the way out of church; she said that she and her husband planned to lead a delegation to see the bishop about putting Father O'Day out to pasture.

After their midday meal, Catherine picked the six or eight tulips that had come up on the sunny side of the house, put them into a Mason jar of water and drove with Hank and Brendan to the cemetery. There were no words at the grave, only the low sounds of Catherine's sobbing as she placed the flowers beside the headstone, and the chattering of the sparrows in the lilac hedge. Later Brendan went to the matinee with Sam: Esther Williams in Technicolor.

In the evening Catherine asked Grandfather and Brendan to come away from the radio for a few minutes—she had something to tell them. She said it wasn't definite yet, but she and Hank were thinking about moving back to the city. They were quite certain of selling the market and house at a profit, with which they might buy a store in the city. She had been offered part-time work at Dayton's. They would try to find a house in the same neighborhood they had left, but because of the housing shortage they might have to rent an apartment temporarily. They hoped to find one within biking distance of St. Bonaventure's. Speaking, she looked frequently to Hank for support and he nodded agreeably, but his eyes were far off. He was trying hard, and without much luck, to see himself in a city market.

When she finished, she turned to her father, whom she expected would be as hard to uproot as he had been last summer, but he put forth no objection. He said, "Give me a day or two notice," and he went back to Jack Benny.

It was Brendan who protested. He asked his parents to think of what he would have to give up. St. Bonaventure's had no athletic program, no coaches, nothing but fussy nuns on the faculty. He said he loved Plum. In arguing against the move he was not being entirely sincere, and he knew it. There were things he missed in the city—the occasional evening with his father at Nicollet Park, watching the Millers play baseball; learning his way around the city by streetcar, which he had begun doing before they moved; the vast choice of movies. And surely Uncle Howard, home from the war, would take him up in planes.

On the day the July issue of *Independent Grocer* appeared Bob Donaldson, the Minneapolis wholesaler, made an unexpected appearance at the market, arriving as Hank was locking up.

"What's going on, Hank? I saw your ad. Why are you selling the store?"

"Family reasons. We've decided to move back to the city."

"Come on next door, I'll buy you supper. We've got business to discuss."

"No, come home with me. My wife's gone to St. Paul and it's my night to cook supper."

Over pork chops, with Brendan listening and Grandfather half-listening, Bob Donaldson spoke of his dream of adding a chain of half a dozen stores to his wholesale enterprise.

"And you want to start with mine?"

"I want you and your store both. I want you to come into partnership with me. We'll use the profits from your store, along with some money of my own, to buy a second one. Then when the second store's on its feet we'll use the profits of those two to buy a third. You'll handle the retail end of things and I'll continue as supplier."

"How could I run half a dozen stores?"

"You won't run them. We'll hire managers, and you'll go around ana oversee them."

"I'm not crazy about living out of a suitcase."

"You'll be on the road less than I will. Two, three nights a week. A couple of the stores I have in mind are close enough to the city so you can make day trips. Have you got a map of Minnesota?"

Brendan went out to the car and brought in the road map. He watched Bob Donaldson pinpoint the towns.

"You know what I want to call our chain, Hank? I want to call it Hank's Markets. It's got a good, honest ring to it."

Hank smiled, picturing his name on the front of six stores. He guessed he'd be proud of that, though not as proud as he had been last September when his name went up on the store in Plum.

"Now here's the clincher, Hank. I know where I can pick up a car just like mine, except it's got fewer miles on it. It'll be yours, on the job and off."

Hank looked as if he didn't believe it.

"Mint condition, Hank. Just come to the city and we'll draw up the papers for our corporation and you'll take the car home with you."

Grandfather excused himself and went to his chair in the living room.

"Of course you'll want a few days to tell your wife and think it over, but don't wait too long. The postwar boom is right around the corner."

Hank was surprised to feel no obligation to consult Catherine, surprised to realize that by leaving town she had opened a rift, not in their marriage but in their partnership as breadwinners. Instead of his wife he consulted his son.

"What do you think, Brendan?"

"What year is your car, Mr. Donaldson?"

" 'Forty-two."

"Jeez, Dad, a 'forty-two Ford."

Summer

30

Sadly taking his leave of Sam and Philip and the other boys on the sun-scorched athletic field, Brendan said nothing about this being his last day in Coach Torborg's summer recreation program. Playing baseball and soccer all summer, he had become bronzed and muscular and grown two inches. His friends knew he would be leaving town before school started, but they had no idea which day. Sam would know it tomorrow morning when he awoke and saw the moving van across the alley.

He climbed the slope to the playground, hopped on his bike, and detoured around several blocks in order to suppress his sadness before arriving at the store. The late-summer elm leaves hung dusty and still. The houses he passed, which had seemed so novel last September when he and Wallace went door to door with handbills, were now too familiar to notice. Without looking left or right he knew every cornice and eave and window curtain. He knew all the people inside.

He entered the store perspiring. He greeted Mrs. Pelzer and Mrs. Flint at the checkout counter. They were loading the day's deliveries into two shopping carts for him. Mrs. Flint, having lost weight and gained stamina, was working longer hours now, and not exclusively in packaging. She took the place, more or less, of Catherine, who, though home from the city for most of the summer, had been working very little in the store. Now and then Wallace, feeling a fit coming on, would phone the store and his mother would rush home. No one but his mother had laid eyes on him since the day of the fire. No one brought up his name in her presence.

On his way to the back door, pushing a cart, Brendan saw his father and Art Nicholi taking inventory of the back-room stock. Hank and Bob Donaldson had chosen Art Nicholi as their manager because he met their four criteria: he was husky, ambitious, polite, and Catholic. An infantryman home from France, he was the eldest son of the barber and married to a daughter of Skeffington the banker. He had black hair, a swarthy complexion, and the military habit of saying "Yes, sir" and "No, sir" more often than necessary—to women and children as well as to men.

"Hot out," said Brendan.

"Yes, sir," said Art Nicholi.

Paul Dimmitburg followed Brendan with the second cart. They carried the orders out the door and lined them up across the back seat of the DeSoto, which was now parked permanently behind the store, delivery its only function. The family car these days was the 'forty-two Ford. They got in, Paul behind the wheel, and set off for the Standard station, the engine popping and coughing.

Len Downie was approaching the pumps and Paul was saying "Two gallons and check the oil," when the fire siren came wailing across town from the post in the Heffernands' back yard. Paul and Brendan got out and looked up and down Main Street for smoke. They saw none.

The Holy Angels churchbell began to ring, and Paul asked Brendan, "What's that all about?"

He was perplexed. Today being August 14, he made a guess: "Tomorrow's a holy day."

"So?"

"So this is the Eve of the Assumption of the Blessed Virgin." Which satisfied Paul, but not Brendan. He had never known of bells to ring on the eve of holy days.

Across the street a man stepped out of Plum Hardware, reached into an open car window and pressed the horn.

The Lutheran bell began to peal.

Downie said, "Call Central and see what the hell's going on."

Brendan went inside and picked up the phone. Melva Heffernand's voice: "Number please?"

"Why are the bells ringing?"

"The war is over."

He ran outside, his stomach turning a somersault. "The war is over," he crowed ecstatically.

Len Downie tossed his long-billed cap into the air and shouted, "Peace at last!" A breeze wafted the cap over the pumps and dropped it into the grease pit.

"Peace at last," Brendan repeated. This was the happy ending he had been urged to pray for since he was eight. It was for this moment he had collected scrap iron, bought war stamps, made novenas and gone without Hershey bars. Now America was in charge of history once again, the enemy crushed forever and every last complication removed from the face of the earth.

"Thank God," said Paul.

With the car fueled and adding its clattering noises to the ringing bells and honking horns, Brendan talked Paul into driving around town to spread the news. Through his open window he shouted, "The war is over!" to a cluster of men outside the pool hall. Gordy waved his bar rag. Next door Hank and his shoppers came spilling out of the market. "The war is over!" Brendan called, and his father clenched his hands over his head. They met Stan Kimball advancing slowly along Main Street in his hearse. He was leading a procession consisting of the county dump truck and the village firetruck, all with their horns blaring. The fire truck was driven by Mayor Brask, who was bowing his head left and right as if taking credit for the victory. "The war is over!" Brendan shouted into the ear of Nicholi the barber, who stood in the middle of the street holding his scissors and comb.

He asked Paul to drive down the alley behind Bean. His mother, airing out curtains and rugs and blankets in preparation for tomorrow's move, was conversing under the clothesline with Mrs. Kimball. Otto was tugging on his leash, digging a hole in the grass. "The war is over!" he called, and his mother threw him several kisses. Mrs. Kimball cupped her ear, not having understood. Behind them, he saw Grandfather, bewildered, groping his way out onto the veranda, mystified by the horns and bells apparently, or by something he had dreamed.

Along Hay and Corn streets people were coming out and standing in their front yards, as though, having heard of the Japanese surrender over their radios and telephones, they were waiting for Brendan to make it official. When he shouted, "The war is over!" they laughed and waved.

Their first stop was the Dombrowski house. "The war is over," he said to the Dombrowskis as he set their carton of groceries on a

kitchen chair. The old couple didn't reply, but looked at him warily, like frightened birds. He said they owed him two dollars and ten cents. They looked aghast, as they always did when he said what was owing. Waiting them out—it was like a game each time—he noticed how much the Dombrowskis resembled one another. They were both lean and ruddy from a lifetime in the sun and wind. They seemed not to have drawn an easy breath since giving up the rigors of farmwork and moving to town. Community life made them tense and suspicious—all this human contact: neighbors passing on the front sidewalk, the delivery boy every few days.

Brendan asked, "Do you want to charge it?" and this horrifying proposal set them in motion. Together they counted out coins.

"The war is over," he said again as he left, but nothing, not even peace on earth, could trick the Dombrowskis into opening their mouths.

Next stop was Holy Angels. Through the open door of the church they saw B. L. Skeffington pulling on the bellrope. As Father O'Day's departure drew near—he was retiring on the first of September—his otherworldliness was becoming more pronounced: he never thought to feed himself, and Mrs. Skeffington came in once a day to fix him a meal. It was she who had phoned in the order which Brendan now carried through the back door of the rectory. The old priest, stalled in the process of packing his belongings, sat at his cluttered kitchen table reading old letters. He ignored Brendan. Setting the groceries on a chair, Brendan noticed that the letters were gauzy and limp from years of handling. The stamps, he noticed, had cost a penny. Who had written them—an angel? Surely this man had never been attached to another mortal.

"Three dollars and thirty-six cents," said Brendan. The priest turned to him, drew out his billfold and paid him. His hands were blue with veins, his face was deathly white. Brendan thanked him and added, "The war is over, Father."

"Oh, I've heard that before," he sighed.

"This time it's true."

He nodded impatiently. "Yes, it was true in 1918 as well."

First the Dombrowskis, and now the priest—would no one rejoice with him? At least Mrs. Clay was on his route today. Mrs. Clay was constantly happy of late, constantly inebriated. When she drank heavily she tended to be careless about her clothes, as Brendan learned two weeks ago when she opened her kitchen door to receive

her groceries dressed in a scanty nightgown that revealed more female skin than Brendan had ever seen in movies or magazines. He had caught sight of a whole breast. He had hurried away to tell Sam and Philip, who accompanied him on his next delivery, but that time she wasn't home.

Paul drove from one church to the other. Waiting in the car while Paul carried groceries in to his mother, Brendan saw Paul's younger brother John pulling on the Lutheran bellrope and thought that peace was proving much more exciting than he had expected it to be. *Dona nobis pacem.* At mass when those words were spoken he had always imagined peace to be quiet and dull, not this loud and exhilarating.

Paul's mother and father followed him out the door. "The war is over!" Brendan called to them. The Reverend Dimmitburg said, "Thank the Lord, Brendan," and raised his arms in a liturgical manner. Mrs. Dimmitburg nodded heavily, as though bestowing her queenly approval on the terms of the armistice.

Next they drove to the Flint house, where the method of delivery, at the request of Wallace's mother, was to set the bag on the porch, knock on the door and leave. Wallace wanted to see no one, she said; he would take in the groceries when no one was looking. Now in his fourth month of seclusion, Wallace was beginning to take on mythic proportions in the collective mind of the village. He was the mad recluse, the bad seed of the unfortunate woman who worked for Hank. All summer Brendan had been glad to leave the groceries and flee, for the house was vaguely spooky, but today he knocked and waited. Even a recluse, it seemed to Brendan, deserved to know the war was over. Also, he harbored the suspicion that Wallace had started the fire; one last glimpse of the man before leaving Plum might help him make up his mind.

There was no sound from inside. He knocked a second time. A third. When Paul honked again he gave up, for surely Wallace would not come to the door knowing the DeSoto was idling in the street. He set down the bag and stepped over to the kitchen window. Shading his eyes, he looked inside. Facing him from the wall over the range were half a dozen enormous faces—popeyed, leering faces painted in shades of red. Were these the movie stars Mrs. Flint had spoken of? The wide, half-smiling, heavy-lidded face next to the stovepipe might have been Peter Lorre, but the others were unrecognizable. Some, in fact, looked scarcely human. One had large

pendulous objects hanging from her cheeks—tears perhaps. Another had cavernous nostrils and vacuous eyes, like Rufus Ottmann's. Paul honked a second time, and Brendan pulled himself away from the window, but not before catching sight of a face that might have been Catherine's. She had snakes for hair.

In the rooming house on Hay Street Brendan finally found someone whose ecstasy matched his own. Mrs. Lansky in number seven was weeping for joy. "It's over," she sobbed in her kitchen, "and now I won't have to imagine my grandchildren dead every day and night. My grandson is in the Seabees and my granddaughter is in the Waves." To the cost of the groceries she added an extra nickel. "That's for my granddaughter who will now live on and on," she said. "Now put out your other hand, this is for my grandson." In his other hand she placed a dime, a Seabee running twice the risk.

Turning to leave, Brendan faced number six across the hall and his joy was interrupted by the memory of Dodger bringing him up here to give him the cap gun. Brendan had never fired it. He didn't know where it was any more. On that same misty afternoon they had gone out into the sticky clay of the plowed field behind Brendan's house and thrown the boomerang until their arms ached. That was when Brendan first saw life as a circle, saw that things came round again. Yet he hadn't foreseen that a year later he would be returning to live in the city. Nor had he foreseen that Dodger would keep coming back, even after death. Not a day passed that Brendan didn't feel Dodger's needy presence at the back of his mind. It had taken him several weeks to understand what Dodger needed. For one thing he needed his name cleared. A whole summer had passed and Brendan had not yet told his parents that Dodger was innocent of the moneybag theft, that he had known about it all along but had said nothing so he could go to the creek with his friends. Would he ever work up the courage to tell them?

Dodger's second need was even more discouraging because it might take a lifetime to fulfill. Dodger needed Brendan's promise never again to be as unkind to anyone as he had been to Dodger, his promise to go through life more openhearted toward others and less concerned with himself. *Atonement* was the term the nuns of St. Bonnie's had been fond of using in cases like this. They said it was never too late to begin making amends. Unfortunately you never knew when your amends were complete. You could go on atoning all your

life and never be sure you were off the hook. But Dodger was giving him no choice, was expecting him to begin atoning at the first opportunity. Luckily Plum, since Dodger's death, seemed to offer no opportunities.

"I know what you're thinking," said Mrs. Lansky behind him.

He turned and saw that the armistice glow in the old woman's face was now overlaid with melancholy. He heard the words before she spoke them: "Poor Dodger."

The Clay delivery was last. Brendan carried the bag around to the back door, knocked and heard Mrs. Clay sing from a distant room, "Who is it?"

"Brendan. Delivery."

"Bring it right on in. I'll be right there." Her melodious voice meant she was pretty well plastered.

He stepped into the kitchen and set the bag on the drainboard. Waiting, he scanned the several clippings pinned to the wallpaper beside the window. Most of the photos came from movie magazines, men and women embracing. They stirred Brendan in the same erotic places that Esther Williams affected when she was wet. After a minute or so he felt a change of atmosphere. He heard no footstep, all was still, yet it was the stillness of a silent human presence. He turned. There across the room, smiling at him with her bathrobe hanging loosely open from her shoulders and wearing nothing underneath and thus revealing to him all her wonders from throat to thigh, was Mrs. Clay. Her feet were bare, her toenails painted the same luscious red as her lips. Her smile was impish. He stood there stunned and learning, absorbed in her flesh until she drew her robe together, tied the belt and said, still beaming, "Charge it please."

Breaking out of his enchantment by force of will, he backed slowly out the door, and his voice was subdued as he left her with the news that no longer seemed so momentous: "The war is over, Mrs. Clay."

He said nothing of this to Paul, but rode beside him in silence, memorizing her rosy contours.

They found Main Street filled with tractors and cars and trucks parked every which way and people milling among them. Villagers were streaming downtown and farmers were coming in from their farms. The honking horns were deafening. Paul stopped in front of the Standard station, for their way was blocked. Brendan climbed up and sat on the roof of the car, his feet on the hood. He followed

the raised eyes of the crowd and saw Constable Heffernand on the roof of the city hall releasing a fiery plane. It made a loop over the street and disintegrated in midair, its wispy remains falling like charred leaves. He sent out another plane and then another. To the delight of the cheering crowd he was launching his entire collection. Only the enemy planes were on fire. The Allied planes circled and dipped and climbed until their rubber bands went slack and they drifted into the outstretched hands of the crowd; most were scuffled over and crushed. Brendan saw Sam in the crowd. He saw Lorraine and Pearl in front of the drugstore, Cokes in their hands. He saw Philip Crowley with his mother. He saw Mrs. Ottmann on the far side of the street under the awning of the hardware store. He saw half a dozen farm children standing in the bed of the Higgins pickup. He saw Norma Nash kissing Andy Romberg. He saw several old men from the poor farm. Edging toward him along the front of the city hall was Rufus Ottmann. Following the example of those around him, Rufus had turned his eyes to the sky without knowing the reason. He was grinning at the sun and making excited little movements with his left hand while trailing the fingers of his right hand along the brick wall to keep his balance. There were cheers and laughter as a Flying Tiger climbed across the street and landed on the roof of the hardware store. For once, thought Brendan, everyone in town looked as happy as Rufus. He watched the idiot reach the corner of the village hall and leave the sidewalk as he followed the side wall back toward the alley. He saw him stumble over one of Len Downie's discarded tires. He kept his balance and continued moving along, heading straight for the grease pit with his eyes still lifted to the sky. "Hey, somebody catch Rufus!" cried Brendan, standing up on the hood of the car and pointing. "He'll fall in that hole!" But his voice was lost in the cheering as a German Fokker climbed to a peak and dropped, trailing smoke. He jumped to the ground and ran to Rufus, who teetered at the verge of the grease pit; he clutched his hand and wrenched him around. He avoided looking into the idiot's repellant face—the gaping nostrils, the cavernous mouth—as he led him back to the street. How docilely he followed. How large his hand was. How soft. The hand tightened painfully on Brendan's as he picked his way through the jostling crowd in the direction of Mrs. Ottmann. Seeing her son advancing toward her, she signaled him with a lavender handkerchief. As Brendan stepped into the shade of the awning and brought Rufus to a halt at his mother's

side, he felt virtuous and mature, felt that Dodger—at least for the moment—was satisfied.

"Thank you very kindly," said Mrs. Ottmann.

"You're welcome," said Brendan, struggling to pry himself free of the idiot's grip.

CHAPEL HILL PUBLIC LIBRARY
TOWN OF CHAPEL HILL

P9-DHQ-528

Chapel Hill
Public Library

'The very thought of it exhausts me,' I muttered as he paid the bill.

*

A wooden foot-ramp had been erected in Byng Place and the traffic was still bad, so we decided to walk. But we had got no further than re-entering Tavistock Square when a young woman came rushing out of the dental practice and straight towards us. Even without her uniform it was easy to recognize her as Jenny, the maid who had admitted us less than two hours ago. She was in a simple black dress and her hair was still tied back.

'Oh, sir, I hoped it was you.' She was red-faced and panting. 'Come quickly, please. Something awful has happened.'

'To your employer, I hope,' my guardian said.

She tugged at her sleeves in agitation. 'Please, sir.'

The front door was wide open and Sidney Grice paused to examine the lintel.

'There is a very strong smell of nitrous oxide,' I said.

'Why, March' – he tapped the wainscoting with his cane – 'you are turning into a veritable bloodhound.'

'Oh, miss, please make him come quickly.'

'If, as I suspect, your employer is dead, there is no hurry whatsoever,' he told her as he ambled down the hallway. He stopped and crouched, then ran his fingers over the parquet.

'Oh, please,' she said.

'Interesting.' He jumped up to look at the unlit gas mantle before following a distraught Jenny towards the surgery.

The smell of gas was very strong by now and almost overpowering as we entered the room. Silas Braithwaite was slumped in his patients' chair. The anaesthetic mask lay upturned in his left hand on his lap. I felt for a pulse.

'I found him like this, sir,' Jenny said and my guardian turned to me.

'Looks dead to me,' he commented. 'What do you think?'

'I think we should open the window,' I replied and Jenny

rushed over to do so. There was a welcome gust of cold air but whatever view there might have been was obscured by a mulberry bush thick with creepers.

Sidney Grice was looking at a framed sepia photograph.

I tapped the gas cylinder with a mirror handle and felt it with the back of my fingers. 'It is ice-cold and empty,' I said and examined the other cylinder. 'But the oxygen is warm and almost full.'

Sidney Grice went to the other side. 'He who lives by the gas…' He lifted Silas Braithwaite's right hand, holding it like a fortune-teller, wiggled the fingers and replaced it on the arm of the chair. 'Stupid man.' And after a while he said to himself, 'But who is doing this to me?'

9

Eagle Beaks and Opium

JENNY WAS SENT to fetch a policeman and found one almost immediately. He was a sturdy middle-aged man who I had seen before, clearing vagrants from the square. It was an offence to sleep out at night and so they were forced to walk the streets in darkness and sleep all day instead.

The constable took one look and marched off to summon help.

'Well, Miss Middleton, we might as well sit in the waiting room,' my guardian said.

'Are you not going to examine him?'

Sidney Grice looked at me as if I were simple. 'What on earth for?'

'To find out how he died?'

'I know how he died and so do you, unless you have one of your bizarre theories,' my guardian said.

'But who do you think killed him?' I asked.

My guardian blinked. 'I know I did not do it and I am confident that you did not. Possibly this maid did.'

And Jenny jumped. 'Not me, sir, honest. I just found him like this.'

Sidney Grice waved an uninterested hand.

'Mr Grice is not accusing you of anything, Jenny,' I said. 'But why did you come back?'

Jenny's eyes jumped about as if she were searching for an

escape route. 'He owed me four months' wages and I came back to ask him for them. I thought if he realized he had no servants at all he might come to his senses. And I was going to threaten him…'

My guardian put on his pince-nez and scrutinized a pair of eagle-beaked forceps.

'Kindly do not make a confession,' he told her. 'I have better things to do than be called as a witness at your trial.'

'What trial?' Jenny reddened. 'Why aren't you looking for clues? I thought you was supposed to be a detective.' And Sidney Grice piffed a little air between his lips.

'I am not *supposed* to be a detective; I *am* the foremost detective in the British Empire. But I am a personal detective and not a public lackey. Your ex-employer was not a client of mine and so his death is no more than an inconvenience for me.'

'Have you no heart?' she asked.

'Certainly.' He prodded his chest with the forceps. 'And it pumps blood to my unequalled brain but does not rule it.'

I touched her shoulder. 'How were you going to threaten him, Jenny?'

She started to sniff. 'Just with being blacklisted by the employment agencies. That's all. You can't expect a girl to work and play games for free.'

'Note how she regresses into her native dialect when she is distressed,' Sidney Grice said. 'The elongated vowels and the burred *r*. I would place it somewhere between Craven Arms and Clun.'

'Are you going to hang her for that?' I asked and my guardian tapped a barometer on the wall.

'It is a small point in her favour,' he said.

'Why?' I demanded. 'Do they not murder people in that part of Shropshire? Have you no cases in your files?'

Sidney Grice ran his finger under the edge of a shelf but did not examine it.

'Several, including one of a wonderfully colourful nature

involving a Serbian engineer.' He wiped his hands on his handkerchief. 'But in my experience people who are lying become more – and not less – careful about how they speak.'

Jenny was crying now. 'I didn't do him no harm.'

'*Any* harm,' he corrected her absently as he opened and closed the forceps.

'Could he really not pay you or was he just being mean?' I asked.

'He couldn't pay no one for he never had no – any patients.' She blew her nose. 'The butcher wouldn't give him any meat. Even the laundry wouldn't let him have his clothes back 'cause he owed them six months.'

'These forceps were designed with an almost complete ignorance of mechanics and human anatomy,' Sidney Grice said. 'The fulcrum is too high and the points are designed more to destroy the jawbone than cleanly extract a tooth. When I have the time I shall design a better pair. You,' he told Jenny, 'will sit in the hallway.' He carefully replaced the forceps, turning them so as to lie exactly as they had before he picked them up. 'Come, March.'

I looked at Silas Braithwaite. His skin was blue.

'There is a red mark on his wrist,' I observed.

'No, there is not,' my guardian called over his shoulder. 'There are three such marks and not one of them is any of our concern.'

I sat in the waiting room in a sagging armchair and Sidney Grice stood with his back to me, staring out of the window, humming the same tuneless few notes over and over again and tapping an erratic beat on the floorboards with his cane. I could see Jenny's feet. They were motionless.

'Stay there,' he snapped without taking his eye off his view. 'You do not work here now.'

The bell rang. 'See to it, Miss Middleton,' he said without turning.

I thought of telling him to do it himself, but it did not seem right to bicker when there was a dead man lying in the next room.

'I see that girl detectives greet callers.' Inspector Quigley stepped inside, leaving his constable to guard the step.

'And I see your powers of observation have not deserted you – yet,' I told him as my guardian came into the hall.

'Well, Mr Grice,' the inspector said, 'I am beginning to think the papers are right. Death follows you like a shadow, according to last night's *Evening News*.'

'If the press are to be believed man will fly in an engine-powered machine one day,' my guardian retorted. 'No, Inspector, I follow death. I learn his secrets; I sometimes forestall him but even my brilliant powers cannot thwart him for ever.'

'So what happened here then?'

'We were called in by this servant.' Sidney Grice indicated Jenny, now on her feet and smoothing down her dress. 'And came in to find her ex-employer, Mr Silas Braithwaite, dead in his dental chair and his surgery filled with nitrous oxide.'

'Laughing gas?' Inspector Quigley asked.

'Quite so.'

'Well, let's take a look then.' The inspector held up his hand in a halt sign to Jenny, who was still standing beside her chair. 'Wait there.'

'I haven't done anything wrong,' she protested and the inspector smiled bleakly.

'If I say you have, you have. If I say you haven't, you haven't,' he said. 'I will let you know in five minutes. In the meantime sit there.' Quigley marched on past me. The smell of nitrous oxide was fainter but still strong. 'I hate dentists,' he said as he stepped into the surgery.

'Well, here is one fewer for you to loathe,' Sidney Grice said as the inspector stood at the foot of the chair.

'Any theories, Mr Grice?'

My guardian opened the filing cabinet and rifled through its contents.

'None whatsoever.' He picked the husk of a spider out by one leg. '*Pardosa amentata* or the spotted wolf spider, so named because it does not build a web but tracks its prey and hunts it down.' He let it fall. 'I am sure you have a solution already, Inspector.'

'Indeed I have,' Quigley said. 'No point in dawdling over these things. Accidental death.'

'How have you decided that?' I asked and Sidney Grice groaned.

'I shall keep this simple for you,' the inspector promised.

'And please try to speak slowly,' I entreated, and he gazed at me as one might a dead rodent.

'Have you ever heard of laughing-gas parties?'

I had attended one in Cabool but I said, 'I think so.' And Inspector Quigley put his hands together and explained, 'Degenerate people, particularly university undergraduates, artists who can't paint and poets who won't rhyme sometimes gather secretly for the purposes of inhaling nitrogen oxide, which by all accounts has a stimulating and intoxicating effect.'

I resisted the urge to ask him to explain what *intoxicating* meant and said, 'I think I understand.'

'What these allegedly intelligent people do not realize is that all drugs can lead to an irresistible hunger for more, what we professionals call an *addiction*.'

'Does that include opium?' I asked.

'Even opium,' the inspector told me. 'There is a dark and terrible underworld based around that seemingly harmless household medicine, which I trust you will never encounter. But, to continue, these misguided youths soon find themselves unable to resist its effects. They start to crave it but their cravings can never be satisfied. This man may have gone to such parties but more likely the amount of gas he inhaled in the course of his work turned him into a laughing-gas fiend. He administered the gas to himself and, in his confused state, forgot to turn on the oxygen. The gas filled his lungs and so he had no air and suffocated himself to death.'

'A neat theory.' Sidney Grice clapped his hands together. 'Now, Inspector, if you have no further need for us we will be about our business.'

Jenny looked up anxiously as we came back into the hall.

'Prepare your soul to meet its maker,' my guardian told her as he passed by.

I turned back to reassure her but she had fainted on to the floor.

'I suppose you think that was funny,' I said as I waved my blue vial of sal volatile under her nose, and her eyelids fluttered.

Sidney Grice considered the matter. 'Do you know, March,' he said, 'I do not believe it was.'

10

French Polish and the Second-best Teapot

THE STUDY AT 125 Gower Street had been tidied while we were away and Horatio Green's body had been removed, as had the rug. The chair he had died in – my usual chair – had been pushed back into place. The smashed crockery was gone and the table wiped clean.

My guardian sighed. 'It will have to be French polished.'

He pulled on the bell rope and sat down but I hovered. 'It does not seem right to use the chair after what has happened.'

Sidney Grice skimmed his hand over the armrest and said, 'Molly clearly thinks like you. Female brains are simple mechanisms but surprisingly often attuned. She has swapped the chairs round.'

'Are you sure?'

'You think I do not know my own chair?'

I sat gingerly and said, 'Inspector Quigley seems very quick to form a conclusion.'

He picked a copy of *The Lancet* from the satinwood lowboy at his side. 'One of the best minds in the force,' he said. 'Not that he has much competition.'

'But in both cases today he has reached the wrong conclusion.'

Sidney Grice leafed through his magazine. 'In seven weeks' time Chief Inspector Newburgh will be retiring. He is going to breed cattle in the desolate hinterlands of Surrey, I believe. The post will fall vacant and our friend Quigley is hotly tipped to fill it, but he is unlikely to gain promotion if, over the next few weeks, he has a string of unsolved murders on his books.'

Molly came in with a tray. 'Cook says begging your pardon, sir, but this is her second-best teapot and please can you not break it.'

'Tell Cook I shall try to restrain myself.' Her employer went back to his journal but I could not let the matter rest.

'So anyone may commit any crime with impunity for the next two months if Inspector Quigley is on the case,' I said.

'Unless he can make an arrest on the spot.' He flipped a page impatiently. 'Obviously, solving cases instantly improves his career prospects.'

'Even if he gets the wrong person?'

'As long as he gets a conviction…' Sidney Grice flapped a hand and went back to his reading.

I poured the tea. 'What about Inspector Pound?' It was a lovely Regency tea set – fine white china with rosy periwinkles and a deep-pink scalloped border on the rims of the cups.

My guardian closed the cover wearily. 'A man would get more peace in Billingsgate Fish Market on a Friday morning,' he said. 'If you want to know whether Pound would let a guilty man go or convict the wrong one to enhance his career prospects, the answer is *no*. Pound has as good a mind as Quigley, if not better, but he lacks that ruthless streak which lifts the scum from the dregs.'

'How cynical you are.'

'If you mean I am sceptical of other people's motives, I would be foolish not to be, in my profession.'

He turned back to his journal but I pressed on. 'Do you have any more theories about how Horatio Green was poisoned?'

My guardian tested the teapot with the back of his fingers and something like approval flashed over his face.

'Not yet,' he said, 'and please do not annoy me with any of yours.'

'I have one thought,' I said and he dropped his *Lancet* into his lap. 'What if Mr Green was sucking on a lozenge?'

'He was not. I would have observed it in the way he spoke.'

'He could have had it in his cheek pouch.'

'Prussic acid, as the name might suggest even to your sluggish mental processes, is an acid. It would have burnt the cheek membranes. I did not observe any ulceration anterior to the oropharynx and, if I do not observe something, it is not there to be observed.'

My guardian popped his eye out and massaged around his socket vigorously.

'Does your eye hurt?'

'My eye is buried in Charlottenburg Cemetery.'

I put the upright chair back at the round table in the middle of the room. 'You had a funeral service for your eye?'

He slid open a drawer and took out a rosewood box. 'The eye was in the throat of a Prussian colonel. He choked to death on it.' He produced a green bottle, clearly not interested in pursuing the subject.

'What do you suppose has happened to Inspector Pound?'

'I do not suppose anything has happened to him that is any of our concern.' Sidney Grice pulled out the cork. 'If anything had he would have told me.' He upended the bottle in a ball of cotton wool.

'Perhaps he cannot. Perhaps he has been hurt or—'

'What? He has been kidnapped by fairies or press-ganged by pirates?' He put the wad to his socket and winced. 'Really, March, you should write shilling shockers for a living. They would sell like saints' fingers in a Roman bazaar.'

'But he is your friend. Are you not even a little concerned?'

'As we have already established, I have no friends.' The cotton wool was stained blue. 'And I doubt that he has either.' It turned red around the edges. 'The life of a criminologist is a lonely one – thank heavens.' Sidney Grice deposited the cotton wool into his wastepaper bin. 'I hope you have a more presentable dress than any I have seen you in so far.' He recorked the bottle. 'We have an appointment tomorrow morning in Kew.'

'Baroness Foskett?'

He wiped his hands with a stained cloth. 'None other.'

From somewhere in the house there was a scream. For a moment I hoped I had imagined it but then there was a second scream, louder and longer and higher.

'If one of the servants is being murdered, I do hope it is Cook,' my guardian said.

Far away there was a crash followed by footsteps rushing up the hallway. I grabbed the coal tongs and raised them over my head as the door flew open. It was Molly – no hat, no apron, hair hanging loose and wild – with a look of utter terror.

'Oh, sir, come quickly!' She struggled for air. 'It's 'orrible.' She forced herself to say the words. 'That dratted cat from number 123 has brought an alive rat in.' She looked at me, the tongs still raised high. 'Oh, miss, if you wanted the fire made up you should've rung.'

'Why am I troubled with these domestic matters? Call the rat catcher immediately.' Sidney Grice touched his cheek and a thin violet tear trickled from his empty eye.

*

I said my prayers, as always, that night, wrote in my journals and opened my writing case. The scent of the sandalwood lining filled my senses and transported me once more.

> *We rarely visited the city but, when my father had to go for supplies, it was too good an opportunity to miss. And, after he had finished his official duties, we had two spare hours before the train. My father took me to Caldebank's cafe – a little piece of England tucked down a side street – for high tea: four different kinds of sandwiches and two of cake, fruit scones with butter and strawberry jam, though we decided not to risk the clotted cream. And afterwards we walked by the shops. It was a happy day. I admired the fabrics and my father invested in a new meerschaum pipe. And then I saw it – a writing box. We went in and had a look.*

The box was beautifully made, polished oak with a lovely grain and brass fittings and inlays, opening out to reveal the compartments for correspondence, stationery and pens. It had a folding-out, green leather writing slope with feathered gold edging and, of course, a 'secret' compartment.

The shopkeeper was a little Frenchman with luxuriant moustaches. He raised his eyebrows politely when I pointed out how easy the compartment was to find. 'Now find zee ozzer one,' he challenged. I pressed every section with no success. My father tried too, turning it upside down and tapping it to no avail. The owner smiled. 'Shall I show mademoiselle?' He pressed the inkwell down and rotated it a quarter-turn, then there was a click and a drawer slid out from the side.

I laughed. 'I shall take it.'

'You already have a serviceable one,' my father pointed out.

'Just as you have a dozen meerschaums,' I countered. 'Besides, it is not for me. It is Edward's birthday next month.'

My father frowned. 'But can you afford it?'

'Of course I can.' I slipped my arm through his. 'With a little help.'

11

The Spike and the Corpulent King

We crossed the Thames but the narrow bridge was so chock-a-block that I could hardly see anything other than the railway bridge to one side and the slow-swaying masts of a clipper disappearing behind the smoking stacks of a paddle steamer on the other. Now and then I glimpsed the red-sailed barges scattered like rose petals on the water. It had been an early start and a long journey.

The Prince of Wales was visiting the Royal Botanical Gardens at Kew and the roads were blocked with the carriages of the gentry. Landaus and barouches converged, while curious onlookers milled around the main entrance, queuing at a coffee stall or chewing ham sandwiches, and bunches of ragged children shouted ironic comments at the visitors making their way to the gate.

We quit our hansom on Lichfield Road and pressed our way through. The royal coach was visible inside the grounds.

'Oh, but we have missed him,' I said.

'We have missed nothing,' Sidney Grice told me, 'but a dull-witted, corpulent, ill-tempered libertine.'

'You do not approve of him?'

'I dislike him intensely.' My guardian barged his way through a group of laundry women and I followed in his wake, trying to ignore their indignant glares. 'And he sometimes treats me as if I were the royal dust collector. But he will make an excellent king if he outlives his bovine mother. Hold on to your impractical bag, March. Where there are crowds there are pickpockets.'

The mass of people thinned out and we saw a tiny boy in a yellow jacket hold out his cap to a young man resplendent in a frock coat and highly brushed beaver-skin top hat. The young man ignored him but when the boy darted in front of him, he raised his cane without warning and whipped it across the child's face. The boy yelped and fell to his knees. I ran over and crouched to look at him. A red weal ran from his mouth to his eye. I looked up.

'If you were a man I would thrash you for that,' I said and the man pulled his lips down.

'I *am* a man.' His voice was as high and thin as his aristocratic nose. 'A gentleman.'

'No,' I said and got to my feet. 'You are a sort of vermin.'

He screwed a monocle into his eye to inspect me. 'Have you any idea whom you are addwessing?'

'Yes,' I said. 'A preening popinjay with the manners of a slattern. I hope your mother never gets to hear of your behaviour.'

The young man inspected me with utter scorn. 'My mother would not have you emptying her bedpan. She—' He stopped abruptly, his face contorted, his monocle fell out and he screeched.

'You will apologize to the lady,' my guardian said as the young man screwed up his face in pain.

'I see no lady.'

'This instant will do.'

I looked down and saw that Sidney Grice was grinding the end of his cane into the top of the young man's highly polished soft shoe.

'I am sowwy.' The tears were rolling from his eyes.

'Will that suffice?' my guardian asked me.

'I accept your apology,' I said. 'On condition that you give that child a sovereign.'

'Anything.' He reached into his trouser pocket. 'But please stop.'

'No need for the money,' Sidney Grice said. There was blood oozing from the young man's shoe. 'That grubby rascal made off with your wallet nearly two minutes ago.'

I laughed.

'And your purse,' Sidney Grice told me, and I looked in my bag to find it gone.

My guardian removed his cane and I saw it had a sharp metal tip on the end. He retracted it by screwing the handle. 'The Grice Patent Spike Stick,' he announced as the young man hopped to a nearby plane tree to support himself and inspect his foot.

'The child has more need of the money than I,' I said and my guardian frowned.

'It is a short tumbril ride from that philosophy to a guillotine in Trafalgar Square.'

We walked away.

'I will wememba you,' the young man yelled. 'Both of you.'

'If there *is* a revolution it is men like him who will ignite it,' I said.

'I recoil from your mixed metaphor,' Sidney Grice told me. The crowd died out as we emerged slightly crumpled into a quiet side street. 'We have made a powerful enemy today.'

'I would not want him for a fwend,' I said and his mouth twitched faintly.

'Nor I, but you must learn to stop interfering.'

'What would Christ have done?' I asked.

'I dread to think.' He gestured to a street sign. 'Not far now.'

The roads of Kew were wide and leafy and the air had lost the stench of factory fumes, though the sky was still strewn with ribbons of smoke from the city. Sidney Grice stopped and pointed with his cane. Through the treetops and a hundred yards away I could just make out a weathervane and the tip of a lead-sheeted turret.

'There it is.' His face fired with excitement.

12

Cutteridge and the Key

MORDENT HOUSE STOOD on the corner enclosed by a high brick wall. We passed a rotting once-solid wooden gate.

'That used to be for the gardeners, but Rupert and I used it once without permission,' my guardian told me.

'You devils,' I said.

'But it is sealed now. They welded a grid behind it after Rupert's grandfather nearly escaped.'

'Escaped?'

But Sidney Grice was looking up beyond the rusting criss-crossed spikes that topped the wall. He stopped and pointed to a high chestnut tree overhanging the pavement.

'I climbed that once,' he said, 'to check the accuracy of our trigonometrical calculations of its height.'

'What larks.'

We walked on and he flipped a twig on to the road with his cane. 'We had underestimated by five eighths of an inch.'

The wall stretched round another corner.

'The extra climb must have been exhausting,' I said and he stopped abruptly.

'Why must you inject levity into every conversation?'

I kept walking and called over my shoulder, 'Why does everything have to be so serious?' The brickwork was bulging quite badly here and supported by five S-shaped iron plates. 'I am only trying to make life pleasant.'

My guardian caught up with me. 'You can try to mask the taste of a lemon' – he sneezed – 'but it will always be sour.' We came to a break in the wall and a pair of tall wrought-iron gates. The pillars were topped by heraldic animals so eroded that I could not tell exactly what they represented. 'The family crest,' my guardian explained as he wrenched on a bell chain.

'How sweet,' I murmured.

On either side stood a small lodge, both of which appeared to be deserted. The roof of one had collapsed and the other was missing several slates, with a sycamore escaping through its sloping hole.

We waited. A robin hopped on the arrowhead tops of the gate. Through the bars I could just make out a gravel driveway thick with tall grass and dandelions. My guardian tutted. 'These grounds were laid out by Simeon Gunwale.'

'I have seen tidier jungles,' I said as a skeletal grey-striped cat wandered across the path, followed by three kittens. 'Shall I ring the bell again? It might not be working.'

'It has worked.' He touched a corroded point with his thumb. 'Somebody will come.' He put out his arm to hold me back. 'Interesting.'

'What is?'

'The condition of these leaves.'

'Fascinating,' I said.

The sun was high but it could not cast light into the garden. Copper beeches and silver birches battled each other for space.

Perhaps five minutes passed.

'Look.' He pointed into the undergrowth but I could see nothing. 'Follow my finger.'

'I am trying.'

'Use your tobacco-damped senses.'

I screwed up my eyes and far away through the mass of vegetation something moved.

'What is it?'

A blackbird sang.

'Cutteridge,' Sidney Grice said, 'the major-domo.'

I watched intently, and the black shape grew and became a man walking slowly but steadily towards us. He disappeared behind a bush but reappeared a moment later, a tall man, shoulders curved by the mould of time, with a mass of white hair trained back behind his ears and a clean-shaven elongated face. He came to the gate carrying a hoop of keys.

'Mr Grice.' His voice rustled drily. 'How nice to see you again.' His manner was dignified and imposing but his eyes were crinkled with kindness.

'I trust you have the dogs under control.'

'Your trust is not misplaced, sir.' Cutteridge selected a large intricate key, straining to turn it as the lock brattled stiffly back. He grasped the octagonal handle, twisted it and heaved, and the high gate squealed jerkily open.

13

Aquinas and the Viper

THE MOMENT WE entered what used to be the front garden the blackbird's song changed to an urgent scolding clatter.

'The cats or us?' I wondered.

'Neither.' Sidney Grice directed my gaze to where a green-brown line was sliding along the trunk of a fallen ash tree. I saw the black zigzag on its back as the tongue whisked out from under its raised snout.

'A viper,' I said.

'I saw an injured female blackbird this morning,' Cutteridge told me. 'The snake is probably after that, miss.'

I watched it slide smoothly over the trunk as the alarm cries of the male grew increasingly urgent, while from the undergrowth came a weaker alarm call and some scuttling.

'*Nature red in tooth and claw*,' I quoted.

'Why, March' – my guardian brushed a leaf from his shoulder – 'that was almost poetical.'

We wound our way through a thicket of rampant rhododendrons, Cutteridge first and Sidney Grice following, slashing some nettles to widen the path for me.

'I refuted every one of Aquinas's seven proofs under that mulberry tree,' my guardian recalled proudly.

'And Master Rupert was chastised for encouraging you as I recall,' Cutteridge chipped in.

'At twenty-two?' My puzzlement went unremarked.

The shrill cries of the blackbirds became frantic, then fell silent, and a flock of crows rose suddenly from a spinney, flapping blackly across our path. Sidney Grice crossed his arms over his head, his cane raised like a sword about him. He darted towards the mulberry and the crows disappeared.

'They will not harm you, sir.' Cutteridge held back a long bramble for us to pass.

'Their very existence harms me.' My guardian put a hand to his right eye and shuddered. 'No wonder they are called *a murder*.'

'Now who is being poetic?' I asked as we rounded a clump of skyward-straining bamboo, the stems as thick as pine trees, and found ourselves in a clearing. The gravel was still tangled with creepers and thistles, but the canopy was gone and ahead of us stood a massive edifice of grey stones. Amongst the confusion of soaring towers and angular turrets were domes and spires, closed balconies and empty niches, jutting ledges, crenelated walls and windows of every shape high overhead – arches rounded and pointed; circular and oval; square and rectangular; many with stained glass, some unglazed, some with panes smashed, some no more than archers' slits. The walls were strewn with ivy, all but obscuring many of the openings.

A clock tower leaned to the right of us, the time fixed at eleven fifty-nine.

'One minute to midnight,' Sidney Grice observed.

'Or noon,' I said.

'Midnight,' he insisted.

There was a dead pigeon under a dock leaf, its breast bursting with wiry red worms.

'The locals call this the Madhouse,' Cutteridge told me. 'They say the architect lost his mind after he built it.'

'After?' I queried and he smiled crookedly.

'Part of the trouble is that every Baron Foskett had his own ideas on remodelling the house, but all of them died before they could realize their intentions. Please follow me, sir, miss.'

We went up the wide marble steps – tilted and cracked, slippery green with algae – that led to massive bleached oak doors, the right-hand one being already open, and into a great hall, lit only by the entrance, the windows being heavily curtained and the central lantern skylight being boarded over from the outside.

'I shall inform the baroness that you have arrived,' Cutteridge said and made his way up the cantilevered stairs, surprisingly strongly for a man of his age, while we stood under the high ribbed ceiling, the plaster blistered and fissured, and looked about us. The walls were grey and tidemarks had crept up and down the sides. The smell of damp and mould was almost suffocating. I pointed to the floor, broad planks with a threadbare Persian rug thrown over, in front of a huge, cobwebbed marble fireplace and littered with droppings.

'Rat?' I suggested.

'And bat.' My guardian's eye was misty. 'I remember liveried footmen on duty night and day, ostlers holding magnificent black horses on the driveway, gold and green coaches with coachmen uniformed to match, French maids dusting these mirrors, and valets bustling with their masters' wardrobes. This hall was filled with flowers – roses from the garden in summer and rare orchids from the hothouse in winter. There was an ornamented spruce in every room at Christmas.'

I had never heard him so lyrical about anything before, not even murder.

'So what happened?'

'Death and decay,' he said. 'When society rots, it rots from the top. The greatest of our families are in decline now – loss of land and power – wealth squandered and bloodstock contaminated by marriages to peasants and Americans, which amount to the same thing.' He lifted back a curtain and a dull rhombus of day fell down the wall and over the floor. 'Look.' The windows were scratched, every pane of glass being filled with columns of numbers – thousands upon thousands of tiny digits in neat rows disappearing behind the cobwebs. 'Rupert loved numbers. He would cram his journals with them. Sometimes he only spoke in equations.'

'How entertaining,' I said.

'Indeed.' He put on his pince-nez and said excitedly, 'What an unusual web. Clearly the spider has a damaged front right leg.' He took out his notebook to sketch an outline of it.

'A useful clue' – I took a look – 'if you wish to track down the killer of that lacewing.'

He let the curtain drop and the daylight scrambled away.

There were panelled doors ajar on the right-hand side of the hall. I wandered over and pushed them apart, the cream paint peeling like birch bark to my touch. They led into a long wide gallery, the full-length windows covered by frayed satin curtains, the walls draped with faded tapestries, the chandeliers bagged in cotton sheets and the floor patterned with snail tracks.

A tall frame hung on the left-hand wall with a clean white sheet over it. I lifted the cloth aside and saw a full-length portrait – a slender, elegant woman in an ivory and silver-threaded gown, with one hand resting lightly on the head of an Afghan hound.

There was an enormous mirror, fixed floor to ceiling and bordered by dull gold ferns. The glass was covered by a dust sheet. I wiped the surface through a triangular rip and something moved, ghost-like, deep behind the tarnished backing.

'Is she not lovely?' Cutteridge said so suddenly behind me that I jumped.

'Quite beautiful,' I said. 'Is that Baroness Foskett?'

'In the first year of her marriage.' He cleared his throat. 'Ah, the balls we had here, the glittering ladies, the aristocratic men, the sparkling conversation, the baths of iced champagne, the music, the laughter... Oh, miss, if you could have been here...' He drifted through his memories for a moment. 'But that was all so very long ago.'

'What happened?' I asked.

'All life is dust, miss.' Cutteridge wheezed long and wearily. 'Dust and vipers.' He straightened his cuff. 'Her ladyship will see you now.'

The three of us ascended the staircase. I refrained from observing that most of life's dust appeared to have settled in that house, for there was not a surface that was not encrusted in it.

'Mind the banister rail.' My guardian reached over and demonstrated how easily it wobbled. I stuck close to the wall, the steps bowing and creaking under our feet as we climbed.

'I expect you used to slide down these,' I said to my guardian.

'That would have been frivolous,' he said.

'I did once,' Cutteridge declared. 'When I was the under-butler, the late Baron Reginald bet me a month's wages to a hundred guineas I could not do it carrying a tray of sherry glasses. I slipped off at the first turn and broke both arms. So I lost six months' wages anyway.' His shoulders quaked in remembered mirth.

'How jolly,' I said.

'Happy times,' Cutteridge agreed as we paused on a half-landing. 'Master Rupert made an attempt as well, but he was disadvantaged by his thumb.'

'The Foskett males had an extra spur of bone...' Sidney Grice explained.

'Is that what he scratched the window with?' I whispered.

'Which made it difficult for them to grip things tightly,' my guardian continued flatly.

'Master Rupert broke his ankle and it never really healed,' Cutteridge continued. 'The game was banned after that.'

'What a shame,' I commented. 'How many servants work here now?'

'I am the last, I fear.'

Sidney Grice was quiet, seemingly lost in wonder at his surroundings. A portrait hung lopsidedly, so darkened that all I could make out was part of an ear and two eyes gaping from the grime. I peered gingerly over the banister. We must have been thirty feet up by the time we reached the first floor.

The stairs wound upwards and a corridor disappeared into the darkness on either side. Here the windows were all shuttered, the light creeping between warped slats, weak and grey on to the bare boards. Even the dust specks floating in numberless argent stars only served to add to the gloom.

My guardian sniffed. '*Serpula lacrymans*,' he said. 'Dry rot.'

'The whole House of Foskett is rotten now, sir.' He led us a few more paces. 'Here we are.' Cutteridge stopped and put a hand on my guardian's arm in an oddly familiar fashion at which he appeared to take no offence whatsoever. 'I must warn you, sir, that the baroness has changed greatly. She has not been well for many years and is unused to visitors now. Even I see her but rarely. Also, she tires very easily so I shall presume upon your good nature not to overtax her.'

'You may rely on it.' Sidney Grice put a finger to his eye, ran a hand through his hair, plumped up his cravat and shone his shoes on the back of his trousers as Cutteridge pushed open the door.

14

Whispers in the Dark

THE ROOM WE entered was in complete darkness. From the dim corridor I could see nothing at all, but Cutteridge strode confidently in and almost immediately disappeared.

'Mr Sidney Grice and Miss March Middleton,' he announced from nowhere into nowhere.

There followed a silence, the distant groan of disturbed floorboards re-settling and then a shallow rasp: 'Light the candle, Cutteridge' – a whisper but louder than any whisper should be and curiously remote and metallic. I looked at my guardian. He was staring intently in the direction of the sound and I thought a shiver rippled over him, but it was not one of fear.

There was a scratching noise and a hiss, and a sudden flare of light as Cutteridge struck a Lucifer and put it to the wick of a half-burnt candle in a frosted glass bowl on an otherwise empty scalloped oval table. He blew the match out and there was only the yellow flame, sinking, then rising fitfully, wavering in the globe, a dull halo fading into nothing. We walked towards it and Cutteridge directed us to two low chairs.

Gradually, my eyes made out the shape of a box on the far side of the room. It was about the size of a four-poster bed and draped in what reminded me of mosquito netting, but was more of a heavy black gauze, hanging from top to floor, so that it was impossible to see the person inside.

'Good afternoon, Lady Foskett,' Sidney Grice said. 'I trust I find you well.'

The same breath and tin voice: 'You will never find me *that,* Sidney. What time has passed until this day?'

'Twenty-nine years, ten months and four days,' he said.

'So brief a span? It seemed to touch eternity.' The words came wheezing from her. 'You must learn to forgive the darkness, but even the conflagration of that waxen taper scorches the lining of my eyes now. I assume the sun still blazes in the ill-named heavens, but I have not confronted it in all these years for here is the realm of endless moonless night.'

'Do you have no visitors?' I asked.

'You will speak when you are spoken to.'

'If I did that I should be almost mute.'

My guardian murmured, 'March.'

But the voice resumed flatly, 'You are the first people I have allowed in this mansion since the great losses.'

'You did not meet a pharmacist by the name of Mr Horatio Green then?' Sidney Grice asked.

'I meet no one and address no soul except to instruct Cutteridge, and my speech is so weak now I must needs use this brass speaking trumpet built into my chair. I passed messages to Mr Green at the gate.'

There was a strong smell in the room like incense, not the frankincense I had smelled in a Roman Catholic Church but more like the masala incenses of India – cedarwood and something sickly.

'It is good of you to allow us in,' I said ironically and she coughed rapidly three times in what may have been a laugh.

'There is no goodness in *me*, young lady, and I am enervated already. Tell me your business.'

'I have come to ask you about a society which we have been told you joined,' Sidney Grice said.

'The Death Club? I did not join it. I conceived, gave birth to and suckled it. It is the bastard child of my unhappy fancies and now I have sent it out into the world.'

My guardian craned forward. 'And may I ask why, Lady Foskett?'

'I have heard about your profession and it does not dumbfound me. You were always an insufferably inquisitive child.'

'I mean no impertinence.'

'It was you who showed my second cousin, Mr Hemingway, his wife's love letters to his father. He shot them and himself as I recall.'

'If I had kept the correspondence from him I should have been an accessory to her deception.'

'You were always an arrant prig, Sidney Grice.'

'I have a love of the truth, Lady Foskett.'

'The truth?' The voice became distorted. 'You may stride around and about this noisome earth until the last fire grows cold upon it and never find such a thing.' She said something inaudible to me and then, 'I formulated the society because it amuses me. I do not read – why be perturbed by the trivial meanderings of men when I can wallow in the depthless mire of my own morbidity? But Cutteridge scours the newspapers on my behalf, clips out the obituaries and delivers them to me on a copper salver. What greater pleasure could I have than to discover obituaries of everyone I knew, all those coruscating perfumed ladies with their gorgeous powerful husbands and their beautiful precocious children. Those strutting, pomaded, shiny-skinned, fine peacocks and their toadying flunkies – what are they now?' Something rattled in her throat. 'Putrefying matter in their marble tombs.' She coughed drily. 'Rotting flesh on crumbling bones in their splendid sarcophagi.' The baroness fought for air. 'But there is a great famine of deaths for me to crow over in this age of steam and drains and telegraphy, and so I must devise some more: people whose complete corporal necrosis will bring me the additional gratification of fiscal advantage.'

'But, Lady Foskett,' Sidney Grice said, 'you must realize that your death is also to *their* advantage.'

Something bumped and the baroness exhaled heavily.

'I cannot die,' she whispered. 'I essayed to quench my thirst for death with a draught of vitriolic oil, but whilst it corroded my voice yet it did not kill me. It flows through my veins now. For two years I took neither food nor water. I willed my vital forces into extinction but whilst this wretched body grew weaker, my aspirations availed me naught and I found I could not die.'

'But surely that is not possible,' I said, and for a while all I could hear was her amplified breathing.

'I feed on my hatred,' she said. 'It is a thin food but pure.'

'But what about your friends?'

'Every man with a pulse, every woman with uncoagulated blood, every infant with a fluttering heart – they are all abominations detestable to me, every one of them my irredeemable enemies now.'

'But I am not your enemy, Lady Foskett,' Sidney Grice said, the shadows dancing on his cheek.

'From henceforth you are.' And for the first time since I had known him, when I looked at my guardian in the candle's flicker, I saw that he was shocked.

He put a hand to his brow and then his scarred ear. 'You know that Mr Edwin Slab died?'

'I rejoiced in my gelidity to hear it.'

'And Horatio Green?' I asked.

'The very fetidness of my soul exults. How and when did he die?'

'Yesterday, of poisoning, in my house.'

'You should take better care of your clients, Sidney' – the whisper was fading now – 'or soon you will have none left.'

'I hope to take care of you, Lady Foskett.'

The air soughed from the speaking tube and as my eyes learned to capture more light, I could just make out the outline of a figure through the black netting, a small woman seated motionless on a high throne. 'Enough...' A long sigh and a longer silence. 'Enough... enough.'

'I am sorry, sir, miss.' For the second time that day Cutteridge made me start. I had forgotten he was still behind us.

'Of course,' Sidney Grice said. 'Thank you for receiving us, Lady Foskett. We shall not tire you any further.'

'How weary, flat, stale and unprofitable seem to me all the uses of this world.' Her words were cracked like old leaves. 'There is no rest for the damned in this world or the next. I shall always be tired even beyond the end of time.'

Cutteridge blew out the candle and we followed his silhouette out of the room. He closed the door and took us down the creaking stairs.

'You will try to save her ladyship, sir?' His old eyes blinked anxiously as we set foot in the hall.

'I will do everything I can to protect her,' my guardian promised.

'May I shake your hand, sir?'

'It would be a privilege.'

Cutteridge's hand was huge. It wrapped around my guardian's and held on. 'We are dependent upon you, sir.'

'One vital question before we go,' Sidney Grice said. 'Where is the nearest tea shop?'

Cutteridge smiled. 'I see you have not lost your affection for that beverage, sir. Might I suggest Trivet's Tea House, just down the road to the right? They serve a good potted meat sandwich as I recall.'

We stepped out, dazzled by the greyness, and Cutteridge followed to lock the gate behind us. I heard the lock clank as we crossed the road, but when I looked back he had gone.

'That was an odd thing for him to say – asking you to save her,' I said, and Sidney Grice chewed his lower lip.

'There was something very wrong in that room,' he told me.

The crowd was thinning outside the gardens and a few cabs were waiting to pick up fares.

'Only one thing?' I asked and he flipped a peach stone into the gutter with his stick.

'Apart from all the obvious oddities that even you would have noticed,' he said, 'there was something else, something I heard but I cannot think what. One thing I do know is that Lady Foskett must be extricated from that awful society at the first opportunity.'

A woman of about my age wobbled past on a velocipede.

'How indecent,' Sidney Grice said.

'It looks like fun to me,' I said.

'Sooner or later you will come to realize that all fun is unfeminine.'

'I hope it is later then,' I said. 'Anyway, I do not think Lady Foskett wants to be removed from the society.'

Sidney Grice put on his gloves. 'Lady Foskett is a woman of the highest breeding and intelligence,' he replied, 'but when all is said and done, that is all she is – a woman.'

'There he is again.'

The boy in the yellow jacket was hurrying towards us.

'Fought you'd come back this way.' He looked up at me with his big child's world-exhausted eyes. 'Can't keep it.' He reached inside his shirt. 'Not after the kindness what you did me.'

He held out my purse and I took it.

'I will wager it is empty,' Sidney Grice said as the boy raced away.

'Every penny is still here.'

'The dirty blighter,' my guardian said. 'He has stolen my handkerchief.'

'Where there are crowds there are pickpockets,' I reminded him.

*

We had only just returned when a black carriage stopped outside with curtained windows and a darker shape on the paintwork where a crest must have been removed.

The groom jumped down and lowered the steps for a tall man to disembark. He reminded me of a frog with his bulbous eyes, thin tight lips and slack throat, but his movements were stately, deliberate and precise as he glided erect across the pavement.

Sidney Grice groaned. 'What the deuce is he up to now?'

'Who?'

I did not have to wait long for an answer, for Molly was dusting the hallway and answered his ring almost immediately.

'It's that Honourable Sir Whatsisname again, sir.' She presented his card on a tray but her employer waved it away.

'Send him in.' He climbed reluctantly to his feet, ran his hand through his hair and checked his cravat and eye patch.

'Mr Grice, how good of you to see me at such short notice.'

My guardian grunted and indicated a chair, but both men remained standing.

'What is it this time?' he demanded and our visitor glanced meaningfully at me. 'You can rely on Miss Middleton's discretion.'

The man's face stretched politely. 'Miss Middleton. My master expressed a wish to meet her, after the newspaper accounts of your last case.'

'It was not my *last* case,' Sidney Grice told him, 'and no such meeting shall take place whilst she is in my care.'

Our caller scrutinized me and turned up his lordly nose. 'Probably just as well to avoid disappointment.'

'Yes,' I said. 'I hate being disappointed.'

His lip quivered with unspoken retorts. 'If you are quite sure...'

'You have my word,' my guardian said and the visitor narrowed his eyes.

'My master finds himself in an embarrassing situation.'

'When does he not?'

The man flushed. 'My master had what I might describe as an indiscreet correspondence with a well-known lady of the theatre. When their... *friendship* ended the lady exacted a large sum of money upon receipt of which she returned all of my master's letters to her and a photograph which he had signed with expressions of an indelicate nature. The letters were burnt but the photograph seems to have disappeared. Were it to fall into the wrong hands…'

Sidney Grice threw his arms into the air. 'When will he ever learn and start behaving like a grown man?'

Our visitor bridled. 'I really cannot allow you to speak of his… my master in such terms.'

Sidney Grice tossed his head. 'I do not have time for all this twaddle. Tell your client to look under the false bottom of his escritoire drawer.'

The man looked flustered. 'Is that the message you wish me to convey?'

'Convey whatever message you choose,' my guardian said. 'Just tell him to be more careful and to stop wasting my time.'

Our visitor tightened his tight lips. 'Very well, Mr Grice. Please ring for me to be seen out.'

'Not your favourite client?' I asked when he had gone.

'I am sick of playing nursemaid to middle-aged children.' Sidney Grice fell back into his chair.

I rang for tea but did not ask him about the Prince of Wales's feathers on the visitor's cravat pin.

15

The Doctor and the Berries

BRYANSTON STREET LOOKED quite similar to Gower Street with its white stone-faced ground floors and the red-brick uppers, alongside the railings and the basement moats of the long Georgian terraces. After fifty yards or so we turned right down a mews, a narrower street with rows of stables to the left and tall, ramshackle houses to the right. My guardian rapped on the roof of our hansom and we came to a halt. He paid the cabby with a large tip.

'I will give you the same again if you wait.'

The cabby showed no sign of hearing him, but lowered his head and allowed his horse to do the same.

Dr Berry's consulting rooms were on the ground floor and a dowdy middle-aged maid with gappy, crooked teeth showed us straight in. A sombrely dressed woman about ten years older than me sat behind a desk, writing notes. She stood and held out her hand, which Sidney Grice took suspiciously.

'You are the doctor's wife?'

'I have no husband,' she said.

'But you are wearing a ring.'

'It wards off unwelcome advances from male patients.' The lady smiled. 'I shall not toy with you, Mr Grice, as I am all too used to the confusion I cause by my choice of profession. I am Dr Berry.'

'A woman.' My guardian put his hand to his mouth. 'How revolting.'

Dr Berry smiled again. 'If you have come to see me about your revulsion for women I can do nothing for you.'

'It is not an illness.'

'That is debatable.'

Sidney Grice recovered with great effort. 'I have come to see you about a Mr Edwin Slab who, I believe, was a patient' – he was unable to disguise his incredulity – 'of yours.'

'Mr Horatio Green told me to expect you,' Dr Berry said. 'I have heard all about their ridiculous club.'

'You certified the cause of death as a seizure,' my guardian said.

'Provisionally,' she agreed. She had short black hair, clipped severely back, but it could not disguise the gentleness of her nature. 'I was not present at Mr Slab's death and his family opposed my request for a full post-mortem examination. Unfortunately, the coroner held the same misguided opinion of women as you, Mr Grice, and respected their opinions more than mine.'

Sidney Grice bristled. 'My opinions are never misguided.'

'Another misguided opinion,' the doctor countered and I laughed. She had a faint accent that I could not place.

'Do you mind if I ask where you are from?' I enquired.

'Everywhere and nowhere,' she told me. 'I have never stayed anywhere long enough to say that I belong there. My parents were travelling performers.'

'Gypsies,' Sidney Grice said.

'Yet another misguided opinion,' Dr Berry responded and Sidney Grice looked at her. I expected him to be indignant at her presumption but he looked, if anything, mildly amused.

'*Gut gesagt*,' he said quietly.

'They ran and acted in a small theatre company,' she continued. 'I was educated in whichever country we toured for a season. You pick up a lot of languages quickly when you have to. So when I found that no British university was willing to award a degree to a member of the superior sex, I studied medicine in Paris and surgery in Bern.'

'Two of the ugliest cities in the ugliest countries in Europe,' my guardian pronounced and Dr Berry laughed.

'Casting your prejudices aside for one moment...'

'The mind of a man without prejudices is a train with no coal,' he asserted. 'It may be on the right track but it goes nowhere. I think you will find that all my prejudices are based on logical processes.'

'Then perhaps the premise on which you found each conclusion is flawed,' she suggested. 'But, to move on, how can I help you?'

Sidney Grice picked up her pen to examine it.

'How long had Edwin Slab been a patient of yours?' I asked.

'Only a few weeks,' she told me. 'I visited him twice because he had a bout of laryngitis which he was convinced was scarlet fever. I gave him a bottle of laudanum, more to calm him down than anything else, and told him to send for me again in a week if he was no better. Five days later I was called in by his housekeeper and told that he had had *an episode*. By the time I got there he was dead.'

'In bed?'

'No. In his workshop. Mr Slab was something of an amateur taxidermist and he appeared to have suffered a fit and fallen into a tank of formalin. His housekeeper and maid were unable to lift him out without help from the gardener and his boy.'

'Was he a big man?' Sidney Grice asked.

'Quite. But the task was made more difficult by the unusual degree of rigor.'

Sidney Grice put the pen back on a brass tray. 'Go on.'

Dr Berry began to pace the room. 'His housekeeper described to me how Mr Slab suffered from occasional epileptic fits, following a head injury in a carriage accident many years ago. He would go into violent convulsions and froth at the mouth, and it was obvious, when I saw his body, that he had had some kind of seizure. There was a great deal of vomit on the floor; he was cyanotic and his eyes were extruded with dilated pupils, but...' Dr Berry stopped by a large rubber plant and peered out of the window.

My guardian clicked his fingers and said, 'You fear the fit may have been induced?'

She spun to face us. 'Two things concern me particularly. The stiffness of his body was extraordinary, especially so soon after death, and I have never seen such a dramatic case of opisthotonus—'

'Which is?' Sidney Grice enquired shortly.

'When a body goes into such violent contractions that it lies arched with only the top of the head and the heels touching the floor,' I said. 'I have seen it in a fatal case of tetanus.'

Dr Berry looked at me. 'And where did you get your medical experience?'

'In India mainly, but also Afghanistan. My father was an army surgeon and he did not trust army nurses to assist him.'

Dr Berry smiled briefly. 'I can sympathize with that.' And her face fell again. 'All of which led me to at least consider the possibility of poisoning with—'

'Of course,' Sidney Grice interjected, 'strychnine.'

Dr Berry raised a crooked finger. 'I have also heard of it occurring with other alkaloids and chemical dyes, but I have never come across it myself.'

My guardian took two halfpennies from his waistcoat pocket. 'And your other concern was?'

She sucked her upper lip. 'When I tapped Mr Slab's chest it did not sound congested.'

'That was thorough of you.' Sidney Grice rattled the coins in his left hand. 'Which would suggest...?' He turned to me.

'That he was dead before he was submerged,' I said.

He tossed the coins and caught them. 'Or that the fluid drained from his lungs as he was hauled out.'

Dr Berry nodded. 'I did point this out to the coroner, but he told me I was letting my imagination run away with me.'

'Perhaps you were overwrought.' My guardian ignored her indignation. 'But I am acquainted with Vernon Harcourt, the Home Secretary, and he owes me nine favours. I shall get the body exhumed.'

'Perhaps you should wait a day before you take that step,' Dr Berry said. 'My concerns were so strong that I took a sample of Mr Slab's vomit and sent it to the pathology department of University College for analysis. The results are due back tomorrow.'

Sidney Grice went down on his haunches to look at her black leather medical bag on the floor by her desk. 'That is an unusual design.' He lifted it and I saw four inch-long legs on the base.

'Yes,' she said. 'I had that made by a man off Charing Cross Road. I have been in houses where raw sewage flows over the floor and my last bag was ruined.'

'Why are there three balls on each foot?' I asked and she laughed.

'Oh yes. They are meant to be berries – just a bit of fun.'

'Fun?' Sidney Grice echoed.

'You are unfamiliar with the word?'

'No. Just the experience,' I said.

*

'What a resourceful person,' my guardian commented as we left the house, 'and such a good clear analytical mind. But what a pity it is wasted on a woman. And what did you mean by implying that I never have any fun? Why, only the other day I got you to calculate some Gaussian eliminations. That was fun.'

'Highly comical,' I said.

'Yes. Especially when you confused co-primes with prime numbers. I... Blast that man!' Our cabby had gone. 'We shall have to walk to Oxford Circus if we are to have any hope of getting a ride.'

'What shall we do tomorrow?' I asked as we made our way back up the mews.

My guardian buttoned his Ulster coat. '*You* are going to do nothing. You have been looking decidedly unattractive in a hearty sort of way recently, so I hope a morning's inactivity might drain the colour from your cheeks. *I*' – he primped up his cravat and ran a hand through his hair – 'shall return in the morning.'

'To see Dr Berry?'

'To see if the laboratory report is back yet.'

'And see Dr Berry.'

Sidney Grice twiddled with his cane. 'Well, I shall need to discuss a few aspects of the case with her, yes.'

And it seemed to me that I was not the only one with colour in their cheeks.

Colour was the first thing I noticed about India before I was overwhelmed. From the deck of the ship I saw the coolies, their black bodies stripped to the waist, clad only in baggy pyjama trousers. But it was the women who really caught my eye. They were dressed in sarees, yards of cloth in one strip wrapped closely around each body and dyed in so many colours – bright saffrons, glowing golds, dazzling crimsons, vivid greens of every hue, some bordered with rich tapestries, some ornamented with silver or glittering with tiny mirrors.

Once we had docked, everything was confusion, a jumble of shouting and jostling all around us, the pleas of beggars and the cries of children, the rattle of rickshaws, the stench of the mob and animal dung and open sewers, the merciless heat of the midday sun, the heaviness of the air saturating my clothes and hair and dragging me down.

Colour was what first attracted you to me, you said, the way I flushed when I was angry – and there was so much to be angry about in India – the living conditions, the corruption, the arrogance, the bureaucracy and you. You were always so optimistic, so nice. It used to drive me to distraction, but... Oh, how I wish I could be angry with you now. I should like to shake you until your buttons flew off, and bury my face in your tunic when you begged for pardon. We always made up but we can never forgive each other anything now.

I carried my gloves. I have always hated wearing gloves but my guardian insisted I brought them. The sun was shining now through the fumes and the rooftops glistened with the remnants of a drizzle, but the people were pallid and their clothes were black and brown and grey as ashes.

16

Quicklime and Velvet

THERE WERE SEVERAL dozen mounds in the field, mostly overgrown and very few with headstones.

The air was still cold and thick with a misty drizzle. My umbrella could not hold it off and the hood of my cape did not stop my hair from clinging damp to my face as I stood and waited for the hearse to arrive.

It came with more speed than was usually considered decent, a low black carriage with one black horse tossing its blinkered head restlessly. The hearse stopped and four undertaker's men climbed out. Close behind came a covered carriage from which emerged a tall, broad woman in full mourning.

'Is this the funeral of Mr Horatio Green?' I asked one of the men as he dusted himself down.

'What there is of it.'

They hauled the coffin out and walked with it, not on their shoulders but holding it low by the handles. It was a fine oak casket with brass fittings and a nameplate on the lid. The woman followed, her head defiantly high and her face fixed, though her dark-ringed eyes belied her lack of expression. She bore little resemblance to her short, plump brother. The ground was boggy and sucked at my sinking boots with every step.

A tarpaulin lay over a long pile of soil beside the straight-cut hole just inside the gate and the pallbearers rested the coffin briefly upon it as they took cords from their velvet coats and looped them through the handles and, with only a brief pause to adjust their grips, they stepped either side of the grave, swinging the coffin over it and lowering it quickly. The cords were pulled away and the oldest bearer clapped his gloved hands twice. From behind a yew hedge two men appeared with shovels, and without further ado began to toss the soil back in.

A small cry escaped from the woman and she clutched her mouth as if to keep another in.

'What, no words?' I asked, and she looked across the filling hole and answered, 'No words, no vicar and no holy ground for the suicide.'

'May God receive his servant Horatio Green and have mercy on his soul,' I said, and the woman stared down and said bitterly, 'There is no mercy for those who quit this world in an act of mortal sin.' A robin landed on a clod of turf, picking through it. 'He loved birds.' She choked back a sob and walked away. I went after her and she stopped suddenly. 'Who are you and what were you to my brother? Must I bear another scandal at his graveside?'

'My name is March Middleton. I—' I began, but she interrupted me urgently. 'You were there. Did you see him kill himself?' She clutched my cloak. 'Did you?'

'No.'

'Then perhaps that weaselly detective of yours did it or maybe you.' She pulled her shawl tight around her.

'No, I—'

Her black-laced hand shot out and snatched my wrist. 'Why have you come here?' She started to pull me back through the gates and I tried to break away, but she was a strong woman and I did not want to fight her at her brother's funeral.

'I came to pay my respects.'

'Respects? To gloat more likely.' She dragged me to the edge of the grave. 'It's you who belongs in there, not him.' She swung me round. My feet were on the edge of the hole now and starting to slide, and I grabbed her arm to stop myself falling into it.

'Please. I do not know who killed your brother, but I tried to save him.' My right foot slid into the air. 'I tried.'

'Miss Green, come now.' The undertaker touched her hand and she let me go. I teetered and the younger of the gravediggers caught my sleeve and steadied me.

One of the pallbearers led Horatio Green's sister away, but she twisted her head and I had never seen such hatred blaze in a woman's eyes. 'You shall have a quicklime grave for this,' she shouted, 'and I shall come and spit on it.'

I stood and watched her being ushered back into her carriage and the pallbearers clamber back into the hearse and the grooms take up their reins and go back up the drive, more slowly and respectfully than they had arrived, and I wondered how she would react when she found she was excluded from her brother's will.

'You all right, miss?' It was the gravedigger who had saved me.

'Yes.' I fumbled in my purse and gave him two shillings. 'Thank you.'

'Only paid to bury 'em one at a time,' he told me with a grin.

You would have loved your funeral – the parade-ground precision, the praise of your courage under fire. You saved a comrade by putting yourself between him and the enemy, they said. They gave you a medal and sent it to your mother. How proud you would have been. How proud I must have been, they told me. They were impressed by my stoicism, not knowing how guilt makes heroes of us all.

I would have shared your grave willingly or taken your place if I could, but life is no fairer than death. And so I stood and watched as my heart was lowered to the accompaniment of a rifle salute, and the red soil thumped in reply. The Union Jack fluttered half-mast, a rectangle of cloth dyed in the three crosses that, we were told by a perspiring padre, you and your comrades died to protect.

It all sounded so noble to those who did not see the surgeon's knife or hear the screams of boys not even pretending to be men.

They did not know you died because of me. If only they could have buried that knowledge so ceremoniously.

17

The Man with No Arms

I WAITED UNTIL the hearse and carriage were out of view and lit a cigarette. My hand was steady but my heart still thumped. It was a long walk back to Bloomsbury but I needed it.

A man came running up to me. 'Spare a copper for a war vet'ran, miss.' He had no arms.

I kept walking because I knew I would be mobbed if I did not, and he trotted alongside. 'Where were you injured?'

'Waterloo, miss.'

I surveyed his face. 'You are about forty years too young for that one.'

'Most foreigners don't know that,' he said. 'They've 'eard of Waterloo, though.'

I laughed. 'What makes you think I'm foreign?'

'You don't live round 'ere,' he said. 'So you're foreign.'

'How did you really lose your arms?'

'Printin' press. I was resettin' it when they switched it on. Bam! Down it comes and splat – my arms is all over the front page.'

'Did your employers compensate you?'

'Oh yeah.' He wiggled his head vigorously. 'They was most generous. Twenty quid they gave me – five weeks' wages 'cause I was skilled, you see.'

I brought out a shilling. 'But how will I give it to you?' He had no pockets in his shabby clothes.

'Toss it in the air, miss.' I did and he caught it in his mouth.

'Gawd bless you, miss.' The coin appeared between his brown teeth. 'I'll keep it 'ere for safety.' The shilling disappeared again. 'You shouldn't be walkin' these streets by yourself.'

'I have been down worse.' I walked on and he fell back.

There was a public house on the corner – The Boar's Head – and I needed a drink, but hearing the drunken arguments going on inside, I dared not go in by myself. I thought about asking the beggar – but how could he have protected me? I was just about to walk on when I saw a man shambling towards the entrance. He was dressed in a grubby suit and his shoes were unlaced. His head was bowed and turned away from me, but there was something about him that I recognized. I hurried over and caught his profile.

'Inspector Pound?'

The man spun round. 'You.' His face was thick with stubble, his collar undone and his trousers splattered with mud. 'Clear off.' He flapped his hand as one might to a persistent stray and stepped backwards.

'But I have been worried about—'

'Take your worries and stuff them.' His voice was hoarse and his eyes bloodshot. 'And keep your trap shut.'

Two men worked their way out, half-supporting and half-pulling each other over in their intoxication. 'Bit of trouble with your strump, mate?' one asked.

'Nothing I can't handle.'

'Give her a bun, did yer?'

The Inspector Pound I knew, the urbane figure of authority, would have rounded on anyone who spoke to me like that. But he laughed coarsely and said, 'Who'd touch that old haddock on a dark night? Not me.'

The two men guffawed and the shorter one was slightly sick down his front.

'How dare—'

'I dare what I dare,' Inspector Pound snapped. 'And keep your trap shut if you don't want a taste of this.' He raised the back of his hand.

I swallowed. 'Very well, Inspector. I will—'

'Inspector?' The taller man burst out and Inspector Pound flinched.

'I used to inspect 'buses,' he said, 'before I found I liked inspecting bottles more.' They all laughed. 'Come inside, mates, and we'll inspect a few together.'

The two men turned unsteadily and with some difficulty, and were just about to go back in when another voice said, ''Buses my backside. I knew there was somefink funny about you.' A tall black-stubbled man with a shaven head and gold-capped teeth had come up behind us. He took a long, narrow butcher's knife from a sheath inside his jacket. 'I knew you was a copper's nark the moment I saw you. Get a nose for crushers when you've been done down and nibbed as often as me.'

'What you talking about, Smith?' the inspector asked. 'Come and have a drink with us.'

'I don't drink with bluebottles.' He adjusted his grip on the knife, holding it at hip level.

Inspector Pound spread his hands innocently. 'What, me? Don't make me laugh. I—'

'You will come home with me this minute,' I said. 'The kids want you and I came to tell you they said you could have your job back at the depot if you turn up sober on Monday.'

Smith sneered. 'Nice try, lady, but I never met a dutch yet who called her old man *inspector*.' With that last word his arm shot forward, the knife flashed, and the blade ripped through Inspector Pound's jacket and shirt, and in one clean movement plunged into his stomach all the way up to the hilt. I heard it cut through him, swishing like a spade in the earth.

We froze, Smith leaning forward clenching the bone handle, the inspector staring into his eyes. A deep stain appeared all at once and Inspector Pound grunted as if he had been punched. He looked down and reached for the knife, but Smith twisted it and pulled it out almost as quickly as it had gone in, and a gush of blood followed it. The inspector clutched at the wound and bent forward. Smith pulled his weapon back, ready to strike again, and I lashed out. I aimed for the eye but Smith was fast. He jerked his head back like a prizefighter and I caught his cheek with the handle of my parasol. He snarled angrily and swung his left arm out, crashing into my neck and sending me sprawling on to the pavement.

The two drunks backed hastily into the pub. Inspector Pound was almost doubled up and I saw his knees buckle as I scrambled up, swinging my handbag wildly and uselessly into Smith's shoulder as he pushed me aside. 'Want some?' he challenged. 'Well, just you wait your turn.'

He raised the knife for a downward blow on the crouching man. Inspector Pound looked at me. His hands were full and overflowing with his life's blood now. 'Run, March,' he gasped. 'Run, my dearest.'

I jabbed Smith in the side with my parasol. 'Drat you.' He wrenched it from my hands. 'Can't wait then?' He threw it into the road and turned to me. The inspector tried to lunge at him but tumbled helplessly to the cobbles. Smith took one step towards me and the knife went back, its blade already wet.

'Leave 'er.' A boot flew up. I saw it clearly – no laces and hardly any sole. But the toe cracked hard into Smith's groin and Smith let out a yelp and grabbed himself, but the knife stayed firmly in his grip. And I saw that the wearer of the boot was the man with no arms, and as Smith spun furiously towards him, the beggar smashed his head hard into Smith's face and Smith blinked and toppled, straight and heavy like a felled tree, cracking the back of his head on the edge of the kerb.

'Run, miss, before 'e comes to.'

'Like hell I will.'

'Go,' Inspector Pound said weakly as I ripped open his shirt. It was a savage cut, gaping wide and pumping steadily. I pulled off my scarf and rammed it into and over the hole, and the inspector groaned and twisted away.

'I am sorry.' I clamped his hands over the scarf.

He gritted his teeth and closed his eyes.

The armless man shouted into the bar. 'We need 'elp 'ere.' But the men inside did not move.

'It's you who'll be needin' 'elp when Smith wakes up with a sore 'ead.'

'You'll all get done if 'e dies – accessories to murder.'

'Where is the nearest hospital?' I asked.

'The London,' the man with no arms told me. 'Ten minutes' walk and you won't never get a cab this way.'

There was a big red-haired man with shaggy sideburns behind the bar.

'Are you sober?' I asked.

'Don't drink, miss,' he said. 'Daren't in my trade or I'd never stop.'

I looked at my watch. 'It is seven minutes to twelve,' I said. 'I will give you ten pounds if you can get this man alive to the hospital before noon.'

'I'll help,' an old black man called from his corner chair, and suddenly the saloon was full of volunteers.

'Just him.' I pointed to the redhead who was vaulting over the bar and out on to the street. He kneeled quickly by Inspector Pound, put one arm under his neck and another under his legs, and heaved him up, getting to his feet as he lifted the inspector like a bride at the threshold. The inspector moaned.

'Oh good Gawd,' the armless man said. 'I've gone and swallered me tin. Ne'er mind. I'll find it in the morning.'

'Out the way,' the redhead shouted. And he was off.

I have watched men run for their lives from a rogue elephant in musk or a wounded tiger in a botched hunt, but I have never seen a man run so fast as that barman went. I was unencumbered but I could not keep up with him as he sprinted along the street and through a court then down a long straight road. There was a massive red-brick building which I hoped was the hospital, but it was so far away and the streets were getting more crowded. On he pelted, hollering, 'Make way. Dyin' man. Make way.'

There was a market with stalls selling rags, buckets and re-caned chairs, and the man weaved between and around them, swerving like a rugby player going for the winning try. I crashed into a rack of battered saucepans and heard it clatter behind me.

'Frebbin' cow,' the woman in charge of it raged. But I had not time to stop and was too winded to apologize.

I was getting a stitch as we turned left into Turner Street and the man was twenty yards ahead of me by now. I could see his back and Inspector Pound's head and feet bobbing up and down as they reached the main gates.

'Man dyin'. Man dyin',' the red-haired man shouted as he forced his way through a heavy queue on the entrance steps.

I caught up with him in the lobby – an immense marbled hall in the palace of disease – both of us fighting for oxygen. The red-headed man slumped down on the bench, scattering a family that was already settled on it. His efforts had finally proved too much and it was all he could do to point to the clock high over the reception desk.

'One minute to twelve,' I gasped.

'Just in time,' he managed to say and looked down. 'Don't know about him, though.'

Inspector Pound's face was waxen white and when I lifted his arm, it was limp and heavy and his skin was clammy cold. I put my fingertips into his wrist, searching for a pulse.

'Oh dear God.' I moved my fingers around and dug them in deep, hunting for the faintest of beats but, hard as I tried, there was nothing but the dark weeping from his wound.

18

The Blood of a Lion

A NURSE CAME over. The red-headed man struggled to his feet and laid his burden on the bench.

The nurse leaned over and I saw she had thick stains on her apron. She pulled up Inspector Pound's top left eyelid with her thumb and peered into it. The pupil was tiny and fixed on the ceiling.

She let the lid go and looked at his other eye.

'He is dead,' she said flatly. 'I'm sorry. Somebody will come and take him.'

'Dead,' I whispered, though nobody heard me, my name in droplets of blood on my face.

She bustled away and I put an ear to the inspector's nose, but the clatter of feet and the cries of the sick were too loud for me to hope to hear anything. I touched the side of his throat and thought I felt a trembling under my third finger, and saw the blood ooze from his wound in time with the flutter of his heart.

I put my mouth to his ear. 'You are not dead,' I said, 'and you are not going to die. If Mr Grice were here he would absolutely forbid it.' And something tickled my cheek. It may have been a wisp of air or perhaps his eyelashes, which were flickering now.

'Nurse,' I called out, but she was dealing with a baby. 'We need a doctor,' I shouted.

'You and two hundred others before you,' a young woman said. She was holding a filthy cloth to her eye.

'Doctor,' the red-headed man bellowed. He had a fine loud voice and several people glared at him. 'Man dyin' 'ere.'

'And a dozen others in this room alone,' the nurse called. 'Hush yourself and wait your turn.'

'He is a policeman,' I said, but she only saw his pretence of a vagrant.

'And I'm the queen of Siam,' she jeered.

The man with no arms came panting into the room. He took one look, threw back his head and crowed like a cockerel. Three times he did it, ear-splittingly loud. And, as if he had been waiting for the summons, a doctor came into the waiting room, his coat off and his sleeves rolled up.

'What in heaven's name is that appalling racket?'

I ran over and grabbed his arm. 'This man is a police inspector working in disguise. He has been stabbed.'

The doctor crouched. 'He certainly has.' He stood. 'You men take a limb each and carry him through there.'

Four bystanders grabbed hold of his arms and legs and marched across the room.

'Be careful,' I said, and was alarmed to see how loosely his head hung back and that he did not even wince. The wound pulled open again and there was another spout of bleeding.

'Through here.' The doctor indicated a side room and they dropped him heavily on his back on a long table and departed.

'Wait out there,' the doctor told me.

'I have nursing experience. Can I help?'

'We have our own proper nurses. Goodbye.'

I went back to the bench. It was occupied now by five crying girls. The man with no arms was crouched in a slurry of Inspector Pound's blood and trying to reassure them. They had vivid pink rashes on their ears and necks.

The red-headed man was standing nearby. 'I 'ope 'e makes it.'

'You did your best.' I reached into my purse. 'Here is my card. If you call tomorrow I will give you the money.'

He took the card and left. The armless man stood up, nodded at me, 'Good luck, miss,' and turned for the exit. I chased after him.

'What is your name?'

'Charles Sawyer. My friends call me Chas.'

'You may have saved a man's life today, Chas, and you certainly saved mine. Thank you.'

Chas looked abashed. 'I don't like to see a lady knocked abart and you was kind to me.'

'Take my card,' I said. 'And if you come tomorrow I will reward you.'

'I don't expect—'

'And I did not expect to be rescued.'

'Show me the card.' He looked down. '125 Gower Street. I won't forget.'

He walked out and I waited and watched the nurse trudging wearily between patients, telling some to wait and others to go. And I wondered if I had been like that, too exhausted to show compassion. A boy with an injured mongrel was chased away. The five girls were herded out to be put in isolation. The doctor returned. 'I have stopped the bleeding but he is very weak. He needs more blood.'

'A transfusion?'

He wiped his hands on his coat. 'I have done a few and sometimes they work, but other times they hasten the patient's death. We think that there are different kinds of human blood and some do not mix well with others, but we have no means of distinguishing between them.'

'Take my blood,' I said. 'It is my fault he was stabbed.'

We went through to the side room where Inspector Pound lay grey as a corpse, his chest hardly rising. 'I have cleaned the wound with carbolic acid,' the doctor told me. 'There is some evidence it prevents suppuration and I have sutured what I could.'

A nurse was sharpening a needle on a stone. She tested it with her finger as I rolled up my sleeve.

'Sit there at his head.' The doctor wrapped a tourniquet crushingly tight round my arm and plunged the needle in at the inside of my elbow. He had some trouble finding a vein in the inspector's arm – they were empty and flat – but eventually he slid a needle in before releasing the pressure on my arm, and I watched my blood run into a sealed jar as the doctor operated a lever to pump it into the patient.

'Dr Lower was doing transfusions two hundred years ago,' he told me. 'He tried putting the blood of a sheep into a patient who had a violent temper in the hope of making him gentle as a lamb.'

The needle was burning in my arm. 'And did it work?'

'According to witnesses, the patient was so ill during the first course that he refused further treatment.' The doctor adjusted a connection in his tubes. 'Apparently Dr Lower was also planning to inject the blood of a lion into a coward to make him braver, but all his suitable cases' – his weary face twitched – 'were too timid to consent to treatment.'

I laughed. 'Perhaps you could give me the blood of a beautiful woman.'

The doctor assessed me. 'I doubt it would help.' It was a long process, but eventually he stopped. 'You must have given a couple of pints by now.'

'I feel fine. You can take more.'

He pulled the needle out and gave me a wad of cotton wool to hold over the site. 'I have enough patients as it is.'

I watched them lift the inspector on to a trolley and wheel him away. And it may have been wishful thinking but I thought he had some colour in his face.

I stood up and felt quite dizzy. The cold outside air helped a little as I made my way cautiously down the steps but, strangely, a nip of gin from my flask only made me feel worse. It took another two nips to fully revive me.

19

Blotting Paper and Goldfish

AN OLD MAN helped me into a cab and I would have been more grateful if he had not taken my brooch in the process. Luckily for me, it was not a favourite and I was too shaken to care. I slouched back in the seat, staring out in front of me, but all I could see was that knife flashing forward and sliding so easily and so deeply into Inspector Pound's stomach, and his look of stunned disbelief.

My guardian came into the hall the moment I got home. He settled me in my chair by the fireplace and went out to pay the driver.

'Let me see your neck… You have a nasty bruise but a high collar will hide that.'

'Inspector Pound—'

'Hush, March.' He touched my shoulder. 'Did you really think something like that could happen without my knowing it? Inspector Grant of the Commercial Road Station was informed by a constable who was questioning an attempted garrotting victim there, and the inspector sent word to me under the illusion that Pound is my friend. I was about to send Molly to collect you when you arrived.'

There was a bottle on a lacquered tray on the round table. 'What on earth were you doing in that area in the first place?'

I struggled to remember. It was so recent but too long ago. 'I attended Horatio Green's funeral.'

He went to the table. 'That was unwise but only what I have come to expect of you. How did you know where and when it was?'

'I stopped one of those girls who are always throwing stones at the house and told her there was a sovereign for whoever could find out which undertaker had the body. Rayner and Sons said that Mr Green's sister was expected to be the only relative in attendance.'

'That shows the best and worst sides of your character.' Sidney Grice took a small penknife off the tray. 'Initiative and extravagance. A shilling would have been more than sufficient. You are inflating the price of bribery, March. On top of which you could have asked me.'

'Would you have told me?'

'No.' He cut the foil on the bottle. 'And, in case you are thinking of traipsing back to the East End, the inspector is not allowed any visitors until he has been moved to a safer area. We shall discuss the incident in the morning when you are recovered.' He put down the knife and took up a corkscrew. 'Now the best thing for anaemia, Dr Berry tells me, is red wine. So...' He twisted the corkscrew in. 'I am afraid you will have to consume several glasses of vintage claret over the next few days to restore yourself.'

'Poor me,' I said.

'You must be brave,' he told me with no hint of irony. 'If I ever manage to get this preposterous' – he held the bottle between his knees and hauled – 'cork...' There was a pop and the wine splashed over his trousers. 'Out.' He poured a generous glassful and handed it to me.

I could see the surface wobble as I raised the glass to my lips. 'So how did your visit go this morning?' Wine was not my favourite drink but this was not at all bad. I drained it in three gulps.

'Exceptionally well.' My guardian touched his cravat and almost smirked. 'Dr Berry is a truly exceptional woman. We had a fascinating chat about Euclidean algorithms. And her geographical knowledge is astonishing. Do you know that she can give you the map reference for almost two hundred cities, towns and villages in England?' He refilled my glass, though not quite as generously this time.

'It sounds like an uproarious morning.' I could feel the effects already. 'And how many can you recite?'

'Oh, I know them all.' He waved his hand airily. 'Guess what she gave me. No you cannot. It—'

'Oh, do let me try,' I begged. 'A goldfish in a bowl.'

'No, she—'

'A coconut?'

'Now you are being silly.'

'A kiss?'

'Now you are being coarse. You remember I was interested in her pen? No, of course you do not. You never remember anything other than soppy poetry. Well, it turns out that Dorna—'

I could not let that pass. 'Dorna?'

'Dr Berry,' he corrected himself, 'designed the nib of that pen herself. It has a fine, flexible point to allow fluid legible handwriting at a much faster rate, and I am going to see if I can adapt it to fit my pen. We shall call it the Grice-Berry Self-Filling Flexible-Nibbed Patent-Pending Pen.'

'It will have to be a very long pen to print all those words on it,' I said and he pursed his lips.

'We have thought of that and agreed that a tasteful copperplate-style G&B embossed on the side will suffice. Just think of it, March. This pen will revolutionize commerce. Think how it would be if every office clerk could effortlessly increase his output by up to twenty per cent a day.'

'But surely the typewriting machine will do that and it produces much more legible results,' I said, and Sidney Grice put his hands together as if in prayer.

'I dare say these novelties have their uses,' he said. 'But try slipping one into your pocket. No, March, the Grice-Berry Pen represents the future of chirography for the next hundred years.'

I swirled the wine in my glass. 'So what did the laboratory tests show?'

My guardian stopped his rhapsody and said, 'Oh, that. The results are not back yet. I shall have to call on Dr Berry again in the next day or two.'

'What a nuisance for you.'

'Yes.'

'Shall I come too?'

'You will not be required.'

'So you will have to be all alone with that monstrous woman,' I sympathized.

Sidney Grice looked at me. 'I shall manage,' he said stiffly as the mantel clock struck. 'But we have no time to squander in brainless chitterchat. Drink your wine, March. You must keep your strength up. Tomorrow we have an appointment at—'

'Edwin Slab's house.'

My guardian looked askance. 'And you acquired that information how?'

'After you wrote a telegram with your wondrous pen,' I explained, 'you blotted it. As I am sure you know, it is a simple thing to read blotting paper in a mirror.' I was feeling dizzy again.

'How inquisitive you are,' he said, not entirely disapprovingly.

'I need to be,' I said, 'if I am to become a personal detective.'

'Dear child,' Sidney Grice selected a journal from the rack beside him, 'that is one thing you shall never be.' I was too worn out to argue with him. My neck ached from the blow and my arm throbbed from the needle. 'There is an interesting paper in this month's *Anatomical News*,' he continued. 'Not only do women have much smaller brains but they have only a quarter of the number of nerve cells per ounce compared to those of a man. Apparently, large areas of the female brain are filled with fluid – not so much grey matter as grey water. Oh, March, you have carelessly splashed your wine in my face. How on earth did you manage that?'

'I cannot imagine.' I closed my eyes and let the sound of sloshing in my head lull me to sleep.

You could never hold your drink and I am not sure you ever really enjoyed it, but a subaltern who did not drink would have been like a vicar who did not pray. I always had a good head for it. My father said I was hardened to alcohol from infancy because my nanny used to put brandy in my milk to get me off to sleep, then top me up if I awoke in the night.

Once, in a silly dispute, I recklessly challenged you to a drinking competition. It would not have mattered really, but I was your guest in the mess and we quickly gathered a crowd of your comrades round us. Only a man could handle whisky, you said, and we matched each other glass for glass. After ten glasses I felt quite woozy, but you were slurring and spilled your eleventh down yourself. You had to take a double drink in forfeit for that and I could see that you were having trouble getting it down, so I dropped my glass and pretended to pass out, and not a moment too soon. I had hardly slumped in my chair when you toppled sideways out of yours.

I was ill the next morning and my father was furious when he found out the cause.

'How irresponsible,' he fumed, 'leading a young innocent astray.' And he stalked out of the house, cane in hand, straight to the junior officers' quarters to commiserate with you.

20

The House of Beasts

EDWIN SLAB HAD lived in a large white house set nicely back from a well-swept street just off Prince Albert Road, the tidy garden secluded from public gaze by a low wall and a high privet hedge. The clatter of traffic was muffled by the tall grand houses overlooking Regent's Park but still audible as Sidney Grice rattled the knocker.

'I wonder why' – he ran the toe of his boot backwards along the path – 'anyone would use shingle from Llandudno beach when there are so many supplies of gravel closer to home.'

'Does it matter?' I asked and he raised an eyebrow.

'The truth always matters, March. If you mean "is it pertinent?" the answer is almost certainly no.' He eyed two pigeons uneasily as they landed in a lilac tree.

We were greeted by a small elderly lady in a grey dress and a voluminous black wig, masses of curls with long ringlets dangling about her face.

'Have you come to evict me?' Her voice quavered.

'No,' I said. 'We just want to talk to you.'

'Do we?' Sidney Grice tapped a stone unicorn with his cane.

'Well, there's nobody else here, sir,' she told him. 'The owner, Mr Slab, has passed away and the rest of his staff have upped and gone.' She made a dipping arc with her arm as if introducing them. 'Maissie and Daisy and Polly and Mrs Prendergast – all skidooddled. But I'm eighty-six, you know, and who would take me on?'

'Not I,' Sidney Grice said. 'Not even in your heyday – if you ever had one.'

The woman swallowed a wounded gulp.

'My name is March Middleton,' I said, and she perked up.

'*The* March Middleton?' Her voice rose excitedly. 'I've read all about you in the papers. You must be the one who works with that horrible Sidney Grice, the man what kills everyone.'

The man what killed everyone scowled, but I laughed and said, 'Not quite everyone. This is Mr Grice in person, and who are you?'

'Miss Flower,' she said. 'I'm eighty-six, you know, and my mother called me Rosie.'

'Then I shall too,' I said. 'Can we come in, Rosie?'

'Of course we can.' Sidney Grice pushed past her into the house. 'What is your position here, old woman?'

'Housekeeper,' she said, 'or at least I used to be until I got too old. Mr Slab only kept me on out of charity.' She dabbed the corners of her eyes with a black-bordered handkerchief which she had tucked into her sleeve. 'Full of kindness, Mr Slab was. He didn't deserve to die like that.'

'To judge him by his taste in furnishings, I am not so sure,' my guardian said. The floor of the entrance hall was scattered with zebra skins and the pine-panelled walls were hung with them. 'Where did your employer die?' He fingered her hairpiece.

'In his workroom,' Miss Flower said, 'if you would like to follow me.'

'I should not like it in the least. Hold still, woman. ' He picked a piece of fluff out of her wig and popped it into an envelope. 'I am most particular about whom I follow, why, when and where, and I shall not have witnesses dictating the sequence in which I collate evidence. At best your suggestion is impertinent. At worst it might be construed as suspicious.'

Rosie Flower blinked. 'Suspicious, sir?'

'But since I am unfamiliar with the topography of this building…' He took off his gloves and dropped them into his hat. 'Show me his study.'

'Study, sir?' She placed his hat on the hall table and my parasol in a stand made of an animal's leg.

'It would seem that Mr Slab, not content with filling up beasts, employed the services of a parrot.'

'Parrot, sir?'

'Study,' he snapped. 'There is not a man in England worth over four thousand pounds who does not possess one. Take me to it... *now*.'

Rosie indicated an open door on the left and Sidney Grice brushed past her again. 'Come along.' And Miss Flower tottered after him with me at the back, scrutinizing the decor.

A zebra's head hung over the interior porch, mouth agape as if remembering the nasty shock it must have endured, and the black-and-white striped curtains were tied back with tasselled tails.

'He called this the Hyena Room,' Rosie Flower announced as we entered.

'I cannot think why,' my guardian murmured. Stuffed hyenas posed self-consciously all around the room, their fur patchily spotted, their black lips pulled back to reveal gapped spikes of orange teeth and dark tongues, their faces a curious cross between bears and wild dogs, with big oval ears and ugly, cold yellow eyes.

'Because—' Rosie Flower began.

'Was this his chair?' Sidney Grice pointed to a hairy armchair with a hyena crouching as a resentful footstool.

'The very one he sat in every evening,' Miss Flower said.

He went down on one knee and patted the seat cushion. 'Left-handed.' He dabbed the tip of his middle finger on the tip of his tongue. 'And a lover of chocolate éclairs.' He lifted the cushion. 'You were not lying about him being kind.'

Rosie Flower looked bewildered. 'But how can you tell?'

'The undersurface of this cushion has not been cleaned since before eighteen seventy-seven. There are five distinct rings of *Erysiphales Espanola* – Spanish mildew also known as oak mould, not because it grows on oak trees, but because it does so in an incremental annual annular fashion.'

'I don't understand, sir.' She sucked her lips in.

'I am merely pointing out that no one other than a soft-hearted dolt would have employed the services of a maid who was so slovenly, nor a housekeeper who was so decrepit as to allow such laxity.'

Rosie's eyes welled up. 'Mr Slab was always very appreciative of our labours.'

Sidney Grice snorted. 'Hence my choice of the word *dolt*. Why are there buckets of sand in every corner?'

'Mr Slab was terrified of being caught in a fire, sir. He had ropes fixed inside all the upstairs windows to climb down but I would die if I tried using one of those.'

I trod on an outstretched paw and jumped. 'Did he kill all these himself?'

'Oh no,' Miss Flower said. 'He did love killing things, but he never travelled further abroad than Winchester. All of these came from the zoo. The man who brought them was most anxious to reassure me that they had all died of old age.'

'But this one is a cub.' The pole of a table lamp projected from its head.

'That one died of young age,' she said.

'If only you had followed its example,' Sidney Grice told her. 'Were you with your lackadaisical employer when he died?'

'No.' Miss Flower polished the tip of a hyena's nose with her sleeve.

'Did you discover him?' I asked.

'Yes.' She ruffled its spiky mane affectionately.

Sidney Grice walked round an onyx table supported on the heads of four sitting hyenas. 'Tell us.' He snapped his fingers.

'Well, I was having my supper downstairs with Maissie and Daisy and Mrs Prendergast when—'

'Where was Polly?' my guardian interrupted.

'It was her afternoon off, sir.' Rosie twisted her handkerchief. 'I expect she was spooning in a pleasure garden with her young man.'

'And his name is?'

'Richard Collins.'

'Then what happened?'

She reddened. 'I'm trying to tell you, sir.'

'Get on with it.' He brought a short pair of tweezers out of his satchel.

Rosie Flower's right hand twizzled in agitation. 'I'm eighty-six,' she remembered. 'Or seven.'

I took her arm. 'Please tell us what happened to Mr Slab the night he died.'

'Well, I was having my supper downstairs with Maissie and Daisy and Mrs Prendergast,' she began as Sidney Grice plucked a tuft of hairs from a snarling hyena's head, 'when Mr Slab rang the bell.'

'How do you know it was Mr Slab?' My guardian dropped his sample into a white envelope.

Rosie Flower twiddled with a ringlet. 'The bell came from his workroom and so—'

'And so you made the illogical but possibly true assumption that it was your employer who rang it.' He scribbled on the envelope and sealed it with a metal clip.

'But there was nobody else in the house, sir.'

'The fact that you did not observe anybody else in the house does not mean there *was* nobody else.' Sidney Grice poked a straight length of wire in the specimen's ear. 'Proceed with your account but do try to gather your senile mind.'

'Just ignore him,' I said.

He grunted and pulled out the wire to scrutinize the end.

'I went to see what he wanted.' She tickled behind a hyena's ear.

'Why you?' he asked as she patted its head.

'Because Maissie was scullery maid, Daisy was having her cow-heel jelly and Mrs Prendergast was Cook.'

'Continue.' Sidney Grice sat behind the desk in a brown leather captain's chair and pulled open the top drawer of the desk. He brought out a stack of letters and undid the string tied round them.

'You shouldn't be looking at those, sir.'

'Which is exactly why I am.' He unfolded the top letter. 'What happened when you answered the call?'

Miss Flower wrapped a string of fur round her finger and said, 'Poor Mr Slab was lying in his tank.'

'What tank?'

'His pickling tank. I can show—' She started towards the hall.

'Stay exactly where you are.' Sidney Grice paused from measuring the hyena's teeth. 'I shall not have you deliberately or inanely misleading me with your false impressions. Was the tank full?'

'Yes, sir. It was full of Mr Slab and overflowing with pickling water.'

'Was he face-down?' I asked.

'Sort of.' She unwrapped her finger. 'He was all bent backwards in a funny way – except it wasn't funny – and the poor man had been sick everywhere.'

'He cannot have been sick on the ceiling,' my guardian pointed out. 'Be more specific, woman.'

'Everywhere,' she said. 'All over the floor. There was a lovely donkey-skin rug soaked all through. We had to throw it away.'

Sidney Grice snatched at the words. 'You admit you destroyed evidence?'

'I was just clearing up, sir, me and—'

'Where else did he vomit?'

'All over his cutting-up table and Veronica too.'

'Who is Veronica?'

'A mangrove.' Miss Flower tapped on the snout of a hyena. 'A sort of otter what kills snakes.'

'I think you mean a mongoose,' I suggested.

'Do not attempt to put words in the witness's mouth,' my guardian snapped.

'Took me all morning to clean her up and she's still damp. And he made a terrible mess of Sidney.' She pointed to an especially mangy wolf near a magazine rack. 'We brought him up here to get dry.'

I laughed. 'Is that really its name?'

'It is now.' Rosie Flower winked.

'What else did you remove from the scene?' Sidney Grice snapped. 'A gun or a knife perhaps? Do not answer that. Proceed with your rambling.'

Rosie Flower pulled down her lips and tensed them for a moment. 'I went over to the tank and he didn't look at all right, sir. Apart from being dead and curved up like a humpback bridge, his eyes were near popped out of his eyeholes like tennis balls, they were, but the worst of it was he had this horrible grin, like a cheddar cat it was, and he had ground his teeth so hard that they were all smashed up.' She shook out her handkerchief. 'Oh, miss, it was most distressing.' Rosie Flower dabbed her eyes.

'Continue,' my guardian said and she raised her chin.

'Pardon my saying so, but you are not a nice man, Mr Grice,' she said as he strolled round her. 'Then I ran to the top of the stairs and shouted down to Maissie, *Go fetch Dr Berry*. She has young legs. *And be sharp about it, you idle good-for-not-very-much*. But he was dead by then. I'm sure of it. Oh, the poor man. He was ...' Rosie Flower's mind strayed far away. 'He was ...' she repeated distractedly.

My guardian clicked his fingers. 'Did he have any callers that day?' And she jolted back to us and said slowly, 'Not a rich man nor a poor man.'

'Or the day before?'

'Not a saint nor a sinner, nor the day before that, nor any other day this side or the other side of any day you trouble yourself with, sir.'

'Why not?' I asked.

'Why, he had no time for callers with all his work, taking innards out and stuffing stuffing in and dealing with all his visitors.'

He regarded her through a glass paperweight. 'You led us to believe that he had no visitors.'

'No *callers*.' She pushed the wig up her forehead. 'Callers come to the front. Visitors go round the back and there was no end of those – people with pets what they wanted done. We had a horse last month, but they were too slow bringing it and the gases exploded it. All its insides were outside.'

'Did he have any visitors on the day he died?' I asked.

'I expect.' She pulled the wig down again. 'But we never really knew who was there or not.'

Sidney Grice folded the letters and tied them in a bundle again. 'Where is the workshop?'

'Down the end of the hall to the left, sir.'

He waved the letters at her. 'Show me.' And let them fall on to the desk top.

21

The Regiment of Cossacks

OFF WE SET back into the hall and down a long colonnaded vestibule, our footsteps clicking on the green marble floor. On either side the walls were plastered and painted with garish jungle scenes. Improbable tigers peeped from behind palm trees and unconvincing lions poked their heads through bamboo screens, and all along the arched ceiling peculiar serpents stretched and coiled in iridescent greens with impossibly daggered fangs. A stuffed black bear stood sullenly in an alcove and a brown one in another. Their paws were probably meant to be slashing, but they looked more like they were waving mournfully to each other.

We got to the end and Rosie Flower unlocked the door. 'Here we are.' It opened into an enormous conservatory. I had not seen anything so big since my father took me to Chatsworth House, and for an instant it was like stepping into an indoor zoo.

There was not a beast I could think of that was not present in that room. Mice played around cats who dabbed at mastiffs and Great Danes. These in turn looked up at ponies and carthorses, an elephant and two giraffes. Panthers, leopards and wolves stood in a peaceful circle, watched happily by a dozen owls perched on the leafless branches of a gnarled olive tree.

Unlike a zoo, however, there was not a cage in sight and every creature there was silently frozen, while our noses were assaulted not by animal odours but by the sting of formalin and the sickly sweet pungency of mothballs.

We made our way through the dead menagerie into a windowless white-distempered room that was more reminiscent of a mortuary. To one side stretched a huge operating table with a rack of gas lamps hanging low over it. Rosie turned the lights up. Surgical saws glinted on hooks along the wall and there was a row of knives arranged in order of size, from scalpels to butchers' skinning knives and cleavers. Four covered bins stood below on the white tiled floor. A stepladder was propped against the wall. To the right was a glass tank about six foot high and five foot square, I estimated. It was three-quarters full of a murky liquid and reeked of formaldehyde.

I tried the handle of the back exit. It was locked. 'Where does this go?' I brushed against a sack and got white powder on my dress.

Rosie blew her nose. 'It opens on to Hatter Street. His visitors came and went this way.'

'And you never saw them?'

'Not unless Mr Slab called me in, which wasn't often enough to be called often.'

'Where is the key?' Sidney Grice took a large femur from a wooden box on a shelf.

'On the wall there, sir.'

He took it off the hook and opened the door. On its outer side was a brass plaque. EDWIN SLAB, TAXIDERMIST TO THE GENTRY. PLEASE RING. The street outside was deserted and it was raining heavily. He stepped out and tested the bell. 'It has been disconnected.'

'Children used to ring it and run away, sir. Customers knew to knock five times.'

He shut the door and locked it. 'This room stinks of bleach.'

'We had to clean up, sir.'

'And destroy evidence.' He pushed his wet hair back. 'That could go very badly against you in court.'

Miss Flower's lower lip quivered. 'Court, sir?'

He picked something off a shelf. 'This syringe is broken and by the small cuts on your right thumb and forefinger you may come under suspicion of having caused the damage.'

Miss Flower bit her lip. 'I picked it up, sir... from the floor over there.'

'Your answer to the next question may have terrible consequences for you.' Sidney Grice put his face very close to hers and peered into her old eyes through his pince-nez. 'Did you bend the needle accidentally or on purpose?'

'Neither, sir. It was already—'

'Who washed the floor?' he asked angrily as I opened a cupboard to find it stacked with pelts steeped in camphor.

'Why I did, sir, with Polly.'

He replaced the syringe. 'Then perhaps you would like to describe every footprint upon it, the size and shape of the boots that made them, any distinctive defects of the soles or heels, the movements conveyed by their patterns but then' – Sidney Grice banged his cane on the table – 'perhaps you cannot. No more than you can tell me where every fibre was, its length, thickness and colour, whether it lay on the dust or partly or completely under it. Of course you cannot because you are a senile and witless short-sighted old—'

I slammed the cupboard door. 'That is enough.'

My guardian jerked his head back as if avoiding a blow. 'Kindly do not interrupt my interrogation of a suspect.'

Rosie Flower quailed. 'Suspect, sir?'

'She is a frail old lady,' I said. 'And please do not trouble to tell me about the frail old lady who single-handedly wiped out a regiment of Cossacks with a cheese wire.'

He looked puzzled. 'I am unfamiliar with that case.' He put his head into an open wall safe and Rosie Flower stepped back uneasily.

'That is all for now, thank you,' I told her as my guardian's head reappeared.

'I have not finished questioning her yet,' he bridled.

'Yes, you have,' I said, and to my surprise he acquiesced,

shutting the safe as if it were delicate, then opening it again and wiping his hands on a white cloth from his satchel. 'Well, congratulations, Miss Flower. You have carried out the most professional obliteration of clues that I have ever been honoured to witness. And I speak as a man who has worked with – or in spite of – the police forces of eight different nations. What a pity for your employer that you were not always so assiduous in your duties.' Rosie Flower opened her mouth in protest but thought better of it. 'There is nothing to be gleaned here.'

We made our way back through the conservatory, skirting a splendid crocodile that I had not noticed before, with a kid goat lying placidly between its jaws.

Miss Flower straightened her wig. 'Shall I see you out, sir?'

He shooed her away. 'We are not leaving yet.' He went back into the study. 'And do not attempt to flee.'

'Where would I go, sir?'

'Are you asking for my advice on how to escape justice?'

'No, sir. I should be glad to see some justice one day.'

He turned his back on us.

'Do not let him upset you,' I told her. 'It is just his way.'

'If he were my charge I should tell him to mend it.'

'What will happen to you now?' I asked and she trembled.

'I'm sure I don't know, miss. I shall stay here until they throw me out. In the meantime I have food and shelter. After that, what is there for my sort? I'm eighty-six, you know, and I have no savings to speak of – just a few shillings I was putting aside for some pretty pink ribbons for my hair – and I shan't go in the workhouse, miss. I shan't.' She stamped her foot and nearly toppled over.

'Have you no family?'

'Brothers and sisters all dead.' She steadied herself on the edge of a zebra-skin stool. 'They never had nice employers like Mr Slab.'

'Are there no charities that can help?'

'Oh, miss,' she exclaimed, 'there's precious little charity in this fine city and what there is goes to fallen women, and the trouble is I never fell.' She smiled shyly. 'Wish I had now.'

I laughed. 'It is a probably a little late for that now.'

Rosie Flower put her hand on my arm. 'Never too late to fall, miss.'

I remembered Harriet Fitzpatrick telling me about a new charity for old servants. 'I shall make some enquiries,' I promised as I turned away.

22

The Hyena in the Room

THERE WAS A stack of paperwork on the captain's chair when I returned. My guardian had pulled all the drawers out of the desk and was on his knees, peering inside its empty shell.

'What are you looking for?'

Mr G emerged, looking a little grubby. 'A scientist records all the information he observes and a good scientist observes everything.' He turned the drawers upside down and banged on them. 'You would be astonished how many people think it is safe to hide things by affixing them under drawers. I have sent two women to prison simply by inspecting their bureaux. But it is difficult to persuade the average policeman to search anything, let alone underneath it.' He slid the drawers back into place. 'Desks are usually a cornucopia of information. They have diaries noting important rendezvous, letters revealing romantic liaisons; incriminating documents, hidden weapons, locks of hair. But this is the most unrewarding piece of furniture I have come across since I searched your bedside cabinet last week.'

I clenched my jaw. 'You searched my bedside cabinet?'

'It would appear that Miss Flower's psittacine tendencies are contagious,' he said and I was just working out that psittacine referred to parrots when he asked, 'What is the first thing you notice about this room?'

'The hyenas,' I replied and waited for a sarcastic response.

'Very good,' he said. 'Grice's third rule of detection is not to ignore the obvious. What else do you notice?'

I thought about it. 'There is only one armchair.'

'Precisely,' he agreed. 'So presumably that scuttle-brained housekeeper was telling the truth about her master never entertaining callers, at least not in this room. Take a look around and see if the other rooms are more sociably equipped, and do try not to destroy any clues.'

'Everything is a clue,' I reminded him.

'Remember that and you might be slightly less of a nuisance.' He crawled round the desk. 'This is only the second time I have come across this type of varnish used on walnut veneer.' He lay on his back with his arms stiff at his sides. 'What is the easiest way to give somebody poison?'

'Put it in their food or drink... providing the flavour is masked.'

He crossed his ankles. 'Would liqueur-filled chocolates do it?'

'I imagine so.'

Sidney Grice pointed lazily and I followed his hand. In plain view on the mantelpiece was a wooden box. 'Open it, but do not touch the contents.'

There were five chocolates in the box with a space just the right size for a sixth.

'So you think—'

My guardian put a finger to his lips.

'Attempt neither to anticipate nor to interpret the complexities of my intellect.' He closed his eyes and began to hum loudly and as tunelessly as ever.

I left him to it and crossed the hall into a dining room, decorated with fish: brown trout over the fireplace; sticklebacks suspended in an aquarium amongst wilted reeds; and a giant tunny fish in a case on a low stand. A rectangular table surrounded by twelve chairs dominated the room. All but the carver at the head were covered in dust sheets.

Further down I found a sitting room. Birds were the theme here – sparrows, owls, hawks and seagulls, two eagles with wings outstretched, an unhappy-looking robin on a twig and a kingfisher frozen in mid-swoop. In this room too there was only one armchair.

From somewhere above me I heard a dull thump and the sound of feet scrabbling. It did not seem likely that Miss Flower would be scurrying about so energetically. I went quickly to the study.

'This room has been searched by someone else and recently.' Sidney Grice had turned a small rug upside down and was dabbing the undersurface with a strip of gummed paper.

'There is somebody upstairs,' I said. 'I heard feet running.'

'Is there any point in telling you to stay here?' My guardian snatched up his cane.

'No,' I said, and we hurried into the hall and up the wide staircase. It turned back on itself on to a well-lit square corridor.

'It was over the sitting room' – I pointed – 'which should be that way.'

The door was ajar but I could hear nothing now. Sidney Grice twisted the handle of his cane until it sprung out to twice its original length, motioned me to stand to one side and prodded the door. It swung open easily. The room we found ourselves in was bright and cheerfully decorated. It had floral wallpaper and a pink Persian carpet. There was a single bed with a red counterpane and a lacquered dressing table with a set of brushes and a cheval mirror on it. The wardrobe was open with one plain dress hanging in it.

'Mr Slab certainly treated his servants well,' my guardian observed.

'There is the rope she spoke of.' There was a thick four-ply cable spliced into a loop and attached to a hook under the sill. The other end hung through the window.

'It is taut.' My guardian ran towards it and I hurried to join him, and the first thing I saw was Rosie's wig in the upper branches of the lilac tree. I leaned out further and straight below me was the back of a bald head and a grey dress billowing in the breeze.

'We must get her down,' I said. 'I hope she is not tangled in those branches.'

'She will pass through,' he assured me. Sidney Grice gripped the rope in both hands and hauled to create a little slack, and I unlooped the rope from the hook. He put a foot on the wall, then leaned back and paid out the rope. 'I have her.' His face was purple with the strain. 'Go to her, March – quick as you can.'

I raced from the room, down the stairs and out into the front garden, almost crashing into the unicorn in my haste. Miss Flower was about four feet from the ground, facing the house and creaking downwards. I ran under the tree and reached up, grasping her under the arms as she descended.

'I have her,' I called up and the rope snaked down, crashing through the branches, her whole weight suddenly in my hands. She was heavier than I expected and I staggered back, almost toppling over with her on top of me, but the trunk steadied me as I laid her supine on the gravel.

Rosie Flower's face was swollen black, her eyes wide and bloodshot, and her chewed tongue stuck out through a bloody froth. I pulled at the knot but it was embedded into the crêpe skin of her bruised neck. Sidney Grice appeared breathlessly. He brought out a clasp knife and sawed, but the rope was tough and it was several minutes before he was able to stop and rip the last few strands apart.

Her body was very hot but lifeless.

'I must have heard her feet drumming on the wall,' I said. 'I did not realize...' I stopped. 'She talked about falling. I thought she meant...'

My guardian touched my shoulder. 'If there *is* a beneficent God, she is happy; if there is not, she is at peace.' He proffered me a big white handkerchief with DB embroidered in one corner. I did not need it, but I accepted it because I knew he was trying to comfort me.

I took some twigs from her sleeve and Sidney Grice lifted the old housekeeper as one might a child, his left arm under her shoulders and his right below her knees, and carried her back to her room. We laid her on her bed and I closed her eyes and crossed her arms, while he fished out her wig with his cane. I raised her head to put it on, but could only create a travesty of the woman we had met little more than an hour ago. I prayed quietly but, though he stood in respect, my guardian's lips did not move.

'I will arrange for an undertaker,' he said, white-faced, and later, in a steadily swaying hansom, he asked, 'Where did you read about the woman who killed a regiment?'

'I was probably confused.'

He sucked his lower lip. 'Yes, you usually are.' He coughed and put a hasty hand to his eye. 'Perhaps Miss Flower was right and I do kill people.'

'It was not you,' I said. 'This Christian world of ours killed Rosie Flower.'

23

Kali and the Toothpick

We went home. Sidney Grice adjourned to his study and I to my room.

I read your letter, the one you wrote when you were sent to the hills. Several British and Indian travellers had gone missing in the district and it was rumoured that the Thuggee cult had been revived in the area. The Thuggees, you told me, were bandits driven by their fanatical devotion to Kali, the goddess of darkness and death. It was their practice to befriend groups of travellers and, having gained their confidence, strangle them with knotted handkerchiefs. The bodies were then mutilated and disposed of in wells.

You were worried that you might not get the chance to confront them. I was worried that you would. I was scared, of course, that you might get killed, but my greatest fear was that you might kill somebody. I could not imagine you doing that. Those big gentle hands that cradled my face were not those of a killer.

As always, we dined by ourselves – cold potatoes and a salad drenched in vinegar. My guardian was occupied with some old case notes, so I turned to Tennyson's 'In Memoriam'. Sometimes it comforted me, but not tonight – the doubts and hopelessness of the verses pressed too heavily upon my heart.

'Ha,' Sidney Grice called out triumphantly. 'Although there are nine known cases of death by nitrous oxide poisoning in this green unpleasant land of ours, four were at the hands of incompetent dentists, another four were accidental overdoses at parties and one was during a demonstration on stage in Piccadilly. Silas Braithwaite could be the first case of murder or suicide by laughing gas ever to be documented. A bit of a feather in my cap, what?'

'Tis better to have loved and lost than never to have loved at all. I closed my book. 'I am so happy for you,' I said.

'Thank you, March.' He clapped his knees.

'And how many cases of elderly housekeepers hanging themselves have you come across?' I asked, and my guardian blew some air between his lips.

'Oh, they are two a penny.' He popped out his eye. 'It would have to be a very quiet week for that to make even the local press.'

There were slug holes in my lettuce.

'So' – he put his eye into its velvet pouch – 'what are we to make of Mr Slab's unpleasant demise?'

'He was probably poisoned with strychnine and possibly drowned in formalin,' I said.

'I am pleased to note that you have qualified your conjectures.' He whipped a folded black patch out of his jacket. 'So how was he poisoned?'

'The chocolates.' I wiped something grey off the surface of a leaf with the corner of my napkin and added hastily, 'Perhaps.'

'Probably not.' He deftly tied the patch behind his head. 'I kept one of them for analysis and gave the rest to Molly. She sucked them up like a McGaffey Whirlwind, well over an hour ago and – to judge by the shrill attempts at civilized speech drifting up the dumbwaiter shaft – she is still alive and as well as she will ever be.'

I swallowed, though I had nothing in my mouth. 'You used Molly as a guinea pig?' And he waved a hand.

'Molly has unwittingly tested five suspect substances without ill effect since she came here, though she did become horrifyingly skittish after sampling an extract of *Cannabis indica* leaves once.'

I knew better than to argue about the morality of his deed. 'So how do you think he was poisoned? With the syringe?'

'That is the most likely.' He straightened his patch. 'You may remember, if you were paying attention, that I questioned the late Miss Flower about the needle and she assured me that she had not bent it.'

'It could have been bent by being dropped.' I cut a black bit out of a potato.

'We have not established that it *was* dropped.' My guardian drummed his forehead with his fingertips. 'But, even if it was, the needle was bent to the left, back on itself and into a sigmoid shape, which would suggest that there was a considerable struggle whilst it was being inserted and, since none of Mr Slab's specimens were capable of active resistance, he would seem to be the most likely recipient of that needle.'

I cut open another piece of potato but that was even worse. 'But if he was injected with strychnine he would have died within a minute or two anyway. So why put him in the tank?'

He refilled his tumbler from his carafe of water. 'To make sure that we knew he was murdered. A fit man would have some difficulty scaling a six-foot high glass wall and the stepladder was at least ten feet away. It is inconceivable that a man in the agonizing muscular contractions that strychnine produces could have done so. Unless we are willing to entertain the idea that he climbed into the tank unaided – and do not forget that Mr Slab was eighty-one years old – then injected himself with the poison.'

'It does not seem likely.' I pushed the potatoes aside.

'Why do you suppose that Mr Slab gave his servant such luxurious accommodation?'

The skin on my tomato was wrinkled and splitting.

'I do not think there was anything untoward going on,' I said and Sidney Grice puffed.

'Neither do I. I suspect it was, as Miss Flower told us, because he was a kind man and kind men are often easy victims.'

'He was not kind to animals.'

'The most gentle man with whom I am acquainted goes to Spain every summer to watch men in gaudy costumes goading bulls to death.' He gestured sharply. 'Dash it all, March. Why does nothing seem to fit together? What am I missing?'

'A good cook,' I said. 'Other than that I do not know. Why were you so hard on Rosie Flower?'

'To find out if she was telling the truth about only trying to clean up when she destroyed the evidence. Guilty people are resentful when confronted with their wrongdoing. They may become truculent and they almost always try to stare you out or fix upon the floor. Miss Flower was upset and confused but said nothing to incriminate herself.'

I turned the plate round but my dinner looked no more attractive from a different angle.

'I have had a message from Dr Berry,' Sidney Grice told me as I forced myself to eat a slice of shrivelled cucumber. 'She will have the results first thing tomorrow.' He speared a radish with a flourish of his fork. 'So you will have to entertain yourself for the day.'

'It will take all day?' I queried as he chewed a stick of limp celery.

'Well,' he said, 'I have promised to take her for lunch so that we can discuss the case at length, and then I intend to consult Mr White Senior of White, Adams and White, in an effort to find a clause that will allow Baroness Foskett to dismantle her society.'

'But Baroness Foskett does not want it dissolved.'

'Baron Foskett saved my life' – my guardian stabbed his tomato so hard that it squirted over his napkin – 'and I have a sacred duty to save his widow's.'

'What happened?' I asked and he wiped his mouth.

'My tomato burst.'

'No, I meant—'

'Besides,' he spoke over me, 'I am half-convinced that Baroness Foskett is a very frightened woman indeed.'

'Why not visit her again?'

He took a drink of water. 'I wrote to her this morning and had a reply by return. She has granted me an audience the day after tomorrow, but only on condition that you come too.'

I nibbled a stalk of watercress. 'She probably wants to gossip about the latest fashions from Paris.'

Sidney Grice looked pensive. 'I think that very unlikely.'

'Silly me.' I slapped the back of my hand.

'Indeed,' he said.

I did not trouble to tell him that he had smeared tomato juice over his cheek.

'Speaking of visits, is it not about time we called upon the other lady member of the club?'

'Ah yes.' He looked towards the ceiling. 'The reputedly merciless and disconcertingly young Miss Primrose McKay.' My guardian rattled his fingernails on his carafe. 'You may be interested to learn that I had news of Pound while you were upstairs.'

'Well, of course I am.'

Was it my imagination or was he hesitating and avoiding my eye?

'It appears' – he smoothed a crease in the tablecloth – 'that the inspector has departed.' I dropped my knife. The room went out of focus and his voice became muffled, but I could just make out the words. '... from the London Hospital and been transferred to the University College Hospital.' I steadied myself on the arms of my chair as he continued. 'And, since it seems ordained by a higher but tedious power, that we talk of nothing but visits this evening, I believe that the Liston Ward is open to public invasion every evening and some mornings.'

'Thank you,' I whispered.

'You are welcome.'

'I was talking to God,' I told him as I retrieved my knife.

'Let me know when he replies.' He turned a chunk of cucumber over.

'He already has,' I said.

24

The Birthday Slaughter

THE HORSE WAS hobbling, stumbling in every dip in the road and scarcely able to lift its feet over the bumps.

'Is Miss McKay very wealthy?' I asked as my guardian gave up his attempts to pour tea from his flask.

'Eight years ago' – he banged the cork home with the heel of his hand – 'Primrose McKay was the sole heiress to a considerable fortune. Her late father's coffers were bloated to the point of pathological obesity with every tube of swine flesh, gristle and sawdust that his factory produced.'

'You are making my mouth water,' I said and he tisked.

'That was not my intention.'

Our horse tripped but just managed to recover its stride, almost throwing us over the flap.

Sidney Grice knocked on the roof. 'Have a care, man.'

'Your horse needs rest,' I called and the hatch shot open.

'Needs a good thrashin', she do.' He cracked his whip. 'Lazy good-for-nuffink bag o' bones.'

'Perhaps you should try feeding her,' I retorted, but the hatch slammed.

'Do you believe that story about her killing a sow on her tenth birthday?' I hung on to a strap as we rounded a corner.

'When I was investigating the disappearance of Canasta – Lord Merrow's prize hog – in '76 I interviewed a slaughter man who mentioned that he held the sow still for little Miss McKay.'

'What an odious creature she must be.'

He caught his satchel as it slid off the seat. 'Hypocrites are always repelled by the lack of hypocrisy in others. You have no objection to pigs being killed on your behalf.'

'Yes, but to enjoy doing it and at such a young age...' I stopped, appalled by the thought.

My guardian put his flask away. 'Not an endearing trait, I grant you, but it does not make her a murderess.'

'It has to make her a more likely suspect.'

He snorted. 'There are few things less likely than a likely suspect.' And while I pondered over that we paused for a funeral cortège to pass by.

By the time we reached Fitzroy Square the horse was struggling so badly that the driver had to pull over to let us off. There was a cold wet stillness in the air.

'You'll be cat meat before this day is out if you don't git goin'.' The driver lashed his mare pointlessly as she crumpled to her knees.

'There is a foul pit in hell for people like you.' I shook with anger and he laughed mockingly.

'Live there already, darlin'. Only it's called Peckham.'

'If I ever see you on Gower Street again I will have your licence.' Sidney Grice flung him his fare.

'Never 'ad one anyways,' the driver shouted after us. 'So don't fink...' but his voice was drowned out by the raucous cries of the newspaper vendor, 'Brave British boys face Russian fret to India.'

My guardian shuddered. 'I knew I should have killed the tzar when I had the chance.'

I looked askance at him but he did not seem to be joking. 'Do you think there will be another war in Afghanistan?'

'Undoubtedly,' he said. 'And when we have won it we should march on to Moscow.'

Miss Primrose McKay lived in a grand house just off the square, the third in a smart Georgian terrace, clad in white stone with a burgundy front door.

'Make an observation,' Sidney Grice said and I looked about me.

'The pavement is uneven.'

'Good. And what conclusion do you draw from that?'

I pulled my cloak tighter around me. 'It needs repairing.'

He clicked his tongue. 'What about the pattern of the unevenness?'

'I cannot see any.' My cloak was heavy with damp.

My guardian sighed. 'Everything has a pattern even if it is random. In this case it is not. The slabs are tilted or even cracked close to the coal holes where sacks of fuel have been dropped carelessly over a period of many years. The pavement outside this dwelling is unscathed which shows…'

My mind raced. 'Either they do not have coal delivered – which seems unlikely for a house of such grandeur – or the servants ensure that the coal merchant takes care.'

'And how will we ascertain the more likely conclusion?'

'By testing their efficiency.' I twisted the bell and scarcely let go before I heard two bolts slide back.

'Case proven,' I said and my guardian put his cane on his shoulder.

'If one ignores the multiple other interpretations which spring immediately to mind.'

We were confronted by a footman in green and gold livery – tall and heavily built with a pox-scarred face.

'Thurston Gates.' Sidney Grice raised his cane as if prepared to use it.

'Mr Grice.' The footman eyed us icily. 'I was told to expect you.'

My guardian lowered his cane. 'What a pity for you that you did not expect me when I exposed your protection racket.'

Thurston sneered lopsidedly. 'It was an insurance scheme. Nothing was proved against me.'

'Only because the shopkeepers were so terrified of your brothers.' Sidney Grice dragged the sole of his boot over the scraper. 'Still, we must not reminisce all day.'

The footman grunted and stood back to admit us.

25

Dead Dogs and Dancing Mandarins

WE WERE TAKEN to the music room, high-ceilinged with full-length windows and ivory silk curtains pulled back. Through the voile I made out a knot garden, the low box hedges laid out in a series of concentric circles within squares.

Chairs were set out on the parquet floor as if for a soirée, facing a raised platform scattered with empty music stands and dominated by an inlaid rosewood piano at which Miss Primrose McKay was seated side-on to us, stabbing out a one-fingered scale. There was something mannered about her posture, her left elbow on the lowered top lid and her forehead resting on her fingertips in a studied pose of pain. Her dusty pink floral dress was arranged in flowing folds as if by a portrait painter. Her yellow tresses hung freely down her back. She did not stand or even raise her head as Thurston announced us.

'Mr Grice,' she said as if I had not been mentioned and was cleverly camouflaged. 'I was beginning to think that you were not coming.'

'We are only five minutes late,' I pointed out as we walked down the aisle towards her.

She struck three middle C's. 'Try holding your breath and tell me five minutes is not a long time.'

'Wait until you are told that you have five minutes to live and then tell me that it is,' I riposted and her right eye met mine in open hostility.

There was an etched glass saucer of champagne on an oval loo table at her side and a folded fan beside it.

'Very few women are blessed with brains *and* beauty.' Her voice was jagged and brittle. 'It would appear that you have neither.'

'There is more to beauty than looks,' I said and she emitted an amused bark.

'Whoever told you that?'

My father did, and Edward, but I was not going to expose them to her ridicule.

'I know ugliness when I see it,' I said as we stopped a few feet away from her.

'You only need a mirror.' She looked me up and down. 'Did you make that dress yourself?'

'You—' I began, but Sidney Grice touched my wrist.

'I am sorry about your dog,' he said, and she struck a clashing chord.

'How did you know about that?'

'Its image is in your locket. Nobody wears the picture of a living pet and the clipping of hair has not had time to fade, hence its loss was recent. Plus few people mourn an animal for more than five months.'

Primrose McKay inclined her head a fraction. 'You are very observant.'

'It is my job,' he said, and she responded scornfully, 'Ah yes, I almost forgot – you *work* – how inexpressibly vulgar.' She sipped her champagne.

'I suppose you think a life of self-indulgent idleness is ennobling?' I said, and my guardian put a finger to steady his eye.

'I am not completely idle.' She tossed her head but in an oddly careful way. 'I have invested in a number of racehorses and a stud farm in somewhere called Suffolk.'

At least that was one interest we had in common, though I could only afford to follow the sport with small wagers. 'And have you had any winners?'

'Not yet.' She pursed her pale pink lips. 'But they shall win because I wish them to. Besides' – she blew me a kiss – 'the noble do not need ennobling.' She played a trill.

'I shall refrain from commenting upon your father's beginnings as a swineherd,' my guardian said, and she slammed the palm of her hand on to the keys. 'What happened to the other figurine?'

'What?' she snapped and he made a flourish towards the yellow, green and white statue of a Chinaman in robes, standing on a black-and-gold oriental table in front of a mirror on the wall.

'Sui dynasty from Henan,' he pronounced. 'I have only seen a dozen dancing mandarins before and never one in such a pristine state, but no lord would dance without his lady and I cannot believe you could not afford the pair.'

'Oh, that old thing.' Miss McKay did not trouble to follow his hand. 'I would not know. Papa collected curios on his travels. I believe we had the lady until a stupid maid smashed it. I had her beaten, of course.'

'You had your maid beaten?' I half thought I must have misheard.

'You could hardly expect me to do it myself.' She rose from the stool in one smooth effortless movement. 'Besides which Thurston is so enthusiastic about his work and knows how not to inflict visible damage.'

Primrose McKay was tall and slender, pale and finely featured, and her hair was combed over the left side of her face, hanging almost to her breast. As if I did not dislike her enough already, I hated her for that hair. Mine is brown and frizzes at the ends. Hers glinted in the light like threads of gold.

My guardian took one step towards her before he spoke. 'The Last Death Club.' He watched her closely.

'What of it?' She picked up the fan.

'Why did you become a member?'

She gazed coolly back at him. 'Why should I not have some fun?'

'Because such *fun* can gain you nothing but money – which as sole heiress to the McKay fortune you surely cannot need – and may very well cost you your life.'

Miss McKay flipped her fan open to reveal a jade-coloured carp swimming beneath pink blossoms. 'I am sorry to contradict you, Mr Grice, but it gives me an interest in life which has been lacking since my dear papa was taken from me.' She peered down at him over her fan. 'Besides, it is unlikely to result in my demise since I am under your protection.'

He separated his hands by a few inches. 'I am not employed to be your bodyguard, Miss McKay.'

She brushed a fly off her forehead with the fan, and the waft of air lifted her hair. At first I thought it was a shadow, but then I realized that she had a birthmark, a dark stain around her left eye spreading over her cheek to her ear and on to her upper lip, which was swollen to her nostril.

'I am aware of that.' Her voice hardened. 'But the fact that you would be certain to capture whoever killed me is surely deterrent enough for any sane man.'

Her hair sank back but was still parted.

'Assuming that the killer is sane and a man,' I pointed out, unable to take my eyes off her blemish. It was as if an expensive porcelain doll had been dropped into mud. 'But surely you know that you have made your death profitable to every other member of the club.'

Miss McKay blinked slowly. 'My death will always be profitable to someone, Miss Middleton. My detestable younger sister stood first in line until I had her committed. A cousin in Canada was next before a wounded grizzly bear tore him asunder.' She swatted the fly off her sleeve and it arced into her glass. 'Beyond that' – she turned languidly to watch its death struggles – 'the surviving McKays may strip my fortune like piranhas with a dead horse.'

'You are very young to be a member of such a club,' Sidney Grice observed. 'What reason could the other members have for expecting to outlive you?'

Miss McKay stretched tiredly. 'The walls of my heart are like tissue paper.' She pushed the fly under with the tip of her finger. 'And they are liable to burst at the slightest exertion. The finest physicians in London have signed certificates to that effect.'

'Then it should be a simple matter to finish you off.' Sidney Grice strolled over to a cello propped on its spike against a beechwood rack.

'You might imagine so.' Miss McKay gave him a sugary smile. 'But I have evolved a clever plan.'

'Clever plans are rarely clever.' Sidney Grice plucked the A string. 'If an idea has occurred to you, it will have occurred to a million other minds. If you had an original thought in your head you would not be wasting your life away, lolling like a solitary basking seal.'

Miss McKay's mouth tightened and the right side of her upper lip blanched. 'I have a good mind to tell Thurston to thrash you for your impudence.'

'Your footman tried to hurt me once before.' He turned the tuning peg and retried the string. 'And you would be inconvenienced were I forced to disable him again.'

Miss McKay stared at my guardian. He had the string tuned to a B flat now.

'May I ask what your plan is?' I enquired as she picked up the saucer.

'It is clever because it is simple.' She looked at the ceiling. 'I shall wait until every other member but one of the club is dead and he has been arrested. At this rate I shall not have to tarry long.'

'There were other members who probably thought they could sit it out,' I told her, 'but they have paid dearly for their mistake.'

She turned her face away. 'They were all sheep.' Her neck was long and white, but I saw another dark stain appear from just above her collar. 'They sat and awaited their fates like tethered ewes, whereas I have made a pact with the wolf.'

'Do you imagine Thurston will keep you safe?' Sidney Grice twanged a C sharp and seemed quite satisfied with the result. 'He would sell you tomorrow if he thought he would be a farthing better off.' He selected a bow and twisted the key to straighten the ribbon.

'That is where you are wrong, Mr Grice,' Primrose purred. 'You see, I give Thurston rather more than mere money.' Her body undulated and my guardian looked nauseous.

'What pleasure can you get out of the club?' I asked and the surface of the champagne trembled in her left hand.

'It is difficult for you who have nothing in the way of looks, style or money to know what life is like for one who was born to everything. Beauty, wealth, taste and intelligence are such a burden, such a bore.'

'How do you bear it?' I asked and she replied with no apparent irony, 'It is a duty, but even I must relax and death amuses me.' She dipped her finger and thumb into her drink and took out the fly.

'Let us hope you die laughing,' I said and she blew my words away as if they were cigarette smoke.

'Harbour no fears on that account, Miss Middleton, for I have no intention of dying.'

'Everybody dies,' I said.

'Yes, but I am not *everybody*.' She popped the fly into her mouth, chewed twice and swallowed. 'I do not want to die and I never do anything that I do not want.'

Sidney Grice replaced the bow and said without raising his voice, 'You may see us out now, Thurston.'

The footman joined us at once and led us out with an insolent swagger. 'Put you in your place,' he remarked to my guardian as he opened the door.

'At least I know mine,' Sidney Grice retorted and Thurston turned puce.

'How are the mighty fallen,' I said as I got to the front step. 'From criminal mastermind to grovelling lackey.'

Thurston Gates jabbed his finger under my nose, livid with fury. 'It is you who will grovel one day, girl.'

'But not to you,' I said as the door slammed.

'There was a time that Thurston would have broken your neck for speaking to him like that,' my guardian told me, 'but he has to keep a lower profile these days. I imagine Miss McKay rewards him handsomely.' He waved to a cab, but it was already pulling over for two men in the Campbell tartan kilts. 'Few will gainsay her with Thurston Gates at her side.'

'What a horrible woman she is,' I said as a line of occupied hansoms passed by.

'For once I quite agree with your assessment.' Sidney Grice waved his cane at a vacant cab but the driver ignored him. 'But I wish there were more like her.' Another cab went by as if we were invisible. 'A quarter of the problems of this world are caused by rich women pretending to be useful and getting in everybody's way. Oh, dash it, there goes another.'

I put my first and second fingers between my lips and blew a good piercing whistle. My guardian stared. 'The word *washer-woman* springs to mind,' he said.

'It did the trick, though,' I told him as the driver tipped his battered bowler and wheeled sharply back to us.

26

Melton Mowbray and Lucinda

THE CORRIDORS WERE crowded as I made my way to the Liston Ward of University College Hospital. I had heard of Robert Liston from my father, who had seen him at work. He was a surgeon who boasted of being able to amputate a leg in less than thirty seconds. He was a great showman but his speed was not just theatricality. The quicker the operation in those days before anaesthesia, the less likely the patient was to die of shock. It was a pity, though, that he held hygiene in contempt, for a great many of his patients died later of infection.

There were about thirty beds on either side of the long ward and most of them were surrounded by visitors. Some patients lay glumly alone and some slept, oblivious to their weeping families.

Inspector Pound was in the end bed on the left-hand side under a window. There was a woman sitting at the head of the bed and a man standing with his back to me.

'Miss Middleton.' The inspector was grey. 'May I introduce my sister, Lucinda?'

My first impression was one of sourness. I went to her and we shook hands. 'Your brother speaks very fondly of you,' I said and she stretched the corners of her mouth briefly, a tiny, pointy-chinned woman with pink cheeks and hair pulled severely back.

'But he has not mentioned you,' she said warily.

'That is because there is nothing to tell,' I assured her and turned to Inspector Pound. 'I have brought you a little whisky for your pain.'

'You should not have troubled,' he said tiredly.

'Oh, it was no trouble,' I assured him. 'I found it in my handbag.'

He snorted in amusement and his sister drew in her thin lips. 'The devil's brew,' she said and I decided that my first impression was correct.

'Did Christ not make alcohol for his first miracle at Canaan and bless it at the last supper?'

'I must be off,' the man said, and I looked across to see that it was Inspector Quigley.

'Good morning, Inspector,' I said. 'And what is your conclusion – attempted suicide or accidental stabbing?'

Inspector Quigley reddened. 'You are getting quite a reputation in the force, Miss Middleton.'

'A good one, I hope.'

'Hope springs eternal.' He picked his hat off the bed. 'Good day, Pound, Miss Pound, Miss Middleton.'

'I suppose it was nice of him to visit you,' I said as he passed into the corridor, and Inspector Pound frowned weakly.

'Much as I admire his detection record, there is not much nice about my colleague.' He put a hand over his stomach and winced. 'He came to make sure I would be out of his way for the next few weeks, and I think he is going away satisfied.'

A child's wails cut through the general chatter.

'I must go, George,' Lucinda said and looked at me sideways.

The sheet was being lifted over a young man's head across the ward.

'I am sure I shall be quite safe with Miss Middleton. You will come again tomorrow?'

'If I can. There is so much to do in the house.' She bent and pecked his forehead. 'Goodbye, Miss Middleton.'

We shook hands.

'You mustn't mind Lucinda,' Inspector Pound said when she was out of earshot. 'My sister had to be a housekeeper for our uncle and a mother to me when she was fourteen. He was a demanding man and I was not the easiest of boys.'

I sat on the vacated chair and leaned towards him. It was difficult to hear above the babble of conversations. 'I do not suppose she will be very fond of the woman who nearly got her brother killed.'

'I haven't told her that bit.'

'I am sorry,' I said. 'It was stupid of me not to realize that you were doing your job.'

Inspector Pound put his finger to his lips. 'You fought to protect me when you could and should have run away. You staunched my bleeding. You got me to hospital and gave me your blood.' He winced. 'I think that more than makes up for it.'

'Does it hurt very much?'

'Not in the least.'

'You have more colour in your cheeks.'

'The doctor has prescribed two pints of stout a day to put iron back in my blood. I would prefer a pint of bitter from the Bull, but it seems to be doing the trick and this will help.' He slipped the bottle of Scotch under his blanket.

A nurse came by with a bowl of broth and I took it from her. 'I will give it to him.'

'Please don't,' he said. 'They moved me here because they thought I would be safer away from the East End, but to go by the food I am not so sure.' And I looked at the greasy globular mess.

'Oh, I see what you mean – but you must eat something.'

'You try it.' He shifted uncomfortably. 'What wouldn't I give for a Melton Mowbray!'

'There is a pie shop down Judd Street. I will bring you something tomorrow – if you do not mind me visiting again.'

'I will be still here – I hope.'

The rain rattled on the windowpane.

'I shall take that as a formal invitation.'

A nurse rang a handbell, shaking it so violently that an old man sitting dozing nearly fell off his pillow.

'Sounds like visiting time is over,' I said.

The ward was emptying swiftly as I stood. Nobody wanted to risk the wrath of Matron. The inspector raised his hand and cleared his throat. 'May I ask you a favour, Miss Middleton?' He spoke haltingly. 'If my men ever found out that you came to my aid in a fight or that I have a woman's blood in my veins...'

'It will be our secret,' I said, and for the first time I wished I was Lucinda and could kiss his forehead. 'Goodbye, Inspector.' I touched the back of his hand.

I glanced back as I reached the exit. His eyes were screwed up and his face was drawn.

'Is there anything more to be done for him?' I asked the matron, who was marching in.

'Everything *is* being done,' she told me.

'I just wondered about the food.'

'The Queen of England does not dine better than the patients here.'

'No wonder she is so skinny.'

Her jaw tensed. 'Goodbye.'

I had lived long enough with Sidney Grice to know when there was no point in arguing.

*

'I have received a correspondence from Mr White Senior of White, Adams and White,' my guardian told me over a parsnip soup, 'and he has confirmed that the terms of the Last Death Club are contractually binding. The only way to quit the society is to quit this life.'

'So your friend the baroness will have to take her chances.' I shook more pepper into my soup but it was not improved.

Sidney Grice lowered his spoon into his bowl. 'Lady Foskett is not my friend,' he informed me coolly. 'Her husband saved me and she did me a great kindness once, but I am trying to forgive them.'

He turned back to his soup and the conversation was at an end.

*

Edward loved his writing box and we had great fun watching him trying to find the hidden drawer. Eventually he too gave up. My father showed him and left. Edward and I were allowed a little time alone together now that we were engaged.

'The very first person I shall write to is you,' Edward promised.

'I shall not hold my breath,' I said. 'It took you three weeks to reply to your brother's last communication.'

'Well, this time you can.' Edward pulled out a chair and sat at the table.

'What?'

'Hold your breath,' he said.

I took a deep gulp and stood peering over his shoulder as he dipped the nib of his pen.

'My Darling March,' he wrote. 'Thank you so much for my wonderful present. I shall treasure it always but not one jot as much...' he re-dipped his pen, 'as I shall treasure you for the rest of my life.' He glanced back and up at me pinching my nose and going red with the effort, as he finished with deliberate slowness. 'With all my heart, your ever-loving...' he paused as I went purple, 'Edward.'

I let out the air and took a deep a breath. 'Beast.' He blotted the paper. 'And you haven't put any kisses on it.'

'I did not think you had enough breath left for those.' Edward smiled and stood up. 'And I have not enough ink to give you all the kisses that I want to. Besides which...' He took me in his arms. 'I wanted to give them to you myself.'

No one can describe love or happiness, but at that moment I had so much of both that I thought I would burst.

27

Poison and Predators

KEW WAS MUCH quieter than it had been for the royal visit and, without the crowds, there were no stalls or beggars – only a crossing boy sweeping the road with a tied bunch of twigs, some fine ladies flaunting their peacock-feathered bonnets in their carriages, and a salt carter clacking his rattle for the kitchen maids to run out of the big houses and purchase a block.

'Why do we alight so far from the house?' I asked as we walked along the side of the gardens.

'It is a question of honour.' Sidney Grice tugged his hat a little lower. 'We cannot turn up at the front in a two-wheeler. It would be an insult to the noble blood of our hostess.'

I stumbled on a loose slab. 'Can I ask what happened to Rupert?'

'You can and you have.' He puffed out his cheeks. 'Rupert was a lion fed to the Christians. He forgot all my refutations and allowed the desperation of hope to drown his logical abilities in the swamp of blind faith.'

'Are you an atheist?' I asked and Sidney Grice paused in his stride.

'When I have the time I shall investigate the matter. If there is a God, be sure of it, I shall track him down. And when I do, he has a great many things to account for. Rupert was a missionary in the tropics, but the natives decided they would rather eat a white man than listen to his sermons. They cooked him live for two days over hot coals, I was told. Apparently they believe that the louder and longer their victim screams, the more evil spirits he frightens away.'

He cupped his nose and mouth in his left hand.

'All the more reason to bring them the word of God,' I said. 'At least he died doing that.'

'I am sure it would have been a great consolation to him.' He closed his eyes briefly. 'A good master looks after his servants. One cannot help but wonder if God is a gentleman.'

'Perhaps he is a she,' I suggested.

We turned the corner.

'What a terrifying thought.' He rang the bell and Cutteridge appeared almost at once from the ruins of the right-hand gatehouse. 'Though it might explain the illogicality of creation.'

'Do you think God could be a woman, Cutteridge?' I asked when he had admitted us.

'I do not imagine that a woman could be so cruel, miss,' he said.

'Also, there are no fashion tips or knitting patterns in the Bible,' my guardian said and I laughed.

'Why, that was almost witty,' I said and he looked mildly indignant.

'It was a serious theological point.'

As we made our way through the undergrowth, Sidney Grice stopped to listen. 'The dogs sound restless.'

'Mastiffs do not like being kennelled, sir. I let them out at night to patrol the grounds.'

A clamour of snarls and yaps cut through the air.

'Are they as aggressive as they sound?' I asked as we rounded a huge flowerless rhododendron.

'A would-be burglar and his boy scaled the wall to the north of the property once,' Cutteridge told me with a small shudder. 'We heard their cries from inside the house. There was a full complement of staff in those days. Three gardeners and two footmen tried to beat them away with poles, but her ladyship was the only one who could command them. By the time she had been roused and called them off, it was difficult to imagine that what was left had been human.'

'But how do you control them now?' I stepped sideways to avoid a patch of thistles and almost trod on the remains of a viper curled in the soil and riddled with maggots. The head was missing. Whatever had taken that – a fox perhaps – would surely be dead by now.

Cutteridge tilted his head in the direction of the barks. 'I don't, miss. I open the cage with a wire from the scullery and I throw horsemeat into it to lure them back. You can see the enclosure from the window. Once I miscounted and one of them got into the house and tried to mount the stairs. I was compelled to run it through with the fourth baron's double-handed sword. Mind your face, miss.' He held back a bramble for me. 'Her ladyship was most annoyed and docked the cost from my wages.'

'How many dogs are there now?' Sidney Grice asked as we came to the gravelled clearing.

'Fifteen, sir.'

We turned another right and all at once it came upon us – Mordent House, tall, bleak and forbidding, its emptiness taking us in as we climbed the algae-green marble steps, its rancid air suffocating me as we entered the decayed hall, its corruption crushing me as we mounted the quivering stairs.

'Did you observe that the lacewing has gone?' my guardian asked me in hushed tones as if still mourning its passing.

'It has probably been eaten.' I hastily stepped up as a board cracked under my weight.

'What a fine portrayal.' Sidney Grice pointed to a darkly varnished painting on a far wall – Actaeon, having been turned into a stag, being torn apart by the goddess Diana's dogs. 'If you look carefully you can still make out gouts of his flesh dripping in the first hound's mouth.'

'And you thought a female god would be kind,' I said, but

Cutteridge made no sign of having heard me. He seemed to age with every step we ascended and his hand was shaking as he tapped on the oak panel.

'Wait here, please.' He entered the darkness, and a match flared and died while the candle flame grew into a glimmering halo, giving just enough glow to show us the outline of our chairs and the gauze box before us.

'Sidney,' the speaking tube hissed the moment we were seated, 'is there no escaping you?'

'Many have tried,' my guardian said.

'And many have succeeded,' the baroness responded and his face fell. 'Perhaps too many to enumerate, but permit me to essay. Thomasina Norton, *exempli gratia*. I am accurately informed that she slew two men whilst entrusted by her progenitors to your incommensurate care. I hope your present ward has no murderous intents.'

'Not yet,' I said and she rasped, 'You have spirit, child, but do not fear. He will soon destroy that as he lays waste all things that are lured into the lair of his existence.'

'Mr Grice has given me his protection,' I said.

'Just as he did with Horatio Green and Edwin Slab? A flimsy shield indeed behind which to shelter.'

'I offered them no protection, Baroness.'

The speaking tube clattered.

'I am bored with you already – stifled and stultified almost to a state of mental paralysis. Why have you come?'

'I am concerned for your safety, Lady Foskett. It does not appear that you can extricate yourself from that death society—'

'I have already made my position clear,' the voice broke in, husky and metallic, 'and you cannot possibly have misconstrued it. The Last Death Club is my whoreson progeny and I mean to sustain it to its sour conclusion. I shall not permit any member to withdraw from their compact with me, nor shall I tolerate any interference with its constitution from you or any other man of woman born.'

I saw Sidney Grice's fingers twitch on his knees. 'At least will you take some steps to protect yourself?'

There was a dry throaty rustling. 'Who can harm me when I cannot harm myself? Do you think Cutteridge will let an assassin into the house?'

'He is only one man,' I said.

'I have a title, child. Kindly use it.'

'And so have I,' I said. 'It is *Miss*. I may be a child to you, Lady Foskett, but you are elderly and I do not address you as *old woman*.'

The baroness wheezed furiously. 'You are an impudent hussy.' She coughed four times. 'But you are right. I am not dependent only on Cutteridge for my security, *Miss* Middleton. I have my dogs of war and when they are unleashed there is not a man on the slime of this earth who can hope to overcome them.'

'Even so, your home is not impregnable, Lady Foskett,' my guardian told her. 'Two members of your society have been poisoned already. Will you at least have your food tasted?'

'I could employ the services of small children.'

'An excellent idea,' my guardian said.

'Ah, what unbridled joy I could obtain in observing their terror, perhaps even watching them writhe and die.'

'I was thinking more of using their sensitive taste buds to detect any toxins.'

There was a thump of boot on wood. 'Stick to the terms of your employment, *Mr* Grice. When, as I so fervently desire, my rancid soul absconds to join the ragged battalions of the damned you will be at liberty to investigate its departure with all your limited powers. But, for so long as the sulphurous fumes of this tortured world continue to flood my alveoli, leave me in my squalid solitude.'

Sidney Grice shrank where he sat. 'Lady Foskett...' he began, but did not seem to know how to continue.

'See them out, Cutteridge,' the voice exhaled and I felt a hand on my shoulder. 'Out... out...' The voice faded.

My eyes were getting accustomed to the light now and I could just make out her figure, tiny and erect in the high-backed chair, a long dress flowing over the platform, a veil over a shadowed face.

'If you please, sir, miss.'

We stood up and in the fluttering candlelight our projected darknesses stretched and bent, separated, twined and swayed, spectres of Sidney Grice and me locked in a *danse macabre* before we were torn apart again.

'Goodbye, Baroness Foskett,' I said, but only an exhalation responded.

The stairs creaked more than ever and twisted under our feet as we made our way down.

The sky was overcast and the path slippery and waterlogged by a shower. 'The wind is getting cold,' I observed as Cutteridge unlocked the gate.

The dogs were clamouring and Cutteridge surveyed the sky. 'There is a storm gathering, if I am not mistaken, miss.'

A crow shrieked.

'Predators.' My guardian buttoned up his coat. 'They are everywhere.'

28

Two Nurses and the Marquess of Salisbury

Two nurses were stripping the bed next to Inspector Pound's when I arrived.

'Nice old chap,' he said. 'Came in with a cut finger and ended up with his arm off. He never recovered.'

'And how are you feeling?'

'Never felt better.'

He did not look it. His face was white again and beaded with sweat, there were dark hollows beneath his eyes and a slight tremor in his hand as he held it out to me.

'I have brought you a pork pie. It is still warm.' I opened my brown paper bag to show him, and he twisted his head but could not lift it to look. 'And two bottles of bitter from the Bull, poured less than twenty minutes ago. Would you like some pie now? I have a knife.'

'Thank you. Perhaps later. I feel a bit green to tell the truth – and hot.'

I pulled the blanket down and saw that his sheet was stained brown with old blood and that his gown was damp and clinging to his shoulders.

'This patient's bedding needs changing,' I told the nurse and she snapped round.

'Did it this morning.'

'She did,' he confirmed. 'I expect the wound is weeping a bit. A couple of stitches pulled out but the surgeon is coming tomorrow.'

'Let me see.'

Inspector Pound clutched his blanket. 'Hold on, Miss Middleton.'

'I have worked as a nurse in three different countries,' I said and took hold of the sheet.

Inspector Pound let go and closed his eyes, as if not seeing me looking at him made it more respectable. Perhaps it did for him. I loosened his bandage and saw the wound was seeping pus. I pressed lightly on his stomach and he yelped involuntarily. His skin was hot and rigid with muscle contractions.

The nurses were going.

'Get me some carbolic acid,' I said and they looked nonplussed. '*Now*.'

'You can't order us about.' They put their hands on their hips.

'I will give you two minutes,' I said and they both hurried away.

The inspector managed a smile. 'I could do with a few of you in the force.'

'Women?'

He shivered and I covered him again.

'I didn't mean that,' he said. 'It's hard to think of you as a woman sometimes.'

He meant it as a compliment, but I knew how he would have reacted if I had told him he was not like a man.

'Do you believe in germs?' I asked as he gingerly put a hand to his side.

'I am not sure. I know Florence Nightingale says they are nonsense.'

'Florence Nightingale is a wonderful woman,' I said, 'but she believes that fresh air cures everything. If that were the case why would agricultural workers be decimated by disease?'

'By the poisonous miasma produced by the smells of cow dung.' His voice was fading as the nurses returned with a blue bottle, a bowl and a stack of cotton squares.

'Hold his arms,' I said. 'I am sorry but this will smart.' I pulled out the cork and the fumes stung my eyes as I poured it on to his stomach. The inspector arched up and cried out.

'Ruddy hell!'

'Kindly moderate your language,' the younger nurse scolded.

'Cripes!' he yelled, writhing as I wiped the muck from the wound.

'I am sorry,' I repeated and tossed a foul-smelling swab into the bowl.

He cried out again and mercifully fainted.

Matron marched over. 'What do you think you are doing?'

'What you should have done,' I said, scooping out what infected matter I could and throwing the wad away.

'You will leave this instant.'

I trickled some of the carbolic over the wound. 'He needs a clean bandage,' I told the older nurse, 'and please wash your hands first.'

I wiped my hands as best I could on the remaining squares. 'You can watch this man die or you can try to kill the cause of his infection.'

She wagged a fat finger at me. 'You are an insolent little madam.'

'I am also the Marquess of Salisbury's goddaughter,' I told her. 'The choice is yours.' And I left.

My father and I had seen the marquess go by in a landau on his way to the India Office once so I was only exaggerating a bit.

'Do not be such a baby,' I said as you clung on to your trousers.

'If I were a baby I should not mind, but I am a man and it is not decent.'

'Very well then,' I said. 'Bleed to death.'

You tried to tell me it was only a scratch, but your trouser leg was saturated and when I eventually managed to coax you and clean the wound I could see your femoral artery exposed, as if by careful dissection rather than the careless slash of a comrade's sabre in a mock duel. I saw your life pulse through it. One sixteenth of an inch more and you would have been dead. They say it takes less than half a minute. My father arrived with his suture needle and you fainted clean away, though we told you afterwards that you had not.

You had a bit of a limp after that but I suspect you played it up, hoping the men and other girls might think you had been injured in action, besides which everyone knew that Lord Byron had a club foot so it was dreadfully romantic. You did not need to fake it for me. There never was a more romantic man. I still have that rose crushed and dried in my journal to prove it. Who else would risk their life because I loved a flower?

*

'I have just been to see Inspector Pound,' I told my guardian on my return.

'I know.' He was fiddling with the levers on a metal box, another of his inventions.

'How?'

'You reek of carbolic acid. It almost masks the smell of tobacco and gin and parma violets. So, since you are clearly anxious to tell me, how is he faring?'

'Not very well,' I said. 'His wound is suppurating and he has a fever.'

He rifled through a tangle of wires and bolts and tools on his desktop and extracted a small screwdriver. 'He is a strong man.'

'Will you not visit him?'

He tightened two screws on the side of his machine and turned it upside down. 'For what reason? He is not involved in any of the cases I am investigating.'

'To see how he is.'

'You have just told me how he is.' He took a bolt out and put it to one side. 'I must find someone who will make a better coiled spring.' He hinged a panel sideways to open a square hole.

'To show your concern,' I suggested.

'How can I show that which does not exist?' He picked up a pair of pliers.

'Do you really not care?'

'He is a good policeman in a world of incompetence and corruption and I should miss that, but my weeping at his bedside will not heal him any the quicker. Give him my regards if you wish.' He poked the pliers through the hole and grasped something. 'Now' – there was a loud click – 'if Cook uses this as instructed we should never have another lump in our creamed potatoes again.'

'Anyway,' I said, 'how was your visit to Dr Berry?'

'Most pleasant.' He twisted the pliers a fraction clockwise. 'She had a pretty blue dress on and—'

'I meant the tests,' I said and he looked up again.

'Oh, those? Yes, they were all positive. Edwin Slab was definitely poisoned with strychnine. She had a frilly collar and matching cuffs too. Something like that would flatter even you, March, if you were not so studiously occupied with looking dowdy.'

'There is nothing studious about my dowdiness,' I retorted, uncertain what I meant but feeling it was probably sufficiently withering to merit flouncing out of the room.

29

Weals, Flares and the Figure of Death

'The trouble is,' Sidney Grice said over breakfast the next morning, 'I have not been focused. There are too many strands in the web of these murders and I have allowed them to lead me in different directions when I should be tracing them all back to the centre.'

'I am not sure I know what that means,' I said.

'Neither am I.' He nonchalantly crumbled his charred toast into his prune juice and over the tablecloth. 'It seems reasonable to assume, though not to take for granted, that the deaths of Messrs Green, Slab and Braithwaite were connected. Horatio Green and Edwin Slab were both members of that ludicrous society, which makes them self-selected targets, but why Braithwaite? His only connection that we know of was that he was Horatio Green's dentist. I rifled through his meagre patients' records and scantily filled appointment book and none of the other members have ever consulted him. So why would he be a victim?'

'Perhaps he knew something that would incriminate the murderer,' I suggested.

'That would seem the most likely explanation.' He felt the teapot and pushed it away. 'Though the fact he said nothing to us indicates that he might not have even realized the significance of his information and, if my profession has taught me anything – which it has – the most likely explanation is often the wrong one.

Perhaps the delightful Quigley was right – and what an unappealing idea that is – and Braithwaite killed himself accidentally.'

'But what about the marks on his wrists?' I reminded him. 'Could he not have been tied to his chair and only released when he was unconscious or dead?'

'The marks on his wrists were at least a few days old,' he declared. 'Long ago I observed that rope marks cause a triple-layered inflammatory response – a red impression, bordered by a paler, less well-delineated flare, bordered by a weal mark. It takes some time for these marks to fade depending on the severity of the trauma. The flare and weal had disappeared, but the inner lurid colouration was still evident even to your poorly trained eye. Hence the marks were not made immediately ante-mortem.'

'So how do you explain them?'

He refilled his cup. 'I was not aware that I was obliged to do so.'

'Do you think that when Jenny referred to Mr Braithwaite wanting her to play games he—'

'Quite possibly.' He opened his egg with a teaspoon but I did not bother with mine. It was crypt cold and my toast was soggy but just about edible.

Molly came in with a copy of the Manchester *Guardian* and her employer dabbed the cover with his middle finger. 'This has not been pressed,' he told her. 'Go and do it immediately.'

'I started to press it,' Molly said, 'but there's a lovely funny picture of you on page four, sir. So I thought you would want to see it straightways. I know how much you love a good hoot.'

Sidney Grice looked at her as if she were a changeling, rustled through the pages, tut-tutting at the ink stain which had miraculously migrated on to his shirt front.

'It's ever so good ain't it, sir?'

'One shilling off your wages,' her employer said absently. His face clouded and he put a finger to his eye. He rammed the paper back at her. 'Take it away and burn it... *now*.'

'Can I see?'

'No, you may not,' he said, but I had already whisked it out of her hand. It was a cleverly executed cartoon and there was no mistaking Sidney Grice with his eye patch on and the cruel exaggeration of his shortened left leg, but even worse were the corpses strewn about his feet, every one of them named – Sarah and William Ashby, Judith Stravinskij, Sir Randolph Cosmo Napier, Alice Hawkins, Horatio Green, Edwin Slab, Silas Braithwaite, Rosie Flower. And Sidney Grice stood over them, holding a scythe and dressed in the hooded robes of Death.

'What in the name of everything unholy has Rosie Flower got to do with me?' Sidney Grice demanded. 'And how the devil did they find out about her?'

'Ten shillings off your wages for strong language,' Molly whispered as she skipped heavily out of the room, and my guardian threw his napkin after her.

'Sarah Ashby was dead before I had even heard her name,' he fumed, 'and William Ashby, who is portrayed as an innocent dupe, was a murderer tried and found guilty by twelve men good and true in an almost fair trial.'

'But he was your client.'

'Then more fool him.' He swept out his hand, sending his egg flying into the coal box. 'He wanted the truth and he got it.' He wiped his fingers on the tablecloth. 'And nobody can blame me because Napier and Hawkins got in the way.'

I put my toast down. 'Got in the way? I can hardly believe you have said that. Alice Hawkins was—'

'A corpse,' he interjected, 'before I even took on the case, and Quarrel – not I – killed them all.' He knocked his teacup but caught it as it spun off the saucer. 'None of the others was ever a client of mine except for that that damned fool Green, and I am in the process of bringing his murderer to book as I speak.'

'I hope so,' I said. 'But who was Judith Stravinskij?'

'I throttled her,' my guardian conceded, 'but it was all an innocent misunderstanding on her part.' He looked at the ceiling for a moment. 'Besides which, it is the unnamed figure that really injures me.'

I looked again and in the bottom right-hand corner was a faceless dead man that I had not noticed before. This body was simply labelled *next client*.

'Will you sue?' I knew of Sidney Grice's predilection for bringing civil actions against his detractors, but he shook his head. 'The editor of the Manchester *Guardian* knows things about me that I would rather he kept to himself, and I have information about him that would destroy his marriage, finish his career and quite possibly put him in prison. We would be like two drowning men, clutching at each other and dragging each other under.'

I remembered Eleanor Quarrel and Father Brewster, and imagined how it must have been for them as the stormy seas closed over their heads. She murdered members of her own family in cold blood, and so many others. Did she repent in her terror or did she only fear for herself? Could her own death make atonement for what she did? I prayed so every night.

'Shall I burn it?'

'No,' he said. 'I shall save this scurrilous rag and the next time I meet Mr Charles Prestwich Scott and his amusing sketch artist, I shall take great pleasure in making them eat their words – preferably literally.' He turned back to the carbonized slurry in his bowl and I tried to shake off my thoughts.

How could she have laid Sarah Ashby on the ground, stabbed and hacked at her and calmly sliced that angelic face through the soft skin and warm muscle down to the teeth and bone?

Sidney Grice let his napkin fall on the floor. 'Come, March.' He scraped back his chair. 'Today we shall visit the displeasingly named Mr Piggety.'

30

Piggety's Cats in Big White Letters

THERE HAD BEEN a fire in Euston Square and the Metropolitan Brigade was still fighting it with water wagons connected to a rattling steam pump, leaving hardly any room for traffic to pass by.

'The subterranean railways were supposed to alleviate our transport problems,' my guardian said, 'but I suspect they have merely added to them by enabling the vulgar herds to invade our capital at will.'

'This is nothing to the chaos I encountered in India.'

He looked away. Firemen were breaking open a window with their axes and the smoke rolled blackly out, stinging the eyes of the onlookers and startling a team of dappled horses harnessed to a stonemason's wagon which skewed across the road, slowing our progress even more.

'There is another approach we could take to these investigations,' Sidney Grice said. I liked the *we*, though I suspected he meant himself rather than me. 'We could just wait until all but one of the club members is dead and arrest the sole survivor. At the rate they are dying it should not take very long.'

'You cannot mean that,' I said as we edged round the obstructions. 'Surely it is your job to protect these people.'

My guardian undid the clips on his satchel and brought out his patent heat-retentive flask.

'On the contrary.' He poured some tea into his new specially designed tin cup, tall with a slight internal lip to discourage spillages. 'If you recall the terms of my engagement, I am employed to investigate the deaths of the members, not to nanny them and, if they do not die, I cannot do my job.'

'But surely your instincts are to save them?'

He recorked his bottle. 'The beasts in the field have instincts. I have intellect and I do not need to exercise it overly much to know that any other deaths will reflect badly on me, and my professional standing has already been battered like the wreck of the Deutschland. Besides, it is an inelegant solution.'

'It helps that we only have five suspects,' I said as he put his flask away.

'Not necessarily.' He steadied his cup as we swung round a fireman carrying a nightgowned old man like a child out of the house. 'Someone who is not even in the society may hold a grudge against the victims. Besides which' – he put his hand over the cup – 'numbers are immaterial. There were one hundred and three suspects when Granny Griggs was sawn in two at four postmeridiem, but I apprehended the culprit before the clock had struck the quarter. Conversely, it took me four years to prove the guilt of Lorraine Merrylegs when she was the only person present at three different murders. If she had remembered to brush behind her teeth, she could still be about her work now.'

'I have never heard of her,' I said, 'and I read all the shilling shockers.'

'The Lord Chancellor begged me to keep the matter quiet for reasons which I am unable to divulge until this century has reached its inglorious conclusion.' He drank a little tea. 'Anyway, you are forgetting there is a sixth suspect.'

I thought about it. 'Who?'

'Myself,' my guardian said. 'I also stand to gain a tidy sum of money pursuant to the deaths of all the members.'

I laughed. 'You cannot seriously suspect yourself.'

'One must always consider all the possibilities,' he said. 'However, I have sufficient intimate knowledge of my actions to enable me to discount myself as the guilty party with a reasonable degree of confidence. You, however, may keep me on your list.'

'I shall bear that in mind,' I told him as we jolted over a pothole that nearly caused him to choke on his tea.

We turned off Euston Road but our rate of progress did not improve. Two men were loading furniture into the back of a van and our cabby had to threaten them with his whip before they would move it to one side. The streets became narrower and shorter and the houses smaller and shabbier the further we went east, and there were fewer carriages and more pedestrians, until ours was the only hansom in view, pushing its way through the bustling crowds.

'What a fine history this place has.' My guardian raised his voice above the general din. 'Over there is The Prospect of Whitby, formerly and more aptly known as The Devil's Tavern. The great Hanging Judge Jefferies frequented it, and his house stands nearby with a noose in the window to commemorate his glorious career. Why, in two particularly productive days of September 1685, he condemned one hundred and forty-nine people to death.'

'What a jolly card he must have been.'

The streets were slightly wider now but more oppressive with their high sides – the towering windowless walls of warehouses, their red bricks blackened by the sooty London air and joined across the road by a mesh of wooden walkways at every level. The alley opened out into a seething mass of porters and lightermen, heading their way to and from the docks, many burdened so heavily that they were bent double under their loads of sacks and crates.

'They used to call this Execution Dock.' He strained to make himself heard. 'It was a favourite site for dispatching pirates and mutineers. They really knew how to hang a man in those days. If the executioner did not pull his legs to finish him off a man could jiggle on a short rope for the best part of an hour – the *Marshal's Dance* as they called it. My father came to watch the last hanging here and told me it was quite wonderful.'

'Like father like son,' I said and he beamed.

The hansom came to a halt. 'That's as far as what I go,' the cabby shouted and my guardian passed up his payment.

'Keep the change and there's a guinea for you if you wait.'

'One hour,' the cabby said and wrenched the reins to urge his horse out of the way.

'Keep your eyes skinned,' Sidney Grice told me. 'We are looking for Piggety's. No need. There it is.'

I followed his hand to see a tarred wooden building, two storeys high, built against the side of a sugar warehouse with a hexagonal tower on top and a row of skylights in the roof, a sign on the side bearing the legend *Piggety's Cats* in white letters three feet high.

We pushed our way through a group of dockers who were bent over a game of Find the Lady. A fat man with a wooden leg was sitting on the cobbles, putting a stone on a tray, then covering it with one of three mugs and shuffling them about while the audience placed bets on which mug he had used. We watched for a while and he was very fast. I could never guess the correct mug.

'Left,' Sidney Grice said and it was. 'Centre.' He was correct again.

The fat man looked up. 'You 'aving a punt, guv?'

'I never gamble,' my guardian told him, 'even on certainties like this. Left again.'

I was aware of a man in a green jacket standing behind us, and turned to see him grasping a wicked-looking cudgel bristling with spikes.

'Time to go before I smash your pretty face.'

Sidney Grice seemed to be engrossed in the game. 'Centre,' he said.

'Thank you,' I said. 'I am not often accused of being pretty.'

'I was talkin' to your old man.' The man in the green jacket moved in close and raised the cudgel. I felt it prick my chin. Instinctively I raised my parasol and accidentally caught him in his right nostril. It was quite a hard jab and he was so taken off-guard that he dropped his weapon and clutched at his nose.

'Centre.' My guardian spun round and I looped my arm through his.

'Take me away from these ruffians, Mr G,' I said as the man scrambled for his club.

Sidney Grice kicked it skittering away. 'Certainly, Miss Middleton,' he said and glanced over his shoulder. The man had retrieved his weapon but made no attempt to follow us.

'Why did you call me Mr G?' he asked as we came up to the shed.

'I was not sure if you wanted them to know who you are,' I said. 'Anyway, I think I quite like it.'

A cesspit was overflowing down the slope towards the water's edge.

'So do I.' He lifted the knocker. 'It manages to be informal and formal simultaneously.' He rapped on the door, which flew open almost immediately, and the stench struck us so forcibly that we both staggered backwards.

31

The Curious Incident of the Cats in the Daytime

'OH, YOU'LL SOON get used to that.' The man who answered our call was so short and onion-shaped that, had he been wearing a peaked cap, I would have been tempted to ask where Tweedledee was.

'I think not.' Sidney Grice put a hand over his mouth and nose.

Our greeter put his hands damply together. 'Think of it as the smell of money.' The front of his head was flattened, sloping downwards, giving him a curiously low brow.

'I shall not be putting it in *my* purse,' I assured him.

'Sidney Grice.' My guardian held out his card. 'And this is Miss Middleton. You must excuse her peculiarities.'

'Prometheus Perseus Piggety.' He took the card and turned it over, as if expecting to find a personal message. 'I can forgive a beautiful lady anything,' he said, quite gallantly, until he added, 'but this one will have to mind her p's and q's.'

'I will tell her that,' I said, 'but I doubt that she ever will.'

Piggety screwed up his eyes and pushed his face quite close to my guardian's. 'How very like your cartoon you are.' And Sidney Grice whipped his card away.

'Were your parents fond of Greek myths, Mr Piggety?' I put in hastily.

All the time we were speaking Mr Piggety was shuffling backwards, like a flunkey in the presence of his monarch, to admit us to his premises.

'I hated them,' he said, 'and they hated me. So they changed my name from Samuel when I was fourteen.'

'How could anyone hate you?' I sprayed some perfume on to my handkerchief.

'Many people have asked me that question and I have yet to provide an answer…' He licked his lips. 'For there is not a more loveable man in this land than me.' He locked the door. 'The only one ever cut' – he held up a long, steel key with rows of teeth set at various angles around the cylindrical shank – 'and one that cannot be copied. Security is my watchword, my guiding light, my beacon, my—'

'A Williams-Hazard deadlock,' Sidney Grice interrupted.

'You know your locks, sir.'

'Mr Hazard paid me three hundred guineas to attempt to pick his prototype.'

'And did you manage?' I asked.

'He paid me another two hundred guineas to keep that information confidential.'

We were standing on a concrete platform with waist-high railings, looking down to a large, well-lit room with four long, parallel rows of cages stacked three high and resting on trestles.

'This used to be a factory for canning soup,' Prometheus Piggety told us, 'until people realized what a useless idea that was.'

'But surely it preserves the food,' I said and Prometheus Piggety snickered. He was neatly if slightly shoddily dressed in a shiny-elbowed, bottle-green coat and good-quality black twill trousers which needed pressing, but his shirt collar was stained a vivid red with a blue tint.

'Yes, dear girl, but how do you get it out again?'

'I am sure I could design an opening device,' my guardian said, half to himself, and Mr Piggety snickered again.

'I should not trouble yourself, sir. It is just a passing frivolity like paraffin. What is the point in that when we have an endless supply of sperm whales already?'

I was about to point out that paraffin was cheaper, cleaner and kinder, but Sidney Grice said, 'You have an interesting business here.'

'Come and see for yourself.' Mr Piggety led the way down a flight of open metal steps into the great hall and stopped at the first cage we came to. It contained five white kittens.

'Aren't they gorgeous?' Mr Piggety opened a cage, lifted one out and handed it gently to me, a tiny thing with big green eyes and soft pink paws. I stroked its head and it nuzzled my hand. I put my finger under its throat and felt nothing.

'How very odd,' I said. 'It seems so happy and yet it does not purr.'

'There is something very curious about the noise these cats are making,' Sidney Grice said.

'I cannot hear anything.' I tickled behind its ears.

'That is what is so curious.' My guardian rattled his cane along the bars of a row of cages and the occupants jumped back and, though some opened their mouths and bared their teeth, not one of them hissed or meowed at him.

Mr Piggety made a high whinnying sound. 'Well spotted, sir. Do you know I have shown countless gentlemen around this establishment and not more than two of them observed that fact until their attention was drawn to it?'

The kitten dabbed a button on my coat.

'Why do they not make any noise?' I asked and Mr Piggety whinnied again, but in a lower register.

'These cats all came from a remote valley in an area of Spain called' – the whinny rose – '*Cat*alonia. Rather good, don't you agree?'

'Not remotely.' Sidney Grice genuflected to peer under a cage.

'I bought a job lot of cats' – more shrill hilarity forewarned of another pun – '*fur* three pounds, but I realized at once these were absolutely *purr*-fect for my purposes: snowy white, wonderfully soft fur and every one of them dumb. What more could you want?'

'Money,' my guardian said and Mr Piggety heehawed.

'You and I could be brothers,' he said and Sidney Grice recoiled. 'For the love of lucre is exactly why I purchased this magnificent edifice.'

'How many cats do you have here?' I asked.

'Four thousand, four hundred and twenty-two,' Mr Piggety replied, taking the kitten from me and putting it back in its cage where it mewed silently. 'I shall start marketing them before the end of next year.'

'But why have you not sold any yet?'

'Two reasons,' Mr Piggety said. 'First, we have to sell by the hundred to make the business viable.'

'But surely people buy cats individually.' I brushed some fine hairs from my collar and Mr Piggety snickered.

'What on earth could you do with one cat?'

I was about to tell him when my guardian said, 'What is the second reason?'

'Why, to let them grow, of course.'

'I would have thought most people want kittens,' I said and Mr Piggety neighed.

'Goodness, miss, but you have a lot to learn. Let me show you.'

We passed between two rows of cages, the occupants pressing their little pink noses out or playfully poking their paws between the bars.

'Every cage has its own bowl of fresh water and a twice-daily supply of minced horsemeat,' Mr Piggety pointed out.

'They seem very well cared for,' I said.

'Indeed they are, miss. Indeed they are,' Mr Piggety agreed. 'We have a system of steam pipes to warm the room in winter and all those skylights can be opened to cool it in the summer. It is important to maintain exactly the right temperature.'

'Sixty-two degrees,' Sidney Grice said, pointing to the far wall and a thermometer so small that I could only just see its outline.

Piggety rubbed his hands together. 'Too cold and they become ill, too hot and they moult and that would be a complete disaster. The steam is piped from my offal-boiling factory on Offal Lane just behind this factory, so I have a constant supply without the need to buy coal or employ a layabout to stoke up a boiler when he feels like bestirring himself.'

'What has happened to your shirt?' I asked. The stain seemed to be spreading and Mr Piggety looked abashed.

'I suffer from *Chromhidrosis*,' he told me, 'an embarrassing condition which stains the sufferer's sweat green, yellow, black or – in my case – bluish-red.' He spoke so sheepishly that I was about to apologize when Sidney Grice gave up examining the hinge of a cage and asked abruptly, 'How many businesses do you own?'

Mr Piggety narrowed his eyes. 'You are not from the ministry of taxation?'

'Do I look like a civil servant?' Sidney Grice bristled as we came to a door at the far end.

'There is not much civil about you,' Mr Piggety observed. 'But since you ask, I have three other businesses, the production and marketing of clockwork animals – mice and dogs mainly – a second-hand sock warehouse, and another factory for the manufacture of false hands – very much in demand in Hungary for some reason. Perhaps they are very...' he smirked '... *Hungary*.' He paused for effect. '*Hand* they eat hands.'

I cringed and my guardian threw him an atrophying look, as Mr Piggety opened up and stood back for us to go through into a smaller rectangular room. Here there were hooks hanging from two parallel belts of chains either side of us, running the length of the room towards two big enamelled circular vats.

'When this is fully functional,' Mr Piggety said, 'four men should be able to put two hundred and forty cats through here in an hour. These,' he picked up a heavy wooden cosh, 'are what we will pretend to kill them with.'

'One moment,' I interrupted his happy flow. 'Why would you want to *pretend* to kill them?'

Mr Piggety shrieked with merriment. 'No, miss. We won't pretend to kill them – we'll pretend to kill them with the clubs.'

'Let me see,' my guardian said and marched over to a vat to peer in and back to us, pausing to examine an array of wheels and levers halfway down. 'So your intention is to tie the cats to the hooks.'

'Using only these silken cords so as not to damage them in any way,' Mr Piggety affirmed.

'I still—' I began but Sidney Grice carried on over me.

'Presumably you will fill the vats with hot water.'

Mr Piggety clapped his hands. 'There you have it, sir. The cats will be transported from here to the tubs in a continuous line to be automatically lowered into the vats.'

'For how long?' Sidney Grice enquired.

'From experiments I have conducted so far, about one minute,' Mr Piggety said. 'As a good rule of thumb, we will just wait until the water stops frothing.'

'So you are going to put live cats into scalding water?' I hoped I had misunderstood him.

'Quite so, miss,' Mr Piggety said proudly. 'The clubs are only there to allay the suspicions of goody-goody milksoppers like the RSPCA should they decide to pay us a visit. I had the room soundproofed for the same reason, though I would not have troubled had I known I would come across such conveniently mute creatures. There are ridiculous laws now based on fanciful ideas that animals are capable of suffering the same as we are. Why, these cats cannot even squeal, and it is a well-known medical fact that a dumb man does not really feel pain.'

'But why not at least stun them first?' I asked.

'Oh, you ladies.' Mr Piggety winked at me and then at my guardian. 'So soft-hearted. Three reasons not to club them, miss. First, it takes time, second, there is a risk of damaging their pelts and, third, the skin is looser on a live cat and the writhing makes it more so. Also, it tenderizes the meat, which we intend to make into a very superior food for the discerning dog owner.'

'Discerning dog owners do not eat the flesh of cats,' Sidney Grice pointed out.

'Perhaps you would like to see the skinning room next.'

I felt queasy. 'What a repellent man you are,' I said, and Mr Piggety flared.

'I wonder if you will be so childishly sentimental when Mr Grice gives you a lovely soft white fur coat for Christmas.'

'You are—'

My guardian stepped between us. '—a member of the Death Club.'

'What is left of it,' Mr Piggety agreed merrily.

'You realize, I assume, that – since some of your members have been murdered already – you must be a suspect yourself?' my guardian enquired, and Prometheus Piggety sniggered sneezily.

'Suspect away,' he said, 'but you would be better employed suspecting the real killer.'

'It causes me no sorrow to tell you that you are going to die, Piggety,' Sidney Grice said, 'horribly and soon. If you are not the murderer you will be murdered, and if you are the murderer I shall experience great *Schadenfreude* in seeing you hanged.'

'I hear you have a fondness for executing innocent clients,' Mr Piggety sneered.

Sidney Grice's grip tightened on his cane.

'Why, you—' he began, but I jumped in with, 'Are you not concerned that the other members are being murdered?'

'Concerned?' Prometheus Piggety took off his gold-rimmed spectacles and hurred on them. 'Delighted, more like. Why, every death brings me closer to a considerable fortune.'

Sidney Grice brought his anger under control and said, 'It does not take a giant stride of the imagination to know that the person most likely to benefit is the murderer himself.'

'Nor does it take a giant stride to know that when there are two of us left, I shall turn the other member in to the very first peeler I bump into. I do hope it's the vicar. I should love to see a vicar swing.'

'But what if you are not his last intended victim?' I asked, and Mr Piggety sniggered yet again.

'Dear girl.' He polished his spectacles with a square of chamois leather and held them up. 'Though I can tell you have taken a shine to me already, you need have no fears on my behalf. I have already taken out an insurance policy which will guarantee Mr Grice will have to do everything in his power to keep me alive. I have placed a notice in tomorrow's *Times*, announcing that I am under his protection.'

Sidney Grice wiped his cheek with the back of his hand. 'Then I shall place a larger notice making it quite clear that you are not.'

Mr Piggety wiggled his fingers as if warming up to play the pianoforte. 'It is of no matter. I had my palm read by an old smelly gypsy woman when I was fifteen and she forecast a number of things correctly, such as that I should grow up irresistible to members of the gentler sex – and please do not trouble to deny it, miss – but also that I should die in my bath before my eightieth birthday, so I am not expecting a visit from the grim reaper for many a year yet.' He hooked his spectacles behind his ears.

'You cannot really think anyone can tell the future by the creases in your palm. If that—' I began, but Prometheus Piggety said over me, 'According to Professor Stone, who has a chair in mathematics at Cambridge, palmists and fortune-tellers are more often correct in their forecasts than economists or weather forecasters.'

'That is like asking who is the most blind man in the country of the blind,' Sidney Grice commented, and Prometheus Piggety giggled.

'I have heard that you are half-blind yourself, Mr Grice.'

My guardian blanched and put a quick finger to his eye. 'I wonder if your gypsy told you what a gullible, conceited, shrivel-brained small man you would become, or if she forecast how odious and malodorous you would be, or perhaps she did not trouble since you possessed all those qualities already.'

'Small?' Mr Piggety clutched the edge of a table to steady himself. 'How dare you, sir? You come barging in with your... dun-headed bat-faced—'

'No wonder your parents did not like you,' I told him. 'I am only astounded that you had parents in the first place.'

Mr Piggety drew himself to his full height, but even then he was a good three inches shorter than me.

'I will thank you to quit my premises.'

'There is no need to thank us,' I said and spun on my heel, trying to pretend I had not caught it in a grating. 'It will be our pleasure.'

'I shall have you closed down by the end of the week,' Sidney Grice told him, but Mr Piggety jeered.

'I think not, sir. Several senior members of the Cabinet have invested heavily into this project,' he called after us as we climbed the stairs.

'To think we are governed by such people,' Sidney Grice bemoaned when we rejoined the swell of dock workers. 'If the British Empire should last a thousand years, men will say this was their most squalid hour.'

'Wotcha, Mr Grice.'

I turned and saw an urchin sitting on an algae-coated mooring post. My guardian did not turn his head towards him but replied through frozen lips, 'If ever you acknowledge me again, you and all your verminous gang can report to Wandsworth for a flogging.' And he spun the boy a shilling as we walked past.

*

'Dr Berry told me something interesting yesterday,' Mr G said as we went in to his study. 'The previous afternoon she was in Tavistock Square on her way to see a patient when she glanced up and saw a woman looking out of a window.' He thumbed through his mail. 'Guess where.' He sliced open an envelope using a wicked little stiletto, the very one – he once told me – that Jimmy Makepeace had used to cut the throat of his father.

'Silas Braithwaite's waiting room,' I exclaimed. He nodded and I thought about it. 'It could have been a cleaning lady sent by a letting agent or a relative looking—'

'Dr Berry could not be sure,' he threw the letter over his shoulder straight into his wastepaper bin, 'but she thought there was a dark stain on the left side of the woman's face.'

'Primrose McKay.'

'Hardly a titan stride of the imagination to imagine so.' He threw another two letters away unopened. 'And she felt that the postulated Miss McKay was watching her, but then you know my views on feelings – they belong in a compendium of fantasies and myths.'

'But why would Primrose go there?'

He tore a letter in half and put one part under his desk lamp. 'You are the one who is besotted with speculation.'

'To check there was no sign of her there – her name in his files, a letter from her or an entry in his diary.'

'Goodness, you *are* feeling creative today.' He sneezed.

'Shall we call and ask Miss McKay about it?'

'You go if you want to.' He blew his nose. 'I do not share your enthusiasm for wasting my days. How many times must I tell them?' He waved a thick document under my nose. 'I do not want to be president of—' But the last word was lost in another sneeze.

32

Chorea and the Whale

THE CRIES WERE reverberating down the corridor as I made my way along it. It sounded like two people, an adult and a child, but it was difficult to tell and none of the visitors was paying any attention. Pain was all too common in the treatments that were supposed to alleviate it.

There was no sign of the matron as I went into the Liston Ward and to Inspector Pound's bed. His eyes were closed and his breathing shallow, and his skin had a waxy glaze to it. I felt his pulse, weak and rapid, and pulled the blanket down. The sheet looked clean at any rate. I lifted it away.

'Don't tell Matron or we'll lose our jobs and never get another,' the older nurse pleaded as the two of them approached, 'but we've been cleaning him up with the carbolic like you said.'

'I can see you have changed his bedding.'

'The wound looks a lot better too,' the younger one said.

'Then I shall not disturb it.' I replaced the sheet and blanket. 'Has he been unconscious long?'

'All day,' said the younger one. 'He had a bit of that pie but he could hardly keep it down.'

His moustaches were damp and ragged.

'Who is his surgeon?'

'Mr Sweeney,' the older nurse said. 'He's Irish but he's very good. I once saw him cut out a live baby unharmed and the mother lived.'

An old man was shouting – something about Lord Raglan. He

repeated the name five times, each time more faintly, the last time breaking up. I saw him struggle to sit up but a nurse pushed him back into his pillow.

'Is he here today?'

'He does a ward round in about half an hour usually, if he hasn't been held up in surgery, but they won't let you stay while he's here.'

I took a card from my handbag – it had a print of a robin on it – and propped it up on the side table.

'How can I recognize him?'

The younger nurse giggled. 'You can't miss him. He nearly fills the corridor and he's got mutton chops like privet hedges.'

'That's no way to speak of a doctor,' the older nurse scolded. 'You won't mention us, will you, miss?'

'No. And thank you for what you are doing.'

I stood a while after they had gone and tidied his hair, and bent over to kiss his brow, but before I could reach him one eye opened a crack.

'Don't fuss, Lucinda,' he mumbled and the eye drifted shut again.

They were covering the old man's face as I left. I went to the chapel and sat at the back, and prayed for the man I never knew and the man I hoped to know again. A couple came in, smiling.

'Thank God,' the husband said. They put some money in the box and left, and I put my face into the cup of my fingers.

'Give me something to thank you for,' I whispered into my hands. People make deals when they want something from God. They promise to be good or give alms or go to church every day, but what could I bargain with that was worth Inspector Pound's life?

I opened a Bible and leafed through to the account of the centurion asking Jesus for help. *Say but the word and my servant shall be healed.* I used to find the words inspirational but now they seemed empty. I looked for something else, opening the book at random, but nothing brought me any comfort. Time passed and I went back up the stairs.

The nurse had not exaggerated. Nobody could have missed Mr Sweeney as he progressed along the corridor. He was a man of truly enormous bulk, swaying side to side, his face almost hidden behind a shrubbery of whiskers, and followed by a gaggle of students and junior staff.

'Might I have a word, Mr Sweeney?'

He lumbered on. 'I never discuss patients with relatives.' His voice boomed like an operatic bass.

'I know how busy you must be. My father was a surgeon.'

He paused in his stride but did not stop rocking. 'What was his name?'

'Colonel Geoffrey Middleton.'

'Never heard of him.'

'He spent most of his time in private practice and the army. He was the first to describe Middleton's Chorea.'

'Was he, by Jupiter?'

'I am Inspector Pound's...' my brain raced, '... fiancée.' *Friend* sounded slightly indecent and he may have met the inspector's sister already. 'I wonder if you would consider giving him some more blood.'

He guffawed and said over his shoulder. 'And how do you suggest I do that – pour him a glass of it?'

The acolytes tittered.

'By transfusion,' I said and the swaying stopped. 'I assisted my father for many years so I know something about it.'

'Then you will also know that three-quarters of patients being given blood go into acute circulatory shock and die during the procedure. Good day, Miss Middleton.'

'I gave him blood at the London Hospital with no ill effect on either of us.'

Mr Sweeney raised one eyebrow. 'Did you, by Jove?'

'Yes, and I was not aware that University College lags so far behind that it is unable to carry out the same procedure.'

The students gasped in a way that would have done credit to the final act of a melodrama, if only they had remembered to throw up their hands. The great bulk of Mr Sweeney tilted alarmingly and examined me. 'You are a highly presumptuous young lady.'

'I am often told that,' I informed him. 'But perhaps in this case I was right to presume things. I presumed that you were one of the finest surgeons in London. You may not have heard of my father but he often spoke highly of your contributions to *The Lancet*. Perhaps it was *his* presumptions which were wrong.'

I could almost swear two juniors threw up their hands, but I was too busy trying to fix his watery brown eyes to show him I was not afraid.

'Do I look like a fish?' He raised the other eyebrow.

I wanted to say *more like a whale* but I settled for 'Not very.'

The students tried to stifle their amusement. He turned to them and they succeeded.

'You think you can throw me the bait of vanity and reel me in?'

I knew I was in danger of going too far. 'I hoped to appeal to your professional pride.'

He growled softly and said, 'How much blood did you donate?'

'Only about half a pint,' I said. 'So I have plenty to spare.'

Mr Sweeney huffed. 'I am much too busy for all of this nonsense,' he told me as he started to lumber on. 'Come back in an hour.'

He was quick and efficient and I was quite relieved that he only took another pint. I would have given more but I was feeling quite woozy.

'Keep the wound clean with carbolic acid,' he told Matron as he slid the needles out.

And as he was leaving he tilted towards me again. 'There is no such thing as Middleton's Chorea and I have never contributed to that vulgar publication *The Lancet*.'

'I had to say something,' I responded and he grunted.

'Let us hope your prevarications have saved a life.'

Inspector Pound shivered.

Outside the rain had lifted and the sun was forcing its way feebly through that grey-beige that Londoners called a sky.

33

The Dead Either Side

ELM ROAD WAS full of life. The baked potato man vied with the cries of the crumpet seller, a boy pulled a block of ice on a handcart and the milkman rolled a churn on its lower rim towards the steps of a cellar.

We turned left down Plane Road and almost immediately the bustle ceased. There were no tradesmen here, only the pig man collecting swill from an imposing house on the corner. I patted his horse and it tried to push its nose into my handbag.

The road had been dug up and some planks laid over two parallel trenches, but the earth was piled so high around the works that it was impossible to cross without our boots becoming caked and the hem of my dress being saturated with wet mud. The workmen were taking a break, leaning on their shovels in their thick coats, except for one in shirtsleeves.

'He must be cold,' I commented, but Sidney Grice was peering into the trench.

'What with all these subterranean railways, passages, cellars, pipes and wires there will soon be more of London below the ground than above.' Mr G scraped some of the sticky clay off his soles against the kerb.

I walked on a few paces. 'Here we are.'

The church grew comfortably from its plot, grey stones, which might have been placed on top of each other three centuries or more ago, rising heavenwards as we walked down the path, the dead either side of us in a small ancient graveyard with the headstones laid flat upon the earth, most of them made illegible by frost and lichen, some half-buried under moss and grass.

'Somebody wept each time these graves were filled,' I said. 'Now nobody even knows who they contain.'

My guardian putted a twig to one side. 'Very few people are worth remembering.'

'They loved and were loved,' I said.

He paused to inspect a footprint on the verge. 'There is nothing clever about that. A flea-bitten cur is capable – and probably more deserving – of affection than the average man.'

We reached the porch and a great oak door strapped to the granite pillars by heavy black hinges studded with square pyramidal iron nails. 'Locked.' Sidney Grice turned the barley-twisted ring handle clockwise. 'It is sobering to reflect that there have only been six periods in the island's blood-soaked history when it has been felt necessary to keep our churches barred and we are living in one of them.' He rapped three times smartly with the handle of his cane and we waited.

'I wonder who will remember me,' I said.

'Nobody at all,' my guardian said, 'unless you put those journals of yours to some use and publish an account of your time with me.'

I was about to tell him that I hoped to mean more than that to somebody some day when a small panel in the woodwork swung inwards and a man's face appeared behind an inset fretwork box.

'Mr Grice?' The voice was high.

'Reverend Jackaman?'

'If you are Mr Grice, prove it by taking your eye out.'

'Step off that kneeler first.'

The face blinked. 'How do you know I am standing on a kneeler?'

'Because I am Sidney Grice.'

The face pondered for a while. 'Very well then. I *am* the Reverend Jackaman and now I should like you to leave.'

'I am Miss Middleton,' I told him and he looked shocked.

'You may be hardly more than a child,' the reverend said, 'but you must know that a lady never introduces herself to a gentleman.'

'If I should meet one I shall remember that,' I told him, 'but you ought to know that it is neither polite nor Christian to lock out a lady when she seeks access to the house of God.'

'My apologies for that,' he said. 'Now kindly go away.'

My guardian leaned towards the hole and it shut. 'What are you frightened of, Reverend Jackaman?' he called through the panel.

'You,' a muffled voice replied. 'I read the papers. Every soul whom you have questioned regarding that accursed death club has met an horrible end.'

'*A* horrible end,' Sidney Grice corrected him and the panel swung open again.

'Henry Alford would not have agreed with you.'

'Henry Alford would never have agreed with anyone,' my guardian retorted. 'He was the epitome of charm, but one of the most disagreeable men I have ever met when discussing linguistic exactitudes.'

'Who was Henry Alford?' I asked.

'Oh, what a meagre education the young receive and what a mean proportion of that they imbibe,' the Reverend Jackaman bemoaned. 'They are too busy dancing in the afternoons and listening to glee singers.'

'And filling their heads with Byronian trash,' my guardian concurred. 'Henry Alford was, amongst other things, a Fellow of Trinity College, a scholar and a textual critic.'

'And why are we talking about him?'

'I suppose you would rather be discussing ribbons and buttons,' Jackaman snapped. 'I see these girls in my church, Mr Grice. They whisper and giggle during my sermons. They pass each other notes. All they have come for is to flaunt their flounces.'

'It makes one despair for the empire,' Sidney Grice tisked. 'But we digress.'

'Surely not,' I murmured.

'You can at least talk to me, Reverend.'

'Can but will not,' Jackaman rejoined. 'Whilst others put their trust in Grice, I put mine in God. I seek his sanctuary in my own church.' The panel closed.

'You may be meeting your creator sooner than you think if you do not let us help you,' Mr G called.

'What's all this then?' We spun round to be confronted by a young man in a dazzling checked suit and bright yellow cravat, waving at us from the roadside. He came hurrying across, neatly leaping over an old man who was lying on the pavement. 'Fretnin' a man of the cloth, Mr Grice? Whatever next? Slaughterin' babes in their mothers' arms?'

'The Lord is my Shepherd,' the vicar was reciting loudly. 'I shall not want...'

'Blast,' my guardian grumbled. 'It is that blighter from the *Evening Standard*. Ignore him, March.' But I could not take my eyes off him.

The man sauntered up the path. He had a large white carnation in his buttonhole and wore white spats over black patent-leather shoes. 'And who is this lovely lady? No, don't tell me. I want to be able to write *Sidney Grice Seen With Mysterious Dark Female Companion*.'

I laughed and said, 'I am March Middleton, Mr Grice's ward.'

My guardian groaned and the young man tipped his natty bowler hat jauntily back with his silver-handled cane, to reveal dark Macassar-oiled hair.

'Yea, though I walk through the shadow of the valley of death,' came from inside the church.

'Wotta disappointin'ly innocent explanation,' the newcomer said. 'Waterloo Trumpington at your service, miss.' He took my hand and clicked his heels together like a Prussian officer at court.

I laughed again. 'Is that your real name?' And Waterloo Trumpington grinned. He had nice white teeth and his face was smooth and boyish.

'Is anyone's?'

'Mine is.'

'Stop jabbering.' Sidney Grice stood listening at the door. 'And listen.' But all I could hear was traffic from Elm Road and the voice of the vicar inside St Jerome's.

'Follow me all the days of my life.'

Sidney Grice tensed. 'Reverend Jackaman,' he called out urgently. 'Listen to me. Your life is in imminent danger.' He rattled and wrenched at the handle. 'For heaven's sake, open up, man.'

'And I shall dwell in the house of the Lord. What?... Who are you? How did you get in here?... What?... No!'

The last word came as a prolonged piteous cry abruptly cut short. There was the sound of a scuffle and then silence.

34

Half-melted Candles and Angels to Smite

Waterloo Trumpington's visage changed in an instant. A moment ago he had been nothing more than a careless cockney dandy, but now the grin was replaced by a tight-lipped determination and the dancing eyes were fixed on the figure of my guardian.

Sidney Grice had his ear to the door and signalled us to stay quiet. There was a bump and a low moan, and then a thump like somebody banging a table.

'No,' Reverend Jackaman cried out. 'For the love of Christ our saviour.'

I heard metal strike metal and a scream and then a series of six duller blows, steady and separate, each one accompanied by another shriek.

Sidney Grice stood back and looked at the window.

'Smash it,' Waterloo Trumpington suggested. His voice was calm and strangely detached.

'With what?' my guardian demanded. 'Anyway, it is too high and barred.'

I banged on the woodwork with the side of my fist and yelled, 'Open this door.' But the only reply was a metallic clash and another cry.

'Mighty Lord, send your angel to smite—' But the words were lost in an agonized sob.

The church was joined between two tall houses.

'That' – Sidney Grice pointed to the house on the left – 'is the rectory. Go, Miss Middleton, and ask if there is a side entrance into the church. Hurry.'

The hammering and shrieking began again, each cry more piteous than the last.

There was a wall between the church grounds and rectory garden, with a gateway set into it. I ran across the graveyard, trying to avoid stepping on the tombstones, but the wooden gate was locked so I zigzagged back. Sidney Grice was rooting through his satchel while Waterloo Trumpington leaned languidly back on his stick, observing him. My guardian brought out a twisted piece of metal and rammed it into the keyhole.

'Breakin' into an 'ouse of God?' Waterloo Trumpington mocked. 'It gets better by the minute.'

'Do something,' I shouted.

'I am.' The reporter grinned. 'I am doing my job and leaving your guardian to his.'

'I have no time for this.' I ran back down the path, calling over my shoulder. 'The *Evening Standard* will be very interested in my account of how you stood back and let a man of God die.'

I did not wait for a response but dashed down the footpath, cursing the impediment of my dress as I whipped though a low gate and to the front of the rectory. Panting heavily, I wrenched the bell. It tinkled merrily in the background and I wrenched it again. Ten times I rang, but there was no reply.

I looked in through the window, cupping my eyes with my hands to the glass, but only saw a dull, unoccupied drawing room with an upright piano with half-melted candles in brass candelabras. I tried the bell again, yanking at the handle until I thought it would come off in my hand, and shouted out, 'Hello. Is anybody there?' And then I heard it, clear and loud from the church of St Jerome.

'Help... Somebody help me... No! Sacrilege. Please God, no!' And that *no* became a wail soaring to the heavens, nothing but terror and pain and then nothing at all.

I ran back. Sidney Grice was wrenching on his lever in the keyhole.

'Now!' he yelled and Waterloo Trumpington ran at an oak panel, flying into it with both boots and landing with great agility on his feet as the door crashed in. He checked his buttonhole and looked over my guardian's shoulder, and the blood drained from his face. His fingers went to his cheek and he half-stepped, half-stumbled backwards.

'Shit me,' he said softly.

'Stay out, March,' Sidney Grice called, not taking his eyes off whatever confronted him. 'And this time I mean it.'

All the more reason to come in, I thought, but, for the first time since I had come to London and ever since that moment, I wished I had obeyed him.

'Sacrilege,' I whispered in an echo of something I had heard a long time ago when I had thought I knew what the word meant.

35

Blood and Water

ST JEROME'S LOOKED normal for a moment – a small austere Norman structure with four rows of benches parted by a central apse and two side aisles, a tapestry-covered footstool lying on its side, and a marble altar with a silver candlestick on each corner, the body of the church being lit by a clumsy stained-glass window at each end. But Sidney Grice was not admiring the architecture. His attention was fixed on a heavy oak screen in front of the organ and what was attached to it.

I gasped and steadied myself on the end of a pew. The thing I saw was a grotesquery, a travesty of a man and his redeemer. The Reverend Jackaman had been stripped to his blood-soaked calico drawers and skewered to the screen in a depraved mockery of the Crucifixion. A nail had been hammered through each of his wrists and a longer one through his overlapped feet. His head hung on to his chest, his scalp pierced by dozens of hat pins, some sticking out through the skin of his forehead, and a wooden spar jutted from where it had been thrust deep into his side and up under his ribcage.

'Forthwith there came out blood and water,' I said and crossed myself, but my guardian showed no sign of having heard me. He stood quite still, the red light of the angels cast across his face as he gazed at this thing, the priest who had become obscenity and suffering.

'Oh, my good Gawd.' Waterloo Trumpington came to stand

beside me and I glanced at him. But instead of the disgust I had expected to see, his eyes flashed with excitement and he narrowed them knowingly, with a peculiar look creeping over his lips.

36

Courcy's Cravat and Sucking Lice

FOR A LONG time Sidney Grice surveyed the monstrosity before us. He put on his pince-nez, leaned forward and took them off again. He whistled seven quick notes softly through closed teeth and crouched. He stood and walked to and fro, not taking his eyes off the body until he turned, paced three steps back and whipped round, as if he were a child playing *statues* and expecting the vicar to have moved. But the Reverend Enoch Jackaman was never again to move on this earth of his own volition.

'May God receive and have mercy on your soul,' I said, and my guardian looked puzzled.

'Mine?' He spoke as if half asleep.

'Reverend Jackaman's.'

He raised an eyebrow and put his pince-nez back on to view the reverend more closely.

'So that is how you did it,' he murmured.

'Surely it is obvious how he was killed,' I said, but my guardian clicked his tongue.

'The truth is rarely obvious and the whole truth never so. Look in your books,' he gestured to a stack of Bibles, 'and tell me how clear it is.'

'There are more answers in the Bible than you seem to think.' I slid on a dark puddle. 'Should you not be chasing the murderer?'

Sidney Grice seemed mildly hurt. 'That is exactly what I am

doing.' He walked round the screen. 'Courcy's cravat,' he said as he emerged.

'But you should be finding out how he escaped.'

Sidney Grice pulled his lower eyelid down a fraction to let his eye drop. 'My dear child—'

'Do *not* call me a child.'

He tightened his mouth. 'Then do not behave like one. You think you can blunder into my life for a few months and tell me how to go about my business?'

I tried to calm myself. 'I am sorry. It is just—' But my guardian shushed me gently.

'I *know* how the murderers escaped. They went through that exit by the side chapel, across the rectory garden and through the back gate into Mulberry Street where they will have been instantly swallowed up in the crowds that attend the Thursday toy market. If they can be tracked, your new friend will be hot on their heels as we speak. Waterloo Trumpington clings to me like a sucking louse sometimes, but once he is on the trail of something he is a veritable pig in a patch. He will turn the whole field over until he finds his turnip.'

'Why more than one murderer?' I asked.

'Because one person could not hold a conscious and struggling vicar still and transfix him at the same time.' Sidney Grice pinched the scar on his ear. 'You need both hands just to hold a nail and hammer it.'

'And you are happy for Waterloo Trumpington to catch them?'

Sidney Grice blew his nose. 'I would be delighted if Trumped-up Trumpington came across the murderers because I have no doubt who would come off the worse for the encounter. Do you seriously imagine that the people who did this could be bested by that jumped-up, slandering, penny-print guttersnipe?' He held out a screwed-up ball of paper and shook off a gelatinous clot. 'I found this crammed into his mouth.'

'What does it say?'

He straightened it out until I could just make out the words: *Eloi El* – a bloodstain – *hani.*

'*Eloi Eloi Lama Sabachthani*,' I said. 'My God, my God, why have you forsaken me?'

'A valid question under the circumstances,' my guardian commented.

I looked around the empty church, the clumsy pillars and the cold statues, and tried to clear the jumble from my mind. A life-sized crucifix lay smashed, wood and plaster in one corner. 'What did you mean by *Courcy's cravat*?'

'Jean-Claude Courcy was a war veteran with a grudge against the Grande Armée. He was paralysed from the waist down by a bullet in the spine, but he had been caught stealing from the mess bar just before battle and forfeited his pension. He killed four officers from his wheelchair whilst going round the streets in uniform. If an officer stopped to give him alms, he would speak very huskily so that the victim had to bend his head towards him to hear. Courcy had a noose on a stick, which he would whip over the victim's head, then pull the rope to tighten round the neck. A strangled man can lose consciousness in under a minute. Sometimes Courcy would toy with them by loosening the noose enough for them to come round before he tightened it again. A captain who he had left for dead recovered and told that story. The last intended victim escaped because he had a very large nose and ears, and Courcy had not opened the noose wide enough to go cleanly over.'

I was feeling very hot and sick, but I forced myself to step forward and look more closely.

'I can see the rope mark round his neck.'

'And under the angle of his left jaw?'

'A circular impression.'

He bobbed down to turn a leaf over. 'Made by the end of the stick.' He jumped up. 'That was the first choking sound we heard. The noose was tightened just enough to incapacitate Jackaman. He could then be led like a stray dog to the screen; the pole was passed through a hole in the screen and wedged the other side. At that stage it could be loosened. The killer wanted him to be fully aware of what was happening to him.'

I closed my eyes in a futile attempt to erase the image before us. 'How can anyone hate people so much?'

Sidney Grice crouched to scrutinize a puddle of blood blotting out most of the Latin inscription on a memorial floor-slab. He took a pipette from his satchel and carefully sucked a scruple of darkness into the bulb. He put a finger over the top, took a test tube in his left hand and deftly removed the cork with his little finger, let the fluid flow into the tube and recorked it.

'They may not have hated Jackaman at all.' He put the test tube and pipette away. 'It may be just me.'

This was intolerable. 'Why does everything have to revolve around you?'

He went down on his knees and crawled with his nose almost on the floor in a wide circle round the blood. 'Ah.' He brought out an envelope and scooped a bit of dirt into it.

'Because,' he said simply, 'it always does.'

I could not bear any more – the disgusting suffering of the man who was dead; the disgusting arrogance of the man who regarded everything that happened as an intellectual jigsaw puzzle made only for him to play with. I went outside where at least the dead were at peace.

Angelica, your youngest sister, the darling of your family, had died of scarlet fever at home in Shropshire, and you were very low and very drunk or you would not have told me about the war. You said that in the Afghan Campaign, when the tribesmen of the Northwest Frontier captured a Christian soldier, they would castrate him and then they would tie him to the ground and prop his mouth open with a stick and the women would crouch over him and drown him in their urine.

I am not sure you believed the stories and I certainly

did not. I could not imagine anyone being so disgustingly cruel – until now.

I sat on a stone bench with my back to the wall of St Jerome's and looked at a gravestone to my side. A whole family lay there, the parents and five children all dead within a three-year span ending in 1785. For almost a century they had lain undisturbed, awaiting the resurrection of their bodies. I could not imagine a soul and yet I knew we all had one. I wanted a cigarette but it seemed disrespectful. I closed my eyes and prayed until I heard hurried footfalls approaching and Waterloo Trumpington came breathlessly back. 'No sign of 'im.'

'Look in the church,' I said. 'There are plenty of signs of him there.' And then I could not stop myself. Everything came welling out of me in uncontrollable sobs. 'I am sorry.' I took his handkerchief and caught myself. I knew how tears embarrassed men, but Waterloo Trumpington showed only concern.

'What you need,' he touched my arm, 'is a good strong drink… What's so funny?'

'I was just thinking' – I wiped my eyes – 'how nice it is to be with a man who does not add *of tea*.'

37

Great Naval Battles in the Snug

THE BLACK BOY was just round the corner, crowded, smoky and noisy, with a huddle of costermongers bantering round the bar.

'Come in the snug,' Waterloo Trumpington said. 'You won't get ogled there... unless, of course, you like being ogled.'

I would not have minded in the least but I said, 'We will go in the snug.' And we passed through to a side room, pine-lined, with three tables made of upturned beer barrels and a fireplace with cold clinker settled in the grate. 'I am sorry I cried.'

Waterloo Trumpington pursed his lips. 'Know why men don't cry? They're frigh'ened to. Women are braver than men.'

'We don't fight in wars.'

He batted the thought away. 'You've got more sense.'

'You have a very good opinion of my sex.'

'I like women. My mother was one.' He clapped his hands together. 'What'll it be? Port? Sherry?'

'A brandy would be nice.'

'That's the spirit.' He went to the bar where it jutted into the room. 'Couple of big Boney's, sweetheart, and one for yourself.' Then he rejoined me with two very large brandies.

'I hope the alcohol kills the germs.' The rim was smeared greasily.

'The drinks 'ere will kill anyfink,' Waterloo Trumpington told me cheerily. 'Good 'ealth.'

We clinked glasses and I took a swig, holding it in my mouth before letting it course down my throat. I blinked. 'I believe you are right, Mr Trumpington.'

'My friends call me Traf,' he said, 'and I 'ope you will do the same.'

'Is that really your name?'

'Waterloo Trafalgar Agincourt Trumpington reporting for duty, ma'am.' He saluted. 'My old man was very patriotic.'

'Traf is certainly less of a mouthful.' I laughed. 'And please call me March.'

'March it is then. Mind if I smoke?'

'Not if you give me one.'

He grinned approvingly. 'You're quite the twist, March.' And, seeing my bemusement, explained. 'Twist and Twirl – girl – rhyming slang.'

'Like *Adam and Eve – believe*,' I said and he chuckled.

'Why, we'll make a cockney of you yet, March. 'Ow long have you known Mr Grice for then?'

'Only a few months,' I said. 'Though it seems a lot longer.'

'I'll bet it does, living with that old devil.'

'You do not like each other, do you?'

Traf leaned back in his chair. 'Our Sidney dislikes the world and the world returns the compliment.'

'I do not think he dislikes everyone. We met a woman doctor recently and I think he holds her in some regard.'

He swigged his brandy. 'A woman doctor?' he asked incredulously.

I nodded. 'Dr Berry.'

'Oh yeah. I've 'eard of that old 'arpy.'

'Dr Berry is neither old nor a harpy. She is still quite young and pretty and I think what she has achieved is quite wonderful. But he does seem to dislike most people. Do you have any idea why?'

'You'll have to ask 'im that one. I 'ave 'eard it said as 'e was disappointed in love.' Waterloo Trumpington snorted. 'Can't imagine 'im being disappointed in anyfink but 'atred myself.'

'But why you especially?'

'Opposite sides of the same coin, me and Sid. We rake around scandals and we uncover things people don't want uncovered. Only 'e's so hoity-toity he can't stand to be reminded of that.' We smoked for a while. 'Having a spot of bother with 'is latest assignment, ain't 'e?'

'Is he?' I finished my brandy.

'Same again?' Waterloo Trumpington picked up both glasses without waiting for a reply.

'I do not mind you trying to get me drunk,' I told him when he returned. 'In fact I do not mind if you succeed. But you will not get me to talk about him.'

Waterloo Trumpington surveyed me in amusement. 'Scratch me, you're a cucumber.'

'How did you come to be here?' I asked.

'Vicar in a deaf club where the members is dyin' like rats in a ring.' His chair creaked as he leaned towards me. 'It 'ad to be worf an interview. Wasn't expectin' nuffin' like that, though.' And from his expression it was clear he was not disappointed.

I sucked the last of my cigarette, downed my brandy in one and stood up. 'Thank you for the drinks. I had better get back to work.'

Traf raised his glass. 'I know when I'm beaten.'

'I cannot imagine anyone getting the better of you.' I stubbed out my cigarette underfoot and left him to it.

The costermongers had gone, leaving only a handful of old men staring into their futures though empty beer mugs. It was drizzling outside now and Sidney Grice was standing in the graveyard. His nose twitched. 'You have been to a public house.'

'The Black Boy.'

'I do not care what colour, sex or age it was. You went unaccompanied into a drinking establishment?'

'No. Traf… Mr Trumpington took me.'

My guardian shot a hand to his eye. 'What did you tell him?'

'Nothing.'

'What did he ask you?'

'How long I had known you. I said a few weeks. Then he tried to get me to talk about these cases, but I told him I would not discuss anything with him.'

'Good. What else did you tell him?'

'Nothing.'

'You are sure?'

'Completely.'

Sidney Grice grunted. 'It is almost impossible to say nothing to the predators of Fleet Street. They could suck the juice from a diamond. However, we shall see what calumnies he begets from your socializing soon enough. I must find somebody to summon the police.'

'At least Inspector Quigley cannot say it is suicide or an accident this time,' I said.

'I would not be too confident of that,' my guardian disagreed, 'but Quigley will not come. He would not want to get embroiled in a case like this at the best of times. No, March, he will send a subordinate or, better still from his point of view, a rival.'

A large middle-aged woman came along with arms full of flowers.

'I am sorry, madam,' I said. 'But the church is closed.'

'Nonsense. I can see it is open from here.' She pushed me aside but Sidney Grice stood his ground.

'One moment, please.' He delved into his satchel like a lady rooting though her handbag. 'Here we are.' He pointed a small, beautifully carved ivory-handled revolver straight at her and said pleasantly. 'If you do not turn round and go away within nine seconds, I will put a bullet into your vestigial brain.'

'How dare—' She clutched her flowers as though expecting to be robbed of them.

'Seven seconds.'

'Well, really.' The woman retreated to the pavement and called back. 'I shall summon the police.'

'Please do.' He pulled back the hammer. 'And tell them to hurry.'

'That was a little extreme,' I commented as she bustled through the gate.

'I disagree.' He lowered the hammer and put his revolver away. 'It was *very* extreme. But she had the glazed eye of a slow-worm and it would have taken half an hour to achieve the same outcome by conventional means.'

We waited until the police came – four constables, a uniformed sergeant and a plainclothed detective, none of whom I had seen before.

'Miss Middleton saw less than I did,' my guardian said. 'I will not have her questioned.'

The detective was ruffled. 'I shall question whosoever I please.' His voice came from somewhere in the back of his throat. 'Stay there,' he said to me.

I sat on the low wall with my feet at the side of a gravestone. It said *John* or *Joan* and *Be*, which I assumed was the start of *beloved*, and the words of Genesis came into my head: *In the sweat of thy face shalt thou eat bread, till thou return unto the ground; for out of it wast thou taken: for dust thou art, and unto dust shalt thou return*. Was that all there was to it? Could God not protect his own servant who had pleaded with him? I thought even the hairs on our heads were numbered.

I heard some clattering and looked up to see my guardian coming out of the church.

'They are taking him down.' He took my arm. 'Come, March. This is no place for you.'

'It is no place for anyone outside of hell.'

We made our way to the path and turned our backs on the dead.

'You are shaking,' my guardian said. 'What you need is a really strong drink,' he patted my hand, 'of tea... What is so amusing?'

'Nothing,' I said. 'Nothing at all.'

*

There was a pretty tea shop at the front of Bailey's Antiquarian Bookstore and they were about to close, but the manageress cheerfully admitted us and seated us beneath a giant aspidistra plant. Sidney Grice swept his arm back to push away a leaf which was tickling his head.

'Did you find out anything else?' I asked as he shifted his chair away from it and me.

'Two things.' The leaf was caressing his cheek now. 'One tangible, the other intangible.' He delved into his satchel for a brown paper bag and whipped out a greasy cloth cap, holding it up for my inspection.

'The tangible clue,' I guessed.

'Quite so.' He placed it on the table. 'I espied it in the garden, caught in the overhanging branch of a fruitless Plymouth pear tree.'

'Perhaps it was swept off the murderer's head as he escaped,' I suggested.

'It is unlikely to have belonged to the vicar,' he concurred, 'and anyone who was not in an extreme hurry would have paused to retrieve it. The branch was only four feet-three inches from the ground, but then…' He looked at me quizzically.

'People bend as they run.'

'Precisely.' He slapped the leaf irritably.

A waitress appeared with our tea in a white china pot with matching cups. 'Shall I hang that up for you, sir?' She viewed the hat with distaste.

'Leave it alone,' he snapped. 'It is not my hat.'

She hurried away and I picked it up. 'The wearer had black hair not pomaded,' I observed, picking out a strand from the lining.

'Or red hair.' Mr G pointed to a few on the underside of the peak.

'One of the men working on the road had red hair and he was not wearing a hat,' I commented.

'And how do you think he got round the back and into the church in the time available?' He rammed the leaf away but it sprang back. 'Plus there would have been mud everywhere from his boots and clothes.'

'I did not say he did,' I defended myself. 'I merely observed—'

'Leave the observations to me.' Mr G leaned back and snapped the leaf off.

'Are you going to show me your intangible clue?' I joked weakly and he huffed.

'I went out through the back gate to the toy fair and, except for Trumpington darting about like a confused whippet, not a soul had noticed anything at all.'

'That is disappointing.' I poured, thinking that I would rather have had another brandy – anything to dull the sights and sounds that crowded through my brain.

'On the contrary.' Sidney Grice stirred his milkless, sugarless tea vigorously clockwise. 'It is one of the most important clues I have discovered so far.'

'I do not understand.'

A look of alarm came over Sidney Grice's face and his hand shot in the air. 'Waitress. I ordered tea, not last week's pencil shavings.'

*

I went to see Inspector Pound. He was still unconscious but his breathing was stronger and steadier. The younger nurse came and wiped his face with a damp flannel.

'He came round a bit this morning,' she told me, 'and said something about the robin on the card and his uncle, but it didn't make much sense.'

'It was just a silly joke. His uncle was a mounted Bow Street Runner,' I told her, 'and they wore red waistcoats.' I touched Inspector Pound's brow. 'His temperature has gone down,' I observed. 'Thank you for tending to him.'

The nurse bowed her head. 'He's a good sort, the inspector,' she told me. 'He arrested my brother once and didn't even beat him up.'

38

Slapped Faces and Torn Remains

WE DID NOT have to wait for the morning. The evening papers were full of the news.

HORRIBLE MURDER OF THE REVEREND ENOCH JACKAMAN, LATE VICAR OF ST JEROME'S CHURCH

But worse was to follow.

THE CURSE OF GRICE STRIKES AGAIN

And:

SIDNEY GRICE, PRIVATE DETECTIVE, WITNESSES TERRIBLE MURDER OF HIS OWN CLIENT

'Personal, personal, personal,' Sidney Grice chanted. 'I am a *personal* detective. There is nothing remotely private about my work at the moment.'

We read them over tea in the study.

'Your new friend devotes a whole column to you, March,' my guardian said quietly and handed me a copy of the *Evening Standard*.

THE TRUTH ABOUT SIDNEY GRICE FROM HIS COMPANION

On the afternoon of the murder while the body of the Reverend Jackaman still hung crucified, dark-haired and dark-eyed Miss March Middletone took our young reporter to one of the many public houses she frequents where she smoked tobacco and consumed great quantities of strong liquor. Only when she was in what we can only refer to as a condition which no lady should be did she consent to give him an interview. Miss Middletone would not comment upon her relationship with Mr Grice at whose address she resides.

'That is disgusting,' I said. 'I shall sue.'

Sidney Grice looked severe. 'What has he said that was untrue?'

'Nothing, but he has implied...'

'He will argue that it is only your depraved mind that imagines anything untoward in his article.'

I read on. 'Nor did she deny that his attentions were not always of a nature one might expect from a man purporting to be her guardian.'

'I did not deny it because I was not asked,' I said, 'and what is this about *purporting*? You *are* my guardian.'

'Not in law,' Sidney Grice said softly. 'There has never been a court order assigning you to my care.'

'If ever I see that man again I shall slap his face.'

'Oh, you will see him again,' my guardian assured me, 'and he would love you to assault him, the more publicly the better.'

'And he has misspelled my name.' I folded the paper. 'I shall not read this filth.'

'Read it later,' he advised. 'You cannot defend yourself from attacks if you do not know what they are.'

I dropped the paper by my chair. 'What kind of a man writes these things?'

'The kind of man with whom you go drinking.'

This seemed a good time to divert the topic.

'How did you know that Reverend Jackaman was standing on a kneeler?' I asked.

'If you were paying attention, you will recall me telling you that I met Jackaman's brother once on the crossing to Calais. He was an exporter of cat-o'-five-tails.'

'Do you not mean nine tails?'

'No. These were considered kinder for flogging children.'

'How soft-hearted he must have been.'

He carefully ripped a strip from his paper and put it on the table face down. 'At present I am more concerned with his stature. He was five foot and three inches before his back was bent and he told me that he was the tallest member of his family, so Jackaman must have stood on something to peer out of the opening.'

'Why not a chair?'

'Because, unlike the rest of mankind, I use my senses. I heard wooden furniture being dragged. It was not as heavy as a pew and a chair would be too tall to stand on and too low for kneeling. It was obvious. A simpleton could have reached the same conclusion.'

'But I did not.'

My guardian allowed himself an ephemeral smile. 'Precisely.' He picked up the *West London Recorder*.

'You seem very relaxed about all this,' I commented.

'I am rarely what I seem.' Sidney Grice folded his arms and leaned back in his chair. 'Besides,' he continued, 'for the first time in my life, I am too angry to be angry. I have come to expect slanders as a professional risk, along with death threats, assaults and damage to my property. But this man has made vile innuendos about a girl – a young woman – in my care and that is insufferable. If I know one thing for certain, Waterloo Trafalgar Trumpington shall rue the day he put his name to such foul falsehoods.' He crunched the *Recorder* and his voice rose. 'How many times do I have to tell them? I am *not* protecting these people.' And the paper bunched up in his grasp. In a seemingly involuntary movement he ripped it apart. 'Perhaps,' he surveyed the torn remains, 'I am not too angry to be angry after all.'

I leafed through the *Hampstead Times* and did not have to go much further than an account of a mugging on the heath of an ebony dealer before I saw:

THE AFFAIRS OF SIDNEY GRICE

Our reporter has been privy to intimate details of a relationship between private detective, Mr Sidney Grice, and Dorna Berry, a married woman posing as a doctor in...

I closed my eyes.

'What is it?'

I handed the paper over and my guardian flushed. 'In a jealous rage, Mr Grice's present female companion revealed that he has developed strong feelings for Mrs Berry, which we have now reason to suspect are not,' his voice rose, 'reciprocated.' He flung the paper down, strewing its pages across the tea tray. 'Apparently I think she is wonderful but refuse to speak of her to you.'

'More lies,' I said, but there was nothing phlegmatic about Sidney Grice's reaction to the papers now.

'What *exactly* did you say to that scoriaceous, grubbing, truth-warping, word-twisting skunk?'

'I only said that I think you like her.'

'*Like?*' He mouthed the word as if it were unclean. '*Like?* You told him I *like* her?'

'Yes.'

'You told that scabrous, excremental—'

'I told him you like her and that was all I said.'

'*All?*' He scrabbled through the pages. 'According to this, I think she is wonderful and beautiful. Explain away that, *Miss Middletone*.'

'I said that *I* thought she has done wonderful things and that she was pretty.'

'Hellfire and blast, March. Why did you not just come out and tell him I was having an illicit relationship with Dr Berry? You have taken that woman's good name and rammed it into the dung heap.'

'You did not mind so much when *my* honour was being impugned.'

He caught his falling eye and clenched his fist around it. 'If your name was sullied it was you who soiled it. I ordered you—'

'Nobody *orders* me to do anything.'

'And more is the pity for that. I told you not to talk to that puffed-up poseur and what did you do? You ran off with him to some sleazy den and confided in him what you salaciously imagined to be my private feelings.'

'I only—'

Sidney Grice stood up. I had never seen him so enraged. 'No, March. You deliberately went behind my back with a man who is my sworn enemy and you smeared excrement over the name of an innocent woman who has done nothing but defend your appalling manners every time I complain about them.'

'So it is all right for you to denigrate me?'

'I wanted advice on how to deal with your waywardness and she suggested tolerance. Well, we see now how her kindness has been repaid. You have turned her life into a freak show for the pavement-scrapings of humanity to gawp at.' His face twisted in pain. 'What you have done to that woman is unforgiveable.' He clutched at his socket and I went to him.

'Is it very painful?'

'Not in the least,' he said. 'It is only ingratitude that hurts me.'

He could have slapped my face and wounded me less. 'I have always been grateful to you for taking me in.'

'And this is how you show it?' He put his handkerchief to the socket and the cotton came away stained straw and red.

'Shall I look at it?'

He twisted his head away. 'I do not want you to look at it and I do not want to look at you.'

I stepped back.

'Then I shall get out of your sight,' I said as Sidney Grice bent and reeled to his desk.

'Damn it,' he said as I left the room and ran upstairs to my memories.

They were fumigating your quarters – a monthly futile battle against the cockroaches, millipedes, columns of ants and innumerable other creatures that crawled into, under, out of and over every surface of every room. Our homes were all raised on wooden piles which helped a little and no one but a griffin – as newcomers were called – put down rugs for horrible things to breed beneath. I learned very early on to shake out my slippers before I put my feet into them. Even then I had a nasty sting from a tenacious scorpion on my great toe once and it was weeks before I could lace up my right boot properly again. But I was lucky, my father told me. The wife of one of the captains had got into a hipbath only for a snake to slither in after her.

You brought a few things to our bungalow for safekeeping. The last time the fumigators had been in your room a penknife had gone missing. The workmen insisted you must have lost it, but you were certain you had left it on your bedside table and you were not usually careless with your things.

Your writing box was slightly scratched and, while you were off on a pig-sticking expedition, I decided to polish it. The wax was fluid in the heat and some of it trickled between the folded doors. I was worried that it would run over your correspondence and spoil it so I opened the lid.

I have always been inquisitive but not a sneaky person. I would never have searched your pockets or steamed open a letter. But it fell out on to the floor and, when I bent to pick it up, I could not help but notice the words.

> With regard to your proposed engagement your mother and I can only express our grievous dismay that you should choose to entangle yourself with a girl whom we have never met and of whose background we know so little. You cannot have forgotten Hester Sandler who waits so patiently and loyally for your return and with whom you have a long-established understanding. For your sake she has spurned all prospective suitors and it is only right that…

I did not see what Edward's father thought was right, but it was not difficult to guess. I put the letter back in the box and went to join my father at the hospital.

'Everything all right?' he asked but I did not reply.

39

Persian Slippers and Maudy Glass

I WENT BACK to Parbold. The Grange had still not been let so Mr Warwick, the land agent, gave me the keys and I walked up the hill while George Carpenter, the old gamekeeper, drove my luggage with Onion, his ancient donkey, wheezing behind me. It was two miles and a steep climb, but we made it just in time to see the sun sink behind Ashurst Beacon with the Douglas Valley glowing in its embers.

For two days I wandered around the house and grounds, unable to settle. I sat in my father's library, staring at his musty books, but could not bring myself even to open them.

Maudy Glass came to stay. As children we had run down the Fairy Glen together or across the pastures to catch sticklebacks in Jackson's pit, but Maudy was married now and heavy with her second child.

'Do you think you will ever have children?' she asked.

'I thought so once,' I said. 'Shall we prepare dinner?'

We cooked together on the ancient range – thick lamb steaks and boiled potatoes with mint from the tangle of my father's old herb garden – and I found a bottle of wine in the cellar. But I remembered Sidney Grice's insistence that animal flesh was no different from human and his account of the cannibals eating Rupert, and I could not put it in my mouth.

We cleared and washed and dried and settled in our armchairs.

Once, when we were sitting by that fireplace, I asked my father if he resented me for killing his wife and he told me that he had 'for fully two minutes until I saw you – a scrunched-up magenta monster struggling to get out of your swaddling – and then what could I do but love you?' He poked a log and the sparks flew into the night. 'And I have never stopped.'

'Not even when I accidentally set fire to my bedroom?'

'Not even then.' He patted my hand. 'Besides, you did not kill your mother. A filthy slaughterer posing as a surgeon did that. I will not call it butchery. Butchery is a skill and he had none. If it had not been for you kicking and caterwauling in my arms I believe I would have beaten him to death.'

'It must be terrifically exciting working with the famous Sidney Grice,' Maudy said, and I rubbed my eyes wearily but she chattered on. 'Remember when we were children? We used to go to the attic and play spies.'

'We made cloaks from old curtains,' I recalled, 'and low-brimmed hats from lampshades. We must have looked ridiculous.'

Maudy laughed and the shadows lit up for a moment. 'And we used to leave each other secret messages in that hole in the old oak tree. It blew down in the gales last year – but why am I telling you that? You have only been away a few months, but it feels like half a lifetime. I don't suppose I shall ever get away from Lancashire.'

'I thought you were happy here.'

Her face fell. 'Jethro is a good man…' Her voice tailed but then she picked it up again. 'You must have had some very exciting adventures.'

'Oh, Maudy, if you only knew… the things I have seen.'

'You are so lucky.'

'Such things,' I whispered.

Maudy Glass was sleepy now but she sat up in expectation of

a thrilling yarn. I could not talk about watching Horatio Green die in the study or finding Silas Braithwaite dead, or lowering Rosie Flowers by the rope round her neck, or seeing Reverend Jackaman crucified, and so I told her about the Ashby case and how Eleanor Quarrel, so alive and so beautiful, had died – drowned when her ship went down and all because of me. I thought that talking might help to heal the wounds but it only burst them open.

'But you acted from the best of motives,' Maudy told me as I sipped my gin by the open fire. Maudy was not taking alcohol even though the doctor had told her she must. She said it made her feel sick, but I managed to persuade her to have a large sherry.

'The road to hell is paved with good intentions,' I said, or think I said, but Maudy was dozing by then, comfortable in the chair that my father had always occupied.

'You would have liked Edward,' I said softly, 'and he would have liked you, Maudy. You would have made each other laugh. I have never told you about him. How could I?'

She began to snore – quite loudly like Bobby, the old retriever we once had.

'I lied to him, Maudy.' I poured myself another drink, almost to the brim. 'I lied without compunction. But I sent him to hell when I thought he had deceived me.'

I raised my glass but the world looked no better through it.

'I lied to everybody. It was my idea and my father went along with it. The army was reluctant to accept the presence of a girl as it was. They would never have accepted what was little more than a child.' I finished my drink and put the glass down a little more heavily than I intended, and Maudy stirred but did not wake. 'So when I met Edward I was sixteen and when we became engaged to be married I was seventeen, though he thought I was twenty and the lie became toxic. I never knew when it would strike my heart or if there would be an antidote. Only he could have told me that.'

'How could you what?' Maudy asked and opened her eyes.

I still lie about it now. It is the only way I can be taken half-seriously – and most of the time I believe it. Sometimes I feel I am an old, old woman – the things I have known – but in my heart all I want is to dance, to waltz with you under those huge Delhi moons, to hold you close and count the countless stars and to be so happy that it hurts.

I damped down the fire and put up the guard and we went to bed, but I could not sleep, so I went down the wooden stairs into the cellars and through the dripping arches, past the wine racks to where Sarah Ashby stood waiting for me. She smiled happily and stepped forwards to greet me, but there was a shadow behind her, Eleanor Quarrel with a knife in her hand, its wicked blade shining, the burnished steel tapered to a lethally fine point, and the edge wavy and razor-thin. I tried to cry out but the hand going over Sarah's mouth somehow gagged me and I saw the blade sweep over and up, plunging into Sarah's chest, and the gush of black blood from her burst heart, and I too doubled up as Eleanor Quarrel rushed towards me, hissing, clawing at my hair and gouging at my eyes.

I jolted out of bed and went to the window to look out at the moon over Hunger Hill. My father had owned this land, and his fathers for over three hundred years, and what had I done with it? My heart was still pounding so I had another gin, and I must have fallen asleep in my chair because the front bell was clattering and I went out to find young Sam Vetch breathlessly presenting me with a telegram.

MARCH RETURN AT ONCE STOP I NEED YOU STOP SIDNEY GRICE

I found a piece of paper and printed in pencil *Will arrive tomorrow stop March*. This left hardly any time even to think about what I had to do, so I crossed out *tomorrow* and wrote *today*.

And so, four days after I had set off for Lancashire, the process was reversed – George Carpenter and Onion, keys to Mr Warwick, then the train, changing at Wigan and disembarking at Euston. London was still quite new to me then – the biggest and wealthiest city on earth, capital of the greatest empire the world had ever known, the noise and bustle crashing around me as I walked towards Gower Street.

I saw a girl, probably no more than ten years old, the skin of her naked limbs tight around her bones, with a sunken-faced baby tied in front of her in a sack. She was crouching in the gutter picking at a rotting fish head, chewing the morsels and feeding the pap to her sibling. I went over to offer her a few coins but she saw me approach and scuttled away, snatching a ride on the back of a coal wagon before the carter saw her and stung her off with his whip.

It was quieter in Gower Street. Two men were carrying a rough pine coffin out of University College Hospital and across the wood-blocked road into the Anatomy Building – another person that no one cared to bury and would get more medical attention dead than he or she would have had while alive. I crossed myself and walked on.

Molly let me in.

'Oh thank Gawd.' She was still snuffly with her head cold and had boot blacking on her hands. 'I've been so worried about him, miss, stuck up in his room, most likely indulging in his secret vice.'

'What *is* his secret vice?'

Molly scratched her neck. 'Why, miss, it is so secret I doubt as even Mr Grice knows and he knows everything.'

'Is he still up there?'

Molly looked at the ceiling as if checking. 'Still is the word,' she said. 'I haven't heard so much as a scamper from him for ever so long and, oh, miss, he hasn't eaten for days. He must be ravished.'

'He certainly must have been desperate to have sent me that telegram,' I said.

'Well—' she began.

'What telegram?' Sidney Grice appeared at the top of the stairs.

He had his paisley dressing gown on and Persian slippers, and a tasselled red velvet fez.

'I came back,' I called up.

'Why?' He adjusted his black patch. 'Where have you been?'

I looked at him and then at Molly who was screwing her apron into a black ball in front of her.

'Nowhere special,' I said, and my guardian humphed and drifted away. I heard his bedroom door close and the four bolts slotting into place.

Molly's face was a fashionable Perkin's mauve.

'You,' I said and she blinked.

'And Cook.' She smudged her hat with four fingerprints. 'She helped with the spelling and grammaticals.'

'I did not know you could be so duplicitous,' I said and she grinned. There was blacking on her nose now.

'Why, thank you, miss.' She attempted a curtsy and scurried away.

40

French Blood and Commodore Bracelet

I DID NOT see Sidney Grice – though I thought I heard him cry out once – until he joined me for dinner. He had his patch on and a smoking jacket, which struck me as a peculiar choice for a man who abhorred tobacco.

'Molly was worried about you,' I told him, 'locking yourself away.'

'It is the only way I can get any peace.'

'But you did not eat.'

'It has long been a habit of mine to fast intermittently. It cleanses the liver and hence the mind.'

'But you are eating tonight?'

My guardian rubbed his hands together. 'Indeed I am. I told Cook, when you wandered off, that you were bored with our usual fare and she was as taken aback as I was. Nevertheless, she has manufactured a special treat in honour of your return.'

'How exciting,' I said uncertainly and added, 'I did not think you knew I had gone.'

He slipped his napkin out of its ring, an ornately carved cross-section of femur from the first man he had brought to the gallows. 'Did you seriously think that I do not know who is or is not in my own home, or that the servants could connive to send a telegram without my knowledge?'

'Not really,' I said. 'Have there been any developments whilst I was away?'

'Very few.' He unfolded his napkin. 'But I have not been entirely idle. After you left I paid three visits, first, to Horatio Green's shop where I made sixty-two observations, three of which may be significant. The shelves were quite high, presumably to stop bottles being accidentally knocked off them; second, the poison book lists strychnine as having been sold the day before he so inconsiderately died, though the name of the person he sold it to is clearly fictitious.'

'How can you be sure of that?'

Mr G shook the napkin vigorously. 'People creating names tend to be a little too creative for their own good. They often give themselves knighthoods or even peerages. This person was a little less ambitious and settled for a commission in the Royal Navy. There are no acting or retired Commodore Bracelets on the naval list.'

'And third?' I inquired.

'Mr Green did not stock prussic acid, making it unlikely that he accidentally gave it to himself. Other than that, it has been very quiet.' He laid the napkin on his lap. 'Perhaps it is you and not I who attracts disaster.'

'Quite possibly.' *I certainly brought it on you, my darling Edward.* 'Where did you go for your second visit?'

'To St Jerome's Rectory.' He corrected the alignment of his cutlery. 'And there I interviewed Reverend Jackaman's old housekeeper – a delightful lady who makes a splendid cup of tea. She told me the rectory was evacuated an hour before we arrived because of a gas leak from the road works.'

Molly came puffing up the stairs, her face still smudged, opened the dumb waiter and brought out two covered plates.

'Can I stay and watch?' She plonked mine in front of me.

'I do not see why not.'

'No,' her employer said and she shuffled away. I saw my face squashed wide in the silver dome. 'Feeling nervous?'

'Yes.' We whipped off the covers and I surveyed the offering. 'It looks very like another vegetable stew to me.'

Sidney Grice was actually smiling. 'What is it on?'

I forked some of the washed-out, grey-green porridge to one side. 'Rice pudding.'

He waited. 'Do you still not know what it is?'

'Vegetable stew on rice pudding.'

'Curry.' He rubbed his hands together. 'We thought it would remind you of your days in India.'

I need no reminding of those. I carry India like your unborn child.

'Curry has spices.'

'Exactly.' He dug into the mound on his plate. 'So Cook put pepper and nutmeg in it.' He chewed a forkful appreciatively. 'And I detect a very generous pinch of mustard powder. Tuck in.'

I speared a flaccid carrot peeling. 'It was a kind thought.'

Sidney Grice swallowed. 'Dr Berry said you needed a more varied diet.'

'She is right about that. Have you seen her since...?'

He waved some sludge around on his fork. 'She is taking advice about their aspersions on her professional qualifications,' he said. 'But she has suffered worse libels than that. She tried to tell me I was harsh with you.'

'I cannot imagine why she would think that.' But, as always, my irony was wasted.

'Exactly what I said.' The sludge splotched back on to his plate. 'You have not asked about my third visit, but I shall not allow that to deter me from describing it to you.' He replenished his fork. 'On the morning you fled this house, I made a call on the last member of that abominable society, the splendidly styled Mr Warrington Tusker Gallop.'

'And did you discover anything?'

'I always discover something.' A sticky brown liquid was dripping between the tines. 'Mr Gallop is allegedly away in France' – his mouth curdled at the last word – 'buying supplies for his snuff shop. According to his housekeeper, he has been absent from our shores since the day before Mr Green died. Do you find that suspicious?' He took another mouthful.

'Not necessarily.' I sniffed my food and wished I had not. 'Though he may have been killed, or he could be in hiding and committing the murders, using the trip to provide him with an alibi.'

He swallowed. 'You know, March, your excursion seems to have done you some good. You have constructed an entire sentence of rational thought.'

'You are the only man I know who can turn a compliment into an insult.'

He looked quite pleased at that remark, but only wiped his mouth and said, 'I am always wary of anyone or anything connected to the land of revolution, infantile paintings, bad cooking and slipshod tailoring, and so, for the time being, I am more inclined to classify Gallop as a suspect than a victim.'

I laughed. 'Because you do not like the French?'

'Because nothing good has come from there since Charles Le Grice in 1066.'

'So you have French blood in your veins.'

Mr G winced. 'Norman blood before it was contaminated by breeding with the French.' He ate some more and smacked his lips. 'I am not partial to this modern fad for giving food flavour, but I shall certainly get Cook to make this again.'

I tasted a sample and wished I had eaten my steak when I had the chance.

41

Pikestaffs and Telegrams

SIDNEY GRICE WAS at the table before me the next morning, engrossed in volume one of Clarke's *Physiognomy of the Criminal and Imbecilic Classes* and huffing to himself.

'Tosh.' He ripped out a page, screwed it up and threw it down. 'Balderdash.' Another page followed. 'These people think you can detect a murderer by the shape of his ears and the length of his nose. Why, Richard Batty had the face of Apollo but he still took a pikestaff to the bridesmaids at his own wedding.' He ripped out two pages at once, quickly rechecked something and threw them away. 'If these sham scientists were correct, then all I should need is a serviceable tape measure and I could round up every ne'er-do-well in London before he or she had even dreamed of transgressing. Molly is on her mettle today – only twenty-eight seconds to answer the summons.'

'How can you be so precise about the time?' I had not heard the bell ring and he had not taken out his watch.

'Because I have a built-in clock.'

'Does it tick?'

'Yes.' He ignored my facetiousness. 'And I am discouraged to learn you have not heard it. It is built into the cabinet behind you.'

'Oh,' I said. 'I had forgotten about that.'

'There is no point in observing things if you do not remember them.'

Molly came in, her hands and sleeves grey. 'Telegram, sir. ' She held out the tray.

'Lower the tray,' her employer told her. 'Raise it.' He scrutinized the undersurface through his pince-nez. 'Why is it covered in scratches?'

'Well, I have to put the ashes on something,' she said.

'What is wrong with the dustpan?'

'Nothing much, sir,' Molly said, ''cept that it was downstairs and I was up.'

Sidney Grice whipped off his pince-nez and said, 'That tray is worth more on the open market than you are.'

'Then perhaps it would like to run up and down with the tea things, make the beds and clean the hall,' I said. 'Perhaps it could answer the bell.'

'And sweep the stairs,' Molly prompted in a stage whisper.

Her employer seized the telegram and ripped it open. 'Tell the boy there is no reply.'

Molly put her hand to her mouth. 'Oh sorry, sir. I told him to go when he came. Do you want me to run after him and tell him not to wait?'

Her employer gazed fixedly at her. 'You have put the cause of female suffrage right back where it belongs,' he told her and she grinned again.

'Thank you, sir. I do my best.'

He opened his mouth but I broke in. 'You had better go now, Molly.' And she wandered uncertainly away.

'What do you make of this?' My guardian passed me the telegram.

I wiped my fingers on my napkin. 'It was sent from—'

'Clearly.' He pushed his plate away. 'But I refer to the content. What do you think it means?'

I read it.

MR GRICE YOU ARE LACKING VITAL INFORMATION COME FACTORY THREE EXACTLY NO LATER OR INDEED ANY EARLIER YOU SHALL GET INSTRUCTIONS BY NEXT POST YOU MUST OPEN LETTER UP IMMEDIATELY RECEIVED KEY HAS

BEEN ATTACHED TO NOTE LEFT DOOR LOCKED SECURELY I SHALL NOT OPEN SO NEED TO OPEN YOURSELF HOPE OBEY ORDERS FROM PROMETHEUS PIGGETY ESQUIRE DONT FORGET KEY OR YOU REALLY CANNOT MAKE AN ENTRY

I spooned some sugar into my tea. 'It is very jumbled but it would appear that Mr Piggety wants—'

He raised his hand. 'How can you possibly make any assumptions about what the odious Piggety does or does not want?'

'Well, his telegram—'

Sidney Grice slapped the table. 'Stop it, March. You are giving me a headache. If you received a telegram signed by the king of the moon would you unquestioningly accept that it came from his lunar majesty?'

'No, but—'

He clutched his forehead. 'No, but there are no *no buts*. The last thing one can do is assume that any telegram was written by the person it purports to be written by. That is part three of my sixteenth law. What is the most utterly dazzlingly manifest thing about this telegram? What is the hyena in the room?'

'Well, it is very long…' I began, and my guardian clapped his hands sarcastically.

'At last,' he said. 'At sixty-seven words it is the third longest telegram I have ever received. Countries have declared war more tersely. What particular word makes it so singular?

'Esquire,' I said, and he threw up his arms.

'Precisely. On average I receive thirteen telegrams a day, which is…?'

'Four thousand, seven hundred and forty-five a year,' I said, and was gratified to see an impressed eyebrow lifted. I did not tell him I knew the figure already because I had done my father's accounts and one of his tenants had paid thirteen pence rent a day.

'And this is the first time I have ever seen anyone use the title. Why pay an extra penny for an unnecessary frill? How would you paraphrase the message?'

'Well, to start with there is no need to use your name,' I said. '*Have vital information stop come to factory three o'clock precisely stop will send key to get in.*'

'Which is fifty words less and four shillings and two pennies cheaper,' Sidney Grice said. 'Did Piggety strike you as a man with no regard for money?'

'I would have thought he was almost as careful as you,' I said.

Sidney Grice crushed his toast to powder. 'And what word did you use twice in your seventeen words that the alleged Piggety did not use even once?'

'*Stop*,' I said. 'Why would anyone be so extravagant with the words and not want to pay for punctuation?'

'I think we can assume – and I loathe to assume anything – that the cost was not a consideration.' He stirred the crumbs into his prune juice with a knife. 'For some reason stops would have interfered with the true import of the message. So who wrote it?'

'Either a lunatic or an inebriate,' I said as he pushed a piece of crust under the surface with the tip of his first finger.

'On the contrary.' He wiped his finger on his napkin. 'I would say it was composed by a highly organized mind. It conveys instructions but conceals a deeper meaning.' He held his spoon to the light. 'It is a riddle wrapped within a riddle.'

I lifted the teapot but it was empty. 'It came from the Copper Lane office. Shall I go and see if they remember who sent it?'

'Oh, they will remember.' He swirled his juice vigorously. 'No clerk would forget that message in a hurry, which leads us to conclude?'

'Whoever sent it wants to be remembered,' I said.

'Or?'

'Got somebody else to send it on his or her behalf.'

'Well done. I am slightly concerned about sending you to such an area unaccompanied, though.'

'I did not know you cared,' I said and his eyebrow fell.

'March, how could you doubt it? You know I shall always

care.' His tones were tender. 'Think how my professional standing would suffer were I unable even to look after my ward.'

I got up from the table. 'And what will *you* do?'

He gave up on his breakfast and rose. 'I shall go to my study and cross-reference my files on matricide – that always relaxes me – while I ponder the implications of this loquacious telegram and await the prophesied arrival of the letter and key. Promise me, March. You will take a cab straight there, get it to wait and come straight home.'

'I shall be careful,' I said.

'That is not what I asked.'

'Goodbye, Mr G,' I said and went down into the hallway to turn the brass handle and run up the flag.

42

Moss Velvet and Black Snow

I PUT ON my faithful moss velvet coat and a new Ardith bonnet with green trim and matching ribbon tie, and selected a parasol. I would not need the last item but, as my friend Harriet once told me, a bonnet is not a bonnet without one. A cab had already pulled up when I stepped out and the horse was trying to lower its head to the water running down the gutter, but the cabby kept pulling it up.

'Why will you not let him drink?' I asked as I clambered through the flaps.

'Thirsty 'orse works 'arder,' he said briefly, setting off at a trot before I was settled into my seat.

The air was grey that day with sour wisps of yellow streaming through it, and the soot hung in big black snowflakes, patting on to my sleeve and lapel. I tried to flick one off but only smudged it.

A gang of street urchins had spotted me and were running after my hansom, chanting,

'Siddie Grice Gower Streeter
'Ad a client couldn't keep 'er.
'Ad another didn't luv 'er.
Killed 'er daugh'er. Killed 'er muvver.'

Once I might have found them amusing, but there was no humour in the deaths that hovered around Sidney Grice and me. I threw them some pennies. Not one of those children would have had a meal half as nutritious as the food I complained about.

We passed through Holborn and into Newgate, once the site of one of seven gates built by the Romans when London was a walled city. Now its most impressive feature was the forbidding massive-stoned structure of the prison.

'Want to visit your dad?' the cabby called down.

'At least I know who my father was,' I said and he whipped the horse.

Cheapside and what Dickens described as the busiest thoroughfare in the world was bustling but strangely quiet. The atmosphere had thickened and was sharp with coal smoke. I could barely see the shops and offices either side of us. Even the rumble of carriage and cart wheels and clipping hooves of straining horses was muffled, and by the time we arrived in Wapping I could see almost nothing at all. The whole of the Thames seemed to be rising out of its basin and creeping over the city, gathering the filth from the air as it advanced.

We came to a stop. 'Four shillin's.'

'That seems rather a lot.'

'Four shillin's.'

I opened my purse. 'I should like to give you some beer money,' I said and was rewarded with a confusion of rotting teeth as I clambered out. 'But a thirsty man works 'arder.' And I pitched him two florins.

He wrenched the reins and swung round so sharply that I thought his cab might topple on to me, before I had the chance to ask him to stay.

I paused to get my bearings. The buildings were fuzzy in the diffuse light, their hazy sides scarcely distinguishable from the vapours they were jutting into, but I only had to turn to find that I was directly outside the telegraphy office. The fog had got in before me and the gaslights scarcely penetrated it as I made my way to the back.

'I received this telegram this morning.'

The woman behind the counter was writing in a long red book. 'You shouldn't 'ave done that.' She stopped writing. 'This is addressed to Mr Sidney Grice the detective and when he finds out 'e'll kill you just like 'e did all them others.'

She had a brown hat on that was much too small for her.

'I am Mr Grice's assistant,' I told her and she perked up, but almost immediately looked incredulous.

'Not 'er,' she said. 'Sidney Grice's assistant is tall and dark. I read it in *The Ashby Slashin's*. She's beautiful and mysterious, but you're like a free-quarters-drownded alley cat. No offence.'

A bored young man was sitting behind her, his finger static on a Morse key, a piece of fruit bread in his free hand.

'I must be his other assistant then,' I said. 'Did you send this telegram?'

'What if I did? I told 'im it was all wrong.'

'It was a man then?' I took the paper back.

'A mudlark, come in off the 'igh tide,' she said. ''E said 'e 'ad been told to make sure it went 'xactly as what it was written.'

'I always sends them 'xactly as they is written.' The young man sprayed crumbs over his desk.

'Did he say who sent him?'

'Did 'e 'eckers. And did I ask? Did I 'eckers.'

'What did he look like?'

'A mudlark.' She stretched to look over my shoulder and called, 'Next,' though the office was otherwise deserted.

There was a rapid series of clicks and the young man jumped to attention. He dropped the remnants of his bread and frantically riffled through the papers on his desk. 'My pencil. Where's my poxy pencil?'

'Behind your cruddin' ear,' the woman said without turning her head.

'Oh, so it is... Oh, sugar me, the lead's broken.' He rooted frantically through a drawer and the clicks stopped.

''Is brain's broken if you ask me.' The woman dipped a splayed nib into her ink pot.

'Oh, well,' he said. 'It was only about someone's mother dyin'. Nuffink you can do about that now.'

I waved the telegram under her nose. 'Do you have the original copy?'

The woman's lips pulled away from her like a braying donkey. ''Course I do,' she said. 'I frame every message to 'ang on the walls of my bleedin' palace.' She indicated the fireplace. 'Got to keep warm some'ow. Next.'

I took the hint and turned to go.

'Not even a tanner for my time,' she grumbled to the young man as the clicker started again.

'And don't you go tryin' to fit us up for nuffink,' he shouted after me as I left. 'I got friends in 'igh places.'

'Monkeys in trees?' I asked politely as I went outside.

The fog had lifted a fraction and the ghostly crew of a spectral clipper filed down the alley towards the dock, the canvas of their duffel bags bulging over their shoulders. Not one man was speaking or looking anywhere but straight ahead to the cabin boy at the front carrying an oil lantern high on a forked stick. I tagged on behind and, where the bottom of the lane opened out, found myself on a quay a few yards from the looming outline of a long shed with a hexagonal tower on top.

43

Mermaids and the Muffled Man

I DO NOT think I fully intended to go to Piggety's Cats. It was just that I thought I had a better chance of finding a cab at a dock than in the confusion of lanes and alleys that led away from it. But now that I was here it seemed a shame not to at least take a look.

The shade of a gentleman was clambering out of a blurred hansom at the foot of a wharf. I hurried over.

'Will you wait while I visit that factory? I shall pay you for your time.'

'All right.' The driver had leather gauntlets on and a leather peaked cap, and was wrapped in a long coat with a scarf around his face.

'Promise?'

'I said *all right*.' He hauled out a huge fob watch on an amulet-laden chain and set it on his lap.

His horse looked well fed and groomed so I decided I could trust him. I wound my way through a labyrinth of packing crates and between two hillocks of stacked sacks. Some girls were playing hopscotch. They threw their stones at the side of the shed and ran away as I slid my feet over slippery cobbles like a nervous ice skater until I got to the entrance. There I hesitated. I knew the telegram had forbidden Sidney Grice from calling before three o'clock, but there was no mention of me. I rapped and waited. Two dockers came by, rolling an enormous barrel up the slope. It was oozing black oil and glistening.

I knocked again but could not hear anything above the cacophony around me. A porter came by with a tray on his head and whistling 'My Mother Was a Mermaid in the Sea'. I put my ear to the door and thought I heard a noise – a creak? a cough? – I could not say what it was but it came from inside the building.

I put my hand to the door and despite Prometheus Piggety's verbose insistence in his telegram, it was unlocked. I pushed it open a foot and called out. 'Hello? Mr Piggety?' But there was no reply. I started forwards but then I hesitated. I knew Mr G would be angry when he found I had been interfering and also I had not really thought about what I was going to say. And then I definitely heard something. To this day I am not sure what. Perhaps it was a rustle or maybe the scrape of a boot on the metal platform, but I had a distinct impression that there was somebody behind that door, hiding from me, and suddenly I was frightened. I turned and rushed away, and when I checked over my shoulder that no one was following, I was almost certain that the door was closed.

'Gotcha!'

I was so busy looking back that I ran straight into a man but, instead of stepping aside, he clutched my wrist and held on tight. I looked up and it was the man in the green jacket, the one who had pulled a cudgel on us the last time we came.

'Let me go.' I took some satisfaction in noting that his nose was still bruised from our last encounter.

He grinned and his breath was like rotting meat. 'Fink you can make a dolly out of me, do you? Well, you won't slip me so easily this time, cod-face.'

'Let me go this instant.' But I knew that all my squirmings and protestations were useless.

'Well, you ain't much of a catch.' His lips were cracked and bleeding. 'And I am 'arf tempted to throw you back.'

I remembered something Inspector Pound had told me about the area and tried to straighten up and look him in his filmy eyes. 'Have you any idea who you are talking to? I am Mick McGregor's niece.'

The man tightened his grip. 'And what? Mick McGregor had a bi' ov a accident last week. Went for a swim and never came up for air. Favourite uncle was 'e? Seein' as he never 'ad no bruvvers or sisters.'

'The police know I am here,' I said.

'Good.' His saliva flecked my face. 'Then it won't take them long to fish you awt.' He had another look at me. 'Shame really, ugly bottle like you. Lay a bob to a wren you've never been kissed.'

'I have never been kissed by a stench-breathed mongrel,' I said, 'and I do not intend to start now.'

I thought about using my parasol again but he knocked it out of my grasp.

'Naughty.' He raised his hand to slap me with the back of it. I slumped as if in a swoon and, as the man leaned over to look at me, jumped straight up again. The top of my head crunched into his chin and cracked my teeth together. I yelped, he grunted, let go of me and staggered two steps back. I picked up my parasol and ran. I did not look to see if he was after me. I was quite good at running as a child, but I had not done much of it since and I was not constricted by several layers of feminine frippery then. I put everything I had into that race as I wound back between the cases. A young Chinaman in black robes and a coolie hat was carrying two baskets on a pole. I swerved to avoid him and nearly collided with a tin bath lying on its side, but just managed to clear it with a desperate leap.

I heard somebody clatter into it close behind and metal-studded boots on the cobbles. It was still quite a way to where the hansom had been parked, but when I lifted my head I could see it heading at a good pace towards me through the clouds. I put on a final spurt and jumped on to the board. A hand reached out from inside and I took it just as I felt my dress being grabbed and myself being dragged backwards. I kicked out and my boot made solid contact, but my assailant only swore and held on.

'Gerroff!' the cabby yelled and with one crack of his whip

dealt with my attacker, and with another propelled his horse forward as I fell through the flaps and collapsed into my seat.

'Careful. You nearly shattered my flask.'

'What are you doing here?'

Sidney Grice tugged his coat out from under me as I straightened myself up. 'You did not seriously think I would let you wander around the docks by yourself?'

'Why did you not come sooner then?'

'We could not see what was going on in the fog. I was just about to get out and look for you when it lifted a little and Gerry saw you brawling with a ganger.'

The cabby pulled his scarf down and grinned broadly. 'I'll put a fiver on you against Gipsy James Mace any day, miss. You certainly got the better of Ted Gallagher there.'

'You know him?'

'Had him by the collar a few times, miss. Got him three years' hard labour once. There's a goodly few round here with grudges against me. That's why I cover my face.'

'Gerry used to be Police Sergeant Dawson,' my guardian told me.

We turned up an alley, the wheels nearly scraping the sides. 'Until I got a taste for the grog,' our driver said. 'I was captain of the Met Cricket Team too – miss that more than the work, I do. Mr Grice put in a word for me to get this job, though. He even paid for—'

'Your hat has not come very well out of the fray,' Sidney Grice said loudly.

'Oh, my poor bonnet.' I took it off and saw the top had been completely crushed. I felt for a bruise and found a gratifyingly large one on my crown. The hansom stopped and we pulled out into a wider road.

An old lady was struggling with a wobbly pram full of rags. I leaned forward and skimmed her my hat and she caught it and grinned gummily. 'Bless yer, darlin',' she called and put it on her head.

'Looks better on her than it did on you,' my guardian said.

You would have disagreed with him about that. You always liked me in hats and almost fell out with Harry Baddington when he said that the one I wore to his brother's wedding made me look like a standard lamp. I told you to forget about it because he was your best friend, but you told me no, he was not, I was – and insisted he apologized. The silly thing was I caught sight of my reflection and thought he was probably right.

I wonder how you would have reacted to my fighting on the docks – probably a mixture of amusement and alarm but I like to think that part of you would have been proud of me.

'Does your head hurt very much?' Sidney Grice asked, and it was only then that I realized I was sighing.

44

The Ninth Sense

'S*MOLLET'S WHALEBONE CORSETS for the distinguished gentleman*,' I read out. We were stuck behind an advertising van with its boards proclaiming in smaller print, *Undetectable Waist Trimming for Every Occasion.* Another van was trying to come down the road, extolling the virtues of *Dr Crambone's Liver Tonic – Never Suffer Biliousness Again*, and there was hardly space for one of them in the road already.

'So.' Sidney Grice pulled the cork out of his flask but, as always, did not have a spare cup to offer me a drink. 'What did you discover – apart from the gentle art of head-butting?'

My scalp was feeling quite tender now. 'The telegram was taken to the office by a river scavenger.' I rubbed my head gingerly. 'A boy. Other than that, they knew nothing about him and they burnt the original copy.'

'And then?' He tapped the cork back into place.

I steeled myself. 'I went to Mr Piggety's factory.' I waited for the onslaught but my guardian only sipped his tea and said, 'I would have been astonished if you had not. So what happened?'

'I knocked,' I said, 'and when there was no answer I tried the handle and the door was not locked.'

His fingers blanched on his cup. 'And then?'

'Shift your frebbin' nag and your festerin' heap of scrap, you bloomin' grut,' Gerry Dawson bellowed, 'or I'll turn your sign to matchwood and stick the splinters up your mother's—'

'Ladies,' Sidney Grice called up.

'Nostrils,' the ex-sergeant muttered.

I said, 'I thought I heard somebody behind the door and I got frightened and ran away. I was probably just imagining it.'

'Not necessarily,' my guardian expounded. 'I am convinced there is something innate in man and many other creatures, which warns them of dangers they cannot detect by more recognized means – a ninth sense perhaps – and you were well advised to pay attention to it.'

I did not trouble to ask what the other extra senses were but said, 'I left the door open but when I looked back, it had been closed.'

Sidney Grice rested the flask on his knee and said, 'That is most intriguing. Either you were indulging in a bout of hyperthermic feminine hysteria or there was somebody behind that door and you were in graver danger than you realize.' He shuddered. 'If anything *had* happened to you, March, I might have blamed myself. But that would require a degree of self-criticism which is alien to my nature.'

'At flippin' last,' our driver shouted. Dr Crambone was reversing and Smollet's Corsets was forcing its way through the gap left on to King William Street, and we followed close on his heels before the Liver Tonic pushed its way back in. 'They likes to cause a jam so more people read their advertisements.'

'And hate their product,' I commented.

'You would have thought so,' Sidney Grice said, 'but when a Winston's Toothpowder board wedged in Mortimer Market for half a day, sales of their alarmingly corrosive dentifrice trebled for a week afterwards.'

We came to another halt.

'Hold on tight,' Gerry warned us, and my guardian hastily swallowed the last of his beverage just as we swung violently to the left again, one wheel mounting the kerb and flinging me over my guardian's lap.

'For goodness sake, man,' Sidney Grice shouted up. 'You will lose your licence.'

I disengaged myself just in time to see a very well-dressed lady and her three equally smartly attired children scatter like driven pheasants from a beater.

'Wanted to get home before Christmas, didn't you?' Gerry answered with a laugh, bumping us back on to the road.

A ginger cat shot out of the way as our horse sidestepped an eel stall and whinnied.

'Were it not for his promise, I would think he has been drinking again,' my guardian said. 'But Gerry is one of the few men I have ever met whose word I can rely on.'

'Are you not angry with me?' I asked and he straightened his collar.

'I myself was sorely tempted to do what you did, but there is no point in trying to sneak into a ball before the orchestra has started to play.'

'On the day I arrived in Gower Street you told me that you disliked metaphors,' I reminded him.

'And so I do.' He shook the last few drops out of his cup. 'But I find them useful devices for communicating with those of meaner mental capacities than my own.'

'By which you mean everybody.'

'It would be immodest of me to respond.'

Gerry started tapping his boots in a kind of dance on the roof.

'What about Chigorin?' I persisted.

'The Russian chess player? I imagine he could give me a game.'

Gerry was whistling tunefully.

'I have never met such an arrogant man in all my life,' I said and Sidney Grice showed polite interest.

'Really?' He put the cup back on his flask. 'I was not aware that you had met him.' And Gerry started singing 'Tell Me Ma' in a rich baritone.

'He is not even Irish.' My guardian rolled his eye.

'They pull my hair and they steal my comb,' Gerry sang and clicked his reins, and the horse shook its mane and lifted its head as it clipped along the side street.

*

After a late lunch I went to the hospital. There had been a fire in one of the operating theatres and they were dragging blackened equipment out into the corridor. The ether had leaked from an anaesthetic machine and an electric light had sparked.

'Was anyone hurt?' I asked a medical student who was helping to carry a half-incinerated table away.

'Just a nurse,' he told me. 'She won't live the night.'

They were wheeling her out as he spoke, a small charred figure hardly recognizable as a woman, and she let out a sob as she heard his words.

'He does not know what he is talking about,' I told her and her eyes swivelled towards me and she wheezed.

'I hope he's right,' she managed as they took her away.

Inspector Pound was conscious when I got to his bed. 'Miss Middleton, I believe I am indebted to you again.'

'If I ever need blood I shall know who to ask for it,' I said. 'At least I know we are compatible.'

He managed a smile. 'Oh, I already knew we were that.' And, before I could think of a response, he added, 'Sounds like I had a lucky escape. They were going to take me down to the operating theatre to clean up my wound today, but it's healing so well they decided not to bother.'

He was shifting constantly.

'Are you in much pain?'

'None at all.' His expression did not convince me. 'And how is Mr Grice?'

I took his hand and turned it to check his pulse.

'Struggling,' I said, and told him about the Last Death Club and the murders of its members.

'For the first time I am glad to be here,' he said when I had finished. 'I can imagine how my superiors would be on my back. How is Inspector Quigley dealing with it all?'

'By pretending that the murders are suicides or accidents.'

The inspector bristled. 'I sometimes wonder why that man became a policeman, other than his personal ambition... I'm sorry. I shouldn't have said that. No doubt he will get his promotion and I shall have to call him sir.'

'I should not have worried you,' I said.

'No.' He moved uncomfortably. 'I like to know what's happening on my patch.' For a moment he drifted but then he shook himself, as if out of a dream. 'It sounds like Miss McKay might be worth questioning again – an extremely unpleasant character if ever there was one. When I was a sergeant I arrested her for what I can only describe as a vile and violent attack on her housekeeper. The victim was anxious to testify and we had an independent witness in the cook. Miss McKay did not trouble to deny the offence and I was confident of a conviction and a stiff sentence. But I reckoned...' He looked blank for a moment, then forced himself awake. 'I reckoned without her father's influence and all charges were suddenly dropped, and – as I discovered later – this was by no means the first time it had happened.'

'But that is disgusting.' I felt his grip sharpen.

'I tendered my resignation.' He was fading. 'But they made hints about my prospects and I told myself I could do more good inside the force than...' We were still holding hands when he fell asleep.

I took some scissors out of my handbag and trimmed his moustaches, but it was more difficult than I expected and, if anything, they looked more ragged than before I had interfered. I put my scissors away, checked that no one was watching and kissed his forehead. One eye popped open and he mumbled, 'Water.'

And on the way out I came across the younger nurse. Her face was pink and she had been crying. 'Oh, miss, I have just heard some terrible news about Hilary Wilkinson.'

'Hilary?'

'The nurse who is usually with me.'

'Was that her in the fire?' She gnawed her lower lip but did not reply. 'I hope she will be all right,' I said.

'Oh, miss.' She burst into tears. 'I don't think she will.'

I took her hand. 'I am so sorry.'

'Oh blimey, here comes Matron. I'll be for it if she sees me like this.'

'Go into the ward and keep your back to her.'

Matron came marching down the corridor and her face darkened when she saw me.

'Flattery,' my father told me, 'is like make-up – cheap and false – but, if you must use it, lay it on thickly or people will see straight through it.'

'Might I have a have a word, Matron?'

'What is it now?'

'I have worked in several military hospitals,' I said, 'and we always prided ourselves on our efficiency.'

Her eyes glinted. 'What of it?'

'I just wanted to say that I have never come across a better run ward in my life.'

I cringed at my own insincerity and hoped she did not think I was mocking her, but Matron grunted and her face softened. 'I am glad you think so but, if you will excuse me, I must talk to Nurse Ramsey. I know she was very attached to Nurse Wilkinson.'

I froze. 'Was?'

Matron's mouth compressed as she controlled herself.

45

Coal Dust, Fingerprints and Death Traps

We were just picking at the remnants of some cold potatoes and re-boiled cabbage when Molly came in, sleeves rolled up and arms coated in flour. 'Special delivery, sir.' And Sidney Grice put down his fork to take a thick white envelope from the tray.

'Why is it special?' He held it by the corner.

She looked skywards for inspiration before deciding. 'I think it's because the boy said it was.'

'Was he a post-office messenger?' I asked

'No, miss. He was a ragamuffin – horrible he was, coughing and spitting. He—'

'Get out,' her employer said, and Molly went pink.

'But—'

'Now.'

Molly pouted. 'Yes, sir.'

'And no pouting,' he said without looking up as she left. 'Come, March. Let us go downstairs and examine this keenly anticipated correspondence in the heart and mind of this house, my study.'

We went down and stood behind his desk, and Sidney Grice shook the envelope. 'Feels and sounds like the key.' He held it up to the light. 'Looks like the outline of a key and therefore quite possibly a key. Plain white envelope with nothing written on it and no impression of anything having been written over it. No hallmark but not cheap paper. Four finger smudges and…' He perched his pince-nez on the tip of his nose. 'What do you make of this, March?'

I went to his side. 'They are a child's prints but the tips look clubbed.'

'What would cause that?' He brought out a pocket magnifying glass to look more closely.

'It can develop with lung diseases. I have seen it in people who work in mines or cotton mills, but never in a child.'

'What about soot?'

'He would have had to inhale a lot of it – a climbing boy could have.'

'An ex-climbing boy in this case,' Sidney Grice said. 'There is not a grain of soot on it, and even Molly would have noticed if he were a sweep's apprentice.'

'He is probably too ill to work. I have seen four-year-olds sent up flues which are still hot from the fires and come down burnt all over and with seared lungs. And it is supposed to be illegal. Something should be done.'

'I seem to have installed a social reformer in the bosom of my home,' my guardian commented. 'Look at that. See how clear the print is? You can make out every whorl. When I have the time I shall make a study of the ridges on fingertips. I am half convinced that very few people share exactly the same patterns.' He opened the envelope carefully with a paperknife and sniffed the flap. 'This has been sealed within the last hour or so. I can smell the gum quite strongly and it is still tacky… what is this stuck to the glue?' He picked at it with a pair of tweezers. 'In that second drawer down you will find a sheet of black card… Put it on my blotter.' He laid his find carefully out, a long white strand.

'It looks very like a hair from one of Mr Piggety's cats,' I said. 'I am still finding them on my coat.'

'Then go and find another one,' he said, and I went into the hall and picked at my lapel. By the time I came back he had dragged the round table to the window and was setting up a microscope, twisting the mirror to catch the light. He took the hair from me, stretched it alongside the other between two glass slides and clipped them on to the stage. 'I have scratched the numbers one and two at the ends of the slides.' He peered down the eyepiece. 'So that even you will not confuse the specimens.' He fiddled with the focus and moved the slides side to side. 'Interesting.' He straightened up sharply. 'Now, you tell me what differences you can see.'

I adjusted the objective lens a fraction to sharpen the image and looked along the hairs. At two hundred magnification they had lost their smoothness and sprouted fibres all over. I touched the slide and the images jumped out of view. 'I cannot see any differences.'

'Look harder.'

I brought the hairs back over the hole in the stage.

'They are the same width and colour.'

'Try harder. Use your eyes.'

I tried again and rotated the slides a few degrees. 'They still look identical to me.' I gave up.

'Good,' Sidney Grice said. 'I could not see any differences either and if I cannot see something it cannot be seen. So what can we deduce from that?'

'That the hair in the envelope came from one of Piggety's cats,' I said.

'Nonsense.' He ran a hand over his head. 'All we can deduce is that the two hairs are indistinguishable under this magnification and so we cannot say with any reasonable certainty that they came from different types of cats, if indeed they *are* cats' hairs. If needs be I shall get Professor James Beart Simonds of the Royal Veterinary College to have a look at it. He was of great help in the Silver Beard goat-swapping scandal.'

We went back to the desk where he looked inside the envelope, turned it upside down and tapped it over the card. 'No dust.' He slipped a letter out, smelled it and held it to the light before opening it out on to his blotting paper. It was a sheet of double foolscap paper and had been folded three times. On the top side it bore a message using cuttings from a newspaper.

GRICE THIS KEY
OPENS
THE OUTER
DOOR
LOCK
TURN
ANTI CLOCKWISE TO
GAIN ENTRY PIG GETY

'The *Hackney Gazette* typeface,' Sidney Grice commented. 'It should be easy enough to find when they last printed *clockwise* as one word, especially as it first appeared in print only four years and twenty-nine weeks ago. And why the *anti* rather the more usual *counter*-clockwise?'

'This message is just as odd as the last one,' I said. 'I cannot make any sense of it. Why explain what the key does when you have already been advised that it was coming? And why tell you how to use it?'

He picked at the top corner of the Y. 'That which appears to be most stupid is sometimes the most clever,' he said.

I looked at the back of the paper. The gum had seeped through but it was otherwise unmarked. 'Also, you have both been reduced to just your surnames in this letter and Mr Piggety has lost his *esquire*.'

'The presence and absence of that word in the two communications is beyond question of immoderate significance.' He rubbed beneath his patch.

'Will you go?' I asked.

'Certainly. You look uneasy.'

'I know you will say—'

'You never know what I will say.'

I often did but I let that pass and restarted. 'I *suspect* you will say that I have been reading too many shockers but, if Mr Piggety is the murderer, it could be a trap.'

'One shocker is too many.' Sidney Grice looked at the reverse of the letter. 'But you may be right, March, and I certainly hope so. It is nearly six months since anybody thought it worth their while to lure me to my death and that was *such* an insultingly opaque attempt. A man can get discouraged so easily when nobody wants to kill him.'

'If you must go, why not go early and take him unawares?'

'Two reasons.' My guardian took the slides from the microscope and wrapped rubber bands round them. 'First, there is no point in trying to spring a trap before it is set. That is Grice's twelfth maxim.'

'And second?'

He looked at his watch. 'We have not yet had our postprandial cup of tea. Ring the bell, March, and I shall tell you the other thirty-nine maxims whilst we are biding our time.'

46

The Long Rows of Death

SIDNEY GRICE TRIED the door.

'Well, it is locked now.' He slipped the key in, turned it easily and rotated the handle. 'Stand well back, March.' He stepped to one side. 'The last time I answered a cryptic summons, Princess Cristobel of Gladbach was waiting in the dark with a primed and loaded musket.' He swung the door open with his cane, took a small rectangular mirror on a stick out of his satchel and checked inside with it. 'Looks clear.' He folded the mirror away, poked his head round the frame and almost immediately recoiled. 'Handkerchief.' He clamped his over his nose and I followed suit.

The stench was even worse than before as we entered Mr Piggety's factory, and the heat hit us immediately. Sidney Grice put out his hand.

'Keep behind me.' I could hardly hear him above the crashing of planks being unloaded from a cargo ship outside.

We stepped on to the platform and looked down at the rows of cages.

'Hello,' he called and rattled the railings, but there was no reply. 'Hello,' he shouted.

We waited a moment before descending and it was immediately obvious that things had gone very wrong indeed. The first cage held about a dozen cats and all of them were dead. We went to the next cage and the same scene greeted us.

'Dear God,' I whispered. It was not until the fifth that I saw any sign of life, a tiny kitten lying on its side, panting weakly and with white-membraned eyes but, even as we watched, the breathing stopped. 'Oh, you poor little thing.'

'The water has been turned off,' my guardian said.

'And the heating up.'

The clatter of timber ceased and Sidney Grice touched my arm. 'Listen.' There was a shrill noise in the background. At first I thought it was a circular saw being used to cut the planks, but the noise was higher than that and changed pitch too much.

'The back room,' my guardian said. 'Wait here.' He ran jerkily between the long rows of death to the far end. There he paused and unsheathed his swordstick. I hurried after him and he rolled his eye. 'Canute had more luck in holding back the sea,' he said.

The sound was louder now and higher and fractured. I stood to one side.

I turned the handle and flung open the door. The room was unlit except through one sealed glass panel in the roof, and it took a while to adjust to the dark and the air heavy with big drops of water and to realize that what we had been listening to was a scream, and that the steam and the scream were both coming from one of the enamelled tubs. There was a tremendous splashing. Perhaps Mr Piggety was having a practice run with a sack full of stray cats. It was difficult to get close with boiling water spraying in every direction, but as we edged nearer I opened my parasol.

'Do *not* flap it.' Sidney Grice hung back.

'I shall try not to.' I held it before us as a shield. The splashing stopped and the scream was silenced, but the machinery still whirred as I peeked round the frilled edge of my parasol. It was then that I saw a head projecting from the bubbling surface of the water and, as I watched, the head turned and I found myself looking at a face. It was barely recognizable under a mask of swelling blisters, but I knew that low brow and flattened head.

Prometheus Piggety stared at me through the slits of his swollen scarlet eyelids. Time was petrified and no sound came now from his gaping mouth. Two ballooned hands broke through the surface, bound at the wrists, reaching out to me in supplication. But then the head went down, the mouth filling with scalding water, desperately trying to spit it out, but the water came over the nose and the tub became a frothing cauldron as the water closed over him.

I cried out something but I do not know what. I probably called to God again. But there was only Sidney Grice, clicking switches and pulling levers behind me. He managed to stop the motor and put it into reverse, and it was only then that I noticed the chains hanging loose into the tub. They straightened and tightened, and the motor whirred and strained before it stopped running. It had been strong enough to lower him but was not able to pull him out.

Sidney Grice ran round the tub and turned a horizontal brass wheel by its handle on top. There was a gurgling noise and the water began to fall, and all I could see was a scalded lump like something in a butcher's shop, lying in the bottom of the tub, trussed with silken cords tied in neat knots to a hook on the chain belt.

Sidney Grice re-sheathed his blade and used the cane to turn Prometheus Piggety's head up, but there was nothing distinguishable as a human face any more except the teeth, still gaping in wordless agony through a bloated fluid-filled purple sac. He withdrew his cane and a long strip of flesh came away with it.

'The gypsy was right about him dying in the bath before he was eighty,' I said.

'And Piggety was right about one thing too,' he observed bleakly. 'Writhing alive in boiling water does loosen the skin.'

47

Touching the Stars

THERE WAS VOMIT on the floor about two yards from the tub and Sidney Grice crouched to survey it.

'Mutton, roast potatoes, carrots and peas, and what looks like plum pudding.'

I turned away. 'Does it matter?' I was aware that my voice was trembling.

'All evidence matters. How important it is remains to be seen. Assuming he produced this, Piggety did not chew his food very thoroughly. Either this was his habit or he was in a hurry today.' He leaned over the pool and breathed in as one might with a rare truffle. 'No smell of wine, beer or spirits, so this was not some drunken escapade.' He took a cigar tube from his satchel and unscrewed the top to bring out a medical thermometer in cotton wool. He unwrapped it, shook the mercury into the bulb, checked the reading and inserted it into a big fatty lump of mutton. He brought out his hunter and flipped open the lid. 'When I was a child I had scarlet fever,' he told me, 'and was kept out of school for several weeks.'

'A sensible precaution,' I said, trying to block out the image of what lay in the tub behind me.

'I have to confess,' he continued, 'that, when the nurse used a thermometer, I deliberately tampered with the results.'

'You warmed it up to get more time off school,' I guessed and he frowned.

'Quite the reverse. I cooled it so as to be able to return to school. I was concerned that the masters were teaching my fellows without me there to correct them.'

'Your teachers must have loved you.' I spoke automatically, glad of anything to distract me.

'I can truthfully say that they did' – he clipped his watch shut – 'not.' He stooped. 'Vomit travels an interesting thermal voyage. The food may be at a higher or, with cooks like mine, lower, temperature than the body. It then reaches equilibrium with the stomach, which is two or three degrees above body temperature of ninety-eight point four. Once expelled it cools to room temperature, the time taken to do so depending on the temperature difference, the flow of air and the insulating properties of the substance ingested. This is at room temperature and therefore produced at least one hour ago.' He wiped the thermometer and put it away. 'What is that?'

There were a thousand stars sparkling on the wooden floor and I crouched to examine them. 'Powdered glass.'

'What sort of glass?'

'How many sorts of glass are there?' I put my finger out.

'Twenty-two. Do *not* touch it.' He came over. 'The glass of my eye is very different from that of a whisky tumbler, a house window, a church window, a pair of spectacles, et cetera, et cetera.' He bobbed down beside me and clipped his pince-nez on. 'Et cetera,' he said absently. 'Note the line here.' I could just make out what he meant – a faint arced impression. 'See how the glass on the concave side is much finer than that on the convex. What does that tell you?'

'The glass was broken and then crushed by something curved,' I suggested.

'Such as?'

'The heel of a boot.'

'Well done.' He brought out a six-inch steel rule and measured the line in both directions. 'Not Mr Piggety's boot. He had unusually large feet and this is small enough to be a woman's—'

'Primrose McKay,' I said. 'She would have enjoyed doing this.'

Sidney Grice put his head to one side briefly before he declared, 'The curve would indicate that the wearer was standing facing the pulley some three and a quarter feet away from it.' He took his rule and scraped the powder either side of the line into two envelopes, then folded and sealed them with four rubber bands, making notes on them with a stubby pencil. 'What are you looking at?'

I bent down. 'Just behind you. It looks like droplets of blood.'

He shuffled round. 'Good perception. They were not easily distinguishable in the shadows, though, of course, I would have observed them myself. Thirty-three drops, the largest being one eighth of an inch in an apparently random pattern over...' he held his ruler above them, 'an area of two foot four inches by one foot nine.' He dabbed a couple with his fingertip. 'And freshly clotted. Clearly from a minor haemorrhage and therefore of major importance. You may write this in your journal as the first clue you have ever discovered, though it will take my intelligence to calculate its significance.'

'Of course.' I spoke automatically.

'Right.' He steadied himself on the wall to get up. 'What now?' And with a shock I remembered.

'Those poor cats,' I said and ran back through.

'I have turned the hot water pipes off,' my guardian said, but the room was stifling and I hastily cupped my handkerchief over my nose again. 'If you try to find the tap which turns the water on, I will open the skylights.'

I ran up the aisle and found a tap, and the moment I turned it there was a clear hiss and water trickled into the bowls of every cage.

'I fear we are too late,' my guardian said.

'I am astonished that you care.'

'I have a degree of respect for cats,' my guardian said. 'They kill for food and they kill for pleasure. It is all the same to them and they make no attempt to wrap their cruelty in sentimental fabrics.'

'Good,' I said. 'Then if we find one alive—'

'No, March.'

'It would get rid of the mice.'

'It is just as likely to bring them into the house.'

I went up and down the aisles. One fluffy white ball was moving slowly, crawling towards the fresh water with sawdust in its fur. It managed to raise its head and flop it over the rim but it seemed that the effort had been too much for it until I saw a pink tongue creep out, curl and scoop up a drink. Four more times it lapped before it struggled to its feet.

'I have a friend who wants a pet,' I said. 'I shall take her.'

'How do you know it is a female?'

There was a box with some straw in the corner and I placed her carefully in it.

'Because,' I said, 'she has spirit. Perhaps my friend will call her that.'

'Spirit,' Sidney Grice repeated thoughtfully. 'What a puerile name. Well…' He bent, reached into his satchel and crouched to pincer something on the floor with a short pair of tweezers. 'What have we here?'

I looked at the pallid soft squirming creature in his grasp. 'A maggot.' I recoiled.

'What a fine fat specimen he is too.' He popped it into a test tube.

I took a bowl of water to put in the box. 'What shall we do now?'

He recorked the tube. 'I shall summon the police. You shall go home. The cab is still outside.'

'But I might be able to help here.'

'Help who? Piggety is beyond help and I do not need any.' He touched my arm. 'Go home, March. I shall wait here. This is no place for anyone with human feelings.'

'And you?'

'Me?' He guided me up the steps. 'I am in my element. This is quite the finest murder I have witnessed in three years.'

'God help you,' I said.

'He is welcome to try.' We stepped outside and the stink of the cesspit suddenly smelled like fresh air.

48

Parasites, Monsters and Fat Hens

MY GUARDIAN SAW me across the jetty to our cab.

'You there,' he shouted at a small boy who was peering out from behind a capstan. 'I paid you to keep a lookout.'

The boy hobbled towards us, using a rough length of wood to support his bandy legs. 'Sorry, mister,' he said. 'We was doin' it like you said, three of us watchin' all the time, but then 'e came and chased us orf and we was too terrorized to 'ang abart.'

'Who chased you?' I said.

'The monster, miss. 'Orrible he was, like Frankunstein, and I ain't larkin'.'

'So why did you come back?' Sidney Grice raised his cane. 'Except for a well-earned thrashing?'

The boy dodged clumsily, almost slipping over on to the wet cobbles. 'I lorst a penny and I fought I might find it 'ere.'

'Here it is.' I reached into my purse. 'Only it was a sixpence.' His hand was gloved in warts.

'Parasites, every one of them.' Sidney Grice checked his pockets as the boy scuttled off. 'Mind they do not bleed you dry as they suck the lifeblood of our nation.'

He helped me into the cab.

'I think we have a few crumbs to spare yet,' I said.

It was a long slow ride home, but I was scarcely aware of anything around me. All I could see through the fog was the torment of the frothing water and all I could hear were the screams and frantic splashes silenced at last by death.

I shook my head, but you cannot shake off memories like ants from an apple. They cling and burrow and they breed in your mind, and I sometimes think they poison it. I closed my eyes and put my thumbs over my ears and my face in my fingers, but the sights and sounds only grew more intense and I was not even aware we had stopped until the cabby leaned down and poked my shoulder with his whip handle.

'All right, miss? Or do you want to go round again? It's your dosh.'

I paid him and went up the steps over the cellar moat and into the house, where Molly was waving a feather duster around lethargically.

'Oh, miss, you look awful, even awfuler than what you usually does. You look like you've seen a phantagasm.'

'Worse than that, Molly,' I whispered. 'Much worse.'

I turned my back on her but she could see my face in the mirror. 'Don't cry, miss.' I spun back to her. 'Why not? Somebody ought to in this godforsaken house.' I brushed past her and ran upstairs, into my room, the only place I could call mine now, and even then only by invitation of a man I hardly knew.

I poured myself a gin and held it in my mouth but it could not wash away the taste and, when I swallowed, it could not warm me.

What would you have done? How could you have comforted me? This was a world more terrible than any battle you ever dreamed of. At least you would have known who you were fighting. At least you believed you would win and could dream of glory. Oh, Edward, I thank God you never had my dreams.

You would have held me, but you could not have helped. Nobody could help me now. We all make our own way into the next world and sometimes there is only the hope that it will be better, and the slippery rocks of faith to cling to.

I went into the bathroom and ripped off my clothes, and sat and waited for the tub to fill. But the rush of water and the rising steam frightened me and I turned off the taps and pulled out the plug and washed myself all over, standing at the sink, but the stench of death was too deep to scrub away and the towel did not seem able to get me dry. I took my bottle of Fougère perfume and put a drop on my face and another on my neck, and slopped it into my cupped hand and rubbed it over my untouched, untouchable body.

Back in my room I put on my black dress, the one Papa bought me to meet Princess Beatrice but which I wore instead to his funeral. I had another gin and went back into the corridor and up to the attic floor where only Molly lived. There was a skylight at the end which served as a fire escape. I hooked down the ladder and climbed on to the roof and sat on the wall, smoking a cigarette and watching the traffic, a line of omnibuses with loud young men on the top deck, throwing apple cores at each other and pedestrians, and the busy people marching past the vendors unheeding of their cries – *Pretty pins for the ladies*, *Buy my fat hens*. A knife grinder was dragging his treadle-stone along the side of the road. *Bring awt yer blades, yer scissors and yer axes.*

I stubbed out my cigarette in the wide, lead-lined gutter and wished I had brought my flask up with me, and that I was somewhere else, anywhere except this seething sulphurous city.

If there had been time to think it over I would probably have handled things better, but you had a regimental dinner so I did not see you that night and the next morning you were off on patrol. In the three weeks you were supposed to be away I would have cooled down. I would probably have discussed the letter with my father, but you came to the hospital just before muster to say goodbye.

I was busy and cross because pilfering was becoming a major problem and a consignment of bandages had disappeared. I went outside to meet you.

'I just came to say—'

But I cut you short. 'What?'

'Goodbye,' you said warily.

'Is that it?'

'Well... yes.'

'Goodbye then.'

You tried to kiss me but I twisted away.

'March, what is it?'

'I was hoping you would tell me that.'

You looked genuinely confused. 'I honestly do not know what you are talking about.' And you were not a good enough actor to have faked it.

'Your father,' I said, and the light dawned. It was one of the rare times I ever saw you angry, and the only time ever with me.

'You read my father's correspondence?'

And instantly I felt guilty. 'I could not help it.'

You raised your voice. 'You could not help opening my writing case, taking out his letter and reading it? Some things are private, March.'

'We do not have secrets from each other.'

Harry Baddington appeared, swaggering down the path towards us. 'Eddy,' he hollered. I hated him calling you that. 'The men are waiting.'

'I have to go. We will talk about it when I get home.' You leaned forward and I turned so that you pecked my cheek.

You stiffened. 'Goodbye, March.'

'Edward,' I called before you had gone three paces. I wanted to say I loved you and to take care, but I only said, 'Who is Hester Sandler?'

'We will talk when I return,' you replied firmly.

How fine you looked as you strode away, your polished boots kicking up the dust, your helmet white in the white sun and your sabre swinging by your side. I think I saw you as you rode off, but the sun and the dust and the tears were in my eyes.

49

The Sleep of the Unjust

THE SUN WAS setting over the rooftops – though I could hardly see it through the tainted air, just the darkening and reddening of the distance – before I clambered down. I changed again into my old mauveine dress and went downstairs.

Sidney Grice sat upright in his armchair. He had taken his eye out and was massaging around it and wincing.

'I used to go on the roof,' he told me without opening his eyes, 'and wonder at this city of mine.'

'Yours?'

'Everything is mine in my world.' He opened his eyes. 'Sit down, March.' His socket was streaked violet and the patch lay on his knee. He rubbed his good eye and looked at me. 'No one should see what you have seen today.'

'You cope.'

He wiped around his socket with the back of his hand. 'If I do not cope nobody else will. Then who will stop these things happening?'

'I could say the same.' I fiddled with a button on my dress.

'But you are a young woman and women have finer feelings than men.'

'And my finer feelings tell me that I can help. Do you think you find murder more abominable than I do?'

'No but—'

'There are no *no buts*,' I reminded him. 'You will not push me out of the house quite as easily as that, Mr G.'

'I was not trying to evict you, merely holding the door open.'

'Then I suggest you close it before we both catch our deaths.'

Sidney Grice's mouth twitched slightly. 'Very well, March, but you must promise to tell me when you have had enough.'

'I will have had enough when there are no more crimes,' I said.

'Which will never happen.'

'Precisely.'

He replaced his patch and tied it behind his head. 'If only your mother could see you now.'

'Tell me about her.'

My guardian frowned. 'You have one failing in common, a sense of humour. She could light up a room with her wit – unfortunately. Otherwise there is no resemblance. You inherited your father's rugged facade but your mother was the loveliest of creatures.' He pinched the dimple in his chin. 'Or so they say.' He thinned his lips and stretched back to pull the bell. 'Quigley came and went. Accidental death, of course. According to our good inspector, Piggety must have been testing his own machinery and got entangled in the silk cords.'

'Nobody can accidentally entangle themselves in several neat knots,' I said.

'He knows that as well as you or I.' My guardian polished his fingernails on his trousers. 'I shall be glad when the promotions are decided next week. The man has never been much of a help, but now he is a positive obstruction.'

'How does he sleep at night?' I asked and Mr G regarded his fingertips.

'People talk about the sleep of the just.' He tugged his earlobe. 'But it is the wicked who have the best nights. Who have they to fear but themselves?' He crooked a finger. 'By the way, you left something at the factory.' He pointed to a tea chest on the floor by his desk.

I went over and something moved. 'Spirit! How could I have

forgotten you?' I bent down and lifted her out, and she opened her eyes and mewed silently.

'I hope your friend takes better care of it,' he said.

'Which friend?'

'The one you are giving it to.'

'Oh yes.'

'The only survivor,' he told me.

I stroked under her chin and Spirit nuzzled her nose into my palm.

You got a letter from your mother and you wept. There was no bad news, just family gossip and wishing you a happy Christmas. You made me swear not to tell anyone but there was no need. I would never have embarrassed you in front of your comrades. After all I never told how the brigadier cried when his pet canary died. He had just taught it to say 'God save the queen' when Dinah, my cat, got it. It was all my father could do to stop him executing her on the spot.

Three days later Dinah went missing and everyone, except the brigadier, made a search for her, but she seemed to have vanished from the face of the earth.

Six weeks later you brought me a cat, a lovely tortoise-shell with one black paw. You had purchased her from your cha walla, *who told you he had heard of my loss and shipped it from England at great expense, and charged you accordingly.*

'I know she can never replace Dinah,' you said, 'but I thought she looked quite similar.'

I picked her out of the basket and held her to me.

'You see. She likes you already,' you said.

'Oh, Edward, you pickle,' I said. 'This is *Dinah.'*

'Well, I'm fried.'

'You certainly have been,' I said and kissed you on the tip of your nose.

50

Three-toed Sloths and Captain Dubois

'LET US IMAGINE,' Sidney Grice said, settling into his armchair, 'what happened at that vile cat factory. And by *imagine*, I mean attempt to logically reconstruct what happened. It is not an invitation to unleash your lurid imagination. First of all, who sent the telegram?'

'Either Mr Piggety or the murderer.'

'And how will you find out which?'

'Me?'

'Yes. You are always whining in your diaries about me not giving you any responsibility.'

'Have you been reading my journal again?'

'Of course.'

'But I keep it hidden and the key is always on my person.'

'It is impossible to hide anything from me,' my guardian said. 'And as for locks…' He piffed. 'A three-toed sloth could open the average diary clasp with a parsnip. Proceed.'

'My journals are personal.'

'Much too personal at times,' Sidney Grice said. 'Proceed.'

I let the matter drop. 'I have already asked the woman at the telegram office, as you know.'

'And how much did you give her?'

'Well, nothing.'

'Nothing?' He could not have been more astonished had I told him I was Cardinal Newman. 'Nobody with an income of below five hundred a year remembers anything for free. A telegrapher requires a shilling to recall facts as accurately as his or her primitive cranium permits. Railway porters' underdeveloped memories can be stimulated for one and sixpence and guards' for a florin. It is all in Beckham's *Financial Inducements of the Lower Orders*, though some of his figures are out of date. He lists three classes of our inferiors who will talk for a farthing, whereas I have never heard anything worth listening to for under a penny.' Molly came in with the tea tray. She was cleanly turned out and had not spilled a drop on the cloth. 'Bring a fresh pot in twenty-four minutes.'

'Certainly, sir.'

'She must be an identical twin,' I joked as she left, and my guardian considered the remark.

'I hope not,' he said. 'Mercy – and never was a child so cruelly misnamed – awaits Her Majesty's pleasure in Broadmoor Criminal Lunatic Asylum, and will still be awaiting it on the day she expires.'

I put a strainer on his cup. 'What did she do?'

'Not a fraction of what she planned to do.'

I could see that he was not going to tell me any more, so I said, 'Are you suggesting that I return to the office and offer the desk clerk a bribe?'

'There is no point in striking when the iron is cold and has been taken away.' He levelled the surface of the sugar with the back of a spoon. 'I mention it only for future reference. So…' He eased the spoon in, taking great care not to disturb the smooth surface. 'We have two possibilities. First, Mr Piggety really did have information.'

'But why instruct us to wait until three o'clock when he described it as *vital*?'

'A moot point which leads us to suspect that the second possibility is more likely to be correct' – he plunged the spoon up to its hilt – 'that the murderer lured us there just in time to witness the crime, but too late to be able to prevent it.'

'How could somebody know this morning exactly what time he would die?' I asked and my guardian pursed his lips.

'How long do you think it would have taken those cats to die?'

'I am not sure.' I poured our teas. 'In that heat and with no water, perhaps two days.'

Sidney Grice straightened the tray. 'Captain François Dubois of the French Foreign Legion did some research on this topic during his country's typically inept intrusion into Mexico. He was concerned about the effects of heat and dehydration on his men, and experimented with dogs in cages in the full sun. He was astonished at how soon they succumbed, some as quickly as two hours. Now cats are hardier than their creepily sycophantic canine counterparts, plus it would take a long time for a room of that size to heat up, even with its insulation and instant hot water supply. According to my mercury thermometer, the water was two hundred and nine degrees Fahrenheit, the pipes were ten inches diameter and, since they go up and down all the rows, two hundred and forty-two feet long – the room must be...' he looked about him as if we were still in it, covering our noses from the stench of nearly five thousand dead cats, 'seven thousand, nine hundred cubic feet. The room temperature was previously set at sixty-two degrees and rose to one hundred and four. So that would take...?' He snapped his fingers at me.

'Four or five hours,' I hazarded.

'Not bad.' Sidney Grice looked mildly impressed. 'So, if we assume that the cats survived for another four or five hours in those conditions...?' He pointed at me.

'We can estimate that the murderer went there some time between six and eight o'clock this morning,' I said. 'But why would he turn the heating up when—'

'Stop,' my guardian protested as if in pain. 'Three logical solecisms in twenty-three words and you have not even finished your sentence. It is more than the human frame can endure.'

'I was only making assumptions, as you have been doing,' I said and he winced.

'I have made twelve assumptions in four minutes, some of them unspoken. The difference being that I know these false friends for what they are, whereas you think of conjecture as fact. First, we cannot know that the murderer turned the heating up, second, we cannot know that it was turned up the moment the murderer arrived and, third, we do not know that the murderer is a man. However, for the sake of linguistic brevity, we will agree to refer to the murderer as *he* for the time being.'

I spooned two sugars into my tea. 'The more I think about it, the more I am convinced we should be saying *she*.' I poured some milk and stirred. 'The cruelty of his death and the senseless killing of all those cats – it all reeks of Primrose McKay to me.'

'I hope so.' Mr G sneezed. 'It would be pleasant indeed to put that young lady into a condemned cell, but I shall stick with *he* for the time being.' He blew his nose. 'To continue – getting into the building was not necessarily a problem. He may have just knocked and been admitted. Perhaps Piggety knew or was expecting him. And, when he left, the killer locked up and posted me the key.'

'Mr Piggety only had one key,' I remembered.

'And, unless you are acquainted with Messrs Frankie Zammit or George Henderson, you cannot get a Williams-Hazard deadlock key made except by the manufacturers, and that is easily checked.'

'The key arrived here just after two and it takes a good half-hour to get here, so—' A thought struck me. 'The murderer was probably at his work when I arrived. But why did he not lock the door?'

Sidney Grice tasted his tea. 'There are two likely reasons. Either he was about to leave or he was waiting for you.'

'But why would he expect me to turn up?'

Mr G rotated his saucer. 'You have heard of Pandora?'

'Of course.' I reached for the milk jug. 'She was told not to look in a box, but she opened it and released chaos into the world.'

He turned the saucer back a fraction. 'Tell a woman not to do something and what will she do?'

'Very often the opposite,' I admitted.

He blew his nose. 'So tell a woman that she must on no account arrive before three?'

'And curiosity might get the better of her.' I splashed myself with the milk. 'But he would have had to hide behind that door for hours on the chance that I would turn up.'

He passed me a napkin to dab my sleeve. 'He may be a very patient man or more likely he had somebody alert him – an accomplice possibly.'

'The children,' I said. 'There were girls throwing stones against the wall. They could have been signalling that I was approaching... But why would he...' I put my hand to my mouth.

'There are two vats.' My guardian's face was sombre.

51

Flash Mobsmen and Royal Garden Parties

It took a while for that thought to sink in and even then I could not imagine it – being stripped and trussed and suspended on that slow ride alongside Prometheus Piggety, watching each other's terror, feeling the first scalding splashes, hearing each other's desperate thrashings, knowing that all I could hope for was what I feared most – death.

I wondered if my guardian was as shocked as I by the thought of what I had escaped but he was humming lightly now, and tapping an irregular rhythm on his leg, and each of his eyes looked as dead as the other.

I stood up unsteadily and he rose from his chair, ready to catch me, but I would not swoon into his arms like the helpless schoolgirl he imagined me to be. He stepped forward but I held out my hand and sat back again with as much dignity as I could salvage.

'You look ill, March. Have you been eating enough vegetables?' He scrutinized me with concern. 'What is so amusing?'

'Enough?' I laughed louder than I intended. 'I have eaten nothing but wretched vegetables since I came here.'

My guardian said, 'Kindly moderate your language.'

'But they *are* wretched,' I insisted. 'They are miserable and soggy and cold. Besides, there is nothing wrong with the word.'

He puffed through his lips. 'You said it as if it were an expletive, and a lady should never say anything that sounds even remotely like an expletive. I had a cousin who once said *affable* in such a way that she was never invited to another royal garden party again.'

'Why are we discussing royal garden parties?'

Sidney Grice brushed an invisible speck from his right shoulder. 'Because it has stopped you shaking. Deliberate verbal distraction is an art usually only practised by flash mobsmen, Whig politicians and the better class of pickpockets, but it can be a useful technique. When Maximilian Hurst was preparing to assassinate me I initiated a conversation about the merits of electrical lighting, which I had to keep going for over an hour before the police arrived.'

'That would never have worked with a woman,' I said.

'Maximilian Hurst *was* a woman,' he told me, 'which was only apparent after she was executed by firing squad in Belarus.'

'Do you really think I would have been boiled alive?' For all his ramblings, I could not get the idea out of my head.

Mr G yawned. 'It is not unlikely that the murderer would have tried, but I would probably have saved you.'

'Only probably?'

'Most probably.'

I lifted the teapot lid and there was only a mound of soggy leaves. 'But why would anybody want to kill me?'

'To wound *me*.'

I was not in the mood to pursue that train of thought. 'So before eight o'clock this morning when the telegram was sent, the murderer had estimated the time of death,' I said. 'He must have been very confident that the chain belt would work, to go off and leave Mr Piggety unattended – and he knew exactly how long it would take. If he had called us too early we could have rescued Mr Piggety and he might have been able to identify his would-be killer.'

My guardian considered the matter, then sprang up and went to his desk. It was littered with the day's envelopes. He took the bands off one and emptied the contents on to his blotter. I went over to look. It was a little heap of the glass fragments. Sidney

Grice spread it out with the edge of a rule and set aside one of the larger pieces.

'Look at this.' He handed me his magnifying glass. 'There is a very slight but definite curve in it.'

He went back and emptied a second envelope of more finely powdered glass next to the first. 'You are a girl and therefore addicted to jigsaws—'

'I quite liked them when I *was* a girl,' I said, 'but I am a woman now.'

My guardian leaned back to look at me. He raised his pince-nez to his nose and let it fall on its string. 'A caterpillar may call itself a butterfly,' he said, 'but it has not the beauty and neither can it fly.' He placed the rule on his blotter. 'So, if you were to indulge in your juvenile passions and assemble these pieces as a disc, what diameter would you expect it to be?'

'It is difficult to say.'

'If it were an easy question, I should have asked Molly.'

'Two inches,' I guessed and he waved the rule in my face.

'What do I have on me that is glass and two inches in diameter?'

'Your eye,' I said, and he rolled his good one.

'My eye is not a flat disc and it is not that wide. I am not a horse. Think, girl. Clear out all that coagulated poetical flotsam with which you clog your brain and concentrate.'

'Your watch face.'

'At last.' He raked his hair back. 'So, armed with our conjectures, I think we can envision the series of events with a reasonable degree of confidence, but first, we have another urgent matter to attend to. That wastrel girl has not brought any more tea.'

He re-crossed the room and grasped the bell rope.

52

The Eternal Scream

SIDNEY GRICE STILL had his hand on the rope when the door flew open and Molly with it, her hat flapping and the tea spilling out of the spout as she rushed to put the tray down on the central table.

'Ever so sorry, Mr G,' she said. 'But—'

He jumped to his feet, tight with indignation. 'If you ever call me that again you will leave this house immediately.'

Molly drew back nervously. 'Sorry, sir, but I heard Miss Middleton call you that and I thought you liked it.'

'When you are my ward you may call me that, but not one particle of a second beforehand.'

Molly's eyes lit up. 'Oh, when shall that be, sir? Someday soon, I trust. Oh, I shall be fienderishly happy to stop this diresome work. The hours are so long and the pay so tiddlerish. Why, Miss Middleton and I will be like sisters. We shall comb each other's hair and I shall call her *March*.'

'Oh, good grief.' Sidney Grice sat down.

'Mr Grice is not going to make you his ward, Molly,' I told her, and she jerked her head sideways as if she had been stung. 'He was just telling you not to call him that.'

'So he's—'

'I am afraid not,' I said and Molly ran her tongue around the inside of her cheek.

'Just as well.' She scratched her arm vigorously. 'I should have to stop cursing and stealing from the kitchen, and I enjoy both those things.' She cleared our tray and replaced it with the new one.

'Why were you so long?' her employer asked and Molly grimaced.

'Oh, sir, it was gruelsome. Cook got her ear caught in that automaticated potato masherer what you invented.'

'But how?' I asked.

'For once in my life I do not want to know.' Sidney Grice put his fingertips to his temples and whisked his hands apart.

'She was trying to hear if there was anything in there.'

'And was there?' I asked.

'Just her ear, miss,' she told me.

'Go away,' her employer said.

'What?' Molly screwed up her face and her apron. 'For ever?'

He half-stood. 'Y—'

'Just until you are called again,' I put in hurriedly. 'Is Cook all right?'

Molly wrinkled her nose. 'As right as a body can be with an ear and half a finger scrungulated.'

'What happened to her finger?'

'She was trying to get her ear back.'

'Does she need a doctor?'

'Yes,' Sidney Grice snapped. 'They both need an alienist.'

'A what, sir?'

'A man who thinks he can cure lunatics and is therefore more delusional than his patients,' he told her. 'Get out... Now... and do not even think about curtsying... Go.'

'Thank you, sir.' Molly froze mid-bob and left the room.

He looked at the tray. 'Give me two half-good reasons why you stopped me sacking that lumpen sluggard?'

'Molly may be scatter brained—'

'There is no *may be* about it.'

'But she is hard-working and loyal. She would die for you.'

He grunted. 'I wish she would get a move on.'

'And besides, nobody else would tolerate your behaviour.'

He tugged at his scarred earlobe. 'That is true. I once got through six servants in a week.'

I righted a tipped teacup and put it on the table. 'So what do you think happened at Mr Piggety's?'

'I can only make preternaturally intelligent guesses at present,' he said as I poured. 'Most probably,' he inspected his tea despondently, 'the murderer or murderers—'

'Why the plural?' I had an itch in the sole of my right foot.

'I will come to that, but I will stick to the masculine singular for now.' He sampled his tea. 'Actually, this is not too bad... The murderer comes to Piggety's Cat Factory. He gains entry without any force, so either Mr Piggety knew or was expecting him or the killer managed to talk his way in. They go through the cattery and into the boiling room.'

I tried to wriggle my toes around but the itch was getting worse.

'Could he have gone in through the skinning room?' I shuddered at the very idea of such a place.

Mr G crossed his legs. 'I looked around after you had gone. It has no means of access other than the door into the killing room.'

I pressed the sole of my boot on to the edge of the hearth and eased my foot up and down. 'So they go through to the boiling room. What then?'

'Mr Piggety undresses himself.' He curled his lips at the unpleasantness of the image. 'The clothes were not ripped off him – they have not been damaged. Indeed, they were neatly folded and his jacket was hung on a peg. So how do you make a man undress himself?'

'By seduction,' I suggested and he coloured.

'What a filthy idea, but one we must consider' – Mr G uncrossed his legs – 'and, I believe, dismiss. A man in what I must call *a state of excitement* does not lay out his attire as if it is on display in a draper's shop.'

The itch was driving me to distraction. 'At gunpoint.' I stamped my foot.

'Temper,' he said absently. 'Possibly, but then he would be even less concerned about sartorial matters.'

'I do not think he was overly concerned about them at the best of times.' I remembered Mr Piggety's shiny-elbowed coat, stained shirt and crumpled trousers.

'Besides which,' Sidney Grice took a sudden interest in the palm of his left hand, running a finger over the creases, 'you would have to put the gun down to tie him up, at which point he is going to struggle.'

'How do you know he did not?' I tickled my palm in the hope that creating another itch would get rid of the first, but my hand did not itch and my foot felt as though I were standing in an ants' nest.

'Because the knots were tied neatly and methodically, which is why we must consider the possibility of a second murderer – one to hold the gun and the other to truss their victim up. Which leads me to the rather alarming thought that these murders may involve at least three different felons – one poisoner for Horatio Green, for poisoners rarely resort to violent means, and two killers for Slab, Jackaman and Piggety.'

The silhouette of an omnibus crossed the room, its top passengers moving in a shadow-puppet display over his bookcase. 'And Braithwaite,' I suggested.

'Not my case.' He folded his arms.

I put the strainer back over my cup, but there was more tea in the tray than in the pot now. 'At this rate the murderers will outnumber the victims.' I got up to fetch a wooden rule from his desk.

'That is not unknown. Most of this peculiar nation murdered Charles I.'

'What if he were knocked out?' I suggested, and Sidney Grice smoothed his hair back.

'He could have been, but I doubt it. If you render a man

unconscious with a blow to the head, you run the risk that he will not regain consciousness. He may even die and whoever killed Mr Piggety did not want him to die peacefully, otherwise he would have been tipped straight into the vat – whereas Mr Piggety knew exactly what was happening to him and probably for a number of hours. That is why he expelled his gastric contents.'

'But who would hate Mr Piggety so much as to kill him so cruelly?' I eased the rule down the side of my boot but could not get it to where it might have helped.

'Every man has his enemies. Possibly a cat-lover who knew what he was intending to do and thought to give him a taste of his own medicine. More likely, they did not hate him at all. I am increasingly convinced that the person the murderer really hates is' – he doodled with his forefinger in a puddle of tea – 'me.'

'Why are you taking it personally? The next victim might easily have been me.'

'I only take things personally when they are.' He eased his head back as if he had a stiff neck. 'And every step that has been taken seems calculated to wreck my career and therefore me, for no man is more than what he does and most people are a great deal less. What on earth are you doing?'

I pulled out the rule. 'I have an itch.'

My guardian looked revolted. 'Ladies,' he declared, '*never* itch.'

'How lucky we are.' I put the rule down with exaggerated care. 'So you think that somebody killed four men so brutally just to harm you?'

He took up the rule. 'It is a possibility that I must bear in mind.'

'But that is inhuman,' I said as my guardian measured his hand at several points.

'Unfortunately, it is all too human. I know of no beast whose savagery can even approach that of mankind, and Mr Piggety's death was one of the most ghastly it has ever been my privilege to witness.'

'You regard it as a cachet?'

'Death is a secretive fellow. It is always an honour to watch him at work.'

I closed my eyes. 'Then I have been privileged a great many times… if only I had realized.' I opened my eyes to see my guardian standing at my side and holding out his hand, and I reached up and he took mine awkwardly, like a bachelor uncle being given a baby and unsure what to do with it.

'The loss of loved ones is never a privilege,' he said, 'but to be with them when they are lost, is.'

'Not always,' I said.

'I know you had loved ones you would rather had not died, but would you want them to have died alone?' His voice was soft and his hand closed on mine, but I pulled away.

'I am sorry,' I whispered as I stood up to leave.

Sidney Grice winced and stepped aside, and I ran up the stairs, threw myself on to my bed and buried my face in my pillow to let the scream escape. But a scream is like an ocean; you can only drain it by creating another, and pain does not end just because you are weary of it.

What passed through your mind as I cradled your head that last time? Did your love turn all at once to a sense of betrayal? 'God bless you,' I said and I thought you nodded. You mouthed my name in flecks of your own blood.

My father stood beside me. 'Dear God in heaven, March.'

'Dead.' I mouthed the word as if not hearing it could make it less true. 'I have killed you.' My lips could not frame that sentence any more than my mind could reject it. I kept it, nurtured it and let it grow, four words which were my birth and became my life.

53

Rabbits and the Marquis de Sade

I WASHED MY face in cold water with a rose-scented soap, smoked a cigarette out of the window, drank a large gin, sucked on a parma violet and was making my way down the stairs as my guardian came up them for dinner. He did not speak and neither did I.

We sat at opposite ends of the table, listening to the dumb waiter creak up from the kitchen. Mr G got up and brought out two plates, and put a dreary khaki slush in front of me.

'I fear you are too distressed to continue.' He returned to his seat. 'It cannot be easy being a member of the weaker sex.'

'I would not know,' I retorted, 'being a woman.' He looked puzzled. 'Anyway,' I continued, 'your concern is misplaced. Please go on with your reconstruction.'

And without the slightest pause he did so. 'Prometheus Piggety is trussed naked in silk cords and fastened to the first hook on the chain track. The killing tub is filled with boiling water and the engine started. This, I suspect, is when the drinking water in the cattery was turned off and the heating turned on.'

'The murderer would not have known how all the valves worked, so perhaps the cats' suffering was accidental,' I suggested with more hope than conviction.

'How did you know which tap turned on their water?' Sidney Grice polished his pince-nez.

'Because it was labelled,' I said.

'I rest my case.' He uncrossed his legs. 'We are not dealing with nice people, March. The suffering of creatures would have given them nothing but pleasure. I shall not soil my lips with the name of the French rascal whose practices they have adopted.'

'I am quite familiar with the story of the Marquis de Sade,' I said and my guardian drew back.

'How have the minds of the young become so polluted?'

'Why do men confuse innocence with ignorance?' I demanded and he wrinkled his brow.

'Because someone who is ignorant of a vice is not tempted to indulge in it.'

'But may be more easily lured into it,' I said.

'In my experience it is more often the women who do the luring,' he retorted. 'But, as always, your inanities are distracting me from the matter in hand.' He rubbed his left cheekbone. 'Where was I?'

'Turning the heating on,' I reminded him.

'Ah yes. Let me see.' Sidney Grice scribbled a few numbers on the tablecloth. 'There were twenty hooks on each chain. According to *Bridlington's Statistics*, the average fully grown cat weighs three pounds and two ounces, which would make a total load of somewhere in the region of one thousand ounces. Piggety must have weighed something like nine stone or two thousand, two hundred and forty ounces, which is more than twenty times the load that the system was designed to carry. Now, one of the many reasons that the electric motor will never replace steam is that it has a poor torque. For every ten per cent you increase the load, the motor will slow by twenty per cent. With the relatively large weight of Piggety, the progress would have been marvellously slow, but how do you calculate how slow it is?'

'You time it over a measured distance,' I said.

'Mr Piggety may have been an unpleasant man but he was no more asinine than average. He would have known what was happening to him. So what does he do?'

'He struggles and kicks out and knocks the watch that his murderer is timing him with on to the floor.'

'Or more likely he catches his persecutor on the nose – hence the blood droplets. The killer then drops the watch and accidentally steps on the glass.'

'So the murderer calculates when Mr Piggety will reach the tub, leaves him to his fate, locks up and sends you a telegram and the key,' I said. 'But why not send the telegram and key together by the same messenger?'

'He sends the telegram early to make sure I get it, and the key later so that I cannot enter the factory too soon and so that I have to stay here waiting for it.' Mr G tucked into his dinner.

'Is it not time we visited the last member of the club?' I proposed, and wondered what he had on his plate that warranted chewing.

'Ah yes, Mr Warrington Tusker Gallop.' He took a sip of water. 'We shall call upon Mr Gallop soon and unexpectedly, in order to catch him unawares at his place of business which is conveniently close by...' He winced.

'In Charlotte Street,' I put in as his fingers went to claw the air an inch from his face.

'Blast this thing.' He squeezed out his eye and cupped a hand over his socket.

'Perhaps if you left it out for a few days it might become less inflamed,' I said. 'Then I could help you make a fresh impression.'

My guardian put out his right hand. 'Stop,' he said. 'I can tolerate the pain but I could not bear it if I thought you cared.'

I did not know what to say. I wanted to reach out but Sidney Grice was, as always, unreachable.

Harry Baddington was devastated by your death. He was very supportive, but then he never knew that I had brought it about.

All of your things went into a packing case but Harry saved the writing box for me. Your father's letter was still in it and also one sheet of paper, a reply. I am sorry, Edward, it was wrong of me to read it but I had to know.

There was no preamble. In an angry hand you had scrawled,

> Dear Father
> I have never understood why you and Mama pretend to think that I have any kind of 'understanding' with Hester Sandler. Though she and I were childhood friends, we were never sweethearts and I have never given her any reason to think otherwise. If I danced with her at the last ball, it was because she was a friend and because you asked me not to leave her unattended at an event where she knew so few other people.

There was more in the same vein, but you never finished that letter. I tore it into little pieces along with your father's and put them in a kidney dish and set them alight, his disapproval and your last written words lost – like me – for ever.

54

Beef Tea and the Hospital Ghost

INSPECTOR POUND WAS propped up on three pillows and listlessly sipping a mug of beef tea when I visited him the next morning, but his expression brightened when he noticed me and even more when I showed him the pies and bottles of ale I had brought along.

'My desk sergeant came this morning with a bag of tea. What on earth am I supposed to do with that here?' He coughed and clutched at his stomach. 'My constables clubbed together for a bag of apples. I hate apples at the best of times and these are crawling with worms. Which is' – he broke off with another fit of coughing – 'the closest you can get to fresh meat here.'

'Has your sister brought you nothing?'

From under his pillows he brought out a battered leather-bound copy of the King James Bible. 'It belonged to my father.'

'Do you read it?'

He covered his mouth in an attempt to smother another cough. 'Don't tell my men or I would never live it down, but I try to read a passage every day.'

The man in the next bed was winking at me. I tried to ignore him. 'I am not sure that Mr Grice believes in God.'

'I have come across so much evil in my profession that I cannot help but believe in the devil and, if he exists, how can there not be a God?' The inspector drained his mug. 'Mr Grice would find more answers in the Bible if he opened it occasionally.'

'I shall tell him you said that.' I put his mug on the side table.

'I would rather you did not.'

Matron came along. 'Mr Sweeney is much impressed by your fiancé's progress.' Inspector Pound hid his surprise at being so described with another cough. 'You must not tire him.'

'I shall only stay a moment,' I assured her, but when we looked back he had already fallen asleep. I stroked the hair off his forehead and bent to kiss his cheek. 'Goodbye, my dear.'

The matron ushered me away, but on the way out she added, 'He has recently been in correspondence with another surgeon in Edinburgh who has had great success with carbolic acid and is very much in favour of its use. My nurses may not thank you for drawing it to our attention for it stings their eyes abominably, but' – the sternness briefly vanished – 'I believe we have saved three lives this week.'

'Thank you,' I said, 'for saving his.'

She touched my arm. 'Do not thank me too soon. That cough of his may be consumptive and we cannot bathe his lungs in antiseptic.'

'I know you will do your best for him.'

I made my way back down the long white corridors and had just reached the stairwell when I saw her, a spectral figure walking through the night air towards me.

'March?'

I spun round.

'I thought that was you.'

'Oh, Dr Berry.'

She came close. 'Why, March, you look like you have seen a ghost.'

For one moment I thought I had. 'I am sorry. I was daydreaming.' And then I added clumsily, 'What are you doing here?'

She laughed as I struggled to collect myself. 'That is like me asking why you are at the scene of a crime. I work here – well, two sessions a week anyway. Not content with outraging all decent people by educating Jews, University College has taken to employing the occasional woman and I am one of the lucky few, albeit on a voluntary basis.'

I felt like hugging her but I took her hand. 'I have been visiting a friend of mine, Inspector Pound.' I told her about the attack on him and how I had brought it upon him.

'The blood transfusion,' she said. 'I heard about that. That was brave of you.'

'It was my fault he needed it.'

Dr Berry squeezed my hand. 'You must not blame yourself. I will take a look at him later – if I can sneak past Matron.'

'She is not such a dragon as she appears,' I said.

'In that case I shall go now.' She hesitated. 'May I visit you tomorrow evening?'

'Oh yes. I am sure Mr Grice will be pleased to see you – and I will too, of course.'

I felt a little happier as I went on my way.

*

Sidney Grice was pasting a cutting into a navy-blue scrapbook.

'An unusual case in the East End.' He squashed the air bubbles with a cylinder rule. 'A man with no arms was fished out of the Thames and his legs were shackled.'

'Chas.' I gripped my handbag and tried to stop shaking. 'Charles Sawyer.'

'An acquaintance of yours?' He closed the book and I nodded weakly. 'Well, you will be interested to learn,' Mr G continued, 'that he survived by hanging on to a mooring rope with his teeth until the river police hauled him out.'

'Oh thank God.'

'What a waste of public resources.' My guardian piffed. 'An armless man is nothing but a drain on society.'

'We could do with a few more drains like him.' I slumped in my chair. 'He saved me from the man who stabbed Inspector Pound.'

My guardian wrinkled his brow and opened his book to pencil a note under the cutting.

'Doubtless expecting a large reward,' he grumbled, 'like some red-haired man who came round claiming he had helped Pound. I told him to go to Marylebone Police Station if he wanted paying, but he did not seem very keen on the idea.'

'But I promised him. He was the barman at the Boar's Head who carried the inspector to hospital.'

'And how was I to know that?' he mumbled as he left the room.

I took a look at what he had written.

Memoranda.

1. *Find and compensate red-headed man.*
2. *Bring would-be killers of* Charles Sawyer *to justice.*

And on his blotter I made out, *3 guineas a day + doctors' fees.*

55

Chocolates and Seaweed

AFTER LUNCH I walked to Huntley Street and the neat house with its green door, and waited for my three quick rings to be answered. A stray dog dragged itself to sit and whimper at me, though I had nothing to give it but a stroke.

The door was opened a crack and then fully by a slender middle-aged lady in a long red gown. 'Eve.' She threw out her arms. We all used false names in those days. An unofficial ladies' club was viewed with grave suspicion by the authorities and prurience by the masculine public.

'Hello, Violet.'

She shooed the dog away, shut it out and gave me a kiss, though her arms remained open.

'We haven't seen you for ages.' Her stiff black hair rasped my face. 'You are quite the celebrity since that murder trial.'

I winced. I never wanted to be well known and certainly not for being associated with so many cruel deaths. I braced myself to peck her cheek. 'Is Harriet here?'

Violet had drenched herself in so much eau de cologne that my nose itched.

'I think she is playing Bezique with the Countess of Bromley.' The *Countess* owned a tobacco shop in Biggin Hill, her tiara was home-made and she had no more right to a title than I, but no one could begrudge it to a woman who had had fourteen children and lost them all in one winter. 'Why don't you step into my parlour and I will let her know you are here?'

I sat on the chintz sofa and picked up a copy of *Myra's Journal of Dress and Fashion*, and was dismayed to see that I needed an eighteen-inch waist to be able to wear anything remotely modern, when Harriet came in. I jumped up and ran into her embrace.

'March, I swear you look more the lady every time I see you. That dress – where did you get it? – could start a colonial war. I thought I turned a few heads in the ticket office at Rugby Station this morning, but I feel positively agricultural next to you in that mantel mirror.' She poured us both a generous Bombay while I lit two Virginians. 'Oh, that awful jumped-up woman. It is positively indecent to put that many aces in a pack. Rooked me for three shillings and sixpence, but don't tell Vi for goodness sake. Gambling on the premises – she'll have us out on the street before you can say chin chin.' She raised her glass.

'Cheerio,' I said and clinked hers, and we settled together on the sofa. 'I know you usually come on the first Tuesday of the month, so I was not sure I would find you here today.'

Harriet swallowed a mouthful of gin. 'Oh, you would find me here every Tuesday of late, and many a day between.'

'Does Mr Fitzpatrick not mind?'

Harriet put her head back and blew three perfect smoke rings. 'To tell you the truth, March, I do not think my husband would notice if I stayed here all year round – not until there was a crisis such as not being able to find his copy of *Wisden*. Do you know, March, I was trapped in the attic last month by a faulty door handle and I was up there all night – and it was the longest, coldest night since the Ice Age – bellowing like a regimental sergeant major and banging like a demented monkey on the floor with his Aunty Helen's bed brick until Sebastian, the youngest offspring and the only one who looks remotely like me, came to investigate and released me. I hurtled downstairs more encrusted in dust than a collier at the end of his shift and draped in more cobwebs than Miss Havisham's wedding cake, my hair hanging over my face like seaweed on the rock of the sirens, gibbering and in absolute floods of saline, and Charles tears himself away from his paper and kedgeree and says, "You really must have a word with the neighbours, Harry. Their builders kept me awake half the night with their hammering." And the really frightening thing, March, is that we share the same bed.'

She tossed back her drink and I refreshed both our glasses.

'Sometimes we do not notice things, but it does not mean we do not care.' I took her hand. 'My father once gave away my favourite chair and it was two days before—'

'That's it.' Harriet seized my words. 'That is exactly it. I am just a piece of furniture to him. I suppose I should be grateful he does not use me as a footstool. Do you know, March, that man pursued and I mean *pursued* me for two years. He sent me barrow-loads of flowers and crates of chocolates and showered me with thoughtful gifts. He wrote me cleverly crafted poems and love letters that simply steamed with adoration. He cajoled my mother and inveigled my sister into speaking on his behalf, and he positively hounded my father into nervous exhaustion for permission to press his pestering to its inevitable doom. He placed me in a shrine and as soon as I let him in, gave me a housekeeping book with a miserly allowance and disappeared into his study for the next quarter-century, reappearing only to work, eat and, very occasionally, have his not very wicked way with me.'

I laughed. 'Oh, Harriet, you are incorrigible, but it cannot really be that bad.'

'I have renovated, emery-papered and put French polish on it.' She leaned towards me. 'Listen to the awful voice of experience, March. Do you know why we have never had slaves in this country? Because we have ten million of them here already, only we call them *women*. If ever a man offers you a ring with one hand and a cup of hemlock with the other, take the poison. The result is the same but less protracted. Why, March, darling, what on earth is the matter? Here I am chattering like a squirrel and you look like you have seen an apparition.'

I had never told her about my engagement and I did not want

to talk about Horatio Green. I had come to Huntley Street to escape such thoughts.

'I am just tired,' I said. 'Dear Harriet, you are my one haven of frivolity in this barbaric world.'

We finished our cigarettes.

'But how is life with the famous Sidney Grice?' she asked. 'If the press are to be believed, he has metamorphosed from the avenging angel into the angel of death.'

'He investigates murders,' I said. 'He does not commit them.'

We were quiet for a moment until Harriet perked up and said, 'Speaking of apparitions – as I was a moment ago – I could have sworn I saw one on Tuesday last week. I was rushing to get on my four thirty – the five fifteen is always packed to the gunnels especially in the smoking compartments – when I saw a very well-dressed lady getting off the train on the next platform, and for one moment I would have sworn it was her.'

'Who?' I asked, but somehow I knew what Harriet was going to say.

'That terrible woman, the murderess. I suppose, after what you told me, I must call her Eleanor Quarrel.' She ground her cigarette into the ashtray. 'It was probably what Charles always calls my overexcited imagination and I only got a glimpse, but she had a very distinctive profile – didn't she? – and you know how you get a feeling. Even when I turned away it felt like she was looking at me. I have to say it sent shivers up and down my spine, but when I looked again she was gone – vanished. Perhaps she has come back to haunt us. Oh, and speaking of coming back to haunt people, one of our housemasters had a very unexpected and unwelcome visitor the other day.'

Her conversation darted to some divorce scandal in Rugby, but I found it difficult to pay attention. My mind was swirling with an image – Eleanor Quarrel rising rotting out of the water, knife in hand, ready to slaughter again.

56

The Fox and the Sparrow

WE HAD JUST finished what was an unusually tasty dinner of fried potatoes and boiled navy beans in a tomato purée when a telegram arrived for Sidney Grice.

'Good heavens.' A cord of vein engorged on his right temple. 'According to Dr Baldwin, my mother is dying and unlikely to last the night.' He drained his tumbler of water.

'Oh, I am sorry,' I said. 'Do you know what is wrong with her?'

He deposited his napkin on the floor. 'It appears she has taken an exorbitant quantity of heroin.'

'Oh dear.' I pushed my plate aside. 'What condition did she have to take it for?'

'Boredom.' He stood up. 'She has so little to do with her time since she came out of prison.'

I listened to him in disbelief. 'Your mother went to prison?'

'She was chairwoman of the Corporal Punishment Society.' He untied his patch. 'But she resigned when they refused to introduce branding of repeat pilferers.'

'I hope she is all right.' I tried to sound more sincere than I felt after that information and he contemplated me with disdain.

'Even with your ragged medical knowledge, I would have thought you would know that people who are dying are not *all right*.'

'I meant—'

'Did you, indeed?' He ran a hand over his brow. 'Well, really.

This is most inconvenient.' He limped down the stairs to summon a cab. 'Try not to set fire to the cherry tree,' he said as he left and I went outside to light a cigarette.

I had hardly settled to enjoy it when Molly stumbled out.

'Oh, miss, I wish I could smoke cigarettes and—'

'Would you like one?'

Molly crossed her feet. 'Not for me, thank you, miss. I meant I wish I could smoke cigarettes and not worry about it being unladylike.' And she beamed as if expecting me to concur.

'Have you come to tell me something?' I asked, as patiently as I could, and leaned back to watch the machinery of her mind operate.

'There is a cabby at the door,' she told me at last.

'What does he want?'

'Funny you should ask that.' Molly reclined against the door frame. 'We had a bit of a chat and he wants to retire and buy a little public house by the sea. He wants a little vegetable plot and a little—'

'Why is he here?'

'He...' She wriggled her nose. 'He has a message to convoy.'

I stubbed out my cigarette, slipped it back into the case to hide the evidence and went to investigate. Gerry was standing on the top step when I opened the door.

'Miss Middleton.' He tipped his leather peaked cap. 'Molly tells me Mr Grice isn't here,' he said.

'Can I take a message?'

Gerry hesitated. 'While we were waiting for you at the docks we were talking about that McKay – excuse my language – bitch. I was on a case against her five or six years ago. I thought he might be interested to know that it looks like she is doing a flit. Her carriage is on Monday Row round the back of her place and the servants were packing all her worldly goods into it when I went by twenty minutes ago.'

I reached for my cloak. 'Take me there, Gerry.' But Gerry held up his hands.

'Not me, miss.'

'I will double your fare.'

Gerry turned his hands palms up. 'It isn't a question of the tin, miss. Old Pudding would kill me if I did.'

Despite my frustration I laughed. 'Why do you call him that?'

'G-rice Pudding,' Gerry explained. 'We all call him that on the ranks, only don't tell him for gawd's sake.' He looked abashed. 'I'm sorry, miss, but Mr Grice did me proud when I was chucked and he'd blow his boiler if I took you into danger.'

'I quite understand.' I hung my cloak up again. 'Thank you, Gerry.'

I waited two minutes, then turned the handle to raise the flag, and I was still turning it when there was a knock on the door.

'Sorry abart the smell,' the driver called as I climbed aboard his hansom and he swung up on top. 'Last gent 'ad four grey'ounds and they weren't particular where they did it. I swilled it awt but it do linger, it do.' It certainly did but I had come to accept that I was living in a city of stinks. I almost envied Mr G his blocked nose.

The streets were still busy, countless pleasure seekers heading for the West End. I would have loved to see *The Corsican Contessa* at the Criterion and I had heard some of the songs being bawled out by song-sheet sellers on the street, but my guardian would never have countenanced me attending such an establishment. I might have been in grave peril of enjoying myself.

Monday Row was a narrow street at right angles to Fitzroy Square. We went along slowly, our horse picking its way through the shadows. A solitary flame glowed in the distance.

'Stop here,' I called out in a stage whisper.

As my eyes became accustomed to the gloom I made out a covered four-wheeler with two horses in harness about thirty feet down the alley, in the glow of a lamp post, and the shape of a groom sitting up at the front. A doorway opened, casting a corridor of light on to the scene, and what looked like a woman and a girl came carrying a trunk out.

'Dunno what you're up to,' my driver said quietly. 'But best we go back now.' His horse shifted uneasily.

'I rarely do what is best,' I declared – how Mr G would have agreed with me there – and clambered down to walk towards the scene.

The road was cobbled unevenly, carpeted with old straw and horse droppings, with wide gutters running along either side. I slithered and splashed through an unexpectedly deep puddle and the pair looked up. As I approached I saw that they were a man and a boy with aprons protecting their servants' uniforms. They balanced the chest on top of four tethering posts and rested their arms.

'Can I help you, miss?' the man enquired but even as he spoke I saw them – Thurston coming out of the door, carrying two bulging carpet bags, followed by Primrose McKay in a long fox-fur coat, lifting her skirts and exposing enough calf to have sent Mr G into an apoplexy.

'Miss Middleton,' she greeted me as she drew near. 'Is your master not with you?'

'I have no master,' I said, 'but Mr Grice has been called away on an urgent matter.'

'If you are touting for business you might do better outside King's Cross,' she advised, 'though you would be best to stand in the shadows.'

Thurston guffawed. 'With a sack over your head.'

'To avoid recognizing your mother?' I asked and he raised the back of his hand.

'It is all right, Thurston,' Primrose promised him. 'I shall let you hurt her very badly one day.'

'His very existence hurts me,' I murmured. 'Are you taking a holiday, Miss McKay?'

Primrose waved a bored hand. 'Life is a holiday for me, Miss Middleton.'

There was a scuttling in the gutter. A rat? I moved sideways.

'May I ask where you are going?'

The man and boy struggled to heave her trunk on to the already laden carriage roof.

'What an inquisitive child you are.' She clicked her tongue in reprimand. 'But I am afraid your curiosity will have to go unsatisfied.' She put the fingertips of her right hand together. 'Your master did not seem very impressed by my plan to sit it out and so I have devised another. It is also simple but even cleverer. Take a good look at me, Miss Middleton, and enjoy my gorgeousness. It may be the last you will see of it for quite some time; for tonight I am going' – she blew on her nails and her hand sprang open, revealing nothing inside – 'to disappear.'

'Disappearing is quite an easy trick,' I told her. 'The poor manage to do it all the time. You may find reappearing a little more difficult.'

The scuttling grew louder and she glanced down. 'What is that?'

The boy darted over and went down on his haunches. 'A bird, miss.'

'Give it to me.' He scooped it up and she took it from him. 'A sparrow,' she said. 'It appears to be injured.' She cradled it in her right hand, its head poking between her circling thumb and first finger and its feet dangling out at the bottom. 'Poor little thing.' She blew it a kiss and the bird opened its beak, but the beak stayed open and the feet curled tight and it squeaked, and I saw that she was clenching her fist.

'Stop it,' I cried out but she only smiled sweetly, and its eyes bulged as her fingers blanched, and I heard a sickening crunching sound and a black liquid was expelled from the sparrow's mouth before its head flopped.

'There,' Primrose McKay opened her hand and let it fall back into the gutter.

'You disgust me,' I railed at her.

'Find me a rag,' she told the boy, 'to clean the blood and excrement from my hand. No, do not worry, I have one.' She reached out and wiped her palm down the front of my cloak. 'Why have you come, Miss Middleton?'

She walked past me to the open carriage door.

'I like to know what our suspects are up to,' I said.

'Suspect?' she repeated scornfully. 'Well, you may tell your master this, girl. When the Last Death Club closes its accounts there will only be one person left alive and that person will be me, and he may draw whatever conclusion he likes from that but he will never prove a thing.'

'But what can you possibly want the money for?' I asked and she put her head to one side.

'For the poor,' she replied. 'I shall take that seventy thousand pounds on to the street and burn it before their very eyes.'

Thurston closed the carriage door and laughed. He turned to me. 'She will kill them all,' he crowed, 'and not you nor your half-blind, dirt-digging cripple can do a thing about it.'

'I only pray that you are an accomplice,' I told him. 'Mr Grice would so love a double hanging.'

Thurston pushed his face close to mine and I forced myself not to flinch.

'One day' – he breathed whisky fumes over me – 'I will crush you just like that little bird in my bare hands.' He stepped into a pile of manure and shook his foot angrily.

'Be sure to clean yourself up,' I advised. 'You will want to look your best in the dock.'

Thurston scraped his boot on the kerb, strode past and climbed into the other side of the carriage. The groom cracked his whip and the horses set off much too fast for such ill-lit conditions.

I dashed back to my cab. 'Follow that coach.'

But the driver shook his head. 'Not likely, miss. That's Bloodthirsty Gates. I know 'im by reputation and that's as much as I wants to.'

He turned his horse and it headed eagerly from the shadows to the light.

*

The lights were on when I returned, and I looked into the study to find Mr G sorting through his filing cabinet.

'I have just found a case of murder with an icicle,' he told me happily.

'I thought you would be with your mother,' I said.

'Oh, that.' He slipped a newspaper cutting into a folder. 'Apparently she had a headache. She has never had one before and assumed the worst.' He printed a number on the cover. 'So it was all a false alarm...' he put the folder away, 'unfortunately.'

'You cannot mean that.'

'I most certainly do.' He took off his pince-nez. 'It was in Norway.'

I told him what had happened.

'And the point of chasing after her was...?' he enquired politely.

'To see what she was up to.'

He ripped a page out of a journal. 'She was hardly likely to be *up to* anything with you peering over her shoulder. Really, March.' He tore the page in two, using his rule as a guide. 'I had four different drivers standing by to follow that woman before you alerted her.'

'Perhaps if you had told me—'

'What?' He slammed down his rule. 'You would not have gone charging round like a dragoon on manoeuvres?'

I was too tired to argue any more. 'She killed a bird,' I told him.

'Thank heavens for that.' He slid the drawer shut. 'By the look of your cloak I thought you had.'

57

Pebbles and the Iceni Hordes

CHARLOTTE STREET WAS ten minutes' walk or twenty minutes by cab on most days. We took a hansom.

'It is estimated,' Sidney Grice said, 'that the Iceni hordes rampaged through Londinium slaughtering the inhabitants at a rate of eight miles per hour. Today they would be lucky to get across Oxford Circus in an afternoon.'

We had been sitting for so long that he had drained his flask of tea while we were still within a few hundred yards of home. This seemed as good a time as any to broach the subject.

'Do you think it possible,' I hardly dared put the idea into words, 'that Eleanor Quarrel is still alive?'

I waited for my guardian to dismiss the idea contemptuously, but he only tapped the cork back into his insulated bottle and enquired, 'Why do you ask?'

'My friend Mrs Fitzpatrick, who knew Eleanor Quarrel quite well from the club in Huntley Street, thought she saw her, at Euston Station.'

A man was juggling three live hens. They flapped and squawked but he passed them hand to hand, high over his head, as easily as if they had been tennis balls.

'When?'

'Tuesday last week at about half past four.'

The man propelled all his hens in the air at once, but one launched itself in a clumsy falling flight and scuttled under a carriage with him scurrying after it.

'Did she speak to her?'

'No. She was alighting from a train as Harriet was boarding another, but she was convinced that Eleanor was looking at her. She thought it might be a ghost.'

Mr G snorted. 'If a fraction of sightings were proved true, you would never get a seat on a Metropolitan Line train for the number of shades already occupying them. Yes.'

'Yes, what?'

A policeman came by on foot, waving his arms and shouting at someone unseen to back up.

'Yes, I do think it possible that Eleanor Quarrel is still alive. The thought occurred to me the moment I read that the *Framlingham Castle* had gone down with all hands and passengers.' He put his flask back into his satchel. 'But I dismissed the idea as too optimistic.'

I shot him a glance. 'But you hated her. Why would you not want her to die?'

'Oh, I wanted her die but not like a bather who had got into difficulties.' Our cab jerked forwards. 'She should have choked and struggled on the end of a rope and I should have been there to watch. She should have been given to the anatomists to dissect. After Corder was hanged for the Red Barn Murder the surgeon tanned his skin for a book binding. Imagine having Mrs Quarrel's hide covering your written account of the case.'

'What a disgusting idea,' I said and he shrugged.

'What she did to the living was worse than anything that could be done to her dead.' He fastened his satchel straps.

'There are four reasonable explanations of what happened to Eleanor Quarrel. First, that she went down with the ship. Second, that she got off the ship, most likely with the pilot, before it went into the open sea. That is easily checked. Third, that she survived the shipwreck and was picked up by a passing vessel when the storm subsided, though this would probably have been widely reported.' We came to a standstill again. 'Fourth, that she was not on the ship when it sailed. Numbers one and four are the most credible events and, when you have a number of options, dismissing the likely ones does not make the unlikely ones any more likely. When this case is settled I shall devote some time to investigating further, but at present we have murderers to apprehend who are all too definitely alive. Let us deal with that first.'

A scrawny boy scrambled under our horse pursued by a skinny girl calling, 'Stop, thief.' They were both almost naked.

'What could she have had that would be worth stealing?' I wondered.

'Everyone has something,' Sidney Grice said, 'a coin or a cup of water, even an idea. Desperate men will fight over pebbles.'

Charlotte Street had developed in an ad hoc fashion but what it lacked in the uniform stylishness of Gower Street, it made up with dozens of different buildings ranging from the quirky to the imposing. The Prince of Wales Theatre stood on the corner, its once-grand facade more than a little tattered now.

'Clear off,' my guardian said to a respectably dressed lady rattling an orphans' charity box. Even by his own standards he was especially ratty that afternoon. 'You might as well throw your money down the drain,' he grunted as I gave her sixpence.

We passed the Sass Academy of Art as a wan young woman came out wrapped in a brown woollen coat, not long enough to hide her bare calves, and Sidney Grice turned away in a horror which I had never seen him display for a slaughtered body.

A police van went by with an old woman standing peering out. She had a clay pipe clenched between her gums and was gripping a bar with one hand and waving merrily to all and sundry with the other.

Gallop's Snuff Emporium had a small bow window crammed with glass jars and coloured pots piled so high that hardly any light filtered through or between them into the shop.

A small bent man stood side-on behind the counter, his head twisted at an odd angle towards us and his back hunched. He had a grey goatee dangling down his chest. 'Good morning, sir, miss.'

'Mr Gallop?' my guardian asked.

'Warrington Tusker Gallop it is, sir,' Mr Gallop confirmed cheerily. 'How may I be of—'

'Who is in the back room?' my guardian demanded.

'Why, nobody.'

'Get down!' Sidney Grice shouted.

'I am not standing on—' Mr Gallop jerked his head away. 'Ouch.' His hand went to his neck.

There was a scuffling noise and I looked across just in time to see a thin tube being withdrawn from a knothole in a cream-painted door behind him. There were running footsteps and another door banged.

'Blowpipe,' my guardian said and scrambled over the counter, ignoring the pyramid of snuffboxes and row of ornamented humidors he scattered in his progress. 'Deal with him.' He jumped down, wrenched open the door and disappeared through it.

Mr Gallop put his hand to his neck. 'Oh dear,' he said and, before I could stop him, pulled out what looked like a bamboo meat skewer. His hand was covered in blood. 'Goodness, that stings.'

I lifted the flap and rushed round. There was a chair behind him and I guided him into it. I reached for my handkerchief to staunch the steady flow down his collar, but when I turned back Warrington Tusker Gallop was dead.

58

Hunting Monkeys

'DO NOT TOUCH it.' Sidney Grice came back into the room. 'It will have been poisoned.' The skewer was still in the dead man's hand.

'But who?'

'He was out of the rear exit before I got into the room and he locked it from the outside. He could be halfway across the city by now.' My guardian put on his pince-nez and bent over. 'This dart has been hollowed out.' He clicked his tongue thoughtfully. 'I have seen blowpipes being used by tribesmen in the Amazon Basin to hunt monkeys and I have heard of them being used in tribal wars, but this is the first case I have ever come across in this country.'

'What a trophy for you,' I said acidly.

'Indeed.' His glass eye glowed red in the light through a jar as he went by the window, bolted the front door and pulled the blind down. I saw the mirror-image *closed* in black through the blue cloth. 'Come here.' I followed him to the doorway behind the counter and he held out an arm to halt me. 'Luckily, Mr Gallop was too mean to employ a cleaner.' The floor was thick with dust. 'What do you make of those?'

'Footprints and scuffmarks.'

'The footprints to the right near the wall are mine, but what do the scuffmarks tell you?' He pointed with his cane.

I looked at the long imprints. 'Something was dragged along the floor.'

'Nonsense.' His cane moved over the outlines. 'The curved front edge is a knee and the trail behind it is a trouser leg.'

'So we know we are dealing with a man.'

'Or a woman dressed as a man – but probably a man. See those?'

'A toe print in front of the knee and to the right of it, and another less distinct one behind the trouser mark.'

'I knew your eyes would be of some use to you one day.' He took hold of the jamb and leaned low into the room over the marks. 'The tip of my little finger to that of my thumb when I stretch my hand is exactly eight inches, so we are looking for a tall man with small feet.'

'Like the print at Piggety's in the crushed glass.'

'Possibly, though the heel shape is different over there, so if it is the same person he has changed his boots.' He looked up and round and pulled himself straight. 'I think we can disturb these now. Lift your skirts as much as is commensurate with decency and go in first.' He ushered me into a low-ceilinged storeroom, with sparsely used shelves on either side – a few old bottles, some rolls of cloth, some curling account books, all covered in grime and clothed in cobwebs. 'First impressions?'

'There is a strong smell in here – a sort of perfume.'

He breathed in through his nose. 'I can just about smell something. A scented snuff?'

'No. It is more like a toiletry but it is difficult to tell with the room being so musty – a sort of cologne, I think. Perhaps it was a woman after all.'

'Or a foreigner,' Mr G muttered. 'Now, let us see the room as the murderer must have.' He pulled the door to. 'Wait a moment for our eyes to adjust. What can you hear outside?'

I listened. 'Very little.' And waited for a sarcastic remark but he only said, 'That is because there is very little to hear – except the two dogs barking and the cries of a ragman above the traffic.'

'I think I can hear the dogs and the man but I cannot hear the traffic.' Four circular cores and two slits of light came through the planks from the shop.

'That is because it is distant so the exit opens into a back alley.' He genuflected to position his knee over the imprint. 'See how much further back the toe is than mine.'

'A good two or three inches.'

'Also, if I were using a blowpipe, I would put it through this lower hole and look through the one above, but the killer used the two top holes. He must be at least five foot ten or eleven. I have a very good view of the shop from here but the side where Gallop stood is slightly obscured. The murderer could much more easily have fired at me or you, so he was clearly intent upon his victim.'

He brought a miniature safety lamp out of his satchel and lit it, the yellow glare momentarily blinding me. I shaded my eyes and turned to see an old packing crate.

'He must have sat on this.'

Sidney Grice came over to inspect it. 'And for quite a while, judging by the amount of shuffling about on the case and floor... and what do you make of those footprints?'

He bent over and held the lamp close, and I peered over his shoulder.

'The right foot is turned in a bit.'

'Good... and it has a less sharp outline, showing that it drags slightly. So he has a limp but not a bad one, more likely a sprained ankle than a game knee or hip.' He strode across to the back door. Hardly any light came in from the outside but a rectangle of day seeped underneath through a gap. 'What do you think happened?'

'The murderer entered through the back door.' He opened his mouth as I added hastily, 'Or else he was known to Mr Gallop and came in through the shop.'

'You must get out of the habit of saying things because you think I want you to say them. I could bring along Cook for that,' he said. 'Just look at the pattern of the prints.'

I followed them carefully with my eye. 'It was the back door.'

'But how did he gain access?'

'Perhaps it was not locked.'

He tutted. 'Who leaves an entrance unlocked in this metropolis? Use your eyes, girl.'

There were more marks on the floor in front of the back door, four of them with long straight edges overlapping. 'Newspaper,' I said. 'I have done it myself as a child. You slide the paper under the door, push the key out with a small length of wire so that it falls on the paper, and pull the paper back.'

Sidney Grice rubbed his hands. 'At this rate I shall be able to leave the business to you and retire to my estate in Dorset by the end of the year. What next?'

'He went and sat on that box and then crept—'

'How do you know he crept?' He stroked a stain on the wall.

'Prints close together and very well delineated – small careful steps.'

'Then what?'

'He kneeled there, looking into the shop through a knothole, pushed his blowpipe through the other hole and fired at Mr Gallop. Either it was just Mr Gallop he intended to kill, or you alerted him and he panicked and ran.'

My guardian blew out his lamp and we went back into the shop where Warrington Tusker Gallop sat in his chair, his head still to one side. Sidney Grice went to him, tried to twist his head and pushed on his shoulders, and Mr Gallop tipped back. 'The spinal curvatures were certainly not feigned,' he said. 'So he could not have carried out the other murders himself or have been of much assistance in them.' He slid his lantern into an asbestos pouch to save his satchel from being scorched and took the dart with his tweezers from the dead man's loose grip. 'This is not from the Amazon. It has been sharpened with a cut-throat razor and the fletch is made from the feathers of a male *Turdus philomelos*, the song thrush. How did he die?'

The eyes were still open and fixed on me. 'Almost instantly, with no pain except from the actual wounding, and no fighting for breath or convulsions.'

He clicked his tongue. 'The tribesmen I came across use curare, which suffocates their prey. He would have died in a similar manner to Horatio Green if that had been used.' He dropped into a crouch and prodded the floors with his finger. 'Blood,' he remarked.

'Mr Gallop did bleed quite heavily when he pulled the dart out,' I informed him.

'Describe the bleeding.' He scrutinized the bare boards through his pince-nez.

'There was a gush and then a steady flow. So it did not hit an artery,' I told him.

'This blood is in droplets.' He jumped up and looked from side to side. 'Where did it come from?'

'Well, surely, Mr Gallop,' I said.

'Nonsense.' He wiped his finger on a cloth. 'I have told you before to look for patterns, whether it be fingermarks or pavements. The droplets form a flattened cone, the base being near Gallop's feet and the apex near the door into the storeroom.'

'So the murderer blew blood through the pipe,' I said and he looked at me questioningly. 'Perhaps he had a wound in his mouth or a severe chest condition such as consumption.'

'Perhaps,' my guardian conceded. He picked up a pot which had been smashed as he vaulted the counter, and sniffed the contents. 'Come,' Mr G said. 'I shall send a message to the inimitable Inspector Quigley from home.' He stopped on the threshold. 'I have had an important thought.'

'About the murderer?'

'Good heavens, no. But it occurs to me,' he pinched the dimple on his chin, 'that a little snuff, possibly a menthol mix, might help clear my nasal passages and restore my olfactory organs to their full and remarkable sensitivities.' He stepped outside. 'Though I shall have to seek another supplier now, of course.'

'How inconvenient.' The bell clinked weakly as I closed the door.

There was no shortage of cabs on the street, and a weak sun came through the clouds and filthy air as we clambered aboard.

'I had thought about visiting Lady Foskett today,' he said, 'but she will never see me at this hour.'

Our horse looked lively and a red plume waved merrily on its head.

'Would you like to know how Inspector Pound is progressing?'

'Not especially.'

A cart in front dropped a bundle of empty sacks, too late for us to avoid, and we bumped over it. Children were already scrambling for salvage.

'I saw Dr Berry this morning.'

'Oh, really?' He tightened a strap on his satchel.

'She said she would call on us this evening.'

'I will probably be out.' He polished the handle of his cane with his glove. 'I must have a second flask manufactured or I shall be forced to go without my tea on every return journey.'

But a moment later he was whistling between his teeth, something which might have been intended to be Beethoven's Fifth but may have been nothing at all.

59

Rubber Boots and Kisses

DR BERRY CAME in very wet.

'I thought I would be safe enough just walking from the hospital but Zeus was waiting behind a cloud with a gigantic bucket of water just for me.' She struggled out of her sopping cape and handed it to Molly. 'They have a very childish sense of humour, these Greek gods.'

'Like most men,' I said.

'Except Mr Grice.' Molly hung the cape on the coat stand, creating an instant puddle on the floor tiles. 'He is too clever to have a sense of humour at all.'

'I am afraid he is out at the moment but he should be back soon.' I directed Dr Berry to the study and into my armchair, pulling up a chair for myself from the table.

'Why do you not use the other armchair?'

'It belongs to Mr G.'

She furrowed her brow. 'He cannot be an easy man to live with.'

'He has his ways,' I said, 'but I am getting used to them. Did you see Inspector Pound?'

She looked very businesslike in a black coat and white blouse.

'He seems to be healing well. I have made him up a tonic.' She produced a brown bottle two thirds full of medicine. 'But please do not tell anybody. We doctors can be very possessive of our patients and if Mr Sweeney found out I was interfering... well, I am there under sufferance as it is.' She looked at me. 'You seem very agitated, March.'

'We witnessed another murder today.' I told her about Warrington Gallop. 'And now we only have two members left.'

'Goodness.' Dr Berry fingered her hair. 'I am getting very worried about you, March. This is no profession for a young girl.'

'I am not as young as I seem, Dr Berry.'

'Call me Dorna, and please do not be offended.'

I shifted in my chair to face her. 'You of all people should understand. You must have seen such horrors as I have, and I believe that I can help save lives by studying the forensic sciences, as surely as you can with the practice of medicine. I would prefer people not to be murdered just as you would prefer your patients not to be mutilated in factories or ravaged by disease.'

'But you put yourself in such danger.' She wiped her right eye.

'Why, Dorna, whatever is wrong.'

'Oh, March, I feel so vacuous.' She took a handkerchief from her handbag. 'When you first came to my house I thought Sidney was one of the most objectionable men I have ever met and I have come across many in my battle for recognition.'

'But what has happened?'

She unfolded the handkerchief. 'As I got to know him I began to see another side.' She blew her nose. 'And I found myself increasingly… attracted to him.'

'But, Dorna, that is lovely.'

'No, March. It is not.'

'But I am sure he has a good opinion of you. You should have seen how angry he was about those newspaper reports.' I looked at the floor and Dorna touched my hand.

'I admire Sidney enormously, March. He is quite the cleverest man I have ever met. Why, he knows more about some aspects of medicine than I do, and I am so very fond of him. But Sidney only loves three things – his work—'

'You cannot blame him for that.'

'I do not blame him for anything.'

'And second?'

She crumpled her handkerchief into a ball. 'He could never love me as much as he loves his past.' She shuddered.

'I do not understand.'

Dr Berry stood up. 'There are things that you should know, March, but it is not for me to tell you.'

I stood too, and she put away the handkerchief and reached out her hand to stroke my cheek.

'What happened that was so terrible that I cannot be told?'

She put two fingers to my lips. 'Oh, dear, sweet March. You have such a heart. It is not only Sidney that I have come to care for.' Her left hand stroked my hair. 'Have you ever been kissed?'

'Yes, of course.'

'I mean really kissed, long and tenderly, like this?'

'Not for a long time,' I said and kissed her back.

Forgive me, Edward, but for one fragment of one second when I closed my eyes I could almost imagine it was you, somehow returned to me whole and beautiful and alive, and that all the pain and guilt and horror had been washed away.

I opened my eyes and it all flooded back.

'Oh, March.' Her face was flushed. 'Put your hand to me.'

'I do not—' She touched my mouth with her fingertips and took my right hand in her left, and placed it on her blouse.

'Feel how fast my heart beats for you.'

I felt the cotton and through it a pendant and a pulse, and her breath short on my cheek.

'Someone might come.'

Dorna sighed and pulled slowly away and pinched the bridge of her nose, pressing hard on the corners of her eyes.

'I have come to tell you that I might be going away, March. A permanent position has come up in Edinburgh and I shall not get such an opportunity again.'

'But when will you go?'

'At the end of the month, if I take it. They want me to start as soon as I can, so I may not see you again, March.'

I shuddered. 'The last woman who said goodbye to me like this was a murderess.'

She raised my jaw and looked deep into me. 'Make sure Inspector Pound gets his medicine.'

'What was the third thing Mr G loves?' I asked, and her hand dropped from my face to the cameo brooch on her jacket.

'Why, you, of course.'

And I smiled unhappily. 'At best he tolerates me.'

'Oh, March.' She put a stray lock of hair behind my ear. 'He has such a good opinion of you, but he is afraid to make you swollen-headed. He loves you more than anyone.'

'Or anything?'

Her face fell. 'I did not say that.' She clipped her bag shut. 'Perhaps you could tell your guardian for me.'

'Surely you can wait and tell him yourself?'

'Tell me what?' I spun round to see my guardian coming into the room. 'Good evening, Dr Berry. I trust you are well.'

Dorna Berry flushed. 'Oh, I did not hear you.'

'I did not mean to startle you, but Molly already had the front door open to polish it and I was trying out my new boots.' I looked down and saw that his feet were clad in two clumsy black lumps. 'They are made of rubber,' he said, 'which means that no cattle have to be slaughtered and skinned to provide them. They also have the advantage of being completely waterproof and, as I have just demonstrated, much quieter than the leather and nails that one is accustomed to clack around in.'

'Excuse me.' I brushed past them both and went upstairs for a gin. I could not flood away the memory of what had just happened, or my disgust with myself, but I could wash away the taste.

I was not trying to replace you – why would I want to and how on earth could I? But I had such a hunger for love. It comes so rarely in this world that, for a broken instant, I thought I had glimpsed it.

I smoked a cigarette. It was my last one and the tobacconist would close soon, but I dare not go down. I could not see her and I was frightened to see him. He might have looked human.

60

Word Games and Pickled Legs

IT WAS A chilly night but Sidney Grice rarely felt the cold. We sat either side of the unlit fire, which only served to cool us with the draught from the chimney.

'My father used to say one sack of coal will keep you warm all year,' he reminisced. 'Whenever it is chilly, you go down to the cellar for it and, by the time you have lugged it up the steps, you are warm enough to take it down again.'

'Why do you speak of your father in the past tense?'

My guardian rubbed his shoulder. 'I have not communicated with him for nine years and three weeks.'

I wrapped a shawl around me. 'But whyever not?'

'We are not worthy of each other.' He folded his arms. 'What were you asking Dr Berry to tell me when I arrived?'

'She said nothing?'

'Nothing of any great import.'

'I think she had some news, but it is not for me to tell it.' I pulled my shawl tighter. 'I was thinking about those messages claiming to be from Mr Piggety.'

'And what conclusion did you arrive at?'

'It may be nothing…'

'Almost certainly.' He picked a speck from his lapel.

'But it struck me that they both read like a children's word game.'

'How so?' A lump of soot fell and burst on to the hearth.

'Well, I cannot remember exactly what they said…'

'I have them here.' We went to his desk where the telegram was folded inside McHugh's *Explosive Devices, Their Construction and Concealment and Divers Means of Discovering Their Whereabouts and Thereafter Rendering Them Impotent.* 'It is patently a code but I find myself as yet unable to break it.'

He flattened the paper out.

MR GRICE YOU ARE LACKING VITAL INFORMATION COME FACTORY THREE EXACTLY NO LATER OR INDEED ANY EARLIER YOU SHALL GET INSTRUCTIONS BY NEXT POST YOU MUST OPEN LETTER UP IMMEDIATELY RECEIVED KEY HAS BEEN ATTACHED TO NOTE LEFT DOOR LOCKED SECURELY I SHALL NOT OPEN SO NEED TO OPEN YOURSELF HOPE OBEY ORDERS FROM PROMETHEUS PIGGETY ESQUIRE DONT FORGET KEY OR YOU REALLY CANNOT MAKE AN ENTRY.

'We used to write messages where the first letter of every word made up other words.'

He grunted and began to print in a hand so small I could hardly read it.

MGYALVICFTENLOIAEYSGIBNPYMOLUIRKHBATNLDLSISNOSN-
TOYHOOFPPEDFKOYRCMAE

'That does not appear to make much sense.'

'What if we reverse it?' I suggested. 'EAMCR… No, that does not work. Sometimes we would use the letter before or after in the alphabet.'

He printed out DZLBQ and then FBNDS.

'It could be two or more letters in either direction.' He tried a few combinations, and as he did so I looked again at the first letters, and then it sprang out at me.

'My life,' I said and he looked down.

'Of course. What a dullard you have been. It uses the first letters of alternate words.' He wrote them down.

MY LIFE LIES IN YOUR HANDS SO NO HOPE FOR ME

'Now the letter that came with the key said...' He had it inside a copy of *Exchange and Mart*.

GRICE THIS KEY
OPENS
THE OUTER
DOOR
LOCK
TURN
ANTI CLOCKWISE TO
GAIN ENTRY PIG GETY

Sidney Grice wrinkled his brow briefly and printed GKT.

'No, that is no use.'

'Try starting with the second word.'

'I was about to.' He wrote TOOLATE. 'Too late.' He cricked his neck to look back and up at me. 'They are toying with me, March. Do you still think I am imagining it?'

We went back to our chairs.

'Is that all it is?' I asked. 'A game?'

My guardian closed his eyes and from his heavy regular chest movements I might have thought that he was asleep, except for the two halfpennies clicking around in his left hand while his right hand massaged his brow. I watched him for twenty minutes while my mind whirled in its search for a solution. Then, without opening his eyes, he spun the coins high in the air, caught them and announced, 'I requested another interview with Baroness Foskett this morning but she refuses to see me.'

'I do not think she believes she is in danger,' I said.

'Who' – my guardian opened his eyes – 'is in danger from whom?'

We heard a thump and turned to see the window splotted with horse manure. 'Botheration.' He blinked and his socket welled with blood. 'A cat-o'-ten-tails would be too good for them.'

61

Macbeth and the Guinea Prize

SIDNEY GRICE WAS usually a dapper dresser but that evening he had excelled himself – white tie and tails and a long black cloak lined in red silk.

'Are you going to the opera?' I asked and his face darkened.

'Almost as bad.' He selected a cane. 'Dorna has invited me to the theatre – some Shakespearean tripe – and she had already obtained the tickets so I did not see how I could get out of it. And you know how I hate to offend people.'

'You would rather kill yourself,' I said.

'And deprive the world of my genius? Never.' He swapped his cane for another.

'Which play are you going to see?'

He frimped up his bow in the mirror. 'Oh, *Hamlet* or something equally dreary – *Macbeth*, I think.'

'Actually, I was thinking about that quotation…'

'Yes, yes.' He polished the nap on his top hat. 'We can discuss your opinions on henpecked Celtic regicides when we are stranded on a desert island and have dredged every other topic of conversation to the apogee of exhaustion. Where is my cab? I shall be even later than I hoped.'

'Yes, but speaking of *Hamlet*, when—'

'*Macbeth*, March. Do pay attention.' There were four sharp raps on the door and Sidney Grice threw it open. 'At last.'

A cabby stood on the steps in a short woollen jacket and

scuffed bowler. He put his arm over his eyes. 'Cripes, Mr Grice, you quite bedazzled me. Goin' to arrest the queen, are we?'

'I do not know where *you* are going,' my guardian said, 'but *I* am going to witness the murder of a Highland king.'

'Blimey. Can't you put a stop to it?'

My guardian shivered. 'I am two hundred and seventy-six years too late, I fear.'

'I wasn't that slow in coming,' the driver protested. 'Oh, and the men wanted me to ask – does the guinea prize still hold?'

'Until further notice.'

'How will we know the other one?'

'She has a large brown birthmark on the left of her face.'

'So does my greyhound,' the cabby grumbled and went back to his cab.

'Do not wait up.' Sidney Grice went down the steps. 'I shall be too depressed for conversation.'

'She got it wrong,' I called after him, and he turned reluctantly.

'Who got what wrong?'

'The baroness. She said *How weary, flat, stale and unprofitable seem to me all the uses of this world*,' I recited. 'But she should have said, *How weary, stale, flat, et cetera*. I do not suppose it matters.'

My guardian's cheek ticked. 'You knew that the first time we saw her?'

'Well, I noticed, but it did not seem important.'

'*Important?*' The wind whipped at his cloak, wrapping it around his legs. 'All clues are important.'

'I did not know it was a clue.'

'For gawdsake,' the cabby complained from his high seat.

'Of course you did not.' He fought to untangle his legs and keep his hat on at the same time. 'That is why you will never be a detective.'

I took two steps back and slammed the door as hard as I could.

'I do that,' Molly said, running up to see what was happening. 'When you are both out and clients call. *Stop botherating him*, I say. *He's got too much to worry about already*.'

'I would advise you not to tell Mr Grice that,' I said and Molly screwed up her nose while she thought about it.

'I will take your advise,' she decided at last and went back down the basement stairs.

I ran upstairs to bring Spirit down and we played with the tassels on a cushion until she grew tired and fell asleep on it, and I tried to read Jane Austen, but it was all simpering girls whose only ambition was to marry. The next thing I knew Sidney Grice was shaking my shoulder.

'Are you awake?'

'Very nearly.' My first thought was to hide Spirit, but she was already standing on her hind legs and trying to claw the hem of his cloak. Somewhat to my surprise, he ignored her.

'You should not sleep upright. It drains blood from the brain.'

He laid his hat on the table.

'I am sorry I did not mention Baroness Foskett's misquotation sooner,' I said and he piffed.

'Perhaps it means nothing.' My guardian unclipped his cloak. 'Perhaps it means everything. I shall find out which.'

'Do you think she was telling us something?'

He puffed. 'I am not even sure she is mentally continent.'

'So how was the play?'

'Unutterably tedious,' he said. 'The only saving grace is that we missed the beginning because Dorna could not find her glove.'

'At least *Macbeth* is one of the shorter plays,' I consoled him. 'You did not have to sit through *Hamlet*. That is a much longer play, though you might have found the murder more…'

Mr G looked at me closely. 'More what?'

'Unusual,' I whispered.

'When you have ceased exhibiting a hitherto unsuspected talent for imitating alabaster statues, perhaps you would like to tell me what you are talking about.'

'Dear God,' I said. 'How could I have been so stupid?'

'I have often asked myself that.'

'Do you know how Hamlet's father was killed?'

'I was not engaged on that case but I suspect you would like to tell me, preferably before I am too decrepit to care.'

'By poison,' I said, 'through his ear.'

Mr G's face tightened. 'You knew that?'

'Of course I did. I have just told you so.'

He took off his scarf. 'And yet you did not tell me?'

'You hate it when I talk about poetry or plays. Besides, it may not really be—'

Sidney Grice flung his cloak and scarf on to the back of his chair and Spirit darted under his desk. 'What affliction did Green suffer from – apart from obnoxiousness and toothache?'

'Earache.' I sat up. 'Do you really think somebody could have put cyanide in his ear?'

'No.' Sidney Grice looked absently at Spirit as she came out with a ball of paper. 'I think that *Mr Green* put cyanide into Mr Green's ear. Remember he had the vicar with the same ailment to whom he showed his medicine? Remember the boys who came into his shop? I remarked that it was an intriguing incident at the time. The only reason a street creature would ransack a shop and not steal anything is because he was under strict instruction and being paid already. The murderer did not want to risk any of them being apprehended with stolen goods. A captured minion points a finger, no matter how vaguely, towards his master.'

'Speaking of fingers,' I said. 'What has happened to yours?'

The top of his right first finger had a cratered ulcer with dead white edges. He looked down as if interested to find it in that condition. 'Oh that. I burnt it. Where was I? Oh yes. What could be easier than to slip a poisoned capsule into his pill box in the confusion?'

'But how could anyone know which one he would use the next day?'

'Simplicity itself. The capsules are made of soft wax. You lightly press them so that they stick together and place the poisoned one on top.' He rang for tea. 'I called in at St Agatha's Rectory on the way back from a nightcap with Dr Berry.'

'I bet they were pleased to see you. It is well after midnight.'

'Well, you would lose your wager.' He sat on the arm of his chair. 'They were most irate and informed me that I shall fare badly on Judgement Day. But, more relevantly, they were adamant that a Reverend Golding did not and never has resided there.'

I thought about it. 'But if a capsule of prussic acid leaked into Mr Green's ear surely he would have been in agony.'

'I shall verify the point, though rather more articulately, with Dorna, but it is probable that Horatio Green had been using oil of cloves for years in his ear, and that you could smell this rather than his dental treatment.'

'I could also smell nitrous oxide,' I said more snappily than I had intended. I knew it was unreasonable but I disliked the thought of him discussing our case with another woman, but he resumed, seemingly unaware. 'In which case the oil would have corroded most of the nerve endings in his ear and Eustachian tube long ago. Also, he had probably administered laudanum to himself before his trip to the late and unlamented Silas Braithwaite, to assuage his anxiety and relieve his pain. On top of this, I believe, some dentists get their patients to rinse with a solution of cocaine for its analgesic effects, so he would not have felt anything much until the acid drained into the back of his throat and down his oesophagus.' He sat on his scarf in the chair. 'I am still not sure if the murderer could know that the capsule would melt while Green was here or if it was pure luck,' he pondered as Spirit, ignoring my warning signals, jumped up beside him.

I clicked my fingers and he winced. 'When you told Mr Green to stop talking twaddle,' I recalled, 'I think he was trying to tell you that he inserted the capsules after breakfast so...'

Sidney Grice tickled Spirit's ear. 'The first cup of tea he had after that would have been hot enough to melt the wax.' He dangled his watch on its chain for Spirit to toy with. 'And, unusually, the pot was steaming that morning.'

'So, if you had not interrupted—'

'What a charming creature,' Mr G interrupted and allowed himself a tiny smile. 'Get rid of it.'

62

Stallions, Sticks and Sandwiches

I WENT BACK to my room and lay on the bed, and looked at the spidery cracks radiating from an old lamp hook in the ceiling, much too tired to even think about sleep.

You rode a black stallion. It reared and I was afraid it would throw you or bring its great metalled hoofs crashing on my head, but you laughed and steadied it and reached down to pull me up, lifting me as if I weighed nothing, almost floating me into the saddle behind you, and I put my arms round your waist and my face against your broad back. I could feel your sword handle dig into my thigh and the roughness of your woollen tunic damp on my cheek, and I could smell it too, like freshly scythed hay. Your horse reared again but I was safe now. I held on tight and knew that you would never let me fall. But even in my happiness I knew that I would betray you and that any moment you would turn, a faceless horror, towards me and that the nightmare would start all over again because the nightmare was always true, but the stirrup was very tight on my boot and it was tugging quite hard. I called out.

'Edward!'

But Molly was shaking my foot and saying, 'Wake up, miss, or his nibs will go without you.'

I stretched. 'Go?'

'Without you,' she repeated.

I forced my eyes open. 'Go where?'

'Baryness Fostick.'

I sat up. 'Give me five minutes and do *not* let him go without me. Hang on to his ankles if necessary.'

Molly looked doubtful. 'I'm not sure he would like that, miss.'

I climbed off the bed. 'Just tell him I am coming.'

Sidney Grice was winding down the flag and Molly was dashing along the hall with his flask as I trotted down the stairs. He looked up at me. 'March.' He had reinserted his eye and his face was fresh and clear. 'I thought you were planning on spending the whole day in bed.'

'What time is it?' I glanced at the clock as I reached the bottom step. 'Why, it is very nearly seven o'clock.'

He took out his watch. 'Six forty-eight and fifteen seconds.'

'Have you eaten?'

He dabbed his lips as if expecting to find crumbs. 'I made do with toast and prune juice and a very good pot of tea, but there was no time for eggs, I am afraid.'

I grabbed my coat. 'But I have had nothing.'

He looked along his cane. 'You have only yourself to blame, if you must slumber your life away.' He dropped his stick back into the rack and chose another, swishing it, handle down as if rehearsing a golf shot.

'I have had less than three hours' sleep.'

'Three hours!' Molly hugged herself. 'What luxurousness. He had me up half the night boiling kettles and making bread sandwiches.'

Sidney Grice hummed atonally as he slipped his arms into his Ulster.

'But we always breakfast at eight.' I grabbed my cloak and shook myself awake. 'Has something happened?'

'There was a possible sighting at about six o'clock.' He selected a bowler.

'Primrose McKay?' I fastened the clasp and he nodded.

'The driver could not be sure, but he thought he spotted her going north from Richmond.'

'Do you think she could be heading for Kew?'

He smacked some dust off the rim with his gloves. 'What I think is irrelevant. It is what might happen that matters.' His face was grim. 'Presumably the baroness is taking my telegraphed report seriously, for she has agreed to see us immediately.'

There was a hammering on the door and Molly opened it to a corpulent blotchy-faced cabby in a long coachman's coat. 'Did you want this cab today or next year?'

'That is a fatuous question if you care to consider it, which I do not,' my guardian told him. 'If you are quite ready, Miss Middleton…' He slipped the flask into his satchel. 'You may sate your epicurean excesses when we return. In the meantime, we have a murderer to catch.'

*

Cutteridge was waiting for us and we were much in need of his lantern for, though the sun had risen to the left of us as we travelled through the city, there was another pea-souper and even the snarls of the mastiffs were dampened in the choking air.

'They have been very restless,' he said, 'especially as you instructed me not to feed them, sir.'

'They will be fed soon enough.' Sidney Grice lit his safety lantern. 'How quiet it is. The whole world might be listening to us.'

We made our way slowly along the path, Cutteridge leading and my guardian to the rear, following the paraffin glares and placing our feet carefully into the shadows.

'I saw a dead adder there last time,' I said and Sidney Grice stopped.

'How did it die?'

'I do not know. It was rotten and its head had been chewed off.'

'Dear God,' he said softly as we reached the gravelled clearing.

Mordent House was half-hidden from us that morning, lost in the heavy fog and only breaking through it into darkness. At the top of the steps Cutteridge paused. 'Have you come to save her ladyship, sir?'

My guardian took off his hat. 'If the baroness can be saved then I shall do it this day, but I fear I may be too late.'

The old butler looked alarmed.

'Has anybody else called?' I questioned him. 'A lady with long golden hair and a mark on her face?'

'No one, miss.' He glanced anxiously at Sidney Grice.

'Is there any way she could have got past you?' I asked as we entered the hall. It was gloomier than I had ever known it.

'Not whilst I have life,' Cutteridge vowed, and we stood in the dank oppressiveness, listening to him make his way up the crooked stairs as the house groaned forbiddingly.

Mr G went to the window, pulled back the curtain and crouched as if to peer out of the lower pane. 'Not only has the lacewing been removed but the entire web has been replaced.'

'What an astonishing turn of events.'

'Do you not understand?' He traced the web with his finger. 'I said *replaced* not *rebuilt*. This web was constructed by a different spider – the same species but with structurally sound legs.'

'Perhaps its leg healed,' I suggested as he scrabbled about in the dust on the floor. 'It might have just sprained it sliding down the banister with a tray of drinks.'

'No. Here it is.' He held up the squashed remains for my inspection.

'I did not realize you were so fond of it.'

But Sidney Grice was not listening. He had shuffled back to the window and was busily pulling the web apart. 'Dear God,' he said again as he crammed his pince-nez on to his nose. 'I fear the murderer is already in the house.'

He let the mildewed satin flop back over the glass and got to his feet.

'Then we must go upstairs immediately.'

Mr G stood and stared out into the garden. 'On the contrary, we must wait.'

'For what?' I thought about my own question. 'But surely the baroness could not have killed them?'

'I have been a fool, March.' He spun round, his lantern almost going out. 'Baroness Foskett is the kindest, most gentle woman I have ever met.'

I coughed. 'That is not the Baroness Foskett I know.'

He turned his back on me. 'Then perhaps you do not know her at all.'

'Perhaps you are seeing her as she was,' I challenged him. 'Perhaps she became embittered by her bereavements.'

He banged his cane on the floor, the impact travelling through the empty hall and passageways, to the masked ceiling and through the faded rooms. 'Lady Foskett's heart was broken by the disappearance of her son and her husband's death, but she turned to good works. She spent her fortune on the charities that you only witter about and, when her fortune was gone, she wrapped herself in mourning so deep that the eye of man could not penetrate it.'

'But why are we discussing this rather than trying to protect her?'

'The numbers are against us,' my guardian said.

Cutteridge returned. 'Her ladyship will see you now, sir, miss.' And my guardian sighed. 'Oh, Cutteridge, good and faithful, I only hope that you are telling the truth.'

The old man stiffened. 'I would never lie to you, sir.'

And Sidney Grice patted his arm just once. 'And I have never doubted your integrity.'

'I must ask you to put your light out, sir.'

Mr G did as he was bidden and slipped it into its pouch before we crept, well apart and close to the wall, up the swaying staircase, not able even to see the floor of the great hall so far below us, while the corridor was filled with a blackness so heavy that Cutteridge's lantern, as he placed it on the boards, could scarcely break through it.

My guardian stopped and crouched so suddenly that I almost toppled over him.

'Fun,' he whispered.

'What is?'

Cutteridge knocked once before pushing the door open to reveal the room, wavering in the candlelight, with the gauze box and the two chairs to which he directed us.

'Sidney,' the speaking horn hissed. 'To what do we owe this allegedly urgent intrusion?'

'The time has come,' my guardian said. 'This great dynasty is swaying on its rotten foundations and is about to come crashing down.'

'Are you presuming to threaten me, you ill-bred—'

'The Grices go back a thousand years,' Sidney Grice interrupted, 'and, should I choose to continue the line, it will survive another millennium. The Fosketts are drowning in their own filth.'

'How dare you—'

'I cannot hear you.'

'I said—'

'I heard what was said,' my guardian broke in. 'Loud and clear. But I cannot hear the voice behind it.'

The smell of incense was even stronger today.

'I do not know what you mean.'

Sidney Grice leaned forward. 'When somebody talks through a speaking tube you hear their voice *and* the magnified sound. I can only hear the sound.'

'You are not making yourself clear.' There was a long pause. 'My acid-corroded vocal cords are very weak.'

'Fifteen point two-two-five-nine-six-six,' my guardian said.

'What are you talking about?' The voice shook a little.

'The logarithm of today's date to the first six decimal points. You must have got up very early to have scratched that on the window, Baroness' – his tone became mocking – 'Lady... Parthena... Foskett.' And as he spoke Sidney Grice undid the straps of his satchel.

'Mr Grice,' Cutteridge said, 'I must ask you not to address her ladyship so disrespectfully.'

'Nor shall I.' There was a slight scuffling noise and Sidney Grice sprang up. Cutteridge snatched the air behind his shoulder, flinging the chair aside as my guardian rushed for the gauze box.

'Save me, Cutteridge.'

Sidney Grice whipped round and I saw in the candlelight that he had his revolver in his hand. 'Stand where you are.'

Cutteridge stopped in his tracks. 'I do not know why you are doing this, sir – I can only assume that you have gone quite mad. But you must know that the threat of death will not deter me from doing my duty.'

Sidney Grice took two steps back and the old servant took two forward. My guardian took aim. 'Do not make me do it, Cutteridge.' And Cutteridge regarded him wonderingly. 'I pushed you on a swing, Master Sidney. I gave you rides on my shoulders.'

'Oh, for heaven's sake,' my guardian said and tossed the gun on the floor. I leaped off my chair but Cutteridge was at it first. It looked so small in his great left fist, that tiny metal bringer of death.

'Move away, please, sir.' He raised the gun and my guardian took one more step back. He was level with the box now. 'Move away.'

'Shoot him, Cutteridge,' the metal voice commanded. 'He will kill me if he can.'

My guardian reached out slowly and grasped the curtain as the major-domo pulled back the hammer. I ran at Cutteridge but he flung me aside with his right arm. 'Please excuse me, miss.'

'Have a care. I am not wearing any protective clothing,' Sidney Grice told him and I thought I saw him tremble. And the gun was pointing straight at my guardian when Cutteridge pulled the trigger.

The flash almost blinded me, but I still saw the impact on Sidney Grice's coat, directly over his heart, and his hand jump convulsively to the hole. And the explosion all but burst my eardrums, but I still heard the curtain rip in his clenched fist and the crash as he toppled over on to the table, sending it flying, and the candle snuffing out mid-air. And I still heard the thin cackle through the speaking trumpet, drowned out by the scream that came from me.

63

The Darkness

THE DARKNESS WAS complete.

'You have killed him!'

From behind and above me. 'I did my duty. He understood that.'

'Oh dear God!' I crawled towards where I saw my guardian fall and felt the tumbled table. 'Get a light. He may still be alive.'

'I fear not, miss. I have always been an excellent shot.'

'Get a light!'

There was a scratching and the flare of a Lucifer was thrown up on Cutteridge's gaunt face as he stooped for the candle and lit it shakily.

'My lady…' He stopped in confusion, shielding the dancing flame with a cupped hand.

The gauze had been torn away and Baroness Foskett sat in her high-backed chair perfectly still, her long black dress arranged carefully over the dais, her jaw hanging in a frozen laugh.

'Get the lantern.'

'Right away, miss.'

The candle blew out as he opened the door. I reached Mr G. 'Do not dare to be dead, you miserable old devil,' I whimpered as Cutteridge returned, turning up the wick on his lantern. My guardian was waxen and his eyes were closed. I slid his sleeve up to feel for a pulse.

'Oh, my lady,' Cutteridge whispered as I unbuttoned my guardian's waistcoat.

'Ouch,' Sidney Grice said, coming up on one elbow and rubbing his chest.

'How on earth...?' I released his wrist.

'It was a blank, but the impact of the wadding had quite a punch.' He scrambled to his feet and checked himself. 'It has torn my favourite Ulster.' He shook himself down and patted his trousers.

I dusted my dress. 'A good job you were wearing it.' And we turned to look at the box.

'My lady,' Cutteridge gasped.

The baroness's hair was fastened back by a silver comb, her hands resting on the arms of her throne, her fingers bare except for one gold band on the left, her eyes unblinking and membranous white, her head thrown back a little. Her skin was grey, blotched with maroon and splattered with dark streaks, a grotesque, shrivelled distortion, white teeth bared in silent mirthlessness.

'Is her ladyship...' Cutteridge could not bring himself to finish.

'Dead,' Sidney Grice said. 'And for quite some time. She is starting to mummify.'

'That perfume,' I said. 'It is myrrh.'

Sidney Grice looked at me. 'You smelled it before and did not mention it?'

'I assumed you—'

'You knew I was incapacitated by a cold. If I had known... Dash it all, Miss Middleton. I would have thought even you would know it is used to preserve bodies.'

Cutteridge set the lantern down heavily on the floor. 'But...'

'The speaking trumpet is connected to this brass pipe.' My guardian indicated with his cane. 'Which goes under the chair and back through that hole in the panelling. Why do you knock before you enter, Cutteridge?'

Cutteridge looked confused. 'Her ladyship instructed me to do so, sir.'

'Servants never knock,' I remembered. 'Not unless the occupant of the room wants some warning to be ready.'

Sidney Grice raised his voice. 'You might as well join us now, Rupert.' And almost immediately a panel in the wall at the back of the box hinged open, and out stepped a man. He was tall with faded and thinning red hair, and had to lower his head slightly to go under the lintel.

'Hello, Sidney.' The voice was husky and quite faint. 'I could never stop myself scratching those numbers. It drove my father almost into a frenzy.'

'We thought you had been eaten by cannibals,' I said.

'If only I had,' he responded. 'Something far worse than that feeds on me now. Oh, Sidney, you have no idea what it was like out there.'

'I have a very good idea,' my guardian said. 'I went looking for you.'

'You knew I was alive?'

'No.' Mr G gazed at him. 'I intended to bring your body home, and I believed I was getting close before I was stricken by malaria and shipped back against my will.'

'Malaria? Oh, fortunate man,' Rupert cried derisively. 'You deserved far worse than that, Sidney. It was because of you I journeyed to that unutterable pit of Hades in the first place. I had everything – a title, wealth – I was one of the most eligible bachelors on the kingdom and you destroyed it all by convincing me that it might all turn to dust.' A brown liquid trickled down Rupert's chin. 'I went looking for God. I thought I could find him by spreading his word.'

'And did you?' I asked and a great sigh came from him.

'I lost him – or rather he lost me – and you cannot be lost by something which does not exist. It was in God's abandonment of me that I found him for certain.'

'That is the biggest perversion of logical syllogism—' my guardian began but Rupert doubled up in spasms of coughing.

'Shut your mouth,' Rupert screeched when he had recovered sufficiently. 'I hate you.'

Mr G flinched. 'It is not my fault that there is no proof for you to cling to.'

'*Do not ask for proof. It shall not be given*,' Rupert quoted.

'I should be out of a job if that were the case,' Sidney Grice said wryly, and Rupert caught his breath.

'Very well then, how about this for evidence?' He raised his head. At first I thought it must be a trick of the light, but his skin was as white as bone and his nose had been eroded so that the turbinate bones were clearly visible through the few shreds of skin remaining. His left lower eyelid was gone too, exposing a raw eyeball.

'*Cochliomyia*,' Sidney Grice said in shock and Rupert laughed hollowly.

'Well diagnosed, Sidney. Most people would think I was a leper and, in every other sense of the word, I am. As it is, I am a modern-day Herod, rich and powerful and being eaten by worms, blowfly maggots burrowing into my putrefying flesh.'

'Can nothing be done?' I asked and he grinned gruesomely.

'When it began I was told it was just a question of picking them out with tweezers. They come up for air sometimes and then you grab them, but they are too numerous for that – and to think it all started with an insect bite. Then the doctors tried surgery, cutting them out of me, but the new wounds only helped them burrow deeper. I have bathed in mercury and been soaked in paraffin. I have been cupped and bled and burnt. The most expensive doctors in England were as effective as the witch doctors' charms I endured in that accursed place. They are inside me now. They burrow into my gut and hatch out in my lungs. I cough them up in gouts of foaming blood. They are destroying my face. I was such a handsome fellow once, was I not, Sidney?'

My guardian did not respond, but Rupert clutched his own head and cried out, 'They are in my brain. I can feel them – loathsome.' He fought for air. 'My mother hid me away and this house became my prison, with Cutteridge the jailor. She could not let the world see what the last Baron Foskett had become and I had no wish to be gawked at by society, pitied and repellent, and with no hope of carrying on our ancient line unless a remedy could be found. She nursed me. Every penny she had went on quack treatments and tricksters. She gave eight thousand pounds to a man who had cured a maharaja and brought him along to show us, but they both turned out to be shipping clerks from Southampton. The Foskett fortune went to swindlers and cranks.'

Sidney Grice said, 'And so you formed this murderous society.'

'It was not meant to be murderous,' Rupert said. 'You were supposed to prevent that.'

'Oh, Rupert.' My guardian straightened his cuffs. 'Every step of the way was calculated to destroy me.'

Rupert coughed. 'I know nothing of that. The only crime that I have committed was to cover up my mother's death. If it were known that she had passed away, then the prize would have gone to one of the other members.' Rupert pinched at his face and tugged and held out a squirming, hook-headed, bloated maggot for our inspection before tossing it away. 'You see what lives in my flesh. My mother tended to me. She spent hours with needles, digging these disgusting creatures out of me, but they were too many for her and they burrowed too deep. I thought that she was safe so long as none of the flies hatched – they do not live long in this climate – but some survived and she got bitten. She did not notice until it was too late. I tried to help. Can you imagine it, Sidney – the last surviving members of one of the greatest families in England sitting picking at each other like monkeys in a cage? In the end she was blind, clawing at her eyes as they tunnelled behind. We called in Dr Simmons. He had treated the family for years and at least we knew he would be discreet, but he was hopeless. He injected caustic soda under her skin and into her stomach. She died horribly, Sidney, beside herself in agony. I could have killed the man but he saved me the trouble and killed himself with his gluttony, and here I was, penniless and alone save for Cutteridge.'

'And so you set up the speaking tube to make it appear that the baroness was still alive,' I said.

Cutteridge was staring at the shrivelled remains of his mistress. 'So I have been serving a ghost.'

Rupert cackled. 'I thought about tying wires to her wrists to make them move, but I was worried you might spot them.'

Cutteridge picked up a long pole from the dais floor. 'And may I ask what this boat hook is for, sir?'

'I tried to turn her head with it when they first visited but it made too much of a clatter.'

Cutteridge exhaled heavily.

'But how would you claim the money?' I asked.

'Once the other members had expired I intended to get Dr Simmons to explain that he had been treating me secretly, and to certify that my mother's heart had failed, but then he died.'

'How inconsiderate of him,' my guardian said. 'But what good would money be to you in your condition?'

'It will buy me a cure. There *is* a cure now, Sidney, but it is expensive.'

'False cures invariably cost more than real ones.' Mr G peered at his old friend. 'Step forward, Rupert.'

'What?'

'Just one step for the lady... Thank you. I see you still drag your foot a little from the broken ankle.'

'What of it?'

'You are wearing a lot of cologne,' I remarked.

'It masks the stench of my decay, and it might even kill a few of the worms.' Rupert had a hole through his hand, an unholy stigmata. 'It deters the blighters from coming to the surface at any rate.'

'That could be why we did not find any in Mr Gallop's storeroom,' I said, and he eyed me sadly.

'Plus I wore a balaclava helmet to attract less attention.' He wheezed in a laugh that I had come to think of as his mother's. 'And to think at one time I craved it. You have no idea how hard I tried to impress you, Sidney.'

'I saw them use blowpipes when I went to look for you,' Sidney Grice said. 'There were footprints in Warrington Gallop's storeroom showing his killer to be a tall man with small feet and a slight limp.'

'Do you really think that any jury will convict an aristocrat of murder on such a sketchy conglomeration of evidence?' Rupert said.

'I have much more evidence than that,' Sidney Grice told him. 'Show me your watch, Rupert.'

But Rupert laughed. 'I have no idea what you are talking about, but how do you think you can even get out of here, Sidney?' he challenged. 'I released the dogs the moment you came in the house.'

Cutteridge cleared his throat. 'I feel it my duty to inform you that I bolted the cage gate this morning. The catch is rusty and I did not want any mishaps while we had visitors.'

'Gerry will be cross,' my guardian said. 'He could have had an extra hour in bed.'

Rupert coughed a spray of black blood into his clawed, torn hand.

'That is why we saw blood droplets on the floor in Mr Gallop's shop,' I realized.

'Precisely.' Mr G wiped his face. 'But tell me, Rupert, how did you plan to divide the money?'

Rupert blinked, but his upper eyelids had been too badly chewed to meet the lowers. 'Divide?'

'You do not think I believe that you alone committed all those crimes?' Sidney Grice poked a finger through the hole in his coat.

'We were to be married.' Rupert smiled ruefully and behind the ravages of his disease I glimpsed the remnants of a shy young man in love, but my guardian flapped his hand in contempt.

'Do you really imagine you would survive twenty-four hours after whatever mockery of a wedding you entered into?'

'She loves me.' Rupert wiped his nose with the back of his sleeve and looked down, as if suddenly realizing the implausibility of his words.

Sidney Grice's face was ashen. 'You are going to hang, Rupert, and your lovely partner in crime will hang with you.'

'I am afraid I cannot allow that, sir.' Cutteridge licked his dry lips. 'I am sure you have not forgotten that you are not the only one who carries a gun, but mine is loaded with bullets.' He brought a revolver out of his inner pocket and Sidney Grice took a step towards him. 'You know I will use it, sir.'

Sidney Grice froze.

'Will you kill me too?' I asked, stepping in front of my guardian.

'Get out of the way, March,' Sidney Grice commanded.

'No.'

'I cannot but salute your loyalty and sacrifice, Miss Middleton,' Cutteridge said, 'for they are qualities which I have always sought to cultivate. And your guardian is the man I admire above all others, but you must realize that my first loyalty is to the house I have served as my father served, since childhood.'

'And you would murder innocent people for this vile creature?' I asked.

'When Baron Rupert was but five years old I dived into the stormy seas at Calais to save him, though I could not swim.' Cutteridge swallowed. 'I shall do my duty to the end, miss.'

'And so shall I.' I straightened my body in an attempt to stop it from shaking.

'Why are you protecting this man, March?' Rupert sneered.

'March, please…' Sidney Grice spoke urgently.

'Because he protects me.'

'Please stand to one side, miss.' Cutteridge steadied the gun with his right hand.

'He is all I have,' I burst out and my guardian took hold of my shoulders.

64

The Web and the Cage

'YOU WILL NEVER get out of London, let alone England,' Sidney Grice told him, and the old servant frowned thinly.

'Be that as it may, sir, I cannot let the last Baron Foskett hang like a common felon.' His hand did not waver and he did not take his eyes off us as he backed away.

'Got you this time, Sidney,' Rupert crowed, stepping off the dais. Close up, I could see writhing under the blackened skin of his cheek. 'You always thought you were cleverer than me.'

'I,' my guardian corrected him. 'Cleverer than *I*. You are using *than* as a conjunction not a preposition. If you are going to make an ass of yourself, you might as well do it grammatically.'

Rupert scrunched his body in a paroxysm of pique. 'You—'

'That aside,' Mr G continued, 'I have always had a very high opinion of your intelligence.' And Rupert exposed more stumps of teeth in what might have been a vestigial smile before my guardian added, 'for a non-Grice.'

Rupert emitted a cry of rage. 'I had you in my sights, Sidney. I should have put a dart in you while I could.'

'Just out of interest,' Sidney Grice said, 'am I correct in assuming that you used viper venom and that you hollowed the dart out to carry a larger dose?'

'The dead adder,' I recalled.

'Which you omitted to mention to me at the time.'

'I see what you are doing.' Rupert spat some blood into a sodden handkerchief. 'You are trying to distract me, but it will do you no good.' He turned to face Cutteridge. 'They will raise the alarm if we leave them. Get rid of them, Cutteridge. Shoot them in the stomachs so they die slowly.'

The old retainer frowned. 'Do you remember when you were six, sir? You used the Devlin Plate as a toboggan and dented it, and I took the blame, though your grandfather laid into me with his riding crop. I have always done everything in my power to protect you and, if I could take your place, I would willingly do so, but this is beyond my powers now.' He cleared his throat. 'And I must do what I can for the family.' Cutteridge swallowed. 'I am so sorry.' His arm jerked up as he raised the pole and thrust the boating hook squelching into his master's shoulder. Rupert instinctively pulled away and howled. 'You will find it hurts a great deal less if do not struggle, my lord.'

Rupert forced himself to hold still. 'Cutteridge, what are you doing?'

'You made a puppet show of my mistress, the finest woman who ever graced this world, Lady Parthena the Dowager Baroness Foskett. You have desecrated her body.'

'She was *my* mother,' Rupert sneered, 'not yours.'

Cutteridge twisted the pole and Rupert shrieked, clutching at his shoulder.

'You might be best not to encourage me to hurt you as much as you deserve,' Cutteridge said. 'Please pick up the lantern, my lord. We shall be needing it.'

Rupert bent gingerly and did as he was told, and Cutteridge backed out of the room, leading Rupert like a bull by its ring.

We waited, craning our ears. I heard the stairs creak and Rupert yelp in pain and Cutteridge saying, 'I am so sorry, sir, but if you keep up, it will be less painful.'

'Stay here,' Sidney Grice whispered and rolled his eye when he saw that I would not. 'Keep behind me then.'

He brought out his safety lantern and lit it, and I looked back at Baroness Foskett as we quit the room. Was this husk really all that was left of the beautiful, wealthy, intelligent woman whose portrait graced the ballroom, who had lost the man she loved and died nursing her monstrous son? The long, lovely hands that must have cosseted her child were leathery claws now.

Mr G picked up his gun and slipped it into his pocket.

'Why did you throw it down?'

'I knew that Cutteridge would be prepared to shoot me if he thought he was protecting his mistress.' We crossed the corridor. 'And I preferred him do it with a blank rather than his own gun.'

'Do you not have any live bullets?'

'Yes, but I shall not shoot Cutteridge.'

'Because he spared our lives?'

My guardian piffed. 'I thought you would have known by now that gratitude is alien to my nature.' There was light coming into the hall when we peered over the banister rail. 'But I have never yet killed an innocent man on purpose.'

'The front door is open,' I said, the stairs swaying alarmingly as we set off down them.

'But they did not go out through it. The cobweb in that archway is ripped.' He raced into the passageway. A rotting velvet curtain had been tied back with what was probably once a golden cord, and it fell to dusty scraps when my shoulder brushed against it.

'Where does this go?'

'To the servants' quarters.' He was running now, his body dipping with his shortened leg and, with the lantern in front of him, I could hardly see to keep up. The passage sloped down, yard after yard, windowless and airless. 'More torn webs.'

There was a light in the distance and we raced towards it, almost tumbling as we emerged into an old kitchen dominated by a long, central pine table and a huge cooking range, copper pans resting empty upon it.

I touched the back of a chair. It had a streak of fresh blood on it. 'They must have come through here,' I said.

'You astonish me.' An open side door led into another

corridor. 'As I recall from when I played here, this wing is more of a maze than Hampton Court.'

We ran along to a flight of stone steps going down and he held out his lantern. 'They did not take this way. The steps are littered with dead beetles and not one of them has been crushed.'

'What—'

'Listen.' Sidney Grice cocked his head and I heard the dogs, their barks hurtling down the passages.

'Something has agitated them,' I said. 'Where is that draught coming from?' He licked his finger and held it up. 'I have never found that works,' I said.

'This way.' My guardian darted to the left. 'The back way is open.'

The barking was nearer and wilder.

The corridor was lit by the day now and a breeze blew along it from outside, carrying the fresh air and the yips of the dogs and a cry that pierced through it all. Sidney Grice broke into a run, drawing his revolver from his pocket as he went, with me close at his heels, out into a courtyard garden, the raised squares of what must have been herb beds overflowing with nettles. The side gate was ajar and, as we rushed round the beds towards it, there was a rattling and clatter and the squeal of rusty wheels.

'Cutteridge. Listen to me. I am Baron Foskett, the master you are sworn to serve.'

We rushed through the gate on to a stone path. 'This way.' My guardian slithered on the wet moss as he swung to the left and round the corner. The clattering was louder now and the barks more frantic.

Rupert stood trapped in an iron-barred run, leading from the dog pound to the garden and gated at either end. He was stooping, the boat hook still jutting from his shoulder and dangling into the ground. Behind him, yapping wildly and throwing their solid bodies at the inner gate, was a pack of huge black mastiffs, teeth bared as they snarled and snapped at the barrier separating them from him.

'I swore to serve your father and your mother,' Cutteridge declared and I looked over to see him standing to one side, turning a corroded metal wheel, and I saw that it was pulling on a wire and that the wire was connected to a heavy bolt which was sliding steadily backwards on the inner gate.

'And, for your mother's sake, I was of service to you, but no man could command my obedience when he has turned my lady into an obscenity.'

The bolt stuck but the old man strained one last quarter-turn and it clunked fully back. And as the gate flew open under the weight of the slavering animals, Rupert turned and flung himself helplessly on to the outer gate, but the first dog was on him the moment he touched the lock. He wrenched at the handle but it would not give and the whole pack tore in behind, ripping at his legs and flailing arms.

'Sidney!' he begged. 'Save me.' And I saw that my guardian was slipping a bullet into the chamber of his revolver and walking forward, taking careful aim, from two feet away.

Rupert fell to his knees and the biggest mastiff leaped over the others, scrambling across their backs as they battled for a share of their quarry. There, at the top of the seething pile, it steadied itself, snuffled at Rupert's hair and licked his ear three times before curling back its lips to take his cheek between its front teeth and tear it away. Sidney Grice took one more step so that the barrel of his gun was between the bars and Rupert's bloodied hand came through and clutched at his trouser leg. Three of Rupert's fingers were missing. One of the mastiffs rammed its jaws out, gripping the hem of Sidney Grice's coat, and he tried to yank away.

'Let go, you filthy animal.' He levelled the gun again and fired, and after the detonation there was a stillness such as I have never witnessed before. The dogs froze in their attack and a black hole appeared in the middle of Rupert's forehead, and it seemed an age before his skull broke.

The silence shattered and a dog behind him yelped and fell back. The rest looked up and then down and set again about their prey, snapping their bloody jaws, squabbling with each other for a portion of his worm-riddled flesh.

Sidney Grice raised his gun again, slowly exhaled and lowered it, uncocking the hammer in one practised movement.

'Filthy animal,' he repeated as he turned away. 'And so the last Baron Foskett dies just as the first, torn apart by a pack of dogs,' my guardian mused aloud and bowed his head. 'Come, March.'

I looked around. 'But where is Cutteridge?'

'He has gone back in and bolted the door but there is a short-cut to the front.'

Our way was tangled with brambles but Sidney Grice scarcely seemed to notice as he trampled round the side of the house, the thorns ripping at his clothes and mine.

'Why did the *Hamlet* quotation matter?' I asked.

He snapped a sapling that blocked our way. 'The baroness was a respected Shakespearean scholar. She would never have got it wrong by mistake, so either she was trying to tell us something or—'

'It was not her.'

'Precisely. Rupert was taunting me.'

Several times I had to stop to wrench my torn dress free, but he marched determinedly ahead until we came out on the gravelled clearing. Sidney Grice put his gun into his satchel.

'The door is still open,' I said. 'Do you think—' But my question was drowned out by a loud hammering.

We ran up the steps and inside, just in time to see the great staircase tipping away from the wall and hanging for a moment before, with a great groan, it collapsed then crashed into the hall, no more than a pile of splintered timber now, and Cutteridge at the top with an axe dangling in his left hand, clouds of dust billowing up around him and the lantern at his feet.

'He did not deserve to be put out of his misery,' he shouted. 'He should have lived to see his rotten heart torn from his breast.'

'Come down, Cutteridge,' my guardian called. 'I shall not tell the police what you have done.'

And Cutteridge tilted his head to one side. 'You were always an honourable boy,' he said, 'and you are a true gentleman, sir, but my mistress needs me one last time. I cannot let her be burnt alone.'

'Burnt?' I queried and Cutteridge bowed.

'I am sorry to have manhandled and threatened you, miss.'

The dust was still rising when he swung the axe back and with hardly a glance let it swing forwards again, sending the lamp flying from the edge of the top step, arcing brightly through the gloom as it fell, smashing into the wreckage and spraying oil in every direction. For a moment it looked like the light had been extinguished, but then a hub of blue appeared and a dozen spokes of yellow ran outwards in every direction, and three more up the wall, where the shards of shattered oak dangled from ancient fixings. The wood was dry and burst into flames like seasoned kindling and soon there was a huge bonfire blazing in the hall. The paintings blistered and the wall hangings smoked and ignited.

Cutteridge stood for a moment peering down at his work.

'Please do not risk your lives by trying to come up the back stairs,' he called. 'I have secured the doors at the top.'

'Go to a window,' I shouted above the crackle of fire. 'You can easily climb down the ivy.' And Cutteridge put a handkerchief over his mouth and nose.

'My place is here,' he said. 'Please excuse my not showing you out. The key for the gate is in the left lodge. Goodbye, sir, miss, and God bless you both.'

The smoke was thick now and it was difficult to see exactly when Cutteridge disappeared, but the ceiling had already taken and the floor was hot beneath our feet as we went out through the front door. We stepped back on the gravel and looked up. The flames were visible through the shattering first-floor windows and as we backed slowly up the path, transfixed by the sight of Mordent House ablaze, we heard it – muffled but unmistakeable – the single shot of a gun.

We made our way to the gatehouse and found the key, and put it in the lock as Cutteridge had done so many times before.

'Shall we call the firefighters?' I suggested.

'What for?' His eye was out and the socket oozing, and his right eye was trickling too. His gaze was fixed on the conflagration. There was a deafening crash and then another and the very building shuddered. He spun round and slashed his stick into a pillar. Again and again he smashed it into the old bricks. The cane cracked and twisted, its steel core bending under the fury of his blows. 'Damn you to eternal damnation!' He raised his arm once more and flung the shattered cane into the undergrowth. It hit a branch and tumbled into the bushes as he turned to me, his face contorted in a strange terrible passion. 'Nothing...' He fought to control himself. '*Nothing* can save the House of Foskett now.'

65

Soggy Messages and the St Leger

We were quiet for most of the way back, our heads down against the wind and drizzle.

'I was supposed to be calling on Dr Berry at half past,' Mr G said, flipping open his hunter, 'but I am not my usual effervescent self. I shall send her a message from home.'

A thought struck me. 'What did you mean about Gerry being disappointed?'

He glanced across. 'I anticipated Rupert releasing the dogs, for he must have known that he was close to being exposed, and arranged with Gerry to use his cricketing skills and toss four dozen poisoned lamb chops over the wall and deep into the grounds. What I did not foresee – for, near miraculous though my powers are, I am not a soothsayer – was Cutteridge's locking the gates of the pound.'

We rounded a sharp corner and I fell heavily against him. I was not sure where we were now. A gas pipe explosion had closed three streets to traffic.

'I am sorry you have lost your friend.' I pulled myself up.

'As I have told you repeatedly, I have no friends.' The corners of his mouth pulled down. 'How could I, being such a *miserable old devil*?'

I laughed involuntarily. 'I am sorry about that.' And he patted my hand.

'I lost Rupert nineteen years ago.' He inspected the torn hem of his Ulster. 'What you saw today was the corruption of a man, not the person I knew.'

'Do you think it possible that he was right and that the maggots *were* in his brain?'

Sidney Grice pulled on a loose thread. 'I think it unlikely. It is too pretty an explanation of what destroyed him and I dislike prettiness in all its manifestations. You cannot trust anything which is appealing if its appeal is the only reason to trust it.'

'So how will we find Miss McKay?'

'We have no need to.' The thread was unravelling. 'There is no one left to kill and if she does not come forward she cannot claim her prize. She will know as well as you or I that we have very little evidence against her.'

I looked out at the ragged people trudging along the drab streets or standing listlessly on corners or sitting on steps. What could they hope for other than sustenance and shelter to keep their souls trapped a little longer in their malformed bodies?

'I lost something else today,' my guardian said suddenly.

'Your faith in God?' I asked and he humphed. 'In human nature?'

'I have never had any faith in that.'

'Yourself?'

'How could I possibly doubt myself?' He snapped the thread. 'No, March. I am not sure what I have lost or where it has gone, but I doubt that I shall ever find it again and I shall always be the poorer for it.'

'Surely not a feeling?' I said, but he was looking out of his window.

I recognized the Edgware Road, and was turning to look at a new hat shop when the hatch shot open and the cabby appeared, his long, lank black hair hanging over his face.

'Before I forget,' he said. 'Joe Dubbins said to let you know 'e picked one of 'em up this mornin'.'

Sidney Grice cricked his head back. 'Which one?'

The driver screwed up his mouth and eyes. 'The one wiv the stained face,' he said.

'Primrose McKay,' I interjected.

'What time and where did he take her?' Mr G demanded.

The hair flopped side to side. 'Dunnow 'cause 'e writ it down and I missed my book learnin' thru 'avin' a kidley fever when I was a pup.'

'Give it to me, man.' My guardian put a finger to his eye, and the driver leaned so far forward that I feared he would fall through as I stood unsteadily to take a folded note from his gloved grasp.

'This is sopping.' It was disintegrating in my hand.

'Swap places and see 'ow dry your pockets is,' the driver challenged me as Sidney Grice tried to unstick and unfold the offering.

'Ridiculous,' he grumbled. 'How can anyone be expected to read that?' He fished out his pince-nez as I leaned over. 'Dash it, the lenses are steamed up.'

'Bryanston,' I said. 'It says Bryanston.'

He polished his pince-nez with a handkerchief and took another look. 'Dr Berry's house.'

'Why would she go there?' I asked, but the thought was already in my head and my guardian pursed his lips.

'Dorna is the only person who can definitely link McKay to the site of a crime.'

'Tavistock Square.' I hardly dared express my conclusion. 'So with Dorna out of the way—'

Sidney Grice jumped up and banged on the roof. 'Bryanston Mews and quick about it.'

'Make your mind up, guv.'

'A sovereign if you make it before the hour is done,' I called.

'Of your money, not mine,' Sidney Grice muttered. And the horse's head turned to the right and all of a sudden we were on one wheel and almost overbalancing, and I was flung across my guardian. 'Mind my flask, March.'

An omnibus was coming straight at us but we just managed to get in front of it.

'Who d'you fink you are? Fred fleckin' Archer?' the omnibus driver bellowed, hauling hard on his reins.

Our driver laughed. 'Wouldn't be sitting on this ole dustcart if I was.' He looked down at my companion. 'You follow the gee-gees, squire?'

Our left wheel came down with a bump, the horse straightened and lifted its head, and set off back down the road.

'I can think of little more tedious.' Sidney Grice unclipped his satchel to check the contents.

'I did get five to two on Silvio at the St Leger,' I told him, and my guardian glared at me.

'You are talking like a flash mobsman.'

I did not dare tell him I got the tip from a barman at The Bull, and we swung sharply across the road again – nearly upsetting a gig this time – and down Bryanston Road into the mews.

The church bell was striking as we pulled up, our horse tossing its head proudly as if it had just crossed the finishing line first at Doncaster.

'I do not imagine Dr Berry is in any real danger,' I said, a little battered, as our driver pulled open the flap. We were a short way down the street from the house as a coal wagon was blocking the way.

'Perhaps not.' Sidney Grice helped me out. 'But—' He gripped my arm and I stepped forward to get a better look.

The door to the house was ajar and, as we hurried towards it, I saw a woman. She was lying face down on the floor in the hall.

66

The Poker and the Cleaver

SIDNEY GRICE LET go of my arm and ran. I rooted around my purse, passed the payment up to the cabby and followed. He was already at the front step and signalled for me to stand clear. For once I obeyed, and watched as he stepped back and pushed the door fully open.

'It is just a servant,' he called and stepped inside. 'All clear.' I hurried in to find him crouched over the prone body of a housemaid. 'See to her.' He stood up and called out, 'Hello? Dorna?' Then he rushed into the consulting room.

I kneeled beside the maid. Her hand was hot with a gold cross on a snapped chain wrapped around her fingers, but I could find no signs of life. Her face was towards me, eyes open and still shining, and mouth agape, showing her small grey teeth. I brushed her eyelid but it did not react. A pool of blood, still wet, had oozed from the back of her head but I could not see any wounds beneath her smashed-in stained hat and thick black hair.

'Just a servant,' I whispered as I closed her eyes.

There was a poker lying nearby and I rose to look at it. It was bent near the end and caked in blood with a clump of hair.

My guardian came back into the hall. 'She is not in there and there are no messages on her desk.' He looked about. 'Good. You have not disturbed anything – except her eyes.'

'She cannot have been dead for very long.'

'And a probable weapon conveniently on display.' He closed

the front door and another door slammed. 'What the…' We set off down the hall, past the stairs and through an open doorway into the back of the house.

The door ahead was closed and Sidney Grice flung it open to reveal a kitchen, small with a central scrubbed table. The moment he did so, we heard a crash and turned to see Dr Berry, hanging by her neck from the ceiling next to a pine dresser.

'Dorna!' I exclaimed.

She had her hands clutching at the noose and her eyes were strained unnaturally wide, turned towards me in desperation, and her pupils were pinpoints. A wooden stool lay upturned beneath her. Sidney Grice snatched it up and scrambled on to it, grabbing a high cupboard door for support. Dorna's feet were in an open cutlery drawer. He bent his knees, put his arms round her waist and straightened up to slacken the rope.

'Untie it,' he commanded. My eye followed the rope from her neck up to a butcher's hook on the ceiling, where it looped through and then down at about thirty degrees from the vertical to an iron ring on the wall by the back door. 'Hurry, March.'

I ran across and tore at the knot. 'It is too tight.'

Dorna was making choking sounds and her face was dark, and I could see my guardian was having trouble holding her and balancing on the stool, which was wobbling beneath him. I snatched a meat cleaver from a rack and slashed at the knot three times as hard as I could, impacting into the whitewashed wall, and ripped the last few frayed strands apart. The rope fell loosely away and I dashed back to steady the stool.

Dorna Berry's eyes were closed as we lowered her to the floor, and she was not breathing, but her fingers between the noose and her chin had taken most of the pressure, and the moment we loosened the rope she shuddered and inhaled noisily.

'You are safe now,' he said, raising her head to take the rope from under it.

Dorna's limbs jerked. 'Thank God,' she gasped hoarsely. 'Thank God you came.'

67

The Poker and the Rope

IN A FEW minutes Dorna was recovered enough to sit up and, shortly afterwards, to be helped on to a chair. I filled a glass of water, but, when she took it from me, she was shaking so badly that she could not drink.

'I really thought…' She rubbed her throat gingerly. 'I really thought…' She broke down in tears.

'Try not to speak,' I said, but my guardian batted my words away.

'Try to if you can.' He steadied her hand and she managed a sip of water.

'If you had not come when you did…' She sobbed again and I took her hand. 'I am sorry.'

'What happened?' Sidney Grice pulled up the stool and sat beside her.

'I hardly know,' she wept, cradling the air around her face with open fingers. 'Somebody came to the door.'

'Was it a ring or a knock?'

She swallowed painfully. 'What?… A ring, I think… Yes, just one ring. Emily answered the door.'

'Where is your usual maid?' I enquired.

'Jane had yesterday off and a half day today. Emily came from an agency. I have used her a few times in the past.'

'Did you see her go to answer the call?' my guardian rattled off.

'No. I was in my consulting room with the door closed, but I heard her footfalls in the hall and the front door open, and she told somebody to wait. Then—'

'How many people?' he asked abruptly and she put a hand to her brow.

'For heaven's sake,' I said. 'Dorna has just escaped death.'

'And her memory of it will never be fresher,' he snapped, but added to her more tenderly, 'If you can manage, it will help enormously.'

'I will try.' Dorna Berry worried at her forehead in quick little pinches. 'I could not tell at that stage because I did not hear any voices except Emily's saying, *Please wait here*. Then there was a sound, a loud thud, and she cried out – no words – just a cry of surprise or pain, and then a crash as if she had fallen over, and three more thuds. I heard them all separately but in rapid succession, the sort of speed that one might...' she hinged her hand down to cover her eye, 'beat a carpet.'

I took her left hand in both of mine. 'Are you sure you can go on?'

Her right hand fell on to mine. 'If it helps to catch them...'

'Them?' He pounced and she nodded twice.

'I went out and saw her.' Her grip spasmed. 'That woman – the one I saw in the square. I am sure it was her – the one with the birthmark.' She touched her cheek silently.

'Primrose McKay,' I said and she nodded again.

'Just her?' my guardian asked.

'At first. Then I saw Emily. She was lying face down towards the front door and it was open, and the McKay woman was standing just behind her with a poker in her hand, raised' – she held out her fist – 'like a weapon.'

'Where could the poker have come from?' I asked. There was no fireplace in the hall. Dorna unclenched her fist.

'Jane kept it in the umbrella stand...' She laughed ironically. 'For our protection as we were frightened, after I saw that woman in Tavistock Square, that she might come for me.'

Sidney Grice caught his eye. 'You never told me.'

She started to rock to and fro. 'I thought you would tell me not to be silly. How could she even know who I am or where I live?'

My guardian touched her shoulder. 'She would have known where *I* live and seen us together. All the world knows where I reside and it would have been a simple matter to have tracked my movements. I am sorry if I led them to you.' Something in his apology sounded hollow. Perhaps it was just that I was unused to hearing him use the word *sorry*. 'What happened next?'

'I stepped into the hall.'

'That was brave of you,' I said and she crinkled her brow.

'Brave or stupid? I think I did not really believe what I was seeing. It was like one of those bad melodramas that my foster parents put me in as the village beauty.' She smiled tightly. 'And that was when I was attacked – a man grabbed me.'

'Thurston Gates—' I began but Mr G hushed me.

'Continue,' he instructed and Mary struggled on.

'He must have been standing behind the door. He got me in a bear hug and lifted me off the ground as easily as I might pick up a pillow. I tried to scream but he clamped his hand over my mouth. I tried to hit him but he did not seem to notice, and then that woman came towards me and raised the poker and I thought...' She put her knuckles to her teeth and tears sprang in her eyes. 'I thought that she would dash my brains out and the first thing I thought about' – she coughed – 'was that I might never see you again.'

'That would have been one blessing for you.' Sidney Grice polished his eye with a square of blue cotton, but Dorna shook her head.

'It was the one thing I could not bear.' She put her hand on his. 'I have seen death so often that I believed I was not afraid of it... He carried me here, down the hall. I kicked and tried to bite his fingers but he held my jaw so tightly. No matter how I struggled, I was no more than a child in his grasp. He pinched my nostrils and I could not breathe, and before I knew it I was standing on a stool while he tied a rope to that ring on the wall.'

'Where did they get the rope from?' I asked and she flared up.

'How should I know? They probably brought it with them.' She forced herself to calm down. 'He slipped the noose over my head and tightened it and' – she closed her eyes – 'kicked the stool away. I only fell a few inches. Either they miscalculated or they wanted me to die slowly. I clutched at the rope and tried to loosen it around my neck.'

'I wonder why they did not tie your hands,' I said.

'Perhaps to prolong the struggle even more.' Sidney Grice prised his eyelids apart and forced his glass eye into its raw socket. He drew a sharp breath but waved away my concern to ask, 'What next?'

'She stood there watching me. Dear Lord, Sidney, the look of pleasure on her face. I have never seen such undisguised evil.' Dorna took a deep breath. 'Then you arrived. They glanced at each other, shrugged and walked very calmly out into the garden. She looked back at me and she was still smiling, almost serene. She blew me a kiss and left... I could not hear any voices then. And I thought whoever had come in might have run off, on seeing Emily, to find a policeman. And I could be left here to die.' She pulled the collar of her dress as if re-enacting her words. 'The drawer was partly open and I managed to pull it out with my feet and stand in it to support myself.'

I gave her my handkerchief. 'That showed great presence of mind.'

'But I could not get my fingers out from under the rope and I was choking and...' She burst into tears. 'Nobody came and I was choking.'

'I think you have had enough,' I said and my guardian concurred.

'Would you like a proper drink?' I asked and she managed a half-smile.

'There is some sherry in that cupboard. Cook was going to make a trifle.'

'Where is Cook?' Sidney Grice stood up and Dorna looked about her as he went to the back door.

'Oh, you don't think...?' Dorna began as he went outside.

He kneeled over the prone form.

'Dead,' he said as he returned, 'in the rose bed – attacked from behind, almost certainly with the cleaver which is lodged in her occiput.'

'Sweet heaven,' Dorna whispered. 'Will it never end?'

'Yes.' My guardian closed the door. 'It will all end today. Stay with Dorna, March, whilst I go next door and summon help.'

68

The Staking of Lives

I SAT WITH Dorna Berry sipping sherry and saying little, while Sidney Grice examined the bodies. He paced round the hall and spent a long time in the garden, apparently taking soil samples and measuring footprints, before rejoining us in the kitchen.

The police came, two constables, a grey-haired sergeant and Inspector Quigley.

'Do not leave me,' Dorna begged and I put my hand on her shoulder.

'Well, you *have* excelled yourself today,' I heard Quigley say as my guardian went to meet them. 'Two brutal murders for the price of one and very nearly a third.'

Dorna buried her face in her hands.

Mr G tucked his thumbs into his waistcoat pocket. 'You seem to forget that whilst I am under no obligation to protect these people, Inspector, you have a sworn duty to do so.' He lowered his voice but it was still clear. 'These women were not clients of mine and I am only here as a courtesy to Dr Berry.'

I walked across and shut the door but could still hear the muffled voices coming from the hallway, intermittently raised as Sidney Grice and the inspector debated heatedly. There was silence for a while and they must have gone out of the front and through the side gate, for I heard them again in the garden, their voices getting angrier, until the back door flew open and they all marched into the kitchen.

Quigley picked up the noose from the dresser and held it out to Dorna. 'Show me how it fits round your neck.' But I snatched it from him and shouted, 'Leave her alone. Can you not see she is in a severe state of shock?'

Quigley coloured indignantly. 'I have to question her.'

'Of course,' Mr G agreed. 'But not today. '

'She will come to the station tomorrow then.'

Dorna buried her face in her hands while the constables poked about, opening and shutting drawers but showing little interest in what they contained. The sergeant lifted the kettle from the side of the range. 'Any chance of a cuppa?' he asked hopefully.

'None at all,' I told him, and the constables grunted in disappointment as they all trudged back into the hall.

'I will have these corpses taken to the morgue,' Quigley announced.

He put on his bowler hat and patted it down, and, bidding us a crisp goodbye, marched out of the house. The constables took the bodies on blankets into the back of a black van and rode off with the sergeant.

'Is it all right to clear up?' I asked, and Mr G shrugged and went back to Dorna. I found a mop and bucket to wash the hall floor and, once the bloodstains were gone, he brought Dorna through to her consulting room.

Jane, the maid, returned and I sat her down in the back parlour and explained what had happened, but there was nothing I could say to lessen the horror of events. She swayed in her seat and for a moment I thought she would vomit but she steadied herself, though her face was white as candle wax.

'Oh, miss, if it had not been my half day...' She did not need to complete her words for us both to know what she had escaped.

I poured her a sherry and for once I did not have another. Sidney Grice came in. 'Ah, Jane, I have convinced your mistress that she needs to eat. She thinks she can manage a ham sandwich.' I glared at him and he returned my look. 'Yes, I know what you are thinking, Miss Middleton, but this is no time for me to preach a civilized diet to her.'

'No.' I stood up. 'Nor any time for you to consider Jane's feelings.'

'Oh.' He waved airily. 'There will never be a time for that. It is inconvenient enough having to be so attentive to my own servants. I will have three peeled raw carrots.'

He wandered away.

'I will make it,' I said, 'if you tell me where the meat safe is.'

But Jane struggled to her feet. 'No, miss. I can't sit back and watch you work. It wouldn't be right.'

'If you feel unable to continue, I can contact the agency,' I offered, but she set her expression.

'My place is with my mistress.'

I tried to help by cutting some bread but Jane put my rough blocks to one side, trimmed the loaf and cut four perfect thin slices.

'And we will take coffee.' My guardian reappeared. 'I have tried to persuade Dr Berry to stay in Gower Street for a few days but she is determined to remain here.'

'Will you and I stay to protect her?' I asked and he flicked his hair back with a jerk of the neck.

'She is adamant that we shall not.'

Jane hung on to the tabletop and I stood by ready to catch her.

'But what if they return, sir?'

'I have given your mistress my word, and you have it too, that they will not,' Sidney Grice told her.

Jane straightened up and let go of the table. 'You are a gentleman, Mr Grice, and your word is good enough for me.'

My guardian crossed the room to view his reflection in the polished base of a hanging saucepan. 'Rest assured.' He tidied his cravat. 'I will stake your life on it.'

69

Salt and the Spiteful Son

I STAYED WITH Jane while she prepared the sandwiches, carrots and coffee, and I double-checked, at her request, that the back door was secured before she took the tray into the front room.

Dorna seemed much cheered. She stood up and embraced Jane and whispered something to her, but Jane said, 'You took me in when no one else would give me an interview. I shall not desert you now, miss.'

Dorna kissed her cheek and took her hands. 'I shall not forget this, Jane.'

'I require salt,' my guardian said, and after her maid had gone, Dorna explained, 'It is a sordid story but all too common I am afraid. The oldest son of her household tried to take advantage of her and, when she spurned him, told his mother that it had been the other way round. Jane was dismissed without a reference and her ex-mistress was vindictive enough to put word about that she had behaved improperly with several guests. After a month of being offered nothing other than virtual prostitution she tried to gas herself, but was rescued and given three months in prison for attempted suicide. After that her position was hopeless.'

'It was good of you to take her on,' I said.

'Or naive,' my guardian grunted, but she addressed me unabashed. 'Sidney has been telling me about *your* morning. It seems we have all had lucky escapes today and we must thank God that none of us was harmed.'

We sat in three padded upright chairs round a low, rectangular table, Dr Berry pulling her chair quite close to his. The rubber plant behind them was wilting and the leaves were yellowed.

'I fear I have been more than a little harmed,' he said. 'I was not paid to protect members of the society, but that is generally assumed to be the case and every person in it met an untimely and violent end. And, if Primrose McKay is hanged, nobody will benefit from their deaths except me. Who is to say that I did not kill the others for personal profit?'

'Why, that is nonsense,' I said. 'I was with you all the time.'

'But you would scarcely be credited as an independent witness,' he pointed out.

'Help yourself to milk and sugar, March.' Dorna poured coffee from a tall pot into three dark pink cups with silver rims. 'But surely, Sidney, there will be no doubt as to Miss McKay's guilt. I may not have had a good view of her in the dentist's window but I certainly had a very good look at her today.'

Sidney Grice cleared his throat. 'Unfortunately, it is your word against hers and I have no doubt that she could buy herself a dozen witnesses, all of good standing, who would swear that she was with them in Penzance from dawn to dusk to dawn again every day this week.'

'But there was that gold cross on the chain,' Dorna reminded him. 'You told me she liked wearing those.'

I picked up the clawed tongs. 'I do not remember that.'

'Have a sandwich, March.' My guardian thrust the plate under my chin. 'She will argue that the cross could have been anybody's. No, Dorna, what we must do is build a body of proof against her in which your evidence is but the keystone that supports our case.'

'But how can we do that?' Dorna was calmer by the minute.

'Let us reason this thing backwards for a moment.' He meditated as Jane came in with his salt. 'I have long been convinced that at least two people were involved in all the killings, except that of Warrington Gallop. If we accept that premise for the time being and that Rupert was one of the murderers, who else – other than the youthful Primrose McKay – could have been involved?'

'Cutteridge could have assisted, especially if he thought that Baroness Foskett was instructing him,' I said, but he held up his hand.

'Cutteridge had not left Mordent House in years. He did not know that Trivet's Tea Shop was demolished eight years ago, and the leaves around the main gate had fallen weeks ago but not been trodden on until we made our first visit. I remarked that they were interesting at the time and I need not remind March how scornful she was.' He took the salt cellar and blew down the hole.

'No, you need not,' I agreed, 'though you have just done so.'

He scratched the back of his hand.

'What about that cat man you told me of – Mr Piggety,' Dorna suggested. 'Could he not have acted with Rupert until Rupert killed him?'

'Which might explain why Rupert committed the last crime alone,' I said, but he shook his head.

'Two people were needed to kill Piggety.'

I took three lumps of sugar. 'What will happen to the money if Miss McKay is executed?'

'A moot point,' he said. 'I suspect the fight for it will go through the courts for years, every distant relative coming forward with a claim, but there is no one who can reasonably expect to inherit everything. The constitution of the society obliged their solicitor to draw up a list of all legal claimants in the unlikely eventuality of the last two members dying simultaneously, and it is a tortuous forest of family trees indeed.' He picked up his coffee and swirled it round. 'What I often do when faced with these conundrums is try to reconstruct the sequence of events in my imagination. I have used March for this in the past but she is pretty hopeless at it.'

'Thank you,' I said and he waved my words aside.

'You are the fourth most intelligent woman I have ever met, Dorna, so perhaps you could assist me this time.'

'Where do I come on your list?' I asked and he blinked.

'You are not on it,' he said, and Dr Berry reached over and rested her hand on his.

'I will do whatever I can to help,' she said.

'I know you will.' He stroked her fingers.

I gazed at them. 'Would you like me to leave?'

'Oh, March,' my guardian said, 'I can see that you are irrationally insulted, but you must allow Dorna to be the murderer just this once.'

70

Playing in the Garden

DORNA LAUGHED IN a way that would not have seemed possible half an hour previously. 'You make it sound like a game.'

'Life *is* a game,' Sidney Grice said, 'and it always ends in tears.'

'Perhaps this one will end happily.' She tried to force a smile. 'And you must feel free to join in, March.'

'Thank you, but I would rather go outside and play,' I retorted.

'Sulking is one of her less attractive qualities' – he held his coffee under his nose and savoured the aroma – 'but preferable to her clumsy attempts at humour.'

'Do not be so hard on March,' Dorna said and sat forward, her green eyes sparkling. 'So how shall we start?'

'Let us begin with the second murder, the man who died in my study, the chemist Horatio Green.' He sipped his beverage and rolled it around his mouth before swallowing. 'How did you kill him?'

Dorna wrinkled her brow. 'I believe you told me he was poisoned with prussic acid.'

'Indeed he was, in one of the wax capsules which he inserted into his ear, but how was it replaced?'

'I do not know, dear.'

Though I knew Dorna was fond of Sidney Grice, I had never imagined her ever calling him *dear*. It seemed an affront to his pomposity, rather like addressing Her Majesty as *ducks*. He appeared to be happy enough with the epithet, though.

'By the man claiming to be Reverend Golding,' I said before they started cooing. 'When the urchins wrecked Mr Green's shop.'

'Who better to impersonate a man of the cloth than another man of the cloth?' He took his hands from hers and unclipped the lid of his snuffbox. 'Remember, March, how Green told us that the vicar picked things up and gave them to him to put away. Perhaps the vicar could not reach the shelves himself.'

'And Reverend Jackaman was a very small man,' I said. 'So whilst they were doing that, his alleged daughter put the poisoned capsule in his pill box. But who was his daughter?'

'Who indeed?' My guardian took a pinch of snuff. 'Jackaman had no children.'

'So let us assume that I – Primrose McKay – am posing as the daughter,' Dorna said. 'But if Reverend Jackaman were the murderer, who murdered him?'

'I was nonplussed by this for a long time.' He wriggled his nose. 'First, I could not understand why he would have done it. The simple explanation is that he hoped to get rid of one of the other members of the society, but how did such a ruthless killer become such an easy victim?' Sidney Grice put another pinch of snuff to his right nostril. 'But then I thought, what if Enoch Jackaman did not know he was helping to kill Mr Green and thought he was merely assisting in a schoolboy jape, perhaps in revenge for a trick that Horatio Green, a notorious practical joker, had played on Miss McKay.'

'Reverend Jackaman did not seem like a prankster,' I pointed out. 'And why did he not go to the police when he realized the consequences of his actions?'

'Who would have believed him against the delightful and powerful Primrose?' Sidney Grice produced a large blue handkerchief with white polka dots. 'The mistake I made was in wondering what Jackaman had to gain by his actions. What I should have been wondering was what he had to lose.'

'Blackmail,' I said.

'Precisely.' He turned to Dr Berry. 'Do you have any observations about that?'

She unfolded a napkin. 'Perhaps I tempted him into improper behaviour – got him to write me a letter, for example. The consequences of that being made public could be ruinous to a clergyman.'

'I can think of no more seductive a temptress.' He dusted his upper lip.

'I feel a little queasy,' I said.

'Is the coffee too strong?' Dorna enquired.

'Not the coffee.' I took another sip to remove the taste in my mouth. 'So Primrose has lured the reverend into a compromising situation and tricked him into helping her with a murder. What next?'

He folded his handkerchief and tucked it away. 'Let us proceed to the third death, that of Silas Braithwaite.'

'The dentist?' Dorna asked. 'I believe you told me he was not even a member of the society.'

'He perplexed me the most,' Sidney Grice said, 'especially as his death was probably suicide.'

'I thought that you said it was an accidental death,' I objected and he tutted.

'I said it *could* have been accidental. He was not killed by Jenny, his Salopian maid. You would need a cool head to carry out a crime like that, but the moment I put her coolness to the test she fainted. I would have been moderately satisfied with the misadventure theory, especially as I was not investigating his death,' he turned the tray and pulled it towards him slightly so that it was exactly in the middle of the table, 'until you, Dorna, spotted Primrose in his house. Let us imagine that Silas Braithwaite had been involved in the murder of the taxidermist Edwin Slab and that he was also acting under duress. Perhaps pressure was being applied to make him commit another murder. There are two kinds of blackmailers. The most common are after a reward, sometimes – how shall I put this? – personal services, but more often money, and they usually increase their demands until they have drained their victims' finances. The cleverer blackmailers operate what I describe in my paper – *A Brief History of Felonious Extortion Techniques in Modern Society* – as a *cascade*. The victim is first caught in or enticed into committing a small offence. It may not even be illegal, but its exposure could be highly embarrassing and socially ruinous. He or she is then coerced by threats of exposure to commit an act which *is* illegal. From then on, the victim is trapped in a descending spiral of offences. The more he does, the more he is compelled to do and, once he has been implicated in murder, why then his very life is in the extortionist's hands. Handing over all his money would be the least of his problems. You, Dorna—'

'In my role as Primrose,' she put in.

'I thought we had established that.' I was getting a little impatient with her coyness.

Sidney Grice continued as if neither of us had spoken. 'Persuaded Silas Braithwaite to take part in the murder of Edwin Slab. The chances are that he did not know what he was letting himself in for until it was too late, but somebody held Mr Slab whilst he was injected.'

'Perhaps Primrose told Silas Braithwaite that she was just going to give Mr Slab a sedative while she hunted for incriminating letters,' I suggested.

'Which would tie in with my observation that the study had been searched.' He rolled his carrots around the plate before selecting the most symmetrical of them.

'They then go back to the workroom where Silas is horrified to find that Mr Slab has suffered a fatal seizure,' I said. 'So he helps to tip Mr Slab into the tank of formaldehyde in the belief that it will make the death look accidental, not realizing that it will do the exact opposite as the lungs will not inhale any liquid.'

'And Primrose makes certain that foul play will be suspected by leaving the syringe on the floor and moving the ladder from the tank' – he dipped his carrot into the salt – 'little knowing that Rosie Flower, the senile housekeeper, will supervise the most thorough destruction of evidence I have ever seen.'

'If I had not had my suspicions, they might have got away with it,' Dorna said.

Mr G straightened his back. 'It is unlikely any murderer could escape my investigations.'

'And Silas Braithwaite is so appalled at what he has done, or so frightened of being made to commit another murder, that he kills himself,' I suggested.

'This is all guesswork.' Dorna finished her coffee. 'What makes you think that Silas Braithwaite was involved at all?'

'His trousers.' Mr G waved his carrot as if conducting the conversation. 'First, they had been splashed with a bleach which smelled very like formaldehyde, though I did not know the significance at the time.'

'But why did he not change them?' I said.

'Because, as Jenny his maid told us – if you were listening and not daydreaming about wandering lonely as a cloud or some such nonsense – his other clothes were at the laundry, which was holding them in lieu of payment.'

'And second?'

'When I picked at them I found traces of a fine white powder, which Dr Manderson of the University College chemistry department analysed as hydrated potassium aluminium sulphate, otherwise known as alum, which is used by taxidermists to tan animal hides.'

'It is also used by unscrupulous millers to adulterate flour and Jenny's father was a miller.' Even as I pointed that out I knew it was a meaningless coincidence.

He clicked his tongue. 'I am afraid that March tends to say the first thing that flits through her head.'

'There was a sack of white powder on the floor of the workroom where he died,' I remembered, and was rewarded with, 'Well done, you have finally bleated out something relevant.'

Dorna put her cup down heavily. 'She is hardly more than a child. Do you have to be so rude to her?'

'No, but I choose to be,' he said. 'She is little enough use as it is without making her any more swollen-headed.'

I was not sure whether his intentional or her unintentional insult wounded me more, but something jogged in my mind, though I could not think what it was.

'But who rang the bell that Rosie Flowers answered before she found Mr Slab's body?' I asked.

'Why, I did, to vex Sidney.' Dorna smiled. 'You know how he hates being teased.'

Mr G tisked. 'It is a pointless exercise, like trying to teach the French to cook.'

Dorna and I looked at each other and raised our eyes, while he smoothed a crease out of the tray cloth.

'A few days after Mr Braithwaite died, I believe you saw somebody in his house,' I said.

'Perhaps it was a patient seeking to destroy any connection with him,' Dorna suggested, 'to avoid any taint of scandal.'

'Or you looking for a suicide note implicating you in the crime,' I said.

'Me?' Dorna queried. 'Goodness, I *have* been busy.' She touched her blouse and I remembered the time when we had been alone in my guardian's study. 'Perhaps it was his shade.'

'Please do not start seeing them,' Mr G beseeched. 'March has friends who see them everywhere.'

'And for a moment I thought I saw the ghost of Eleanor Quarrel in the hospital once,' I admitted, and Dorna shivered.

'Well, I hope she does not reappear. I think I have seen enough murderesses for one day.'

'Be careful, March.' My guardian handed me his napkin. 'You have spilled your coffee.'

71

Gas Leaks and Crumbs

DORNA PASSED ME two napkins.

'I hope I did not get any on the rug.' I mopped my dress.

'Do not worry.' She refilled all our cups.

'Shall we continue?' Sidney Grice looked at his watch.

'Where were we?' Dorna asked.

'Well, so far,' I counted them off on my fingers, 'you have killed Edwin Slab with the aid of Silas Braithwaite, Horatio Green assisted by Reverend Jackaman, driven Silas Braithwaite to suicide and searched his house.'

Dorna laughed a little too loudly. 'It seems quite a hectic life being a murderess.'

He huffed. 'Do try to take this seriously.'

She trembled and I stood to put my shawl around her. 'If I did that I should have to take to my bed for a year.' Her voice became shaky again.

'Can you go on?' I sat down and she nodded silently.

My guardian bit off the tip of his carrot. 'Let us consider the peculiarly cruel death of the diminutive Reverend Enoch Jackaman.'

'Well,' Dorna shook herself, 'you told me how he died but did I kill him by myself or with yet another accomplice?'

'One moment.' We watched in silence as he re-dipped his carrot and nibbled it slowly. 'Delicious.' He dabbed his lips. 'And all the way from Lincolnshire, if I am not mistaken.' He put the carrot down. 'Here is where you strike a bit of luck. You find a man who is greedy, lacks any kind of compassion and is not in the least bit squeamish.'

'Prometheus Piggety,' I said.

'The cat man?' Dorna lowered a lump of sugar into her coffee and opened the tongs to let it sink.

'The very same.' He twisted his chain and let the watch spin round. 'I cannot imagine that he would have needed much persuasion to participate in a murder that was very much to his advantage. If he could dispose of the vicar and Warrington Gallop, there would only be Miss McKay and Baroness Foskett left. Whoever won the duel between Prometheus and Primrose could probably anticipate waiting for the baroness to predecease him or her naturally. After all, she was an old woman and to kill her would have made the survivor the only suspect.'

'So how do we dispose of the vicar?' Dorna stirred her beverage and clinked the spoon dry.

'You make him sound like a waste product,' I objected.

'Perhaps that is all he was – to Mr Piggety,' she said despondently.

'The greatest problem is getting into the church,' Sidney Grice said. 'The front door is locked but the back door lock was faulty and could not be used. This would not have worried Jackaman overly as it led into a high-walled garden with a securely bolted solid gate, leading on to Mulberry Street, and the only other entrance was through the rectory, which was also locked, with his trusted housekeeper inside. But she is the weakest point of his defences. It takes a rare level of expertise to break into a house from the front on a busy street unobserved in broad daylight – I have only managed it twice myself. But servants are almost invariably dull-witted. Why else would they be servants?'

'Perhaps they have not had our advantages,' I suggested.

A furniture van paused outside the window, cutting the daylight, and then reversed.

'Indeed they have not,' he agreed, 'our greatest advantage being our superior minds. Remember I found that cloth cap? Piggety, wearing an old coat with the collar up and the cap low over his face—'

'He must have bought them from that road digger with red hair,' I interrupted. 'I said at the time that the—'

'Piggety rings the rectory doorbell,' Mr G carried on tetchily, 'and tells the housekeeper that there is a gas leak from the roadworks. She must evacuate the house immediately, taking the cook and maids with her, to the safety of nearby St Michael's Church until she is told it is safe to return.'

'She must have been told that her employer had already gone or she would not have left without him,' I speculated.

'Of course,' he said. 'Now, where was I? Piggety tells her he must come into the house to secure the gas supply. She goes out and leaves him to it. He lets you in. You both exit the rectory into the garden, enter St Jerome's through the back and perform the deed – whilst we are helpless to assist on the other side of the church door. You put a noose over Jackaman's neck, lead him to the screen, nail him to it, pierce his scalp with a crown of needles, and finally his side with a spar of wood from the smashed crucifix.'

Dorna swallowed. 'I have seen some terrible injuries in my profession but they were all industrial or road accidents. I have never heard of anything so cruel as that.'

Sidney Grice touched her arm. 'Would you like to stop?'

'Not if I can be of any help. This woman must be brought to justice.' She looked down. 'And who is to say she will not make another attempt to kill me?'

My guardian raised her chin and held her gaze. 'I guarantee it.' And she forced a small smile.

'How did they get out?' I asked.

'Piggety went through the back gate.' Mr G selected another carrot, leaving his half-eaten one aside. 'He threw his bloodstained overclothes into the bushes and went out on to Mulberry Street where, if he was noticed, no one would think it worth mentioning as he has a stall there, selling…' He pointed at me with the carrot.

'Clockwork mice and dogs,' I said.

'Just so. He would not have run the stall himself but no doubt he visited it often. He was not a man to leave his employees unsupervised. Remember he told us that he would not trust a boiler man to work unattended.'

'So how did Primrose leave?' Dorna asked. 'Presumably she was somebody who might stand out in a toy market.'

'Through the rectory,' I said, 'either after we had gone or when we went into the church.'

'But what grounds do you have for suspecting Mr Piggety?' she asked.

'They are threefold.' Mr G swung his watch like a mesmerist. 'First, there is a limited number of suspects and he is one of them; second, I took a sample of mud from the floor of St Jerome's. It had an elongated moulded shape and I intended to keep it in case it fitted the defect in a suspect's boot, but it dried and crumbled in the envelope so that when I came to re-examine it I found a small white hair imbedded inside.'

'Like the cat hairs?' I asked.

'Very like,' he confirmed. 'Third, I was so intent on examining the torn page of the Bible which was forced into the vicar's mouth that I paid insufficient attention to the book from which it was torn. On scrutinizing it later, I found a number of what at first appeared to be bloody fingermarks, but there was an odd bluish tinge to them.'

'And Mr Piggety suffered with coloured sweat,' I recalled as he put his watch away.

'*Chromhidrosis*,' he confirmed.

'I told you there were still answers to be found in the Bible,' I reminded him.

'You cannot pretend that is what you had in mind.' He nibbled the tip of his carrot.

'*The Lord works in mysterious ways*,' Dorna quoted. 'This

coffee is cold. Let me ring for some more.' She got up and went to the bell pull. 'Oh, March.' She was a little drawn now. 'I would not have your job for all the tea in China.'

'Imagine you could cut cancer out of your patients,' I posited. 'The process might be painful and gory, but you do it to save lives. I hope to save lives by ridding the world of something just as insidious as cancer, the calculating murderer.'

'Why, March,' my guardian crooned, 'you almost make it sound worthwhile.'

72

Four Minutes and Forty-eight Seconds

JANE CAME AND cleared the tray.

'Are you all right?' Dorna asked and Jane's head went back.

'Yes, thank you, ma'am.' She was clearly close to tears.

'I know this has been a great shock,' her mistress commiserated. 'Would you like me to request a police guard?'

Jane looked at my guardian, who said firmly, 'There is no need.'

There was an uncomfortable silence until Dorna said, 'Then you shall sleep with me tonight.'

'Thank you, ma'am.'

'Why do you not come to Gower Street?' I urged. 'I am sure we can fit you both in.'

'That is a kind offer but I hope you will be the first to agree that, just because we are women, we are not helpless,' Dorna retorted.

'But I am frightened for you,' I burst out and Jane looked at us all.

'Bring a fresh tray,' Dorna told her.

'Yes, ma'am.' She bobbed and left.

Sidney Grice stretched his arms up as if about to dive. 'There is something quite addictive about sleep. Hardly a night goes by without me craving it in one form or another and I had none last night. However...' He lowered his arms and rotated his shoulders. 'Since you are not helpless, let us consider the penultimate murder.'

Dorna held her head. 'Remind me, dear.'

'Mr Piggety,' I said. 'I suppose there was some kind of natural justice in what happened to him since he intended to do the same to thousands of innocent animals but, even if he did kill Reverend Jackaman, I would not wish that death on any man.'

'The manner of his death was exceedingly unpleasant,' my guardian conceded, 'and the greatest proof yet that the deaths were planned in such a way as to taunt me.'

'The coded messages seemed to serve little other purpose,' I said, 'except to make sure we arrived at the right time. Do you think Rupert wrote them?"

'Probably.' He rested his right heel on the toe of his left foot. 'Whilst few men could equal the last Baron Foskett's numerical prowess, his lyrical skills were rather more limited, which is why I was so slow decoding them.' He waggled his right foot from side to side. 'I was looking for something clever, but they were so elementary that even March was able to work them out.'

'*Even?*' I seethed.

'Sulk later,' he told me.

'Do not worry, I will.'

Dorna rubbed her neck uneasily. 'So presumably I was responsible for killing Mr Piggety too.' A strand of hair fell forwards from behind her ear but she let it stay. 'Did I have an accomplice? Thurston Gates, perhaps?'

But Mr G shook his head. 'Rupert,' he said.

'How can you be sure?' I asked, and Sidney Grice looked at the carrot in his grasp as if surprised to find it there.

'Quite simply, because he was seen, or rather he deliberately showed himself.'

'To the boys who were supposed to be keeping watch,' I remembered. 'He frightened them off by pretending to be a monster.'

'And there were few men more monstrous than Rupert in their appearance.' He put the carrot on to the table as if it were an exhibit.

'Or in their actions,' I said.

My guardian tugged at his earlobe. 'And, whilst he was sending the boys packing, you, Dorna, were bribing a gaggle of gutter girls to warn if anybody else came near.'

'Which they did when I turned up,' I said.

'By yourself?' Dorna looked alarmed. 'You did not let March go by herself?'

My guardian put his third finger to his eye and rotated it a fraction. 'First, I forbade her to go but, as I am sure you are aware, March may not have much of a mind but it is very definitely her own.'

'Why are you always so rude about me?' I asked.

'I cannot be blamed if the truth offends you.' He twisted his eye a little the other way.

'Sidney would not tell a lie to save his own mother,' Dorna said.

'And she would be the first to condemn me if I did. Second, I took the precaution of waiting nearby with a cab and a burly ex-policeman.' Jane returned with another tray of coffee and a plate of shortbread. 'Four minutes and forty-eight seconds,' he observed when she had gone. 'We are lucky if Molly brings our tea in twice that time, no matter how much I shout at her.'

'Perhaps your shouting flusters her,' Dorna suggested.

'Nonsense.' He coaxed his lower right eyelid up. 'She likes being bullied.'

'I think she probably does,' I agreed.

'In that case I shall stop it immediately,' he said. 'Happy servants are lazy servants. Where was I?'

Dorna touched the coffee pot but did not pour. 'You were about to tell me how I killed Mr Piggety.'

'Simple enough.' He drummed his fingertips on the arm of his chair. 'You rang the doorbell. He was either expecting you on some pretext or you bluffed your way in. Either way you go down to his killing room. One of you points a gun at Piggety and tells him to undress. The other binds him – probably not Rupert, who was hopeless at knots as a youth – fixes him to a hook, turns on the hot water supply and starts the motor. You time his progress for a while. He kicks out wildly and knocks the watch out of Rupert's hands, smashes it and one of you steps on the broken glass. At some point March turns up, probably as you are about to leave, since the building is unlocked. She takes fright, runs away and becomes embroiled in a pugilistic match on the docks. You write a telegram and give it to a street urchin to deliver. Later you send the letter and key with another boy. You pay well and scare them to be sure they carry out your instructions.'

I tested the pot but it was so hot that I decided to leave it. 'How can we be sure the monster was Rupert? There is no shortage of men who look like ghouls in this city.'

He scratched his cheek. 'Would you say Piggety was neat in his person?'

'No. He had a scruffy air about him.'

'What man carefully folds his clothes when he is being forced to undress, let alone a man who has little interest in sartorial matters already. Rupert, however, was an obsessive man. Apart from being driven to write numbers he was compulsively tidy. He could not have abided seeing a messy heap of clothing and would have had to rearrange them. Also...' He stood and took out his hunter. 'Knock this out of my hands – and that is not an invitation to perform an act of violence.'

I got up and swiped his watch from his grasp. It fell six inches, swinging on its chain, and he flipped it open.

'Undamaged,' I said. 'So why did the murderer's watch get smashed on the floor?'

'Rupert could not tolerate chains.' He clipped the lid shut. 'They hang untidily and clink, and he drove himself to distraction forever trying to straighten the links.' Mr G put his watch away. 'In the end he decided to forgo the chain and so, if the watch was knocked out of his hand, it would have fallen to the ground. I asked to see his watch – which used to be his father's – and was about to press the matter when Cutteridge intervened. Also, I found this.' He picked his satchel from the floor and delved inside to produce a test tube.

'The maggot,' I recalled.

'And not just any old maggot, of which there is no shortage is this hub of empire, but a specimen of *Cochliomyia*. They are not native to our shores, but by this stage Rupert was shedding them liberally.'

'And the last murder?' Dorna asked.

'Warrington Gallop, the snuff seller,' I said.

'Gallop was killed by Rupert alone.' Sidney Grice put the test tube away. 'There was only one set of footprints in the room from which the dart was fired and they were those of a man with a slight limp who exhaled blood. The type of dart used is typical of the region where he was disseminating his Christian doctrines and I do not doubt that, if Mordent House had not been razed to the ground, we would have discovered his blowpipe. Rupert could not bear to throw anything away. He saved every finger- and toenail clipping from the age of four – all these and many other things in labelled boxes. He loved organizing his files.'

'I cannot think why he was your friend.' I helped myself to a biscuit.

'Everyone who has ever pretended to be my friend has betrayed me.'

Dorna reached across. 'Poor Sidney, but surely...' she said, and he smiled wryly.

'All of them,' he said, 'without exception.'

73

The Ashes of Mordent House

DORNA WENT RED. 'But I have never—'

He silenced her with a glare. 'I would be more flattered by your concern if I did not know you have deceived me already.' And she looked at him blankly.

'But what—' I began.

'I tried to get a copy of your nib made by Harrington's,' he butted in, 'but they told me there was no need to put in a special order.' He reached inside his coat and scattered a dozen nibs on the table. 'They already make them.'

Dr Berry picked one up. 'They are very like mine.'

'Identical,' he said and she grimaced.

'Oh, Sidney,' she said, 'you were so overbearing and dismissive of my status when we met. The only thing you admired was my pen so when you asked who designed it, I unthinkingly blurted out that I had. It was a harmless deception.'

'That is an oxymoron,' he said. 'All untruths harm somebody, if only the people who cheapen themselves by spawning them.'

I am sorry I deceived you. It was almost a joke when I started.

'Everybody tells fibs,' she said and he humphed.

'I do not.'

'You told a mob they had cut your eye out once,' I reminded him.

'No, I did not. I told them it was an offence to do so.'

'I am sorry. It was stupid of me.' Dorna blushed.

My guardian leaned forward and scooped the nibs off the table with the side of his hand into his other palm. 'If that were your only deception I could probably forgive you. After all, it is not unknown for March to treat the truth as a toy to be broken and thrown away whenever she is bored with it.'

'Perhaps I can redeem myself by pouring the coffee,' I said.

'You may pour but it will not redeem you,' he told me as I picked up the pot.

'I am sorry,' Dorna Berry said in the awkward silence. 'I hope that we can still be friends.'

Sidney Grice watched her closely. 'If only your other lies were so easily discounted.'

And Dorna bristled. 'What lies? I have never—'

'You told me your parents were actors but I have consulted Jonathon Furbish, the foremost theatrical historian in Europe, and he could find no trace of them.'

'Then tell him to look harder. They worked under the stage name of Marlowe, after the playwright.'

'When and where were you born?' he fired off.

'Paris, April the first, 1850. I would imagine that all the records were destroyed in the crushing of the commune.'

He blinked. 'How convenient.'

'Yes, it is, because I generally add a few years to my age to give me more gravitas.'

'We are both guilty of that offence,' I told her.

Dorna dabbed her mouth with a little triangular napkin. 'Now, if you will forgive my playful deception over the nibs, I will consider forgiving your unwarranted attack on my parentage.'

Sidney Grice puffed his lips and exhaled. 'You have a capacity for rebuttal which would do you credit in the Oxford Union.' He surveyed her coolly. 'Why did you not tell me you were Rupert Foskett's medical attendant?'

She held out her cup for me to refill. 'I did not know you had any interest in Baron Foskett until today.'

'I do find it a little odd that you did not mention it while we were discussing him just now,' I said and she looked at me sadly.

'Oh, March, do not let living with him make you as cynical as he is. First of all, I did not wish to interrupt your story and, second, there is the question of professional ethics. I am obliged to keep the details of my patients confidential. The Hippocratic Oath says—'

'*All that may come to my knowledge in the exercise of my profession or in daily commerce with men, which ought not to be spread abroad, I will keep secret and will never reveal,*' Sidney Grice quoted. 'The case of Harkness versus the Crown established that this duty expires with the patient, and you are presumably well aware of this since you exhibited no such reticence when it came to discussing Edwin Slab with us.'

'I would have told you, had you given me a chance,' she snapped. 'Anyway, how did you know?'

'I use my eye,' he told her. 'And I saw an imprint in the dust at Mordent House when Cutteridge set his lamp down at the top of the stairs. Four clusters of berries in the corners of a rectangle, the same design you have on the feet of your case. I believe you told me it was *fun*.'

'And so it seemed,' she said. 'Perhaps you would like to recite the names of all your clients for me now so that, if we have anyone else in common, *I* can accuse *you* of withholding information.'

Sidney Grice drank thoughtfully. 'I have accused you of no such thing,' he said, 'yet.' He took a longer drink. 'What concerns me more, though, Dr Berry—'

'Dr Berry? Since when have we become so formal?'

He replaced his cup as if it were a delicate artefact. 'I am always formal when I interview suspects.'

'That is rather harsh,' I said, and Dorna Berry's cup rattled in the saucer as she struggled to put it down. 'Interview? Suspects?'

You have gone too far this time, *Mr* Grice.' She rose from her chair. 'I am afraid I must ask you to leave my house.'

My guardian laughed flatly. 'That is the last thing you need be afraid of,' he said. 'If you choose not to talk to me I shall be forced to divulge my concerns to Inspector Quigley, who will no doubt wish to discuss the issues with you at great length in the comfort of Marylebone Police Station.'

She froze. 'Are you threatening me?'

He smiled briefly. 'Of course.'

Dr Berry sat down gracefully. 'Very well. Let us get this over with and then you may quit my house' – her voice trembled – 'never to return.'

Sidney Grice leaned back. 'I am not overly concerned with your having been Rupert's physician.' He crossed his legs. 'For there is no doubt he was in need of medical assistance, though it might have been better for him had you consulted Professor Stockton who is the foremost expert in tropical parasitology and, as I am sure you are aware, lives less than two hundred yards from here.'

'Baron Rupert forbade me to discuss his case with anyone,' she said.

'But he told us that his doctor had sought every expert's opinion,' I recalled.

'He was confused,' she said.

'What concerns me more...' my guardian produced his snuff-box, 'is the fact that you must also have been attending his mother, the baroness.'

'What of it?' She smoothed her dress.

'At what stage did you inform Cutteridge that she was dead?'

She flushed. 'Since when does a doctor discuss her patients with their servants?'

'Since when does a doctor allow the servants to believe that they are receiving instructions from their dead mistress and allow that deception to carry on for weeks on end?' I asked and she turned on me.

'Oh, how you have changed. The last time we met it was all affection, but how you snap at my heels now. My first duty was to my living patient, Rupert.'

'Concealing a death is a serious crime,' Sidney Grice said, 'particularly for somebody in your profession.'

'I wrote a death certificate. It is probably in the ashes of Mordent House.'

'Your answers are very neat,' Mr G said sharply and she looked hurt.

'That is because they are true.' She peered across the corner of the table at him. 'Your socket is still oozing. You must let me clean it up before you go.'

He closed both eyes and rubbed his good one. 'Oh, Dorna,' he said. 'Why did it have to be you?'

She put her cup down and reached across to touch his wrist and he opened his eyes and looked at her.

'And why did it have to be *you*?' she asked, and he raised his left hand and let it fall on hers and his fingers curled inwards to give it a little squeeze.

'I am tired of these games,' he said and she smiled encouragingly.

'So am I, dear. Tell me what you know.'

74

Shellfish and the Foskett Thumb

'IT IS A simple tale,' Sidney Grice said, 'though not a happy one and largely inspired by shellfish – the countless millions that petrify into limestone and one bad oyster. The Honourable Rupert Foskett had a crisis of religious faith, which began when I was able to demonstrate that many things he had accepted as true were in fact unprovable. Doubt is common enough since the geologists started chipping at limestone and finding fossils, and his beliefs were undermined further when historians had the temerity to study the Bible in a rational way.

'Rupert found the possibility of mortality impossible to accept and decided to immerse himself in missionary work, presumably in the hope that, if he could convince others that the gospels were gospel truths, he could convince himself in the process, and so he set off for the tropics. At first things went well. He wrote letters to his parents and to me that were full of hope and enthusiasm. He contracted jungle fever but recovered quickly. He was going to move deeper inland to convert natives who had never even seen a white man, let alone heard of Jesus the Christ, and then the letters stopped.

'Nobody was overly concerned at first. The chain of mail delivery was long and tortuous. A runner might get killed or simply not bother to carry out his task; a canoe might overturn; countless letters are eaten by rats before they reach the coast; but the weeks turned into months and two years went by without word.

'At the request of the family and because of my own friendship with Rupert, I went in search of him. It was not easy. The crossing was appalling and, when the ship reached port, the heat and humidity were almost intolerable. However, I assembled a team of porters and a guide, and went into the jungle. The trail was overgrown and, to make matters worse, I was struck by a particularly virulent form of malaria. Apparently, I was raving like a madman for a while.'

'Only a while?' I queried, but he ploughed on regardless.

'When I was recovered sufficiently we pressed on, crossing rivers and tangled ravines, until eventually we came to a squalid village in a clearing where I was told that Rupert had been roasted alive and eaten. I was given to believe that human flesh tastes very like pork and have been unable to tolerate the smell of it since.'

'Is that why you became a vegetarian?' I asked.

'One of the nine reasons,' he concurred. 'In this fetid settlement I was shown an item which I recognized as Rupert's signet ring and a thumb bone which I was assured was his. I did not doubt it as it had an extra spur of bone, which was a characteristic peculiar to the male line of the Fosketts. I purchased them both – they are presently in the family crypt – and set off for England, arriving, after another awful voyage, almost a year to the day after I had set off.'

He picked up a finger of shortbread. 'However, as we are all aware, I had been deceived. And here I am obliged to conjecture a little – during my outward voyage Rupert came secretly back to Mordent House, riddled with blowfly and wasted by fevers. His parents could not bear for the world to know that their fine son, the last of a long and noble line, was no more than food for maggots and so they hid him away. Their only dishonesty would have been to charter a clipper to overtake my ship, carrying the bone taken from an ancestor's coffin and Rupert's ring, and bribe the natives to say that he was dead.'

'But why did they not tell you the truth, Sidney?' Dorna asked. 'The Fosketts must have known they could trust you.'

'That was exactly why. They knew I could be trusted never to tell a lie, and their whole lives had become founded in deception.' Mr G snapped his shortcake in two, spraying crumbs over himself and the table. 'Baron Reginald Foskett had a weak heart – it came from taking exercise as a child – and he died soon after his son's return. His wife, who adored him, was devastated but determined to do everything she could for her son. She called on every so-called expert she could find. They took her money and left her son to rot, and in the end her care of him was so unstinting that she came under attack herself. Dr Simmons, the family physician, was worse than useless. One might – as Rupert did – argue that he hastened her ladyship's death with his incompetence, and that it was more agonizing than it would have been if he had left her alone. Let us return to shellfish.

'Dr Simmons was a glutton with a particular predilection for oysters. He ate them with such a passion that he did not pause to check if they were fresh or not, and died of food poisoning. His practice is taken over by an ambitious young doctor by the name of Berry. She is only too pleased to have a baroness on her books, though she is sworn to secrecy about Baron Rupert. There is little she can do, but she has a reassuring manner and gives Rupert hope. There is a cure for his condition but the drugs required are rare and very expensive, she tells him. What fortune the Fosketts have left is tied up in their property, but Dr Berry comes up with a plan to make money. All they have to do is form a last death club and ensure that the other members die before the baroness. The baroness would then die of her infestation and Rupert would come forward and claim his inheritance.'

'But how would he explain where he has been?' I asked.

'By telling the truth. No crime has been committed in keeping him hidden. There was no attempt to have Rupert's death registered or to make any insurance claims. He was not hiding from debtors or a fugitive from justice.' He rattled his halfpennies in his left hand. 'His illness was a shame upon the family. It made the last of the line unmarriageable, but once he has his inheritance he can be cured. And who better to marry than the beautiful young woman who rid him of his affliction, the woman he loves and who he believes loves him – Dr Berry.'

Dorna raised her eyebrows. 'Why, Sidney, you are wasted in detection with such a talent for romantic gothic horror stories.'

'A good detective needs an imagination' – he flung his halfpennies in the air and caught them with a downward scoop – 'but only for imagining the truth. Bear with me a little longer. I have almost finished. At some point Baroness Foskett dies. This is most unfortunate for, if she is not the last survivor of the club, the winnings will go to the unpleasant Piggety or the crook-backed Mr Gallop, or whoever else is still alive at the time. Luckily for our conspirators, Lady Foskett is a recluse. Who is to know that she has died other than her last surviving retainer? All Rupert has to do is embalm her in spices. Perhaps he sought the help of Edwin Slab, though that would have made him more vulnerable to exposure. It is an easy matter then to sit her in a curtained chamber and fake her hoarse whisper through a speaking trumpet. At the rate the members are dying, the deception need not be maintained for long. Once the last member has been disposed of, it is merely a question of forging the baroness's signature on the society's contract to claim the prize and, after a suitable interval, declaring her dead.'

'This is a very silly game,' Dorna said. 'I do not wish to play it any more. I shall get Jane to see you out.' She rose but my guardian caught hold of her by the arm. 'Your blotting paper,' he said. 'It is smudged with the ink of eight letters and a death certificate.'

Dorna flapped her hand. 'What of it?'

'Oh, Dorna,' he said softly, 'the certificate is for Baroness Lady Parthena Foskett and it is dated today.'

'Rupert sent me a message that his mother had died. I was in no doubt as to the cause and quite happily filled out a form. I planned to visit Mordent House later today.'

'But she died weeks ago,' I objected.

'I had not seen her for weeks.'

'When did you last visit the house?' Mr G challenged.

'I do not know… about a month ago. It was—'

'Yesterday,' he said, 'at a quarter past three.'

Dorna paled. 'You were having me followed?'

'There was no need.' He let go of her arm. 'I put out word that any driver who reported where he had taken you or Primrose McKay would be paid a guinea.'

'There you have it. They would say they took me anywhere for a guinea.'

'Another driver reported picking you up there just over an hour later.'

'They were in collusion to earn two guineas between them. Who would take the word of a common cabby?'

Sidney Grice stood to face her. 'The second driver was a Mr Gerry Dawson. He was in the area because I planned to visit Lady Foskett that afternoon and I wanted him to deal with the dogs if necessary, but we were delayed by the murder of Warrington Gallop and Gerry was just about to leave when he picked up a fare – you.'

'Gerry is a retired policeman,' I informed her, 'and his word will carry some weight in court.'

Dorna touched her forehead. 'I remember. I did visit yesterday but only to attend to Rupert. He told me his mother was asleep and did not wish to be disturbed.'

Sidney Grice raised an eyebrow. 'You are quick on your feet, my dear. Be careful you do not trip yourself up.'

Dorna laughed scornfully. 'What evidence do you have? The imprint of my case on a floor which has gone up in flames? Blotting paper, which I have explained? The fact that I visited my patient? The hearsay of a dead, worm-riddled mad baron? Juries do not like to convict beautiful women of murder and, as you said yourself, I *am* beautiful.' She ran her fingers under his chin. 'Nobody can resist my charms.' She turned to me. 'Can they, March?' She blew me a little kiss.

Swollen-headed, I thought. And then I remembered when she

had first used those words – in my guardian's study. 'Whose ring do you have around your neck?' I got up to look her in the eye.

'What?'

'When you kissed me—'

'When *I* kissed *you*?'

'When we kissed—' I restarted.

'What the devil has been going on?' My guardian stared at us both and we all sat down.

'I felt a ring on a chain,' I continued. 'It was an odd shape – like an animal.'

'I do not know what you are talking about.'

'Show us the ring, Dr Berry,' Sidney Grice said. 'Or I shall summon the police to search you by force.'

Dorna's eyes filled with tears. 'You would not humiliate me so.'

'There are three women in my household,' he said. 'If I paid any attention to weeping I should be immured in a mental asylum by now.'

Dorna reached under her collar and produced a fine-linked gold chain.

'A jackal,' he said. 'The insignia of the Fosketts.'

'Rupert asked me to look after it,' she protested. 'He suspected Cutteridge of pilfering.'

'He prised it off his dead mother's finger,' Mr G said.

'I do not know where he got it from.'

Sidney Grice looked about him as if for inspiration.

'The tonic,' I remembered. 'You made up a tonic for Inspector Pound but I have not given it to him yet.'

'And what will we find when it is analysed?' Mr G asked and she jumped up.

'Damn you,' she said. 'Damn you and your meddling girl.' She darted sideways towards the door but we were both there before her.

'Oh, Dorna,' Sidney Grice said gently. 'It is *you* who is damned.'

75

The Economics of Hope

'SHALL WE SIT down again?' Sidney Grice turned their two chairs so that they were facing each other, and guided Dorna Berry back into hers. He sat opposite her and took her hands. 'Why Inspector Pound?' he asked.

Dorna shivered. 'Can you not guess?'

'It is apparent that you have a grudge against me – though I do not know why yet. Presumably you have some grievance against the police too, though I do not believe you have a criminal record.'

'I had a perfect plan,' she said. 'I would have been rich and titled. I would not have had to tolerate Rupert for long. The maggots had entered his body cavity and it was only a matter of time before they fed off his vital organs.'

'Did you care for him at all?' I asked and she snorted.

'He was a self-pitying, obsessional child. He would talk for hours about numbers.'

'He was a mathematical genius,' my guardian said, 'on the verge of disproving Pythagoras' Theorem before he decided to squander his life on religion.'

'And Lord, how he hated you, Sidney, for making him doubt it. Hour after hour he would pour bile upon your name. He told me he had almost spared Warrington Gallop and used his dart on you, but he knew how angry I would be and how desperately he needed that money.'

'For a cure that does not exist,' I said.

'*I* was his cure.' She raised her head. 'I gave him something he had never had before – hope.'

'False hope,' I insisted.

'I gave him something to live for.'

'You gave him something to kill for,' Sidney Grice said, 'and something to die for and, ultimately, you made him more corrupt than those filthy worms had done in all those years.'

'You did not do this for yourself,' I said.

'Now you are talking nonsense. I do not know why you involve that stupid little slut in your enquiries, Sidney. No wonder your reputation has suffered so much since she arrived.'

Sidney Grice sat watching me. 'Go on,' he said.

'Have you ever told Dr Berry about Eleanor Quarrel?' I asked.

'Never,' he said. 'It is not a case I am proud of.'

'Neither have I,' I told him. 'And yet...'

'I read about her.' Dorna pulled her hands away.

'Where?' he demanded and she struggled for words.

'Eleanor Quarrel has never been mentioned in any newspapers,' I said. 'She was never convicted of any crimes and we did not know her real name until after she disappeared.'

'Until she died fleeing you.' She swept her arm to indicate us both and I stood up.

'What lovely green eyes you have,' I said and she looked deep into mine, and at that moment I knew. 'Oh, Dorna, did you really do it all to avenge your mother?'

'Can you think of a better reason?' She jumped up to face me. 'Mrs Marlowe was a dull-witted, vain dipsomaniac and I hated her. I had no parents and then my real mother found me about a year ago. She was beautiful and clever and witty, and we were just getting to really know each other when you took her away from me.'

'She died fleeing justice,' my guardian said.

'Justice?' she echoed bitterly. 'What justice did she ever have? For pity's sake, she was sent to prison for defending herself from a policeman's advances when she was hardly more than a child.'

'She probably encouraged him,' Sidney Grice said and I rounded on him.

'That is a filthy thing to say.'

Dorna shushed me. 'All men are vile, March – however they choose to present themselves.'

'I believe Inspector Pound to be a good man at heart, but you set fire to the operating theatre and tried to kill him,' I said and she looked at me with disdain.

'Now you are being ridiculous. Even if I did you cannot prove it.'

'Carry on.' Sidney Grice leaned back in his chair and surveyed her.

'But I qualified and found employment and my private practice was expanding, and when my mother turned up I was so happy. I loved her from the first and she loved me.'

'She never loved anyone,' I said, 'and no more do you.'

She eyed me with contempt. 'You know nothing about love.'

I let that pass.

'But surely when you found out what she had done—' Mr G began.

'*What* had she done?' she shouted. 'Other than be an innocent pawn in a sordid affair! She told me that you hated her for exposing you as a fraud, an incompetent who sent an innocent man to his death, and that you and the police were trying to destroy her. The day I heard that she had died I made a vow: I would destroy you all, and what better way to do it than make myself rich in the process. I assumed that Pound would be involved in the case too, but he avoided that by being put on another investigation.' She smiled grimly. 'Imagine my joy when he fell into my hands, utterly helpless. I could have smothered him where he lay and no one would have suspected me, but why should I let him die peacefully in his sleep when he could die painfully and at your hand, dear March?'

'Do you really hate us that much?' I asked.

'As a matter of a fact I have become quite fond of you both

over the last few weeks, but by then the wheels were set in motion.' She looked around the room. 'Oh, March, if you had truly known her as I did. We were so alike. I do not mean in appearance – she told me I looked like my father.'

'Did she tell you who your father was?' I asked.

'He was a captain in the Guards who was going to marry her when she came of age, but then he was sent abroad and died.'

'Dear Dorna,' Sidney Grice said. 'How like a small child you are to believe that.'

She turned on him furiously. 'What now? Are you going to tell me he was a corporal or a private? I do not care what he was.'

'Dorna.' I went over and touched her shoulder, but she brushed me away. 'Your father was your grandfather.'

She flinched. 'You are talking nonsense.'

'I wish I was.'

She stood up, grasping the chair to steady herself. 'No wonder she never told me his name. Oh, my poor mother... She was *thirteen*.' She cradled her mouth in her free hand.

My guardian took her elbow. 'Sit down please, Dorna.'

She obeyed meekly, and suddenly she looked very small and vulnerable. I went over and crouched before her. 'I have something else to tell you.'

She looked confused. 'Have you found him? I do not want to meet him if you have.'

'No,' I said. 'Your father died a long time ago but your mother is *not* dead.'

Her face twisted into one contorted word, so tangled with hate that I had difficulty understanding it. 'Liar!' She leaped up to stand over me.

I spoke slowly as I rose. 'A friend of mine, a lady who knew your mother quite well, saw her a few days ago boarding a train at Euston.'

Dorna looked at me blankly. 'But I have avenged her.'

'And now she might as well have died for you shall never see her again,' Sidney Grice said. 'She has abandoned you, Dorna.'

And she covered her face and for a while we were silent and, when she took her hands away, her expression was calm again. She unclipped her bag and brought out a scent bottle.

'Was that how you were going to destroy me – getting me to kill the inspector?' I asked, and she put her head to one side.

'That and this.' She pulled out the stopper. 'Though I planned to do it at night when you could not see me.'

'Perfume?' I said as her hand went back. Sidney Grice was watching her with interest but made no effort to intervene.

'Sulphuric acid.' Her hand darted forward, dashing it into my face.

I screamed and clutched my face, curled over, but I was too late. I felt it splash into my eyes with the first throw and over my hands, cheeks and neck with each succeeding cast.

76

The Frequency of Unvoiced Wonderment

SIDNEY GRICE SPRANG to his feet and pulled my fingers away.

'Take this.' He pressed something into my palm. 'It is all right. Open your eyes.'

I forced myself to do so and found that I could perfectly well see the white handkerchief he had given to me.

'It does not sting.' I fought down my panic.

'But I filled it myself.' Dorna sniffed the empty bottle in wonder.

I dabbed myself dry.

'So you did,' he said. 'But last night when we went to the play – and you only took me there to mock me – I hid your glove and when you went to help Emily find another, I looked in your handbag.

'My suspicions were aroused when I saw a bottle of Fougère. I do not know which perfume you wear – for I have yet to study the subject in depth – but March uses Fougère and your scent is very different. I shook the bottle and touched the rim.' He held up his finger, the tip still raw. 'If there had not been a carafe of water on your desk to plunge my digit into, I could have lost the end of it. I thought perhaps you carried it for self-defence as you go into some very shady corners, but then I saw the little handgun and I decided that was security enough. So, to play it safe, I poured the acid into your plant pot and rinsed and refilled the bottle from the carafe.'

'I wondered what had happened to that rubber tree,' I said.

'Unvoiced wonderment is rare in the young,' he said, 'but almost always welcome. I also took the bullets out of your rather lovely little revolver while I was at it. I am never happy socializing with anyone who possesses the means of killing me.'

'Oh, Sidney,' she protested. 'How could you ever think I truly meant to harm you?'

He reinserted his eye. 'Apart from the particularly cruel murders you have committed or your attempts to destroy my reputation, my ward and my police colleague – I cannot imagine what makes me so suspicious of your intentions.'

'But you will not hand me over to the police,' she said, 'after everything we have been to each other.'

'Oh, Dorna.' Sidney Grice ran his fingers through his hair. 'It was all built on nibs and lies.'

77

Clocks and the Atoms of Decency

THERE WAS LITTLE to say after that. Mr G rang for Jane and Dorna put her hand up.

'I am still mistress here.' And when Jane came, Dorna instructed her to fetch the police without saying why.

'Inspector Quigley of Marylebone Police Station,' my guardian told the young constable who marched in ten minutes later. 'Mr Sidney Grice requires him at his earliest convenience.'

For half an hour or more we sat, listening to the clocks tick and chime. I hardly dared look at my companions but whenever I did Dorna's eyes were downcast, whilst Sidney Grice was gazing at her with a peculiar intentness. In the end I could stand that and the silence no longer.

'But why did you kill Emily and your cook and pretend to hang yourself?' I asked.

'Did I?' Her face was a mask.

'Partly because they were witnesses to the charade Dr Berry had planned and partly to cast more victims at Miss McKay's door,' my guardian answered. 'If there is an atom of decency in all of this, she did at least wait until it was Jane's day off and kill a virtual stranger instead.'

Dorna Berry shrugged. 'Perhaps it just happened to be Jane's day off.'

'Not an atom then.' He pinched his ear lobe. 'The murders of the servants and the fake hanging were all designed to put a noose round Primrose McKay's neck when she came out of hiding to claim her winnings. It would have been your word against hers and she had every motive for all the killings whereas you, apparently, had none.'

I clicked my fingers to his obvious disapproval. 'But what about Thurston, her manservant?'

'If you were a man, which you very nearly are in some ways,' my guardian brought out his Mordan mechanical pencil, 'who would you rather have as a mistress, the hypochondriac and dangerously sadistic heiress to a failing business...?'

'Failing?' I queried and he waved the pencil at me.

'I have advised you before to read the business pages. McKay Sausages has taken a tumble with the deteriorating quality of their product since death wrenched Mr McKay's hand from the tiller eight years ago. Coupled with his daughter's unwise forays into the equine world – and I am surprised you did not look into that aspect of her affairs, Miss Middleton, eighty-four horses which she would have been better putting into her product – she is on the brink of bankruptcy. Why, even that figurine of a mandarin was a cheap fake. She put the original pair up for auction along with a number of valuable paintings last year. She needed the money. Why else do you think she joined the society? And Thurston could choose between her and an alluring young doctor who was about to acquire one of the oldest titles in the country.'

'What a filthy mind you have,' Dorna told him bitterly.

'The world I deal with is filthy but I remain pure,' he responded. 'In case you are interested, you made three major mistakes this morning.'

She leaned back in her chair and closed her eyes. 'My only mistake was in trusting you. It is that McKay trollop who should be facing these accusations, not me.'

Sidney Grice turned the pencil between his fingers as if he were rolling a cigarette. 'First, the noose – luckily, March had to cut it so I could judge the length of the rope to the inch. It was much too short. If you had stood on the stool it would have been above your head. It was only when you climbed into the drawer that you could put it round your neck.'

'He lifted me up.'

'You told us he kicked the stool from under you,' I reminded her and she breathed out slowly.

'I was confused. I wonder how clearly you would remember things when you have seen your maid horribly killed and almost been murdered yourself.'

'The knot was quite interesting, as knots very often are.' Sidney Grice lowered the pencil to point it like a rapier towards her. 'A reverse reef knot.'

She looked at him coldly. 'What of it?'

'The same sort of knot was also used to tie up Piggety.'

'And?' She yawned ostentatiously.

'And is otherwise known as a surgeon's knot.'

'I am a physician, not a surgeon.'

'Even I know how to tie a suture,' I said and she eyed me sourly.

'Lastly' – my guardian lowered the pencil – 'the gold cross on the snapped chain in the hall. Primrose McKay never wore one.'

Dorna opened her eyes. 'But you told me she did.'

'I never lie.' He looked at her with his pencil at arm's length, as if about to start a portrait. 'I merely asked a few days ago if March had mentioned that Miss McKay liked wearing little gold crosses on chains, and then by some strange coincidence one appears in Emily's dead grasp. It was one clue too many, Dr Berry, and perhaps the final nail in the scaffold.'

Quigley came at last and Mr G spoke to him in the hall before ushering him into the room.

'At this gentleman's request I shall not manacle you,' the inspector told her.

'This is an outrage,' Dorna protested, but followed him to the door without resisting.

'Take a good look, Dr Berry,' Sidney Grice said. 'You shall never know these comforts again.'

She forced a tense smile. 'Oh, I shall be back,' she vowed, but Sidney Grice demurred.

'Dear Doctor' – he crunched on his last piece of carrot – 'the last person you shall see is the man who is about to choke you to death for a fee of two guineas.'

She spun away and let Inspector Quigley lead her out and into a Black Maria.

'You see,' my guardian told me, 'I said you must allow Dorna to be the murderer.' He clambered aboard the van. 'I shall send you a cab.'

'Not yet,' I said, turning back to the house. 'Somebody has to talk to Jane.'

*

It was almost midnight before Sidney Grice returned, grey with exhaustion.

'I shall not talk about it tonight.' He took two sniffs of snuff and threw back his head with his eyes closed. At last he bowed his head and I watched him for a while, staring into the open snuff-box as if waiting for something to happen. 'You should go to bed.'

'We both should.'

My guardian patted my shoulder awkwardly and I thought he shivered.

And, as I lay in bed that night looking out into the starless sky, I thought about that shadow on my guardian's face. The sadness had been there since the day I met Sidney Grice and it was never to go away.

*

When I returned to the hospital the next day, the screens were pulled round Inspector Pound's bed and my first thought was that something dreadful had happened, but the nurse told me that he had visitors and was playing cards, and they did not want Matron to see.

'He must be feeling better,' I said and, as I neared the end of the ward, I heard a stranger chuckle and say, 'Got you that time, Baker.'

Somebody else grunted and said, 'No sign of your fiancée today, Pound?'

'Miss Middleton isn't actually my fiancée.' The inspector's voice was weak. 'It was just something she told Matron so she could visit me.'

And someone else laughed but this time with a hard edge. 'Give him some credit, pal. He's not that desperate.' And the men roared in mirth and one of them leaned back, and the screen parted and I saw Inspector Pound propped up in bed. He was not laughing but he was not speaking, and at that moment he glanced up and our eyes met.

I spun round as if he had struck me and I almost wished he had.

'That was quick,' the nurse said.

'I just remembered something,' I said.

I lifted my skirt – how my guardian would have fussed about that – and ran.

78

The Trial

THE TRIAL OF Dr Dorna Berry was not a prolonged affair. There were so few witnesses left. Sidney Grice and I told the court what we knew and Inspector Quigley turned up to pick what scratchings of glory he could from the case. My guardian had briefed the prosecuting counsel well. Valiantly though the defence tried to shift all the blame on to Baron Rupert Foskett, they could not make a convincing account of it.

Dorna was demure and her replies were quick and seductive, but they were crushed under the weight of evidence against her.

The only time she seemed about to break down was when it was revealed that Rupert's cousin, the Earl of Bocking, had recently died childless, leaving him all his estate via the baroness. Had Dorna been content with merely seducing and marrying Rupert, she would have come into two titles and a considerable fortune.

The jury deliberated for a long time, doubtless desperate in their attempts to believe her. As Dorna Berry had said, nobody wanted to sentence a beautiful woman to death. The judge, however, showed no such reluctance.

*

There was none of the crowing triumphalism that I had witnessed in Sidney Grice when he had seen William Ashby condemned. He sat throughout, rattling his halfpennies and ignoring the attentions of the press. I had thought Waterloo Trumpington might be there but apparently he had been sent to report on a gasworks explosion in Derbyshire.

'I have an appointment with the patent office,' Sidney Grice told me in a strange monotone. 'A fraudulent American is claiming to have invented the Grice-ophone before me – some stupid device with wax cylinders.'

He saw me to a cab and wandered away, deep in thought. I got the driver to drop me off at Tavistock Square and sat watching Silas Braithwaite's empty house. Once I thought I saw a woman in the waiting-room window and an insane thought shot through me that Dorna might have been telling the truth, and that she had seen somebody in there. But the figure moved and I saw that it was just the reflection of a dray driver.

I walked slowly back to 125 Gower Street, paying little attention to my surroundings or the masses of people bustling by.

Molly admitted me and took one look at my face. 'Oh, miss,' she said in dismay as she took my cloak and hat. She touched my arm.

'Thank you, Molly,' I said and trudged upstairs to my bottle of oblivion.

Not an hour goes by without me thinking of him repeatedly. Edward, so young and brave and caring and foolish. Dear God, how we loved.

He did not put me on a pedestal; he put me in his eyes and – for all my plainness – I saw myself in them as more lovely than is humanly possible.

But Edward was not handsome. He was beautiful. He blushed when I told him that but it was true. He was so very beautiful.

He was a subaltern in India. There had been some trouble in the area and he went on patrol, him and eleven others. I thought he was safe, miles away, but we had had that argument and he wanted to see me. So he persuaded his commanding officer to let him join the group that was coming to our camp... They were ambushed. Four of them died on the spot and four were seriously wounded, but their comrades managed to fight their way through and get them home.

The normal practice was for the officers to be dealt with before the men but I had persuaded my father, who was the camp surgeon, to allow me to triage casualties so that those who would benefit the most received treatment first.

His face had been blown off by a musket shot at close range. I thought he was a hopeless case and that we would be better treating his juniors. I left him for the padre, so disfigured that I did not know him. He was unrecognizable, my father said, but it was always with me, the thought – if I had truly loved, I would have known him through a mountain. And a voice in the night whispered to me, 'You knew it was him all along and did not want him when he was no longer pretty.'

'Liar!' I screamed. 'You damnable, sick, perverted liar.' And I woke up drenched with my father shaking my shoulder. He hugged me for the first time and I sobbed until I thought I could sob no more. How very wrong I was. But then I was born wrong.

79

The Corridors of Perdition

DORNA BERRY WAS simply attired in a black dress with a white lace trim. Her hair was neatly tied back and at first sight she looked so cheerful and relaxed that we might have been meeting for afternoon tea in Hyde Park, but there was nothing elegant about her surroundings: a stone sepulchre, dripping condensation, and lit only by a high, barred window and the traces of day seeping past the silhouette of the warder standing in the open doorway.

'March' – her voice was acrid with irony – 'how lovely.' She gestured to the bed and we sat side by side a foot or two apart and, as we turned to each other, I saw that her complexion was grey and her eyes darkly ringed.

I hesitated. 'I was not sure you would want to see me.'

'I have nothing else to occupy my time.' Her left fingers tremored in her lap. 'And I am curious as to why you wanted to come.'

'To see if there is anything you need.'

She twitched in grisly amusement. 'A ticket to America might be nice.'

I watched her fingers. 'Is there anything you need that I can get you?'

'No. Is that all?'

There was a tic in her right cheek. It crawled under her skin like one of Rupert's maggots. I shuddered and burst out with, 'Oh, Dorna, why did you have to do it?'

She inhaled sharply. 'I came from nothing, March, and I was no one. The Marlowes dragged me round the fleapits and louse-riddled hostelries of every decaying principality in Europe. Before I could even speak they had me on the stage. I hated it and I hated them. My earliest memories are of being exhibited like a prize pig, being laughed at when I tripped and hit my head, being booed when I forgot my lines or derided when the Marlowes made me sing.'

Her arm shook. 'I lost count of the times we sneaked out of inns before dawn because we could not pay bills, or were put into prison for debts. I was reared in a morass but I scrambled my way out of it by my own determination. I fought tooth and nail for my professional qualifications and even then I was spurned. Only one hospital would employ me occasionally and then only because I worked for free.'

She quivered. 'And then I saw my chance to escape and rise above them all. Rupert fell in love with me. Imagine it, March. I could have been a baroness. Who knows what suitors I would have attracted? And then my mother found me. The club was her idea.'

'It would be,' I said.

'When I heard that she had died it felt like everything that I wished for had lost its savour. It was Rupert who suggested bringing Sidney Grice into the club. Why not make our fortunes and be avenged at the same time? He hated Sidney for destroying what is most precious in any man – the sure and certain hope of immortality – but it is always a mistake to mix business with pleasure.'

'Pleasure?' I whispered and her expression lit up.

'You have no idea, March, how exquisite is the joy of taking a life slowly and deliberately, the power and pitilessness of it.'

I leaned away from her.

'You are a monster.'

But she smiled gently. 'You are the monster, March – putting human suffering under the microscope, glorying in every detail and then pretending to be shocked. We are not so very different, you and I.'

'No,' I protested. 'I tried to stop what you did.'

'Did you really?' Her voice was low and mocking. 'Well, perhaps you should have tried harder. We scattered clues like rice at a wedding. Or did you merely follow what we did with a horrible fascination?'

'No. I wept for those poor men.'

'Poor men?' she repeated. 'Those *poor men* who so willingly killed for profit and jostled with each other to be seduced.'

'How could you give yourself so cheaply?' I asked and she chuckled.

'I never gave myself to any man,' she told me. 'A hungry man who smells dinner is much more obliging than a man who has eaten and will very often move on.'

'That is disgusting.'

'Oh, March,' she said softly, 'I know the passion of your kisses.'

The warder coughed, either in embarrassment or to remind us he was there.

'Why did you tell me and not Mr Grice that you were going to Edinburgh?' I asked as she picked a stray hair from my cheek.

'So that you would not be suspicious if I went away. Things were coming to a head and I could see that Sidney was starting to pull the strands together. I did not tell him because he would have asked probing questions whereas you, March, you are a trusting child.'

'And yet you would have thrown acid in my face.'

She snorted. 'It might have been an improvement.'

'I would never have been as ugly as you have become,' I retorted and the warder stepped forward.

'No fighting, ladies.'

Dorna laughed. 'Why, my visitor and I have been doing battle since the day we met.'

'And all the time I thought you were my friend.'

'The murderer and the detective have one thing in common,' she told me. 'They have no friends. There are only victims or prospective victims.'

I shivered. 'When I saw you in the glass at the hospital I thought you were your mother's ghost.'

Dorna's eyelid quivered. 'Even my mother is not her own ghost yet.' The tic shot up her cheek, twisting it sideways. 'And now I shall never see her again. She can hardly visit me here.'

'Oh, Dorna,' I said, 'surely you set out to cure, not to kill?'

'And you?' She clenched her left fist in her right. 'What did you set out to do?'

'To love and be loved.'

Dorna put her head back and sucked in the thick, moist air. 'That is too much to hope for, March.'

'It is the hope that keeps me alive.' I stood up. 'I shall pray for you, Dorna.'

She lowered her head very slowly. 'Do not waste your words. It is too late for me and it was always too late for Sidney Grice. Pray for yourself, March, while there is still somebody to pray for.'

I started to go.

'They will not hang me,' she cried with sudden fire. 'I am too beautiful. Can you imagine it? I hear there are petitions to the Home Secretary. He owes favours to Sidney and Sidney will speak up for me. I shall pick ochre until my nails are torn from their roots. I may be transported, but in the end I shall be reprieved and survive to start again.'

'Again?' I could hardly speak the word.

'March.' Dorna pressed something into my hand. 'Give him this.'

I did not need to ask who she meant. The warder looked at what she had given me but I had no reason to. I felt the hard metal and it bit into me.

The warder turned sideways to let me pass.

'I cared for you, Dorna. I cared so much,' I just managed before the door clanged. 'We both did.' And the lock clashed and I walked in a dream down the corridors of perdition, through the gates which would never open for Dorna Berry again and into the explosion of life which was condemned to be extinguished in her.

80

Eight Minutes

SIDNEY GRICE WAS invited to the execution and attended with some alacrity, always keen to see his work completed, but he was quiet when he returned.

'I never saw a woman face death with greater courage.' He massaged his eye. 'From her demeanour she might have been promenading along the Strand. They went to bind her ankles but she waved them away, saying, *I shall not run off.* She caught sight of me in the audience and called out *I...*' Here his voice faltered a little. '*I loved you.* A damnable lie, of course... Then they put the hood over her head and the noose round her neck. I had had a word with the executioner and persuaded him to try a long drop to break her neck instantly but, as he pulled the lever, Dorna jumped sideways, presumably to try to make sure of it.' He stopped, mouthed something silently and cleared his throat. 'But her foot caught on the edge of the platform and the fall broke her leg – I heard it snap – and it slowed her enough to be sure that she struggled for eight long minutes in agony.'

He shivered and did not raise any objections when I went to light the fire except to say, 'Molly should do that.'

'I like to do it.' I poured his tea and brought out my father's hip flask and held it out, but he put his hand over his cup.

'Just a spoonful. Just this once,' I said, but he kept his hand in place.

He drank slowly and in silence, the fire glinting in the jackal ring on his watch chain.

'Did you love her very much?' I asked and he peered at me as if I were a new species.

'What on earth would I want to do that for?' He took out his eye and the socket was raw with inflammation.

'People cannot choose whom they love.'

'Then why do they bother doing it? Is it, by any chance, because they are witless and undisciplined?' He swilled the last of his tea, staring deep into the dregs. 'There is a decanter in the sideboard. I keep it for over-excited clients.'

I got it out with two tumblers and poured us each a generous measure of brandy.

'You seemed very fond of her.'

'I was gaining her confidence.' He raised the glass in an unspoken toast. 'How could you think I would love a woman who committed such crimes?' He put on his black eye patch. 'For heaven's sake, March – she preferred coffee to tea.' His face froze and his lips struggled with each other, but even his silence could not muffle the howling of his soul.

'She was so lovely,' I said and the very life seemed to dwindle in him.

'Quicklime.' He looked around the room. 'She is in quicklime now.'

He put the tumbler to his mouth but, in a sudden movement, hurled it smashing into the fireplace.

81

Witchcraft, Tea and Crumpets

TWO DAYS AFTER the hanging a black carriage with curtained windows pulled up outside 125 Gower Street. It was the same frog-like equerry my guardian had sent away in such a pique only a few weeks ago.

I offered him a seat but again he preferred to remain standing, while Sidney Grice stayed in his chair, his feet crossed on the table.

'My master has asked me to extend his warmest gratitude to you, Mr Grice, and this small reward.' He handed my guardian a little velvet-covered box. 'The photograph was exactly where you said it would be.' The equerry smiled. 'In another age you might have been burnt for witchcraft. In these more enlightened times, we stand in awe of your genius and my master requests that you accept the appointment as his official private detective.'

'*Personal*,' Sidney Grice grunted. 'Tell your master I shall be happy to be of service – if I have no other pressing business.' And when we were alone he flipped open the lid and I glanced over. It was the largest ruby I had ever seen.

'But how did you know where it would be?' I asked and he twisted his lips wryly.

'My remark was meant to be ironic because that is exactly where I found a compromising letter at the end of last year. I did not think even he would be such a dunderhead as to use the same hiding place or to forget for a second time that he had done so.'

We had tea, crumpets, muffins and fruit cake that afternoon, with our chairs pulled close to the glowing fire. This was the nearest thing to luxury I had known since I arrived.

'I am still not clear—'

'You will never be that.'

I let the insult pass. 'Are the New Chartists really such a threat?'

Sidney Grice stretched lavishly. 'The New Chartists are an unimaginative invention of our very good friend, Inspector Quigley. He planned to arrest a few would-be rabble-rousers, have them deported and announce that he had saved the empire.'

'Was Inspector Pound trying to infiltrate their organization then?' I hoped he would not be involved in such a shabby plot.

My guardian yawned. 'Pound had real criminals to tackle. There were reliable rumours of a planned assault on Coutts Bank and he was trying to get into the gang.'

'And I ruined it for him.'

Mr G selected a muffin carefully, though they all looked the same to me. 'On the contrary, the gang thought they had been infiltrated and, with the attempted murder of a police officer over their heads, fled to Canada and Australia where their violent ways will be properly appreciated.' He nibbled his dry muffin. 'So it would seem that your clog-footed intervention did the inspector's job for him.'

'I do not suppose he will thank me.' I saw his look of disgust as I spread the butter on my crumpet and said, 'I did not know you had had malaria.'

'I still get occasional bouts. That is one reason I lock myself away.'

I cut my crumpet in half. 'Next time I will look after you.'

'I do not need any fuss.'

'Perhaps I need to.'

He massaged his brow. 'I will think about it.'

'And, while you are thinking about it, we will get that eye cleaned up.'

He wiped his fingers. 'Yes, Nurse.'

'That is better. Now, would you like the last slice of cake?'

'No,' Sidney Grice said. 'Let us share – and then we have work to do.'

'We?' I cut it in two and he raised an eyebrow.

'You cannot spend your entire life lounging about and preening yourself if you are to be London's first female personal detective.'

'Do you think I could?'

Sidney Grice leaned back and surveyed me lazily. 'Time will tell,' he said with something very nearly like a smile.

POSTSCRIPT

PRIMROSE MCKAY DID not reappear until after the hanging, though she did write a letter asking if she could attend. Sidney Grice got his three thousand pounds for every murder and the rest of the fortune was hers. Much good did it do her. With breathtaking misjudgement she married her footman, the notorious Thurston Gates, and had her neck broken in an unwitnessed riding accident within the month.

The affair of the Fosketts was over and the discreet recognition of Sidney Grice in royal circles was of enormous help in restoring his professional pride and standing, but there was one affair which did not seem likely to be resolved – until I received a letter.

I went back to University College Hospital that evening and I had not even reached Liston Ward when I saw him – Inspector Pound, leaning lightly on the arm of Nurse Ramsey and heavily on a walking stick.

'Should you be out of bed?' I asked. He still looked haggard. His suit hung loosely on his frame and he wore a shirt open at the top with no collar.

'No, he should not.' She tried to sound cross as she steadied him. 'You can use this side room – only don't be too long or I'll be in trouble.'

She sat him on a wooden chair and left us alone together.

'You look so much better,' I said.

'Now that my moustaches have recovered.' He smiled.

'I am sorry about that.'

We fell into an awkward silence, but he broke it with, 'They want to move me into a private cottage hospital in Dorset. They think the fresh air might do me good, but I'm not sure my lungs would know what to do with it.'

I looked up. 'But can you afford it?' And he shook his head.

'At three guineas a day plus doctor's fees? I'm on the wrong side of the law for that,' he observed wryly. 'It appears that a gentleman who wishes to remain anonymous offered to foot the bill, but I like to know who I am in debt to.'

I could make a very good guess but I only said, 'I am glad I shall still be able to visit you.'

'I should miss that,' he admitted and a shaft of pain shot up the side of his face.

'Can I get you anything?'

The inspector shook his head and cleared his throat. 'I believe you may have overheard my colleagues.' He struggled for words.

'I was with the army,' I reminded him. 'I know how men talk.' I took a slow breath. 'But it was not what I heard that hurt me.'

Inspector Pound's gaze fell away and he rubbed the stubble on his chin. 'If I had said anything, they would have mocked you and I could not face that.'

'So I am to believe that you did not defend me in order to defend me?' My voice shook.

His hand went to the back of his neck. 'I was weak and I am sorry for that.'

I remembered a letter and a man striding away through the dust, taking my last chance to forgive him.

'You have been staring at death,' I said.

'That is no excuse.' The inspector coughed from deep in his chest. 'The next time I see them I shall tell them exactly how I feel.'

'I would rather you told me.'

He flopped his arms. 'You are a remarkable woman and I have

come to respect and… admire you.' He put his palm gingerly over his wound. 'Miss Middleton…'

'Call me March.'

'March' – he looked at his hands – 'there is a favour I need to ask of you.'

'I shall do my best.'

'I know that.' He shifted uncomfortably. 'I have my mother's wedding ring around my neck and it is my fear that I shall be robbed of it whilst I am asleep. So many people come and go in the ward.'

I chewed my lower lip. 'Why not ask your sister?'

He fiddled with his jacket buttons. 'I would never get it back. Lucinda is of the opinion that it would be best sold to improve our situation.'

'Not when it means so much,' I said.

'It means a great deal to me.' He reached under his shirt and pulled out a black cord with a plain gold band round it. 'I wonder…' he looked into my eyes and I saw that his were dark blue, 'if you would consent to' – he cleared his throat again – 'wear it for me?'

He looked down.

'Around my neck?' I asked and he looked at me again, and all at once his face was alive.

'For the time being,' he said.

'Put it on for me.' I leaned over him and he slipped the cord over my head, and my hair brushed against his.

Inspector Pound shivered. 'How lovely you are,' he whispered. 'Have you ever been kissed?' I closed my eyes and when I opened them I was happy to find myself held closely in his.

*

There were two letters on the desk for me when I returned, one from Mr Warwick, the land agent, saying he had found a tenant for the Grange. I was glad that the house would be looked after but I hated the idea of strangers living there.

The other was in a plain brown, badly creased and grubby envelope with no stamp upon it. The handwriting was small and fluid, and I hardly dared recognize it as I ripped the flap open and sat in my usual chair.

Mr G was buried behind a newspaper and grunted absently to acknowledge my presence.

My Dear March,

I know that I have no right to address you thus but I cannot call you anything else for I have truly come to love you in the short time we had.

I cannot ask you to think well of me, but only to believe that I spent my whole life seeking to heal before I met that woman. Perhaps you were lucky never to have known your mother for it was meeting mine that set me on this terrible course.

I make no excuses and ask no forgiveness, but if anybody can bring Eleanor Quarrel to justice I truly believe it is you.

I do not add 'and your guardian' for, if I have one wish before they take me from here into the executioner's shed, it is that you see him for what he is.

This is the last letter I shall ever write, the last there shall ever be of me, and I shall not waste it in idle words.

Be strong, March, as I tried to be: be true as I know you are and I once was: but most of all guard your heart.

I am afraid for you, March. You must leave that house. Leave it today or Sidney Grice will destroy you, just as he destroyed me and just as surely as he murdered your mother.

I shall bear you in my last breath.

Ever yours

Dorna.

I stared at the letter and reread it twice.

'Oh, Dorna,' I whispered and let the paper fall. It seemed to hang a while before it sailed, swishing from side to side across the hearth and settling face up upon the glowing coals. The middle blackened and the edges curled and it rose a little before falling back, the paper as black as the words upon it, and the flames crept yellow around it, shot red through it with white wisps and then blue rising high into shadows flickering over the dark tragedy of the accursed House of Foskett.

I had destroyed the letter but those words could never be erased: 'Just as surely as he murdered your mother.'

Sidney Grice lowered his newspaper.

'Is everything all right?' he said.